THE PSALMS OF DAVID
IN METRE

ACCORDING TO THE VERSION APPROVED BY

THE CHURCH OF SCOTLAND

AND APPOINTED TO BE USED IN WORSHIP

KT-368-779

DOMI NUS ILLU MINA TIO MEA

LONDON

OXFORD UNIVERSITY PRESS

GLASGOW MELBOURNE

3R. Nonpareil

Oxford University Press, Walton Street, Oxford OX2 6DP

OXFORD LONDON GLASGOW
NEW YORK TORONTO MELBOURNE WELLINGTON
KUALA LUMPUR SINGAPORE JAKARTA HONG KONG TOKYO
DELHI BOMBAY CALCUTTA MADRAS KARACHI
IBADAN NAIROBI DAR ES SALAAM CAPE TOWN

PRINTED IN GREAT BRITAIN AT THE UNIVERSITY PRESS, OXFORD
BY VIVIAN RIDLER, PRINTER TO THE UNIVERSITY

THE
PSALMS OF DAVID
IN METRE.

PSALM 1.

1 THAT man hath perfect blessed-
    who walketh not astray [ness
In counsel of ungodly men,
    nor stands in sinners' way,
Nor sitteth in the scorner's chair:
2   But placeth his delight
Upon God's law, and meditates
    on his law day and night.

3 He shall be like a tree that grows
    near planted by a river,
Which in his season yields his fruit,
    and his leaf fadeth never:
And all he doth shall prosper well.
4   The wicked are not so;
But like they are unto the chaff,
    which wind drives to and fro.

5 In judgment therefore shall not stand
    such as ungodly are;
Nor in th' assembly of the just
    shall wicked men appear.
6 For why? the way of godly men
    unto the Lord is known:
Whereas the way of wicked men
    shall quite be overthrown.

PSALM 2.

1 WHY rage the heathen? and vain
    things
why do the people mind?
2 Kings of the earth do set themselves,
    and princes are combin'd,
To plot against the Lord, and his
    Anointed, saying thus,
3 Let us asunder break their bands,
    and cast their cords from us.

4 He that in heaven sits shall laugh;
    the Lord shall scorn them all.
5 Then shall he speak to them in wrath,
    in rage he vex them shall.
6 Yet, notwithstanding, I have him
    to be my King appointed;
And over Sion, my holy hill,
    I have him King anointed.

7 The sure decree I will declare;
    the Lord hath said to me,
Thou art mine only Son; this day
    I have begotten thee.

8 Ask of me, and for heritage
    the heathen I'll make thine;
And, for possession, I to thee
    will give earth's utmost line.
9 Thou shalt, as with a weighty rod
    of iron, break them all;
And, as a potter's sherd, thou shalt
    them dash in pieces small.
10 Now therefore, kings, be wise; be
    ye judges of the earth: [taught,
11 Serve God in fear, and see that ye
    join trembling with your mirth.
12 Kiss ye the Son, lest in his ire
    ye perish from the way,
If once his wrath begin to burn:
    bless'd all that on him stay.

PSALM 3.

1 O LORD, how are my foes in-
    against me many rise. [creas'd?
2 Many say of my soul, For him
    In God no succour lies.
3 Yet thou my shield and glory art,
    th' uplifter of mine head.
4 I cry'd, and, from his holy hill,
    the Lord me answer made.

5 I laid me down and slept, I wak'd;
    for God sustained me.
6 I will not fear though thousands ten
    set round against me be.
7 Arise, O Lord; save me, my God;
    for thou my foes hast stroke
All on the cheek-bone, and the teeth
    of wicked men hast broke.

8 Salvation doth appertain
    unto the Lord alone:
Thy blessing, Lord, for evermore
    thy people is upon.

PSALM 4.

1 GIVE ear unto me when I call,
    God of my righteousness:
Have mercy, hear my pray'r; thou
    enlarg'd me in distress. [hast
2 O ye the sons of men! how long
    will ye love vanities?
How long my glory turn to shame,
    and will ye follow lies?

3 But know, that for himself the Lord
   the godly man doth chuse:
The Lord, when I on him do call,
   to hear will not refuse.
4 Fear, and sin not; talk with your
   on bed, and silent be.   [heart
5 Off'rings present of righteousness,
   and in the Lord trust ye.

6 O who will show us any good?
   is that which many say:
But of thy countenance the light,
   Lord, lift on us alway.
7 Upon my heart, bestow'd by thee,
   more gladness I have found
Than they, ev'n then, when corn and
   did most with them abound. [wine
8 I will both lay me down in peace,
   and quiet sleep will take;
Because thou only me to dwell
   in safety, Lord, dost make.

PSALM 5.

1 GIVE ear unto my words, O Lord,
   my meditation weigh.
2 Hear my loud cry, my King, my
   for I to thee will pray.   [God;
3 Lord, thou shalt early hear my voice:
   I early will direct
My pray'r to thee; and, looking up,
   an answer will expect.

4 For thou art not a God that doth
   in wickedness delight;
Neither shall evil dwell with thee,
5 Nor fools stand in thy sight.
All that ill-doers are thou hat'st;
6 Cutt'st off that liars be:
The bloody and deceitful man
   abhorred is by thee.

7 But I into thy house will come
   in thine abundant grace;
And I will worship in thy fear
   toward thy holy place.
8 Because of those mine enemies,
   Lord, in thy righteousness
Do thou me lead; do thou thy way
   make straight before my face.

9 For in their mouth there is no truth,
   their inward part is ill;
Their throat's an open sepulchre,
   their tongue doth flatter still.
10 O God, destroy them; let them be
   by their own counsel quell'd;
Them for their many sins cast out,
   for they 'gainst thee rebell'd.

11 But let all joy that trust in thee,
   and still make shouting noise;

For them thou sav'st: let all that love
   thy name in thee rejoice.
12 For, Lord, unto the righteous man
   thou wilt thy blessing yield:
With favour thou wilt compass him
   about, as with a shield.

PSALM 6.

1 LORD, in thy wrath rebuke me not;
   Nor in thy hot rage chasten me.
2 Lord, pity me, for I am weak:
   Heal me, for my bones vexed be.
3 My soul is also vexed sore;
   But, Lord, how long stay wilt thou
   make?
4 Return, O Lord, my soul set free;
   O save me, for thy mercies' sake.
5 Because those that deceased are
   Of thee shall no remembrance have;
And who is he that will to thee
   Give praises lying in the grave?
6 I with my groaning weary am,
   I also all the night my bed
Have caused for to swim; and I
   With tears my couch have watered.

7 Mine eye, consum'd with grief, grows
   Because of all mine enemies.   [old,
8 Hence from me, wicked workers all;
   For God hath heard my weeping
   cries.
9 God hath my supplication heard,
   My pray'r received graciously.
10 Sham'd and sore vex'd be all my foes,
   Sham'd and back turned suddenly.

Another of the same.

1 IN thy great indignation,
   O Lord, rebuke me not;
Nor on me lay thy chast'ning hand,
   in thy displeasure hot.
2 Lord, I am weak, therefore on me
   have mercy, and me spare:
Heal me, O Lord, because thou
   know'st
   my bones much vexed are.

3 My soul is vexed sore: but, Lord,
   how long stay wilt thou make?
4 Return, Lord, free my soul; and save
   me, for thy mercies' sake.
5 Because of thee in death there shall
   no more remembrance be:
Of those that in the grave do lie,
   who shall give thanks to thee?
6 I with my groaning weary am,
   and all the night my bed
I caused for to swim; with tears
   my couch I watered.

4

7 By reason of my vexing grief
   mine eye consumed is;
It waxeth old, because of all
   that be mine enemies.

8 But now, depart from me all ye
   that work iniquity:
For why? the Lord hath heard my
   voice,
   when I did mourn and cry.

9 Unto my supplication
   the Lord did hearing give:
When I in him my prayer make,
   the Lord will it receive.

10 Let all be sham'd and troubled sore,
   that en'mies are to me;
Let them turn back, and suddenly
   ashamed let them be.

PSALM 7.

1 O LORD my God, in thee do I
   my confidence repose:
Save and deliver me from all
   my persecuting foes;

2 Lest that the enemy my soul
   should, like a lion, tear,
In pieces rending it, while there
   is no deliverer.

3 O Lord my God, if it be so
   that I committed this;
If it be so that in my hands
   iniquity there is:

4 If I rewarded ill to him
   that was at peace with me;
(Yea, ev'n the man that without cause
   my foe was I did free;)

5 Then let the foe pursue and take
   my soul, and my life thrust
Down to the earth, and let him lay
   mine honour in the dust.

6 Rise in thy wrath, Lord, raise thyself,
   for my foes raging be;
And, to the judgment which thou
   commanded, wake for me.   [hast

7 So shall th' assembly of thy folk
   about encompass thee:
Thou, therefore, for their sakes, re-
   unto thy place on high.   [turn

8 The Lord he shall the people judge:
   my judge, JEHOVAH, be,
After my righteousness, and mine
   integrity in me.

9 O let the wicked's malice end;
   but stablish stedfastly
The righteous: for the righteous God
   the hearts and reins doth try.

10 In God, who saves th' upright in
   is my defence and stay.   [heart,

11 God just men judgeth, God is wroth
   with ill men ev'ry day.

12 If he do not return again,
   then he his sword will whet;
His bow he hath already bent,
   and hath it ready set:

13 He also hath for him prepar'd
   the instruments of death;
Against the persecutors he
   his shafts ordained hath.

14 Behold, he with iniquity
   doth travail, as in birth;
A mischief he conceived hath,
   and falsehood shall bring forth.

15 He made a pit, and digg'd it deep,
   another there to take;
But he is fall'n into the ditch
   which he himself did make.

16 Upon his own head his mischief
   shall be returned home;
His vi'lent dealing also down
   on his own pate shall come.

17 According to his righteousness
   the Lord I'll magnify;
And will sing praise unto the name
   of God that is most high.

PSALM 8.

1 HOW excellent in all the earth,
   Lord, our Lord, is thy name!
Who hast thy glory far advanc'd
   above the starry frame.

2 From infants' and from sucklings'
   mouth
   thou didest strength ordain,
For thy foes' cause, that so thou
   might'st
   th' avenging foe restrain.

3 When I look up unto the heav'ns,
   which thine own fingers fram'd,
Unto the moon, and to the stars,
   which were by thee ordain'd;

4 Then say I, What is man, that he
   remember'd is by thee?
Or what the son of man, that thou
   so kind to him should'st be?

5 For thou a little lower hast
   him than the angels made;
With glory and with dignity
   thou crowned hast his head.

6 Of thy hands' works thou mad'st him
   all under's feet didst lay;   [lord,

7 All sheep and oxen, yea, and beasts
   that in the field do stray;

8 Fowls of the air, fish of the sea,
   all that pass through the same.
9 How excellent in all the earth,
   Lord, our Lord, is thy name!

PSALM 9.

1 LORD, thee I'll praise with all my
   heart,
   thy wonders all proclaim.
2 In thee, most High, I'll greatly joy,
   and sing unto thy name.
3 When back my foes were turn'd, they
   and perish'd at thy sight: [fell,
4 For thou maintain'dst my right and
   cause;
   on throne sat'st judging right.

5 The heathen thou rebuked hast,
   the wicked overthrown;
   Thou hast put out their names, that
   may never more be known.   [they
6 O en'my! now destructions have
   an end perpetual:
   Thou cities raz'd, perish'd with them
   is their memorial.

7 God shall endure for aye; he doth
   for judgment set his throne;
8 In righteousness to judge the world,
   justice to give each one.
9 God also will a refuge be
   for those that are oppress'd;
   A refuge will he be in times
   of trouble to distress'd.

10 And they that know thy name, in thee
   their confidence will place:
   For thou hast not forsaken them
   that truly seek thy face.
11 O sing ye praises to the Lord
   that dwells in Sion hill;
   And all the nations among
   his deeds record ye still.

12 When he enquireth after blood,
   he then remem'b'reth them:
   The humble folk he not forgets
   that call upon his name.
13 Lord, pity me; behold the grief
   which I from foes sustain; .
   Ev'n thou, who from the gates of
   dost raise me up again;   [death
14 That I, in Sion's daughters' gates,
   may all thy praise advance;
   And that I may rejoice always
   in thy deliverance.
15 The heathen are sunk in the pit
   which they themselves prepar'd;
   And in the net which they have hid
   their own feet fast are snar'd.

16 The Lord is by the judgment known
   which he himself hath wrought:
   The sinners' hands do make the snares
   wherewith themselves are caught.
17 They who are wicked into hell
   each one shall turned be;
   And all the nations that forget
   to seek the Lord most high.
18 For they that needy are shall not
   forgotten be alway;
   The expectation of the poor
   shall not be lost for aye.
19 Arise, Lord, let not man prevail;
   judge heathen in thy sight:
20 That they may know themselves but
   the nations, Lord, affright.   [men,

PSALM 10.

1 WHEREFORE is it that thou, O
   dost stand from us afar? [Lord,
   And wherefore hidest thou thyself
   when times so troublous are?
2 The wicked in his loftiness
   doth persecute the poor:
   In these devices they have fram'd
   let them be taken sure.

3 The wicked of his heart's desire
   doth talk with boasting great;
   He blesseth him that's covetous,
   whom yet the Lord doth hate.
4 The wicked, through his pride of
   on God he doth not call;   [face,
   And in the counsels of his heart
   the Lord is not at all.

5 His ways they always grievous are;
   thy judgments from his sight
   Removed are: at all his foes
   he puffeth with despight.
6 Within his heart he thus hath said,
   I shall not moved be;
   And no adversity at all
   shall ever come to me.

7 His mouth with cursing, fraud, de-
   is fill'd abundantly;   [ceit,
   And underneath his tongue there is
   mischief and vanity.
8 He closely sits in villages;
   he slays the innocent:
   Against the poor that pass him by
   his cruel eyes are bent.
9 He, lion-like, lurks in his den;
   he waits the poor to take;
   And when he draws him in his net,
   his prey he doth him make.
10 Himself he humbleth very low,
   he croucheth down withal,

That so a multitude of poor
    may by his strong ones fall.
11 He thus hast said within his heart,
    The Lord hath quite forgot;
He hides his countenance, and he
    for ever sees it not.
12 O Lord, do thou arise; O God,
    lift up thine hand on high:
Put not the meek afflicted ones
    out of thy memory.
13 Why is it that the wicked man
    thus doth the Lord despise?
Because that God will it require
    he in his heart denies.
14 Thou hast it seen; for their mischief
    and spite thou wilt repay:
The poor commits himself to thee;
    thou art the orphan's stay.
15 The arm break of the wicked man,
    and of the evil one;
Do thou seek out his wickedness,
    until thou findest none.
16 The Lord is king through ages all,
    ev'n to eternity;
The heathen people from his land
    are perish'd utterly.
17 O Lord, of those that humble are
    thou the desire didst hear;
Thou wilt prepare their heart, and
    to hear wilt bend thine ear; [thou
18 To judge the fatherless, and those
    that are oppressed sore;
That man, that is but sprung of
    earth,
    may them oppress no more.

PSALM 11.

1 I IN the Lord do put my trust:
    how is it then that ye
Say to my soul, Flee, as a bird,
    unto your mountain high?
2 For, lo, the wicked bend their bow,
    their shafts on string they fit,
That those who upright are in heart
    they privily may hit.
3 If the foundations be destroy'd,
    what hath the righteous done?
4 God in his holy temple is,
    in heaven is his throne:
His eyes do see, his eyelids try
5   men's sons. The just he proves:
But his soul hates the wicked man,
    and him that vi'lence loves.
6 Snares, fire and brimstone, furious
    on sinners he shall rain: [storms,
This, as the portion of their cup,
    doth unto them pertain.

7 Because the Lord most righteous
    in righteousness delight; [doth
And with a pleasant countenance
    beholdeth the upright.

PSALM 12.

1 HELP, Lord, because the godly
    doth daily fade away; [man
And from among the sons of men
    the faithful do decay.
2 Unto his neighbour ev'ry one
    doth utter vanity:
They with a double heart do speak,
    and lips of flattery.
3 God shall cut off all flatt'ring lips,
    tongues that speak proudly thus,
4 We'll with our tongue prevail, our
    are ours : who's lord o'er us? [lips
5 For poor oppress'd, and for the sighs
    of needy, rise will I,
Saith God, and him in safety set
    from such as him defy.
6 The words of God are words most
    they be like silver try'd [pure;
In earthen furnace, seven times
    that hath been purify'd.
7 Lord, thou shalt them preserve and
    for ever from this race. [keep
8 On each side walk the wicked, when
    vile men are high in place.

PSALM 13.

1 HOW long wilt thou forget me,
    shall it for ever be? [Lord?
O how long shall it be that thou
    wilt hide thy face from me?
2 How long take counsel in my soul,
    still sad in heart, shall I?
How long exalted over me
    shall be mine enemy?
3 O Lord my God, consider well,
    and answer to me make:
Mine eyes enlighten, lest the sleep
    of death me overtake:
4 Lest that mine enemy should say,
    Against him I prevail'd;
And those that trouble me rejoice,
    when I am mov'd and fail'd.
5 But I have all my confidence
    thy mercy set upon;
My heart within me shall rejoice
    in thy salvation.
6 I will unto the Lord my God
    sing praises cheerfully,
Because he hath his bounty shown
    to me abundantly.

PSALM 14.

1 THAT there is not a God, the fool
  doth in his heart conclude:
They are corrupt, their works are
    vile;
  not one of them doth good.
2 Upon men's sons the Lord from
    did cast his eyes abroad, [heav'n
To see if any understood,
  and did seek after God.
3 They altogether filthy are,
    they all aside are gone;
And there is none that doeth good,
  yea, sure there is not one.
4 These workers of iniquity
    do they not know at all,
That they my people eat as bread,
  and on God do not call?
5 There fear'd they much; for God is
    the whole race of the just. [with
6 You shame the counsel of the poor,
    because God is his trust.
7 Let Isr'el's help from Sion come:
    when back the Lord shall bring
His captives, Jacob shall rejoice,
  and Israel shall sing.

PSALM 15.

1 WITHIN thy tabernacle, Lord,
    who shall abide with thee?
And in thy high and holy hill
  who shall a dweller be?
2 The man that walketh uprightly,
    and worketh righteousness,
And as he thinketh in his heart,
  so doth he truth express.
3 Who doth not slander with his
    tongue,
  nor to his friend doth hurt;
Nor yet against his neighbour doth
  take up an ill report.
4 In whose eyes vile men are despis'd;
    but those that God do fear
He honoureth; and changeth not,
  though to his hurt he swear.
5 His coin puts not to usury,
    nor take reward will he
Against the guiltless. Who doth thus
  shall never moved be.

PSALM 16.

1 LORD, keep me; for I trust in thee.
2   To God thus was my speech,
Thou art my Lord; and unto thee
  my goodness doth not reach:

3 To saints on earth, to th' excellent,
    where my delight's all plac'd.
4 Their sorrows shall be multiply'd
    to other gods that haste:

Of their drink-offerings of blood
  I will no off'ring make;
Yea, neither I their very names
  up in my lips will take.
5 God is of mine inheritance
    and cup the portion;
The lot that fallen is to me
  thou dost maintain alone.
6 Unto me happily the lines
    in pleasant places fell;
Yea, the inheritance I got
  in beauty doth excel.
7 I bless the Lord, because he doth
    by counsel me conduct;
And in the seasons of the night
  my reins do me instruct.
8 Before me still the Lord I set:
    sith it is so that he
Doth ever stand at my right hand,
  I shall not moved be.
9 Because of this my heart is glad,
    and joy shall be exprest
Ev'n by my glory; and my flesh
  in confidence shall rest.
10 Because my soul in grave to dwell
    shall not be left by thee;
Nor wilt thou give thine Holy One
  corruption to see.
11 Thou wilt me show the path of life:
    of joys there is full store
Before thy face; at thy right hand
  are pleasures evermore.

PSALM 17.

1 LORD, hear the right, attend my
    unto my pray'r give heed, [cry,
That doth not in hypocrisy
  from feigned lips proceed.
2 And from before thy presence forth
    my sentence do thou send:
Toward these things that equal are
  do thou thine eyes intend.
3 Thou prov'dst mine heart, thou
    visit'dst me
  by night, thou didst me try,
Yet nothing found'st; for that my
  shall not sin, purpos'd I. [mouth
4 As for men's works, by the word
    that from thy lips doth flow,
Did me preserve out of the paths
  wherein destroyers go.

8

5 Hold up my goings, Lord, me guide
    in those thy paths divine,
So that my footsteps may not slide
    out of those ways of thine.

6 I called have on thee, O Lord,
    because thou wilt me hear:
That thou may'st hearken to my
    to me incline thine ear. [speech,

7 Thy wondrous loving-kindness show,
    thou that, by thy right hand,
Sav'st them that trust in thee from
    that up against them stand. [those

8 As th' apple of the eye me keep;
    in thy wings' shade me close

9 From lewd oppressors, compassing
    me round, as deadly foes.

10 In their own fat they are inclos'd;
    their mouth speaks loftily.

11 Our steps they compass'd; and to
    ground
down bowing set their eye.

12 He like unto a lion is
    that's greedy of his prey,
Or lion young, which lurking doth
    in secret places stay.

13 Arise, and disappoint my foe,
    and cast him down, O Lord;
My soul save from the wicked man,
    the man which is thy sword.

14 From men, which are thy hand, O
    Lord,
from worldly men me save.
Which only in this present life
    their part and portion have.

Whose belly with thy treasure hid
    thou fill'st: they children have
In plenty; of their goods the rest
    they to their children leave.

15 But as for me, I thine own face
    in righteousness will see;
And with thy likeness, when I wake,
    I satisfy'd shall be.

PSALM 18.

1 THEE will I love, O Lord, my
    strength.

2   My fortress is the Lord,
My rock, and he that doth to me
    deliverance afford:
My God, my strength, whom I will
    a buckler unto me,   [trust,
The horn of my salvation,
    and my high tow'r, is he.

3 Upon the Lord, who worthy is
    of praises, will I cry;
And then shall I preserved be
    safe from mine enemy.

4 Floods of ill men affrighted me,
    death's pangs about me went;

5 Hell's sorrows me environed;
    death's snares did me prevent.

6 In my distress I call'd on God,
    cry to my God did I;
He from his temple heard my voice,
    to his ears came my cry.

7 Th' earth, as affrighted, then did
    trembling upon it seiz'd: [shake,
The hills' foundations moved were,
    because he was displeas'd.

8 Up from his nostrils came a smoke,
    and from his mouth there came
Devouring fire, and coals by it
    were turned into flame.

9 He also bowed down the heav'ns,
    and thence he did descend;
And thickest clouds of darkness did
    under his feet attend.

10 And he upon a cherub rode,
    and thereon he did fly;
Yea, on the swift wings of the wind
    his flight was from on high.

11 He darkness made his secret place:
    about him, for his tent,
Dark waters were, and thickest clouds
    of th' airy firmament.

12 And at the brightness of that light,
    which was before his eye,
His thick clouds pass'd away, hail-
    and coals of fire did fly.   [stones

13 The Lord God also in the heav'ns
    did thunder in his ire;
And there the Highest gave his voice,
    hailstones and coals of fire.

14 Yea, he his arrows sent abroad,
    and them he scattered;
His lightnings also he shot out,
    and them discomfited.

15 The waters' channels then were seen,
    the world's foundations vast
At thy rebuke discover'd were,
    and at thy nostrils' blast.

16 And from above the Lord sent down,
    and took me from below;
From many waters me drew,
    which would me overflow.

17 He me reliev'd from my strong foes,
    and such as did me hate;
Because he saw that they for me
    too strong were, and too great.

18 They me prevented in the day
    of my calamity;
But even then the Lord himself
    a stay was unto me.

19 He to a place where liberty
   and room was hath me brought;
   Because he took delight in me,
   he my deliv'rance wrought.

20 According to my righteousness
   he did me recompense,
   He me repaid according to
   my hands' pure innocence.

21 For I God's ways kept, from my God
   did not turn wickedly.

22 His judgments were before me, I
   his laws put not from me.

23 Sincere before him was my heart;
   with him upright was I;
   And watchfully I kept myself
   from mine iniquity.

24 After my righteousness the Lord
   hath recompensed me,
   After the cleanness of my hands
   appearing in his eye.

25 Thou gracious to the gracious art,
   to upright men upright:

26 Pure to the pure, froward thou
   kyth'st
   unto the froward wight.

27 For thou wilt the afflicted save
   in grief that low do lie:
   But wilt bring down the countenance
   of them whose looks are high.

28 The Lord will light my candle so,
   that it shall shine full bright:
   The Lord my God will also make
   my darkness to be light.

29 By thee through troops of men I
   and them discomfit all;   [break,
   And, by my God assisting me,
   I overleap a wall.

30 As for God, perfect is his way:
   the Lord his word is try'd;
   He is a buckler to all those
   who do in him confide.

31 Who but the Lord is God? but he
   who is a rock and stay?

32 'Tis God that girdeth me with
   strength,
   and perfect makes my way.

33 He made my feet swift as the hinds,
   set me on my high places.

34 Mine hands to war he taught, mine
   arms
   brake bows of steel in pieces.

35 The shield of thy salvation
   thou didst on me bestow:
   Thy right hand held me up, and
   great
   thy kindness made me grow.

36 And in my way my steps thou hast
   enlarged under me,
   That I go safely, and my feet
   are kept from sliding free.

37 Mine en'mies I pursued have,
   and did them overtake;
   Nor did I turn again till I
   an end of them did make.

38 I wounded them, they could not rise;
   they at my feet did fall.

39 Thou girdedst me with strength for
   war;
   my foes thou brought'st down all:

40 And thou hast giv'n to me the necks
   of all mine enemies;
   That I might them destroy and slay,
   who did against me rise.

41 They cried out, but there was none
   that would or could them save;
   Yea, they did cry unto the Lord,
   but he no answer gave.

42 Then did I beat them small as dust
   before the wind that flies;
   And I did cast them out like dirt
   upon the street that lies.

43 Thou mad'st me free from people's
   and heathen's head to be: [strife,
   A people whom I have not known
   shall service do to me.

44 At hearing they shall me obey,
   to me they shall submit.

45 Strangers for fear shall fade away,
   who in close places sit.

46 God lives, bless'd be my Rock; the
   of my health praised be.   [God

47 God doth avenge me, and subdues
   the people under me.

48 He saves me from mine enemies;
   yea, thou hast lifted me
   Above my foes; and from the man
   of vi'lence set me free.

49 Therefore to thee will I give thanks
   the heathen folk among;
   And to thy name, O Lord, I will
   sing praises in a song.

50 He great deliv'rance gives his king:
   he mercy doth extend
   To David, his anointed one,
   and his seed without end.

PSALM 19.

1 THE heav'ns God's glory do declare,
   the skies his hand-works preach:

2 Day utters speech to day, and night
   to night doth knowledge teach.

3 There is no speech nor tongue to which
    their voice doth not extend:
4 Their line is gone through all the earth,
    their words to the world's end.
    In them he set the sun a tent;
5   Who, bridegroom-like, forth goes
   From 's chamber, as a strong man
    to run his race rejoice.   [doth
6 From heav'n's end is his going forth,
    circling to th' end again;
  And there is nothing from his heat
    that hidden doth remain.
7 God's law is perfect, and converts
    the soul in sin that lies:
  God's testimony is most sure,
    and makes the simple wise.
8 The statutes of the Lord are right,
    and do rejoice the heart:
  The Lord's command is pure, and
    light to the eyes impart.   [doth
9 Unspotted is the fear of God,
    and doth endure for ever:
  The judgments of the Lord are true
    and righteous altogether.
10 They more than gold, yea, much fine
    to be desired are: [gold,
  Than honey, honey from the comb
    that droppeth, sweeter far.
11 Moreover, they thy servant warn
    how he his life should frame:
  A great reward provided is
    for them that keep the same.
12 Who can his errors understand?
    O cleanse thou me within
13 From secret faults. Thy servant keep
    from all presumptuous sin:
  And do not suffer them to have
    dominion over me:
  Then, righteous and innocent,
    I from much sin shall be.
14 The words which from my mouth proceed,
    the thoughts sent from my heart,
  Accept, O Lord, for thou my   [strength
    and my Redeemer art.

PSALM 20.

1 JEHOVAH hear thee in the day
    when trouble he doth send:
  And let the name of Jacob's God
    thee from all ill defend.
2 O let him help send from above,
    out of his sanctuary:
  From Sion, his own holy hill,
    let him give strength to thee.

3 Let him remember all thy gifts,
    accept thy sacrifice:
4 Grant thee thine heart's wish, and fulfil
    thy thoughts and counsel wise.
5 In thy salvation we will joy;
    In our God's name we will
  Display our banners: and the Lord
    thy prayers all fulfil.
6 Now know I God his king doth save:
    he from his holy heav'n
  Will hear him, with the saving strength
    by his own right hand giv'n.
7 In chariots some put confidence,
    some horses trust upon:
  But we remember will the name
    of our Lord God alone.
8 We rise, and upright stand, when   [they
    are bowed down, and fall.
9 Deliver, Lord; and let the King
    us hear, when we do call.

PSALM 21.

1 THE king in thy great strength, O   [Lord,
    shall very joyful be:
  In thy salvation rejoice
    how veh'mently shall he!
2 Thou hast bestowed upon him
    all that his heart would have;
  And thou from him didst not with-   [hold
    whate'er his lips did crave.
3 For thou with blessings him pre-   [vent'st
    of goodness manifold;
  And thou hast set upon his head
    a crown of purest gold.
4 When he desired life of thee,
    thou life to him didst give;
  Ev'n such a length of days, that he
    for evermore should live.
5 In thy salvation wrought by thee
    his glory is made great;
  Honour and comely majesty
    thou hast upon him set.
6 Because that thou for evermore
    most blessed hast him made;
  And thou hast with thy countenance
    made him exceeding glad.
7 Because the king upon the Lord
    his confidence doth lay;
  And through the grace of the most   [High
    shall not be mov'd away.
8 Thine hand shall all those men find
    that en'mies are to thee;   [out
  Ev'n thy right hand shall find out
    of thee that haters be.   [those

9 Like fiery ov'n thou shalt them make,
    when kindled is thine ire;
God shall them swallow in his wrath,
    devour them shall the fire.

10 Their fruit from earth thou shalt
    destroy,
    their seed men from among:

11 For they beyond their might 'gainst
    thee
    did plot mischief and wrong.

12 Thou therefore shalt make them turn
    back,
    when thou thy shafts shalt place
Upon thy strings, made ready all
    to fly against their face.

13 In thy great pow'r and strength, O
    be thou exalted high;   [Lord,
So shall we sing with joyful hearts,
    thy power praise shall we.

PSALM 22.

1 MY God, my God, why hast thou
    forsaken? why so far   [me
Art thou from helping me, and from
    my words that roaring are?

2 All day, my God, to thee I cry,
    yet am not heard by thee;
And in the season of the night
    I cannot silent be.

3 But thou art holy, thou that dost
    inhabit Isr'el's praise.

4 Our fathers hop'd in thee, they hop'd,
    and thou didst them release.

5 When unto thee they sent their cry,
    to them deliv'rance came:
Because they put their trust in thee,
    they were not put to shame.

6 But as for me, a worm I am,
    and as no man am priz'd:
Reproach of men I am, and by
    the people am despis'd.

7 All that me see laugh me to scorn;
    shoot out the lip do they;
They nod and shake their heads at
    and, mocking, thus do say,   [me,

8 This man did trust in God, that he
    would free him by his might:
Let him deliver him, sith he
    had in him such delight.

9 But thou art he out of the womb
    that didst me safely take;
When I was on my mother's breasts
    thou me to hope didst make.

10 And I was cast upon thy care,
    ev'n from the womb till now;
And from my mother's belly, Lord,
    my God and guide art thou.

11 Be not far off, for grief is near,
    and none to help is found.

12 Bulls many compass me, strong bulls
    of Bashan me surround.

13 Their mouths they open'd wide on
    upon me gape did they,   [me,
Like to a lion ravening
    and roaring for his prey.

14 Like water I'm pour'd out, my bones
    all out of joint do part:
Amidst my bowels, as the wax,
    so melted is my heart.

15 My strength is like a potsherd dry'd;
    my tongue it cleaveth fast
Unto my jaws; and to the dust
    of death thou brought me hast.

16 For dogs have compass'd me about:
    the wicked, that did meet
In their assembly, me inclos'd;
    they pierc'd my hands and feet.

17 I all my bones may tell; they do
    upon me look and stare.

18 Upon my vesture lots they cast,
    and clothes among them share.

19 But be not far, O Lord, my strength;
    haste to give help to me.

20 From sword my soul, from pow'r o'
    my darling set thou free.   [dogs

21 Out of the roaring lion's mouth
    do thou me shield and save:
For from the horns of unicorns
    an ear to me thou gave.

22 I will show forth thy name unto
    those that my brethren are;
Amidst the congregation
    thy praise I will declare.

23 Praise ye the Lord, who do him fear;
    him glorify all ye
The seed of Jacob: fear him all
    that Isr'el's children be.

24 For he despis'd not nor abhorr'd
    th' afflicted's misery;
Nor from him hid his face, but heard
    when he to him did cry.

25 Within the congregation great
    my praise shall be of thee;
My vows before them that him fear
    shall be perform'd by me.

26 The meek shall eat, and shall be
    they also praise shall give   [fill'd;
Unto the Lord that do him seek:
    your heart shall ever live.

27 All ends of th' earth remember shall,
    and turn the Lord unto;
All kindreds of the nations
    to him shall homage do:

28 Because the kingdom to the Lord
doth appertain as his;
Likewise among the nations
the Governor he is.

29 Earth's fat ones eat, and worship
all who to dust descend [shall:
Shall bow to him; none of them can
his soul from death defend.

30 A seed shall service do to him;
unto the Lord it shall
Be for a generation
reckon'd in ages all.

31 They shall come, and they shall de-
his truth and righteousness [clare
Unto a people yet unborn,
and that he hath done this.

PSALM 23.

1 THE Lord's my shepherd, I'll not
2 He makes me down to lie [want.
In pastures green: he leadeth me
the quiet waters by.

3 My soul he doth restore again;
and me to walk doth make
Within the paths of righteousness,
ev'n for his own name's sake.

4 Yea, though I walk in death's dark
yet will I fear none ill: [vale,
For thou art with me; and thy rod
and staff me comfort still.

5 My table thou hast furnished
in presence of my foes;
My head thou dost with oil anoint,
and my cup overflows.

6 Goodness and mercy all my life
shall surely follow me:
And in God's house for evermore
my dwelling-place shall be.

PSALM 24.

1 THE earth belongs unto the Lord,
and all that it contains;
The world that is inhabited,
and all that there remains.

2 For the foundations thereof
he on the seas did lay,
And he hath it established
upon the floods to stay.

3 Who is the man that shall ascend
into the hill of God?
Or who within his holy place
shall have a firm abode?

4 Whose hands are clean, whose heart
and unto vanity [is pure,
Who hath not lifted up his soul,
nor sworn deceitfully.

5 He from th' Eternal shall receive
the blessing him upon,
And righteousness, ev'n from the
of his salvation. [God

6 This is the generation
that after him enquire,
O Jacob, who do seek thy face
with their whole heart's desire.

7 Ye gates, lift up your heads on high;
ye doors that last for aye,
Be lifted up, that so the King
of glory enter may.

8 But who of glory is the King?
The mighty Lord is this;
Ev'n that same Lord, that great in
and strong in battle is. [might

9 Ye gates, lift up your heads; ye doors,
doors that do last for aye,
Be lifted up, that so the King
of glory enter may.

10 But who is he that is the King
of glory? who is this?
The Lord of hosts, and none but he,
the King of glory is.

PSALM 25.

1 TO thee I lift my soul:
2 O Lord, I trust in thee:
My God, let me not be asham'd,
nor foes triumph o'er me.

3 Let none that wait on thee
be put to shame at all;
But those that without cause trans-
let shame upon them fall. [gress,

4 Show me thy ways, O Lord;
thy paths, O teach thou me:

5 And do thou lead me in thy truth,
therein my teacher be:
For thou art God that dost
to me salvation send,
And I upon thee all the day
expecting do attend.

6 Thy tender mercies, Lord,
I pray thee to remember,
And loving-kindnesses; for they
have been of old for ever.

7 My sins and faults of youth
do thou, O Lord, forget:
After thy mercy think on me,
and for thy goodness great.

8 God good and upright is:
the way he'll sinners show.

9 The meek in judgment he will guide,
and make his path to know.

10 The whole paths of the Lord
are truth and mercy sure,

To those that do his cov'nant keep,
and testimonies pure.

11 Now, for thine own name's sake,
O Lord, I thee entreat
To pardon mine iniquity;
for it is very great.

12 What man is he that fears
the Lord, and doth him serve?
Him shall he teach the way that he
shall chuse, and still observe.

13 His soul shall dwell at ease;
and his posterity
Shall flourish still, and of the earth
inheritors shall be.

14 With those that fear him is
the secret of the Lord;
The knowledge of his covenant
he will to them afford.

15 Mine eyes unto the Lord
continually are set;
For he it is that shall bring forth
my feet out of the net.

16 Turn unto me thy face,
and to me mercy show;
Because that I am desolate,
and am brought very low.

17 My heart's griefs are increas'd:
me from distress relieve.

18 See mine affliction and my pain,
and all my sins forgive.

19 Consider thou my foes,
because they many are;
And it a cruel hatred is
which against me bear.

20 O do thou keep my soul,
do thou deliver me:
And let me never be asham'd,
because I trust in thee.

21 Let uprightness and truth
keep me, who thee attend.

22 Redemption, Lord, to Israel
from all his troubles send.

Another of the same.

1 TO thee I lift my soul, O Lord:
2 My God, I trust in thee:
Let me not be asham'd; let not
my foes triumph o'er me.

3 Yea, let thou none ashamed be
that do on thee attend:
Ashamed let them be, O Lord,
who without cause offend.

4 Thy ways, Lord, show; teach me thy
paths:

5 Lead me in truth, teach me:
For my safety thou art God;
all day I wait on thee.

6 Thy mercies, that most tender are,
do thou, O Lord, remember,
And loving-kindnesses; for they
have been of old for ever.

7 Let not the errors of my youth,
nor sins, remember'd be:
In mercy, for thy goodness' sake,
O Lord, remember me.

8 The Lord is good and gracious,
he upright is also:
He therefore sinners will instruct
in ways that they should go.

9 The meek and lowly he will guide
in judgment just alway:
To meek and poor afflicted ones
he'll clearly teach his way.

10 The whole paths of the Lord our
are truth and mercy sure, [God
To such as keep his covenant,
and testimonies pure.

11 Now, for thine own name's sake, O
I humbly thee entreat [Lord,
To pardon mine iniquity;
for it is very great.

12 What man fears God? him shall he
the way that he shall chuse. [teach

13 His soul shall dwell at ease; his seed
the earth, as heirs, shall use.

14 The secret of the Lord is with
such as do fear his name;
And he his holy covenant
will manifest to them.

15 Towards the Lord my waiting eyes
continually are set;
For he it is that shall bring forth
my feet out of the net.

16 O turn thee unto me, O God,
have mercy me upon;
Because I solitary am,
and in affliction.

17 Enlarg'd the griefs are of mine heart;
me from distress relieve.

18 See mine affliction and my pain,
and all my sins forgive.

19 Consider thou mine enemies,
because they many are;
And it a cruel hatred is
which they against me bear.

20 O do thou keep my soul; O God,
do thou deliver me:
Let me not be asham'd; for I
do put my trust in thee.

21 O let integrity and truth
keep me, who thee attend.

22 Redemption, Lord, to Israel
from all his troubles send.

PSALM 26.

1 JUDGE me, O Lord, for I have
in mine integrity: [walk'd
I trusted also in the Lord;
  slide therefore shall not I.

2 Examine me, and do me prove;
  try heart and reins, O God:

3 For thy love is before mine eyes,
  thy truth's paths I have trode.

4 With persons vain I have not sat,
  nor with dissemblers gone:

5 Th' assembly of ill men I hate;
  to sit with such I shun.

6 Mine hands in innocence, O Lord,
  I'll wash and purify;
So to thine holy altar go,
  and compass it will I:

7 That I, with voice of thanksgiving,
  may publish and declare,
And tell of all thy mighty works,
  that great and wondrous are.

8 The habitation of thy house,
  Lord, I have loved well;
Yea, in that place I do delight
  where doth thine honour dwell.

9 With sinners gather not my soul,
  and such as blood would spill:

10 Whose hands mischievous plots, right
  corrupting bribes do fill.   [hand

11 But as for me, I will walk on
  in mine integrity:
Do thou redeem me, and, O Lord,
  be merciful to me.

12 My foot upon an even place
  doth stand with stedfastness:
Within the congregations
  th' Eternal I will bless.

PSALM 27.

1 THE Lord's my light and saving
  health,
who shall make me dismay'd?
My life's strength is the Lord, of
  then shall I be afraid?   [whom

2 When as mine enemies and foes,
  most wicked persons all,
To eat my flesh against me rose,
  they stumbled and did fall.

3 Against me though an host encamp,
  my heart yet fearless is:
Though war against me rise, I will
  be confident in this.

4 One thing I of the Lord desir'd,
  and will seek to obtain,
That all days of my life I may
  within God's house remain;

That I the beauty of the Lord
  behold may and admire,
And that I in his holy place
  may rev'rently enquire.

5 For he in his pavilion shall
  me hide in evil days;
In secret of his tent me hide,
  and on a rock me raise.

6 And now, ev'n at this present time,
  mine head shall lifted be
Above all those that are my foes,
  and round encompass me:
Therefore unto his tabernacle
  I'll sacrifices bring
Of joyfulness; I'll sing, yea, I
  to God will praises sing.

7 O Lord, give ear unto my voice,
  when I do cry to thee;
Upon me also mercy have,
  and do thou answer me.

8 When thou didst say, Seek ye my
  then unto thee reply   [face,
Thus did my heart, Above all things
  thy face, Lord, seek will I.

9 Far from me hide not thou thy face;
  put not away from thee
Thy servant in thy wrath: thou hast
  an helper been to me.
O God of my salvation,
  leave me not, nor forsake:

10 Though me my parents both should
  the Lord will me up take. [leave,

11 O Lord, instruct me in thy way,
  to me a leader be
In a plain path, because of those
  that hatred bear to me.

12 Give me not to mine en'mies' will;
  for witnesses that lie
Against me risen are, and such
  as breathe out cruelty.

13 I fainted had, unless that I
  believed had to see
The Lord's own goodness in the land
  of them that living be.

14 Wait on the Lord, and be thou
  strong,
and he shall strength afford
Unto thine heart; yea, do thou wait,
  I say, upon the Lord.

PSALM 28.

1 TO thee I'll cry, O Lord, my rock;
  hold not thy peace to me;
Lest like those that to pit descend
  I by thy silence be.

15

2 The voice hear of my humble pray'rs,
    when unto thee I cry;
When to thine holy oracle
    I lift mine hands on high.

3 With ill men draw me not away
    that work iniquity;
That speak peace to their friends,
    while in
    their hearts doth mischief lie.

4 Give them according to their deeds
    and ills endeavoured:
And as their handy-works deserve,
    to them be rendered.

5 God shall not build, but them de-
    who would not understand [stroy,
The Lord's own works, nor did
    the doing of his hand.   [regard

6 For ever blessed be the Lord,
    for graciously he heard
The voice of my petitions,
    and prayers did regard.

7 The Lord's my strength and shield;
    upon him did rely;   [my heart
And I am helped: hence my heart
    doth joy exceedingly,
And with my song I will him praise.

8 Their strength is God alone:
He also is the saving strength
    of his anointed one.

9 O thine own people do thou save,
    bless thine inheritance;
Them also do thou feed, and them
    for evermore advance.

PSALM 29.

1 GIVE ye unto the Lord, ye sons
    that of the mighty be,
All strength and glory to the Lord
    with cheerfulness give ye.

2 Unto the Lord the glory give
    that to his name is due;
And in the beauty of holiness
    unto JEHOVAH bow.

3 The Lord's voice on the waters is;
    the God of majesty
Doth thunder, and on multitudes
    of waters sitteth he.

4 A pow'rful voice it is that comes
    out from the Lord most high;
The voice of that great Lord is full
    of glorious majesty.

5 The voice of the Eternal doth
    asunder cedars tear;
Yea, God the Lord doth cedars break
    that Lebanon doth bear.

6 He makes them like a calf to skip,
    ev'n that great Lebanon,
And, like to a young unicorn,
    the mountain Sirion.

7 God's voice divides the flames of fire;
8   The desert it doth shake:
The Lord doth make the wilderness
    of Kadesh all to quake.

9 God's voice doth make the hinds to
    it makes the forest bare: [calve,
And in his temple ev'ry one
    his glory doth declare.

10 The Lord sits on the floods; the Lord
    sits King, and ever shall.
11 The Lord will give his people
    strength,
    and with peace bless them all.

PSALM 30.

1 LORD, I will thee extol, for thou
    hast lifted me on high,
And over me thou to rejoice
    mad'st not mine enemy.

2 O thou who art the Lord my God,
    I in distress to thee,
With loud cries lifted up my voice,
    and thou hast healed me.

3 O Lord, my soul thou hast brought
    and rescu'd from the grave; [up,
That I to pit should not go down,
    alive thou didst me save.

4 O ye that are his holy ones,
    sing praise unto the Lord;
And give unto him thanks, when ye
    his holiness record.

5 For but a moment lasts his wrath;
    life in his favour lies:
Weeping may for a night endure,
    at morn doth joy arise.

6 In my prosperity I said,
    that nothing shall me move.

7 O Lord, thou hast my mountain
    made
    to stand strong by thy love:
But when that thou, O gracious God,
    didst hide thy face from me,
Then quickly was my prosp'rous
    turn'd into misery.   [state
8 Wherefore unto the Lord my cry
    I caused to ascend:
My humble supplication
    I to the Lord did send.

9 What profit is there in my blood,
    when I go down to pit?
Shall unto thee the dust give praise?
    thy truth declare shall it?

16

10 Hear, Lord, have mercy; help me,
    Lord:
11 Thou turned hast my sadness
    To dancing; yea, my sackcloth loos'd,
      and girded me with gladness;
12 That sing thy praise my glory may,
    and never silent be.
    O Lord my God, for evermore
      I will give thanks to thee.

PSALM 31.

1 IN thee, O Lord, I put my trust,
    sham'd let me never be;
    According to thy righteousness
      do thou deliver me.
2 Bow down thine ear to me, with
    send me deliverance: [speed
    To save me, my strong rock be thou,
      and my house of defence.
3 Because thou art my rock, and thee
    I for my fortress take;
    Therefore do thou me lead and guide,
      ev'n for thine own name's sake.
4 And sith thou art my strength, there-
    pull me out of the net,   [fore
    Which they in subtilty for me
      so privily have set.
5 Into thine hands I do commit
    my sp'rit: for thou art he,
    O thou, JEHOVAH, God of truth,
      that hast redeemed me.
6 Those that do lying vanities
    regard, I have abhorr'd:
    But as for me, my confidence
      is fixed on the Lord.
7 I'll in thy mercy gladly joy:
    for thou my miseries
    Consider'd hast; thou hast my soul
      known in adversities:
8 And thou hast not inclosed me
    within the en'my's hand;
    And by thee have my feet been made
      in a large room to stand.
9 O Lord, upon me mercy have,
    for trouble is on me:
    Mine eye, my belly, and my soul,
      with grief consumed be.
10 Because my life with grief is spent,
    my years with sighs and groans:
    My strength doth fail; and for my sin
      consumed are my bones.
11 I was a scorn to all my foes,
    and to my friends a fear;
    And specially reproach'd of those
      that were my neighbours near:
    When they me saw they from me fled.
12 Ev'n so I am forgot,

As men are out of mind when dead:
    I'm like a broken pot.
13 For slanders I of many heard;
    fear compass'd me, while they
    Against me did consult, and plot
      to take my life away.
14 But as for me, O Lord, my trust
    upon thee I did lay;
    And I to thee, Thou art my God,
      did confidently say.
15 My times are wholly in thine hand:
    do thou deliver me
    From their hands that mine enemies
      and persecutors be.
16 Thy countenance to shine do thou
    upon thy servant make:
    Unto me give salvation,
      for thy great mercies' sake.
17 Let me not be asham'd, O Lord,
    for on thee call'd I have:
    Let wicked men be sham'd, let them
      be silent in the grave.
18 To silence put the lying lips,
    that grievous things do say,
    And hard reports, in pride and scorn,
      on righteous men do lay.
19 How great 's the goodness thou for
    them
      that fear thee keep'st in store,
    And wrought'st for them that trust
      the sons of men before!   [in thee
20 In secret of thy presence thou
    shalt hide them from man's pride:
    From strife of tongues thou closely
      as in a tent, them hide.   [shalt,
21 All praise and thanks be to the Lord;
    for he hath magnify'd
    His wondrous love to me within
      a city fortify'd.
22 For from thine eyes cut off I am,
    I in my haste had said;
    My voice yet heard'st thou, when to
      with cries my moan I made.   [thee
23 O love the Lord, all ye his saints;
    because the Lord doth guard
    The faithful, and he plenteously
      proud doers doth reward.
24 Be of good courage, and he strength
    unto your heart shall send,
    All ye whose hope and confidence
      doth on the Lord depend.

PSALM 32.

1 O BLESSED is the man to whom
    is freely pardoned
    All the transgression he hath done,
      whose sin is covered.

2 Bless'd is the man to whom the Lord
    imputeth not his sin,
And in whose sp'rit there is no guile,
    nor fraud is found therein.

3 When as I did refrain my speech,
    and silent was my tongue,
My bones then waxed old, because
    I roared all day long.
4 For upon me both day and night
    thine hand did heavy lie,
So that my moisture turned is
    in summer's drought thereby.

5 I thereupon have unto thee
    my sin acknowledged,
And likewise mine iniquity
    I have not covered:
I will confess unto the Lord
    my trespasses, said I;
And of my sin thou freely didst
    forgive th' iniquity.

6 For this shall ev'ry godly one
    his prayer make to thee;
In such a time he shall thee seek,
    as found thou mayest be.
Surely, when floods of waters great
    do swell up to the brim,
They shall not overwhelm his soul,
    nor once come near to him.

7 Thou art my hiding-place, thou shalt
    from trouble keep me free:
Thou with songs of deliverance
    about shalt compass me.
8 I will instruct thee, and thee teach
    the way that thou shalt go;
And, with mine eye upon thee set,
    I will direction show.

9 Then be not like the horse or mule,
    which do not understand;
Whose mouth, lest they come near to
    a bridle must command.   [thee,
10 Unto the man that wicked is
    his sorrows shall abound;
But him that trusteth in the Lord
    mercy shall compass round.

11 Ye righteous, in the Lord be glad,
    in him do ye rejoice:
All ye that upright are in heart,
    for joy lift up your voice.

PSALM 33.

1 YE righteous, in the Lord rejoice;
    it comely is and right,
That upright men, with thankful
    voice,
    should praise the Lord of might.

2 Praise God with harp, and unto him
    sing with the psaltery;
Upon a ten-string'd instrument
    make ye sweet melody.

3 A new song to him sing, and play
    with loud noise skilfully;
4 For right is God's word, all his works
    are done in verity.

5 To judgment and to righteousness
    a love he beareth still;
The loving-kindness of the Lord
    the earth throughout doth fill.

6 The heavens by the word of God
    did their beginning take;
And by the breathing of his mouth
    he all their hosts did make.
7 The waters of the seas he brings
    together as an heap;
And in storehouses, as it were,
    he layeth up the deep.

8 Let earth, and all that live therein,
    with rev'rence fear the Lord;
Let all the world's inhabitants
    dread him with one accord.
9 For he did speak the word, and done
    it was without delay;
Established it firmly stood,
    whatever he did say.

10 God doth the counsel bring to nought
    which heathen folk do take;
And what the people do devise
    of none effect doth make.
11 O but the counsel of the Lord
    doth stand for ever sure;
And of his heart the purposes
    from age to age endure.

12 That nation blessed is, whose God
    JEHOVAH is, and those
A blessed people are, whom for
    his heritage he chose.

13 The Lord from heav'n sees and be-
    all sons of men full well: [holds
14 He views all from his dwelling-place
    that in the earth do dwell.

15 He forms their hearts alike, and all
    their doings he observes.
16 Great hosts save not a king, much
    strength
    no mighty man preserves.

17 An horse for preservation
    is a deceitful thing;
And by the greatness of his strength
    can no deliv'rance bring.
18 Behold, on those that do him fear
    the Lord doth set his eye;
Ev'n those who on his mercy do
    with confidence rely.

19 From death to free their soul, in
  life unto them to yield.   [dearth
20 Our soul doth wait upon the Lord;
  he is our help and shield.

21 Sith in his holy name we trust,
  our heart shall joyful be.
22 Lord, let thy mercy be on us,
  as we do hope in thee.

PSALM 34.

1 GOD will I bless all times; his
    praise
  my mouth shall still express.
2 My soul shall boast in God: the meek
  shall hear with joyfulness.
3 Extol the Lord with me, let us
  exalt his name together.
4 I sought the Lord, he heard, and did
  me from all fears deliver.

5 They look'd to him, and lighten'd
    were:
  not shamed were their faces.
6 This poor man cry'd, God heard, and
  him from all his distresses. [sav'd
7 The angel of the Lord encamps,
  and round encompasseth
All those about that do him fear,
  and them delivereth.

8 O taste and see that God is good:
  who trusts in him is bless'd.
9 Fear God his saints: none that him
  shall be with want oppress'd. [fear
10 The lions young may hungry be,
  and they may lack their food:
But they that truly seek the Lord
  shall not lack any good.

11 O children, hither do ye come,
  and unto me give ear;
I shall you teach to understand
  how ye the Lord should fear.
12 What man is he that life desires,
  to see good would live long?
13 Thy lips refrain from speaking guile
  and from ill words thy tongue.

14 Depart from ill, do good, seek peace,
  pursue it earnestly.
15 God's eyes are on the just; his ears
  are open to their cry.
16 The face of God is set against
  those that do wickedly,
That he may quite out from the earth
  cut off their memory.

17 The righteous cry unto the Lord,
  he unto them gives ear;
And they out of their troubles all
  by him deliver'd are.

18 The Lord is ever nigh to them
  that be of broken sp'rit;
To them he safety doth afford
  that are in heart contrite.
19 The troubles that afflict the just
  in number many be;
But yet at length out of them all
  the Lord doth set him free.
20 He carefully his bones doth keep,
  whatever can befall;
That not so much as one of them
  can broken be at all.

21 Ill shall the wicked slay; laid waste
  shall be who hate the just.
22 The Lord redeems his servants'
    souls;
  none perish that him trust.

PSALM 35.

1 PLEAD, Lord, with those that
    plead; and fight
  with those that fight with me.
2 Of shield and buckler take thou hold,
  stand up mine help to be.
3 Draw also out the spear, and do
  against them stop the way
That me pursue: unto my soul,
  I'm thy salvation, say.

4 Let them confounded be and sham'd
  that for my soul have sought:
Who plot my hurt turn'd back be
  and to confusion brought. [they,
5 Let them be like unto the chaff
  that flies before the wind;
And let the angel of the Lord
  pursue them hard behind.

6 With darkness cover thou their way,
  and let it slipp'ry prove;
And let the angel of the Lord
  pursue them from above.
7 For without cause have they for me
  their net hid in a pit,
They also have without a cause
  for my soul digged it.

8 Let ruin seize him unawares;
  his net he hid withal
Himself let catch; and in the same
  destruction let him fall.
9 My soul in God shall joy; and glad
  in his salvation be:
10 And all my bones shall say, O Lord,
  who is like unto thee,

Which dost the poor set free from
  that is for him too strong;   [him
The poor and needy from the man
  that spoils and does him wrong?

11 False witnesses rose; to my charge
  things I not knew they laid.
12 They, to the spoiling of my soul,
  me ill for good repaid.
13 But as for me, when they were sick,
  in sackcloth sad I mourn'd:
  My humbled soul did fast, my pray'r
  into my bosom turn'd.
14 Myself I did behave as he
  had been my friend or brother;
  I heavily bow'd down, as one
  that mourneth for his mother.
15 But in my trouble they rejoic'd,
  gath'ring themselves together;
  Yea, abjects vile together did
  themselves against me gather:
  I knew it not; they did me tear,
  and quiet would not be.
16 With mocking hypocrites, at feasts
  they gnash'd their teeth at me.
17 How long, Lord, look'st thou on? from those
  destructions they intend
  Rescue my soul, from lions young
  my darling do defend.
18 I will give thanks to thee, O Lord,
  within th' assembly great;
  And where much people gather'd are
  thy praises forth will set.
19 Let not my wrongful enemies
  proudly rejoice o'er me;
  Nor who me hate without a cause,
  let them wink with the eye.
20 For peace they do not speak at all;
  but crafty plots prepare
  Against all those within the land
  that meek and quiet are.
21 With mouths set wide, they 'gainst
  Ha, ha! our eye doth see. [me said,
22 Lord, thou hast seen, hold not thy
  Lord, be not far from me. [peace;
23 Stir up thyself; wake, that thou
  judgment to me afford, [may'st
  Ev'n to my cause, O thou that art
  my only God and Lord.
24 O Lord my God, do thou me judge
  after thy righteousness;
  And let them not their joy 'gainst me
  triumphantly express:
25 Nor let them say within their hearts,
  Ah, we would have it thus;
  Nor suffer them to say, that he
  is swallow'd up by us.
26 Sham'd and confounded be they all
  that at my hurt are glad;
  Let those against me that do boast
  with shame and scorn be clad.

27 Let them that love my righteous
  cause
  be glad, shout, and not cease
  To say, The Lord be magnify'd,
  who loves his servant's peace.
28 Thy righteousness shall also be
  declared by my tongue;
  The praises that belong to thee
  speak shall it all day long.

PSALM 36.

1 THE wicked man's transgression
  within my heart thus says,
  Undoubtedly the fear of God
  is not before his eyes.
2 Because himself he flattereth
  in his own blinded eye,
  Until the hatefulness be found
  of his iniquity.
3 Words from his mouth proceeding
  fraud and iniquity: [are,
  He to be wise, and to do good,
  hath left off utterly.
4 He mischief, lying on his bed,
  most cunningly doth plot:
  He sets himself in ways not good,
  ill he abhorreth not.
5 Thy mercy, Lord, is in the heav'ns;
  thy truth doth reach the clouds:
6 Thy justice is like mountains great;
  thy judgments deep as floods:
  Lord, thou preservest man and beast.
7 How precious is thy grace!
  Therefore in shadow of thy wings
  men's sons their trust shall place.
8 They with the fatness of thy house
  shall be well satisfy'd;
  From rivers of thy pleasures thou
  wilt drink to them provide.
9 Because of life the fountain pure
  remains alone with thee;
  And in that purest light of thine
  we clearly light shall see.
10 Thy loving-kindness unto them
  continue that thee know;
  And still on men upright in heart
  thy righteousness bestow.
11 Let not the foot of cruel pride
  come, and against me stand;
  And let me not removed be,
  Lord, by the wicked's hand.
12 There fallen are they, and ruined,
  that work iniquities:
  Cast down they are, and never shall
  be able to arise.

PSALM 37.

1 FOR evil doers fret thou not
thyself unquietly;
Nor do thou envy bear to those
that work iniquity.

2 For, even like unto the grass,
soon be cut down shall they;
And, like the green and tender herb,
they wither shall away.

3 Set thou thy trust upon the Lord,
and be thou doing good;
And so thou in the land shalt dwell,
and verily have food.

4 Delight thyself in God; he'll give
thine heart's desire to thee.

5 Thy way to God commit, him trust,
it bring to pass shall he.

6 And, like unto the light, he shall
thy righteousness display;
And he thy judgment shall bring [forth
like noon-tide of the day.

7 Rest in the Lord, and patiently
wait for him: do not fret
For him who, prosp'ring in his way,
success in sin doth get.

8 Do thou from anger cease, and wrath
see thou forsake also:
Fret not thyself in any wise,
that evil thou should'st do.

9 For those that evil doers are
shall be cut off and fall:
But those that wait upon the Lord
the earth inherit shall.

10 For yet a little while, and then
the wicked shall not be;
His place thou shalt consider well,
but it thou shalt not see.

11 But by inheritance the earth
the meek ones shall possess:
They also shall delight themselves
in an abundant peace.

12 The wicked plots against the just,
and at him whets his teeth:

13 The Lord shall laugh at him, because
his day he coming seeth.

14 The wicked have drawn out the
sword,
and bent their bow, to slay
The poor and needy, and to kill
men of an upright way.

15 But their own sword, which they
have drawn,
shall enter their own heart:
Their bows which they have bent
shall break,
and into pieces part.

16 A little that a just man hath
is more and better far
Than is the wealth of many such
as lewd and wicked are.

17 For sinners' arms shall broken be;
but God the just sustains.

18 God knows the just man's days, and
their heritage remains. [still

19 They shall not be asham'd when they
the evil time do see;
And when the days of famine are,
they satisfy'd shall be.

20 But wicked men, and foes of God,
as fat of lambs, decay;
They shall consume, yea, into smoke
they shall consume away.

21 The wicked borrows, but the same
again he doth not pay;
Whereas the righteous mercy shows,
and gives his own away.

22 For such as blessed be of him
the earth inherit shall;
And they that cursed are of him
shall be destroyed all.

23 A good man's footsteps by the Lord
are ordered aright;
And in the way wherein he walks
he greatly doth delight.

24 Although he fall, yet shall he not
be cast down utterly;
Because the Lord with his own hand
upholds him mightily.

25 I have been young, and now am old,
yet have I never seen
The just man left, nor that his seed
for bread have beggars been.

26 He's ever merciful, and lends:
his seed is bless'd therefore.

27 Depart from evil, and do good,
and dwell for evermore.

28 For God loves judgment, and his
leaves not in any case; [saints
They are kept ever: but cut off
shall be the sinner's race.

29 The just inherit shall the land,
and ever in it dwell:

30 The just man's mouth doth wisdom
speak;
his tongue doth judgment tell.

31 In 's heart the law is of his God,
his steps slide not away.

32 The wicked man doth watch the just,
and seeketh him to slay.

33 Yet him the Lord will not forsake,
nor leave him in his hands:
The righteous will he not condemn,
when he in judgment stands.

34 Wait on the Lord, and keep his way,
  and thee exalt shall he
Th' earth to inherit; when cut off
  the wicked thou shalt see.

35 I saw the wicked great in pow'r,
  spread like a green bay-tree:

36 He pass'd, yea, was not; him I
  sought,
    but found he could not be.

37 Mark thou the perfect, and behold
  the man of uprightness;
Because that surely of this man
  the latter end is peace.

38 But those men that transgressors are
  shall be destroy'd together;
The latter end of wicked men
  shall be cut off for ever.

39 But the salvation of the just
  is from the Lord above;
He in the time of their distress
  their stay and strength doth prove.

40 The Lord shall help, and them
  deliver:
    he shall them free and save
From wicked men; because in him
  their confidence they have.

PSALM 38.

1 IN thy great indignation,
  O Lord, rebuke me not;
Nor on me lay thy chast'ning hand,
  in thy displeasure hot.

2 For in me fast thine arrows stick,
  thine hand doth press me sore:

3 And in my flesh there is no health,
  nor soundness any more.

  This grief I have, because thy wrath
  is forth against me gone;
And in my bones there is no rest,
  for sin that I have done.

4 Because gone up above mine head
  my great transgressions be;
And, as a weighty burden, they
  too heavy are for me.

5 My wounds do stink, and are cor-
  my folly makes it so.   [rupt;

6 I troubled am, and much bow'd
  all day I mourning go.   [down;

7 For a disease that loathsome is
  so fills my loins with pain,
That in my weak and weary flesh
  no soundness doth remain.

8 So feeble and infirm am I,
  and broken am so sore,
That, through disquiet of my heart,
  I have been made to roar.

9 O Lord, all that I do desire
  is still before thine eye;
And of my heart the secret groans
  not hidden are from thee.

10 My heart doth pant incessantly
  my strength doth quite decay;
As for mine eyes, their wonted light
  is from me gone away.

11 My lovers and my friends do stand
  at distance from my sore;
And those do stand aloof that were
  kinsmen and kind before.

12 Yea, they that seek my life lay snares:
  who seek to do me wrong
Speak things mischievous, and de-
  imagine all day long.   [ceits

13 But, as one deaf, that heareth not,
  I suffer'd all to pass;
I as a dumb man did become,
  whose mouth not open'd was:

14 As one that hears not, in whose
  are no reproofs at all.   [mouth

15 For, Lord, I hope in thee; my God,
  thou'lt hear me when I call.

16 For I said, Hear me, lest they should
  rejoice o'er me with pride;
And o'er me magnify themselves,
  when as my foot doth slide.

17 For I am near to halt, my grief
  is still before mine eye:

18 For I'll declare my sin, and grieve
  for mine iniquity.

19 But yet mine en'mies lively are,
  and strong are they beside;
And they that hate me wrongfully
  are greatly multiply'd.

20 And they for good that render ill,
  as en'mies me withstood;
Yea, ev'n for this, because that I
  do follow what is good.

21 Forsake me not, O Lord; my God,
  far from me never be.

22 O Lord, thou my salvation art,
  haste to give help to me.

PSALM 39.

1 I SAID, I will look to my ways,
  lest with my tongue I sin:
In sight of wicked men my mouth
  with bridle I'll keep in.

2 With silence I as dumb became,
  I did myself restrain
From speaking good; but then the
  increased was my pain.   [more

3 My heart within me waxed hot;
  and, while I musing was,

22

The fire did burn; and from my
tongue
  these words I did let pass:
4 Mine end, and measure of my days,
    O Lord, unto me show
What is the same; that I thereby
    my frailty well may know.

5 Lo, thou my days an handbreadth
    mad'st;
  mine age is in thine eye
As nothing: sure each man at best
    is wholly vanity.

6 Sure each man walks in a vain show;
    they vex themselves in vain:
He heaps up wealth, and doth not
    to whom it shall pertain.   [know

7 And now, O Lord, what wait I for?
    my hope is fix'd on thee.
8 Free me from all my trespasses,
    the fool's scorn make not me.
9 Dumb was I, op'ning not my mouth,
    because this work was thine.
10 Thy stroke take from me; by the
    of thine hand I do pine.   [blow
11 When with rebukes thou dost correct
    man for iniquity,
Thou wastes his beauty like a moth:
    sure each man's vanity.

12 Attend my cry, Lord, at my tears
    and pray're not silent be;
I sojourn as my fathers all,
    and stranger am with thee.

13 O spare thou me, that I my strength
    recover may again,
Before me hence I do depart,
    and here no more remain.

1 I WAITED for the Lord my God,
    and patiently did bear;
At length to me he did incline
    my voice and cry to hear.

2 He took me from a fearful pit,
    and from the miry clay,
And on a rock he set my feet,
    establishing my way.

3 He put a new song in my mouth,
    our God to magnify:
Many shall see it, and shall fear,
    and on the Lord rely.

4 O blessed is the man whose trust
    upon the Lord relies;
Respecting not the proud, nor such
    as turn aside to lies.

5 O Lord my God, full many are
    the wonders thou hast done;

Thy gracious thoughts to us-ward far
    above all thoughts are gone;
In order none can reckon them
    to thee: if them declare,
And speak of them I would, they
    than can be number'd are. [more

6 No sacrifice nor offering
    didst thou at all desire;
Mine ears thou bor'd: sin-off'ring
    thou
  and burnt didst not require:
7 Then to the Lord these were my
    I come, behold and see;   [words,
Within the volume of the book
    it written is of me:
8 To do thy will I take delight,
    O thou my God that art;
Yea, that most holy law of thine
    I have within my heart.
9 Within the congregation great
    I righteousness did preach:
Lo, thou dost know, O Lord, that I
    refrained not my speech.

10 I never did within my heart
    conceal thy righteousness;
I thy salvation have declar'd,
    and shown thy faithfulness:
Thy kindness, which most loving is,
    concealed have not I,
Nor from the congregation great
    have hid thy verity.

11 Thy tender mercies, Lord, from me
    O do thou not restrain;
Thy loving-kindness, and thy truth,
    let them me still maintain.

12 For ills past reck'ning compass me,
    and mine iniquities
Such hold upon me taken have,
    I cannot lift mine eyes:

They more than hairs are on mine
    head,
  thence is my heart dismay'd.
13 Be pleased, Lord, to rescue me;
    Lord, hasten to mine aid.
14 Sham'd and confounded be they all
    that seek my soul to kill;
Yea, let them backward driven be,
    and sham'd, that wish me ill.

15 For a reward of this their shame
    confounded let them be,
That in this manner scoffing say,
    Aha, aha! to me.
16 In thee let all be glad, and joy,
    who seeking thee abide;
Who thy salvation love, say still,
    The Lord be magnify'd.

17 I'm poor and needy, yet the Lord
of me a care doth take:
Thou art my help and saviour,
my God, no tarrying make.

PSALM 41.

1 BLESSED is he that wisely doth
the poor man's case consider;
For when the time of trouble is,
the Lord will him deliver.
2 God will him keep, yea, save alive;
on earth he bless'd shall live;
And to his enemies' desire
thou wilt him not up give.

3 God will give strength when he on
of languishing doth mourn; [bed
And in his sickness sore, O Lord,
thou all his bed wilt turn.
4 I said, O Lord, do thou extend
thy mercy unto me;
O do thou heal my soul; for why?
I have offended thee.

5 Those that to me are enemies,
of me do evil say,
When shall he die, that so his name
may perish quite away?
6 To see me if he comes, he speaks
vain words: but then his heart
Heaps mischief to it, which he tells,
when forth he doth depart.

7 My haters jointly whispering,
'gainst me my hurt devise.
8 Mischief, say they, cleaves fast to
him;
he li'th, and shall not rise.
9 Yea, ev'n mine own familiar friend,
on whom I did rely,
Who ate my bread, ev'n he his heel
against me lifted high.

10 But, Lord, be merciful to me,
and up again me raise,
That I may justly them requite
according to their ways.
11 By this I know that certainly
I favour'd am by thee;
Because my hateful enemy
triumphs not over me.

12 But as for me, thou me uphold'st
in mine integrity;
And me before thy countenance
thou sett'st continually.
13 The Lord, the God of Israel,
be bless'd for ever then,
From age to age eternally.
Amen, yea, and amen.

PSALM 42.

1 LIKE as the hart for water-brooks
in thirst doth pant and bray;
So pants my longing soul, O God,
that come to thee I may.
2 My soul for God, the living God,
doth thirst: when shall I near
Unto thy countenance approach,
and in God's sight appear?

3 My tears have unto me been meat,
both in the night and day,
While unto me continually,
Where is thy God? they say.
4 My soul is poured out in me,
when this I think upon;
Because that with the multitude
I heretofore had gone:

With them into God's house I went,
with voice of joy and praise;
Yea, with the multitude that kept
the solemn holy days.
5 O why art thou cast down, my soul?
why in me so dismay'd?
Trust God, for I shall praise him yet,
his count'nance is mine aid.

6 My God, my soul's cast down in me;
thee therefore mind I will
From Jordan's land, the Hermonites,
and ev'n from Mizar hill.
7 At the noise of thy water-spouts
deep unto deep doth call;
Thy breaking waves pass over me,
yea, and thy billows all.

8 His loving-kindness yet the Lord
command will in the day,
His song's with me by night; to God,
by whom I live, I'll pray:
9 And I will say to God my rock,
Why me forgett'st thou so?
Why, for my foes' oppression,
thus mourning do I go?

10 'Tis as a sword within my bones,
when my foes me upbraid;
Ev'n when by them, Where is thy
God?
'tis daily to me said.
11 O why art thou cast down, my soul?
why, thus with grief opprest,
Art thou disquieted in me?
in God still hope and rest:

For yet I know I shall him praise,
who graciously to me
The health is of my countenance,
yea, mine own God is he.

PSALM 43.

1 JUDGE me, O God, and plead my cause
against th' ungodly nation;
From the unjust and crafty man,
O be thou my salvation.
2 For thou the God art of my strength;
why thrusts thou me thee fro'?
For th' enemy's oppression
why do I mourning go?

3 O send thy light forth and thy truth;
let them be guides to me,
And bring me to thine holy hill,
ev'n where thy dwellings be.
4 Then will I to God's altar go,
to God my chiefest joy:
Yea, God, my God, thy name to
my harp I will employ.   [praise

5 Why art thou then cast down, my soul?
what should discourage me?
And why with vexing thoughts art
disquieted in me?   [thou
Still trust in God; for him to praise
good cause I yet shall have:
He of my count'nance is the health,
my God that doth me save.

PSALM 44.

1 O GOD, we with our ears have
our fathers have us told, [heard,
What works thou in their days hadst
ev'n in the days of old.   [done,
2 Thy hand did drive the heathen out,
and plant them in their place;
Thou didst afflict the nations,
but them thou didst increase.

3 For neither got their sword the land,
nor did their arm them save;
But thy right hand, arm, counte-
for thou them favour gave. [nance;
4 Thou art my King: for Jacob, Lord,
deliv'rances command.
5 Through thee we shall push down
our foes,
that do against us stand:

We, through thy name, shall tread
down those
that ris'n against us have.
6 For in my bow I shall not trust,
nor shall my sword me save.
7 But from our foes thou hast us sav'd,
our haters put to shame.
8 In God we all the day do boast,
and ever praise thy name.

9 But now we are cast off by thee,
and us thou putt'st to shame;
And when our armies do go forth,
thou go'st not with the same.
10 Thou mak'st us from the enemy,
faint-hearted, to turn back;
And they who hate us for themselves
our spoils away do take.

11 Like sheep for meat thou gavest us;
'mong heathen cast we be.
12 Thou didst for nought thy people
sell;
their price enrich'd not thee.
13 Thou mak'st us a reproach to be
unto our neighbours near;
Derision and a scorn to them
that round about us are.

14 A by-word also thou dost us
among the heathen make;
The people, in contempt and spite
at us their heads do shake.
15 Before me my confusion
continually abides;
And of my bashful countenance
the shame me ever hides;

16 For voice of him that doth reproach,
and speaketh blasphemy;
By reason of th' avenging foe,
and cruel enemy.
17 All this is come on us, yet we
have not forgotten thee;
Nor falsely in thy covenant
behav'd ourselves have we.

18 Back from thy way our heart not
turn'd;
our steps no straying made;
19 Though us thou brak'st in dragons'
place,
and cover'dst with death's shade.
20 If we God's name forgot, or stretch'd
to a strange god our hands,
21 Shall not God search this out? for he
heart's secrets understands.

22 Yea, for thy sake we're kill'd all day,
counted as slaughter-sheep.
23 Rise, Lord, cast us not ever off;
awake, why dost thou sleep?
24 O wherefore hidest thou thy face?
forgett'st our cause distress'd,
25 And our oppression? For our soul
is to the dust down press'd:

Our belly also on the earth
fast cleaving, hold doth take.
26 Rise for our help, and us redeem,
ev'n for thy mercies' sake.

PSALM 45.

1 MY heart brings forth a goodly
    my words that I indite [thing;
Concern the King: my tongue's a pen
    of one that swift doth write.

2 Thou fairer art than sons of men:
    into thy lips is store
Of grace infus'd; and God therefore thee
    hath bless'd for evermore.

3 O thou that art the mighty One,
    thy sword gird on thy thigh;
Ev'n with thy glory excellent,
    and with thy majesty.

4 For meekness, truth, and righteous-
    in state ride prosp'rously;   [ness,
And thy right hand shall thee instruct
    in things that fearful be.

5 Thine arrows sharply pierce the heart
    of th' en'mies of the King;
And under thy subjection
    the people down do bring.

6 For ever and for ever is,
    O God, thy throne of might;
The sceptre of thy kingdom is
    a sceptre that is right.

7 Thou lovest right, and hatest ill;
    for God, thy God, most high,
Above thy fellows hath with th' oil
    of joy anointed thee.

8 Of aloes, myrrh, and cassia,
    a smell thy garments had,
Out of the iv'ry palaces,
    whereby they made thee glad.

9 Among thy women honourable
    kings' daughters were at hand:
Upon thy right hand did the queen
    in gold of Ophir stand.

10 O daughter, hearken and regard,
    and do thine ear incline;
Likewise forget thy father's house,
    and people that are thine.

11 Then of the King desir'd shall be
    thy beauty veh'mently:
Because he is thy Lord, do thou
    him worship rev'rently.

12 The daughter there of Tyre shall be
    with gifts and off'rings great:
Those of the people that are rich
    thy favour shall entreat.

13 Behold, the daughter of the King
    all glorious is within:
And with embroideries of gold
    her garments wrought have been.

14 She shall be brought unto the King
    in robes with needle wrought;

Her fellow-virgins following
    shall unto thee be brought.

15 They shall be brought with gladness
    and mirth on ev'ry side,   [great,
Into the palace of the King,
    and there they shall abide.

16 Instead of those thy fathers dear,
    thy children thou may'st take,
And in all places of the earth
    them noble princes make.

17 Thy name remember'd I will make
    through ages all to be:
The people therefore evermore
    shall praises give to thee.

Another of the same.

1 MY heart inditing is
    good matter in a song:
I speak the things that I have made,
    which to the King belong:
My tongue shall be as quick,
    his honour to indite,
As is the pen of any scribe
    that useth fast to write.

2 Thou'rt fairest of all men;
    grace in thy lips doth flow:
And therefore blessings evermore
    on thee doth God bestow.

3 Thy sword gird on thy thigh,
    thou that art most of might:
Appear in dreadful majesty,
    and in thy glory bright.

4 For meekness, truth, and right,
    ride prosp'rously in state;
And thy right hand shall teach to thee
    things terrible and great.

5 Thy shafts shall pierce their hearts
    that foes are to the King;
Whereby into subjection
    the people thou shalt bring.

6 Thy royal seat, O Lord,
    for ever shall remain:
The sceptre of thy kingdom doth
    all righteousness maintain.

7 Thou lov'st right, and hat'st ill;
    for God, thy God, most high,
Above thy fellows hath with th' oil
    of joy anointed thee.

8 Of myrrh and spices sweet
    a smell thy garments had,
Out of the iv'ry palaces,
    whereby they made thee glad.

9 And in thy glorious train
    kings' daughters waiting stand;
And thy fair queen, in Ophir gold,
    doth stand at thy right hand.

10 O daughter, take good heed,
 incline, and give good ear;
Thou must forget thy kindred all,
 and father's house most dear.

11 Thy beauty to the King
 shall then delightful be:
And do thou humbly worship him,
 because thy Lord is he.

12 The daughter then of Tyre
 there with a gift shall be,
And all the wealthy of the land
 shall make their suit to thee.

13 The daughter of the King
 all glorious is within;
And with embroideries of gold
 her garments wrought have been.

14 She cometh to the King
 in robes with needle wrought;
The virgins that do follow her
 shall unto thee be brought.

15 They shall be brought with joy,
 and mirth on ev'ry side,
Into the palace of the King,
 and there they shall abide.

16 And in thy fathers' stead,
 thy children thou may'st take,
And in all places of the earth
 them noble princes make.

17 I will show forth thy name
 to generations all:
Therefore the people evermore
 to thee give praises shall.

PSALM 46.

1 GOD is our refuge and our
 strength,
 in straits a present aid;

2 Therefore, although the earth re-
 we will not be afraid: [move,
Though hills amidst the seas be cast;

3 Though waters roaring make,
And troubled be; yea, though the
 by swelling seas do shake.   [hills

4 A river is, whose streams do glad
 the city of our God;
The holy place, wherein the Lord
 most high hath his abode.

5 God in the midst of her doth dwell;
 nothing shall her remove:
The Lord to her an helper will,
 and that right early, prove.

6 The heathen rag'd tumultuously,
 the kingdoms moved were:
The Lord God uttered his voice,
 the earth did melt for fear.

7 The Lord of hosts upon our side
 doth constantly remain:

The God of Jacob's our refuge,
 us safely to maintain.

8 Come, and behold what wondrous
 works
 have by the Lord been wrought;
Come, see what desolations
 he on the earth hath brought.

9 Unto the ends of all the earth
 wars into peace he turns:
The bow he breaks, the spear he cuts,
 in fire the chariot burns.

10 Be still, and know that I am God;
 among the heathen I
Will be exalted; I on earth
 will be exalted high.

11 Our God, who is the Lord of hosts,
 is still upon our side;
The God of Jacob our refuge
 for ever will abide.

PSALM 47.

1 ALL people, clap your hands; to
 God
 with voice of triumph shout:

2 For dreadful is the Lord most high,
 great King the earth throughout.

3 The heathen people under us
 he surely shall subdue;
And he shall make the nations
 under our feet to bow.

4 The lot of our inheritance
 chuse out for us shall he,
Of Jacob, whom he loved well,
 ev'n the excellency.

5 God is with shouts gone up, the Lord
 with trumpets sounding high.

6 Sing praise to God, sing praise, sing
 praise,
 praise to our King sing ye.

7 For God is King of all the earth;
 with knowledge praise express.

8 God rules the nations: God sits on
 his throne of holiness.

9 The princes of the people are
 assembled willingly;
Ev'n of the God of Abraham
 they who the people be.
For why? the shields that do defend
 the earth are only his:
They to the Lord belong; yea, he
 exalted greatly is.

PSALM 48.

1 GREAT is the Lord, and greatly he
 is to be praised still,
Within the city of our God,
 upon his holy hill.

27

2 Mount Sion stands most beautiful,
   the joy of all the land;
The city of the mighty King
   on her north side doth stand.

3 The Lord within her palaces
   is for a refuge known.
4 For, lo, the kings that gather'd were
   together, by have gone.

5 But when they did behold the same,
   they, wond'ring, would not stay;
But, being troubled at the sight,
   they thence did haste away.

6 Great terror there took hold on them,
   they were possess'd with fear;
Their grief came like a woman's pain,
   when she a child doth bear.

7 Thou Tarshish ships with east wind
8   As we have heard it told, [break'st:
So, in the city of the Lord,
   our eyes did it behold;
In our God's city, which his hand
   for ever stablish will.

9 We of thy loving-kindness thought,
   Lord, in thy temple still.
10 O Lord, according to thy name,
   through all the earth's thy praise;
And thy right hand, O Lord, is full
   of righteousness always.

11 Because thy judgments are made
   let Sion mount rejoice; [known,
Of Judah let the daughters all
   send forth a cheerful voice.

12 Walk about Sion, and go round;
   the high tow'rs thereof tell:
13 Consider ye her palaces,
   and mark her bulwarks well;

That ye may tell posterity.
14   For this God doth abide
Our God for evermore; he will
   ev'n unto death us guide.

PSALM 49.

1 HEAR this, all people, and give ear,
   all in the world that dwell;
2 Both low and high, both rich and
   poor.
3   My mouth shall wisdom tell:
My heart shall knowledge meditate.
4   I will incline mine ear
To parables, and on the harp
   my sayings dark declare.

5 Amidst those days that evil be,
   why should I, fearing, doubt?
When of my heels th' iniquity
   shall compass me about.
6 Whoe'er they be that in their wealth
   their confidence do pitch,

And boast themselves, because they
   become exceeding rich: [are
7 Yet none of these his brother can
   redeem by any way;
Nor can he unto God for him
   sufficient ransom pay,
8 (Their soul's redemption precious is,
   and it can never be,)
9 That still he should for ever live,
   and not corruption see.

10 For why? he seeth that wise men die,
   and brutish fools also
Do perish; and their wealth, when
   to others they let go.   [dead,
11 Their inward thought is, that their
   and dwelling-places shall [house
Stand through all ages; they their
   by their own names do call. [lands

12 But yet in honour shall not man
   abide continually;
But passing hence, may be compar'd
   unto the beasts that die.
13 Thus brutish folly plainly is
   their wisdom and their way;
Yet their posterity approve
   what they do fondly say.

14 Like sheep they in the grave are laid,
   and death shall them devour;
And in the morning upright men
   shall over them have pow'r:
Their beauty from their dwelling
   consume within the grave. [shall
15 But from hell's hand God will me
   for he shall me receive.   [free,

16 Be thou not then afraid when one
   enriched thou dost see,
Nor when the glory of his house
   advanced is on high:
17 For he shall carry nothing hence
   when death his days doth end;
Nor shall his glory after him
   into the grave descend.

18 Although he his own soul did bless
   whilst he on earth did live;
(And when thou to thyself dost well,
   men will thee praises give;)
19 He to his fathers' race shall go,
   they never shall see light.
20 Man honour'd wanting knowledge is
   like beasts that perish quite.

PSALM 50.

1 THE mighty God, the Lord,
   hath spoken, and did call
The earth, from rising of the sun,
   to where he hath his fall.

2 From out of Sion hill,
  which of excellency
And beauty the perfection is,
  God shined gloriously.

3 Our God shall surely come,
  keep silence shall not he:
Before him fire shall waste, great
  shall round about him be. [storms

4 Unto the heavens clear
  he from above shall call,
And to the earth likewise, that he
  may judge his people all.

5 Together let my saints
  unto me gather'd be,
Those that by sacrifice have made
  a covenant with me.

6 And then the heavens shall
  his righteousness declare:
Because the Lord himself is he
  by whom men judged are.

7 My people Isr'el hear,
  speak will I from on high,
Against thee I will testify;
  God, ev'n thy God, am I.

8 I for thy sacrifice
  no blame will on thee lay,
Nor for burnt-off'rings, which to me
  thou offer'dst ev'ry day.

9 I'll take no calf nor goats
  from house or fold of thine:

10 For beasts of forests, cattle all
  on thousand hills, are mine.

11 The fowls on mountains high
  are all to me well known;
Wild beasts which in the fields do lie,
  ev'n they are all mine own.

12 Then, if I hungry were,
  I would not tell it thee;
Because the world, and fulness all
  thereof, belongs to me.

13 Will I eat flesh of bulls?
  or goats' blood drink will I?

14 Thanks offer thou to God, and pay
  thy vows to the most High.

15 And call upon me when
  in trouble thou shalt be;
I will deliver thee, and thou
  my name shalt glorify.

16 But to the wicked man
  God saith, My laws and truth
Should'st thou declare? how dar'st
  thou take
  my cov'nant in thy mouth?

17 Sith thou instruction hat'st,
  which should thy ways direct;
And sith my words behind thy back
  thou cast'st, and dost reject.

18 When thou a thief didst see,
  with him thou didst consent;
And with the vile adulterers
  partaker on thou went.

19 Thou giv'st thy mouth to ill,
  thy tongue deceit doth frame;

20 Thou sitt'st, and 'gainst thy brother
  speak'st,
  thy mother's son dost shame.

21 Because I silence kept,
  while thou these things hast
That I was altogether like [wrought;
  thyself, hath been thy thought;
Yet I will thee reprove,
  and set before thine eyes,
In order ranked, thy misdeeds,
  and thine iniquities.

22 Now, ye that God forget,
  this carefully consider;
Lest I in pieces tear you all,
  and none can you deliver.

23 Whoso doth offer praise
  me glorifies; and I
Will show him God's salvation,
  that orders right his way.

Another of the same.

1 THE mighty God, the Lord, hath
  and call'd the earth upon, [spoke,
Ev'n from the rising of the sun
  unto his going down.

2 From out of Sion, his own hill,
  where the perfection high
Of beauty is, from thence the Lord
  hath shined gloriously.

3 Our God shall come, and shall no
  be silent, but speak out: [more
Before him fire shall waste, great
  shall compass him about. [storms

4 He to the heavens from above,
  and to the earth below,
Shall call, that he his judgments may
  before his people show.

5 Let all my saints together be
  unto me gathered;
Those that by sacrifice with me
  a covenant have made.

6 And then the heavens shall declare
  his righteousness abroad:
Because the Lord himself doth come;
  none else is judge but God.

7 Hear, O my people, and I'll speak;
  O Israel by name,
Against thee I will testify;
  God, ev'n thy God, I am.

8 I for thy sacrifices few
  reprove thee never will,

29

Nor for burnt-off'rings to have been
   before me offer'd still.
9 I'll take no bullock nor he-goats
   from house nor folds of thine:
10 For beasts of forests, cattle all
   on thousand hills, are mine.
11 The fowls are all to me well known
   that mountains high do yield;
   And I do challenge as mine own
   the wild beasts of the field.
12 If I were hungry, I would not
   to thee for need complain;
   For earth, and all its fulness, doth
   to me of right pertain.
13 That I to eat the flesh of bulls
   take pleasure dost thou think?
   Or that I need, to quench thy thirst,
   the blood of goats to drink?
14 Nay, rather unto me, thy God,
   thanksgiving offer thou:
   To the most High perform thy word,
   and fully pay thy vow:
15 And in the day of trouble great
   see that thou call on me;
   I will deliver thee, and thou
   my name shalt glorify.
16 But God unto the wicked saith,
   Why should'st thou mention make
   Of my commands? how dar'st thou
   thy mouth my cov'nant take? [in
17 Sith it is so that thou dost hate
   all good instruction;
   And sith thou cast'st behind thy back,
   and slight'st my words each one.
18 When thou a thief didst see, then
   straight
   thou join'dst with him in sin,
   And with the vile adulterers
   thou hast partaker been.
19 Thy mouth to evil thou dost give,
   thy tongue deceit doth frame.
20 Thou sitt'st, and 'gainst thy brother
   speak'st,
   thy mother's son to shame.
21 These things thou wickedly hast
   and I have silent been: [done,
   Thou thought'st that I was like thy-
   and did approve thy sin: [self,
   But I will sharply thee reprove,
   and I will order right
   Thy sins and thy transgressions
   in presence of thy sight.
22 Consider this, and be afraid,
   ye that forget the Lord,
   Lest I in pieces tear you all,
   when none can help afford.

23 Who off'reth praise me glorifies:
   I will show God's salvation
   To him that ordereth aright
   his life and conversation.

PSALM 51.

1 AFTER thy loving-kindness, Lord,
   have mercy upon me:
   For thy compassions great, blot out
   all mine iniquity.
2 Me cleanse from sin, and throughly
   from mine iniquity: [wash
3 For my transgressions I confess;
   my sin I ever see.
4 'Gainst thee, thee only, have I sinn'd,
   in thy sight done this ill;
   That when thou speak'st thou may'st
   and clear in judging still. [be just,
5 Behold, I in iniquity
   was form'd the womb within;
   My mother also me conceiv'd
   in guiltiness and sin.
6 Behold, thou in the inward parts
   with truth delighted art;
   And wisdom thou shalt make me
   within the hidden part. [know
7 Do thou with hyssop sprinkle me,
   I shall be cleansed so;
   Yea, wash thou me, and then I shall
   be whiter than the snow.
8 Of gladness and of joyfulness
   make me to hear the voice;
   That so these very bones which thou
   hast broken may rejoice.
9 All mine iniquities blot out,
   thy face hide from my sin.
10 Create a clean heart, Lord, renew
   a right sp'rit me within.
11 Cast me not from thy sight, nor take
   thy Holy Sp'rit away.
12 Restore me thy salvation's joy;
   with thy free Sp'rit me stay.
13 Then will I teach thy ways unto
   those that transgressors be;
   And those that sinners are shall then
   be turned unto thee.
14 O God, of my salvation God,
   me from blood-guiltiness
   Set free; then shall my tongue aloud
   sing of thy righteousness.
15 My closed lips, O Lord, by thee
   let them be opened;
   Then shall thy praises by my mouth
   abroad be published.
16 For thou desir'st not sacrifice,
   else would I give it thee;

Nor wilt thou with burnt-offering
at all delighted be.
17 A broken spirit is to God
a pleasing sacrifice:
A broken and a contrite heart,
Lord, thou wilt not despise.
18 Show kindness, and do good, O Lord,
to Sion, thine own hill:
The walls of thy Jerusalem
build up of thy good will.
19 Then righteous off'rings shall thee
please,
and off'rings burnt, which they
With whole burnt-off'rings, and with
shall on thine altar lay. [calves,

PSALM 52.

1 WHY dost thou boast, O mighty
of mischief and of ill? [man,
The goodness of Almighty God
endureth ever still.
2 Thy tongue mischievous calumnies
deviseth subtilely,
Like to a razor sharp to cut,
working deceitfully.
3 Ill more than good, and more than
thou lovest to speak wrong: [truth
4 Thou lovest all-devouring words,
O thou deceitful tongue.
5 So God shall thee destroy for aye,
remove thee, pluck thee out
Quite from thy house, out of the land
of life he shall thee root.
6 The righteous then shall see, and fear,
and laugh at him they shall:
7 Lo, this the man is that did not
make God his strength at all:
But he in his abundant wealth
his confidence did place;
And he took strength unto himself
from his own wickedness.
8 But I am in the house of God
like to an olive green:
My confidence for ever hath
upon God's mercy been.
9 And I for ever will thee praise,
because thou hast done this:
I on thy name will wait; for good
before thy saints it is.

PSALM 53.

1 THAT there is not a God, the fool
doth in his heart conclude:
They are corrupt, their works are
not one of them doth good. [vile,
2 The Lord upon the sons of men
from heav'n did cast his eyes,

To see if any one there was
that sought God, and was wise.
3 They altogether filthy are,
they all are backward gone;
And there is none that doeth good,
no, not so much as one.
4 These workers of iniquity,
do they not know at all,
That they my people eat as bread,
and on God do not call?
5 Ev'n there they were afraid, and stood
with trembling, all dismay'd,
Whereas there was no cause at all
why they should be afraid:
For God his bones that thee besieg'd
hath scatter'd all abroad;
Thou hast confounded them, for they
despised are of God.
6 Let Isr'el's help from Sion come:
when back the Lord shall bring
His captives, Jacob shall rejoice,
and Israel shall sing.

PSALM 54.

1 SAVE me, O God, by thy great
name,
and judge me by thy strength:
2 My prayer hear, O God; give ear
unto my words at length.
3 For they that strangers are to me
do up against me rise;
Oppressors seek my soul, and God
set not before their eyes.
4 The Lord my God my helper is,
lo, therefore I am bold:
He taketh part with ev'ry one
that doth my soul uphold.
5 Unto mine enemies he shall
mischief and ill repay:
O for thy truth's sake cut them off,
and sweep them clean away.
6 I will a sacrifice to thee
give with free willingness;
Thy name, O Lord, because 'tis
with praise I will confess. [good,
7 For he hath me delivered
from all adversities;
And his desire mine eye hath seen
upon mine enemies.

PSALM 55.

1 LORD, hear my pray'r, hide not
thyself
from my entreating voice:
2 Attend and hear me; in my plaint
I mourn and make a noise.

31

3 Because of th' en'my's voice, and for
    lewd men's oppression great:
On me they cast iniquity,
    and they in wrath me hate.

4 Sore pain'd within me is my heart:
    death's terrors on me fall.

5 On me comes trembling, fear and
    o'erwhelmed me withal.   [dread

6 O that I, like a dove, had wings,
    said I, then would I flee
Far hence, that I might find a place
    where I in rest might be.

7 Lo, then far off I wander would,
    and in the desert stay;

8 From windy storm and tempest I
    would haste to 'scape away.

9 O Lord, on them destruction bring,
    and do their tongues divide;
For in the city violence
    and strife I have espy'd.

10 They day and night upon the walls
    do go about it round:
There mischief is, and sorrow there
    in midst of it is found.

11 Abundant wickedness there is
    within her inward part;
And from her streets deceitfulness
    and guile do not depart.

12 He was no foe that me reproach'd,
    then that endure I could;
Nor hater that did 'gainst me boast,
    from him me hide I would.

13 But thou, man, who mine equal,
    guide,
and mine acquaintance wast:

14 We join'd sweet counsels, to God's
    in company we past.   [house

15 Let death upon them seize, and down
    let them go quick to hell;
For wickedness doth much abound
    among them where they dwell.

16 I'll call on God: God will me save.

17   I'll pray, and make a noise
At ev'ning, morning, and at noon;
    and he shall hear my voice.

18 He hath my soul delivered,
    that in it peace might be
From battle that against me was;
    for many were with me.

19 The Lord shall hear, and them afflict,
    of old who hath abode:
Because they never changes have,
    therefore they fear not God.

20 'Gainst those that were at peace with
    he hath put forth his hand: [him
The covenant that he had made,
    by breaking he profan'd.

21 More smooth than butter were his
    while in his heart was war; [words,
His speeches were more soft than oil,
    and yet drawn swords they are.

22 Cast thou my burden on the Lord,
    and he shall thee sustain;
Yea, he shall cause the righteous man
    unmoved to remain.

23 But thou, O Lord my God, those
    in justice shalt o'erthrow, [men
And in destruction's dungeon dark
    at last shalt lay them low:
The bloody and deceitful men
    shall not live half their days:
But upon thee with confidence
    I will depend always.

PSALM 56.

1 SHOW mercy, Lord, to me, for man
    would swallow me outright;
He me oppresseth, while he doth
    against me daily fight.

2 They daily would me swallow up
    that hate me spitefully;
For they be many that do fight
    against me, O most High.

3 When I'm afraid I'll trust in thee:

4   In God I'll praise his word;
I will not fear what flesh can do,
    my trust is in the Lord.

5 Each day they wrest my words; their
    thoughts
'gainst me are all for ill.

6 They meet, they lurk, they mark my
    waiting my soul to kill. [steps,

7 But shall they by iniquity
    escape thy judgments so?
O God, with indignation down
    do thou the people throw.

8 My wand'rings all what they have
    been
thou know'st; their number took;
Into thy bottle put my tears:
    are they not in thy book?

9 My foes shall, when I cry, turn back;
    I know 't, God is for me.

10 In God his word I'll praise; his word
    in God shall praised be.

11 In God I trust; I will not fear
    what man can do to me.

12 Thy vows upon me are, O God:
    I'll render praise to thee.

13 Wilt thou not, who from death me
    sav'd,
my feet from falls keep free,
To walk before God in the light
    of those that living be?

PSALM 57.

1 BE merciful to me, O God;
thy mercy unto me
Do thou extend; because my soul
doth put her trust in thee:
Yea, in the shadow of thy wings
my refuge I will place,
Until these sad calamities
do wholly overpass.

2 My cry I will cause to ascend
unto the Lord most high;
To God, who doth all things for me
perform most perfectly.

3 From heav'n he shall send down, and
from his reproach defend [me
That would devour me: God his
and mercy forth shall send. [truth

4 My soul among fierce lions is,
I firebrands live among,
Men's sons, whose teeth are spears
and darts,
a sharp sword is their tongue.

5 Be thou exalted very high
above the heav'ns, O God;
Let thou thy glory be advanc'd
o'er all the earth abroad.

6 My soul's bow'd down; for they a net
have laid, my steps to snare:
Into the pit which they have digg'd
for me, they fallen are.

7 My heart is fix'd, my heart is fix'd,
O God; I'll sing and praise.

8 My glory wake; wake psalt'ry, harp;
myself I'll early raise.

9 I'll praise thee 'mong the people,
'mong nations sing will I: [Lord;

10 For great to heav'n thy mercy is,
thy truth is to the sky.

11 O Lord, exalted by thy name
above the heav'ns to stand:
Do thou thy glory far advance
above both sea and land.

PSALM 58.

1 DO ye, O congregation,
indeed speak righteousness?
O ye that are the sons of men,
judge ye with uprightness?

2 Yea, ev'n within your very hearts
ye wickedness have done;
And ye the vi'lence of your hands
do weigh the earth upon.

3 The wicked men estranged are,
ev'n from the very womb;
They, speaking lies, do stray as soon
as to the world they come.

4 Unto a serpent's poison like
their poison doth appear;
Yea, they are like the adder deaf,
that closely stops her ear;

5 That so she may not hear the voice
of one that charm her would,
No, not though he most cunning
were,
and charm most wisely could.

6 Their teeth, O God, within their
mouth
break thou in pieces small;
The great teeth break thou out, O
of these young lions all.   [Lord,

7 Let them like waters melt away,
which downward still do flow;
In pieces cut his arrows all,
when he shall bend his bow.

8 Like to a snail that melts away,
let each of them be gone;
Like woman's birth untimely, that
they never see the sun.

9 He shall them take away before
your pots the thorns can find,
Both living, and in fury great,
as with a stormy wind.

10 The righteous, when he vengeance
he shall be joyful then;   [sees,
The righteous one shall wash his feet
in blood of wicked men.

11 So men shall say, The righteous man
reward shall never miss:
And verily upon the earth
a God to judge there is.

PSALM 59.

1 MY God, deliver me from those
that are mine enemies;
And do thou me defend from those
that up against me rise.

2 Do thou deliver me from them
that work iniquity;
And give me safety from the men
of bloody cruelty.

3 For, lo, they for my soul lay wait:
the mighty do combine
Against me, Lord; not for my fault,
nor any sin of mine.

4 They run, and, without fault in me,
themselves do ready make:
Awake to meet me with thy help;
and do thou notice take.

5 Awake therefore, Lord God of hosts,
thou God of Israel,
To visit heathen all: spare none
that wickedly rebel.

6 At ev'ning they go to and fro;
   they make great noise and sound,
   Like to a dog, and often walk
      about the city round.

7 Behold, they belch out with their
      mouth,
   and in their lips are swords:
   For they do say thus, Who is he
      that now doth hear our words?

8 But thou, O Lord, shalt laugh at
      them,
      the heathen mock.

9 While he's in pow'r I'll wait on thee;
   for God is my high rock.

10 He of my mercy that is God
      betimes shall me prevent;
   Upon mine en'mies God shall let
      me see mine heart's content.

11 Them slay not, lest my folk forget;
      but scatter them abroad
   By thy strong pow'r; and bring them
      down,
      O thou our shield and God.

12 For their mouth's sin, and for the
   that from their lips do fly, [words
   Let them be taken in their pride;
   because they curse and lie.

13 In wrath consume them, them con-
   that so they may not be: [sume,
   And that in Jacob God doth rule
   to th' earth's ends let them see.

14 At ev'ning let thou them return,
      making great noise and sound,
   Like to a dog, and often walk
      about the city round.

15 And let them wander up and down,
      in seeking food to eat;
   And let them grudge when they shall
      be satisfy'd with meat.   [not

16 But of thy pow'r I'll sing aloud;
      at morn thy mercy praise:
   For thou to me my refuge wast,
      and tow'r, in troublous days.

17 O God, thou art my strength, I will
      sing praises unto thee;
   For God is my defence, a God
      of mercy unto me.

PSALM 60.

1 O LORD, thou hast rejected us,
      and scatter'd us abroad;
   Thou justly hast displeased been;
      return to us, O God.

2 The earth to tremble thou hast made;
      therein didst breaches make:
   Do thou thereof the breaches heal,
      because the land doth shake.

3 Unto thy people thou hard things
      hast show'd, and on them sent;
   And thou hast caused us to drink
      wine of astonishment.

4 And yet a banner thou hast giv'n
      to them who thee do fear;
   That it by them, because of truth,
      displayed may appear.

5 That thy beloved people may
      deliver'd be from thrall,
   Save with the pow'r of thy right
      and hear me when I call.   [hand,

6 God in his holiness hath spoke;
      Herein I will take pleasure:
   Shechem I will divide, and forth
      will Succoth's valley measure.

7 Gilead I claim as mine by right;
      Manasseh mine shall be;
   Ephraim is of mine head the strength;
      Judah gives laws for me;

8 Moab's my washing-pot; my shoe
      I'll over Edom throw;
   And over Palestina's land
      I will in triumph go.

9 O who is he will bring me to
      the city fortify'd?
   O who is he that to the land
      of Edom will me guide?

10 O God, which hadest us cast off,
      this thing wilt thou not do?
   Ev'n thou, O God, which didest not
      forth with our armies go?

11 Help us from trouble; for the help
      is vain which man supplies.

12 Through God we'll do great acts; he
      tread down our enemies.   [shall

PSALM 61.

1 O GOD, give ear unto my cry;
      unto my pray'r attend.

2 From th' utmost corner of the land
      my cry to thee I'll send.
   What time my heart is overwhelm'd,
      and in perplexity,
   Do thou me lead unto the Rock
      that higher is than I.

3 For thou hast for my refuge been
      a shelter by thy pow'r;
   And for defence against my foes
      thou hast been a strong tow'r.

4 Within thy tabernacle I
      for ever will abide;
   And under covert of thy wings
      with confidence me hide.

5 For thou the vows that I did make,
      O Lord my God, didst hear:

Thou hast giv'n me the heritage
of those thy name that fear.

6 A life prolong'd for many days
thou to the king shalt give;
Like many generations be
the years which he shall live.

7 He in God's presence his abode
for evermore shall have:
O do thou truth and mercy both
prepare, that may him save.

8 And so will I perpetually
sing praise unto thy name;
That having made my vows, I may
each day perform the same.

PSALM 62.

1 MY soul with expectation
depends on God indeed;
My strength and my salvation doth
from him alone proceed.

2 He only my salvation is,
and my strong rock is he:
He only is my sure defence;
much mov'd I shall not be.

3 How long will ye against a man
plot mischief? ye shall all
Be slain; ye as a tott'ring fence
shall be, and bowing wall.

4 They only plot to cast him down
from his excellency:
They joy in lies; with mouth they
but they curse inwardly. [bless,

5 My soul, wait thou with patience
upon thy God alone;
On him dependeth all my hope
and expectation.

6 He only my salvation is,
and my strong rock is he;
He only is my sure defence:
I shall not moved be.

7 In God my glory placed is,
and my salvation sure;
In God the rock is of my strength,
my refuge most secure.

8 Ye people, place your confidence
in him continually;
Before him pour ye out your heart:
God is our refuge high.

9 Surely mean men are vanity,
and great men are a lie;
In balance laid, they wholly are
more light than vanity.

10 Trust ye not in oppression,
in robb'ry be not vain;
On wealth set not your hearts, when
increased is your gain. [as

11 God hath it spoken once to me,
yea, this I heard again,
That power to Almighty God
alone doth appertain.

12 Yea, mercy also unto thee
belongs, O Lord, alone:
For thou according to his work
rewardest ev'ry one.

PSALM 63.

1 LORD, thee my God, I'll early seek:
my soul doth thirst for thee;
My flesh longs in a dry parch'd land,
wherein no waters be:

2 That I thy power may behold,
and brightness of thy face,
As I have seen thee heretofore
within thy holy place.

3 Since better is thy love than life,
my lips thee praise shall give.

4 I in thy name will lift my hands,
and bless thee while I live.

5 Ev'n as with marrow and with fat
my soul shall filled be;
Then shall my mouth with joyful lips
sing praises unto thee:

6 When I do thee upon my bed
remember with delight,
And when on thee I meditate
in watches of the night.

7 In shadow of thy wings I'll joy;
for thou mine help hast been.

8 My soul thee follows hard; and me
thy right hand doth sustain.

9 Who seek my soul to spill shall sink
down to earth's lowest room.

10 They by the sword shall be cut off,
and foxes' prey become.

11 Yet shall the king in God rejoice,
and each one glory shall
That swear by him: but stopp'd shall
the mouth of liars all. [be

PSALM 64.

1 WHEN I to thee my prayer make,
Lord, to my voice give ear;
My life save from the enemy,
of whom I stand in fear.

2 Me from their secret counsel hide
who do live wickedly;
From insurrection of those men
that work iniquity:

3 Who do their tongues with malice
whet,
and make them cut like swords;
In whose bent bows are arrows set,
ev'n sharp and bitter words:

4 That they may at the perfect man
   in secret aim their shot;
Yea, suddenly they dare at him
   to shoot, and fear it not.

5 In ill encourage they themselves,
   and their snares close do lay:
Together conference they have;
   Who shall them see? they say.

6 They have search'd out iniquities,
   a perfect search they keep:
Of each of them the inward thought,
   and very heart, is deep.

7 God shall an arrow shoot at them,
   and wound them suddenly:

8 So their own tongue shall them con-
   all who them see shall fly. [found;

9 And on all men a fear shall fall,
   God's works they shall declare;
For they shall wisely notice take
   what these his doings are.

10 In God the righteous shall rejoice,
   and trust upon his might;
Yea, they shall greatly glory all
   in heart that are upright.

PSALM 65.

1 PRAISE waits for thee in Sion,
   Lord:
   to thee vows paid shall be.

2 O thou that hearer art of pray'r,
   all flesh shall come to thee.

3 Iniquities, I must confess,
   prevail against me do:
But as for our transgressions,
   them purge away shalt thou.

4 Bless'd is the man whom thou dost
   chuse,
   and mak'st approach to thee,
That he within thy courts, O Lord,
   may still a dweller be:
We surely shall be satisfy'd
   with thy abundant grace,
And with the goodness of thy house,
   ev'n of thy holy place.

5 O God of our salvation,
   thou, in thy righteousness,
By fearful works unto our pray'rs
   thine answer dost express:
Therefore the ends of all the earth,
   and those afar that be
Upon the sea, their confidence,
   O Lord, will place in thee.

6 Who, being girt with pow'r, sets fast
   by his great strength the hills.

7 Who noise of seas, noise of their
   and people's tumult, stills. [waves,

8 Those in the utmost parts that dwell
   are at thy signs afraid:
Th' outgoings of the morn and ev'n
   by thee are joyful made.

9 The earth thou visit'st, wat'ring it;
   thou mak'st it rich to grow
With God's full flood; thou corn pre-
   when thou provid'st it so. [par'st,

10 Her rigs thou wat'rest plenteously,
   her furrows settelest:
With show'rs thou dost her mollify,
   her spring by thee is blest.

11 So thou the year most lib'rally
   dost with thy goodness crown;
And all thy paths abundantly
   on us drop fatness down.

12 They drop upon the pastures wide,
   that do in deserts lie;
The little hills on ev'ry side
   rejoice right pleasantly.

13 With flocks the pastures clothed be,
   the vales with corn are clad;
And now they shout and sing to thee,
   for thou hast made them glad.

PSALM 66.

1 ALL lands to God, in joyful sounds,
   aloft your voices raise.

2 Sing forth the honour of his name,
   and glorious make his praise.

3 Say unto God, How terrible
   in all thy works art thou!
Through thy great pow'r thy foes to
   shall be constrain'd to bow. [thee

4 All on the earth shall worship thee,
   they shall thy praise proclaim
In songs: they shall sing cheerfully
   unto thy holy name.

5 Come, and the works that God hath
   with admiration see: [wrought
In 's working to the sons of men
   most terrible is he.

6 Into dry land the sea he turn'd,
   and they a passage had;
Ev'n marching through the flood on
   there we in him were glad. [foot,

7 He ruleth ever by his pow'r;
   his eyes the nations see:
O let not the rebellious ones
   lift up themselves on high.

8 Ye people, bless our God; aloud
   the voice speak of his praise:

9 Our soul in life who safe preserves,
   our foot from sliding stays.

10 For thou didst prove and try us,
   as men do silver try;   [Lord,

36

11 Brought'st us into the net, and mad'st
bands on our loins to lie.
12 Thou hast caus'd men ride o'er our
heads;
and though that we did pass
Through fire and water, yet thou
us to a wealthy place. [brought'st
13 I'll bring burnt-off'rings to thy
to thee my vows I'll pay, [house;
14 Which my lips utter'd, my mouth
when trouble on me lay. [spake,
15 Burnt-sacrifices of fat rams
with incense I will bring;
Of bullocks and of goats I will
present an offering.
16 All that fear God, come, hear, I'll tell
what he did for my soul.
17 I with my mouth unto him cry'd,
my tongue did him extol.
18 If in my heart I sin regard,
the Lord me will not hear:
19 But surely God me heard, and to
my prayer's voice gave ear.
20 O let the Lord, our gracious God,
for ever blessed be,
Who turned not my pray'r from him,
nor yet his grace from me.

PSALM 67.

1 LORD, bless and pity us,
shine on us with thy face:
2 That th' earth thy way, and nations
may know thy saving grace. [all
3 Let people praise thee, Lord;
let people all thee praise.
4 O let the nations be glad,
in songs their voices raise:
Thou'lt justly people judge,
on earth rule nations all.
5 Let people praise thee, Lord; let
them
praise thee, both great and small.
6 The earth her fruit shall yield,
our God shall blessing send.
7 God shall us bless; men shall him
unto earth's utmost end. [fear

Another of the same.

1 LORD, unto us be merciful,
do thou us also bless;
And graciously cause shine on us
the brightness of thy face:
2 That so thy way upon the earth
to all men may be known;
Also among the nations all
thy saving health be shown.

3 O let the people praise thee, Lord;
let people all thee praise.
4 O let the nations be glad,
and sing for joy always:
For rightly thou shalt people judge,
and nations rule on earth.
5 Let people praise thee, Lord; let all
the folk praise thee with mirth.
6 Then shall the earth yield her increase;
God, our God, bless us shall.
7 God shall us bless; and of the earth
the ends shall fear him all.

PSALM 68.

1 LET God arise, and scattered
let all his en'mies be;
And let all those that do him hate
before his presence flee.
2 As smoke is driv'n, so drive thou
as fire melts wax away, [them;
Before God's face let wicked men
so perish and decay.
3 But let the righteous be glad:
let them before God's sight
Be very joyful; yea, let them
rejoice with all their might.
4 To God sing, to his name sing praise;
extol him with your voice,
That rides on heav'n, by his name
before his face rejoice. [JAH,
5 Because the Lord a father is
unto the fatherless;
God is the widow's judge, within
his place of holiness.
6 God doth the solitary set
in fam'lies: and from bands
The chain'd doth free; but rebels do
inhabit parched lands.
7 O God, what time thou didst go forth
before thy people's face;
And when through the great wilder-
thy glorious marching was; [ness
8 Then at God's presence shook the
earth,
then drops from heaven fell;
This Sinai shook before the Lord,
the God of Israel.
9 O God, thou to thine heritage
didst send a plenteous rain,
Whereby thou, when it weary was,
didst it refresh again.
10 Thy congregation then did make
their habitation there:
Of thine own goodness for the poor,
O God, thou didst prepare.

11 The Lord himself did give the word,
  the word abroad did spread;
Great was the company of them
  the same who published.
12 Kings of great armies foiled were,
  and forc'd to flee away;
And women, who remain'd at home,
  did distribute the prey.
13 Though ye have lien among the pots,
  like doves ye shall appear,
Whose wings with silver, and with
  whose feathers cover'd are. [gold
14 When there th' Almighty scatter'd
  kings,
  like Salmon's snow 'twas white.
15 God's hill is like to Bashan hill,
  like Bashan hill for height.
16 Why do ye leap, ye mountains high?
  this is the hill where God
Desires to dwell; yea, God in it
  for aye will make abode.
17 God's chariots twenty thousand are,
  thousands of angels strong;
In 's holy place God is, as in
  mount Sinai, them among.
18 Thou hast, O Lord, most glorious,
  ascended up on high;
And in triumph victorious led
  captive captivity:
Thou hast received gifts for men,
  for such as did rebel;
Yea, ev'n for them, that God the Lord
  in midst of them might dwell.
19 Bless'd be the Lord, who is to us
  of our salvation God;
Who daily with his benefits
  us plenteously doth load.
20 He of salvation is the God,
  who is our God most strong;
And unto God the Lord from death
  the issues do belong.
21 But surely God shall wound the head
  of those that are his foes;
The hairy scalp of him that still
  on in his trespass goes.
22 God said, My people I will bring
  again from Bashan hill;
Yea, from the sea's devouring depths
  them bring again I will;
23 That in the blood of enemies
  thy foot imbru'd may be,
And of thy dogs dipp'd in the same
  the tongues thou mayest see.
24 Thy goings they have seen, O God;
  the steps of majesty
Of my God, and my mighty King,
  within the sanctuary.

25 Before went singers, players next
  on instruments took way;
And them among the damsels were
  that did on timbrels play.
26 Within the congregations
  bless God with one accord:
From Isr'el's fountain do ye bless
  and praise the mighty Lord.
27 With their prince, little Benjamin,
  princes and council there
Of Judah were, there Zabulon's
  and Napht'li's princes were.
28 Thy God commands thy strength;
  make strong
  what thou wrought'st for us, Lord.
29 For thy house at Jerusalem
  kings shall thee gifts afford.
30 The spearmen's host, the multitude
  of bulls, which fiercely look,
Those calves which people have forth
  O Lord our God, rebuke, [sent,
Till ev'ry one submit himself,
  and silver pieces bring:
The people that delight in war
  disperse, O God and King.
31 Those that be princes great shall then
  come out of Egypt lands;
And Ethiopia to God
  shall soon stretch out her hands.
32 O all ye kingdoms of the earth,
  sing praises to this King;
For he is Lord that ruleth all,
  unto him praises sing.
33 To him that rides on heav'ns of
  heav'ns,
  which he of old did found;
Lo, he sends out his voice, a voice
  in might that doth abound.
34 Strength unto God do ye ascribe;
  for his excellency
Is over Israel, his strength
  is in the clouds most high.
35 Thou'rt from thy temple dreadful,
  Isr'el's own God is he, [Lord:
Who gives his people strength and
  O let God blessed be. [pow'r:

PSALM 69.

1 SAVE me, O God, because the
  do so environ me, [floods
That ev'n unto my very soul
  come in the waters be.
2 I downward in deep mire do sink,
  where standing there is none:
I am into deep waters come,
  where floods have o'er me gone.

3 I weary with my crying am,
   my throat is also dry'd;
Mine eyes do fail, while for my God
   I waiting do abide.

4 Those men that do without a cause
   bear hatred unto me,
Than are the hairs upon my head
   in number more they be:

They that would me destroy, and are
   mine en'mies wrongfully,
Are nighty: so what I took not,
   to render forc'd was I.

5 Lord, thou my folly know'st, my sins
   not cover'd are from thee.

6 Let none that wait on thee be sham'd,
   Lord God of hosts, for me.

O Lord, the God of Israel,
   let none, who search me, make,
And seek thee, be at any time
   confounded for my sake.

7 For I have borne reproach for thee,
   my face is hid with shame.

8 To brethren strange, to mother's
   an alien I became.   [sons

9 Because the zeal did eat me up,
   which to thine house I bear;
And the reproaches cast at thee,
   upon me fallen are.

10 My tears and fasts, t' afflict my soul,
   were turned to my shame.

11 When sackcloth I did wear, to them
   a proverb I became.

12 The men that in the gate do sit
   against me evil spake;
They also that vile drunkards were,
   of me their song did make.

13 But, in an acceptable time,
   my pray'r, Lord, is to thee:
In truth of thy salvation, Lord,
   and mercy great, hear me.

14 Deliver me out of the mire,
   from sinking do me keep;
Free me from those that do me hate,
   and from the waters deep.

15 Let not the flood on me prevail,
   whose water overflows;
Nor deep me swallow, nor the pit
   her mouth upon me close.

16 Hear me, O Lord, because thy love
   and kindness is most good;
Turn unto me, according to
   thy mercies' multitude.

17 Nor from thy servant hide thy face:
   I'm troubled, soon attend.

18 Draw near my soul, and it redeem;
   me from my foes defend.

19 To thee is my reproach well known,
   my shame, and my disgrace:
Those that mine adversaries be
   are all before thy face.

20 Reproach hath broke my heart; I'm
   of grief: I look'd for one   [full
To pity me, but none I found;
   comforters found I none.

21 They also bitter gall did give
   unto me for my meat:
They gave me vinegar to drink,
   when as my thirst was great.

22 Before them let their table prove
   a snare; and do thou make
Their welfare and prosperity
   a trap themselves to take.

23 Let thou their eyes so darken'd be,
   that sight may them forsake;
And let their loins be made by thee
   continually to shake.

24 Thy fury pour thou out on them,
   and indignation;
And let thy wrathful anger, Lord,
   fast hold take them upon.

25 All waste and desolate let be
   their habitation;
And in their tabernacles all
   inhabitants be none.

26 Because him they do persecute,
   whom thou didst smite before;
They talk unto the grief of those
   whom thou hast wounded sore.

27 Add thou iniquity unto
   their former wickedness;
And do not let them come at all
   into thy righteousness.

28 Out of the book of life let them
   be raz'd and blotted quite;
Among the just and righteous
   let not their names be writ.

29 But now become exceeding poor
   and sorrowful am I:
By thy salvation, O my God,
   let me be set on high.

30 The name of God I with a song
   most cheerfully will praise;
And I, in giving thanks to him,
   his name shall highly raise.

31 This to the Lord a sacrifice
   more gracious shall prove
Than bullock, ox, or any beast
   that hath both horn and hoof.

32 When this the humble men shall see,
   it joy to them shall give:
O all ye that do seek the Lord,
   your hearts shall ever live.

33 For God the poor hears, and will not
 his prisoners contemn.
34 Let heav'n, and earth, and seas, him
 praise,
  and all that move in them.
35 For God will Judah's cities build,
 and he will Sion save,
 That they may dwell therein, and it
  in sure possession have.
36 And they that are his servants' seed
 inherit shall the same;
 So shall they have their dwelling
  that love his blessed name. [there

PSALM 70.

1 LORD, haste me to deliver;
 with speed, Lord, succour me.
2 Let them that for my soul do seek
 sham'd and confounded be:
 Turn'd back be they, and sham'd,
  that in my hurt delight.
3 Turn'd back be they, Ha, ha! that
 their shaming to requite. [say,
4 In thee let all be glad,
 and joy that seek for thee:
 Let them who thy salvation love
  say still, God praised be.
5 I poor and needy am;
 come, Lord, and make no stay:
 My help thou and deliv'rer art;
  O Lord, make no delay.

Another of the same.

1 MAKE haste, O God, me to preserve;
 with speed, Lord, succour me.
2 Let them that for my soul do seek,
 sham'd and confounded be:
 Let them be turned back, and
  that in my hurt delight. [sham'd,
3 Turn'd back be they, Ha, ha! that
 their shaming to requite. [say,
4 O Lord, in thee let all be glad,
 and joy that seek for thee:
 Let them who thy salvation love
  say still, God praised be.
5 But I both poor and needy am;
 come, Lord, and make no stay:
 My help thou and deliv'rer art:
  O Lord, make no delay.

PSALM 71.

1 O LORD, my hope and confidence
 is plac'd in thee alone;
 Then let thy servant never be
 put to confusion.

2 And let me, in thy righteousness,
 from thee deliv'rance have;
 Cause me escape, incline thine ear
  unto me, and me save.
3 Be thou my dwelling-rock, to which
 I ever may resort:
 Thou gav'st commandment me to
  save,
  for thou'rt my rock and fort.
4 Free me, my God, from wicked
 hands cruel and unjust; [hands,
5 For thou, O Lord God, art my hope,
 and from my youth my trust.
6 Thou from the womb didst hold me
 thou art the same that me [up,
 Out of my mother's bowels took;
  I ever will praise thee.
7 To many I a wonder am;
 but thou'rt my refuge strong.
8 Fill'd let my mouth be with thy
 and honour all day long. [praise
9 O do not cast me off, when as
 old age doth overtake me;
 And when my strength decayed is,
  then do not thou forsake me.
10 For those that are mine enemies
 against me speak with hate;
 And they together counsel take
  that for my soul lay wait.
11 They said, God leaves him; him
 pursue
 and take: none will him save.
12 Be thou not far from me, my God:
 thy speedy help I crave.
13 Confound, consume them, that unto
 my soul are enemies:
 Cloth'd be they with reproach and
  that do my hurt devise. [shame
14 But I with expectation
 will hope continually;
 And yet with praises more and more
  I will thee magnify.
15 Thy justice and salvation
 my mouth abroad shall show,
 Ev'n all the day; for I thereof
  the numbers do not know.
16 And I will constantly go on
 in strength of God the Lord;
 And thine own righteousness, ev'n
  alone, I will record. [thine
17 For even from my youth, O God,
 by thee I have been taught;
 And hitherto I have declar'd
  the wonders thou hast wrought.
18 And now, Lord, leave me not, when I
 old and gray-headed grow:

19 And thy most perfect righteousness,
    O Lord, is very high,
Who hast so great things done: O
    who is like unto thee?   [God,

20 Thou, Lord, who great adversities,
    and sore, to me didst show,
Shalt quicken, and bring me again
    from depths of earth below.

21 My greatness and my pow'r thou wilt
    increase, and far extend:
On ev'ry side against all grief
    thou wilt me comfort send.

22 Thee, ev'n thy truth, I'll also praise,
    my God, with psaltery:
Thou Holy One of Israel,
    with harp I'll sing to thee.

23 My lips shall much rejoice in thee,
    when I thy praises sound;
My soul, which thou redeemed hast,
    in joy shall much abound.

24 My tongue thy justice shall proclaim,
    continuing all day long;
For they confounded are, and sham'd,
    that seek to do me wrong.

PSALM 72.

1 O LORD, thy judgments give the
    his son thy righteousness. [king,
2 With right he shall thy people judge,
    thy poor with uprightness.
3 The lofty mountains shall bring forth
    unto the people peace;
Likewise the little hills the same
    shall do by righteousness.

4 The people's poor ones he shall
    the needy's children save; [judge,
And those shall he in pieces break
    who them oppressed have.
5 They shall thee fear, while sun and
    do last, through ages all.   [moon
6 Like rain on mown grass he shall
    or show'rs on earth that fall. [drop,

7 The just shall flourish in his days,
    and prosper in his reign:
He shall, while doth the moon en-
    abundant peace maintain.   [dure,
8 His large and great dominion shall
    from sea to sea extend:
It from the river shall reach forth
    unto earth's utmost end.
9 They in the wilderness that dwell
    bow down before him must;
And they that are his enemies
    shall lick the very dust.

10 The kings of Tarshish, and the isles,
    to him shall presents bring;
And unto him shall offer gifts
    Sheba's and Seba's king.
11 Yea, all the mighty kings on earth
    before him down shall fall;
And all the nations of the world
    do service to him shall.
12 For he the needy shall preserve,
    when he to him doth call;
The poor also, and him that hath
    no help of man at all.
13 The poor man and the indigent
    in mercy he shall spare;
He shall preserve alive the souls
    of those that needy are.
14 Both from deceit and violence
    their soul he shall set free;
And in his sight right precious
    and dear their blood shall be.
15 Yea, he shall live, and giv'n to him
    shall be of Sheba's gold:
For him still shall they pray, and he
    shall daily be extoll'd.
16 Of corn an handful in the earth
    on tops of mountains high,
With prosp'rous fruit shall shake,
    on Lebanon like trees [like trees
The city shall be flourishing,
    her citizens abound
In number shall, like to the grass
    that grows upon the ground.
17 His name for ever shall endure;
    last like the sun it shall:
Men shall be bless'd in him, and
    all nations shall him call. [bless'd
18 Now blessed be the Lord our God,
    the God of Israel,
For he alone doth wondrous works,
    in glory that excel.
19 And blessed be his glorious name
    to all eternity:
The whole earth let his glory fill.
    Amen, so let it be.

PSALM 73.

1 YET God is good to Israel,
    to each pure-hearted one.
2 But as for me, my steps near slipp'd,
    my feet were almost gone.
3 For I envious was, and grudg'd
    the foolish folk to see,
When I perceiv'd the wicked sort
    enjoy prosperity.
4 For still their strength continueth
    their death of bands is free. [firm;

5 They are not toil'd like other men,
   nor plagu'd, as others be.
6 Therefore their pride, like to a chain,
   them compasseth about;
   And, as a garment, violence
   doth cover them throughout.
7 Their eyes stand out with fat; they
   have
   more than their hearts could wish.
8 They are corrupt; their talk of wrong
   both lewd and lofty is.
9 They set their mouth against the
   heav'ns
   in their blasphemous talk;
   And their reproaching tongue
   throughout
   the earth at large doth walk.
10 His people oftentimes for this
   look back, and turn about;
   Sith waters of so full a cup
   to these are poured out.
11 And thus they say, How can it be
   that God these things doth know?
   Or, Can there in the Highest be
   knowledge of things below?
12 Behold, these are the wicked ones,
   yet prosper at their will
   In worldly things; they do increase
   in wealth and riches still.
13 I verily have done in vain
   my heart to purify;
   To no effect in innocence
   washed my hands have I.
14 For daily, and all day throughout,
   great plagues I suffer'd have;
   Yea, ev'ry morning I of new
   did chastisement receive.
15 If in this manner foolishly
   to speak I would intend,
   Thy children's generation,
   behold, I should offend.
16 When I this thought to know, it was
   too hard a thing for me;
17 Till to God's sanctuary I went,
   then I their end did see.
18 Assuredly thou didst them set
   a slipp'ry place upon;
   Them suddenly thou castedst down
   into destruction.
19 How in a moment suddenly
   to ruin brought are they!
   With fearful terrors utterly
   they are consum'd away.
20 Ev'n like unto a dream, when one
   from sleeping doth arise;
   So thou, O Lord, when thou awak'st,
   their image shalt despise.

21 Thus grieved was my heart in me,
   and me my reins opprest:
22 So rude was I, ignorant,
   and in thy sight a beast.
23 Nevertheless continually,
   O Lord, I am with thee:
   Thou dost me hold by my right hand,
   and still upholdest me.
24 Thou, with thy counsel, while I live,
   wilt me conduct and guide;
   And to thy glory afterward
   receive me to abide.
25 Whom have I in the heavens high
   but thee, O Lord, alone?
   And in the earth whom I desire
   besides thee there is none.
26 My flesh and heart doth faint and
   but God doth fail me never: [fail,
   For of my heart God is the strength
   and portion for ever.
27 For, lo, they that are far from thee
   for ever perish shall;
   Them that a whoring from thee go
   thou hast destroyed all.
28 But surely it is good for me
   that I draw near to God:
   In God I trust, that all thy works
   I may declare abroad.

PSALM 74.

1 O GOD, why hast thou cast us off?
     is it for evermore?
   Against thy pasture-sheep why doth
   thine anger smoke so sore?
2 O call to thy remembrance
   thy congregation,
   Which thou hast purchased of old;
   still think the same upon:
   The rod of thine inheritance,
   which thou redeemed hast,
   This Sion hill, wherein thou hadst
   thy dwelling in times past.
3 To these long desolations
   thy feet lift, do no' tarry;
   For all the ills thy foes have done
   within thy sanctuary.
4 Amidst thy congregations
   thine enemies do roar:
   Their ensigns they set up for signs
   of triumph thee before.
5 A man was famous, and was had
   in estimation,
   According as he lifted up
   his axe thick trees upon.
6 But all at once with axes now
   and hammers they go to,

And down the carved work thereof
   they break, and quite undo.
7 They fired have thy sanctuary,
   and have defil'd the same,
By casting down unto the ground
   the place where dwelt thy name.

8 Thus said they in their hearts, Let us
   destroy them out of hand:
They burnt up all the synagogues
   of God within the land.
9 Our signs we do not now behold;
   there is not us among
A prophet more, nor any one
   that knows the time how long.

10 How long, Lord, shall the enemy
   thus in reproach exclaim?
And shall the adversary thus
   always blaspheme thy name?
11 Thy hand, ev'n thy right hand of
   might,
   why dost thou thus draw back?
O from thy bosom pluck it out
   for our deliv'rance' sake.

12 For certainly God is my King,
   ev'n from the times of old,
Working in midst of all the earth
   salvation manifold.
13 The sea, by thy great pow'r, to part
   asunder thou didst make;
And thou the dragons' heads, O
   within the waters brake.   [Lord,
14 The leviathan's head thou brak'st
   in pieces, and didst give
Him to be meat unto the folk
   in wilderness that live.
15 Thou clav'st the fountain and the
   flood,
   which did with streams abound:
Thou dry'dst the mighty waters up
   unto the very ground.
16 Thine only is the day, O Lord,
   thine also is the night;
And thou alone prepared hast
   the sun and shining light.
17 By thee the borders of the earth
   were settled ev'ry where:
The summer and the winter both
   by thee created were.
18 That th' enemy reproached hath,
   O keep it in record;
And that the foolish people have
   blasphem'd thy name, O Lord.
19 Unto the multitude do not
   thy turtle's soul deliver:
The congregation of thy poor
   do not forget for ever.

20 Unto thy cov'nant have respect;
   for earth's dark places be
Full of the habitations
   of horrid cruelty.
21 O let not those that be oppress'd
   return again with shame:
Let those that poor and needy are
   give praise unto thy name.
22 Do thou, O God, arise and plead
   the cause that is thine own:
Remember how thou art reproach'd
   still by the foolish one.
23 Do not forget the voice of those
   that are thine enemies:
Of those the tumult ever grows
   that do against thee rise.

PSALM 75.

1 TO thee, O God, do we give thanks,
   we do give thanks to thee;
Because thy wondrous works declare
   thy great name near to be.
2 I purpose, when I shall receive
   the congregation,
That I shall judgment uprightly
   render to ev'ry one.

3 Dissolved is the land, with all
   that in the same do dwell;
But I the pillars thereof do
   bear up, and stablish well.
4 I to the foolish people said,
   Do not deal foolishly;
And unto those that wicked are,
   Lift not your horn on high.

5 Lift not your horn on high, nor speak
6   with stubborn neck. But know,
That not from east, nor west, nor
   promotion doth flow.   [south,
7 But God is judge; he puts down one,
   and sets another up.
8 For in the hand of God most high
   of red wine is a cup:
'Tis full of mixture; he pours forth,
   and makes the wicked all
Wring out the bitter dregs thereof;
   yea, and they drink them shall.
9 But I for ever will declare,
   I Jacob's God will praise.
10 All horns of lewd men I'll cut off;
   but just men's horns will raise.

PSALM 76.

1 IN Judah's land God is well known,
   his name's in Isr'el great:
2 In Salem is his tabernacle,
   in Sion is his seat.

3 There arrows of the bow he brake,
  the shield, the sword, the war.
4 More glorious thou than hills of prey,
  more excellent art far.

5 Those that were stout of heart are
  spoil'd,
  they slept their sleep outright;
  And none of those their hands did
  that were the men of might. [find,
6 When thy rebuke, O Jacob's God,
  had forth against them past,
  Their horses and their chariots both
  were in a dead sleep cast.

7 Thou, Lord, ev'n thou art he that
  be fear'd; and who is he [should
  That may stand up before thy sight,
  if once thou angry be?
8 From heav'n thou judgment caus'd
  be heard;
  the earth was still with fear,
9 When God to judgment rose, to save
  all meek on earth that were.

10 Surely the very wrath of man
   unto thy praise redounds:
   Thou to the remnant of his wrath
   wilt set restraining bounds.
11 Vow to the Lord your God, and pay:
   all ye that near him be,
   Bring gifts and presents unto him;
   for to be fear'd is he.
12 By him the sp'rits shall be cut off
   of those that princes are:
   Unto the kings that are on earth
   he fearful doth appear.

PSALM 77.

1 UNTO the Lord I with my voice,
  I unto God did cry;
  Ev'n with my voice, and unto me
  his ear he did apply.
2 I in my trouble sought the Lord,
  my sore by night did run,
  And ceased not; my grieved soul
  did consolation shun.

3 I to remembrance God did call,
  yet trouble did remain;
  And overwhelm'd my spirit was,
  whilst I did sore complain.
4 Mine eyes, debarr'd from rest and
  thou makest still to wake; [sleep,
  My trouble is so great that I
  unable am to speak.
5 The days of old to mind I call'd,
  and oft did think upon
  The times and ages that are past
  full many years agone.

6 By night my song I call to mind,
  and commune with my heart;
  My sp'rit did carefully enquire
  how I might ease my smart.
7 For ever will the Lord cast off,
  and gracious be no more?
8 For ever is his mercy gone?
  fails his word evermore?
9 Is't true that to be gracious
  the Lord forgotten hath?
  And that his tender mercies he
  hath shut up in his wrath?

10 Then did I say, That surely this
   is mine infirmity:
   I'll mind the years of the right hand
   of him that is most High.
11 Yea, I remember will the works
   performed by the Lord:
   The wonders done of old by thee
   I surely will record.
12 I also will of all thy works
   my meditation make;
   And of thy doings to discourse
   great pleasure I will take.
13 O God, thy way most holy is
   within thy sanctuary;
   And what god is so great in pow'r
   as is our God most high?

14 Thou art the God that wonders do'st
   by thy right hand most strong:
   Thy mighty pow'r thou hast declar'd
   the nations among.
15 To thine own people with thine arm
   thou didst redemption bring;
   To Jacob's sons, and to the tribes
   of Joseph that do spring.
16 The waters, Lord, perceived thee,
   the waters saw thee well;
   And they for fear aside did flee;
   the depths on trembling fell.
17 The clouds in water forth were
   sound loudly did the sky; [pour'd,
   And swiftly through the world
   thine arrows fierce did fly. [abroad
18 Thy thunder's voice alongst the
   a mighty noise did make; [heav'n
   By lightnings lighten'd was the
   world,
   th' earth tremble did and shake.
19 Thy way is in the sea, and in
   the waters great thy path;
   Yet are thy footsteps not, O Lord,
   none knowledge thereof hath.
20 Thy people thou didst safely lead,
   like to a flock of sheep;
   By Moses' hand and Aaron's thou
   didst them conduct and keep.

PSALM 78.

1 ATTEND, my people, to my law;
　　thereto give thou an ear;
The words that from my mouth pro-
　　attentively do hear.　　　[ceed

2 My mouth shall speak a parable,
　　and sayings dark of old;

3 The same which we have heard and
　　and us our fathers told.　　[known,

4 We also will them not conceal
　　from their posterity;
Them to the generation
　　to come declare will we:
The praises of the Lord our God,
　　and his almighty strength,
The wondrous works that he hath
　　done,
　　we will show forth at length.

5 His testimony and his law
　　in Isr'el he did place,
And charg'd our fathers it to show
　　to their succeeding race;

6 That so the race which was to come
　　might well them learn and know;
And sons unborn, who should arise,
　　might to their sons them show:

7 That they might set their hope in
　　and suffer not to fall　　　[God,
His mighty works out of their mind,
　　but keep his precepts all:

8 And might not, like their fathers, be
　　a stiff rebellious race;
A race not right in heart; with God
　　whose sp'rit not stedfast was.

9 The sons of Ephraim, who nor bows
　　nor other arms did lack,
When as the day of battle was,
　　they faintly turned back,

10 They brake God's cov'nant, and
　　refus'd
　　in his commands to go;

11 His works and wonders they forgot,
　　which he to them did show.

12 Things marvellous he brought to
　　their fathers them beheld　　[pass;
Within the land of Egypt done,
　　yea, ev'n in Zoan's field.

13 By him divided was the sea,
　　he caus'd them through to pass;
And made the waters so to stand,
　　as like an heap it was.

14 With cloud by day, with light of fire
　　all night, he did them guide.

15 In desert rocks he clave, and drink,
　　as from great depths, supply'd.

16 He from the rock brought streams,
　　like floods
　　made waters to run down.

17 Yet sinning more, in desert they
　　provok'd the Highest One.

18 For in their heart they tempted God,
　　and, speaking with mistrust,
They greedily did meat require
　　to satisfy their lust.

19 Against the Lord himself they spake,
　　and, murmuring, said thus,
A table in the wilderness
　　can God prepare for us?

20 Behold, he smote the rock, and
　　thence
　　came streams and waters great;
But can he give his people bread?
　　and send them flesh to eat?

21 The Lord did hear, and waxed
　　so kindled was a flame　　[wroth:
'Gainst Jacob, and 'gainst Israel
　　up indignation came.

22 For they believ'd not God, nor trust
　　in his salvation had;

23 Though clouds above he did com-
　　mand,
　　and heav'n's doors open made,

24 And manna rain'd on them, and gave
　　them corn of heav'n to eat.

25 Man angels' food did eat; to them
　　he to the full sent meat.

26 And in the heaven he did cause
　　an eastern wind to blow;
And by his power he let out
　　the southern wind to go.

27 Then flesh as thick as dust he made
　　to rain down them among;
And feather'd fowls, like as the sand
　　which li'th the shore along.

28 At his command amidst their camp
　　these show'rs of flesh down fell,
All round about the tabernacles
　　and tents where they did dwell.

29 So they did eat abundantly,
　　and had of meat their fill;
For he did give to them what was
　　their own desire and will.

30 They from their lust had not
　　estrang'd
　　their heart and their desire;
But while the meat was in their
　　mouths,
　　which they did so require,

31 God's wrath upon them came, and
　　the fattest of them all;　　[slew
So that the choice of Israel,
　　o'erthrown by death, did fall.

32 Yet, notwithstanding of all this,
       they sinned still the more;
   And though he had great wonders
       wrought,
   believ'd him not therefore:

33 Wherefore their days in vanity
       he did consume and waste;
   And by his wrath their wretched
       away in trouble past.   [years

34 But when he slew them, then they
       to seek him show desire;   [did
   Yea, they return'd, and after God
       right early did enquire.

35 And that the Lord had been their
       they did remember then;   [Rock
   Ev'n that the high almighty God
       had their Redeemer been.

36 Yet with their mouth they flatter'd
       and spake but feignedly;   [him,
   And they unto the God of truth
       with their false tongues did lie.

37 For though their words were good,
       their heart
   with him was not sincere;
   Unstedfast and perfidious
       they in his cov'nant were.

38 But, full of pity, he forgave
       their sin, them did not slay;
   Nor stirr'd up all his wrath, but oft
       his anger turn'd away.

39 For that they were but fading flesh
       to mind he did recall;
   A wind that passeth soon away,
       and not returns at all.

40 How often did they him provoke
       within the wilderness!
   And in the desert did him grieve
       with their rebelliousness!

41 Yea, turning back, they tempted
       and limits set upon   [God,
   Him, who in midst of Isr'el is
       the only Holy One.

42 They did not call to mind his pow'r,
       nor yet the day when he
   Deliver'd them out of the hand
       of their fierce enemy.

43 Nor how great signs in Egypt land
       he openly had wrought;
   What miracles in Zoan's field
       his hand to pass had brought.

44 How lakes and rivers ev'ry where
       he turned into blood;
   So that nor man nor beast could
       of standing lake or flood.   [drink

45 He brought among them swarms of
       which did them sore annoy; [flies,

And divers kinds of filthy frogs
       he sent them to destroy.

46 He to the caterpillar gave
       the fruits of all their soil;
   Their labours he deliver'd up
       unto the locusts' spoil.

47 Their vines with hail, their syca-
       he with the frost did blast: [mores

48 Their beasts to hail he gave; their
       hot thunderbolts did waste. [flocks

49 Fierce burning wrath he on them
       and indignation strong,   [cast,
   And troubles sore, by sending forth
       ill angels them among.

50 He to his wrath made way; their soul
       from death he did not save;
   But over to the pestilence
       the lives of them he gave.

51 In Egypt land the first-born all
       he smote down ev'ry where;
   Among the tents of Ham, ev'n these
       chief of their strength that were.

52 But his own people, like to sheep,
       thence to go forth he made;
   And he, amidst the wilderness,
       them, as a flock, did lead.

53 And he them safely on did lead,
       so that they did not fear;
   Whereas their en'mies by the sea
       quite overwhelmed were.

54 To borders of his sanctuary
       the Lord his people led,
   Ev'n to the mount which his right
       for them had purchased.   [hand

55 The nations of Canaan,
       by his almighty hand,
   Before their face he did expel
       out of their native land;
   Which for inheritance to them
       by line he did divide,
   And made the tribes of Israel
       within their tents abide.

56 Yet God most high they did provoke,
       and tempted ever still;
   And to observe his testimonies
       did not incline their will:

57 But, like their fathers, turned back,
       and dealt unfaithfully:
   Aside they turned, like a bow
       that shoots deceitfully.

58 For they to anger did provoke
       him with their places high;
   And with their graven images
       mov'd him to jealousy.

59 When God heard this, he waxed
       wroth,
       and much loath'd Isr'el then:

46

60 So Shiloh's tent he left, the tent
    which he had plac'd with men.

61 And he his strength delivered
    into captivity;
He left his glory in the hand
    of his proud enemy.

62 His people also he gave o'er
    unto the sword's fierce rage:
So sore his wrath inflamed was
    against his heritage.

63 The fire consum'd their choice young
    men;
    their maids no marriage had;

64 And when their priests fell by the
    sword,
    their wives no mourning made.

65 But then the Lord arose, as one
    that doth from sleep awake;
And like a giant that, by wine
    refresh'd, a shout doth make:

66 Upon his en'mies' hinder parts
    he made his stroke to fall;
And so upon them he did put
    a shame perpetual.

67 Moreover, he the tabernacle
    of Joseph did refuse;
The mighty tribe of Ephraim
    he would in no wise chuse:

68 But he did chuse Jehudah's tribe
    to be the rest above;
And of mount Sion he made choice,
    which he so much did love.

69 And he his sanctuary built
    like to a palace high,
Like to the earth which he did found
    to perpetuity.

70 Of David, that his servant was,
    he also choice did make,
And even from the folds of sheep
    was pleased him to take:

71 From waiting on the ewes with
    young,
    he brought him forth to feed
Israel, his inheritance,
    his people, Jacob's seed.

72 So after the integrity
    he of his heart them fed;
And by the good skill of his hands
    them wisely governed.

PSALM 79.

1 O GOD, the heathen enter'd have
    thine heritage; by them
Defiled is thy house: on heaps
    they laid Jerusalem.

2 The bodies of thy servants they
    have cast forth to be meat
To rav'nous fowls; thy dear saints'
    they gave to beasts to eat. [flesh

3 Their blood about Jerusalem
    like water they have shed;
And there was none to bury them
    when they were slain and dead.

4 Unto our neighbours a reproach
    most base become are we;
A scorn and laughingstock to them
    that round about us be.

5 How long, Lord, shall thine anger
    last?
    wilt thou still keep the same?
And shall thy fervent jealousy
    burn like unto a flame?

6 On heathen pour thy fury forth,
    that have thee never known,
And on those kingdoms which thy
    have never call'd upon. [name

7 For these are they who Jacob have
    devoured cruelly;
And they his habitation
    have caused waste to lie.

8 Against us mind not former sins;
    thy tender mercies show;
Let them prevent us speedily,
    for we're brought very low.

9 For thy name's glory help us, Lord,
    who hast our Saviour been:
Deliver us; for thy name's sake,
    O purge away our sin.

10 Why say the heathen, Where's their
    let him to them be known; [God?
When those who shed thy servants'
    are in our sight o'erthrown. [blood

11 O let the pris'ner's sighs ascend
    before thy sight on high;
Preserve those in thy mighty pow'r
    that are design'd to die.

12 And to our neighbours' bosom cause
    it sev'n-fold render'd be,
Ev'n the reproach wherewith they
    O Lord, reproached thee. [have,

13 So we thy folk, and pasture-sheep,
    shall give thee thanks always;
And unto generations all
    we will shew forth thy praise.

PSALM 80.

1 HEAR, Isr'el's Shepherd! like a
    flock
    thou that dost Joseph guide;
Shine forth, O thou that dost be-
    the cherubims abide. [tween

2 In Ephraim's, and Benjamin's,
   and in Manasseh's sight,
O come for our salvation;
   stir up thy strength and might.

3 Turn us again, O Lord our God,
   and upon us vouchsafe
To make thy countenance to shine,
   and so we shall be safe.

4 O Lord of hosts, almighty God,
   how long shall kindled be
Thy wrath against the prayer made
   by thine own folk to thee?

5 Thou tears of sorrow giv'st to them
   instead of bread to eat;
Yea, tears instead of drink thou giv'st
   to them in measure great.

6 Thou makest us a strife unto
   our neighbours round about;
Our enemies among themselves
   at us do laugh and flout.

7 Turn us again, O God of hosts,
   and upon us vouchsafe
To make thy countenance to shine,
   and so we shall be safe.

8 A vine from Egypt brought thou hast,
   by thine outstretched hand;
And thou the heathen out didst cast,
   to plant it in their land.

9 Before it thou a room didst make,
   where it might grow and stand;
Thou causedst it deep root to take,
   and it did fill the land.

10 The mountains vail'd were with its
   as with a covering;   [shade,
Like goodly cedars were the boughs
   which out from it did spring.

11 Upon the one hand to the sea
   her boughs she did out send;
On th' other side unto the flood
   her branches did extend.

12 Why hast thou then thus broken
   and ta'en her hedge away? [down,
So that all passengers do pluck,
   and make of her a prey.

13 The boar who from the forest comes
   doth waste it at his pleasure;
The wild beast of the field also
   devours it out of measure.

14 O God of hosts, we thee beseech,
   return now unto thine;
Look down from heav'n in love, be-
   and visit this thy vine: [hold,

15 This vineyard, which thine own right
   hath planted us among;
And that same branch, which for thy-
   thou hast made to be strong. [self

16 Burnt up it is with flaming fire,
   it also is cut down:
They utterly are perished,
   when as thy face doth frown.

17 O let thy hand be still upon
   the Man of thy right hand,
The Son of man, whom for thyself
   thou madest strong to stand.

18 So henceforth we will not go back,
   nor turn from thee at all:
O do thou quicken us, and we
   upon thy name will call.

19 Turn us again, Lord God of hosts,
   and upon us vouchsafe
To make thy countenance to shine,
   and so we shall be safe.

PSALM 81.

1 SING loud to God our strength;
      with joy
   to Jacob's God do sing.

2 Take up a psalm, the pleasant harp,
   timbrel and psalt'ry bring.

3 Blow trumpets at new-moon, what
   our feast appointed is: [day

4 For charge to Isr'el, and a law
   of Jacob's God was this.

5 To Joseph this a testimony
   he made, when Egypt land
He travell'd through, where speech I
   I did not understand.   [heard

6 His shoulder I from burdens took,
   his hands from pots did free.

7 Thou didst in trouble on me call,
   and I deliver'd thee:

   In secret place of thundering
   I did thee answer make;
And at the streams of Meribah
   of thee a proof did take.

8 O thou, my people, give an ear,
   I'll testify to thee;
To thee, O Isr'el, if thou wilt
   but hearken unto me.

9 In midst of thee there shall not be
   any strange god at all;
Nor unto any god unknown
   thou bowing down shalt fall.

10 I am the Lord thy God, which did
   from Egypt land thee guide;
I'll fill thy mouth abundantly,
   do thou it open wide.

11 But yet my people to my voice
   would not attentive be;
And ev'n my chosen Israel
   he would have none of me.

12 So to the lust of their own hearts
　　I them delivered;
　And then in counsels of their own
　　they vainly wandered.

13 O that my people had me heard,
　　Isr'el my ways had chose!

14 I had their en'mies soon subdu'd,
　　my hand turn'd on their foes.

15 The haters of the Lord to him
　　submission should have feign'd;
　But as for them, their time should
　　for evermore remain'd.　　[have

16 He should have also fed them with
　　the finest of the wheat;
　Of honey from the rock thy fill
　　I should have made thee eat.

PSALM 82.

1 IN gods' assembly God doth stand;
　　he judgeth gods among.

2 How long, accepting persons vile,
　　will ye give judgment wrong?

3 Defend the poor and fatherless;
　　to poor oppress'd do right.

4 The poor and needy ones set free;
　　rid them from ill men's might.

5 They know not, nor will understand;
　　in darkness they walk on:
　All the foundations of the earth
　　out of their course are gone.

6 I said that ye are gods, and are
　　sons of the Highest all:

7 But ye shall die like men, and as
　　one of the princes fall.

8 O God, do thou raise up thyself,
　　the earth to judgment call:
　For thou, as thine inheritance,
　　shalt take the nations all.

PSALM 83.

1 KEEP not, O God, we thee entreat,
　　O keep not silence now:
　Do thou not hold thy peace, O God,
　　and still no more be thou.

2 For, lo, thine enemies a noise
　　tumultuously have made;
　And they that haters are of thee
　　have lifted up the head.

3 Against thy chosen people they
　　do crafty counsel take;
　And they against thy hidden ones
　　do consultations make.

4 Come, let us cut them off, said they,
　　from being a nation,
　That of the name of Isr'el may
　　no more be mention.

5 For with joint heart they plot, in
　　league
　　against thee they combine.

6 The tents of Edom, Ishm'elites,
　　Moab's and Hagar's line;

7 Gebal, and Ammon, Amalek,
　　Philistines, those of Tyre;

8 And Assur join'd with them, to help
　　Lot's children they conspire.

9 Do to them as to Midian,
　　Jabin at Kison strand;

10 And Sis'ra, which at En-dor fell,
　　as dung to fat the land.

11 Like Oreb and like Zeeb make
　　their noble men to fall;
　Like Zeba and Zalmunna like,
　　make thou their princes all;

12 Who said, For our possession
　　let us God's houses take.

13 My God, them like a wheel, as chaff
　　before the wind, them make.

14 As fire consumes the wood, as flame
　　doth mountains set on fire,

15 Chase and affright them with the
　　and tempest of thine ire.　　[storm

16 Their faces fill with shame, O Lord,
　　that they may seek thy name.

17 Let them confounded be, and vex'd,
　　and perish in their shame:

18 That men may know that thou, to
　　alone doth appertain　　　[whom
　The name JEHOVAH, dost most
　　o'er all the earth remain.　　[high

PSALM 84.

1 HOW lovely is thy dwelling-place,
　　O Lord of hosts, to me!
　The tabernacles of thy grace
　　how pleasant, Lord, they be!

2 My thirsty soul longs veh'mently,
　　yea faints, thy courts to see:
　My very heart and flesh cry out,
　　O living God, for thee.

3 Behold, the sparrow findeth out
　　an house wherein to rest;
　The swallow also for herself
　　hath purchased a nest;
　Ev'n thine own altars, where she safe
　　her young ones forth may bring,
　O thou almighty Lord of hosts,
　　who art my God and King.

4 Bless'd are they in thy house that
　　they ever give thee praise.　　[dwell,

5 Bless'd is the man whose strength
　　thou art,
　　in whose heart are thy ways:

6 Who passing thorough Baca's vale,
 therein do dig up wells;
Also the rain that falleth down
 the pools with water fills.

7 So they from strength unwearied go
 still forward unto strength,
Until in Sion they appear
 before the Lord at length.

8 Lord God of hosts, my prayer hear;
 O Jacob's God, give ear.

9 See God our shield, look on the face
 of thine anointed dear.

10 For in thy courts one day excels
 a thousand; rather in
My God's house will I keep a door,
 than dwell in tents of sin.

11 For God the Lord 's a sun and shield:
 he'll grace and glory give;
And will withhold no good from
 that uprightly do live.   [them

12 O thou that art the Lord of hosts,
 that man is truly blest,
Who by assured confidence
 on thee alone doth rest.

PSALM 85.

1 O LORD, thou hast been favour-
 to thy beloved land: [able
Jacob's captivity thou hast
 recall'd with mighty hand.

2 Thou pardoned thy people hast
 all their iniquities;
Thou all their trespasses and sins
 hast cover'd from thine eyes.

3 Thou took'st off all thine ire, and
 turn'dst
from thy wrath's furiousness.

4 Turn us, God of our health, and cause
 thy wrath 'gainst us to cease.

5 Shall thy displeasure thus endure
 against us without end?
Wilt thou to generations all
 thine anger forth extend?

6 That in thee may thy people joy,
 wilt thou not us revive?

7 Show us thy mercy, Lord, to us
 do thy salvation give.

8 I'll hear what God the Lord will
 speak:
to his folk he'll speak peace,
And to his saints; but let them not
 return to foolishness.

9 To them that fear him surely near
 is his salvation;
That glory in our land may have
 her habitation.

10 Truth met with mercy, righteousness
 and peace kiss'd mutually:

11 Truth springs from earth, and righteousness
looks down from heaven high.

12 Yea, what is good the Lord shall
 give;
our land shall yield increase:

13 Justice, to set us in his steps,
 shall go before his face.

PSALM 86.

1 O LORD, do thou bow down thine
 and hear me graciously;   [ear,
Because I sore afflicted am,
 and am in poverty.

2 Because I'm holy, let my soul
 by thee preserved be:
O thou my God, thy servant save,
 that puts his trust in thee.

3 Sith unto thee I daily cry,
 be merciful to me.

4 Rejoice thy servant's soul; for, Lord,
 I lift my soul to thee.

5 For thou art gracious, O Lord,
 and ready to forgive;
And rich in mercy, all that call
 upon thee to relieve.

6 Hear, Lord, my pray'r; unto the
 of my request attend;   [voice

7 In troublous times I'll call on thee;
 for thou wilt answer send.

8 Lord, there is none among the gods
 that may with thee compare;
And like the works which thou hast
 not any work is there.   [done,

9 All nations whom thou mad'st shall
 and worship rev'rently   [come
Before thy face; and they, O Lord,
 thy name shall glorify.

10 Because thou art exceeding great,
 and works by thee are done
Which are to be admir'd; and thou
 art God thyself alone.

11 Teach me thy way, and in thy truth,
 O Lord, then walk will I;
Unite my heart, that I thy name
 may fear continually.

12 O Lord my God, with all my heart
 to thee I will give praise;
And I the glory will ascribe
 unto thy name always:

13 Because thy mercy toward me
 in greatness doth excel;
And thou deliver'd hast my soul
 out from the lowest hell.

14 O God, the proud against me rise,
    and vi'lent men have met,
That for my soul have sought; and
    before them have not set.   [thee

15 But thou art full of pity, Lord,
    a God most gracious,
Long-suffering, and in thy truth
    and mercy plenteous.

16 O turn to me thy countenance,
    and mercy on me have;
Thy servant strengthen; and the son
    of thine own handmaid save.

17 Show me a sign for good, that they
    which do me hate may see,
And be asham'd; because thou, Lord,
    didst help and comfort me.

PSALM 87.

1 UPON the hills of holiness
    he his foundation sets.

2 God, more than Jacob's dwellings all,
    delights in Sion's gates.

3 Things glorious are said of thee,
    thou city of the Lord.

4 Rahab and Babel I, to those
    that know me, will record:

Behold ev'n Tyrus, and with it
    the land of Palestine,
And likewise Ethiopia;
    this man was born therein.

5 And it of Sion shall be said,
    This man and that man there
Was born; and he that is most High
    himself shall stablish her.

6 When God the people writes, he'll
    count
    that this man born was there.

7 There be that sing and play; and all
    my well-springs in thee are.

PSALM 88.

1 LORD God, my Saviour, day and
    before thee cry'd have I. [night

2 Before thee let my prayer come;
    give ear unto my cry.

3 For troubles great do fill my soul;
    my life draws nigh the grave.

4 I'm counted with those that go down
    to pit, and no strength have.

5 Ev'n free among the dead, like them
    that slain in grave do lie;
Cut off from thy hand, whom no
    thou hast in memory.   [more

6 Thou hast me laid in lowest pit,
    in deeps and darksome caves.

7 Thy wrath lies hard on me, thou hast
    me press'd with all thy waves.

8 Thou hast put far from me my
    friends,
    thou mad'st them to abhor me;
And I am so shut up, that I
    find no evasion for me.

9 By reason of affliction
    mine eye mourns dolefully:
To thee, Lord, do I call, and stretch
    my hands continually.

10 Wilt thou show wonders to the dead?
    shall they rise, and thee bless?

11 Shall in the grave thy love be told?
    in death thy faithfulness?

12 Shall thy great wonders in the dark,
    or shall thy righteousness
Be known to any in the land
    of deep forgetfulness?

13 But, Lord, to thee I cry'd; my pray'r
    at morn prevent shall thee.

14 Why, Lord, dost thou cast off my
    soul,
    and hid'st thy face from me?

15 Distress'd am I, and from my youth
    I ready am to die;
Thy terrors I have borne, and am
    distracted fearfully.

16 The dreadful fierceness of thy wrath
    quite over me doth go:
Thy terrors great have cut me off,
    they did pursue me so.

17 For round about me ev'ry day,
    like water, they did roll;
And, gathering together, they
    have compassed my soul.

18 My friends thou hast put far from
    and him that did me love;   [me,
And those that mine acquaintance
    to darkness didst remove.   [were

PSALM 89.

1 GOD's mercies I will ever sing;
    and with my mouth I shall
Thy faithfulness make to be known
    to generations all.

2 For mercy shall be built, said I,
    for ever to endure;
Thy faithfulness, ev'n in the heav'ns,
    thou wilt establish sure.

3 I with my chosen One have made
    a cov'nant graciously;
And to my servant, whom I lov'd,
    to David sworn have I;

4 That I thy seed establish shall
    for ever to remain,

51

And will to generations all
  thy throne build and maintain.

5 The praises of thy wonders, Lord,
  the heavens shall express;
And in the congregation
  of saints thy faithfulness.

6 For who in heaven with the Lord
  may once himself compare?
Who is like God among the sons
  of those that mighty are?

7 Great fear in meeting of the saints
  is due unto the Lord;
And he of all about him should
  with rev'rence be ador'd.

8 O thou that art the Lord of hosts,
  what Lord in mightiness
Is like to thee? who compass'd round
  art with thy faithfulness.

9 Ev'n in the raging of the sea
  thou over it dost reign;
And when the waves thereof do swell,
  thou stillest them again.

10 Rahab in pieces thou didst break,
  like one that slaughter'd is;
And with thy mighty arm thou hast
  dispers'd thine enemies.

11 The heav'ns are thine, thou for thine
  the earth dost also take;   [own
The world, and fulness of the same,
  thy pow'r did found and make.

12 The north and south from thee alone
  their first beginning had;
Both Tabor mount and Hermon hill
  shall in thy name be glad.

13 Thou hast an arm that's full of pow'r,
  thy hand is great in might;
And thy right hand exceedingly
  exalted is in height.

14 Justice and judgment of thy throne
  are made the dwelling-place;
Mercy, accompany'd with truth,
  shall go before thy face.

15 O greatly bless'd the people are
  the joyful sound that know;
In brightness of thy face, O Lord,
  they ever on shall go.

16 They in thy name shall all the day
  rejoice exceedingly;
And in thy righteousness shall they
  exalted be on high.

17 Because the glory of their strength
  doth only stand in thee;
And in thy favour shall our horn
  and pow'r exalted be.

18 For God is our defence; and he
  to us doth safety bring:

The Holy One of Israel
  is our almighty King.

19 In vision to thy Holy One
  thou saidst, I help upon
A strong one laid; out of the folk
  I rais'd a chosen one;

20 Ev'n David, I have found him out
  a servant unto me;
And with my holy oil my King
  anointed him to be.

21 With whom my hand shall stablish'd
  be;
  mine arm shall make him strong.

22 On him the foe shall not exact,
  nor son of mischief wrong.

23 I will beat down before his face
  all his malicious foes;
I will them greatly plague who do
  with hatred him oppose.

24 My mercy and my faithfulness
  with him yet still shall be;
And in my name his horn and pow'r
  men shall exalted see.

25 His hand and pow'r shall reach afar;
  I'll set it in the sea;
And his right hand established
  shall in the rivers be.

26 Thou art my Father, he shall cry,
  thou art my God alone;
And he shall say, Thou art the Rock
  of my salvation.

27 I'll make him my first-born, more
  than kings of any land.   [high

28 My love I'll ever keep for him,
  my cov'nant fast shall stand.

29 His seed I by my pow'r will make
  for ever to endure;
And, as the days of heav'n, his throne
  shall stable be, and sure.

30 But if his children shall forsake
  my laws, and go astray,
And in my judgments shall not walk,
  but wander from my way:

31 If they my laws break, and do not
  keep my commandments;

32 I'll visit then their faults with rods,
  their sins with chastisements.

33 Yet I'll not take my love from him,
  nor false my promise make.

34 My cov'nant I'll not break, nor change
  what with my mouth I spake.

35 Once by my holiness I sware,
  to David I'll not lie;

36 His seed and throne shall, as the sun,
  before me last for aye.

37 It, like the moon, shall ever be
  establish'd stedfastly;

And like to that which in the heav'n
    doth witness faithfully.

38 But thou, displeased, hast cast off,
    thou didst abhor and loathe;
  With him that thine anointed is
    thou hast been very wroth.

39 Thou hast thy servant's covenant
    made void, and quite cast by;
  Thou hast profan'd his crown, while
    cast on the ground doth lie.   [it

40 Thou all his hedges hast broke down,
    his strong holds down hast torn.

41 He to all passers-by a spoil,
    to neighbours is a scorn.

42 Thou hast set up his foes' right hand;
    mad'st all his en'mies glad:

43 Turn'd his sword's edge, and him to
    in battle hast not made.   [stand

44 His glory thou hast made to cease,
    his throne to ground down cast;

45 Shorten'd his days of youth, and him
    with shame thou cover'd hast.

46 How long, Lord, wilt thou hide thy-
    for ever, in thine ire?   [self?
  And shall thine indignation
    burn like unto a fire?

47 Remember, Lord, how short a time
    I shall on earth remain:
  O wherefore is it so that thou
    hast made all men in vain?

48 What man is he that liveth here,
    and death shall never see?
  Or from the power of the grave
    what man his soul shall free?

49 Thy former loving-kindnesses,
    O Lord, where be they now?
  Those which in truth and faithfulness
    to David sworn hast thou?

50 Mind, Lord, thy servant's sad re-
    how I in bosom bear   [proach:
  The scornings of the people all,
    who strong and mighty are.

51 Wherewith thy raging enemies
    reproach'd, O Lord, think on;
  Wherewith they have reproach'd the
    of thine anointed one.   [steps

52 All blessing to the Lord our God
    let be ascribed then:
  For evermore so let it be.
    Amen, yea, and amen.

PSALM 90.

1 LORD, thou hast been our dwelling-
    in generations all.   [place

2 Before thou ever hadst brought forth
    the mountains great or small;

Ere ever thou hadst form'd the earth,
    and all the world abroad;
Ev'n thou from everlasting art
    to everlasting God.

3 Thou dost to destruction
    man that is mortal turn;
  And unto them thou say'st, Again,
    ye sons of men, return.

4 Because a thousand years appear
    no more before thy sight
  Than yesterday, when it is past,
    or than a watch by night.

5 As with an overflowing flood
    thou carry'st them away:
  They like a sleep are, like the grass
    that grows at morn are they.

6 At morn it flourishes and grows,
    cut down at ev'n doth fade.

7 For by thine anger we're consum'd,
    thy wrath makes us afraid.

8 Our sins thou and iniquities
    dost in thy presence place,
  And sett'st our secret faults before
    the brightness of thy face.

9 For in thine anger all our days
    do pass on to an end;
  And as a tale that hath been told,
    so we our years do spend.

10 Threescore and ten years do sum up
    our days and years, we see;
  Or if, by reason of more strength,
    in some fourscore they be:
  Yet doth the strength of such old
    but grief and labour prove; [men
  For it is soon cut off, and we
    fly hence, and soon remove.

11 Who knows the power of thy wrath?
    according to thy fear

12 So is thy wrath: Lord, teach thou us
    our end in mind to bear;
  And so to count our days, that we
    our hearts may still apply
  To learn thy wisdom and thy truth,
    that we may live thereby.

13 Turn yet again to us, O Lord,
    how long thus shall it be?
  Let it repent thee now for those
    that servants are to thee.

14 O with thy tender mercies, Lord,
    us early satisfy;
  So we rejoice shall all our days,
    and still be glad in thee.

15 According as the days have been,
    wherein we grief have had,
  And years wherein we ill have seen,
    so do thou make us glad.

16 O let thy work and pow'r appear
 thy servants' face before;
And show unto their children dear
 thy glory evermore:

17 And let the beauty of the Lord
 our God be us upon:
Our handy-works establish thou,
 establish them each one.

PSALM 91.

1 HE that doth in the secret place
 of the most High reside,
Under the shade of him that is
 th' Almighty shall abide.

2 I of the Lord my God will say,
 He is my refuge still,
He is my fortress, and my God,
 and in him trust I will.

3 Assuredly he shall thee save,
 and give deliverance
From subtile fowler's snare, and
 the noisome pestilence. [from

4 His feathers shall thee hide; thy trust
 under his wings shall be:
His faithfulness shall be a shield
 and buckler unto thee.

5 Thou shalt not need to be afraid
 for terrors of the night;
Nor for the arrow that doth fly
 by day, while it is light;

6 Nor for the pestilence, that walks
 in darkness secretly;
Nor for destruction, that doth waste
 at noon-day openly.

7 A thousand at thy side shall fall,
 on thy right hand shall lie
Ten thousand dead; yet unto thee
 it shall not once come nigh.

8 Only thou with thine eyes shalt look,
 and a beholder be;
And thou therein the just reward
 of wicked men shalt see.

9 Because the Lord, who constantly
 my refuge is alone,
Ev'n the most High, is made by thee
 thy habitation;

10 No plague shall near thy dwelling
 no ill shall thee befall: [come;

11 For thee to keep in all thy ways
 his angels charge he shall.

12 They in their hands shall bear thee
 still waiting thee upon; [up,
Lest thou at any time should'st dash
 thy foot against a stone.

13 Upon the adder thou shalt tread,
 and on the lion strong;

Thy feet on dragons trample shall,
 and on the lions young.

14 Because on me he set his love,
 I'll save and set him free;
Because my great name he hath
 I will him set on high. [known,

15 He'll call on me, I'll answer him;
 I will be with him still
In trouble, to deliver him,
 and honour him I will.

16 With length of days unto his mind
 I will him satisfy;
I also my salvation
 will cause his eyes to see.

PSALM 92.

1 TO render thanks unto the Lord
 it is a comely thing,
And to thy name, O thou most High,
 due praise aloud to sing.

2 Thy loving-kindness to show forth
 when shines the morning light;
And to declare thy faithfulness
 with pleasure ev'ry night,

3 On a ten-stringed instrument,
 upon the psaltery,
And on the harp with solemn sound,
 and grave sweet melody.

4 For thou, Lord, by thy mighty works
 hast made my heart right glad;
And I will triumph in the works
 which by thine hands were made.

5 How great, Lord, are thy works! each
 of thine a deep it is: [thought

6 A brutish man it knoweth not;
 fools understand not this.

7 When those that lewd and wicked are
 spring quickly up like grass,
And workers of iniquity
 do flourish all apace;

It is that they for ever may
 destroyed be and slain:

8 But thou, O Lord, art the most High,
 for ever to remain.

9 For, lo, thine enemies, O Lord,
 thine en'mies perish shall;
The workers of iniquity
 shall be dispersed all.

10 But thou shalt, like unto the horn
 of th' unicorn, exalt
My horn on high: thou with fresh oil
 anoint me also shalt.

11 Mine eyes shall also my desire
 see on mine enemies;
Mine ears shall of the wicked hear,
 that do against me rise.

12 But like the palm-tree flourishing
    shall be the righteous one;
He shall like to the cedar grow
    that is in Lebanon.

13 Those that within the house of God
    are planted by his grace,
They shall grow up, and flourish all
    in our God's holy place.

14 And in old age, when others fade,
    they fruit still forth shall bring;
They shall be fat, and full of sap,
    and aye be flourishing;

15 To show that upright is the Lord:
    he is a rock to me;
And he from all unrighteousness
    is altogether free.

PSALM 93.

1 THE Lord doth reign, and cloth'd
    with majesty most bright; [is he
His works do show him cloth'd to be,
    and girt about with might.
The world is also stablished,
    that it cannot depart.

2 Thy throne is fix'd of old, and thou
    from everlasting art.

3 The floods, O Lord, have lifted up,
    they lifted up their voice;
The floods have lifted up their waves,
    and made a mighty noise.

4 But yet the Lord, that is on high,
    is more of might by far
Than noise of many waters is,
    or great sea-billows are.

5 Thy testimonies ev'ry one
    in faithfulness excel;
And holiness for ever, Lord,
    thine house becometh well.

PSALM 94.

1 O LORD God, unto whom alone
    all vengeance doth belong;
O mighty God, who vengeance
    own'st,
shine forth, avenging wrong.

2 Lift up thyself, thou of the earth
    the sov'reign Judge that art;
And unto those that are so proud
    a due reward impart.

3 How long, O mighty God, shall they
    who lewd and wicked be,
How long shall they who wicked are
    thus triumph haughtily?

4 How long shall things most hard by
    be uttered and told? [them
And all that work iniquity
    to boast themselves be bold?

5 Thy folk they break in pieces, Lord,
    thine heritage oppress:

6 The widow they and stranger slay,
    and kill the fatherless.

7 Yet say they, God it shall not see,
    nor God of Jacob know.

8 Ye brutish people! understand;
    fools! when wise will ye grow?

9 The Lord did plant the ear of man,
    and hear then shall not he?
He only form'd the eye, and then
    shall he not clearly see?

10 He that the nations doth correct,
    shall he not chastise you?
He knowledge unto man doth teach,
    and shall himself not know?

11 Man's thoughts to be but vanity
    the Lord doth well discern.

12 Bless'd is the man thou chast'nest,
    Lord,
and mak'st thy law to learn:

13 That thou may'st give him rest from
    of sad adversity, [days
Until the pit be digg'd for those
    that work iniquity.

14 For sure the Lord will not cast off
    those that his people be,
Neither his own inheritance
    quit and forsake will he:

15 But judgment unto righteousness
    shall yet return again;
And all shall follow after it
    that are right-hearted men.

16 Who will rise up for me against
    those that do wickedly?
Who will stand up for me 'gainst
    that work iniquity? [those

17 Unless the Lord had been my help
    when I was sore opprest,
Almost my soul had in the house
    of silence been at rest.

18 When I had uttered this word,
    My foot doth slip away,
Thy mercy held me up, O Lord,
    thy goodness did me stay.

19 Amidst the multitude of thoughts
    which in my heart do fight,
My soul, lest it be overcharg'd,
    thy comforts do delight.

20 Shall of iniquity the throne
    have fellowship with thee,
Which mischief, cunningly contriv'd,
    doth by a law decree?

21 Against the righteous souls they join,
    they guiltless blood condemn.

22 But of my refuge God's the rock,
    and my defence from them.

23 On them their own iniquity
    the Lord shall bring and lay,
And cut them off in their own sin;
    our Lord God shall them slay.

PSALM 95.

1 O COME, let us sing to the Lord:
    come, let us ev'ry one
A joyful noise make to the Rock
    of our salvation.

2 Let us before his presence come
    with praise and thankful voice;
Let us sing psalms to him with grace,
    and make a joyful noise.

3 For God, a great God, and great
    above all gods he is.   [King,
4 Depths of the earth are in his hand,
    the strength of hills is his.
5 To him the spacious sea belongs,
    for he the same did make;
The dry land also from his hands
    its form at first did take.

6 O come, and let us worship him,
    let us bow down withal,
And on our knees before the Lord
    our Maker let us fall.
7 For he's our God, the people we
    of his own pasture are,
And of his hand the sheep; to-day,
    if ye his voice will hear,
8 Then harden not your hearts, as in
    the provocation,
As in the desert, on the day
    of the tentation:
9 When me your fathers tempt'd and
    and did my working see; [prov'd,
10 Ev'n for the space of forty years
    this race hath grieved me.

    I said, This people errs in heart,
        my ways they do not know:
11 To whom I sware in wrath, that to
        my rest they should not go.

PSALM 96.

1 O SING a new song to the Lord:
    sing all the earth to God.
2 To God sing, bless his name, show
    his saving health abroad.   [still
3 Among the heathen nations
    his glory do declare;
And unto all the people show
    his works that wondrous are.

4 For great's the Lord, and greatly he
    is to be magnify'd;
Yea, worthy to be fear'd is he
    above all gods beside.

5 For all the gods are idols dumb,
    which blinded nations fear;
But our God is the Lord, by whom
    the heav'ns created were.

6 Great honour is before his face,
    and majesty divine;
Strength is within his holy place,
    and there doth beauty shine.
7 Do ye ascribe unto the Lord,
    of people ev'ry tribe,
Glory do ye unto the Lord,
    and mighty pow'r ascribe.

8 Give ye the glory to the Lord
    that to his name is due;
Come ye into his courts, and bring
    an offering with you.
9 In beauty of his holiness,
    O do the Lord adore;
Likewise let all the earth throughout
    tremble his face before.

10 Among the heathen say, God reigns;
    the world shall stedfastly
Be fix'd from moving; he shall judge
    the people righteously.
11 Let heav'ns be glad before the Lord,
    and let the earth rejoice;
Let seas, and all that is therein,
    cry out, and make a noise.
12 Let fields rejoice, and ev'ry thing
    that springeth of the earth:
Then woods and ev'ry tree shall sing
    with gladness and with mirth
13 Before the Lord; because he comes,
    to judge the earth comes he:
He'll judge the world with righteous-
    the people faithfully.   [ness,

PSALM 97.

1 GOD reigneth, let the earth be
    glad,
    and isles rejoice each one.
2 Dark clouds him compass; and in
    right
    with judgment dwells his throne.
3 Fire goes before him, and his foes
    it burns up round about:
4 His lightnings lighten did the world;
    earth saw, and shook throughout.
5 Hills at the presence of the Lord,
    like wax, did melt away;
Ev'n at the presence of the Lord
    of all the earth, I say.
6 The heav'ns declare his righteous-
    all men his glory see.   [ness,
7 All who serve graven images,
    confounded let them be.

Who do of idols boast themselves,
    let shame upon them fall:
Ye that are called gods, see that
    ye do him worship all.

8 Sion did hear, and joyful was,
    glad Judah's daughters were;
They much rejoic'd, O Lord, because
    thy judgments did appear.

9 For thou, O Lord, art high above
    all things on earth that are;
Above all other gods thou art
    exalted very far.

10 Hate ill, all ye that love the Lord:
    his saints' souls keepeth he;
And from the hands of wicked men
    he sets them safe and free.

11 For all those that be righteous
    sown is a joyful light,
And gladness sown is for all those
    that are in heart upright.
12 Ye righteous, in the Lord rejoice;
    express your thankfulness,
When ye into your memory
    do call his holiness.

PSALM 98.

1 O SING a new song to the Lord,
    for wonders he hath done:
His right hand and his holy arm
    him victory hath won.
2 The Lord God his salvation
    hath caused to be known;
His justice in the heathen's sight
    he openly hath shown.

3 He mindful of his grace and truth
    to Isr'el's house hath been;
And the salvation of our God
    all ends of th' earth have seen.
4 Let all the earth unto the Lord
    send forth a joyful noise;
Lift up your voice aloud to him,
    sing praises, and rejoice.

5 With harp, with harp, and voice of
    psalms,
    unto JEHOVAH sing:
6 With trumpets, cornets, gladly sound
    before the Lord the King.
7 Let seas and all their fulness roar;
    the world, and dwellers there;
8 Let floods clap hands, and let the hills
    together joy declare

9 Before the Lord; because he comes,
    to judge the earth comes he:
He'll judge the world with righteous-
    his folk with equity.   [ness,

PSALM 99.

1 TH' eternal Lord doth reign as king,
    let all the people quake;
He sits between the cherubims,
    let th' earth be mov'd and shake.
2 The Lord in Sion great and high
    above all people is;
3 Thy great and dreadful name (for it
    is holy) let them bless.

4 The king's strength also judgment
    thou settlest equity: [loves;
Just judgment thou dost execute
    in Jacob righteously.
5 The Lord our God exalt on high,
    and rev'rently do ye
Before his footstool worship him:
    the Holy One is he.

6 Moses and Aaron 'mong his priests,
    Samuel, with them that call
Upon his name: these call'd on God,
    and he them answer'd all.
7 Within the pillar of the cloud
    he unto them did speak:
The testimonies he them taught,
    and laws, they did not break.

8 Thou answer'dst them, O Lord our
    God;
    thou wast a God that gave
Pardon to them, though on their deeds
    thou wouldest vengeance have.
9 Do ye exalt the Lord our God,
    and at his holy hill
Do ye him worship: for the Lord
    our God is holy still.

PSALM 100.

1 ALL people that on earth do dwell,
    Sing to the Lord with cheerful
    voice.
2 Him serve with mirth, his praise forth
    tell,
    Come ye before him and rejoice.
3 Know that the Lord is God indeed;
    Without our aid he did us make:
We are his flock, he doth us feed,
    And for his sheep he doth us take.

4 O enter then his gates with praise,
    Approach with joy his courts unto:
Praise, laud, and bless his name
    always,
    For it is seemly so to do.
5 For why? the Lord our God is good,
    His mercy is for ever sure;
His truth at all times firmly stood,
    And shall from age to age endure.

Another of the same.

1 O ALL ye lands, unto the Lord
   make ye a joyful noise.
2 Serve God with gladness, him before
   come with a singing voice.
3 Know ye the Lord that he is God;
   not we, but he us made:
  We are his people, and the sheep
   within his pasture fed.
4 Enter his gates and courts with praise,
   to thank him go ye thither:
  To him express your thankfulness,
   and bless his name together.
5 Because the Lord our God is good,
   his mercy faileth never;
  And to all generations
   his truth endureth ever.

PSALM 101.

1 I MERCY will and judgment sing,
   Lord, I will sing to thee.
2 With wisdom in a perfect way
   shall my behaviour be.
  O when, in kindness unto me,
   wilt thou be pleas'd to come?
  I with a perfect heart will walk
   within my house at home.
3 I will endure no wicked thing
   before mine eyes to be:
  I hate their work that turn aside,
   it shall not cleave to me.
4 A stubborn and a froward heart
   depart quite from me shall;
  A person giv'n to wickedness
   I will not know at all.
5 I'll cut him off that slandereth
   his neighbour privily:
  The haughty heart I will not bear,
   nor him that looketh high.
6 Upon the faithful of the land
   mine eyes shall be, that they
  May dwell with me: he shall me serve
   that walks in perfect way.
7 Who of deceit a worker is
   in my house shall not dwell;
  And in my presence shall he not
   remain that lies doth tell.
8 Yea, all the wicked of the land
   early destroy will I;
  All from God's city to cut off
   that work iniquity.

PSALM 102.

1 O LORD, unto my pray'r give ear,
   my cry let come to thee;
2 And in the day of my distress
   hide not thy face from me.

  Give ear to me; what time I call,
   to answer me make haste:
3 For, as an hearth, my bones are burnt,
   my days, like smoke, do waste.
4 My heart within me smitten is,
   and it is withered
  Like very grass; so that I do
   forget to eat my bread.
5 By reason of my groaning voice
   my bones cleave to my skin.
6 Like pelican in wilderness
   forsaken I have been:

  I like an owl in desert am,
   that nightly there doth moan;
7 I watch, and like a sparrow am
   on the house-top alone.
8 My bitter en'mies all the day
   reproaches cast on me;
  And, being mad at me, with rage
   against me sworn they be.
9 For why? I ashes eaten have
   like bread, in sorrows deep;
  My drink I also mingled have
   with tears that I did weep.
10 Thy wrath and indignation
   did cause this grief and pain;
  For thou hast lift me up on high,
   and cast me down again.
11 My days are like unto a shade,
   which doth declining pass;
  And I am dry'd and withered,
   ev'n like unto the grass.
12 But thou, Lord, everlasting art,
   and thy remembrance shall
  Continually endure, and be
   to generations all.
13 Thou shalt arise, and mercy have
   upon thy Sion yet;
  The time to favour her is come,
   the time that thou hast set.
14 For in her rubbish and her stones
   thy servants pleasure take;
  Yea, they the very dust thereof
   do favour for her sake.
15 So shall the heathen people fear
   the Lord's most holy name;
  And all the kings on earth shall dread
   thy glory and thy fame.
16 When Sion by the mighty Lord
   built up again shall be,
  In glory then and majesty
   to men appear shall he.
17 The prayer of the destitute
   he surely will regard;
  Their prayer will he not despise,
   by him it shall be heard.

18 For generations yet to come
 this shall be on record:
So shall the people that shall be
 created praise the Lord.

19 He from his sanctuary's height
 hath downward cast his eye;
And from his glorious throne in
 heav'n
  the Lord the earth did spy;

20 That of the mournful prisoner
 the groanings he might hear,
To set them free that unto death
 by men appointed are:

21 That they in Sion may declare
 the Lord's most holy name,
And publish in Jerusalem
 the praises of the same:

22 When as the people gather shall
 in troops with one accord,
When kingdoms shall assembled be
 to serve the highest Lord.

23 My wonted strength and force he
 abated in the way,   [hath
And he my days hath shortened:

24 Thus therefore did I say,
My God, in mid-time of my days
 take thou me not away:
From age to age eternally
 thy years endure and stay.

25 The firm foundation of the earth
 of old time thou hast laid;
The heavens also are the work
 which thine own hands have made.

26 Thou shalt for evermore endure,
 but they shall perish all;
Yea, ev'ry one of them wax old,
 like to a garment, shall:

Thou, as a vesture, shalt them change,
 and they shall changed be:

27 But thou the same art, and thy years
 are to eternity.

28 The children of thy servants shall
 continually endure;
And in thy sight, O Lord, their seed
 shall be establish'd sure.

Another of the same.

1 LORD, hear my pray'r, and let my
 cry
Have speedy access unto thee;

2 In day of my calamity
O hide not thou thy face from me.
Hear when I call to thee; that day
An answer speedily return:

3 My days, like smoke, consume away,
And, as an hearth, my bones do burn.

4 My heart is wounded very sore,
And withered, like grass doth fade:
I am forgetful grown therefore
To take and eat my daily bread.

5 By reason of my smart within,
And voice of my most grievous
 groans,
My flesh consumed is, my skin,
All parch'd, doth cleave unto my
 bones.

6 The pelican of wilderness,
The owl in desert, I do match;

7 And, sparrow-like, companionless,
Upon the house's top, I watch.

8 I all day long am made a scorn,
Reproach'd by my malicious foes:
The madmen are against me sworn,
The men against me that arose.

9 For I have ashes eaten up,
To me as if they had been bread;
And with my drink I in my cup
Of bitter tears a mixture made.

10 Because thy wrath was not appeas'd,
And dreadful indignation:
Therefore it was that thou me rais'd,
And thou again didst cast me down.

11 My days are like a shade alway,
Which doth declining swiftly pass;
And I am withered away,
Much like unto the fading grass.

12 But thou, O Lord, shalt still endure,
From change and all mutation free,
And to all generations sure
Shall thy remembrance ever be.

13 Thou shalt arise, and mercy yet
Thou to mount Sion shalt extend:
Her time for favour which was set,
Behold, is now come to an end.

14 Thy saints take pleasure in her stones,
Her very dust to them is dear.

15 All heathen lands and kingly thrones
On earth thy glorious name shall fear.

16 God in his glory shall appear,
When Sion he builds and repairs.

17 He shall regard and lend his ear
Unto the needy's humble pray'rs:
Th' afflicted's pray'r he will not
 scorn.

18 All times this shall be on record:
And generations yet unborn
Shall praise and magnify the Lord.

19 He from his holy place look'd down,
The earth he view'd from heav'n on
 high;

20 To hear the pris'ner's mourning
 groan,
And free them that are doom'd to die;

21 That Sion, and Jerus'lem too,
  His name and praise may well record,
22 When people and the kingdoms do
  Assemble all to praise the Lord.

23 My strength he weaken'd in the way,
  My days of life he shortened.
24 My God, O take me not away
  In mid-time of my days, I said:
  Thy years throughout all ages last.
25 Of old thou hast established
  The earth's foundation firm and fast:
  Thy mighty hands the heav'ns have
  made.

26 They perish shall, as garments do,
  But thou shalt evermore endure;
  As vestures, thou shalt change them
  so;
  And they shall all be changed sure:
27 But from all changes thou art free;
  Thy endless years do last for aye.
28 Thy servants, and their seed who be,
  Establish'd shall before thee stay.

PSALM 103.

1 O THOU my soul, bless God the
  and all that in me is   [Lord;
  Be stirred up his holy name
  to magnify and bless.
2 Bless, O my soul, the Lord thy God,
  and not forgetful be
  Of all his gracious benefits
  he hath bestow'd on thee.

3 All thine iniquities who doth
  most graciously forgive:
  Who thy diseases all and pains
  doth heal, and thee relieve.
4 Who doth redeem thy life, that thou
  to death may'st not go down;
  Who thee with loving-kindness doth
  and tender mercies crown:
5 Who with abundance of good things
  doth satisfy thy mouth;
  So that, ev'n as the eagle's age,
  renewed is thy youth.
6 God righteous judgment executes
  for all oppressed ones.
7 His ways to Moses, he his acts
  made known to Isr'el's sons.

8 The Lord our God is merciful,
  and he is gracious,
  Long-suffering, and slow to wrath,
  in mercy plenteous.
9 He will not chide continually,
  nor keep his anger still.
10 With us he dealt not as we sinn'd,
  nor did requite our ill.

11 For as the heaven in its height
  the earth surmounteth far;
  So great to those that do him fear
  his tender mercies are:
12 As far as east is distant from
  the west, so far hath he
  From us removed, in his love,
  all our iniquity.

13 Such pity as a father hath
  unto his children dear;
  Like pity shows the Lord to such
  as worship him in fear.
14 For he remembers we are dust,
  and he our frame well knows.
15 Frail man, his days are like the grass,
  as flow'r in field he grows:
16 For over it the wind doth pass,
  and it away is gone;
  And of the place where once it was
  it shall no more be known.

17 But unto them that do him fear
  God's mercy never ends;
  And to their children's children still
  his righteousness extends:
18 To such as keep his covenant,
  and mindful are alway
  Of his most just commandments,
  that they may them obey.
19 The Lord prepared hath his throne
  in heavens firm to stand;
  And ev'ry thing that being hath
  his kingdom doth command.

20 O ye his angels, that excel
  in strength, bless ye the Lord;
  Ye who obey what he commands,
  and hearken to his word.
21 O bless and magnify the Lord,
  ye glorious hosts of his;
  Ye ministers, that do fulfil
  whate'er his pleasure is.
22 O bless the Lord, all ye his works,
  wherewith the world is stor'd
  In his dominions ev'ry where.
  My soul, bless thou the Lord.

PSALM 104.

1 BLESS God, my soul. O Lord my
  thou art exceeding great; [God,
  With honour and with majesty
  thou clothed art in state.
2 With light, as with a robe, thyself
  thou coverest about;
  And, like unto a curtain, thou
  the heavens stretchest out.

3 Who of his chambers doth the **beams**
  within the waters lay;

60

Who doth the clouds his chariot make,
on wings of wind make way.

4 Who flaming fire his ministers,
his angels sp'rits, doth make:

5 Who earth's foundations did lay,
that it should never shake.

6 He didst it cover with the deep,
as with a garment spread:
The waters stood above the hills,
when thou the word but said.

7 But at the voice of thy rebuke
they fled, and would not stay;
They at thy thunder's dreadful voice
did haste them fast away.

8 They by the mountains do ascend,
and by the valley-ground
Descend, unto that very place
which thou for them didst found.

9 Thou hast a bound unto them set,
that they may not pass over,
That they do not return again
the face of earth to cover.

10 He to the valleys sends the springs,
which run among the hills:

11 They to all beasts of field give drink,
wild asses drink their fills.

12 By them the fowls of heav'n shall
their habitation, [have
Which do among the branches sing
with delectation.

13 He from his chambers watereth
the hills, when they are dry'd:
With fruit and increase of thy works
the earth is satisfy'd.

14 For cattle he makes grass to grow,
he makes the herb to spring
For th' use of man, that food to him
he from the earth may bring;

15 And wine, that to the heart of man
doth cheerfulness impart,
Oil that his face makes shine, and
that strengtheneth his heart. [bread

16 The trees of God are full of sap;
the cedars that do stand
In Lebanon, which planted were
by his almighty hand.

17 Birds of the air upon their boughs
do chuse their nests to make;
As for the stork, the fir-tree she
doth for her dwelling take.

18 The lofty mountains for wild goats
a place of refuge be;
The conies also to the rocks
do for their safety flee.

19 He sets the moon in heav'n, thereby
the seasons to discern:

From him the sun his certain time
of going down doth learn.

20 Thou darkness mak'st, 'tis night, then
of forests creep abroad. [beasts

21 The lions young roar for their prey,
and seek their meat from God.

22 The sun doth rise, and home they
down in their dens they lie. [flock,

23 Man goes to work, his labour he
doth to the ev'ning ply.

24 How manifold, Lord, are thy works!
in wisdom wonderful
Thou ev'ry one of them hast made;
earth's of thy riches full:

25 So is this great and spacious sea,
wherein things creeping are,
Which number'd cannot be; and
beasts
both great and small are there.

26 There ships go; there thou mak'st to
that leviathan great. [play

27 These all wait on thee, that thou
may'st
in due time give them meat.

28 That which thou givest unto them
they gather for their food;
Thine hand thou open'st lib'rally,
they filled are with good.

29 Thou hid'st thy face; they troubled
are,
their breath thou tak'st away;
Then do they die, and to their dust
return again do they.

30 Thy quick'ning spirit thou send'st
then they created be; [forth,
And then the earth's decayed face
renewed is by thee.

31 The glory of the mighty Lord
continue shall for ever:
The Lord JEHOVAH shall rejoice
in all his works together.

32 Earth, as affrighted, trembleth all,
if he on it but look;
And if the mountains he but touch,
they presently do smoke.

33 I will sing to the Lord most high,
so long as I shall live;
And while I being have I shall
to my God praises give.

34 Of him my meditation shall
sweet thoughts to me afford;
And as for me, I will rejoice
in God, my only Lord.

35 From earth let sinners be consum'd,
let ill men no more be.
O thou my soul, bless thou the Lord.
Praise to the Lord give ye.

PSALM 105.

1 GIVE thanks to God, call on his
name;
  to men his deeds make known.

2 Sing ye to him, sing psalms; proclaim
his wondrous works each one.

3 See that ye in his holy name
to glory do accord;
And let the heart of ev'ry one
rejoice that seeks the Lord.

4 The Lord Almighty, and his strength,
with stedfast hearts seek ye:
His blessed and his gracious face
seek ye continually.

5 Think on the works that he hath
which admiration breed;   [done,
His wonders, and the judgments all
which from his mouth proceed:

6 O ye that are of Abr'ham's race,
his servant well approv'n;
And ye that Jacob's children are,
whom he chose for his own.

7 Because he, and he only, is
the mighty Lord our God;
And his most righteous judgments
in all the earth abroad.   [are

8 His cov'nant he remember'd hath,
that it may ever stand:
To thousand generations
the word he did command.

9 Which covenant he firmly made
with faithful Abraham,
And unto Isaac, by his oath,
he did renew the same:

10 And unto Jacob, for a law,
he made it firm and sure,
A covenant to Israel,
which ever should endure.

11 He said, I'll give Canaan's land
for heritage to you;

12 While they were strangers there, and
in number very few: [few,

13 While yet they went from land to
without a sure abode;   [land
And while through sundry kingdoms
did wander far abroad;   [they

14 Yet, notwithstanding, suffer'd he
no man to do them wrong:
Yea, for their sakes, he did reprove
kings, who were great and strong.

15 Thus did he say, Touch ye not those
that mine anointed be,
Nor do the prophets any harm
that do pertain to me.

16 He call'd for famine on the land,
he brake the staff of bread:

17 But yet he sent a man before,
by whom they should be fed;

Ev'n Joseph, whom unnat'rally
sell for a slave did they;

18 Whose feet with fetters they did hurt,
and he in irons lay;

19 Until the time that his word came
to give him liberty;
The word and purpose of the Lord
did him in prison try.

20 Then sent the king, and did com-
that he enlarg'd should be: [mand
He that the people's ruler was
did send to set him free.

21 A lord to rule his family
he rais'd him, as most fit;
To him of all that he possess'd
he did the charge commit:

22 That he might at his pleasure bind
the princes of the land;
And he might teach his senators
wisdom to understand.

23 The people then of Israel
down into Egypt came;
And Jacob also sojourned
within the land of Ham.

24 And he did greatly by his pow'r
increase his people there;
And stronger than their enemies
they by his blessing were.

25 Their heart he turned to envy
his folk maliciously,
With those that his own servants
to deal in subtilty.   [were

26 His servant Moses he did send,
Aaron his chosen one.

27 By these his signs and wonders great
in Ham's land were made known.

28 Darkness he sent, and made it dark
his word they did obey.

29 He turn'd their waters into blood,
and he their fish did slay.

30 The land in plenty brought forth
in chambers of their kings.   [frogs

31 His word all sorts of flies and lice
in all their borders brings.

32 He hail for rain, and flaming fire
into their land he sent:

33 And he their vines and fig-trees
smote;
trees of their coasts he rent.

34 He spake, and caterpillars came,
locusts did much abound;

35 Which in their land all herbs consum'd,
and all fruits of their ground.

36 He smote all first-born in their land,
    chief of their strength each one.
37 With gold and silver brought them
    forth,
    weak in their tribes were none.

38 Egypt was glad when forth they went,
    their fear on them did light.
39 He spread a cloud for covering,
    and fire to shine by night.
40 They ask'd, and he brought quails:
    with bread
    of heav'n he filled them.
41 He open'd rocks, floods gush'd, and
    in deserts like a stream.   [ran

42 For on his holy promise he,
    and servant Abr'ham, thought.
43 With joy his people, his elect
    with gladness, forth he brought.
44 And unto them the pleasant lands
    he of the heathen gave;
    That of the people's labour they
    inheritance might have.

45 That by his statutes might observe
    according to his word;
    And that they might his laws obey.
    Give praise unto the Lord.

PSALM 106.

1 GIVE praise and thanks unto the
    for bountiful is he;   [Lord,
    His tender mercy doth endure
    unto eternity.
2 God's mighty works who can express?
    or show forth all his praise?
3 Blessed are they that judgment keep,
    and justly do always.

4 Remember me, Lord, with that love
    which thou to thine dost bear;
    With thy salvation, O my God,
    to visit me draw near:
5 That I thy chosen's good may see,
    and in their joy rejoice;
    And may with thine inheritance
    triumph with cheerful voice.

6 We with our fathers sinned have,
    and of iniquity
    Too long we have the workers been;
    we have done wickedly.
7 The wonders great, which thou, O
    didst work in Egypt land,   [Lord,
    Our fathers, though they saw, yet
    they did not understand: [them
    And they thy mercies' multitude
    kept not in memory;
    But at the sea, ev'n the Red sea,
    provok'd him grievously.

8 Nevertheless he saved them,
    ev'n for his own name's sake;
    That so he might to be well known
    his mighty power make.

9 When he the Red sea did rebuke,
    then dried up it was:
    Through depths, as through the wil-
    derness,
    he safely made them pass.

10 From hands of those that hated them
    he did his people save;
    And from the en'my's cruel hand
    to them redemption gave.
11 The waters overwhelm'd their foes
    not one was left alive.
12 Then they believ'd his word, and
    to him in songs did give.   [praise
13 But soon did they his mighty works
    forget unthankfully,
    And on his counsel and his will
    did not wait patiently.

14 But much did lust in wilderness,
    and God in desert tempt.
15 He gave them what they sought, but
    their soul he leanness sent.   [to
16 And against Moses in the camp
    their envy did appear;
    At Aaron they, the saint of God,
    envious also were.

17 Therefore the earth did open wide,
    and Dathan did devour,
    And all Abiram's company
    did cover in that hour.
18 Likewise among their company
    a fire was kindled then;
    And so the hot consuming flame
    burnt up these wicked men.
19 Upon the hill of Horeb they
    an idol-calf did frame,
    A molten image they did make,
    and worshipped the same.
20 And thus their glory, and their God,
    most vainly changed they
    Into the likeness of an ox
    that eateth grass or hay.

21 They did forget the mighty God,
    that had their saviour been,
    By whom such great things brought
    they had in Egypt seen.   [to pass
22 In Ham's land he did wondrous
    things terrible did he,   [works,
    When he his mighty hand and arm
    stretch'd out at the Red sea.
23 Then said he, He would them de-
    had not, his wrath to stay.   [stroy,
    His chosen Moses stood in breach,
    that them he should not slay.

24 Yea, they despis'd the pleasant land,
   believed not his word:
25 But in their tents they murmured,
   not heark'ning to the Lord.
26 Therefore in desert them to slay
   he lifted up his hand:
27 'Mong nations to o'erthrow their
   and scatter in each land.   [seed,
28 They unto Baal-peor did
   themselves associate;
   The sacrifices of the dead
   they did profanely eat.
29 Thus, by their lewd inventions,
   they did provoke his ire;
   And then upon them suddenly
   the plague brake in as fire.
30 Then Phin'has rose, and justice did,
   and so the plague did cease;
31 That to all ages counted was
   to him for righteousness.
32 And at the waters, where they strove,
   they did him angry make,
   In such sort, that it fared ill
   with Moses for their sake:
33 Because they there his spirit meek
   provoked bitterly,
   So that he utter'd with his lips
   words unadvisedly.
34 Nor, as the Lord commanded them,
   did they the nations slay:
35 But with the heathen mingled were,
   and learn'd of them their way.
36 And their idols serv'd, which
   a snare unto them turn.   [did
37 Their sons and daughters they to
   in sacrifice did burn.   [dev'ls
38 In their own children's guiltless blood
   their hands they did imbrue,
   Whom to Canaan's idols they
   for sacrifices slew:
   So was the land defil'd with blood.
39 They stain'd with their own way,
   And with their own inventions
   a whoring they did stray.
40 Against his people kindled was
   the wrath of God therefore,
   Insomuch that he did his own
   inheritance abhor.
41 He gave them to the heathen's hand;
   their foes did them command.
42 Their en'mies them oppress'd, they
   made subject to their hand.   [were
43 He many times deliver'd them;
   but with their counsel so
   They him provok'd, that for their sin
   they were brought very low.

44 Yet their affliction he beheld,
   when he did hear their cry:
45 And he for them his covenant
   did call to memory;
   After his mercies' multitude
46 he did repent: And made
   Them to be pity'd of all those
   who did them captive lead.
47 O Lord our God, us save, and gather
   the heathen from among,
   That we thy holy name may praise
   in a triumphant song.
48 Bless'd be JEHOVAH, Isr'el's God,
   to all eternity:
   Let all the people say, Amen.
   Praise to the Lord give ye.

PSALM 107.

1 PRAISE God, for he is good: for
   his mercies lasting be.   [still
2 Let God's redeem'd say so, whom he
   from th' en'my's hand did free;
3 And gather'd them out of the lands,
   from north, south, east, and west.
4 They stray'd in desert's pathless way,
   no city found to rest.
5 For thirst and hunger in them faints
6 their soul. When straits them
   press,
   They cry unto the Lord, and he
   them frees from their distress.
7 Them also in a way to walk
   that right is he did guide,
   That they might to a city go,
   wherein they might abide.
8 O that men to the Lord would give
   praise for his goodness then,
   And for his works of wonder done
   unto the sons of men!
9 For he the soul that longing is
   doth fully satisfy;
   With goodness he the hungry soul
   doth fill abundantly.
10 Such as shut up in darkness deep,
   and in death's shade abide,
   Whom strongly hath affliction bound,
   and irons fast have ty'd:
11 Because against the words of God
   they wrought rebelliously,
   And they the counsel did contemn
   of him that is most High:
12 Their heart he did bring down with
   grief,
   they fell, no help could have.
13 In trouble then they cry'd to God,
   he them from straits did save.

14 He out of darkness did them bring,
　　and from death's shade them take;
These bands, wherewith they had
　　　been bound,
　　asunder quite he brake.

15 O that men to the Lord would give
　　praise for his goodness then,
And for his works of wonder done
　　unto the sons of men!

16 Because the mighty gates of brass
　　in pieces he did tear,
By him in sunder also cut
　　the bars of iron were.

17 Fools, for their sin, and their offence,
　　do sore affliction bear;

18 All kind of meat their soul abhors;
　　they to death's gates draw near.

19 In grief they cry to God; he saves
　　them from their miseries.

20 He sends his word, them heals, and
　　　them
　　from their destructions frees.

21 O that men to the Lord would give
　　praise for his goodness then,
And for his works of wonder done
　　unto the sons of men!

22 And let them sacrifice to him
　　off'rings of thankfulness;
And let them show abroad his works
　　in songs of joyfulness.

23 Who go to sea in ships, and in
　　great waters trading be,

24 Within the deep these men God's
　　and his great wonders see. [works

25 For he commands, and forth in haste
　　the stormy tempest flies,
Which makes the sea with rolling
　　aloft to swell and rise. [waves

26 They mount to heav'n, then to the
　　they do go down again; [depths
Their soul doth faint and melt away
　　with trouble and with pain.

27 They reel and stagger like one drunk,
　　at their wit's end they be:

28 Then they to God in trouble cry,
　　who them from straits doth free.

29 The storm is chang'd into a calm
　　at his command and will;
So that the waves, which rag'd be-
　　now quiet are and still. [fore,

30 Then are they glad, because at rest
　　and quiet now they be:
So to the haven he them brings,
　　which they desir'd to see.

31 O that men to the Lord would give
　　praise for his goodness then,

And for his works of wonder done
　　unto the sons of men!

32 Among the people gathered
　　let them exalt his name;
Among assembled elders spread
　　his most renowned fame.

33 He to dry land turns water-springs,
　　and floods to wilderness;

34 For sins of those that dwell therein,
　　fat land to barrenness.

35 The burnt and parched wilderness
　　to water-pools he brings;
The ground that was dry'd up before
　　he turns to water-springs:

36 And there, for dwelling, he a place
　　doth to the hungry give,
That they a city may prepare
　　commodiously to live.

37 There sow they fields, and vineyards
　　to yield fruits of increase. [plant,

38 His blessing makes them multiply,
　　lets not their beasts decrease.

39 Again they are diminished,
　　and very low brought down,
Through sorrow and affliction,
　　and great oppression.

40 He upon princes pours contempt,
　　and causeth them to stray,
And wander in a wilderness,
　　wherein there is no way.

41 Yet setteth he the poor on high
　　from all his miseries,
And he, much like unto a flock,
　　doth make him families.

42 They that are righteous shall rejoice,
　　when they the same shall see;
And, as ashamed, stop her mouth
　　shall all iniquity.

43 Whoso is wise, and will these things
　　observe, and them record,
Ev'n they shall understand the love
　　and kindness of the Lord.

PSALM 108.

1 MY heart is fix'd, Lord; I will sing
　　and with my glory praise.

2 Awake up psaltery and harp;
　　myself I'll early raise.

3 I'll praise thee 'mong the people,
　　'mong nations sing will I: [Lord;

4 For above heav'n thy mercy's great,
　　thy truth doth reach the sky.

5 Be thou above the heavens, Lord,
　　exalted gloriously;
Thy glory all the earth above
　　be lifted up on high.

6 That those who thy beloved are
  delivered may be,
  O do thou save with thy right hand,
  and answer give to me.
7 God in his holiness hath said,
  Herein I will take pleasure;
  Shechem I will divide, and forth
  will Succoth's valley measure.
8 Gilead I claim as mine by right;
  Manasseh mine shall be;
  Ephraim is of my head the strength;
  Judah gives laws for me;
9 Moab's my washing-pot; my shoe
  I'll over Edom throw;
  Over the land of Palestine
  I will in triumph go.
10 O who is he will bring me to
  the city fortify'd?
  O who is he that to the land
  of Edom will me guide?
11 O God, thou who hadst cast us off,
  this thing wilt thou not do?
  And wilt not thou, ev'n thou, O God.
  forth with our armies go?
12 Do thou from trouble give us help,
  for helpless is man's aid.
13 Through God we shall do valiantly;
  our foes he shall down tread.

PSALM 109.

1 O THOU the God of all my praise,
  do thou not hold thy peace;
2 For mouths of wicked men to speak
  against me do not cease:
  The mouths of vile deceitful men
  against me open'd be;
  And with a false and lying tongue
  they have accused me.
3 They did beset me round about
  with words of hateful spight;
  And though to them no cause I gave,
  against me they did fight.
4 They for my love became my foes,
  but I me set to pray.
5 Evil for good, hatred for love,
  to me they did repay.
6 Set thou the wicked over him;
  and upon his right hand
  Give thou his greatest enemy,
  ev'n Satan, leave to stand.
7 And when by thee he shall be judg'd,
  let him condemned be;
  And let his pray'r be turn'd to sin,
  when he shall call on thee.
8 Few be his days, and in his room
  his charge another take.

9 His children let be fatherless,
  his wife a widow make.
10 His children let be vagabonds,
  and beg continually;
  And from their places desolate
  seek bread for their supply.
11 Let covetous extortioners
  catch all he hath away:
  Of all for which he labour'd hath
  let strangers make a prey.
12 Let there be none to pity him,
  let there be none at all
  That on his children fatherless
  will let his mercy fall.
13 Let his posterity from earth
  cut off for ever be,
  And in the foll'wing age their name
  be blotted out by thee.
14 Let God his father's wickedness
  still to remembrance call;
  And never let his mother's sin
  be blotted out at all.
15 But let them all before the Lord
  appear continually,
  That he may wholly from the earth
  cut off their memory.
16 Because he mercy minded not,
  but persecuted still
  The poor and needy, that he might
  the broken-hearted kill.
17 As he in cursing pleasure took,
  so let it to him fall;
  As he delighted not to bless,
  so bless him not at all.
18 As cursing he like clothes put on,
  into his bowels so,
  Like water, and into his bones,
  like oil, down let it go.
19 Like to the garment let it be
  which doth himself array,
  And for a girdle, wherewith he
  is girt about alway.
20 From God let this be their reward
  that en'mies are to me,
  And their reward that speak against
  my soul maliciously.
21 But do thou, for thine own name's
  O God the Lord, for me: [sake,
  Sith good and sweet thy mercy is,
  from trouble set me free.
22 For I am poor and indigent,
  afflicted sore am I,
  My heart within me also is
  wounded exceedingly.
23 I pass like a declining shade,
  am like the locust tost:

24 My knees through fasting weaken'd
     my flesh hath fatness lost.   [arc,
25 I also am a vile reproach
     unto them made to be;
     And they that did upon me look
     did shake their heads at me.

26 O do thou help and succour me,
     who art my God and Lord:
     And, for thy tender mercy's sake,
     safety to me afford:
27 That thereby they may know that
     is thy almighty hand;   [this
     And that thou, Lord, hast done the
     they may well understand.   [same,

28 Although they curse with spite, yet,
     bless thou with loving voice: [Lord,
     Let them asham'd be when they rise;
     thy servant let rejoice.
29 Let thou mine adversaries all
     with shame be clothed over;
     And let their own confusion
     them, as a mantle, cover.

30 But as for me, I with my mouth
     will greatly praise the Lord;
     And I among the multitude
     his praises will record.
31 For he shall stand at his right hand
     who is in poverty,
     To save him from all those that
     condemn his soul to die.   [would

PSALM 110.

1 THE Lord did say unto my Lord,
     Sit thou at my right hand,
     Until I make thy foes a stool,
     whereon thy feet may stand.
2 The Lord shall out of Sion send
     the rod of thy great pow'r:
     In midst of all thine enemies
     be thou the governor.

3 A willing people in thy day
     of pow'r shall come to thee,
     In holy beauties from morn's womb;
     thy youth like dew shall be.
4 The Lord himself hath made an oath,
     and will repent him never,
     Of th' order of Melchisedec
     thou art a priest for ever.

5 The glorious and mighty Lord,
     that sits at thy right hand,
     Shall, in his day of wrath, strike
     through
     kings that do him withstand.
6 He shall among the heathen judge,
     he shall with bodies dead
     The places fill: o'er many lands
     he wound shall ev'ry head.

7 The brook that runneth in the way
     with drink shall him supply;
     And, for this cause, in triumph he
     shall lift his head on high.

PSALM 111.

1 PRAISE ye the Lord: with my
     whole heart
     I will God's praise declare,
     Where the assemblies of the just
     and congregations are.
2 The whole works of the Lord our
     are great above all measure, [God
     Sought out they are of ev'ry one
     that doth therein take pleasure.

3 His work most honourable is,
     most glorious and pure,
     And his untainted righteousness
     for ever doth endure.
4 His works most wonderful he hath
     made to be thought upon:
     The Lord is gracious, and he is
     full of compassion.

5 He giveth meat unto all those
     that truly do him fear;
     And evermore his covenant
     he in his mind will bear.
6 He did the power of his works
     unto his people show,
     When he the heathen's heritage
     upon them did bestow.

7 His handy-works are truth and right;
     all his commands are sure:
8 And, done in truth and uprightness,
     they evermore endure.
9 He sent redemption to his folk;
     his covenant for aye
     He did command: holy his name
     and rev'rend is alway.

10 Wisdom's beginning is God's fear:
     good understanding they
     Have all that his commands fulfil:
     his praise endures for aye.

PSALM 112.

1 PRAISE ye the Lord. The man is
     bless'd
     that fears the Lord aright,
     He who in his commandements
     doth greatly take delight.
2 His seed and offspring powerful
     shall be the earth upon:
     Of upright men blessed shall be
     the generation.

3 Riches and wealth shall ever be
     within his house in store;

And his unspotted righteousness
    endures for evermore.
4 Unto the upright light doth rise,
    though he in darkness be:
Compassionate, and merciful,
    and righteous, is he.

5 A good man doth his favour show,
    and doth to others lend:
He with discretion his affairs
    will guide unto the end.

6 Surely there is not any thing
    that ever shall him move:
The righteous man's memorial
    shall everlasting prove.

7 When he shall evil tidings hear,
    he shall not be afraid:
His heart is fix'd, his confidence
    upon the Lord is stay'd.

8 His heart is firmly stablished,
    afraid he shall not be,
Until upon his enemies
    he his desire shall see.

9 He hath dispers'd, giv'n to the poor;
    his righteousness shall be
To ages all; with honour shall
    his horn be raised high.

10 The wicked shall it see, and fret,
    his teeth gnash, melt away:
What wicked men do most desire
    shall utterly decay.

PSALM 113.

1 PRAISE God: ye servants of the
    Lord,
    O praise, the Lord's name praise.
2 Yea, blessed be the name of God
    from this time forth always.
3 From rising sun to where it sets,
    God's name is to be prais'd.
4 Above all nations God is high,
    'bove heav'ns his glory rais'd.

5 Unto the Lord our God that dwells
    on high, who can compare?
6 Himself that humbleth things to see
    in heav'n and earth that are.

7 He from the dust doth raise the poor,
    that very low doth lie;
And from the dunghill lifts the man
    oppress'd with poverty;

8 That he may highly him advance,
    and with the princes set;
With those that of his people are
    the chief, ev'n princes great.

9 The barren woman house to keep
    he maketh, and to be
Of sons a mother full of joy.
    Praise to the Lord give ye.

PSALM 114.

1 WHEN Isr'el out of Egypt went,
    and did his dwelling change,
When Jacob's house went out from
    those
    that were of language strange,
2 He Judah did his sanctuary,
    his kingdom Isr'el make:
3 The sea it saw, and quickly fled,
    Jordan was driven back.

4 Like rams the mountains, and like
    the hills skipp'd to and fro. [lambs
5 O sea, why fledd'st thou? Jordan,
    why wast thou driven so?   [back
6 Ye mountains great, wherefore was it
    that ye did skip like rams?
And wherefore was it, little hills,
    that ye did leap like lambs?

7 O at the presence of the Lord,
    earth, tremble thou for fear,
While as the presence of the God
    of Jacob doth appear:
8 Who from the hard and stony rock
    did standing water bring;
And by his pow'r did turn the flint
    into a water-spring.

PSALM 115.

1 NOT unto us, Lord, not to us,
    but do thou glory take
Unto thy name, ev'n for thy truth,
    and for thy mercy's sake.
2 O wherefore should the heathen say,
    Where is their God now gone?
3 But our God in the heavens is,
    what pleas'd him he hath done.

4 Their idols silver are and gold,
    work of men's hands they be.
5 Mouths have they, but they do not
    and eyes, but do not see; [speak,
6 Ears have they, but they do not hear;
    noses, but savour not;
7 Hands, feet, but handle not, nor
    walk;
    nor speak they through their
    throat.

8 Like them their makers are, and all
    on them their trust that build.
9 O Isr'el, trust thou in the Lord,
    he is their help and shield.
10 O Aaron's house, trust in the Lord,
    their help and shield is he.
11 Ye that fear God, trust in the Lord,
    their help and shield he'll be.

12 The Lord of us hath mindful been,
    and he will bless us still:

He will the house of Isr'el bless,
bless Aaron's house he will.
13 Both small and great, that fear the
he will them surely bless. [Lord,
14 The Lord will you, you and your
aye more and more increase. [seed,
15 O blessed are ye of the Lord,
who made the earth and heav'n.
16 The heav'n, ev'n heav'ns, are God's,
but he
earth to men's sons hath giv'n.
17 The dead, nor who to silence go,
God's praise do not record.
18 But henceforth we for ever will
bless God. Praise ye the Lord.

PSALM 116.

1 I LOVE the Lord, because my voice
and prayers he did hear.
2 I, while I live, will call on him,
who bow'd to me his ear.
3 Of death the cords and sorrows did
about me compass round;
The pains of hell took hold on me,
I grief and trouble found.
4 Upon the name of God the Lord
then did I call, and say,
Deliver thou my soul, O Lord,
I do thee humbly pray.
5 God merciful and righteous is,
yea, gracious is our Lord.
6 God saves the meek: I was brought
he did me help afford.   [low,
7 O thou my soul, do thou return
unto thy quiet rest;
For largely, lo, the Lord to thee
his bounty hath exprest.
8 For my distressed soul from death
deliver'd was by thee:
Thou didst my mourning eyes from
my feet from falling, free. [tears,
9 I in the land of those that live
will walk the Lord before.
10 I did believe, therefore I spake:
I was afflicted sore.
11 I said, when I was in my haste,
that all men liars be.
12 What shall I render to the Lord
for all his gifts to me?
13 I'll of salvation take the cup,
on God's name will I call:
14 I'll pay my vows now to the Lord
before his people all.
15 Dear in God's sight is his saints'
16 Thy servant, Lord, am I; [death.
Thy servant sure, thine handmaid's
my bands thou didst untie. [son:

17 Thank-off'rings I to thee will give,
and on God's name will call.
18 I'll pay my vows unto the Lord
before his people all;
19 Within the courts of God's own
within the midst of thee, [house
O city of Jerusalem.
Praise to the Lord give ye.

PSALM 117.

1 O GIVE ye praise unto the Lord,
all nations that be:
Likewise, ye people all, accord
his name to magnify.
2 For great to us-ward ever are
his loving-kindnesses:
His truth endures for evermore.
The Lord O do ye bless.

PSALM 118.

1 O PRAISE the Lord, for he is
his mercy lasteth ever. [good;
2 Let those of Israel now say,
His mercy faileth never.
3 Now let the house of Aaron say,
His mercy lasteth ever.
4 Let those that fear the Lord now say,
His mercy faileth never.
5 I in distress call'd on the Lord;
the Lord did answer me:
He in a large place did me set,
from trouble made me free.
6 The mighty Lord is on my side,
I will not be afraid;
For any thing that man can do
I shall not be dismay'd.
7 The Lord doth take my part with
that help to succour me: [them
Therefore on those that do me hate
I my desire shall see.
8 Better it is to trust in God
than trust in man's defence:
9 Better to trust in God than make
princes our confidence.
10 The nations, joining all in one,
did compass me about:
But in the Lord's most holy name
I shall them all root out.
11 They compass'd me about; I say,
they compass'd me about:
But in the Lord's most holy name
I shall them all root out.
12 Like bees they compass'd me about;
like unto thorns that flame
They quenched are: for them shall I
destroy in God's own name.

69

13 Thou sore hast thrust, that I might
    but my Lord helped me.   [fall,
14 God my salvation is become,
    my strength and song is he.
15 In dwellings of the righteous
    is heard the melody
    Of joy and health: the Lord's right
    doth ever valiantly.   [hand
16 The right hand of the mighty Lord
    exalted is on high;
    The right hand of the mighty Lord
    doth ever valiantly.
17 I shall not die, but live, and shall
    the works of God discover.
18 The Lord hath me chastised sore,
    but not to death giv'n over.
19 O set ye open unto me
    the gates of righteousness;
    Then will I enter into them,
    and I the Lord will bless.
20 This is the gate of God, by it
    the just shall enter in.
21 Thee will I praise, for thou me
    and hast my safety been. [heard'st,
22 That stone is made head corner-
    stone,
    which builders did despise:
23 This is the doing of the Lord,
    and wondrous in our eyes.
24 This is the day God made, in it
    we'll joy triumphantly.
25 Save now, I pray thee, Lord; I pray,
    send now prosperity.
26 Blessed is he in God's great name
    that cometh us to save:
    We, from the house which to the
    pertains, you blessed have. [Lord
27 God is the Lord, who unto us
    hath made light to arise:
    Bind ye unto the altar's horns
    with cords the sacrifice.
28 Thou art my God, I'll thee exalt;
    my God, I will thee praise.
29 Give thanks to God, for he is good:
    his mercy lasts always.

PSALM 119.

ALEPH. The First Part.

1 BLESSED are they that undefil'd,
    and straight are in the way;
    Who in the Lord's most holy law
    do walk, and do not stray.
2 Blessed are they who to observe
    his statutes are inclin'd;
    And who do seek the living God
    with their whole heart and mind.

3 Such in his ways do walk, and they
    do no iniquity.
4 Thou hast commanded us to keep
    thy precepts carefully.
5 O that thy statutes to observe
    thou would'st my ways direct!
6 Then shall I not be sham'd, when I
    thy precepts all respect.
7 Then with integrity of heart
    thee will I praise and bless,
    When I thy judgments all have
    learn'd
    of thy pure righteousness.
8 That I will keep thy statutes all
    firmly resolv'd have I:
    O do not then, most gracious God,
    forsake me utterly.

BETH. The Second Part.

9 By what means shall a young man
    his way to purify?   [learn
    If he according to thy word
    thereto attentive be.
10 Unfeignedly thee have I sought
    with all my soul and heart:
    O let me not from the right path
    of thy commands depart.
11 Thy word I in my heart have hid,
    that I offend not thee.
12 O Lord, thou ever blessed art,
    thy statutes teach thou me.
13 The judgments of thy mouth each
    my lips declared have: [one
14 More joy thy testimonies' way
    than riches all me gave.
15 I will thy holy precepts make
    my meditation;
    And carefully I'll have respect
    unto thy ways each one.
16 Upon thy statutes my delight
    shall constantly be set:
    And, by thy grace, I never will
    thy holy word forget.

GIMEL. The Third Part.

17 With me thy servant, in thy grace,
    deal bountifully, Lord;
    That by thy favour I may live,
    and duly keep thy word.
18 Open mine eyes, that of thy law
    the wonders I may see.
19 I am a stranger on this earth,
    hide not thy laws from me.
20 My soul within me breaks, and doth
    much fainting still endure,
    Through longing that it hath all
    unto thy judgments pure. [times

21 Thou hast rebuk'd the cursed proud,
    who from thy precepts swerve.
22 Reproach and shame remove from
    for I thy laws observe.   [me,
23 Against me princes spake with spite,
    while they in council sat:
    But I thy servant did upon
    thy statutes meditate.
24 My comfort, and my heart's delight,
    thy testimonies be;
    And they, in all my doubts and fears,
    are counsellors to me.

DALETH. *The Fourth Part.*

25 My soul to dust cleaves: quicken me,
    according to thy word.
26 My ways I show'd, and me thou
    heard'st:
    teach me thy statutes, Lord.
27 The way of thy commandments
    make me aright to know;
    So all thy works that wondrous are
    I shall to others show.
28 My soul doth melt, and drop away,
    for heaviness and grief:
    To me, according to thy word,
    give strength, and send relief.
29 From me the wicked way of lies
    let far removed be;
    And graciously thy holy law
    do thou grant unto me.
30 I chosen have the perfect way
    of truth and verity:
    Thy judgments that most righteous
    before me laid have I.   [are
31 I to thy testimonies cleave;
    shame do not on me cast.
32 I'll run thy precepts' way, when thou
    my heart enlarged hast.

HE. *The Fifth Part.*

33 Teach me, O Lord, the perfect way
    of thy precepts divine,
    And to observe it to the end
    I shall my heart incline.
34 Give understanding unto me,
    so keep thy law shall I;
    Yea, ev'n with my whole heart I shall
    observe it carefully.
35 In thy law's path make me to go;
    for I delight therein.
36 My heart unto thy testimonies,
    and not to greed, incline.
37 Turn thou away my sight and eyes
    from viewing vanity;
    And in thy good and holy way
    be pleas'd to quicken me.

38 Confirm to me thy gracious word,
    which I did gladly hear,
    Ev'n to thy servant, Lord, who is
    devoted to thy fear.
39 Turn thou away my fear'd reproach;
    for good thy judgments be.
40 Lo, for thy precepts I have long'd;
    in thy truth quicken me.

VAU. *The Sixth Part.*

41 Let thy sweet mercies also come
    and visit me, O Lord;
    Ev'n thy benign salvation,
    according to thy word.
42 So shall I have wherewith I may
    give him an answer just,
    Who spitefully reproacheth me;
    for in thy word I trust.
43 The word of truth out of my mouth
    take thou not utterly;
    For on thy judgments righteous
    my hope doth still rely.
44 So shall I keep for evermore
    thy law continually.
45 And, sith that I thy precepts seek,
    I'll walk at liberty.
46 I'll speak thy word to kings, and I
    with shame shall not be mov'd;
47 And will delight myself always
    in thy laws, which I lov'd.
48 To thy commandments, which I
    my hands lift up I will;   [lov'd,
    And I will also meditate
    upon thy statutes still.

ZAIN. *The Seventh Part.*

49 Remember, Lord, thy gracious word
    thou to thy servant spake,
    Which, for a ground of my sure hope,
    thou causedst me to take.
50 This word of thine my comfort is
    in mine affliction:
    For in my straits I am reviv'd
    by this thy word alone.
51 The men whose hearts with pride are
    did greatly me deride;   [stuff'd
    Yet from thy straight commande-
    I have not turn'd aside.   [ments
52 Thy judgments righteous, O Lord,
    which thou of old forth gave,
    I did remember, and myself
    by them comforted have.
53 Horror took hold on me, because
    ill men thy law forsake.
54 I in my house of pilgrimage
    thy laws my songs do make.

55 Thy name by night, Lord, I did
 and I have kept thy law. [mind,
56 And this I had, because thy word
 I kept, and stood in awe.

CHETH. *The Eighth Part.*

57 Thou my sure portion art alone,
 which I did chuse, O Lord:
I have resolv'd, and said, that I
 would keep thy holy word.
58 With my whole heart I did entreat
 thy face and favour free:
According to thy gracious word
 be merciful to me.
59 I thought upon my former ways,
 and did my life well try;
And to thy testimonies pure
 my feet then turned I.
60 I did not stay, nor linger long,
 as those that slothful are;
But hastily thy laws to keep
 myself I did prepare.
61 Bands of ill men me robb'd; yet I
 thy precepts did not slight.
62 I'll rise at midnight thee to praise,
 ev'n for thy judgments right.
63 I am companion to all those
 who fear, and thee obey.
64 O Lord, thy mercy fills the earth:
 teach me thy laws, I pray.

TETH. *The Ninth Part.*

65 Well hast thou with thy servant dealt,
 as thou didst promise give.
66 Good judgment me, and knowledge
 for I thy word believe. [teach,
67 Ere I afflicted was I stray'd;
 but now I keep thy word.
68 Both good thou art, and good thou
 teach me thy statutes, Lord. [do'st:
69 The men that are puff'd up with
 against me forg'd a lie; [pride
Yet thy commandements observe
 with my whole heart will I.
70 Their hearts, through worldly ease
 and wealth,
 as fat as grease they be;
But in thy holy law I take
 delight continually.
71 It hath been very good for me
 that I afflicted was,
That I might well instructed be,
 and learn thy holy laws.
72 The word that cometh from thy
 is better unto me [mouth
Than many thousands and great
 of gold and silver be. [sums

JOD. *The Tenth Part.*

73 Thou mad'st and fashion'dst me: thy
 to know thy wisdom, Lord. [laws
74 So who thee fear shall joy to see
 me trusting in thy word.
75 That very right thy judgments are
 I know, and do confess;
And that thou hast afflicted me
 in truth and faithfulness.
76 O let thy kindness merciful,
 I pray thee, comfort me,
As to thy servant faithfully
 was promised by thee.
77 And let thy tender mercies come
 to me, that I may live;
Because thy holy laws to me
 sweet delectation give.
78 Lord, let the proud ashamed be;
 for they, without a cause,
With me perversely dealt: but I
 will muse upon thy laws.
79 Let such as fear thee, and have
 thy statutes, turn to me. [known
80 My heart let in thy laws be sound,
 that sham'd I never be.

CAPH. *The Eleventh Part.*

81 My soul for thy salvation faints;
 yet I thy word believe.
82 Mine eyes fail for thy word: I say,
 When wilt thou comfort give?
83 For like a bottle I'm become,
 that in the smoke is set:
I'm black, and parch'd with grief;
 thy statutes not forget. [yet I
84 How many are thy servant's days?
 when wilt thou execute
Just judgment on these wicked men
 that do me persecute?
85 The proud have digged pits for me,
 which is against thy laws.
86 Thy words all faithful are: help me,
 pursu'd without a cause.
87 They so consum'd me, that on earth
 my life they scarce did leave:
Thy precepts yet forsook I not,
 but close to them did cleave.
88 After thy loving-kindness, Lord,
 me quicken, and preserve:
The testimony of thy mouth
 so shall I still observe.

LAMED. *The Twelfth Part.*

89 Thy word for ever is, O Lord,
 in heaven settled fast;
90 Unto all generations
 thy faithfulness doth last:

The earth thou hast established,
and it abides by thee.

91 This day they stand as thou or-
for all thy servants be. [dain'dst;

92 Unless in thy most perfect law
my soul delights had found,
I should have perished, when as
my troubles did abound.

93 Thy precepts I will ne'er forget;
they quick'ning to me brought.

94 Lord, I am thine; O save thou me:
thy precepts I have sought.

95 For me the wicked have laid wait,
me seeking to destroy:
But I thy testimonies true
consider will with joy.

96 An end of all perfection
here have I seen, O God:
But as for thy commandment,
it is exceeding broad.

MEM. The Thirteenth Part.

97 O how love I thy law! it is
my study all the day:

98 It makes me wiser than my foes;
for it doth with me stay.

99 Than all my teachers now I have
more understanding far;
Because my meditation
thy testimonies are.

100 In understanding I excel
those that are ancients;
For I endeavoured to keep
all thy commandments.

101 My feet from each ill way I stay'd,
that I may keep thy word.

102 I from thy judgments have not
swerv'd;
for thou hast taught me, Lord.

103 How sweet unto my taste, O Lord,
are all thy words of truth!
Yea, I do find them sweeter far
than honey to my mouth.

104 I through thy precepts, that are
do understanding get; [pure,
I therefore ev'ry way that's false
with all my heart do hate.

NUN. The Fourteenth Part.

105 Thy word is to my feet a lamp,
and to my path a light.

106 I sworn have, and I will perform,
to keep thy judgments right.

107 I am with sore affliction
ev'n overwhelm'd, O Lord:
In mercy raise and quicken me,
according to thy word.

108 The free-will-off'rings of my mouth
accept, I thee beseech;
And unto me thy servant, Lord,
thy judgments clearly teach.

109 Though still my soul be in my hand,
thy laws I'll not forget.

110 I err'd not from them, though for
the wicked snares did set. [me

111 I of thy testimonies have
above all things made choice,
To be my heritage for aye;
for they my heart rejoice.

112 I carefully inclined have
my heart still to attend;
That I thy statutes may perform
alway unto the end.

SAMECH. The Fifteenth Part.

113 I hate the thoughts of vanity,
but love thy law do I.

114 My shield and hiding-place thou
I on thy word rely. [art:

115 All ye that evil-doers are
from me depart away;
For the commandments of my God
I purpose to obey.

116 According to thy faithful word
uphold and stablish me,
That I may live, and of my hope
ashamed never be.

117 Hold thou me up, so shall I be
in peace and safety still;
And to thy statutes have respect
continually I will.

118 Thou tread'st down all that love to
stray;
false their deceit doth prove.

119 Lewd men, like dross, away thou
therefore thy law I love. [putt'st;

120 For fear of thee my very flesh
doth tremble, all dismay'd;
And of thy righteous judgments,
my soul is much afraid. [Lord,

AIN. The Sixteenth Part.

121 To all men I have judgment done,
performing justice right;
Then let me not be left unto
my fierce oppressors' might.

122 For good unto thy servant, Lord,
thy servant's surety be:
From the oppression of the proud
do thou deliver me.

123 Mine eyes do fail with looking long
for thy salvation,
The word of thy pure righteousness
while I do wait upon.

124 In mercy with thy servant deal,
    thy laws me teach and show.
125 I am thy servant, wisdom give,
    that I thy laws may know.
126 'Tis time thou work, Lord; for they
    made void thy law divine. [have
127 Therefore thy precepts more I love
    than gold, yea, gold most fine.
128 Concerning all things thy commands
    all right I judge therefore;
    And ev'ry false and wicked way
    I perfectly abhor.

PE. *The Seventeenth Part.*

129 Thy statutes, Lord, are wonderful,
    my soul them keeps with care.
130 The entrance of thy words gives
    light,
    makes wise who simple are.
131 My mouth I have wide opened,
    and panted earnestly,
    While after thy commandements
    I long'd exceedingly.
132 Look on me, Lord, and merciful
    do thou unto me prove,
    As thou art wont to do to those
    thy name who truly love.
133 O let my footsteps in thy word
    aright still order'd be:
    Let no iniquity obtain
    dominion over me.
134 From man's oppression save thou
    so keep thy laws I will. [me;
135 Thy face make on thy servant shine;
    teach me thy statutes still.
136 Rivers of waters from mine eyes
    did run down, when I saw
    How wicked men run on in sin,
    and do not keep thy law.

TSADDI. *The Eighteenth Part.*

137 O Lord, thou art most righteous;
    thy judgments are upright.
138 Thy testimonies thou command'st
    most faithful are and right.
139 My zeal hath ev'n consumed me,
    because mine enemies
    Thy holy words forgotten have,
    and do thy laws despise.
140 Thy word's most pure, therefore on
    thy servant's love is set. [it
141 Small, and despis'd I am, yet I
    thy precepts not forget.
142 Thy righteousness is righteousness
    which ever doth endure:
    Thy holy law, Lord, also is
    the very truth most pure.

143 Trouble and anguish have me
    and taken hold on me: [found,
    Yet in my trouble my delight
    thy just commandments be.
144 Eternal righteousness is in
    thy testimonies all:
    Lord, to me understanding give,
    and ever live I shall.

KOPH. *The Nineteenth Part.*

145 With my whole heart I cry'd, Lord,
    I will thy word obey. [hear;
146 I cry'd to thee; save me, and I
    will keep thy laws alway.
147 I of the morning did prevent
    the dawning, and did cry:
    For all mine expectation
    did on thy word rely.
148 Mine eyes did timeously prevent
    the watches of the night,
    That in thy word with careful mind
    then meditate I might.
149 After thy loving-kindness hear
    my voice, that calls on thee:
    According to thy judgment, Lord,
    revive and quicken me.
150 Who follow mischief they draw
    they from thy law are far: [nigh;
151 But thou art near, Lord; most firm
    truth
    all thy commandments are.
152 As for thy testimonies all,
    of old this have I try'd,
    That thou hast surely founded them
    for ever to abide.

RESH. *The Twentieth Part.*

153 Consider mine affliction,
    in safety do me set:
    Deliver me, O Lord, for I
    thy law do not forget.
154 After thy word revive thou me:
    save me, and plead my cause.
155 Salvation is from sinners far;
    for they seek not thy laws.
156 O Lord, both great and manifold
    thy tender mercies be:
    According to thy judgments just,
    revive and quicken me.
157 My persecutors many are,
    and foes that do combine;
    Yet from thy testimonies pure
    my heart doth not decline.
158 I saw transgressors, and was griev'd;
    for they keep not thy word.
159 See how I love thy law! as thou
    art kind, me quicken, Lord.

160 From the beginning all thy word
hath been most true and sure:
Thy righteous judgments ev'ry one
for evermore endure.

SCHIN. *The Twenty-first Part.*

161 Princes have persecuted me,
although no cause they saw:
But still of thy most holy word
my heart doth stand in awe.

162 I at thy word rejoice, as one
of spoil that finds great store.

163 Thy law I love; but lying all
I hate and do abhor.

164 Sev'n times a day it is my care
to give due praise to thee;
Because of all thy judgments, Lord,
which righteous ever be.

165 Great peace have they who love thy
law;
offence they shall have none.

166 I hop'd for thy salvation, Lord,
and thy commands have done.

167 My soul thy testimonies pure
observed carefully;
On them my heart is set, and them
I love exceedingly.

168 Thy testimonies and thy laws
I kept with special care;
For all my works and ways each one
before thee open are.

TAU. *The Twenty-second Part.*

169 O let my earnest pray'r and cry
come near before thee, Lord:
Give understanding unto me,
according to thy word.

170 Let my request before thee come:
after thy word me free.

171 My lips shall utter praise, when thou
hast taught thy laws to me.

172 My tongue of thy most blessed word
shall speak, and it confess;
Because all thy commandements
are perfect righteousness.

173 Let thy strong hand make help to
thy precepts are my choice. [me:

174 I long'd for thy salvation, Lord,
and in thy law rejoice.

175 O let my soul live, and it shall
give praises unto thee;
And let thy judgments gracious
be helpful unto me.

176 I, like a lost sheep, went astray;
thy servant seek, and find:
For thy commands I suffer'd not
to slip out of my mind.

PSALM 120.

1 IN my distress to God I cry'd,
and he gave ear to me.

2 From lying lips, and guileful tongue,
O Lord, my soul set free.

3 What shall be giv'n thee? or what
shall
be done to thee, false tongue?

4 Ev'n burning coals of juniper,
sharp arrows of the strong.

5 Woe's me that I in Mesech am
a sojourner so long;
That I in tabernacles dwell
to Kedar that belong.

6 My soul with him that hateth peace
hath long a dweller been.

7 I am for peace; but when I speak,
for battle they are keen.

PSALM 121.

1 I TO the hills will lift mine eyes,
from whence doth come mine aid.

2 My safety cometh from the Lord,
who heav'n and earth hath made.

3 Thy foot he'll not let slide, nor will
he slumber that thee keeps.

4 Behold, he that keeps Israel,
he slumbers not, nor sleeps.

5 The Lord thee keeps, the Lord thy
shade
on thy right hand doth stay:

6 The moon by night thee shall not
nor yet the sun by day. [smite,

7 The Lord shall keep thy soul; he
preserve thee from all ill. [shall

8 Henceforth thy going out and in
God keep for ever will.

PSALM 122.

1 I JOY'D when to the house of God,
Go up, they said to me.

2 Jerusalem, within thy gates
our feet shall standing be.

3 Jerus'lem, as a city, is
compactly built together:

4 Unto that place the tribes go up,
the tribes of God go thither:

To Isr'el's testimony, there
to God's name thanks to pay.

5 For thrones of judgment, ev'n the
thrones
of David's house, there stay.

6 Pray that Jerusalem may have
peace and felicity:
Let them that love thee and thy peace
have still prosperity.

7 Therefore I wish that peace may still
  within thy walls remain,
And ever may thy palaces
  prosperity retain.
8 Now, for my friends' and brethren's
  Peace be in thee, I'll say. [sakes,
9 And for the house of God our Lord,
  I'll seek thy good alway.

PSALM 123.

1 O THOU that dwellest in the
    heav'ns,
  I lift mine eyes to thee.
2 Behold, as servants' eyes do look
  their masters' hand to see,
As handmaid's eyes her mistress'
  so do our eyes attend   [hand;
Upon the Lord our God, until
  to us he mercy send.
3 O Lord, be gracious to us,
  unto us gracious be;
Because replenish'd with contempt
  exceedingly are we.
4 Our soul is fill'd with scorn of those
  that at their ease abide,
And with the insolent contempt
  of those that swell in pride.

PSALM 124.

1 HAD not the Lord been on our
    may Israel now say; [side,
2 Had not the Lord been on our side,
  when men rose us to slay;
3 They had us swallow'd quick, when as
  their wrath 'gainst us did flame:
4 Waters had cover'd us, our soul
  had sunk beneath the stream.
5 Then had the waters, swelling high,
  over our soul made way.
6 Bless'd be the Lord, who to their
  us gave not for a prey. [teeth
7 Our soul 's escaped, as a bird
  out of the fowler's snare;
The snare asunder broken is,
  and we escaped are.
8 Our sure and all-sufficient help
  is in JEHOVAH's name;
His name who did the heav'n create,
  and who the earth did frame.

Another of the same.

1 NOW Israel
    may say, and that truly,
If that the Lord
  had not our cause maintain'd;
2 If that the Lord
  had not our right sustain'd,

When cruel men
  against us furiously
Rose up in wrath,
  to make of us their prey;
3 Then certainly
  they had devour'd us all,
And swallow'd quick,
  for ought that we could deem;
Such was their rage,
  as we might well esteem.
4 And as fierce floods
  before them all things drown,
So had they brought
  our soul to death quite down.
5 The raging streams,
  with their proud swelling waves,
Had then our soul
  o'erwhelmed in the deep.
6 But bless'd be God,
  who doth us safely keep,
And hath not giv'n
  us for a living prey
Unto their teeth,
  and bloody cruelty.
7 Ev'n as a bird
  out of the fowler's snare
Escapes away,
  so is our soul set free:
Broke are their nets,
  and thus escaped we.
8 Therefore our help
  is in the Lord's great name,
Who heav'n and earth
  by his great pow'r did frame.

PSALM 125.

1 THEY in the Lord that firmly trust
  shall be like Sion hill,
Which at no time can be remov'd,
  but standeth ever still.
2 As round about Jerusalem
  the mountains stand alway,
The Lord his folk doth compass so,
  from henceforth and for aye.
3 For ill men's rod upon the lot
  of just men shall not lie;
Lest righteous men stretch forth
  unto iniquity. [their hands
4 Do thou to all those that be good
  thy goodness, Lord, impart;
And do thou good to those that are
  upright within their heart.
5 But as for such as turn aside
  after their crooked way,
God shall lead forth with wicked
  on Isr'el peace shall stay. [men:

PSALM 126.

1 WHEN Sion's bondage God turn'd
      back,
    as men that dream'd were we.
2 Then fill'd with laughter was our
      our tongue with melody: [mouth,
    They 'mong the heathen said, The
      Lord
    great things for them hath wrought.
3 The Lord hath done great things for
    whence joy to us is brought. [us,

4 As streams of water in the south,
    our bondage, Lord, recall.
5 Who sow in tears, a reaping time
    of joy enjoy they shall.
6 That man who, bearing precious
    in going forth doth mourn, [seed,
    He doubtless, bringing back his
    rejoicing shall return. [sheaves,

PSALM 127.

1 EXCEPT the Lord do build the
      house,
    the builders lose their pain:
    Except the Lord the city keep,
    the watchmen watch in vain.
2 'Tis vain for you to rise betimes,
    or late from rest to keep,
    To feed on sorrows' bread; so gives
    he his beloved sleep.

3 Lo, children are God's heritage,
    the womb's fruit his reward.
4 The sons of youth as arrows are,
    for strong men's hands prepar'd.
5 O happy is the man that hath
    his quiver fill'd with those;
    They unashamed in the gate
    shall speak unto their foes.

PSALM 128.

1 BLESS'D is each one that fears the
      and walketh in his ways; [Lord,
2 For of thy labour thou shalt eat,
    and happy be always.
3 Thy wife shall as a fruitful vine
    by thy house' sides be found:
    Thy children like to olive-plants
    about thy table round.
4 Behold, the man that fears the Lord,
    thus blessed shall he be.
5 The Lord shall out of Sion give
    his blessing unto thee:
    Thou shalt Jerus'lem's good behold
    whilst thou on earth dost dwell.
6 Thou shalt thy children's children
    and peace on Israel. [see,

PSALM 129.

1 OFT did they vex me from my
      may Isr'el now declare; [youth,
2 Oft did they vex me from my youth,
    yet not victorious were.
3 The plowers plow'd upon my back;
    they long their furrows drew.
4 The righteous Lord did cut the cords
    of the ungodly crew.
5 Let Sion's haters all be turn'd
    back with confusion.
6 As grass on houses' tops be they,
    which fades ere it be grown:
7 Whereof enough to fill his hand
    the mower cannot find;
    Nor can the man his bosom fill,
    whose work is sheaves to bind.
8 Neither say they who do go by,
    God's blessing on you rest:
    We in the name of God the Lord
    do wish you to be blest.

PSALM 130.

1 LORD, from the depths to thee I
      cry'd,
2 My voice, Lord, do thou hear:
    Unto my supplication's voice
    give an attentive ear.
3 Lord, who shall stand, if thou, O
    should'st mark iniquity? [Lord,
4 But yet with thee forgiveness is,
    that fear'd thou mayest be.

5 I wait for God, my soul doth wait,
    my hope is in his word.
6 More than they that for morning
      watch,
    my soul waits for the Lord;
    I say, more than they that do watch
    the morning light to see.
7 Let Israel hope in the Lord,
    with him his mercies be;

    And plenteous redemption
    is ever found with him.
8 And from all his iniquities
    he Isr'el shall redeem.

PSALM 131.

1 MY heart not haughty is, O Lord,
      mine eyes not lofty be;
    Nor do I deal in matters great,
    or things too high for me.
2 I surely have myself behav'd
    with quiet sp'rit and mild,
    As child of mother wean'd: my soul
    is like a weaned child.

3 Upon the Lord let all the hope
    of Israel rely,
  Ev'n from the time that present is
    unto eternity.

PSALM 132.

1 DAVID, and his afflictions all,
    Lord, do thou think upon;
2 How unto God he sware, and vow'd
    to Jacob's mighty One.
3 I will not come within my house,
    nor rest in bed at all;
4 Nor shall mine eyes take any sleep,
    nor eyelids slumber shall;

5 Till for the Lord a place I find,
    where he may make abode;
  A place of habitation
    for Jacob's mighty God.
6 Lo, at th eplace of Ephratah
    of it we understood;
  And we did find it in the fields,
    and city of the wood.

7 We'll go into his tabernacles,
    and at his footstool bow.
8 Arise, O Lord, into thy rest,
    th' ark of thy strength, and thou.
9 O let thy priests be clothed, Lord,
    with truth and righteousness;
  And let all those that are thy saints
    shout loud for joyfulness.

10 For thine own servant David's sake,
    do not deny thy grace;
  Nor of thine own anointed one
    turn thou away the face.
11 The Lord in truth to David sware,
    he will not turn from it,
  I of thy body's fruit will make
    upon thy throne to sit.

12 My cov'nant if thy sons will keep,
    and laws to them made known,
  Their children then shall also sit
    for ever on thy throne.
13 For God of Sion hath made choice;
    there he desires to dwell.
14 This is my rest, here still I'll stay;
    for I do like it well.

15 Her food I'll greatly bless; her poor
    with bread will satisfy.
16 Her priests I'll clothe with health;
    her saints
    shall shout forth joyfully.
17 And there will I make David's horn
    to bud forth pleasantly:
  For him that mine anointed is
    a lamp ordain'd have I.

18 As with a garment I will clothe
    with shame his en'mies all:
  But yet the crown that he doth wear
    upon him flourish shall.

PSALM 133.

1 BEHOLD, how good a thing it is,
    and how becoming well,
  Together such as brethren are
    in unity to dwell!
2 Like precious ointment on the head,
    that down the beard did flow,
  Ev'n Aaron's beard, and to the skirts
    did of his garments go.
3 As Hermon's dew, the dew that doth
    on Sion' hills descend:
  For there the blessing God com-
    life that shall never end. [mands,

PSALM 134.

1 BEHOLD, bless ye the Lord, all ye
    that his attendants are,
  Ev'n you that in God's temple be,
    and praise him nightly there.
2 Your hands within God's holy place
    lift up, and praise his name.
3 From Sion' hill the Lord thee bless,
    that heav'n and earth did frame.

PSALM 135.

1 PRAISE ye the Lord, the Lord's
    name praise;
    his servants, praise ye God.
2 Who stand in God's house, in the
    of our God make abode. [courts
3 Praise ye the Lord, for he is good;
    unto him praises sing:
  Sing praises to his name, because
    it is a pleasant thing.

4 For Jacob to himself the Lord
    did chuse of his good pleasure,
  And he hath chosen Israel
    for his peculiar treasure.
5 Because I know assuredly
    the Lord is very great,
  And that our Lord above all gods
    in glory hath his seat.
6 What things soever pleas'd the Lord,
    that in the heav'n did he,
  And in the earth, the seas, and all
    the places deep that be.
7 He from the ends of earth doth make
    the vapours to ascend;
  With rain he lightnings makes, and
    wind
    doth from his treasures send.

78

8 Egypt's first-born, from man to beast
9 who smote. Strange tokens he
On Phar'oh and his servants sent,
Egypt, in midst of thee.

10 He smote great nations, slew great
11 Sihon of Heshbon king, [kings:
And Og of Bashan, and to nought
did Canaan's kingdoms bring:

12 And for a wealthy heritage
their pleasant land he gave,
An heritage which Israel,
his chosen folk, should have.

13 Thy name, O Lord, shall still endure,
and thy memorial
With honour shall continu'd be
to generations all.

14 For why? the righteous God will
his people righteously; [judge
Concerning those that do him serve,
himself repent will he.

15 The idols of the nations
of silver are and gold,
And by the hands of men is made
their fashion and mould.

16 Mouths have they, but they do not
eyes, but they do not see; [speak,
17 Ears have they, but hear not; and in
their mouths no breathing be.

18 Their makers are like them; so are
all that on them rely.

19 O Isr'el's house, bless God; bless
O Aaron's family. [God,

20 O bless the Lord, of Levi's house
ye who his servants are ;
And bless the holy name of God,
all ye the Lord that fear.

21 And blessed be the Lord our God
from Sion's holy hill,
Who dwelleth at Jerusalem.
The Lord O praise ye still.

PSALM 136.

1 GIVE thanks to God, for good is
for mercy hath he ever. [he:
2 Thanks to the God of gods give ye:
for his grace faileth never.
3 Thanks give the Lord of lords unto:
for mercy hath he ever.
4 Who only wonders great can do:
for his grace faileth never.
5 Who by his wisdom made heav'ns
for mercy hath he ever. [high:
6 Who stretch'd the earth above the
for his grace faileth never. [sea:
7 To him that made the great lights
for mercy hath he ever. [shine:

8 The sun to rule till day decline:
for his grace faileth never.

9 The moon and stars to rule by night:
for mercy hath he ever.

10 Who Egypt's first-born kill'd out-
for his grace faileth never. [right:

11 And Isr'el brought from Egypt land:
for mercy hath he ever.

12 With stretch'd-out arm, and with
strong hand:
for his grace faileth never.

13 By whom the Red sea parted was:
for mercy hath he ever.

14 And through its midst made Isr'el
for mercy hath he ever. [pass:

15 But Phar'oh and his host did drown:
for mercy hath he ever.

16 Who through the desert led his own:
for his grace faileth never.

17 To him great kings who overthrew:
for he hath mercy ever.

18 Yea, famous kings in battle slew:
for his grace faileth never.

19 Ev'n Sihon king of Amorites:
for he hath mercy ever.

20 And Og the king of Bashanites:
for his grace faileth never.

21 Their land in heritage to have:
for mercy hath he ever.

22 His servant Isr'el right he gave:
for his grace faileth never.

23 In our low state who on us thought:
for he hath mercy ever.

24 And from our foes our freedom
wrought:
for his grace faileth never.

25 Who doth all flesh with food relieve:
for he hath mercy ever.

26 Thanks to the God of heaven give:
for his grace faileth never.

Another of the same.

1 PRAISE God, for he is kind:
His mercy lasts for aye.
2 Give thanks with heart and mind
To God of gods alway:
For certainly
His mercies dure
Most firm and sure
Eternally.

3 The Lord of lords praise ye,
Whose mercies still endure.
4 Great wonders only he
Doth work by his great pow'r:
For certainly, &c.

5 Which God omnipotent,
By might and wisdom high,
The heav'n and firmament
Did frame, as we may see:
    For certainly, &c.

6 To him who did outstretch
This earth so great and wide,
Above the waters' reach
Making it to abide:
    For certainly, &c.

7 Great lights he made to be;
For his grace lasteth aye:

8 Such as the sun we see,
To rule the lightsome day:
    For certainly, &c.

9 Also the moon so clear,
Which shineth in our sight;
The stars that do appear,
To guide the darksome night:
    For certainly, &c.

10 To him that Egypt smote,
Who did his message scorn;
And in his anger hot
Did kill all their first-born:
    For certainly, &c.

11 Thence Isr'el out he brought;
For his grace lasteth ever.

12 With a strong hand he wrought,
And stretch'd-out arm deliver:
    For certainly, &c.

13 The sea he cut in two;
For his grace lasteth still.

14 And through its midst to go
Made his own Israel:
    For certainly, &c.

15 But overwhelm'd and lost
Was proud king Pharaoh,
With all his mighty host,
And chariots there also:
    For certainly, &c.

16 To him who pow'rfully
His chosen people led,
Ev'n through the desert dry,
And in that place them fed:
    For certainly, &c.

17 To him great kings who smote;
For his grace hath no bound.

18 Who slew, and spared not
Kings famous and renown'd:
    For certainly, &c.

19 Sihon the Am'rites' king;
For his grace lasteth ever:

20 Og also, who did reign
The land of Bashan over:

21 Their land by lot he gave;
For his grace faileth never,

22 That Isr'el might it have
In heritage for ever:
    For certainly, &c.

23 Who hath remembered
Us in our low estate;

24 And us delivered
From foes which did us hate:
    For certainly, &c.

25 Who to all flesh gives food;
For his grace faileth never.

26 Give thanks to God most good,
The God of heav'n, for ever:
    For certainly, &c.

PSALM 137.

1 BY Babel's streams we sat and wept,
    when Sion we thought on.

2 In midst thereof we hang'd our harps
    the willow-trees upon.

3 For there a song required they,
    who did us captive bring:
Our spoilers call'd for mirth, and
    A song of Sion sing.   [said,

4 O how the Lord's song shall we sing
    within a foreign land?

5 If thee, Jerus'lem, I forget,
    skill part from my right hand.

6 My tongue to my mouth's roof let
    if I do thee forget,   [cleave,
Jerusalem, and thee above
    my chief joy do not set.

7 Remember Edom's children, Lord,
    who in Jerus'lem's day,
Ev'n unto its foundation,
    Raze, raze it quite, did say.

8 O daughter thou of Babylon,
    near to destruction;
Bless'd shall he be that thee rewards,
    as thou to us hast done.

9 Yea, happy surely shall he be
    thy tender little ones
Who shall lay hold upon, and them
    shall dash against the stones.

PSALM 138.

1 THEE will I praise with all my
    I will sing praise to thee   [heart,

2 Before the gods: And worship will
    toward thy sanctuary.
I'll praise thy name, ev'n for thy
    and kindness of thy love;   [truth,
For thou thy word has magnify'd
    all thy great name above.

3 Thou didst me answer in the day
  when I to thee did cry;
  And thou my fainting soul with
    strength
  didst strengthen inwardly.

4 All kings upon the earth that are
  shall give thee praise, O Lord;
  When as they from thy mouth shall
  thy true and faithful word. [hear

5 Yea, in the righteous ways of God
  with gladness they shall sing:
  For great's the glory of the Lord,
  who doth for ever reign.

6 Though God be high, yet he respects
  all those that lowly be;
  Whereas the proud and lofty ones
  afar off knoweth he.

7 Though I in midst of trouble walk,
  I life from thee shall have:
  'Gainst my foes' wrath thou'lt stretch
    thine hand;
  thy right hand shall me save.

8 Surely that which concerneth me
  the Lord will perfect make:
  Lord, still thy mercy lasts; do not
  thine own hands' works forsake.

PSALM 139.

1 O LORD, thou hast me search'd
    and known.

2   Thou know'st my sitting down,
  And rising up; yea, all my thoughts
  afar to thee are known.

3 My footsteps, and my lying down,
  thou compassest always;
  Thou also most entirely art
  acquaint with all my ways.

4 For in my tongue, before I speak,
  not any word can be,
  But altogether, lo, O Lord,
  it is well known to thee.

5 Behind, before, thou hast beset,
  and laid on me thine hand.

6 Such knowledge is too strange for
  too high to understand.   [me,

7 From thy Sp'rit whither shall I go?
  or from thy presence fly?

8 Ascend I heav'n, lo, thou art there;
  there, if in hell I lie.

9 Take I the morning wings, and dwell
  in utmost parts of sea;

10 Ev'n there, Lord, shall thy hand me
  thy right hand hold shall me. [lead,

11 If I do say that darkness shall
  me cover from thy sight,
  Then surely shall the very night
  about me be as light.

12 Yea, darkness hideth not from thee,
  but night doth shine as day:
  To thee the darkness and the light
  are both alike alway.

13 For thou possessed hast my reins,
  and thou hast cover'd me,
  When I within my mother's womb
  inclosed was by thee.

14 Thee will I praise; for fearfully
  and strangely made I am;
  Thy works are marv'llous, and right
  my soul doth know the same. [well

15 My substance was not hid from thee,
  when as in secret I
  Was made; and in earth's lowest
    parts
  was wrought most curiously.

16 Thine eyes my substance did behold,
  yet being unperfect;
  And in the volume of thy book
  my members all were writ;

  Which after in continuance
  were fashion'd ev'ry one,
  When as they yet all shapeless were,
  And of them there was none.

17 How precious also are thy thoughts,
  O gracious God, to me!
  And in their sum how passing great
  and numberless they be!

18 If I should count them, than the sand
  they more in number be:
  What time soever I awake,
  I ever am with thee.

19 Thou, Lord, wilt sure the wicked
  hence from me bloody men. [slay:

20 Thy foes against thee loudly speak,
  and take thy name in vain.

21 Do not I hate all those, O Lord,
  that hatred bear to thee?
  With those that up against thee rise
  can I but grieved be?

22 With perfect hatred them I hate,
  my foes I them do hold.

23 Search me, O God, and know my
    heart,
  try me, my thoughts unfold:

24 And see if any way wicked
  there be at all in me;
  And in thine everlasting way
  to me a leader be.

PSALM 140.

1 LORD, from the ill and froward man
    give me deliverance,
  And do thou safe preserve me from
  the man of violence:

2 Who in their heart mischievous
are meditating ever;   [things
And they for war assembled are
continually together.

3 Much like unto a serpent's tongue
their tongues they sharp do make;
And underneath their lips there lies
the poison of a snake.

4 Lord, keep me from the wicked's
from vi'lent men me save; [hands,
Who utterly to overthrow
my goings purpos'd have.

5 The proud for me a snare have hid,
and cords; yea, they a net
Have by the way-side for me spread;
they gins for me have set.

6 I said unto the Lord, Thou art
my God: unto the cry
Of all my supplications,
Lord, do thine ear apply.

7 O God the Lord, who art the strength
of my salvation:
A cov'ring in the day of war
my head thou hast put on.

8 Unto the wicked man, O Lord,
his wishes do not grant;
Nor further thou his ill device,
lest they themselves should vaunt.

9 As for the head and chief of those
about that compass me,
Ev'n by the mischief of their lips
let thou them cover'd be.

10 Let burning coals upon them fall,
them throw in fiery flame,
And in deep pits, that they no more
may rise out of the same.

11 Let not an evil speaker be
on earth established:
Mischief shall hunt the vi'lent man,
till he be ruined.

12 I know God will th' afflicted's cause
maintain, and poor men's right.

13 Surely the just shall praise thy name;
th' upright dwell in thy sight.

PSALM 141.

1 O LORD, I unto thee do cry,
do thou make haste to me,
And give an ear unto my voice,
when I cry unto thee.

2 As incense let my prayer be
directed in thine eyes;
And the uplifting of my hands
as th' ev'ning sacrifice.

3 Set, Lord, a watch before my mouth,
keep of my lips the door.

4 My heart incline thou not unto
the ills I should abhor,
To practise wicked works with men
that work iniquity;
And with their delicates my taste
let me not satisfy.

5 Let him that righteous is me smite,
it shall a kindness be;
Let him reprove, I shall it count
a precious oil to me:
Such smiting shall not break my
for yet the time shall fall, [head;
When I in their calamities
to God pray for them shall.

6 When as their judges down shall be
in stony places cast,
Then shall they hear my words; for
shall sweet be to their taste. [they

7 About the grave's devouring mouth
our bones are scatter'd round,
As wood which men do cut and cleave
lies scatter'd on the ground.

8 But unto thee, O God the Lord,
mine eyes uplifted be:
My soul do not leave destitute;
my trust is set on thee.

9 Lord, keep me safely from the snares
which they for me prepare;
And from the subtile gins of them
that wicked workers are.

10 Let workers of iniquity
into their own nets fall,
Whilst I do, by thine help, escape
the danger of them all.

PSALM 142.

1 I WITH my voice cry'd to the Lord,
with it made my request:

2 Pour'd out to him my plaint, to him
my trouble I exprest.

3 When in me was o'erwhelm'd my
sp'rit,
then well thou knew'st my way;
Where I did walk a snare for me
they privily did lay.

4 I look'd on my right hand, and view'd,
but none to know me were;
All refuge failed me, no man
did for my soul take care.

5 I cry'd to thee; I said, Thou art
my refuge, Lord, alone;
And in the land of those that live
thou art my portion.

6 Because I am brought very low,
attend unto my cry:
Me from my persecutors save,
who stronger are than I.

7 From prison bring my soul, that I
   thy name may glorify:
The just shall compass me, when
   with me deal'st bounteously. [thou

PSALM 143.

1 LORD, hear my pray'r, attend my
   and in thy faithfulness   [suits;
Give thou an answer unto me,
   and in thy righteousness.

2 Thy servant also bring thou not
   in judgment to be try'd:
Because no living man can be
   in thy sight justify'd.

3 For th' en'my hath pursu'd my soul,
   my life to ground down tread:
In darkness he hath made me dwell,
   as who have long been dead.

4 My sp'rit is therefore overwhelm'd
   in me perplexedly;
Within me is my very heart
   amazed wondrously.

5 I call to mind the days of old,
   to meditate I use
On all thy works; upon the deeds
   I of thy hands do muse.

6 My hands to thee I stretch; my soul
   thirsts, as dry land, for thee.

7 Haste, Lord, to hear, my spirit fails:
   hide not thy face from me;
Lest like to them I do become
   that go down to the dust.

8 At morn let me thy kindness hear;
   for in thee do I trust.
Teach me the way that I should
   I lift my soul to thee.   [walk:

9 Lord, free me from my foes; I flee
   to thee to cover me.

10 Because thou art my God, to do
   thy will do me instruct:
Thy Sp'rit is good, me to the land
   of uprightness conduct.

11 Revive and quicken me, O Lord,
   ev'n for thine own name's sake;
And do thou, for thy righteousness,
   my soul from trouble take.

12 And of thy mercy slay my foes;
   let all destroyed be
That do afflict my soul: for I
   a servant am to thee.

Another of the same.

1 OH, hear my prayer, Lord,
   And unto my desire
To bow thine ear accord,
   I humbly thee require;

And, in thy faithfulness,
   Unto me answer make,
And, in thy righteousness,
   Upon me pity take.

2 In judgment enter not
   With me thy servant poor;
For why, this well I wot,
   No sinner can endure
The sight of thee, O God:
   If thou his deeds shalt try,
He dare make none abode
   Himself to justify.

3 Behold, the cruel foe
   Me persecutes with spite,
My soul to overthrow:
   Yea, he my life down quite
Unto the ground hath smote,
   And made me dwell full low
In darkness, as forgot,
   Or men dead long ago.

4 Therefore my sp'rit much vex'd,
   O'erwhelm'd is me within;
My heart right sore perplex'd
   And desolate hath been.

5 Yet I do call to mind
   What ancient days record,
Thy works of ev'ry kind
   I think upon, O Lord.

6 Lo, I do stretch my hands
   To thee, my help alone;
For thou well understands
   All my complaint and moan:
My thirsting soul desires,
   And longeth after thee,
As thirsty ground requires
   With rain refresh'd to be.

7 Lord, let my pray'r prevail,
   To answer it make speed;
For, lo, my sp'rit doth fail:
   Hide not my face in need;
Lest I be like to those
   That do in darkness sit,
Or him that downward goes
   Into the dreadful pit.

8 Because I trust in thee,
   O Lord, cause me to hear
Thy loving-kindness free,
   When morning doth appear:
Cause me to know the way
   Wherein my path should be;
For why, my soul on high
   I do lift up to thee.

9 From my fierce enemy
   In safety do me guide,
Because I flee to thee,
   Lord, that thou may'st me hide.

10 My God alone art thou,
Teach me thy righteousness:
Thy Sp'rit's good, lead me to
The land of uprightness.

11 O Lord, for thy name's sake,
Be pleas'd to quicken me;
And, for thy truth, forth take
My soul from misery.

12 And of thy grace destroy
My foes, and put to shame
All who my soul annoy;
For I thy servant am.

PSALM 144.

1 O BLESSED ever be the Lord,
who is my strength and might,
Who doth instruct my hands to war,
my fingers teach to fight.

2 My goodness, fortress, my high
deliverer, and shield,   [tow'r,
In whom I trust: who under me
my people makes to yield.

3 Lord, what is man, that thou of him
dost so much knowledge take?
Or son of man, that thou of him
so great account dost make?

4 Man is like vanity; his days,
as shadows, pass away.

5 Lord, bow thy heav'ns, come down,
touch thou
the hills, and smoke shall they.

6 Cast forth thy lightning, scatter them;
thine arrows shoot, them rout.

7 Thine hand send from above, me
save;
from great depths draw me out;
And from the hand of children
strange,

8 Whose mouth speaks vanity;
And their right hand is a right hand
that works deceitfully.

9 A new song I to thee will sing,
Lord, on a psaltery;
I on a ten-string'd instrument
will praises sing to thee.

10 Ev'n he it is that unto kings
salvation doth send;
Who his own servant David doth
from hurtful sword defend.

11 O free me from strange children's
hand,
whose mouth speaks vanity;
And their right hand a right hand is
that works deceitfully.

12 That, as the plants, our sons may be
in youth grown up that are;

Our daughters like to corner-stones,
carv'd like a palace fair.

13 That to afford all kind of store
our garners may be fill'd;
That our sheep thousands, in our
streets
ten thousands they may yield.

14 That strong our oxen be for work,
that no in-breaking be,
Nor going out; and that our streets
may from complaints be free.

15 Those people blessed are who be
in such a case as this;
Yea, blessed all those people are,
whose God JEHOVAH is.

PSALM 145.

1 I'LL thee extol, my God, O King;
I'll bless thy name always.

2 Thee will I bless each day, and will
thy name for ever praise.

3 Great is the Lord, much to be
prais'd;
his greatness search exceeds.

4 Race unto race shall praise thy works,
and show thy mighty deeds.

5 I of thy glorious majesty
the honour will record;
I'll speak of all thy mighty works,
which wondrous are, O Lord.

6 Men of thine acts the might shall
show,
thine acts that dreadful are;
And I, thy glory to advance,
thy greatness will declare.

7 The mem'ry of thy goodness great
they largely shall express;
With songs of praise they shall extol
thy perfect righteousness.

8 The Lord is very gracious;
in him compassions flow;
In mercy he is very great,
and is to anger slow.

9 The Lord JEHOVAH unto all
his goodness doth declare;
And over all his other works
his tender mercies are.

10 Thee all thy works shall praise, O
Lord,
and thee thy saints shall bless;

11 They shall thy kingdom's glory show,
thy pow'r by speech express:

12 To make the sons of men to know
his acts done mightily,
And of his kingdom th' excellent
and glorious majesty.

13 Thy kingdom shall for ever stand,
    thy reign through ages all.
14 God raiseth all that are bow'd down,
    upholdeth all that fall.

15 The eyes of all things wait on thee,
    the giver of all good;
    And thou, in time convenient,
    bestow'st on them their food:
16 Thine hand thou open'st lib'rally,
    and of thy bounty gives
    Enough to satisfy the need
    of ev'ry thing that lives.

17 The Lord is just in all his ways,
    holy in his works all.
18 God's near to all that call on him,
    in truth that on him call.
19 He will accomplish the desire
    of those that do him fear:
    He also will deliver them,
    and he their cry will hear.

20 The Lord preserves all who him love,
    that nought can them annoy:
    But all those that wicked are
    will utterly destroy.
21 My mouth the praises of the Lord
    to publish cease shall never:
    Let all flesh bless his holy name
    for ever and for ever.

Another of the same.

1 O LORD, thou art my God and
    King;
    Thee will I magnify and praise:
    I will thee bless, and gladly sing
    Unto thy holy name always.
2 Each day I rise I will thee bless,
    And praise thy name time without
    end.
3 Much to be prais'd, and great God is;
    His greatness none can comprehend.
4 Race shall thy works praise unto race,
    The mighty acts show done by thee.
5 I will speak of the glorious grace,
    And honour of thy majesty;
    Thy wondrous works I will record.
6 By men the might shall be extoll'd
    Of all thy dreadful acts, O Lord:
    And I thy greatness will unfold.
7 They utter shall abundantly
    The mem'ry of thy goodness great;
    And shall sing praises cheerfully,
    Whilst they thy righteousness relate.
8 The Lord our God is gracious,
    Compassionate is he also;
    In mercy he is plenteous,
    But unto wrath and anger slow.

9 Good unto all men is the Lord:
    O'er all his works his mercy is.
10 Thy works all praise to thee afford:
    Thy saints, O Lord, thy name shall
    bless.
11 The glory of thy kingdom show
    Shall they, and of thy power tell:
12 That so men's sons his deeds may
    know,
    His kingdom's grace that doth excel.

13 Thy kingdom hath none end at all,
    It doth through ages all remain.
14 The Lord upholdeth all that fall,
    The cast-down raiseth up again.
15 The eyes of all things, Lord, attend,
    And on thee wait that here do live,
    And thou, in season due, dost send
    Sufficient food them to relieve.
16 Yea, thou thine hand dost open wide,
    And ev'ry thing dost satisfy
    That lives, and doth on earth abide,
    Of thy great liberality.

17 The Lord is just in his ways all,
    And holy in his works each one.
18 He's near to all that on him call,
    Who call in truth on him alone.
19 God will the just desire fulfil
    Of such as do him fear and dread:
    Their cry regard, and hear he will,
    And save them in the time of need.
20 The Lord preserves all, more and
    less,
    That bear to him a loving heart:
    But workers all of wickedness
    Destroy will he, and clean subvert.
21 Therefore my mouth and lips I'll
    frame
    To speak the praises of the Lord:
    To magnify his holy name
    For ever let all flesh accord.

PSALM 146.

1 PRAISE God. The Lord praise, O
    my soul.
2   I'll praise God while I live;
    While I have being to my God
    in songs I'll praises give.
3 Trust not in princes, nor man's son,
    in whom there is no stay:
4 His breath departs, to 's earth he
    turns;
    that day his thoughts decay.
5 O happy is that man and blest,
    whom Jacob's God doth aid;
    Whose hope upon the Lord doth rest,
    and on his God is stay'd:

6 Who made the earth and heavens high,
  who made the swelling deep,
  And all that is within the same;
  who truth doth ever keep:

7 Who righteous judgment executes
  for those oppress'd that be,
  Who to the hungry giveth food;
  God sets the pris'ners free.

8 The Lord doth give the blind their
  the bowed down doth raise: [sight,
  The Lord doth dearly love all those
  that walk in upright ways.

9 The stranger's shield, the widow's
  the orphan's help, is he: [stay,
  But yet by him the wicked's way
  turn'd upside down shall be.

10 The Lord shall reign for evermore:
  thy God, O Sion, he
  Reigns to all generations.
  Praise to the Lord give ye.

PSALM 147.

1 PRAISE ye the Lord; for it is good
  praise to our God to sing:
  For it is pleasant, and to praise
  it is a comely thing.

2 God doth build up Jerusalem;
  and he it is alone
  That the dispers'd of Israel
  doth gather into one.

3 Those that are broken in their heart,
  and grieved in their minds,
  He healeth, and their painful wounds
  he tenderly up-binds.

4 He counts the number of the stars;
  he names them ev'ry one.

5 Great is our Lord, and of great pow'r;
  his wisdom search can none.

6 The Lord lifts up the meek; and casts
  the wicked to the ground.

7 Sing to the Lord, and give him
  on harp his praises sound; [thanks;

8 Who covereth the heav'n with clouds,
  who for the earth below
  Prepareth rain, who maketh grass
  upon the mountains grow.

9 He gives the beast his food, he feeds
  the ravens young that cry.

10 His pleasure not in horses' strength,
  nor in man's legs, doth lie.

11 But in all those that do him fear
  the Lord doth pleasure take;
  In those that to his mercy do
  by hope themselves betake.

12 The Lord praise, O Jerusalem;
  Sion, thy God confess:

13 For thy gates' bars he maketh strong;
  thy sons in thee doth bless.

14 He in thy borders maketh peace;
  with fine wheat filleth thee.

15 He sends forth his command on
  his word runs speedily.   [earth,

16 Hoar-frost, like ashes, scatt'reth he;
  like wool he snow doth give:

17 Like morsels casteth forth his ice;
  who in its cold can live?

18 He sendeth forth his mighty word,
  and melteth them again;
  His wind he makes to blow, and then
  the waters flow amain.

19 The doctrine of his holy word
  to Jacob he doth show;
  His statutes and his judgments he
  gives Israel to know.

20 To any nation never he
  such favour did afford;
  For they his judgments have not
  O do ye praise the Lord. [known.

PSALM 148.

1 PRAISE God. From heavens praise
  the Lord,
  in heights praise to him be.

2 All ye his angels, praise ye him;
  his hosts all, praise him ye.

3 O praise ye him, both sun and moon;
  praise him, all stars of light.

4 Ye heav'ns of heav'ns him praise, and
  above the heavens' height. [floods

5 Let all the creatures praise the name
  of our almighty Lord:
  For he commanded, and they were
  created by his word.

6 He also, for all times to come,
  hath them establish'd sure;
  He hath appointed them a law,
  which ever shall endure.

7 Praise ye JEHOVAH from the earth,
  dragons, and ev'ry deep:

8 Fire, hail, snow, vapour, stormy
  his word that fully keep.   [wind,

9 All hills and mountains, fruitful trees,
  and all ye cedars high:

10 Beasts, and all cattle, creeping things,
  and all ye birds that fly.

11 Kings of the earth, all nations,
  princes, earth's judges all:

12 Both young men, yea, and maidens
  old men, and children small. [too,

13 Let them God's name praise; for his
  alone is excellent: [name
  His glory reacheth far above
  the earth and firmament.

14 His people's horn, the praise of all
  his saints, exalteth he;
  Ev'n Isr'el's seed, a people near
  to him. The Lord praise ye.

Another of the same.

1 THE Lord of heav'n confess,
    On high his glory raise.
2 Him let all angels bless,
    Him all his armies praise.
3   Him glorify
      Sun, moon, and stars;
4   Ye higher spheres,
      And cloudy sky.

5 From God your beings are,
    Him therefore famous make;
  You all created were,
    When he the word but spake.
6   And from that place,
        Where fix'd you be
        By his decree,
        You cannot pass.

7 Praise God from earth below,
    Ye dragons, and ye deeps:
8 Fire, hail, clouds, wind, and snow,
    Whom in command he keeps.
9   Praise ye his name,
        Hills great and small,
        Trees low and tall;
10 Beasts wild and tame;
  All things that creep or fly.
11 Ye kings, ye vulgar throng,
  All princes mean or high;
12 Both men and virgins young,
    Ev'n young and old,
13   Exalt his name;
        For much his fame
        Should be extoll'd.

  O let God's name be prais'd
  Above both earth and sky;
14 For he his saints hath rais'd,
  And set their horn on high;
      Ev'n those that be
      Of Isr'el's race,
      Near to his grace.
      The Lord praise ye.

PSALM 149.

1 PRAISE ye the Lord: unto him sing
    a new song, and his praise
  In the assembly of his saints
    in sweet psalms do ye raise.

2 Let Isr'el in his Maker joy,
    and to him praises sing:
  Let all that Sion's children are
    be joyful in their King.

3 O let them unto his great name
    give praises in the dance;
  Let them with timbrel and with harp
    in songs his praise advance.

4 For God doth pleasure take in those
    that his own people be;
  And he with his salvation
    the meek will beautify.

5 And in his glory excellent
    let all his saints rejoice:
  Let them to him upon their beds
    aloud lift up their voice.

6 Let in their mouth aloft be rais'd
    the high praise of the Lord,
  And let them have in their right hand
    a sharp two-edged sword;

7 To execute the vengeance due
    upon the heathen all,
  And make deserved punishment
    upon the people fall.

8 And ev'n with chains, as pris'ners,
    bind
    their kings that them command;
  Yea, and with iron fetters strong,
    the nobles of their land.

9 On them the judgment to perform
    found written in his word:
  This honour is to all his saints.
    O do ye praise the Lord.

PSALM 150.

1 PRAISE ye the Lord. God's praise
    his sanctuary raise;   [within
  And to him in the firmament
    of his pow'r give ye praise.

2 Because of all his mighty acts,
    with praise him magnify:
  O praise him, as he doth excel
    in glorious majesty.

3 Praise him with trumpet's sound; his
    with psaltery advance: [praise
4 With timbrel, harp, string'd instru-
    and organs, in the dance.   [ments,
5 Praise him on cymbals loud; him
    praise
    on cymbals sounding high.
6 Let each thing breathing praise the
    Praise to the Lord give ye. [Lord.

END OF THE PSALMS.

INDEX

	Psalm		Psalm
AFTER thy loving-kindness, Lord,	51	I to the hills will lift mine eyes,	121
All lands to God, in joyful sounds,	66	I waited for the Lord my God,	40
All people, clap your hands; to God	47	I with my voice cry'd to the Lord,	142
All people that on earth do dwell,	100	I'll thee extol, my God, O King;	145
Attend, my people, to my law;	78	In gods' assembly God doth stand;	82
		In Judah's land God is well known,	76
Be merciful to me, O God;	57	In my distress to God I cry'd,	120
Behold, bless ye the Lord, all ye	134	In thee, O Lord, I put my trust,	31
Behold, how good a thing it is,	133	In thy great indignation,	6
Bless God, my soul. O Lord my God,	104	In thy great indignation,	38
Blessed are they that undefil'd,	119	Jehovah hear thee in the day	20
Bless'd is each one that fears the Lord,	128	Judge me, O God, and plead my cause	43
Blessed is he that wisely doth	41	Judge me, O Lord, for I have walk'd	26
By Babel's streams we sat and wept,	137	Keep not, O God, we thee entreat,	83
David, my afflictions all,	132	Let God arise, and scattered	68
Do ye, O congregation,	58	Like as the hart for water-brooks	42
		Lord, bless and pity us,	67
Except the Lord do build the house,	127	Lord, from the depths to thee I cry'd.	130
For evil doers fret thou not	37	Lord, from the ill and froward man	140
		Lord God, my Saviour, day and night	88
Give ear unto me when I call,	4	Lord, haste me to deliver;	70
Give ear unto my words, O Lord,	5	Lord, hear my pray'r, and let my cry	102
Give praise and thanks unto the Lord,	106	Lord, hear my pray'r, attend my suits;	143
Give thanks to God, call on his name:	105	Lord, hear my pray'r, hide not thyself	55
Give thanks to God, for good is he:	136	Lord, hear the right, attend my cry,	17
Give ye unto the Lord, ye sons	29	Lord, I will thee extol, for thou	30
God is our refuge and our strength,	46	Lord, in thy wrath rebuke me not;	6
God reigneth, let the earth be glad,	97	Lord, keep me; for I trust in thee.	16
God will I bless all times; his praise	34	Lord, thee I'll praise with all my heart,	9
God's mercies I will ever sing;	89	Lord, thee my God, I'll early seek:	63
Great is the Lord, and greatly he	48	Lord, thou hast been our dwelling-place	90
Had not the Lord been on our side,	124	Lord, unto us be merciful,	67
He that doth in the secret place	91		
Hear, Isr'el's Shepherd! like a flock	80	Make haste, O God, me to preserve;	70
Hear this, all people, and give ear,	49	My God, deliver me from those	59
Help, Lord, because the godly man	12	My God, my God, why hast thou me	22
How excellent in all the earth,	8	My heart brings forth a goodly thing;	45
How long wilt thou forget me, Lord?	13	My heart inditing is	45
How lovely is thy dwelling-place,	84	My heart is fix'd, Lord; I will sing,	108
		My heart not haughty is, O Lord,	131
I in the Lord do put my trust:	11	My soul with expectation	62
I joy'd when to the house of God,	122		
I love the Lord, because my voice	116	Not unto us, Lord, not to us,	115
I mercy and judgment sing,	101	Now Israel may say,	124
I said, I will look to my ways,	39		

INDEX

	Psalm		Psalm
O all ye lands, unto the Lord	100	Save me, O God, because the floods	69
O blessed ever be the Lord,	144	Save me, O God, by thy great name,	54
O blessed is the man to whom	32	Show mercy, Lord, to me, for man	56
O come, let us sing to the Lord:	95	Sing loud to God our strength; with	
O give ye praise unto the Lord,	117	joy	81
O God, give ear unto my cry;	61		
O God, the heathen enter'd have	79	That man hath perfect blessedness	1
O God, we with our ears have heard,	44	That there is not a God, the fool	14
O God, why hast thou cast us off?	74	That there is not a God, the fool	53
O Lord, do thou bow down thine ear,	86	The earth belongs unto the Lord,	24
O Lord God, unto whom alone	94	Th' eternal Lord doth reign as king,	99
O Lord, how are my foes increas'd?	3	The heav'ns God's glory do declare,	19
O Lord, I unto thee do cry,	141	The king in thy great strength, O	
O Lord my God, in thee do I	7	Lord,	21
O Lord, my hope and confidence	71	The LORD did say unto my Lord,	110
O Lord, thou art my God and King;	145	The LORD doth reign, and cloth'd	
O Lord, thou hast been favourable	85	is he	93
O Lord, thou hast me search'd and		The Lord's my light and saving	
known.	139	health,	27
O Lord, thou hast rejected us,	60	The Lord's my shepherd, I'll not	
O Lord, thy judgments give the king,	72	want.	23
O Lord, unto my pray'r give ear,	102	The Lord of heav'n confess,	148
O praise the Lord, for he is good:	118	The mighty God, the Lord,	50
O sing a new song to the Lord:	96	The mighty God, the Lord, hath	
O sing a new song to the Lord,	98	spoke,	50
O thou my soul, bless God the Lord;	103	The wicked man's transgression	36
O thou that dwellest in the heav'ns,	123	Thee will I love, O Lord, my	
O thou the God of all my praise,	109	strength.	18
Oft did they vex me from my youth,	129	Thee will I praise with all my heart,	138
Oh, hear my prayer, Lord,	143	They in the Lord that firmly trust	125
		To render thanks unto the Lord	92
Plead, Lord, with those that plead;		To thee I lift my soul:	25
and fight	35	To thee I lift my soul, O Lord:	25
Praise God, for he is good: for still	107	To thee I'll cry, O Lord, my rock;	28
Praise God, for he is kind:	136	To thee, O God, do we give thanks,	75
Praise God. From heavens praise			
the Lord,	148	Unto the Lord, I with my voice,	77
Praise God. The Lord praise, O my		Upon the hills of holiness	87
soul.	146		
Praise God: ye servants of the Lord,	113	When I to thee my prayer make,	64
Praise waits for thee in Sion, Lord:	65	When Isr'el out of Egypt went,	114
Praise ye the Lord; for it is good	147	When Sion's bondage God turn'd	
Praise ye the Lord. God's praise		back,	126
within	150	Wherefore is it that thou, O Lord,	10
Praise ye the Lord, the Lord's name		Why dost thou boast, O mighty man,	52
praise;	135	Why rage the heathen? and vain	
Praise ye the Lord. The man is		things	2
bless'd	112	Within thy tabernacle, Lord,	15
Praise ye the Lord: unto him sing	149		
Praise ye the Lord: with my whole		Ye righteous, in the Lord rejoice;	33
heart	111	Yet God is good to Israel,	73

DOXOLOGIES OR CONCLUSIONS.

May be sung at the close of a Psalm or portion of a Psalm.

1.   L.M.

TO Father, Son, and Holy Ghost,
    The God whom earth and heaven
        adore,
Be glory, as it was of old,
Is now, and shall be evermore. AMEN.

2.   C.M.

TO Father, Son, and Holy Ghost,
    the God whom we adore,
Be glory, as it was, and is,
    and shall be evermore. AMEN.

3.   S.M.

TO Thee be glory, Lord,
    whom heaven and earth adore,
To Father, Son, and Holy Ghost,
    one God for evermore. AMEN.

4.   10 10 10 10 10 10
     PSALM 124, second version.

GLORY to God
    the Father, God the Son,
And unto God
    the Spirit, Three in One.
From age to age
    let saints his name adore,
His power and love
    proclaim from shore to shore,
And spread his fame,
    till time shall be no more. AMEN.

5.   8 7 8 7
     PSALM 136, first version.

TO Father, Son, and Holy Ghost,
    whose mercy faileth never,
Be praise and glory, as it was,
    is now, and shall be ever. AMEN.

6.   6 6 6 6 8 8
     PSALMS 136, second version; 148,
        second version.

TO God the Father, Son,
    And Spirit ever bless'd,
Eternal Three in One,
    All worship be address'd,
      As heretofore
        It was, is now,
      And still shall be
        For evermore. AMEN.

7.   6 6 6 6 D.
     PSALM 143, second version.

NOW glory be to God
    The Father, and the Son,
And to the Holy Ghost,
    All-glorious Three in One.
And his most holy name
    Let all his saints adore,
As it hath been, is now,
    And shall be evermore. AMEN.

TRANSLATIONS AND PARAPHRASES,

IN VERSE,

OF SEVERAL PASSAGES OF

SACRED SCRIPTURE.

1. GENESIS i.

1 LET heav'n arise, let earth appear,
   said the Almighty Lord:
The heav'n arose, the earth appear'd,
   at his creating word.

2 Thick darkness brooded o'er the deep:
   God said, 'Let there be light:'
The light shone forth with smiling ray,
   and scatter'd ancient night.

3 He bade the clouds ascend on high;
   the clouds ascend, and bear
A wat'ry treasure to the sky,
   and float upon the air.

4 The liquid element below
   was gather'd by his hand;
The rolling seas together flow,
   and leave the solid land.

5 With herbs, and plants, and fruitful
   trees,
   the new-form'd globe he crown'd,
Ere there was rain to bless the soil,
   or sun to warm the ground.

6 Then high in heav'n's resplendent
   arch
   he plac'd two orbs of light,
He set the sun to rule the day,
   the moon to rule the night.

7 Next, from the deep, th' Almighty
   King
   did vital beings frame;
Fowls of the air of ev'ry wing,
   and fish of ev'ry name.

8 To all the various brutal tribes
   he gave their wondrous birth;
At once the lion and the worm
   sprung from the teeming earth.

9 Then, chief o'er all his works below,
   at last was Adam made;
His Maker's image bless'd his soul,
   and glory crown'd his head.

10 Fair in th' Almighty Maker's eye
   the whole creation stood.
He view'd the fabric he had rais'd;
   his word pronounc'd it good.

2. GENESIS xxviii. 20–22.

1 O GOD of Bethel! by whose hand
   thy people still are fed;
Who through this weary pilgrimage
   hast all our fathers led:

2 Our vows, our pray'rs, we now present
   before thy throne of grace:
God of our fathers! be the God
   of their succeeding race.

3 Through each perplexing path of life
   our wand'ring footsteps guide;
Give us each day our daily bread,
   and raiment fit provide.

4 O spread thy cov'ring wings around,
   till all our wand'rings cease,
And at our Father's lov'd abode
   our souls arrive in peace.

5 Such blessings from thy gracious
   hand
   our humble pray'rs implore;
And thou shalt be our chosen God,
   and portion evermore.

3. JOB i. 21.

1 NAKED as from the earth we
   came,
   and enter'd life at first;
Naked we to the earth return,
   and mix with kindred dust.

2 Whate'er we fondly call our own
   belongs to heav'n's great Lord;
The blessings lent us for a day
   are soon to be restor'd.

3 'Tis God that lifts our comforts high,
   or sinks them in the grave:
He gives; and, when he takes away,
   he takes but what he gave.

4 Then, ever blessed be his name!
   his goodness swell'd our store;
His justice but resumes its own;
   'tis ours still to adore.

4. JOB iii. 17–20.

1 HOW still and peaceful is the grave!
   where, life's vain tumults past,
Th' appointed house, by Heav'n's
   decree,
   receives us all at last.

2 The wicked there from troubling
   cease,
   their passions rage no more;
And there the weary pilgrim rests
   from all the toils he bore.

3 There rest the pris'ners, now releas'd
   from slav'ry's sad abode;

No more they hear th' oppressor's voice,
    or dread the tyrant's rod.   [voice,
4 There servants, masters, small and great,
    partake the same repose;   [great,
And there, in peace, the ashes mix
    of those who once were foes.
5 All, levell'd by the hand of Death,
    lie sleeping in the tomb;
Till God in judgment calls them forth,
    to meet their final doom.   [forth,

5. Job v. 6–12.

1 THOUGH trouble springs not
    from the dust,
    nor sorrow from the ground;
Yet ills on ills, by Heav'n's decree,
    in man's estate are found.
2 As sparks in close succession rise,
    so man, the child of woe,
Is doom'd to endless cares and toils
    through all his life below.
3 But with my God I leave my cause;
    from him I seek relief;
To him, in confidence of pray'r,
    unbosom all my grief.
4 Unnumber'd are his wondrous works,
    unsearchable his ways;
'Tis his the mourning soul to cheer,
    the bowed down to raise.

6. Job viii. 11–22.

1 THE rush may rise where waters
    flow,
    and flags beside the stream;
But soon their verdure fades and dies
    before the scorching beam:
2 So is the sinner's hope cut off;
    or, if it transient rise,
'Tis like the spider's airy web,
    from ev'ry breath that flies.
3 Fix'd on his house he leans; his house
    and all its props decay:
He holds it fast; but, while he holds,
    the tott'ring frame gives way.
4 Fair, in his garden, to the sun
    his boughs with verdure smile;
And, deeply fix'd, his spreading roots
    unshaken stand a while.
5 But forth the sentence flies from
    Heav'n,
    that sweeps him from his place;
Which then denies him for its lord,
    nor owns it knew his face.
6 Lo! this the joy of wicked men,
    who Heav'n's high laws despise:
They quickly fall; and in their room
    as quickly others rise.

7 But, for the just, with gracious care,
    God will his pow'r employ;
He'll teach their lips to sing his
    praise,
    and fill their hearts with joy.

7. Job ix. 2–10.

1 HOW should the sons of Adam's
    be pure before their God? [race
If he contends in righteousness,
    we sink beneath his rod.
2 If he should mark my words and
    thoughts
    with strict enquiring eyes,
Could I for one of thousand faults
    the least excuse devise?
3 Strong is his arm, his heart is wise;
    who dares with him contend?
Or who, that tries th' unequal strife,
    shall prosper in the end?
4 He makes the mountains feel his
    wrath,
    and their old seats forsake;
The trembling earth deserts her
    and all her pillars shake.   [place,
5 He bids the sun forbear to rise;
    th' obedient sun forbears:
His hand with sackcloth spreads the
    and seals up all the stars.   [skies,
6 He walks upon the raging sea;
    flies on the stormy wind:
None can explore his wondrous way,
    or his dark footsteps find.

8. Job xiv. 1–15.

1 FEW are thy days, and full of woe,
    O man, of woman born!
Thy doom is written, 'Dust thou art,
    and shalt to dust return.'
2 Behold the emblem of thy state
    in flow'rs that bloom and die,
Or in the shadow's fleeting form,
    that mocks the gazer's eye.
3 Guilty and frail, how shalt thou stand
    before thy sov'reign Lord?
Can troubled and polluted springs
    a hallow'd stream afford?
4 Determin'd are the days that fly
    successive o'er thy head;
The number'd hour is on the wing
    that lays thee with the dead.
5 Great God! afflict not in thy wrath
    the short allotted span,
That bounds the few and weary days
    of pilgrimage to man.
6 All nature dies, and lives again:
    the flow'r that paints the field,

The trees that crown the mountain's
    brow,
    and boughs and blossoms yield,
7 Resign the honours of their form
    at Winter's stormy blast,
And leave the naked leafless plain
    a desolated waste.
8 Yet soon reviving plants and flow'rs
    anew shall deck the plain;
The woods shall hear the voice of
    and flourish green again. [Spring,
9 But man forsakes this earthly scene,
    ah! never to return:
Shall any foll'wing spring revive
    the ashes of the urn?
10 The mighty flood that rolls along
    its torrents to the main,
Can ne'er recall its waters lost
    from that abyss again.
11 So days, and years, and ages past,
    descending down to night,
Can henceforth never more return
    back to the gates of light;
12 And man, when laid in lonesome
    grave,
    shall sleep in Death's dark gloom,
Until th' eternal morning wake
    the slumbers of the tomb.
13 O may the grave become to me
    the bed of peaceful rest,
Whence I shall gladly rise at length,
    and mingle with the blest!
14 Cheer'd by this hope, with patient
    mind,
I'll wait Heav'n's high decree,
Till the appointed period come,
    when death shall set me free.

9. JOB xxvi. 6, to the end.

1 WHO can resist th' Almighty arm
    that made the starry sky?
Or who elude the certain glance
    of God's all-seeing eye?
2 From him no cov'ring vails our
    hell opens to his sight; [crimes;
And all Destruction's secret snares
    lie full disclos'd in light.
3 Firm on the boundless void of space
    he pois'd the steady pole,
And in the circle of his clouds
    bade secret waters roll.
4 While nature's universal frame
    its Maker's pow'r reveals,
His throne, remote from mortal eyes,
    an awful cloud conceals.
5 From where the rising day ascends,
    to where it sets in night,

He compasses the floods with bounds,
    and checks their threat'ning might.
6 The pillars that support the sky
    tremble at his rebuke;
Through all its caverns quakes the
    as though its centre shook. [earth,
7 He brings the waters from their beds,
    although no tempest blows,
And smites the kingdom of the proud
    without the hand of foes.
8 With bright inhabitants above
    he fills the heav'nly land,
And all the crooked serpent's breed
    dismay'd before him stand.
9 Few of his works can we survey;
    these few our skill transcend:
But the full thunder of his pow'r
    what heart can comprehend?

10. PROV. i. 20-31.

1 IN streets, and op'nings of the gates,
    where pours the busy crowd,
Thus heav'nly Wisdom lifts her
    and cries to men aloud: [voice,
2 How long, ye scorners of the truth,
    scornful will ye remain?
How long shall fools their folly love,
    and hear my words in vain?
3 O turn, at last, at my reproof!
    and, in that happy hour,
His bless'd effusions on your heart
    my Spirit down shall pour.
4 But since so long, with earnest voice,
    to you in vain I call,
Since all my counsels and reproofs
    thus ineffectual fall;
5 The time will come, when humbled
    in Sorrow's evil day, [low,
Your voice by anguish shall be taught,
    but taught too late, to pray.
6 When, like the whirlwind, o'er me
    comes Desolation's blast; [deep
Pray'rs then extorted shall be vain,
    the hour of mercy past.
7 The choice you made has fix'd your
    for this is Heav'n's decree, [doom;
That with the fruits of what he sow'd
    the sinner fill'd shall be.

11. PROV. iii. 13-17.

1 O HAPPY is the man who hears
    Instruction's warning voice;
And who celestial Wisdom makes
    his early, only choice.
2 For she has treasures greater far
    than east or west unfold;

And her rewards more precious are
  than all their stores of gold.

3 In her right hand she holds to view
  a length of happy days;
Riches, with splendid honours join'd,
  are what her left displays.

4 She guides the young with innocence,
  in pleasure's paths to tread,
A crown of glory she bestows
  upon the hoary head.

5 According as her labours rise,
  so her rewards increase;
Her ways are ways of pleasantness,
  and all her paths are peace.

12.   PROV. vi. 6–12.

1 YE indolent and slothful! rise,
  View the ant's labours, and be
    wise;
She has no guide to point her way,
  No ruler chiding her delay:

2 Yet see with what incessant cares
  She for the winter's storm prepares;
In summer she provides her meat,
  And harvest finds her store complete.

3 But when will slothful man arise?
  How long shall sleep seal up his eyes?
Sloth more indulgence still demands;
  Sloth shuts the eyes, and folds the
    hands.

4 But mark the end; want shall assail,
  When all your strength and vigour
    fail;
Want, like an armed man, shall rush
  The hoary head of age to crush.

13.   PROV. viii. 22, to the end.

1 KEEP silence, all ye sons of men,
  and hear with rev'rence due;
Eternal Wisdom from above
  thus lifts her voice to you:

2 I was th' Almighty's chief delight
  from everlasting days,
Ere yet his arm was stretched forth
  the heav'ns and earth to raise.

3 Before the sea began to flow,
  and leave the solid land,
Before the hills and mountains rose,
  I dwelt at his right hand.

4 When first he rear'd the arch of
    heav'n,
  and spread the clouds on air,
When first the fountains of the deep
  he open'd, I was there.

5 There I was with him, when he
    stretch'd
  his compass o'er the deep,

And charg'd the ocean's swelling
    waves
  within their bounds to keep.

6 With joy I saw th' abode prepar'd
  which men were soon to fill:
Them from the first of days I lov'd,
  unchang'd, I love them still.

7 Now therefore hearken to my words,
  ye children, and be wise:
Happy the man that keeps my ways;
  the man that shuns them dies.

8 Where dubious paths perplex the
    mind,
  direction I afford;   [mind,
Life shall be his that follows me,
  and favour from the Lord.

9 But he who scorns my sacred laws
  shall deeply wound his heart,
He courts destruction who contemns
  the counsel I impart.

14.   ECCLES. vii. 2–6.

1 WHILE others crowd the house of
    mirth,
  and haunt the gaudy show,
Let such as would with Wisdom
    dwell,
  frequent the house of woe. [dwell,

2 Better to weep with those who weep,
  and share th' afflicted's smart,
Than mix with fools in giddy joys
  that cheat and wound the heart.

3 When virtuous sorrow clouds the
    face,
  and tears bedim the eye,   [face,
The soul is led to solemn thought,
  and wafted to the sky.

4 The wise in heart revisit oft
  grief's dark sequester'd cell;
The thoughtless still with levity
  and mirth delight to dwell.

5 The noisy laughter of the fool
  is like the crackling sound
Of blazing thorns, which quickly fall
  in ashes to the ground.

15.   ECCLES. ix. 4, 5, 6, 10.

1 AS long as life its term extends,
  Hope's blest dominion never
    ends;
For while the lamp holds on to burn,
  The greatest sinner may return.

2 Life is the season God hath giv'n
  To fly from hell, and rise to heav'n;
That day of grace fleets fast away,
  And none its rapid course can stay.

3 The living know that they must die;
  But all the dead forgotten lie:
Their mem'ry and their name is gone,
  Alike unknowing and unknown.

94

4 Their hatred and their love is lost,
   Their envy bury'd in the dust;
   They have no share in all that's done
   Beneath the circuit of the sun.

5 Then what thy thoughts design to do,
   Still let thy hands with might pursue;
   Since no device nor work is found,
   Nor wisdom underneath the ground.

6 In the cold grave, to which we haste,
   There are no acts of pardon past:
   But fix'd the doom of all remains,
   And everlasting silence reigns.

16. ECCLES. xii. 1.

1 IN life's gay morn, when sprightly
      with vital ardour glows,   [youth
   And shines in all the fairest charms
      which beauty can disclose;

2 Deep on thy soul, before its pow'rs
      are yet by vice enslav'd,
   Be thy Creator's glorious name
      and character engrav'd.

3 For soon the shades of grief shall
      the sunshine of thy days;   [cloud
   And cares, and toils, in endless round,
      encompass all thy ways.

4 Soon shall thy heart the woes of age
      in mournful groans deplore,
   And sadly muse on former joys,
      that now return no more.

17. ISAIAH i. 10-19.

1 RULERS of Sodom! hear the voice
      of heav'n's eternal Lord;
   Men of Gomorrah! bend your ear
      submissive to his word.

2 'Tis thus he speaks: To what intent
      are your oblations vain?
   Why load my altars with your gifts,
      polluted and profane?

3 Burnt-off'rings long may blaze to
      heav'n,
      and incense cloud the skies;
   The worship and the worshipper
      are hateful in my eyes.

4 Your rites, your fasts, your pray'rs, I
      and pomp of solemn days: [scorn,
   I know your hearts are full of guile,
      and crooked are your ways.

5 But cleanse your hands, ye guilty
      and cease from deeds of sin; [race,
   Learn in your actions to be just,
      and pure in heart within.

6 Mock not my name with honours
      but keep my holy laws;   [vain,
   Do justice to the friendless poor,
      and plead the widow's cause.

7 Then though your guilty souls are
      with sins of crimson dye, [stain'd
   Yet, through my grace, with snow
      in whiteness they shall vie.   [itself

18. ISAIAH ii. 2-6.

1 BEHOLD! the mountain of the
      in latter days shall rise   [Lord
   On mountain tops above the hills,
      and draw the wond'ring eyes.

2 To this the joyful nations round,
      all tribes and tongues shall flow;
   Up to the hill of God, they'll say,
      and to his house we'll go.

3 The beam that shines from Sion hill
      shall lighten ev'ry land;
   The King who reigns in Salem's
      tow'rs
      shall all the world command.

4 Among the nations he shall judge;
      his judgments truth shall guide;
   His sceptre shall protect the just,
      and quell the sinner's pride.

5 No strife shall rage, nor hostile feuds
      disturb those peaceful years;
   To ploughshares men shall beat their
      swords,
      to pruning-hooks their spears.

6 No longer hosts encount'ring hosts
      shall crowds of slain deplore:
   They hang the trumpet in the hall,
      and study war no more.

7 Come then, O house of Jacob! come
      to worship at his shrine;
   And, walking in the light of God,
      with holy beauties shine.

19. ISAIAH ix. 2-8.

1 THE race that long in darkness
      have seen a glorious light; [pin'd
   The people dwell in day, who dwelt
      in death's surrounding night.

2 To hail thy rise, thou better Sun!
      the gath'ring nations come,
   Joyous, as when the reapers bear
      the harvest treasures home.

3 For thou our burden hast remov'd,
      and quell'd th' oppressor's sway,
   Quick as the slaughter'd squadrons
      in Midian's evil day.   [fell

4 To us a Child of hope is born;
      to us a Son is giv'n;
   Him shall the tribes of earth obey,
      him all the hosts of heav'n.

5 His name shall be the Prince of
      for evermore ador'd,   [Peace,

The Wonderful, the Counsellor,
  the great and mighty Lord.
6 His pow'r increasing still shall spread,
  his reign no end shall know;
Justice shall guard his throne above,
  and peace abound below.

20. ISAIAH xxvi. 1-7.

1 HOW glorious Sion's courts ap-
  the city of our God! [pear,
His throne he hath establish'd here,
  here fix'd his lov'd abode.
2 Its walls, defended by his grace,
  no pow'r shall e'er o'erthrow,
Salvation is its bulwark sure
  against th' assailing foe.
3 Lift up the everlasting gates,
  the doors wide open fling;
Enter, ye nations, who obey
  the statutes of our King.
4 Here shall ye taste unmingled joys,
  and dwell in perfect peace,
Ye, who have known JEHOVAH's
  and trusted in his grace. [name,
5 Trust in the Lord, for ever trust,
  and banish all your fears;
Strength in the Lord JEHOVAH
  eternal as his years. [dwells
6 What though the wicked dwell on
  high,
  his arm shall bring them low;
Low as the caverns of the grave
  their lofty heads shall bow.
7 Along the dust shall then be spread
  their tow'rs, that brave the skies:
On them the needy's feet shall tread,
  and on their ruins rise.

21. ISAIAH xxxiii. 13-18.

1 ATTEND, ye tribes that dwell remote,
  ye tribes at hand, give ear;
Th' upright in heart alone have hope,
  the false in heart have fear.
2 The man who walks with God in
  and ev'ry guile disdains; [truth,
Who hates to lift oppression's rod,
  and scorns its shameful gains;
3 Whose soul abhors the impious bribe
  that tempts from truth to stray,
And from th' enticing snares of vice
  who turns his eyes away:
4 His dwelling, 'midst the strength of
  shall ever stand secure; [rocks,
His Father will provide his bread,
  his water shall be sure.

5 For him the kingdom of the just
  afar doth glorious shine;
And he the King of kings shall see
  in majesty divine.

22. ISAIAH xl. 27, to the end.

1 WHY pour'st thou forth thine
  anxious plaint,
  despairing of relief,
As if the Lord o'erlook'd thy cause,
  and did not heed thy grief?
2 Hast thou not known, hast thou not
  that firm remains on high [heard,
The everlasting throne of Him
  who form'd the earth and sky?
3 Art thou afraid his pow'r shall fail
  when comes thy evil day?
And can an all-creating arm
  grow weary or decay?
4 Supreme in wisdom as in pow'r
  the Rock of ages stands;
Though him thou canst not see, nor
  the working of his hands. [trace
5 He gives the conquest to the weak,
  supports the fainting heart;
And courage in the evil hour
  his heav'nly aids impart.
6 Mere human pow'r shall fast decay,
  and youthful vigour cease;
But they who wait upon the Lord,
  in strength shall still increase.
7 They with unweary'd feet shall tread
  the path of life divine;
With growing ardour onward move,
  with growing brightness shine.
8 On eagles' wings they mount, they
  their wings are faith and love, [soar,
Till, past the cloudy regions here,
  they rise to heav'n above.

23. ISAIAH xlii. 1-13.

1 BEHOLD my Servant! see him rise
  exalted in my might!
Him have I chosen, and in him
  I place supreme delight.
2 On him, in rich effusion pour'd,
  my Spirit shall descend;
My truths and judgments he shall
  to earth's remotest end. [show
3 Gentle and still shall be his voice,
  no threats from him proceed;
The smoking flax he shall not quench,
  nor break the bruised reed.
4 The feeble spark to flames he'll raise;
  the weak will not despise;
Judgment he shall bring forth to
  and make the fallen rise. [truth,

5 The progress of his zeal and pow'r
    shall never know decline,
Till foreign lands and distant isles
    receive the law divine.

6 He who erected heav'n's bright arch,
    and bade the planets roll,
Who peopled all the climes of earth,
    and form'd the human soul,

7 Thus saith the Lord, Thee have I
    my Prophet thee install;   [rais'd,
In right I've rais'd thee, and in
    I'll succour whom I call. [strength

8 I will establish with the lands
    a covenant in thee,
To give the Gentile nations light,
    and set the pris'ners free:

9 Asunder burst the gates of brass;
    the iron fetters fall;
And gladsome light and liberty
    are straight restor'd to all.

10 I am the Lord, and by the name
    of great JEHOVAH known;
No idol shall usurp my praise,
    nor mount into my throne.

11 Lo! former scenes, predicted once,
    conspicuous rise to view;
And future scenes, predicted now,
    shall be accomplish'd too.

12 Sing to the Lord in joyful strains!
    let earth his praise resound,
Ye who upon the ocean dwell,
    and fill the isles around!

13 O city of the Lord! begin
    the universal song;
And let the scatter'd villages
    the cheerful notes prolong.

14 Let Kedar's wilderness afar
    lift up its lonely voice;
And let the tenants of the rock
    with accents rude rejoice;

15 Till 'midst the streams of distant
    lands
    the islands sound his praise;
And all combin'd, with one accord,
    JEHOVAH's glories raise.

24. ISAIAH xlix. 13–17.

1 YE heav'ns, send forth your song of
    praise!
    earth, raise your voice below!
Let hills and mountains join the
    hymn,
    and joy through nature flow.

2 Behold how gracious is our God!
    hear the consoling strains,
In which he cheers our drooping
    and mitigates our pains.   [hearts,

3 Cease ye, when days of darkness
    in sad dismay to mourn,   [come,
As if the Lord could leave his saints
    forsaken or forlorn?

4 Can the fond mother e'er forget
    the infant whom she bore?
And can its plaintive cries be heard,
    nor move compassion more?

5 She may forget: nature may fail
    a parent's heart to move;
But Sion on my heart shall dwell
    in everlasting love.

6 Full in my sight, upon my hands
    I have engrav'd her name:
My hands shall build her ruin'd walls,
    and raise her broken frame.

25. ISAIAH liii.

1 HOW few receive with cordial faith
    the tidings which we bring?
How few have seen the arm reveal'd
    of heav'n's eternal King?

2 The Saviour comes! no outward
    pomp
    bespeaks his presence nigh;
No earthly beauty shines in him
    to draw the carnal eye.

3 Fair as a beauteous tender flow'r
    amidst the desert grows,
So slighted by a rebel race
    the heav'nly Saviour rose.

4 Rejected and despis'd of men,
    behold a man of woe!
Grief was his close companion still
    through all his life below.

5 Yet all the griefs he felt were ours,
    ours were the woes he bore:
Pangs, not his own, his spotless soul
    with bitter anguish tore.

6 We held him as condemn'd by
    an outcast from his God, [Heav'n,
While for our sins he groan'd, he
    beneath his Father's rod.   [bled,

7 His sacred blood hath wash'd our
    from sin's polluted stain;   [souls
His stripes have heal'd us, and his
    reviv'd our souls again.   [death

8 We all, like sheep, had gone astray
    in ruin's fatal road:
On him were our transgressions laid;
    he bore the mighty load.

9 Wrong'd and oppress'd, how meekly
    in patient silence stood!   [he
Mute, as the peaceful harmless lamb,
    when brought to shed its blood.

10 Who can his generation tell?
    from prison see him led!

With impious show of law con-
    demn'd,
    and number'd with the dead.

11 'Midst sinners low in dust he lay;
    the rich a grave supply'd:
Unspotted was his blameless life;
    unstain'd by sin he dy'd.

12 Yet God shall raise his head on high,
    though thus he brought him low;
His sacred off'ring, when complete,
    shall terminate his woe.

13 For, saith the Lord, my pleasure then
    shall prosper in his hand;
His shall a num'rous offspring be,
    and still his honours stand.

14 His soul, rejoicing, shall behold
    the purchase of his pain;
And all the guilty whom he sav'd
    shall bless Messiah's reign.

15 He with the great shall share the
    spoil, [spoil,
    and baffle all his foes;
Though rank'd with sinners, here he
    a conqueror he rose. [fell,

16 He dy'd to bear the guilt of men,
    that sin might be forgiv'n:
He lives to bless them and defend,
    and plead their cause in heav'n.

26. Isaiah lv.

1 HO! ye that thirst, approach the
    spring
    where living-waters flow:
Free to that sacred fountain all
    without a price may go.

2 How long to streams of false delight
    will ye in crowds repair?
How long your strength and sub-
    stance waste
    on trifles, light as air?

3 My stores afford those rich supplies
    that health and pleasure give:
Incline your ear, and come to me;
    the soul that hears shall live.

4 With you a cov'nant I will make,
    that ever shall endure;
The hope which gladden'd David's
    heart
    my mercy hath made sure.

5 Behold he comes! your leader comes,
    with might and honour crown'd;
A witness who shall spread my name
    to earth's remotest bound.

6 See! nations hasten to his call
    from ev'ry distant shore;
Isles, yet unknown, shall bow to him,
    and Isr'el's God adore.

7 Seek ye the Lord while yet his ear
    is open to your call;
While offer'd mercy still is near,
    before his footstool fall.

8 Let sinners quit their evil ways,
    their evil thoughts forego:
And God, when they to him return,
    returning grace will show.

9 He pardons with o'erflowing love:
    for, hear the voice divine!
My nature is not like to yours,
    nor like your ways are mine:

10 But far as heav'n's resplendent orbs
    beyond earth's spot extend,
As far my thoughts, as far my ways,
    your ways and thoughts transcend.

11 And as the rains from heav'n distil,
    nor thither mount again,
But swell the earth with fruitful juice,
    and all its tribes sustain:

12 So not a word that flows from me
    shall ineffectual fall;
But universal nature prove
    obedient to my call.

13 With joy and peace shall then be led
    the glad converted lands;
The lofty mountains then shall sing,
    the forests clap their hands.

14 Where briers grew 'midst barren
    wilds,
    shall firs and myrtles spring;
And nature, through its utmost
    bounds, [bounds,
    eternal praises sing.

27. Isaiah lvii. 15, 16.

1 THUS speaks the high and lofty
    One;
    ye tribes of earth, give ear;
The words of your Almighty King
    with sacred rev'rence hear:

2 Amidst the majesty of heav'n
    my throne is fix'd on high;
And through eternity I hear
    the praises of the sky.

3 Yet, looking down, I visit oft
    the humble hallow'd cell;
And with the penitent who mourn
    'tis my delight to dwell:

4 The downcast spirit to revive,
    the sad in soul to cheer;
And from the bed of dust the man
    of heart contrite to rear.

5 With me dwells no relentless wrath
    against the human race;
The souls which I have form'd shall
    find [find
    a refuge in my grace.

28. ISAIAH lviii. 5-9.

1 ATTEND, and mark the solemn fast
    which to the Lord is dear;
Disdain the mask unhallow'd mask
    which vain dissemblers wear.

2 Do I delight in sorrow's dress?
    saith he who reigns above;
The hanging head and rueful look,
    will they attract my love?

3 Let such as feel oppression's load
    thy tender pity share:
And let the helpless, homeless poor,
    be thy peculiar care.

4 Go, bid the hungry orphan be
    with thy abundance blest;
Invite the wand'rer to thy gate,
    and spread the couch of rest.

5 Let him who pines with piercing cold
    by thee be warm'd and clad;
Be thine the blissful task to make
    the downcast mourner glad.

6 Then, bright as morning, shall come
    in peace and joy, thy days; [forth,
And glory from the Lord above
    shall shine on all thy ways.

29. LAMENT. iii. 37-40.

1 AMIDST the mighty, where is he
    who saith, and it is done?
Each varying scene of changeful life
    is from the Lord alone.

2 He gives in gladsome bow'rs to dwell,
    or clothes in sorrow's shroud;
His hand hath form'd the light, his
    hand
    hath form'd the dark'ning cloud.

3 Why should a living man complain
    beneath the chast'ning rod?
Our sins afflict us; and the cross
    must bring us back to God.

4 O sons of men! with anxious care
    your hearts and ways explore;
Return from paths of vice to God:
    return, and sin no more!

30. HOSEA vi. 1-4.

1 COME, let us to the Lord our God
    with contrite hearts return;
Our God is gracious, nor will leave
    the desolate to mourn.

2 His voice commands the tempest
    and stills the stormy wave; [forth,
And though his arm be strong to
'tis also strong to save.   [smite,

3 Long hath the night of sorrow
    reign'd;
    the dawn shall bring us light:

God shall appear, and we shall rise
    with gladness in his sight.

4 Our hearts, if God we seek to know,
    shall know him, and rejoice;
His coming like the morn shall be,
    like morning songs his voice.

5 As dew upon the tender herb,
    diffusing fragrance round;
As show'rs that usher in the spring,
    and cheer the thirsty ground:

6 So shall his presence bless our souls,
    and shed a joyful light;
That hallow'd morn shall chase away
    the sorrows of the night.

31. MICAH vi. 6-9.

1 THUS speaks the heathen: How
    shall man
    the Pow'r Supreme adore?
With what accepted off'rings come
    his mercy to implore?

2 Shall clouds of incense to the skies
    with grateful odour speed?
Or victims from a thousand hills
    upon the altar bleed?

3 Does justice nobler blood demand
    to save the sinner's life?
Shall, trembling, in his offspring's
    the father plunge the knife? [side

4 No: God rejects the bloody rites
    which blindfold zeal began;
His oracles of truth proclaim
    the message brought to man.

5 He what is good hath clearly shown,
    O favour'd race! to thee;
And what doth God require of those
    who bend to him the knee?

6 Thy deeds, let sacred justice rule;
    thy heart, let mercy fill;
And, walking humbly with thy God,
    to him resign thy will.

32. HABAK. iii. 17, 18.

1 WHAT though no flow'rs the fig-
    tree clothe,
    though vines their fruit deny,
The labour of the olive fail,
    and fields no meat supply?

2 Though from the fold, with sad sur-
    my flock cut off I see;   [prise,
Though famine pine in empty stalls,
    where herds were wont to be?

3 Yet in the Lord will I be glad,
    and glory in his love;
In him I'll joy, who will the God
    of my salvation prove.

4 He to my tardy feet shall lend
 the swiftness of the roe;
Till, rais'd on high, I safely dwell
 beyond the reach of woe.

5 God is the treasure of my soul,
 the source of lasting joy;
A joy which want shall not impair,
 nor death itself destroy.

33. MATTH. vi. 9-14.

1 FATHER of all! we bow to thee,
 who dwell'st in heav'n ador'd;
But present still through all thy
 the universal Lord. [works,

2 For ever hallow'd be thy name
 by all beneath the skies;
And may thy kingdom still advance,
 till grace to glory rise.

3 A grateful homage may we yield,
 with hearts resign'd to thee;
And as in heav'n thy will is done,
 on earth so let it be.

4 From day to day we humbly own
 the hand that feeds us still
Give us our bread, and teach to rest
 contented in thy will.

5 Our sins before thee we confess;
 O may they be forgiv'n!
As we to others mercy show,
 we mercy beg from Heav'n.

6 Still let thy grace our life direct;
 from evil guard our way;
And in temptation's fatal path
 permit us not to stray.

7 For thine the pow'r, the kingdom
 all glory's due to thee: [thine;
Thine from eternity they were,
 and thine shall ever be.

34. MATTH. xi. 25, to the end.

1 THUS spoke the Saviour of the
 world
and rais'd his eyes to heav'n:
To thee, O Father! Lord of all,
 eternal praise be giv'n.

2 Thou to the pure and lowly heart
 hast heav'nly truth reveal'd;
Which from the self-conceited mind
 thy wisdom hath conceal'd.

3 Ev'n so! thou, Father, hast ordain'd
 thy high decree to stand;
Nor men nor angels may presume
 the reason to demand.

4 Thou only know'st the Son: from
 my kingdom I receive; [thee

And none the Father know but they
 who in the Son believe.

5 Come then to me, all ye who groan,
 with guilt and fears opprest;
Resign to me the willing heart,
 and I will give you rest.

6 Take up my yoke, and learn of me
 the meek and lowly mind;
And thus your weary troubled souls
 repose and peace shall find.

7 For light and gentle is my yoke;
 the burden I impose
Shall ease the heart, which groan'd
 beneath a load of woes. [before

35. MATTH. xxvi. 26-29.

1 'TWAS on that night, when doom'd
 to know
The eager rage of ev'ry foe,
That night in which he was betray'd,
The Saviour of the world took bread:

2 And, after thanks and glory giv'n
To him that rules in earth and heav'n,
That symbol of his flesh he broke,
And thus to all his foll'wers spoke:

3 My broken body thus I give
For you, for all; take, eat, and live;
And oft the sacred rite renew,
That brings my wondrous love to
 view.

4 Then in his hands the cup he rais'd,
And God anew he thank'd and
 prais'd;
While kindness in his bosom glow'd,
And from his lips salvation flow'd:

5 My blood I thus pour forth, he cries,
To cleanse the soul in sin that lies;
In this the covenant is seal'd,
And Heav'n's eternal grace reveal'd.

6 With love to man this cup is fraught,
Let all partake the sacred draught;
Through latest ages let it pour,
In mem'ry of my dying hour.

36. LUKE i. 46-56.

1 MY soul and spirit, fill'd with joy,
 my God and Saviour praise,
Whose goodness did from poor estate
 his humble handmaid raise.

2 Me bless'd of God, the God of might,
 all ages shall proclaim;
From age to age his mercy lasts,
 and holy is his name.

3 Strength with his arm th' Almighty
 shew'd;
the proud his looks abas'd;

He cast the mighty to the ground,
the meek to honour rais'd.

4 The hungry with good things were
the rich with hunger pin'd: [fill'd,
He sent his servant Isr'el help,
and call'd his love to mind;

5 Which to our fathers' ancient race
his promise did ensure,
To Abrah'm and his chosen seed
for ever to endure.

37. LUKE ii. 8–15.

1 WHILE humble shepherds watch'd
their flocks
in Bethleh'm's plains by night,
An angel sent from heav'n appear'd,
and fill'd the plains with light.

2 Fear not, he said, (for sudden dread
had seiz'd their troubled mind;)
Glad tidings of great joy I bring
to you, and all mankind.

3 To you, in David's town, this day
is born, of David's line,
The Saviour, who is Christ the Lord;
and this shall be the sign:

4 The heav'nly Babe you there shall
to human view display'd, [find
All meanly wrapt in swaddling-
and in a manger laid. [bands,

5 Thus spake the seraph; and forth-
appear'd a shining throng [with
Of angels, praising God; and thus
address'd their joyful song:

6 All glory be to God on high,
and to the earth be peace;
Good-will is shown by Heav'n to
and never more shall cease. [men,

38. LUKE ii. 25–33.

1 JUST and devout old Simeon liv'd;
to him it was reveal'd,
That Christ, the Lord, his eyes should
ere death his eyelids seal'd. [see

2 For this consoling gift of Heav'n
to Isr'el's fallen state,
From year to year, with patient hope
the aged saint did wait.

3 Nor did he wait in vain; for, lo!
revolving years brought round,
In season due, the happy day,
which all his wishes crown'd.

4 When Jesus, to the temple brought
by Mary's pious care,
As Heav'n's appointed rites requir'd,
to God was offer'd there;

5 Simeon into those sacred courts
a heav'nly impulse drew;

He saw the Virgin hold her Son,
and straight his Lord he knew.

6 With holy joy upon his face
the good old father smil'd;
Then fondly in his wither'd arms
he clasp'd the promis'd child:

7 And while he held the heav'n-born
ordain'd to bless mankind, [Babe,
Thus spoke, with earnest look, and
exulting, yet resign'd: [heart

8 Now, Lord! according to thy word,
let me in peace depart;
Mine eyes have thy salvation seen,
and gladness fills my heart.

9 At length my arms embrace my Lord,
now let their vigour cease;
At last my eyes my Saviour see,
now let them close in peace.

10 This great salvation, long prepar'd,
and now disclos'd to view,
Hath prov'd thy love was constant
and promises were true. [still,

11 That Sun I now behold, whose light
shall heathen darkness chase,
And rays of brightest glory pour
around thy chosen race.

39. LUKE iv. 18, 19.

1 HARK, the glad sound, the Saviour
comes!
the Saviour promis'd long;
Let ev'ry heart exult with joy,
and ev'ry voice be song!

2 On him the Spirit, largely shed,
exerts its sacred fire;
Wisdom and might; and zeal and
his holy breast inspire. [love,

3 He comes! the pris'ners to relieve,
in Satan's bondage held;
The gates of brass before him burst,
the iron fetters yield.

4 He comes! from dark'ning scales of
to clear the inward sight; [vice
And on the eye-balls of the blind
to pour celestial light.

5 He comes! the broken hearts to bind,
the bleeding souls to cure;
And with the treasures of his grace
t' enrich the humble poor.

6 The sacred year has now revolv'd,
accepted of the Lord,
When Heav'n's high promise is ful-
and Isr'el is restor'd. [fill'd,

7 Our glad hosannahs, Prince of Peace!
thy welcome shall proclaim;
And heav'n's exalted arches ring
with thy most honour'd name.

40. LUKE xv. 13–25.

1 THE wretched prodigal behold
  in mis'ry lying low,
Whom vice had sunk from high estate,
  and plung'd in want and woe.

2 While I, despis'd and scorn'd, he
      starve in a foreign land, [cries,
The meanest in my father's house
  is fed with bounteous bread:

3 I'll go, and with a mourning voice,
  fall down before his face:
Father! I've sinn'd 'gainst Heav'n and
  nor can deserve thy grace. [thee,

4 He said, and hasten'd to his home,
  to seek his father's love:
The father sees him from afar,
  and all his bowels move.

5 He ran, and fell upon his neck,
  embrac'd and kiss'd his son:
The grieving prodigal bewail'd
  the follies he had done.

6 No more, my father, can I hope
  to find paternal grace;
My utmost wish is to obtain
  a servant's humble place.

7 Bring forth the fairest robe for him,
  the joyful father said;
To him each mark of grace be shown,
  and ev'ry honour paid.

8 A day of feasting I ordain;
  let mirth and song abound:
My son was dead, and lives again!
  was lost, and now is found!

9 Thus joy abounds in paradise
  among the hosts of heav'n,
Soon as the sinner quits his sins,
  repents, and is forgiv'n.

41. JOHN iii. 14–19.

1 AS when the Hebrew prophet rais'd
  the brazen serpent high,
The wounded look'd, and straight
      were cur'd,
  the people ceas'd to die:

2 So from the Saviour on the cross
  a healing virtue flows;
Who looks to him with lively faith
  is sav'd from endless woes.

3 For God gave up his Son to death,
  so gen'rous was his love,
That all the faithful might enjoy
  eternal life above.

4 Not to condemn the sons of men
  the Son of God appear'd;
No weapons in his hand are seen,
  nor voice of terror heard:

5 He came to raise our fallen state,
  and our lost hopes restore:
Faith leads us to the mercy-seat,
  and bids us fear no more.

6 But vengeance just for ever lies
  on all the rebel race,
Who God's eternal Son despise,
  and scorn his offer'd grace.

42. JOHN xiv. 1–7.

1 LET not your hearts with anxious
      thoughts
  be troubled or dismay'd;
But trust in Providence divine,
  and trust my gracious aid.

2 I to my Father's house return;
  there num'rous mansions stand,
And glory manifold abounds
  through all the happy land.

3 I go your entrance to secure,
  and your abode prepare;
Regions unknown are safe to you,
  when I, your friend, am there.

4 Thence shall I come, when ages close,
  to take you home with me;
There we shall meet to part no more,
  and still together be.

5 I am the way, the truth, the life:
  no son of human race,
But such as I conduct and guide,
  shall see my Father's face.

43. JOHN xiv. 25–28.

1 YOU now must hear my voice no
      my Father calls me home; [more;
But soon from heav'n the Holy Ghost,
  your Comforter, shall come.

2 That heav'nly Teacher, sent from
      God,
  shall your whole soul inspire;
Your minds shall fill with sacred
  your hearts with sacred fire. [truth,

3 Peace is the gift I leave with you;
  my peace to you bequeath;
Peace that shall comfort you through
      life,
  and cheer your souls in death.

4 I give not as the world bestows,
  with promise false and vain;
Nor cares, nor fears, shall wound the
  in which my words remain. [heart

44. JOHN xix. 30.

1 BEHOLD the Saviour on the cross,
  a spectacle of woe!
See from his agonizing wounds
  the blood incessant flow;

2 Till death's pale ensigns o'er his cheek
    and trembling lips were spread;
Till light forsook his closing eyes,
    and life his drooping head!

3 'Tis finish'd—was his latest voice;
    these sacred accents o'er,
He bow'd his head, gave up the ghost,
    and suffer'd pain no more.

4 'Tis finish'd—The Messiah dies
    for sins, but not his own;
The great redemption is complete,
    and Satan's pow'r o'erthrown.

5 'Tis finish'd—All his groans are past;
    his blood, his pain, and toils,
Have fully vanquish'd our foes,
    and crown'd him with their spoils.

6 'Tis finish'd—Legal worship ends,
    and gospel ages run;
All old things are now past away,
    and a new world begun.

45. ROMANS ii. 4-8.

1 UNGRATEFUL sinners! whence
    this scorn
of God's long-suff'ring grace?
And whence this madness that insults
th' Almighty to his face?

2 Is it because his patience waits,
    and pitying bowels move,
You multiply transgressions more,
    and scorn his offer'd love?

3 Dost thou not know, self-blinded
    his goodness is design'd   [man!
To wake repentance in thy soul,
    and melt thy harden'd mind?

4 And wilt thou rather chuse to meet
    th' Almighty as thy foe,
And treasure up his wrath in store
    against the day of woe?

5 Soon shall that fatal day approach
    that must thy sentence seal,
And righteous judgments, now un-
    in awful pomp reveal;   [known,

6 While they, who full of holy deeds
    to glory seek to rise,
Continuing patient to the end,
    shall gain th' immortal prize.

46. ROMANS iii. 19-22.

1 VAIN are the hopes the sons of men
    upon their works have built;
Their hearts by nature are unclean,
    their actions full of guilt.

2 Silent let Jew and Gentile stand,
    without one vaunting word;
And, humbled low, confess their guilt
    before heav'n's righteous Lord.

3 No hope can on the law be built
    of justifying grace;
The law, that shows the sinner's guilt,
    condemns him to his face.

4 Jesus! how glorious is thy grace!
    when in thy name we trust,
Our faith receives a righteousness
    that makes the sinner just.

47. ROMANS vi. 1-7.

1 AND shall we then go on to sin,
    that grace may more abound?
Great God, forbid that such a thought
    should in our breast be found!

2 When to the sacred font we came,
    did not the rite proclaim,
That, wash'd from sin, and all its
    new creatures we became?   [stains,

3 With Christ the Lord we dy'd to sin;
    with him to life we rise,
To life, which now begun on earth,
    is perfect in the skies.

4 Too long enthrall'd to Satan's sway,
    we now are slaves no more;
For Christ hath vanquish'd death
    our freedom to restore.   [and sin,

48. ROMANS viii. 31, to the end.

1 LET Christian faith and hope dispel
    the fears of guilt and woe;
The Lord Almighty is our friend,
    and who can prove a foe?

2 He who his Son, most dear and lov'd,
    gave up for us to die.
Shall he not all things freely give
    that goodness can supply?

3 Behold the best, the greatest gift,
    of everlasting love!
Behold the pledge of peace below,
    and perfect bliss above!

4 Where is the judge who can con-
    since God hath justify'd?   [demn,
Who shall charge those with guilt or
    crime
for whom the Saviour dy'd?

5 The Saviour dy'd, but rose again
    triumphant from the grave;
And pleads our cause at God's right
    omnipotent to save.   [hand,

6 Who then can e'er divide us more
    from Jesus and his love,
Or break the sacred chain that binds
    the earth to heav'n above?

7 Let troubles rise, and terrors frown,
    and days of darkness fall;
Through him all dangers we'll defy,
    and more than conquer all.

8 Nor death nor life, nor earth nor hell,
nor time's destroying sway,
Can e'er efface us from his heart,
or make his love decay.

9 Each future period that will bless,
as it has bless'd the past;
He lov'd us from the first of time,
he loves us to the last.

49. 1 CORINTH. xiii.

1 THOUGH perfect eloquence a-
dorn'd
my sweet persuading tongue,
Though I could speak in higher
than ever angel sung; [strains

2 Though prophecy my soul inspir'd,
and made all myst'ries plain:
Yet, were I void of Christian love,
these gifts were all in vain.

3 Nay, though my faith with boundless
pow'r
ev'n mountains could remove
I still am nothing, if I'm void
of charity and love.

4 Although with lib'ral hand I gave
my goods the poor to feed,
Nay, gave my body to the flames,
still fruitless were the deed.

5 Love suffers long; love envies not;
but love is ever kind;
She never boasteth of herself,
nor proudly lifts the mind.

6 Love harbours no suspicious thought,
is patient to the bad;
Griev'd when she hears of sins and
and in the truth is glad. [crimes,

7 Love no unseemly carriage shows,
nor selfishly confin'd;
She glows with social tenderness,
and feels for all mankind.

8 Love beareth much, much she be-
and still she hopes the best; [lieves,
Love meekly suffers many a wrong,
though sore with hardship press'd.

9 Love still shall hold an endless reign
in earth and heav'n above,
When tongues shall cease, and pro-
and ev'ry gift but love. [phets fail,

10 Here all our gifts imperfect are;
but better days draw nigh,
When perfect light shall pour its rays,
and all those shadows fly.

11 Like children here we speak and
amus'd with childish toys; [think,
But when our pow'rs their manhood
reach,
we'll scorn our present joys.

12 Now dark and dim, as through a
are God and truth beheld; [glass,
Then shall we see as face to face,
and God shall be unvail'd.

13 Faith, Hope, and Love, now dwell on
earth,
and earth by them is blest;
But Faith and Hope must yield to
of all the graces best. [Love,

14 Hope shall to full fruition rise,
and Faith be sight above:
These are the means, but this the
for saints for ever love. [end;

50. 1 CORINTH. xv. 52, to the end.

1 WHEN the last trumpet's awful
voice
this rending earth shall shake,
When op'ning graves shall yield their
and dust to life awake; [charge,

2 Those bodies that corrupted fell
shall incorrupted rise,
And mortal forms shall spring to life
immortal in the skies.

3 Behold what heav'nly prophets sung
is now at last fulfill'd,
That Death should yield his ancient
reign,
and, vanquish'd, quit the field.

4 Let Faith exalt her joyful voice,
and thus begin to sing;
O Grave! where is thy triumph now?
and where, O Death! thy sting?

5 Thy sting was sin, and conscious guilt,
'twas this that arm'd thy dart;
The law gave sin its strength and
to pierce the sinner's heart: [force

6 But God, whose name be ever bless'd!
disarms that foe we dread,
And makes us conqu'rors when we
die,
through Christ our living head.

7 Then stedfast let us still remain,
though dangers rise around,
And in the work prescrib'd by God
yet more and more abound;

8 Assur'd that though we labour now,
we labour not in vain,
But, through the grace of heav'n's
great Lord,
th' eternal crown shall gain.

51. 2 CORINTH. v. 1–11.

1 SOON shall this earthly frame, dis-
in death and ruins lie; [solv'd,
But better mansions wait the just,
prepar'd above the sky.

2 An house eternal, built by God,
    shall lodge the holy mind,
When once those prison-walls have
    by which 'tis now confin'd. [fall'n

3 Hence, burden'd with a weight of
    we groan beneath the load, [clay,
Waiting the hour which sets us free,
    and brings us home to God.

4 We know, that when the soul, un-
    shall from this body fly, [cloth'd,
'Twill animate a purer frame
    with life that cannot die.

5 Such are the hopes that cheer the just;
    these hopes their God hath giv'n;
His Spirit is the earnest now,
    and seals their souls for heav'n.

6 We walk by faith of joys to come,
    faith grounded on his word;
But while this body is our home,
    we mourn an absent Lord.

7 What faith rejoices to believe,
    we long and pant to see;
We would be absent from the flesh,
    and present, Lord! with thee.

8 But still, or here, or going hence,
    to this our labours tend,
That, in his service spent, our life
    may in his favour end.

9 For, lo! before the Son, as judge,
    th' assembled world shall stand,
To take the punishment or prize
    from his unerring hand.

10 Impartial retributions then
    our diff'rent lives await;
Our present actions, good or bad,
    shall fix our future fate.

52. PHILIP. ii. 6–12.

1 YE who the name of Jesus bear,
    his sacred steps pursue;
And let that mind which was in him
    be also found in you.

2 Though in the form of God he was,
    his only Son declar'd,
Nor to be equally ador'd
    as robb'ry did regard.

3 His greatness he for us abas'd,
    for us his glory vail'd;
In human likeness dwelt on earth,
    his majesty conceal'd:

4 Nor only as a man appears,
    but stoops a servant low;
Submits to death, nay, bears the
    in all its shame and woe. [cross,

5 Hence God this gen'rous love to men
    with honours just hath crown'd,

And rais'd the name of Jesus far
    above all names renown'd:

6 That at this name, with sacred awe,
    each humble knee should bow,
Of hosts immortal in the skies,
    and nations spread below:

7 That all the prostrate pow'rs of hell
    might tremble at his word,
And ev'ry tribe, and ev'ry tongue,
    confess that he is Lord.

53. 1 THESSAL. iv. 13, to the end.

1 TAKE comfort, Christians, when
    your friends
    in Jesus fall asleep;
Their better being never ends;
    why then dejected weep?

2 Why inconsolable, as those
    to whom no hope is giv'n?
Death is the messenger of peace,
    and calls the soul to heav'n.

3 As Jesus dy'd, and rose again
    victorious from the dead;
So his disciples rise, and reign
    with their triumphant Head.

4 The time draws nigh, when from the
    clouds
Christ shall with shouts descend,
And the last trumpet's awful voice
    the heav'ns and earth shall rend.

5 Then they who live shall changed be,
    and they who sleep shall wake;
The graves shall yield their ancient
    charge,
    and earth's foundations shake.

6 The saints of God, from death set free,
    with joy shall mount on high;
The heav'nly hosts with praises loud
    shall meet them in the sky.

7 Together to their Father's house
    with joyful hearts they go;
And dwell for ever with the Lord,
    beyond the reach of woe.

8 A few short years of evil past,
    we reach the happy shore,
Where death-divided friends at last
    shall meet, to part no more.

54. 2 TIM. i. 12.

1 I'M not asham'd to own my Lord,
    or to defend his cause,
Maintain the glory of his cross,
    and honour all his laws.

2 Jesus, my Lord! I know his name,
    his name is all my boast;
Nor will he put my soul to shame,
    nor let my hope be lost.

3 I know that safe with him remains,
   protected by his pow'r,
What I've committed to his trust,
   till the decisive hour.
4 Then will he own his servant's name
   before his Father's face,
And in the New Jerusalem
   appoint my soul a place.

55. 2 TIM. iv. 6, 7, 8, 18.

1 MY race is run; my warfare 's o'er;
   the solemn hour is nigh,
When, offer'd up to God, my soul
   shall wing its flight on high.
2 With heav'nly weapons I have fought
   the battles of the Lord;
Finish'd my course, and kept the
   faith,
   depending on his word.
3 Henceforth there is laid up for me
   a crown which cannot fade;
The righteous Judge at that great day
   shall place it on my head.
4 Nor hath the Sov'reign Lord decreed
   this prize for me alone;
But for all such as love like me
   th' appearance of his Son.
5 From ev'ry snare and evil work
   his grace shall me defend,
And to his heav'nly kingdom safe
   shall bring me in the end.

56. TITUS iii. 3-9.

1 HOW wretched was our former
   state,
   when, slaves to Satan's sway,
With hearts disorder'd and impure,
   o'erwhelm'd in sin we lay!
2 But, O my soul! for ever praise,
   for ever love his name,
Who turn'd thee from the fatal paths
   of folly, sin, and shame.
3 Vain and presumptuous is the trust
   which in our works we place,
Salvation from a higher source
   flows to the human race.
4 'Tis from the mercy of our God
   that all our hopes begin;
His mercy sav'd our souls from death,
   and wash'd our souls from sin.
5 His Spirit, through the Saviour shed,
   its sacred fire imparts,
Refines our dross, and love divine
   rekindles in our hearts.
6 Thence rais'd from death, we live
   and, justify'd by grace,   [anew;
We hope in glory to appear,
   and see our Father's face.

7 Let all who hold this faith and hope
   in holy deeds abound;
Thus faith approves itself sincere,
   by active virtue crown'd.

57. HEB. iv. 14, to the end.

1 JESUS, the Son of God, who once
   for us his life resign'd,
Now lives in heav'n, our great High
   and never-dying friend.   [Priest,
2 Through life, through death, let us to
   with constancy adhere;   [him
Faith shall supply new strength, and
   shall banish ev'ry fear.   [hope
3 To human weakness not severe
   is our High Priest above;
His heart o'erflows with tenderness,
   his bowels melt with love.
4 With sympathetic feelings touch'd,
   he knows our feeble frame;
He knows what sore temptations are,
   for he has felt the same.
5 But though he felt temptation's
   unconquer'd he remain'd; [pow'r,
Nor, 'midst the frailty of our frame,
   by sin was ever stain'd.
6 As, in the days of feeble flesh,
   he pour'd forth cries and tears;
So, though exalted, still he feels
   what ev'ry Christian bears.
7 Then let us, with a filial heart,
   come boldly to the throne
Of grace supreme, to tell our griefs,
   and all our wants make known:
8 That mercy we may there obtain
   for sins and errors past,
And grace to help in time of need,
   while days of trial last.

58. Another Version of the same Passage.

1 WHERE high the heav'nly temple
   stands,
   The house of God not made with
   hands,
A great High Priest our nature wears,
   The guardian of mankind appears.
2 He who for men their surety stood,
   And pour'd on earth his precious
   blood,
Pursues in heav'n his mighty plan,
   The Saviour and the friend of man.
3 Though now ascended up on high,
   He bends on earth a brother's eye;
Partaker of the human name,
   He knows the frailty of our frame.

4 Our fellow-suff'rer yet retains
    A fellow-feeling of our pains;
    And still remembers in the skies
    His tears, his agonies, and cries.

5 In ev'ry pang that rends the heart,
    The Man of sorrows had a part;
    He sympathizes with our grief,
    And to the suff'rer sends relief.

6 With boldness, therefore, at the throne,
    Let us make all our sorrows known;
    And ask the aids of heav'nly pow'r
    To help us in the evil hour.

59. HEB. xii. 1-13.

1 BEHOLD what witnesses unseen
    encompass us around;
Men, once like us, with suff'ring try'd,
    but now with glory crown'd.

2 Let us, with zeal like theirs inspir'd,
    begin the Christian race,
And, freed from each encumb'ring weight,
    their holy footsteps trace.

3 Behold a witness nobler still,
    who trod affliction's path,
Jesus, at once the finisher
    and author of our faith.

4 He for the joy before him set,
    so gen'rous was his love,
Endur'd the cross, despis'd the shame,
    and now he reigns above.

5 If he the scorn of wicked men
    with patience did sustain,
Becomes it those for whom he dy'd
    to murmur or complain?

6 Have ye like him to blood, to death,
    the cause of truth maintain'd?
And is your heav'nly Father's voice
    forgotten or disdain'd?

7 My son, saith he, with patient mind
    endure the chast'ning rod;
Believe, when by afflictions try'd,
    that thou art lov'd by God.

8 His children thus most dear to him,
    their heav'nly Father trains,
Through all the hard experience led
    of sorrows and of pains.

9 We know he owns us for his sons,
    when we correction share;
Nor wander as a bastard race,
    without our Father's care.

10 A father's voice with rev'rence we
    on earth have often heard;
The Father of our spirits now
    demands the same regard.

11 Parents may err; but he is wise,
    nor lifts the rod in vain;
His chast'nings serve to cure the soul
    by salutary pain.

12 Affliction, when it spreads around,
    may seem a field of woe;
Yet there, at last, the happy fruits
    of righteousness shall grow.

13 Then let our hearts no more despond,
    our hands be weak no more;
Still let us trust our Father's love,
    his wisdom still adore.

60. HEB. xiii. 20, 21.

1 FATHER of peace, and God of love!
    we own thy pow'r to save,
That pow'r by which our Shepherd rose
    victorious o'er the grave.

2 Him from the dead thou brought'st again,
    when, by his sacred blood,
Confirm'd and seal'd for evermore,
    th' eternal cov'nant stood.

3 O may thy Spirit seal our souls,
    and mould them to thy will,
That our weak hearts no more may stray,
    but keep thy precepts still;

4 That to perfection's sacred height
    we nearer still may rise,
And all we think, and all we do,
    be pleasing in thine eyes.

61. I PET. i. 3-5.

1 BLESS'D be the everlasting God,
    the Father of our Lord;
Be his abounding mercy prais'd,
    his majesty ador'd.

2 When from the dead he rais'd his Son,
    and call'd him to the sky,
He gave our souls a lively hope
    that they should never die.

3 To an inheritance divine
    he taught our hearts to rise;
'Tis uncorrupted, undefil'd,
    unfading in the skies.

4 Saints by the pow'r of God are kept
    till the salvation come:
We walk by faith as strangers here;
    but Christ shall call us home.

62. 2 PET. iii. 3-14.

1 LO! in the last of days behold
    a faithless race arise;
Their lawless lust their only rule;
    and thus the scoffer cries,

2 Where is the promise, deem'd so true,
    that spoke the Saviour near?

E'er since our fathers slept in dust,
  no change has reach'd our ear.

3 Years roll'd on years successive glide,
  since first the world began,
And on the tide of time still floats,
  secure, the bark of man.

4 Thus speaks the scoffer; but his
  conceal the truth he knows, [words
That from the waters' dark abyss
  the earth at first arose.

5 But when the sons of men began
  with one consent to stray,
At Heav'n's command a deluge swept
  the godless race away.

6 A diff'rent fate is now prepar'd
  for Nature's trembling frame;
Soon shall her orbs be all enwrapt
  in one devouring flame.

7 Reserv'd are sinners for the hour
  when to the gulf below,
Arm'd with the hand of sov'reign
  the Judge consigns his foe. [pow'r,

8 Though now, ye just! the time ap-
  protracted, dark, unknown, [pears
An hour, a day, a thousand years,
  to heav'n's great Lord are one.

9 Still all may share his sov'reign grace,
  in ev'ry change secure;
The meek, the suppliant contrite
  shall find his mercy sure. [race,

10 The contrite race he counts his friends
  forbids the suppliant's fall;
Condemns reluctant, but extends
  the hope of grace to all.

11 Yet as the night-wrapp'd thief who
  to seize th' expected prize, [lurks
Thus steals the hour when Christ
  shall come,
  and thunder rend the skies.

12 Then at the loud, the solemn peal,
  the heav'ns shall burst away;
The elements shall melt in flame,
  at Nature's final day.

13 Since all this frame of things must
  as Heav'n has so decreed, [end,
How wise our inmost thoughts to
  and watch o'er ev'ry deed; [guard,

14 Expecting calm th' appointed hour,
  when, Nature's conflict o'er,
A new and better world shall rise,
  where sin is known no more.

63. 1 JOHN iii. 1-4.

1 BEHOLD th' amazing gift of love
  the Father hath bestow'd
On us, the sinful sons of men,
  to call us sons of God!

2 Conceal'd as yet this honour lies,
  by this dark world unknown,
A world that knew not when he came,
  ev'n God's eternal Son.

3 High is the rank we now possess;
  but higher we shall rise;
Though what we shall hereafter be
  is hid from mortal eyes:

4 Our souls, we know, when he appears,
  shall bear his image bright;
For all his glory, full disclos'd,
  shall open to our sight.

5 A hope so great, and so divine,
  may trials well endure;
And purge the soul from sense and
  as Christ himself is pure. [sin,

64. REV. i. 5-9.

1 TO him that lov'd the souls of men,
  and wash'd us in his blood,
To royal honours rais'd our head,
  and made us priests to God;

2 To him let ev'ry tongue be praise,
  and ev'ry heart be love!
All grateful honours paid on earth,
  and nobler songs above!

3 Behold, on flying clouds he comes!
  his saints shall bless the day;
While they that pierc'd him sadly
  in anguish and dismay. [mourn

4 I am the First, and I the Last;
  time centres all in me;
Th' Almighty God, who was, and is,
  and evermore shall be.

65. REV. v. 6, to the end.

1 BEHOLD the glories of the Lamb
  amidst his Father's throne;
Prepare new honours for his name,
  and songs before unknown.

2 Lo! elders worship at his feet;
  the church adores around,
With vials full of odours rich,
  and harps of sweetest sound.

3 These odours are the pray'rs of saints,
  these sounds the hymns they raise;
God bends his ear to their requests,
  he loves to hear their praise.

4 Who shall the Father's record search,
  and hidden things reveal?
Behold the Son that record takes,
  and opens ev'ry seal.

5 Hark how th' adoring hosts above
  with songs surround the throne!
Ten thousand thousand are their
  tongues;
  but all their hearts are one.

6 Worthy the Lamb that dy'd, they cry,
  to be exalted thus;
  Worthy the Lamb, let us reply,
  for he was slain for us.

7 To him be pow'r divine ascrib'd,
  and endless blessings paid;
  Salvation, glory, joy, remain
  for ever on his head!

8 Thou hast redeem'd us with thy
    [blood,
  and set the pris'ners free;
  Thou mad'st us kings and priests to
    God,
  and we shall reign with thee.

9 From ev'ry kindred, ev'ry tongue,
  thou brought'st thy chosen race;
  And distant lands and isles have
  the riches of thy grace.   [shar'd

10 Let all that dwell above the sky,
   or on the earth below,
   With fields, and floods, and ocean's
     shores,
   to thee their homage show.

11 To Him who sits upon the throne,
   the God whom we adore,
   And to the Lamb that once was slain,
   be glory evermore.

66. Rev. vii. 13, to the end.

1 HOW bright these glorious spirits
     shine!
  whence all their white array?
  How came they to the blissful seats
  of everlasting day?

2 Lo! these are they from suff'rings
     great,
  who came to realms of light,
  And in the blood of Christ have
     wash'd
  those robes which shine so bright.

3 Now, with triumphal palms, they
    [stand
  before the throne on high,
  And serve the God they love, amidst
  the glories of the sky.

4 His presence fills each heart with joy,
  tunes ev'ry mouth to sing:
  By day, by night, the sacred courts
  with glad hosannahs ring.

5 Hunger and thirst are felt no more,
  nor suns with scorching ray;
  God is their sun, whose cheering
    [beams
  diffuse eternal day.

6 The Lamb which dwells amidst the
     throne
  shall o'er them still preside;
  Feed them with nourishment divine,
  and all their footsteps guide.

7 'Mong pastures green he'll lead his
    [flock,
  where living streams appear;
  And God the Lord from ev'ry eye
  shall wipe off ev'ry tear.

67. Rev. xxi. 1-9.

1 LO! what a glorious sight appears
     to our admiring eyes!
  The former seas have pass'd away,
  the former earth and skies.

2 From heav'n the New Jerus'lem
    [comes,
  all worthy of its Lord;
  See all things now at last renew'd,
  and paradise restor'd!

3 Attending angels shout for joy,
  and the bright armies sing;
  Mortals! behold the sacred seat
  of your descending King!

4 The God of glory down to men
  removes his bless'd abode;
  He dwells with men; his people they,
  and he his people's God.

5 His gracious hand shall wipe the tears
  from ev'ry weeping eye:
  And pains and groans, and griefs and
    [fears,
  and death itself, shall die.

6 Behold, I change all human things!
  saith he, whose words are true;
  Lo! what was old is pass'd away,
  and all things are made new!

7 I am the First, and I the Last,
  through endless years the same;
  I AM, is my memorial still,
  and my eternal name.

8 Ho, ye that thirst! to you my grace
  shall hidden streams disclose,
  And open full the sacred spring,
  whence life for ever flows.

9 Bless'd is the man that overcomes;
  I'll own him for a son;
  A rich inheritance rewards
  the conquests he hath won.

10 But bloody hands and hearts unclean,
   and all the lying race,
   The faithless, and the scoffing crew,
   who spurn at offer'd grace;

11 They, seiz'd by justice, shall be
   in dark abyss to lie,   [doom'd
   And in the fiery burning lake
   the second death shall die.

12 O may we stand before the Lamb,
   when earth and seas are fled,
   And hear the Judge pronounce our
     name,
   with blessings on our head!

HYMNS.

HYMN I.

1 WHEN all thy mercies, O my God!
 my rising soul surveys,
Transported with the view, I'm lost
 in wonder, love, and praise.

2 O how shall words, with equal
 the gratitude declare   [warmth,
That glows within my ravish'd heart!
 but Thou canst read it there.

3 Thy Providence my life sustain'd,
 and all my wants redrest,
When in the silent womb I lay,
 and hung upon the breast.

4 To all my weak complaints and cries
 thy mercy lent an ear,
Ere yet my feeble thoughts had
  learn'd
 to form themselves in pray'r.

5 Unnumber'd comforts to my soul
 thy tender care bestow'd,
Before my infant heart conceiv'd
 from whom these comforts flow'd.

6 When in the slipp'ry paths of youth
 with heedless steps I ran;
Thine arm, unseen, convey'd me
 and led me up to man: [safe,

7 Through hidden dangers, toils, and
  deaths,
 it gently clear'd my way;
And through the pleasing snares of
 more to be fear'd than they. [vice,

8 When worn with sickness, oft hast
  thou
 with health renew'd my face;
And, when in sins and sorrows sunk,
 reviv'd my soul with grace.

9 Thy bounteous hand with worldly
 hath made my cup run o'er; [bliss
And, in a kind and faithful friend,
 hath doubled all my store.

10 Ten thousand thousand precious
 my daily thanks employ;   [gifts
Nor is the least a cheerful heart,
 that tastes these gifts with joy.

11 Through ev'ry period of my life
 thy goodness I'll proclaim;
And after death, in distant worlds,
 resume the glorious theme.

12 When nature fails, and day and night
 divide thy works no more,
My ever grateful heart, O Lord,
 thy mercy shall adore.

13 Through all eternity to thee
 a joyful song I'll raise;
For, oh! eternity's too short
 to utter all thy praise.

HYMN 2.

1 THE spacious firmament on high,
 With all the blue ethereal sky,
And spangled heav'ns, a shining
  frame,
Their great Original proclaim.

2 Th' unweary'd sun, from day to day,
Does his Creator's pow'r display;
And publishes to ev'ry land
The work of an Almighty hand.

3 Soon as the ev'ning shades prevail,
The moon takes up the wondrous
  tale,
And, nightly to the list'ning earth,
Repeats the story of her birth;

4 While all the stars that round her
  burn,
And all the planets in their turn,
Confirm the tidings as they roll,
And spread the truth from pole to
  pole.

5 What though in solemn silence all
Move round the dark terrestrial ball?
What though no real voice, nor
  sound,
Amidst their radiant orbs be found?

6 In Reason's ear they all rejoice,
And utter forth a glorious voice;
For ever singing, as they shine:
'The hand that made us is divine.'

HYMN 3.

1 WHEN rising from the bed of
  death,
 o'erwhelm'd with guilt and fear,
I see my Maker face to face,
 O how shall I appear!

2 If yet while pardon may be found,
 and mercy may be sought,
My heart with inward horror shrinks,
 and trembles at the thought;

3 When thou, O Lord! shalt stand dis-
 in majesty severe,   [clos'd
And sit in judgment on my soul,
 O how shall I appear!

4 But thou hast told the troubled mind,
 who doth her sins lament,

That timely grief for errors past
    shall future woe prevent.

5 Then see the sorrows of my heart,
    ere yet it be too late;
And hear my Saviour's dying groans,
    to give those sorrows weight.

6 For never shall my soul despair
    of mercy at thy throne,
Who knows thine only Son has dy'd
    thy justice to atone.

HYMN 4.

1 BLEST morning! whose first dawn-
    beheld the Son of God   [ing rays
Arise triumphant from the grave,
    and leave his dark abode.

2 Wrapt in the silence of the tomb
    the great Redeemer lay,
Till the revolving skies had brought
    the third, th' appointed day.

3 Hell and the grave combin'd their
    to hold our Lord in vain;   [force
Sudden the Conqueror arose,
    and burst their feeble chain.

4 To thy great name, Almighty Lord!
    we sacred honours pay,
And loud hosannahs shall proclaim
    the triumphs of the day.

5 Salvation and immortal praise
    to our victorious King!
Let heav'n and earth, and rocks and
    with glad hosannahs ring.   [seas,

6 To Father, Son, and Holy Ghost,
    the God whom we adore,
Be glory, as it was, and is,
    and shall be evermore.

HYMN 5.

1 THE hour of my departure's come;
    I hear the voice that calls me
    home:
At last, O Lord! let trouble cease,
And let thy servant die in peace.

2 The race appointed I have run;
The combat's o'er, the prize is won;
And now my witness is on high,
And now my record's in the sky.

3 Not in mine innocence I trust;
I bow before thee in the dust;
And through my Saviour's blood
    alone
I look for mercy at thy throne.

4 I leave the world without a tear,
Save for the friends I held so dear;
To heal their sorrows, Lord, descend,
And to the friendless prove a friend.

5 I come, I come, at thy command,
I give my spirit to thy hand;
Stretch forth thine everlasting arms,
And shield me in the last alarms.

6 The hour of my departure's come;
I hear the voice that calls me home:
Now, O my God! let trouble cease;
Now let thy servant die in peace.

FINIS.

PASSAGES OF SCRIPTURE PARAPHRASED.

1. Genesis i.
2. Genesis xxviii. 20–22.
3. Job i. 21.
4. Job iii. 17–20.
5. Job v. 6–12.
6. Job viii. 11–22.
7. Job ix. 2–10.
8. Job xiv. 1–15.
9. Job xxvi. 6, to the end.
10. Prov. i. 20–31.
11. Prov. iii. 13–17.
12. Prov. vi. 6–12.
13. Prov. viii. 22, to the end.
14. Eccles. vii. 2–6.
15. Eccles. ix. 4, 5, 6, 10.
16. Eccles. xii. 1.
17. Isaiah i. 10–19.
18. Isaiah ii. 2–6.
19. Isaiah ix. 2–8.
20. Isaiah xxvi. 1–7.
21. Isaiah xxxiii. 13–18.
22. Isaiah xl. 27, to the end.
23. Isaiah xlii. 1–13.
24. Isaiah xlix. 13–17.
25. Isaiah liii.
26. Isaiah lv.
27. Isaiah lvii. 15, 16.
28. Isaiah lviii. 5–9.
29. Lament. iii. 37–40.
30. Hosea vi. 1–4.
31. Micah vi. 6–9.
32. Habak. iii. 17, 18.
33. Matth. vi. 9–14.
34. Matth. xi. 25, to the end.
35. Matth. xxvi. 26–29.
36. Luke i. 46–56.
37. Luke ii. 8–15.
38. Luke ii. 25–33.
39. Luke iv. 18, 19.
40. Luke xv. 13–25.
41. John iii. 14–19.
42. John xiv. 1–7.
43. John xiv. 25–28.
44. John xix. 30.
45. Romans ii. 4–8.
46. Romans iii. 19–22.
47. Romans vi. 1–7.
48. Romans viii. 31, to the end.
49. 1 Corinth. xiii.
50. 1 Corinth. xv. 52, to the end.
51. 2 Corinth. v. 1–11.
52. Philip. ii. 6–12.
53. 1 Thessal. iv. 13, to the end.
54. 2 Tim. i. 12.
55. 2 Tim. iv. 6, 7, 8, 18.
56. Titus iii. 3–9.
57. Heb. iv. 14, to the end.
58. Another version of the same passage.
59. Heb. xii. 1–13.
60. Heb. xiii. 20, 21.
61. 1 Peter i. 3–5.
62. 2 Peter iii. 3–14.
63. 1 John iii. 1–4.
64. Rev. i. 5–9.
65. Rev. v. 6, to the end.
66. Rev. vii. 13, to the end.
67. Rev. xxi. 1–9.

HYMNS.

Hymn 1.
Hymn 2.
Hymn 3.
Hymn 4.
Hymn 5.

THE CHURCH HYMNARY

REVISED EDITION

THE CHURCH HYMNARY

REVISED EDITION

Authorized for Use in Public Worship

by

THE CHURCH OF SCOTLAND
THE UNITED FREE CHURCH OF SCOTLAND
THE PRESBYTERIAN CHURCH IN IRELAND
THE PRESBYTERIAN CHURCH OF ENGLAND
THE PRESBYTERIAN CHURCH OF WALES
THE PRESBYTERIAN CHURCH OF AUSTRALIA
THE PRESBYTERIAN CHURCH OF NEW ZEALAND
THE PRESBYTERIAN CHURCH
OF SOUTHERN AFRICA

OXFORD UNIVERSITY PRESS

3 R. Nonpareil

Oxford University Press, Walton Street, Oxford OX2 6DP

Oxford New York Toronto
Delhi Bombay Calcutta Madras Karachi
Kuala Lumpur Singapore Hong Kong Tokyo
Nairobi Dar es Salaam Cape Town
Melbourne Auckland

and associated companies in
Beirut Berlin Ibadan Nicosia

Oxford is a trade mark of Oxford University Press

Printed by the Oxford University Press in Scotland

PREFACE

THE original edition of the Church Hymnary appeared in 1898, and its wide circulation has been the best proof of its popularity. In 1922 the General Assemblies of the Churches interested, the Church of Scotland, the United Free Church of Scotland, and the Presbyterian Church in Ireland, recognizing that the time had come for the preparation of a revised edition, instructed their Praise Committees to proceed with the revision of the Hymnary both as to words and music.

The work was entrusted to a Joint Revision Committee formed of representatives from these Committees; but the Presbyterian Church of England and the Presbyterian Church of Wales having expressed a desire to co-operate, the General Assemblies of 1923 of the Scottish and Irish Churches instructed the Committees to admit representatives of these Churches to take part in the work, and the Joint Revision Committee was augmented accordingly. The Presbyterian Churches of South Africa, Australia, and New Zealand also appointed Committees to co-operate with the revisers, and two of the members of the Committee acted in the interests of these Churches. In 1925 the General Assemblies approved the draft of the words of the Revised Hymnary and, subject to adjustments, authorized its publication on the completion of the choice and arrangement of the music.

In the revision of the music the Committee has been fortunate in having the co-operation of representatives of the Societies of Organists in Edinburgh, Glasgow, Aberdeen, and Ulster, and musicians from England and Wales. Thanks are due to these gentlemen, whose practical experience has been of the utmost value, and particularly to Dr. David Evans, Professor of Music in the University of Wales, who has not only acted as chief musical editor, but has transcribed the tunes for the sol-fa and melody editions. The Committee desires likewise to put on record its special indebtedness to the secretary, Mr. W. M. Page, who has spared neither time nor labour in its service. Great care has been taken to trace the authors or proprietors of words and music. If there has been any infringement of copyright or omission of acknowledgement it is unintentional, and the Committee trusts that it will be pardoned.

The Church Hymnary in this revised form is issued with the prayer that its use may be to the glory of God and the good of His people.

April 1927.

Full copyright acknowledgements of words and tunes will be found in the principal harmonized music editions; also acknowledgements for the words in the Pica (No. 6 R.) words edition.

CONTENTS

                                        HYMNS

GOD : HIS BEING, WORKS, AND WORD—

The Holy Trinity	1–7
God in Creation, Providence, and Redemption	8–39
The Lord Jesus Christ—	
His Incarnation	40–66
His Life and Example	67–93
His Sufferings and Death	94–114
His Resurrection	115–127
His Ascension and Exaltation	128–139
His Sympathy and Intercession	140–148
His Coming in Power	149–163
His Praise	164–179
The Holy Spirit	180–196
The Holy Scriptures	197–204

THE CHURCH—

The Communion of Saints	205–227
Worship { The Sanctuary	228–255
Morning	256–270
Evening	271–294
Close of Worship	295–303
The Sacraments—	
Baptism	304–310
The Lord's Supper	311–324
Marriage	325–327
Burial of the Dead	328–332
The Service of the Kingdom	333–363
Missions	364–389

CONTENTS

		HYMNS
THE CHRISTIAN LIFE—		
The Gospel Call	. . . .	390–398
Penitence and Faith	. . .	399–415
Love and Gratitude	. . .	416–437
Peace and Joy	. . . .	438–448
Prayer, Aspiration, and Holiness	. .	449–483
Brotherly Love	. . . .	484–493
Consecration and Discipleship	. .	494–522
Conflict and Victory	. . .	523–538
Trust and Resignation	. . .	539–561
Pilgrimage and Rest	. . .	562–584
Death, Resurrection, and the Life Everlasting	.	585–600
TIMES AND SEASONS	. . .	601–623
TRAVELLERS AND THE ABSENT	.	624–630
NATIONAL HYMNS	. . .	631–647
HOME AND SCHOOL	. . .	648–678
MISSION SERVICES	. . .	679–707
DOXOLOGIES	. . . .	708–713
ANCIENT HYMNS AND CANTICLES	.	714–728
LIST OF HYMNS FOR THE YOUNG	.	p. 229
INDEX OF FIRST WORDS	. .	p. 233

GOD: HIS BEING, WORKS, AND WORD

THE HOLY TRINITY

1

11 12. 12 10.

HOLY, holy, holy, Lord God
   Almighty!
Early in the morning our song
      shall rise to Thee;
Holy, holy, holy, merciful and
      mighty,
   God in Three Persons, blessèd
      Trinity!

2 Holy, holy, holy! all the saints adore
      Thee,
   Casting down their golden crowns
      around the glassy sea,
Cherubim and seraphim falling down
      before Thee,
   Which wert, and art, and ever-
      more shalt be.

3 Holy, holy, holy! though the dark-
      ness hide Thee,
   Though the eye of sinful man Thy
      glory may not see,
Only Thou art holy; there is none
      beside Thee,
   Perfect in power, in love, and
      purity.

4 Holy, holy, holy, Lord God
      Almighty!
   All Thy works shall praise Thy
      Name in earth and sky and sea;
Holy, holy, holy, merciful and
      mighty,
   God in Three Persons, blessèd
      Trinity!

REGINALD HEBER, 1783–1826.

2

87. 87. and refrain.

ROUND the Lord in glory seated,
   Cherubim and seraphim
Filled His temple, and repeated
   Each to each the alternate hymn:
'Lord, Thy glory fills the heaven;
   Earth is with its fulness stored;
Unto Thee be glory given,
   Holy, holy, holy Lord.'

2 Heaven is still with glory ringing,
   Earth takes up the angels' cry,
'Holy, holy, holy,' singing,
   'Lord of hosts, the Lord most high.

Lord, Thy glory fills the heaven;
   Earth is with its fulness
      stored;
Unto Thee be glory given,
   Holy, holy, holy Lord.'

3 With His seraph train before Him,
   With His holy Church below,
Thus conspire we to adore Him,
   Bid we thus our anthem flow:
'Lord, Thy glory fills the
      heaven;
   Earth is with its fulness
      stored;
Unto Thee be glory given,
   Holy, holy, holy Lord.'
      RICHARD MANT, 1776–1848.

3

L. M.

WE praise, we worship Thee, O
   God;
Thy sovereign power we sound
      abroad;
All nations bow before Thy throne,
And Thee the great Jehovah own.

2 Loud hallelujahs to Thy Name
Angels and seraphim proclaim;
By all the powers and thrones in
      heaven
Eternal praise to Thee is given.

3 O holy, holy, holy Lord,
Thou God of hosts, by all adored,
Earth and the heavens are full of
      Thee,
Thy light, Thy power, Thy majesty.

4 Apostles join the glorious throng,
And swell the loud triumphant song;
Prophets and martyrs hear the sound,
And spread the hallelujah round.

5 Glory to Thee, O God most high!
Father, we praise Thy majesty:
The Son, the Spirit we adore—
One Godhead, blest for evermore.

Tr. in PHILIP GELL'S *Psalms
      and Hymns*, 1815.

GOD : HIS BEING, WORKS, AND WORD

4   L. M.

Ö TRINITY, O blessèd Light,
  Ö Unity, most principal,
Thë fiery sun now leaves öur sight :
  Cäuse in our hearts Thy beams tö
    fall.

2 Lët us with songs of praise divine
  At morn and evening Thee implore ;
And let our glory, bowèd tö Thine,
  Thëe glorify for evermore.

3 To God the Father, glöry great,
  And glory to His only Son,
And to the Holy Paraclete,
  Both now and still while ages run.
            Amen.

        ST. AMBROSE, 340–97;
        tr. by WM. DRUMMOND OF
        HAWTHORNDEN, 1585–1649.

5   L. M.

FATHER of heaven, whose love
   profound
A ransom for our souls hath found,
Before Thy throne we sinners bend ;
To us Thy pardoning love extend.

2 Almighty Son, Incarnate Word,
Our Prophet, Priest, Redeemer,
   Lord,
Before Thy throne we sinners bend ;
To us Thy saving grace extend.

3 Eternal Spirit, by whose breath
The soul is raised from sin and death,
Before Thy throne we sinners bend ;
To us Thy quickening power extend.

4 Jehovah—Father, Spirit, Son—
Mysterious Godhead, Three in One,
Before Thy throne we sinners bend ;
Grace, pardon, life to us extend.

        EDWARD COOPER, 1770–1833.

6   88. 88. 88.

O KING of kings, before whose
   throne
The angels bow, no gift can we
Present that is indeed our own,
  Since heaven and earth belong to
    Thee :

Yet this our souls through grace
   impart,
The offering of a thankful heart.

2 O Jesus, set at God's right hand,
With Thine eternal Father plead
For all Thy loyal-hearted band,
  Who still on earth Thy succour
    need :
For them in weakness strength pro-
   vide,
And through the world their foot-
   steps guide.

3 O Holy Spirit, Fount of breath,
  Whose comforts never fail nor fade,
Vouchsafe the life that knows no
   death,
  Vouchsafe the light that knows no
    shade ;
And grant that we, through all our
   days,
May share Thy gifts and sing Thy
   praise.

        JOHN QUARLES, 1624–65 ; and
        THOMAS DARLING, 1816–93.

7   87. 87. 87.

GLORY be to God the Father,
  Glory be to God the Son,
Glory be to God the Spirit,—
  Great Jehovah, Three in One !
    Glory, glory
  While eternal ages run !

2 Glory be to Him who loved us,
  Washed us from each spot and
   stain !
Glory be to Him who bought us,
  Made us kings with Him to reign !
    Glory, glory
  To the Lamb that once was slain !

3 Glory to the King of angels,
  Glory to the Church's King,
Glory to the King of nations !
  Heaven and earth, your praises
   bring ;
    Glory, glory
  To the King of Glory bring !

4 ' Glory, blessing, praise eternal ! '
  Thus the choir of angels sings ;
' Honour, riches, power, dominion ! '
  Thus its praise creation brings ;
    Glory, glory,
  Glory to the King of kings !

        HORATIUS BONAR, 1808–89.

GOD IN CREATION, PROVIDENCE, AND REDEMPTION

8   C. M.

THERE is a book, who runs may
    read,
  Which heavenly truth imparts,
And all the lore its scholars need,
  Pure eyes and Christian hearts.

2 The works of God, above, below,
    Within us and around,
  Are pages in that book, to show
    How God Himself is found.

3 The glorious sky, embracing all,
    Is like the Maker's love,
  Wherewith encompassed, great and
      small
    In peace and order move.

4 The dew of heaven is like Thy grace :
    It steals in silence down ;
  But, where it lights, the favoured
      place
    By richest fruits is known.

5 One Name, above all glorious names,
    With its ten thousand tongues
  The everlasting sea proclaims,
    Echoing angelic songs.

6 Two worlds are ours ; 'tis only sin
    Forbids us to descry
  The mystic heaven and earth within,
    Plain as the sea and sky.

7 Thou who hast given me eyes to see
    And love this sight so fair,
  Give me a heart to find out Thee,
    And read Thee everywhere.

                    JOHN KEBLE, 1792–1866.

9   *From Psalm civ.*   10 10. 11 11.

O WORSHIP the King all-
    glorious above,
O gratefully sing His power and His
    love,
Our Shield and Defender, the
    Ancient of Days,
Pavilioned in splendour, and girded
    with praise.

2 O tell of His might, O sing of His
    grace,
  Whose robe is the light, whose
    canopy space.
  His chariots of wrath the deep thun-
    der-clouds form,
  And dark is His path on the wings
    of the storm.

3 The earth with its store of wonders
    untold,
  Almighty, Thy power hath founded
    of old,
  Hath stablished it fast by a change-
    less decree,
  And round it hath cast, like a mantle,
    the sea.

4 Thy bountiful care what tongue can
    recite ?
  It breathes in the air ; it shines in the
    light ;
  It streams from the hills ; it descends
    to the plain,
  And sweetly distils in the dew and the
    rain.

5 Frail children of dust, and feeble as
    frail,
  In Thee do we trust, nor find Thee
    to fail ;
  Thy mercies how tender, how firm
    to the end,
  Our Maker, Defender, Redeemer,
    and Friend !

6 O measureless Might ! ineffable Love !
  While angels delight to hymn Thee
    above,
  The humbler creation, though feeble
    their lays,
  With true adoration shall lisp to Thy
    praise.

                    ROBERT GRANT, 1779–1838.

10   *From Psalm xix.*   D. L. M.

THE spacious firmament on high,
  With all the blue ethereal sky,
And spangled heavens, a shining
    frame,
Their great Original proclaim.
The unwearied sun, from day to **day,**
Does his Creator's power display,
And publishes to every land
The work of an almighty hand.

3

2 Soon as the evening shades prevail,
The moon takes up the wondrous
    tale,
And nightly to the listening earth
Repeats the story of her birth ;
While all the stars that round her
    burn,
And all the planets, in their turn,
Confirm the tidings, as they roll,
And spread the truth from pole to
    pole.

3 What though in solemn silence all
Move round the dark terrestrial ball ?
What though no real voice nor sound
Amidst their radiant orbs be found ?
In reason's ear they all rejoice,
And utter forth a glorious voice,
For ever singing, as they shine,
' The hand that made us is divine.'
        JOSEPH ADDISON, 1672–1719.

11 *From Psalm* cxxxvi.   77. 77.

LET us with a gladsome mind
Praise the Lord, for He is kind :
  For His mercies aye endure,
  Ever faithful, ever sure.

2 Let us blaze His Name abroad,
For of gods He is the God :
  For His mercies aye endure,
  Ever faithful, ever sure.

3 He, with all-commanding might,
Filled the new-made world with
    light :
  For His mercies aye endure,
  Ever faithful, ever sure.

4 All things living He doth feed ;
His full hand supplies their need :
  For His mercies aye endure,
  Ever faithful, ever sure.

5 He His chosen race did bless
In the wasteful wilderness :
  For His mercies aye endure,
  Ever faithful, ever sure.

6 He hath with a piteous eye
Looked upon our misery :
  For His mercies aye endure,
  Ever faithful, ever sure.

7 Let us then with gladsome mind
Praise the Lord, for He is kind :
  For His mercies aye endure,
  Ever faithful, ever sure.

        JOHN MILTON, 1608–74.

12   11 11. 11 11.

IMMORTAL, invisible, God only
    wise.
In light inaccessible hid from our
    eyes,
Most blessèd, most glorious, the
    Ancient of Days,
Almighty, victorious, Thy great
    Name we praise.

2 Unresting, unhasting, and silent as
    light,
Nor wanting, nor wasting, Thou
    rulest in might ;
Thy justice like mountains high
    soaring above
Thy clouds which are fountains of
    goodness and love.

3 To all, life Thou givest—to both great
    and small :
In all life Thou livest, the true life of
    all ;
We blossom and flourish as leaves
    on the tree,
And wither and perish—but nought
    changeth Thee.

4 Great Father of Glory, pure Father
    of Light,
Thine angels adore Thee, all veiling
    their sight ;
All laud we would render : O help
    us to see
'Tis only the splendour of light
    hideth Thee.

        WALTER CHALMERS SMITH,
                  1824–1908.

13   88. 44. 88. and refrain.

ALL creatures of our God and
    King,
Lift up your voice and with us sing
    Alleluia, Alleluia !
Thou burning sun with golden beam,
Thou silver moon with softer gleam,
  O praise Him, O praise Him,
  Alleluia, Alleluia, Alleluia !

2 Thou rushing wind that art so strong,
Ye clouds that sail in heaven along,
    O praise Him, Alleluia !
Thou rising morn, in praise rejoice,
Ye lights of evening, find a voice.

CREATION, PROVIDENCE, REDEMPTION

3 Thou flowing water, pure and clear,
Make music for thy Lord to hear,
  Alleluia, Alleluia!
Thou fire so masterful and bright,
That givest man both warmth and
  light.

4 Dear mother earth, who day by day
Unfoldest blessings on our way,
  O praise Him, Alleluia!
The flowers and fruits that in thee
  grow,
Let them His glory also show.

5 And all ye men of tender heart,
Forgiving others, take your part,
  O sing ye, Alleluia!
Ye who long pain and sorrow bear,
Praise God and on Him cast your
  care.

6 And thou, most kind and gentle
  death,
Waiting to hush our latest breath,
  O praise Him, Alleluia!
Thou leadest home the child of God,
And Christ our Lord the way hath
  trod.

7 Let all things their Creator bless,
And worship Him in humbleness,
  O praise Him, Alleluia!
Praise, praise the Father, praise the
  Son,
And praise the Spirit, Three in One.
  ST. FRANCIS OF ASSISI, 1182-1226;
      tr. by WILLIAM HENRY
        DRAPER, 1855-1933.

14   Irr.

THE strain upraise of joy and
  praise,   Alleluia!
To the glory of their King
Let the ransomed people sing
                          Alleluia!

2 And the choirs that dwell on high
Swell the chorus in the sky,
                          Alleluia!

3 Ye through the fields of Paradise
    that roam,
Ye blessèd ones, repeat through that
  bright home,   Alleluia!

4 Ye planets, glittering on your
    heavenly way,
Ye shining constellations, join and
  say   Alleluia!

5 Ye clouds that onward sweep,
  Ye winds on pinions light,
Ye thunders, echoing loud and deep,
  Ye lightnings wildly bright,
In sweet consent unite your
                          Alleluia!

6 Ye floods and ocean billows,
  Ye storms and winter snow,
Ye days of cloudless beauty,
  Hoar frost and summer glow,
Ye groves that wave in spring,
And glorious forests, sing
                          Alleluia!

7 First let the birds, with painted
    plumage gay,
Exalt their great Creator's praise,
  and say   Alleluia!

8 Then let the beasts of earth, with
    varying strain,
Join in creation's hymn, and cry
  again   Alleluia!

9 Here let the mountains thunder
    forth sonorous   Alleluia!
There let the valleys sing in gentler
  chorus,   Alleluia!

10 Thou jubilant abyss of ocean, cry
                          Alleluia!
Ye tracts of earth and continents,
  reply   Alleluia!

11 To God, who all creation made,
The frequent hymn be duly paid,
                          Alleluia!

12 This is the strain, the eternal strain,
  the Lord of all things loves:
                          Alleluia!
This is the song, the heavenly song,
  that Christ Himself approves:
                          Alleluia!

13 Wherefore we sing, both heart and
  voice awaking,   Alleluia!
And children's voices echo, answer
  making,   Alleluia!

14 Now from all men be outpoured
Alleluia to the Lord.
With Alleluia evermore
The Son and Spirit we adore.

15 Praise be done to the Three in One,
  Alleluia! Alleluia! Alleluia!
  Attributed to BALBULUS NOTKER,
    840-912; tr. by JOHN MASON
        NEALE, 1818-66.

5

GOD : HIS BEING, WORKS, AND WORD

15   10 4. 66. 66. 10 4.

LET all the world in every corner
     sing,
     ' My God and King ! '
The heavens are not too high,
His praise may thither fly ;
The earth is not too low,
His praises there may grow.
Let all the world in every corner sing,
     ' My God and King ! '

2 Let all the world in every corner sing,
     ' My God and King ! '
The Church with psalms must
     shout,
No door can keep them out ;
But, above all, the heart
Must bear the longest part.
Let all the world in every corner sing,
     ' My God and King ! '

GEORGE HERBERT, 1593-1632.

16 *From Psalm* cl.   77. 77.

PRAISE the Lord, His glories
     show,   *Hallelujah !*
Saints within His courts below,
                           Hallelujah !
Angels round His throne above,
                           Hallelujah !
All that see and share His love.
                           Hallelujah !

2 Earth to heaven, and heaven to earth,
Tell His wonders, sing His worth ;
Age to age and shore to shore,
Praise Him, praise Him evermore !

3 Praise the Lord, His mercies trace ;
Praise His providence and grace,
All that He for man hath done,
All He sends us through His Son.

4 Strings and voices, hands and hearts,
In the concert bear your parts ;
All that breathe, your Lord adore,
Praise Him, praise Him evermore !

HENRY FRANCIS LYTE,
1793-1847.

17   77. 77. 77.

FOR the beauty of the earth,
     For the beauty of the skies,
For the love which from our birth
     Over and around us lies,
Christ, our God, to Thee we raise
This our sacrifice of praise.

2 For the beauty of each hour
     Of the day and of the night,
Hill and vale, and tree and flower,
     Sun and moon and stars of light,
Christ, our God, to Thee we raise
This our sacrifice of praise.

3 For the joy of ear and eye,
     For the heart and mind's delight,
For the mystic harmony
     Linking sense to sound and sight,
Christ, our God, to Thee we raise
This our sacrifice of praise.

4 For the joy of human love,
     Brother, sister, parent, child,
Friends on earth and friends above,
     For all gentle thoughts and mild,
Christ, our God, to Thee we raise
This our sacrifice of praise.

5 For each perfect gift of Thine
     To our race so freely given,
Graces human and divine,
     Flowers of earth and buds of
        heaven,
Christ, our God, to Thee we raise
This our sacrifice of praise.

FOLLIOTT SANDFORD PIERPOINT,
1835-1917.

18   76. 76.

ALL things bright and beautiful,
     All creatures great and small,
All things wise and wonderful,—
     The Lord God made them all.

2 Each little flower that opens,
     Each little bird that sings,—
He made their glowing colours,
     He made their tiny wings.

3 The purple-headed mountain,
     The river running by,
The sunset, and the morning
     That brightens up the sky,

4 The cold wind in the winter,
     The pleasant summer sun,
The ripe fruits in the garden,—
     He made them every one.

5 The tall trees in the greenwood,
     The meadows where we play,
The rushes, by the water,
     We gather every day,—

6

6 He gave us eyes to see them,
    And lips that we might tell
How great is God Almighty,
    Who has made all things well.
          CECIL FRANCES ALEXANDER,
                    1818-95.

19   88. 84.

O LORD of heaven and earth and
    sea,
To Thee all praise and glory be ;
How shall we show our love to Thee,
    Who givest all ?

2 The golden sunshine, vernal air,
Sweet flowers and fruits Thy love
    declare ;
Where harvests ripen, Thou art
    there,
      Who givest all.

3 For peaceful homes and healthful
    days,
For all the blessings earth displays,
We owe Thee thankfulness and
    praise,
      Who givest all.

4 Thou didst not spare Thine only Son,
But gav'st Him for a world undone,
And freely with that blessèd One
    Thou givest all.

5 Thou giv'st the Spirit's blessèd
    dower,
Spirit of life and love and power,
And dost His sevenfold graces
    shower
      Upon us all.

6 For souls redeemed, for sins for-
    given,
For means of grace and hopes of
    heaven,
Father, all praise to Thee be given,
    Who givest all.
          CHRISTOPHER WORDSWORTH,
                    1807-85.

20   56. 64.

G OD, who made the earth,
    The air, the sky, the sea,
Who gave the light its birth,
    Careth for me.

2 God, who made the grass,
    The flower, the fruit, the tree,
The day and night to pass,
    Careth for me.

3 God, who made the sun,
    The moon, the stars, is He
Who, when life's clouds come on,
    Careth for me.

4 God, who made all things,
    On earth, in air, in sea,
Who changing seasons brings,
    Careth for me.

5 God, who sent His Son
    To die on Calvary,
He, if I lean on Him,
    Will care for me.

6 When in heaven's bright land
    I all His loved ones see,
I'll sing with that blest band,
    'God cared for me.'
          SARAH BETTS RHODES, 1829-1904.

21   *From Psalm ciii.*   87. 87. 87.

PRAISE, my soul, the King of
    heaven ;
To His feet thy tribute bring ;
Ransomed, healed, restored, for-
    given,
Who like me His praise should
    sing ?
      Praise Him ! Praise Him !
      Praise Him ! Praise Him !
Praise the everlasting King.

2 Praise Him for His grace and favour
    To our fathers in distress ;
Praise Him, still the same for ever,
    Slow to chide and swift to bless :
      Praise Him ! Praise Him !
      Praise Him ! Praise Him !
Glorious in His faithfulness.

3 Father-like He tends and spares us
    Well our feeble frame He knows
In His hands He gently bears us,
    Rescues us from all our foes :
      Praise Him ! Praise Him !
      Praise Him ! Praise Him !
Widely as His mercy flows.

4 Frail as summer's flower we flourish
    Blows the wind and it is gone ;
But, while mortals rise and perish,
    God endures unchanging on :
      Praise Him ! Praise Him !
      Praise Him ! Praise Him !
Praise the high eternal One.

GOD : HIS BEING, WORKS, AND WORD

5 Angels, help us to adore Him ;
  Ye behold Him face to face ;
Sun and moon, bow down before
    Him ;
  Dwellers all in time and space.
    Praise Him ! Praise Him !
    Praise Him ! Praise Him !
Praise with us the God of grace.
        HENRY FRANCIS LYTE,
          1793–1847.

22   *From Psalms ciii, cl.* 14 14. 478.

PRAISE to the Lord, the Al-
  mighty, the King of creation ;
O my soul, praise Him, for He is thy
  health and salvation ;
  All ye who hear,
  Now to His temple draw near,
Joining in glad adoration.

2 Praise to the Lord, who o'er all things
  so wondrously reigneth,
Shieldeth thee gently from harm, or
  when fainting sustaineth ;
  Hast thou not seen
  How thy heart's wishes have
    been
Granted in what He ordaineth ?

3 Praise to the Lord, who doth prosper
  thy work and defend thee ;
Surely His goodness and mercy shall
  daily attend thee ;
  Ponder anew
  What the Almighty can do,
If with His love He befriend thee.

4 Praise to the Lord ! O let all that is
  in me adore Him !
All that hath life and breath, come
  now with praises before Him !
  Let the Amen
  Sound from His people again :
Gladly for aye we adore Him.
      JOACHIM NEANDER, 1650–80 ;
     tr. by CATHERINE WINKWORTH,
        1827–78, and others.

23   L. M.

SING to the Lord a joyful song,
  Lift up your hearts, your voices
  raise ;
To us His gracious gifts belong,
  To Him our songs of love and
  praise.

2 For life and love, for rest and food,
  For daily help and nightly care,
Sing to the Lord, for He is good,
  And praise His Name, for it is fair.

3 For strength to those who on Him
  wait
  His truth to prove, His will to do,
Praise ye our God, for He is great,
  Trust in His Name, for it is true.

4 For joys untold, that from above
  Cheer those who love His sweet
  employ,
Sing to our God, for He is love,
  Exalt His Name, for it is joy.

5 For He is Lord of heaven and earth,
  Whom angels serve and saints
  adore,
The Father, Son, and Holy Ghost,
  To whom be praise for evermore.
    JOHN SAMUEL BEWLEY MONSELL,
            1811–75.

24   L. M.

LORD of all being, throned afar,
  Thy glory flames from sun and
  star ;
Centre and soul of every sphere,
Yet to each loving heart how near !

2 Sun of our life, Thy quickening ray
Sheds on our path the glow of day ;
Star of our hope, Thy softened light
Cheers the long watches of the night.

3 Our midnight is Thy smile with-
  drawn,
Our noontide is Thy gracious dawn,
Our rainbow arch Thy mercy's sign ;
All, save the clouds of sin, are Thine.

4 Lord of all life, below, above,
Whose light is truth, whose warmth
  is love,
Before Thy ever-blazing throne
We ask no lustre of our own.

5 Grant us Thy truth to make us free,
  And kindling hearts that burn for
  Thee,
Till all Thy living altars claim
One holy light, one heavenly flame.
        OLIVER WENDELL HOLMES,
            1809–94.

8

CREATION, PROVIDENCE, REDEMPTION

25 L. M.

THE Lord is King! lift up thy
    voice,
O earth, and, all ye heavens, rejoice;
From world to world the joy shall
    ring,
    ' The Lord Omnipotent is King!'

2 The Lord is King! who then shall
    dare
Resist His will, distrust His care,
Or murmur at His wise decrees,
Or doubt His royal promises?

3 The Lord is King! child of the dust,
The Judge of all the earth is just;
Holy and true are all His ways:
Let every creature speak His praise.

4 He reigns! ye saints, exalt your
    strains;
Your God is King, your Father
    reigns;
And He is at the Father's side,
The Man of Love, the Crucified.

5 Come, make your wants, your bur-
    dens known;
He will present them at the throne;
And angel bands are waiting there
His messages of love to bear.

6 One Lord, one empire, all secures;
He reigns, and life and death are
    yours:
Through earth and heaven one song
    shall ring,
    ' The Lord Omnipotent is King!'
        JOSIAH CONDER, 1789–1855.

26 C. M.

WHEN all Thy mercies, O my
    God!
    My rising soul surveys,
Transported with the view, I'm lost
In wonder, love, and praise.

2 O how shall words, with equal
    warmth,
    The gratitude declare
That glows within my ravished heart!
But Thou canst read it there.

3 Unnumbered comforts to my soul
    Thy tender care bestowed,
Before my infant heart conceived
From whom these comforts flowed.

4 When in the slippery paths of youth
    With heedless steps I ran,
Thine arm, unseen, conveyed me
    safe,
    And led me up to man.

5 When worn with sickness, oft hast
    Thou
With health renewed my face;
And, when in sins and sorrows sunk,
Revived my soul with grace.

6 Ten thousand thousand precious
    gifts
    My daily thanks employ;
Nor is the least a cheerful heart,
    That tastes those gifts with joy.

7 Through every period of my life
    Thy goodness I'll pursue;
And after death, in distant worlds,
    The glorious theme renew.
        JOSEPH ADDISON, 1672–1719.

27 C. M.

MY God, how wonderful Thou
    art,
    Thy majesty how bright!
How beautiful Thy mercy-seat,
    In depths of burning light!

2 How dread are Thine eternal years,
    O everlasting Lord,
By prostrate spirits day and night
    Incessantly adored!

3 O how I fear Thee, living God,
    With deepest, tenderest fears,
And worship Thee with trembling
    hope
    And penitential tears!

4 Yet I may love Thee too, O Lord,
    Almighty as Thou art,
For Thou hast stooped to ask of me
    The love of my poor heart.

5 No earthly father loves like Thee;
    No mother, e'er so mild,
Bears and forbears as Thou hast done
    With me, Thy sinful child.

6 How beautiful, how beautiful
    The sight of Thee must be,
Thine endless wisdom, boundless
    power,
    And awful purity!
        FREDERICK WILLIAM FABER,
            1814–63.

9

GOD : HIS BEING, WORKS, AND WORD

28
87. 87.

A GLADSOME hymn of praise
we sing,
And thankfully we gather
To bless the love of God above,
Our everlasting Father.

2 In Him rejoice with heart and voice,
Whose glory fadeth never,
Whose providence is our defence,
Who lives and loves for ever.

3 Full in His sight His children stand,
By His strong arm defended,
And He whose wisdom guides the
world
Our footsteps hath attended.

4 For nothing falls unknown to Him,
Or care or joy or sorrow,
And He whose mercy ruled the past
Will be our stay to-morrow.

5 Then praise the Lord with one
accord,
To His great Name give glory,
And of His never-changing love
Repeat the wondrous story.

AMBROSE NICHOLS BLATCHFORD,
1842–1924.

29
67. 67. 66. 66.

N OW thank we all our God,
With heart and hands and voices,
Who wondrous things hath done,
In whom His world rejoices,—
Who, from our mothers' arms,
Hath blessed us on our way
With countless gifts of love,
And still is ours to-day.

2 O may this bounteous God
Through all our life be near us,
With ever-joyful hearts
And blessèd peace to cheer us,
And keep us in His grace,
And guide us when perplexed,
And free us from all ills
In this world and the next.

3 All praise and thanks to God
The Father now be given,
The Son, and Him who reigns
With Them in highest heaven,—

The one, eternal God,
Whom earth and heaven adore;
For thus it was, is now,
And shall be evermore.

MARTIN RINKART, 1586–1649;
tr. by CATHERINE WINKWORTH,
1827–78.

30
10 10. 11 11.

T HOUGH troubles assail and
dangers affright,
Though friends should all fail and
foes all unite,
Yet one thing secures us, whatever
betide,
The Scripture assures us the Lord
will provide.

2 The birds without barn or storehouse
are fed;
From them let us learn to trust for
our bread;
His saints what is fitting shall ne'er
be denied,
So long as 'tis written, ' The Lord
will provide.'

3 His call we obey, like Abram of old,
Not knowing our way, but faith
makes us bold;
For, though we are strangers, we
have a good guide,
And trust, in all dangers, the Lord
will provide.

4 No strength of our own or goodness
we claim;
Yet, since we have known the
Saviour's great Name,
In this our strong tower for safety we
hide,—
The Lord is our power, the Lord
will provide.

JOHN NEWTON, 1725–1807.

31
C. M.

G OD moves in a mysterious way,
His wonders to perform;
He plants His footsteps in the sea,
And rides upon the storm.

2 Deep in unfathomable mines
Of never-failing skill
He treasures up His bright designs,
And works His sovereign will.

10

3 Ye fearful saints, fresh courage take ;
   The clouds ye so much dread
Are big with mercy, and shall break
   In blessings on your head.

4 Judge not the Lord by feeble sense,
   But trust Him for His grace ;
Behind a frowning providence
   He hides a smiling face.

5 His purposes will ripen fast,
   Unfolding every hour ;
The bud may have a bitter taste,
   But sweet will be the flower.

6 Blind unbelief is sure to err,
   And scan His work in vain ;
God is His own interpreter,
   And He will make it plain.

WILLIAM COWPER,
1731–1800.

32   C. M.

PRAISE to the Holiest in the
      height,
   And in the depth be praise,—
In all His words most wonderful,
   Most sure in all His ways.

2 O loving wisdom of our God !
   When all was sin and shame,
A second Adam to the fight
   And to the rescue came.

3 O wisest love ! that flesh and blood,
   Which did in Adam fail,
Should strive afresh against the foe,
   Should strive and should prevail ;

4 And that a higher gift than grace
   Should flesh and blood refine,
God's presence, and His very self
   And essence all-divine.

5 O generous love ! that He who smote
   In Man, for man, the foe,
The double agony in Man,
   For man, should undergo,

6 And in the garden secretly,
   And on the Cross on high,
Should teach His brethren, and
      inspire
   To suffer and to die.

7 Praise to the Holiest in the height,
   And in the depth be praise,—
In all His words most wonderful,
   Most sure in all His ways.

JOHN HENRY NEWMAN,
1801–90

33   87. 87.

GOD is love : His mercy brightens
   All the path in which we rove ;
Bliss He wakes, and woe He lightens :
   God is wisdom, God is love.

2 Chance and change are busy ever ;
   Man decays, and ages move ;
But His mercy waneth never :
   God is wisdom, God is love.

3 Even the hour that darkest seemeth
   Will His changeless goodness prove ;
From the mist His brightness stream-
      eth :
   God is wisdom, God is love.

4 He with earthly cares entwineth
   Hope and comfort from above ;
Everywhere His glory shineth :
   God is wisdom, God is love !

JOHN BOWRING, 1792–1872.

34   11 10. 11 10.

PRAISE ye Jehovah, praise the
      Lord most holy,
Who cheers the contrite, girds with
      strength the weak ;
Praise Him who will with glory
      crown the lowly,
   And with salvation beautify the
      meek.

2 Praise ye the Lord for all His loving-
      kindness,
   And all the tender mercy He hath
      shown ;
Praise Him who pardons all our sin
      and blindness,
   And calls us sons, and takes us for
      His own.

3 Praise ye Jehovah, Source of all our
      blessing ;
   Before His gifts earth's richest
      boons wax dim ;
Resting in Him, His peace and joy
      possessing,
   All things are ours, for we have
      all in Him.

4 Praise ye the Father, God the Lord,
      who gave us,
   With full and perfect love, His
      only Son ;
Praise ye the Son, who died Himself
      to save us ;
   Praise ye the Spirit : praise the
      Three in One.

MARGARET COCKBURN-CAMPBELL,
1808–41.

GOD : HIS BEING, WORKS, AND WORD

35 *From Psalm cxlviii.* 87. 87.

PRAISE the Lord ! ye heavens,
  adore Him ;
Praise Him, angels, in the height ;
Sun and moon, rejoice before Him,
Praise Him, all ye stars and light.

2 Praise the Lord ! for He hath spoken ;
Worlds His mighty voice obeyed ;
Laws which never shall be broken
For their guidance hath He made.

3 Praise the Lord ! for He is glorious ;
Never shall His promise fail ;
God hath made His saints victorious ;
Sin and death shall not prevail.

4 Praise the God of our salvation !
Hosts on high, His power proclaim ;
Heaven, and earth, and all creation,
Laud and magnify His Name.
Foundling Hospital Hymns,
1809.

36 86. 886.

ETERNAL Light ! eternal Light !
  How pure the soul must be,
When, placed within Thy searching
    sight,
It shrinks not, but, with calm delight,
Can live, and look on Thee !

2 The spirits that surround Thy throne
May bear the burning bliss ;
But that is surely theirs alone,
Since they have never, never known
A fallen world like this.

3 O how shall I, whose native sphere
  Is dark, whose mind is dim,
Before the Ineffable appear,
And on my naked spirit bear
  The uncreated beam ?

4 There is a way for man to rise
  To that sublime abode :
An offering and a sacrifice,
A Holy Spirit's energies,
  An Advocate with God.

5 These, these prepare us for the sight
Of holiness above :
The sons of ignorance and night
May dwell in the eternal Light,
  Through the eternal Love !
THOMAS BINNEY, 1798–1874.

37 6666. 4444.

ABOVE the clear blue sky,
  In heaven's bright abode,
The angel host on high
  Sing praises to their God.
    Hallelujah !
  They love to sing
  To God their King,
    ' Hallelujah ! '

2 But God from children's tongues
  On earth receiveth praise ;
We then our cheerful songs
  In sweet accord will raise.
    Hallelujah !
  We too will sing
  To God our King,
    ' Hallelujah ! '

3 O blessèd Lord, Thy truth
  In love to us impart,
And teach us in our youth
  To know Thee as Thou art.
    Hallelujah !
  Then shall we sing
  To God our King,
    ' Hallelujah ! '

4 O may Thy holy word
  Spread all the world around ;
All then with one accord
  Uplift the joyful sound.
    Hallelujah !
  All then shall sing
  To God our King,
    ' Hallelujah ! '
JOHN CHANDLER, 1806–76.

38 77. 77.

SONGS of praise the angels sang,
  Heaven with hallelujahs rang,
When creation was begun,
When God spake, and it was done.

2 Songs of praise awoke the morn
When the Prince of Peace was born ;
Songs of praise arose when He
Captive led captivity.

3 Heaven and earth must pass away :
Songs of praise shall crown that day ;
God will make new heavens, **new
    earth :**
Songs of praise shall hail their birth.

4 And can man alone be dumb,
Till that glorious Kingdom come ?
No ! the Church delights to raise
Psalms, and hymns, and songs of
    praise.

5 Saints below, with heart and voice,
Still in songs of praise rejoice,
Learning here, by faith and love,
Songs of praise to sing above.

6 Borne upon their latest breath,
Songs of praise shall conquer death ;
Then, amidst eternal joy,
Songs of praise their powers employ.
    JAMES MONTGOMERY, 1771–1854.

39   66. 66. 44. 44.

YE holy angels bright,
    Who wait at God's right hand,
Or through the realms of light
Fly at your Lord's command,
        Assist our song,
        Or else the theme
        Too high doth seem
    For mortal tongue.

2 Ye blessèd souls at rest,
    Who ran this earthly race,
And now, from sin released,
    Behold the Saviour's face,
        His praises sound,
        As in His light
        With sweet delight
    Ye do abound.

3 Ye saints, who toil below,
    Adore your heavenly King,
And, onward as ye go,
    Some joyful anthem sing ;
        Take what He gives,
        And praise Him still
        Through good and ill,
    Who ever lives.

4 My soul, bear thou thy part,
    Triumph in God above,
And with a well-tuned heart
    Sing thou the songs of love.
        Let all thy days
        Till life shall end,
        Whate'er He send,
    Be filled with praise.
        RICHARD BAXTER, 1615–91.
                    and others.

THE LORD JESUS CHRIST

HIS INCARNATION

40 *From St. Luke* iv. 18–19.   C. M.

HARK, the glad sound ! the
    Saviour comes,
The Saviour promised long ;
Let every heart exult with joy,
And every voice be song !

2 On Him the Spirit, largely shed,
    Exerts its sacred fire ;
Wisdom and might, and zeal and love,
    His holy breast inspire.

3 He comes, the prisoners to relieve,
    In Satan's bondage held ;
The gates of brass before Him burst,
    The iron fetters yield.

4 He comes, from darkening scales of
    vice
To clear the inward sight ;

And on the eye-balls of the blind
    To pour celestial light.

5 He comes, the broken hearts to
    bind,
The bleeding souls to cure ;
And with the treasures of His
    grace
To enrich the humble poor.

6 The sacred year has now revolved,
    Accepted of the Lord,
When heaven's high promise is ful-
    filled,
And Israel is restored.

7 Our glad hosannas, Prince of Peace,
    Thy welcome shall proclaim ;
And heaven's exalted arches ring
    With Thy most honoured Name.
    PHILIP DODDRIDGE, 1702–51, as in
        Scottish Paraphrases, 1781.

13

THE LORD JESUS CHRIST

41
8336. 8336.

ALL my heart this night rejoices,
   As I hear, far and near,
      Sweetest angel voices,
' Christ is born ! ' their choirs are
         singing,
   Till the air, everywhere,
      Now with joy is ringing.

2 Hark ! a voice from yonder manger,
   Soft and sweet, doth entreat :
      ' Flee from woe and danger ;
Brethren, come : from all doth grieve
         you
   You are freed ; all you need
      I will surely give you.'

3 Come, then, let us hasten yonder ;
   Here let all, great and small,
      Kneel in awe and wonder.
Love Him who with love is yearning ;
   Hail the Star that, from far,
      Bright with hope is burning.

4 Thee, O Lord, with heed I'll cherish,
   Live to Thee, and with Thee
      Dying, shall not perish,
But shall dwell with Thee for ever
   Far on high, in the joy
      That can alter never.
            PAUL GERHARDT, 1607–76;
            tr. by CATHERINE WINKWORTH,
                           1827–78.

42 *From St. Luke* ii. 8–15. D. C. M.

WHILE humble shepherds
      watched their flocks
In Bethlehem's plains by night,
An angel sent from heaven appeared,
   And filled the plains with light.
' Fear not,' he said, for sudden dread
   Had seized their troubled mind ;
' Glad tidings of great joy I bring
   To you and all mankind.

2 ' To you, in David's town, this day,
   Is born, of David's line,
The Saviour, who is Christ the Lord ;
   And this shall be the sign :
' The heavenly Babe you there shall
         find
   To human view displayed,
All meanly wrapped in swaddling-
         bands,
   And in a manger laid.'

3 Thus spake the seraph ; and forth-
         with
   Appeared a shining throng
Of angels, praising God, and thus
   Addressed their joyful song :
' All glory be to God on high,
   And to the earth be peace ;
Good will is shown by heaven to men,
   And never more shall cease.'
         NAHUM TATE, 1652–1715, as in
            Scottish Paraphrases, 1781.

43
Irr.

IN the field with their flocks abiding,
   They lay on the dewy ground,
And glimmering under the starlight
   The sheep lay white around,
When the light of the Lord streamed
         o'er them,
   And lo ! from the heaven above,
An angel leaned from the glory,
   And sang his song of love ;
      He sang, that first sweet Christ-
         mas,
         The song that shall never
            cease,—
   ' Glory to God in the highest,
      On earth goodwill and peace !

2 ' To you in the city of David
   A Saviour is born to-day.'
And sudden a host of the heavenly
         ones
   Flashed forth to join the lay.
O never hath sweeter message
   Thrilled home to the souls of men ;
And the heavens themselves had
         never heard
   A gladder choir till then ;
      For they sang that Christmas
         carol
         That never on earth shall
            cease,—
   ' Glory to God in the highest,
      On earth goodwill and peace !'

3 And the shepherds came to the man-
         ger,
   And gazed on the Holy Child :
And calmly o'er that rude cradle
   The virgin mother smiled ;
And the sky, in the starlit silence,
   Seemed full of the angel lay,—
' To you in the city of David
   A Saviour is born to-day.'

HIS INCARNATION

O they sang—and I ween that
never
The carol on earth shall cease,—
' Glory to God in the highest,
On earth goodwill and peace ! '
FREDERIC WILLIAM FARRAR,
1831–1903.

44   87. 87. D.

LITTLE children, wake and listen !
  Songs are breaking o'er the
earth ;
While the stars in heaven glisten,
  Hear the news of Jesus' birth.
Long ago, to lonely meadows,
  Angels brought the message down ;
Still, each year, through midnight
shadows,
  It is heard in every town.

2 What is this that they are telling,
  Singing in the quiet street ?
While their voices high are swelling,
  What sweet words do they repeat ?
Words to bring us greater gladness,
  Though our hearts from care are
free ;
Words to chase away our sadness,
  Cheerless though our hearts may
be.

3 Christ has left His throne of glory,
  And a lowly cradle found ;
Well might angels tell the story,
  Well may we their words resound.
Little children, wake and listen !
  Songs are ringing through the
earth ;
While the stars in heaven glisten,
  Hail with joy your Saviour's birth.
         S.P.C.K. Appendix, 1869.

45   Irr.

THE first Nowell the angel did say
  Was to certain poor shepherds in
fields as they lay :
In fields where they lay a-keeping
their sheep
On a cold winter's night that was so
deep.
  *Nowell, Nowell, Nowell, Nowell,
  Born is the King of Israel.*

2 They lookèd up and saw a star,
Shining in the east, beyond them far,
And to the earth it gave great light,
And so it continued both day and
night.

3 And by the light of that same star,
Three wise men came from country
far ;
To seek for a King was their intent,
And to follow the star wherever it
went.

4 This star drew nigh to the north-
west,
O'er Bethlehem it took its rest,
And there it did both stop and stay
Right over the place where Jesus lay.

5 Then entered in those wise men three,
Full reverently upon their knee,
And offered there in His presence
Their gold and myrrh and frankin-
cense.

6 Then let us all with one accord
Sing praises to our Heavenly Lord,
That hath made heaven and earth of
nought,
And with His blood mankind hath
bought.
         Traditional Carol.

46   77. 77. D. and refrain.

HARK ! the herald angels sing,
  ' Glory to the new-born King,
Peace on earth, and mercy mild,
God and sinners reconciled ! '
Joyful, all ye nations, rise,
Join the triumph of the skies,
With the angelic host proclaim,
' Christ is born in Bethlehem.'
  *Hark ! the herald angels sing,
  ' Glory to the new-born King.'*

2 Christ, by highest heaven adored,
Christ, the everlasting Lord,
Late in time behold Him come,
Offspring of a virgin's womb.
Veiled in flesh the Godhead see ;
Hail, the Incarnate Deity,
Pleased as Man with man to dwell,
Jesus, our Immanuel !

3 Hail, the heaven-born Prince of
Peace !
Hail, the Sun of Righteousness !
Light and life to all He brings,
Risen with healing in His wings.
Mild He lays His glory by,
Born that man no more may die,
Born to raise the sons of earth,
Born to give them second birth.
       CHARLES WESLEY, 1707–88.

THE LORD JESUS CHRIST

47
D. C. M.

IT came upon the midnight clear,
That glorious song of old,
From angels bending near the earth
To touch their harps of gold :—
'Peace on the earth, good will to
men,
From heaven's all-gracious King !'
The world in solemn stillness lay
To hear the angels sing.

2 Still through the cloven skies they
come
With peaceful wings unfurled ;
And still their heavenly music floats
O'er all the weary world ;
Above its sad and lowly plains
They bend on hovering wing,
And ever o'er its Babel sounds
The blessèd angels sing.

3 But with the woes of sin and strife
The world has suffered long ;
Beneath the angel strain have rolled
Two thousand years of wrong ;
And man, at war with man, hears not
The love song which they bring ;
O hush the noise, ye men of strife,
And hear the angels sing.

4 And ye, beneath life's crushing load
Whose forms are bending low,
Who toil along the climbing way
With painful steps and slow,
Look now ! for glad and golden
hours
Come swiftly on the wing ;
O rest beside the weary road,
And hear the angels sing.

5 For, lo ! the days are hastening on,
By prophet bards foretold,
When with the ever-circling years
Comes round the Age of Gold,
When peace shall over all the earth
Its ancient splendours fling,
And the whole world give back the
song
Which now the angels sing.
EDMUND HAMILTON SEARS,
1810–76.

48
D. C. M.

O LITTLE town of Bethlehem,
How still we see thee lie !
Above thy deep and dreamless sleep
The silent stars go by :

Yet in thy dark streets shineth
The everlasting Light ;
The hopes and fears of all the
years
Are met in thee to-night.

2 For Christ is born of Mary ;
And, gathered all above,
While mortals sleep, the angels keep
Their watch of wondering love.
O morning stars, together
Proclaim the holy birth,
And praises sing to God the King,
And peace to men on earth.

3 How silently, how silently,
The wondrous gift is given !
So God imparts to human hearts
The blessings of His heaven.
No ear may hear His coming ;
But in this world of sin,
Where meek souls will receive Him,
still
The dear Christ enters in.

4 O Holy Child of Bethlehem,
Descend to us, we pray ;
Cast out our sin, and enter in ;
Be born in us to-day.
We hear the Christmas angels
The great glad tidings tell ;
O come to us, abide with us,
Our Lord Immanuel.
PHILLIPS BROOKS, 1835–93.

49
Irr.

STILL the night, holy the night !
Sleeps the world ; hid from sight,
Mary and Joseph in stable bare
Watch o'er the Child beloved and fair,
Sleeping in heavenly rest.

2 Still the night, holy the night !
Shepherds first saw the light,
Heard resounding clear and long,
Far and near, the angel-song,
'Christ the Redeemer is here !'

3 Still the night, holy the night !
Son of God, O how bright
Love is smiling from Thy face !
Strikes for us now the hour of grace,
Saviour, since Thou art born !
JOSEPH MOHR, 1792–1848.

16

50
Irr.

IN the bleak mid-winter,
    Frosty wind made moan,
Earth stood hard as iron,
    Water like a stone ;
Snow had fallen, snow on snow,
    Snow on snow,
In the bleak mid-winter,
    Long ago.

2 Our God, heaven cannot hold Him,
    Nor earth sustain ;
Heaven and earth shall flee away
    When He comes to reign :
In the bleak mid-winter
    A stable-place sufficed
The Lord God Almighty,
    Jesus Christ.

3 Angels and archangels
    May have gathered there,
Cherubim and seraphim
    Thronged the air ;
But His mother only,
    In her maiden bliss,
Worshipped the Belovèd
    With a kiss.

4 What can I give Him,
    Poor as I am ?
If I were a shepherd,
    I would bring a lamb ;
If I were a wise man,
    I would do my part ;
Yet what I can I give Him—
    Give my heart.

CHRISTINA GEORGINA ROSSETTI,
1830–94.

51
77. 77. and refrain.

SEE ! in yonder manger low,
    Born for us on earth below,
See ! the tender Lamb appears,
Promised from eternal years.
    Hail, thou ever-blessèd morn !
    Hail, redemption's happy dawn !
    Sing through all Jerusalem,
    ' Christ is born in Bethlehem !'

2 Lo ! within a manger lies
He who built the starry skies,
He who, throned in height sublime,
Sits amid the cherubim.

3 Say, ye holy shepherds, say,
What your joyful news to-day ;
Wherefore have ye left your sheep
On the lonely mountain steep ?

4 ' As we watched at dead of night,
Lo ! we saw a wondrous light :
Angels, singing peace on earth,
Told us of the Saviour's birth.'

5 Sacred Infant, all Divine,
What a tender love was Thine,
Thus to come from highest bliss
Down to such a world as this !

6 Teach, O teach us, Holy Child,
By Thy face so meek and mild,
Teach us to resemble Thee
In Thy sweet humility.

EDWARD CASWALL, 1814–78.

52
67. 67.

LOVE came down at Christmas,
    Love all lovely, Love Divine ;
Love was born at Christmas,
    Star and angels gave the sign.

2 Worship we the Godhead,
    Love Incarnate, Love Divine ;
Worship we our Jesus :
    But wherewith for sacred sign ?

3 Love shall be our token,
    Love be yours and love be mine,
Love to God and all men,
    Love for plea and gift and sign.

CHRISTINA GEORGINA ROSSETTI,
1830–94.

53
55. 53. D.

CHILD in the manger,
    Infant of Mary ;
Outcast and stranger,
    Lord of all !
Child who inherits
    All our transgressions,
All our demerits
    On Him fall.

2 Once the most holy
    Child of salvation
Gently and lowly
    Lived below ;
Now, as our glorious
    Mighty Redeemer,
See Him victorious
    O'er each foe.

3 Prophets foretold Him,
　　Infant of wonder ;
　Angels behold Him
　　On His throne ;
　Worthy our Saviour
　　Of all their praises ;
　Happy for ever
　　Are His own.

MARY MACDONALD, 1817–c. 1890;
tr. by LACHLAN MACBEAN, 1853–1931.

54
10 10. 10 10. 10 10.

CHRISTIANS, awake, salute the
　happy morn,
Whereon the Saviour of the world
　was born ;
Rise to adore the mystery of love,
Which hosts of angels chanted from
　above ;
With them the joyful tidings first be-
　gun
Of God Incarnate and the Virgin's
　Son :

2 Then to the watchful shepherds it was
　told,
Who heard the angelic herald's voice,
　' Behold,
I bring good tidings of a Saviour's
　birth
To you and all the nations upon earth;
This day hath God fulfilled His pro-
　mised word,
This day is born a Saviour, Christ the
　Lord.'

3 He spake ; and straightway the celes-
　tial choir,
In hymns of joy unknown before, con-
　spire.
The praises of redeeming love they
　sang,
And heaven's whole orb with hallelu-
　jahs rang :
God's highest glory was their anthem
　still,
Peace upon earth, and mutual good-
　will.

4 To Bethlehem straight the en-
　lightened shepherds ran,
To see the wonder God had wrought
　for man,

And found, with Joseph and the
　blessèd Maid,
Her Son, the Saviour, in a manger
　laid ;
Amazed, the wondrous story they
　proclaim,
The first apostles of His infant fame.

5 Like Mary, let us ponder in our mind
God's wondrous love in saving lost
　mankind ;
Trace we the Babe, who has retrieved
　our loss,
From His poor manger to His bitter
　Cross ;
Treading His steps, assisted by His
　grace,
Till man's first heavenly state again
　takes place.

6 Then may we hope, the angelic
　thrones among,
To sing, redeemed, a glad triumphal
　song.
He that was born upon this joyful day
Around us all His glory shall display ;
Saved by His love, incessant we shall
　sing
Of angels and of angel men the King.

JOHN BYROM, 1691–1763.

55
Irr.

FIRST FORM.

O COME, all ye faithful,
　　Joyful and triumphant,
O come ye, O come ye to Bethlehem ;
　Come and behold Him
　Born the King of angels ;
O come, let us adore Him, Christ the
　Lord.

2　　God of God,
　　Light of Light,
Lo ! He abhors not the Virgin's
　womb ;
　Very God,
　Begotten, not created ;
O come, let us adore Him, Christ the
　Lord.

3　　Sing, choirs of angels,
　　Sing in exultation,
Sing, all ye citizens of heaven above,
　' Glory to God
　In the highest.'
O come, let us adore Him, Christ the
　Lord.

HIS INCARNATION

4
Yea, Lord, we greet Thee,
Born this happy morning;
Jesus, to Thee be glory given:
Word of the Father,
Now in flesh appearing;
O come, let us adore Him, Christ the
Lord.

18th century;
tr. by FREDERICK OAKELEY, 1802–80.

55   Irr.

SECOND FORM.

O COME, all ye faithful,
Joyfully triumphant,
To Bethlehem hasten now with glad
accord;
Lo! in a manger
Lies the King of angels;
O come, let us adore Him, Christ the
Lord.

2
Though true God of true God,
Light of Light eternal,
The womb of a virgin He hath not
abhorred;
Son of the Father,
Not made, but begotten;
O come, let us adore Him, Christ the
Lord.

3
Raise, raise, choirs of angels,
Songs of loudest triumph,
Through heaven's high arches be
your praises poured,
'Now to our God be
Glory in the highest.'
O come, let us adore Him, Christ the
Lord.

4
Amen! Lord, we bless Thee,
Born for our salvation!
O Jesus, for ever be Thy Name
adored;
Word of the Father,
Now in flesh appearing;
O come, let us adore Him, Christ the
Lord.

18th century;
tr. by WILLIAM MERCER, 1811–73.

56   L. M.

'FROM heaven above to earth I
come,
To bear good news to every home;
Glad tidings of great joy I bring,
Whereof I now will say and sing,—

2 ' " To you this night is born a Child
Of Mary, chosen mother mild ";
This little Child, of lowly birth,
Shall be the joy of all your earth.

3 ''Tis Christ our God, who far on
high
Hath heard your sad and bitter cry;
Himself will your salvation be;
Himself from sin will make you free.'

4 Welcome to earth, Thou noble Guest,
Through whom even wicked men
are blest!.
Thou com'st to share our misery;
What can we render, Lord, to Thee?

5 Were earth a thousand times as fair,
Beset with gold and jewels rare,
She yet were far too poor to be
A narrow cradle, Lord, for Thee.

6 Ah! dearest Jesus, Holy Child,
Make Thee a bed, soft, undefiled,
Within my heart, that it may be
A quiet chamber kept for Thee.

7 My heart for very joy doth leap;
My lips no more can silence keep;
I too must raise with joyful tongue
That sweetest ancient cradle song,—

8 ' Glory to God in highest heaven,
Who unto man His Son hath given!'
While angels sing with pious mirth
A glad New Year to all the earth.

MARTIN LUTHER, 1483–1546;
tr. by CATHERINE WINKWORTH,
1827–78.

57 *From Isaiah ix. 2–7.*   C. M.

THE race that long in darkness
pined
Have seen a glorious light;
The people dwell in day, who dwelt
In death's surrounding night.

2 To hail Thy rise, Thou better Sun!
The gathering nations come,
Joyous, as when the reapers bear
The harvest treasures home.

3 For Thou our burden hast removed,
And quelled the oppressor's sway,
Quick as the slaughtered squadrons
fell
In Midian's evil day.

4 To us a Child of hope is born;
To us a Son is given;
Him shall the tribes of earth obey,
Him all the hosts of heaven.

19

THE LORD JESUS CHRIST

5 His name shall be the Prince of Peace,
    For evermore adored,
The Wonderful, the Counsellor,
    The great and mighty Lord.

6 His power increasing still shall spread,
    His reign no end shall know ;
Justice shall guard His throne above,
    And peace abound below.

      JOHN MORISON, 1750–98, as in
      Scottish Paraphrases, 1781.

58
                  Irr.

GOOD Christian men, rejoice
  With heart and soul and voice !
Give ye heed to what we say :
    News ! News !
Jesus Christ is born to-day.
Ox and ass before Him bow,
And He is in the manger now :
    Christ is born to-day.

2 Good Christian men, rejoice
With heart and soul and voice !
    Now ye hear of endless bliss :
    Joy ! Joy !
Jesus Christ was born for this.
He hath oped the heavenly door,
And man is blessed for evermore.
    Christ was born for this.

3 Good Christian men, rejoice
With heart and soul and voice !
    Now ye need not fear the grave :
    Peace ! Peace !
Jesus Christ was born to save ;
Calls you one, and calls you all,
To gain His everlasting hall.
    Christ was born to save.

      JOHN MASON NEALE, 1818–66.

59
              87. 87.

GOD and Father, we adore Thee
  For the Son, Thine image bright,
In whom all Thy holy nature
    Dawned on our once hopeless
      night.

2 Far from Thee our footsteps wan-
    dered,
  On dark paths of sin and shame ;
But our midnight turned to morning,
  When the Lord of Glory came.

3 Word Incarnate, God revealing,
    Longed-for while dim ages ran,
Love Divine, we bow before Thee,
    Son of God and Son of Man.

4 Let our life be new created,
    Ever-living Lord, in Thee,
Till we wake with Thy pure likeness,
    When Thy face in heaven we see ;

5 Where the saints of all the ages,
    Where our fathers glorified,
Clouds and darkness far beneath
    them,
    In unending day abide.

6 God and Father, now we bless Thee
    For the Son, Thine image bright,
In whom all Thy nature
    Dawns on our adoring sight.

    Verse 1 attributed to JOHN NELSON
    DARBY, 1800–82 ; verses 2–5 and
    adaptation of verse 6, HUGH FAL-
    CONER, 1859–1931.

60
              87. 87. 877.

OF the Father's love begotten
  Ere the worlds began to be,
He is Alpha and Omega,
  He the source, the ending He,
Of the things that are, that have been,
  And that future years shall see,
    Evermore and evermore.

2 O that birth for ever blessèd,
  When the Virgin, full of grace,
By the Holy Ghost conceiving,
  Bare the Saviour of our race,
And the Babe, the world's Redeemer,
  First revealed His sacred face,
    Evermore and evermore !

3 This is He whom seers in old time
  Chanted of with one accord,
Whom the voices of the prophets
  Promised in their faithful word ;
Now He shines, the Long-expected ;
  Let creation praise its Lord,
    Evermore and evermore.

20

4 O ye heights of heaven, adore Him !
    Angel hosts, His praises sing ;
All dominions, bow before Him,
    And extol our God and King ;
Let no tongue on earth be silent,
    Every voice in concert ring,
            Evermore and evermore.

5 Christ, to Thee, with God the Father,
    And, O Holy Ghost, to Thee,
Hymn, and chant, and high thanks-
            giving,
    And unwearied praises be,
Honour, glory, and dominion,
    And eternal victory,
            Evermore and evermore.
                    Amen.
        AURELIUS CLEMENS PRUDENTIUS,
                        348–413 ;
    tr by JOHN MASON NEALE, 1818–66.

61

66 10. 66 10 8 12.

RING out, ye crystal spheres !
    Once bless our human ears,
If ye have power to touch our
        senses so :
And let your silver chime
Move in melodious time :
    And let the bass of heaven's deep
        organ blow :
And with your ninefold harmony
Make up full consort to the angelic
        symphony.

2 For, if such holy song
    Enwrap our fancy long,
Time will run back, and fetch the
        Age of Gold,
And speckled Vanity
Will sicken soon and die,
    And leprous Sin will melt from
        earthly mould ;
And Hell itself will pass away,
And leave her dolorous mansions to
        the peering day.

3 Yea, Truth and Justice then
    Will down return to men,
        Orbed in a rainbow ; and, like
            glories wearing,
    Mercy will sit between,
    Throned in celestial sheen,

With radiant feet the tissued clouds
        down steering :
And Heaven, as at some festival,
Will open wide the gates of her high
        palace-hall.
                JOHN MILTON, 1608–74.

62

77. 77.

' JESUS !' Name of wondrous love;
    Name all other names above,
Unto which must every knee
    Bow in deep humility.

2 ' Jesus !' Name of priceless worth
    To the fallen sons of earth,—
    For the promise that it gave,—
    ' Jesus shall His people save.'

3 ' Jesus !' Name of mercy mild,
    Given to the Holy Child
    When the cup of human woe
    First He tasted here below.

4 ' Jesus !' only Name that 's given
    Under all the mighty heaven
    Whereby man, to sin enslaved,
    Bursts his fetters, and is saved.

5 ' Jesus !' Name of wondrous love ;
    Human Name of God above ;
    Pleading only this, we flee,
    Helpless, O our God, to Thee.
            WILLIAM WALSHAM HOW, 1823–97.

63

77. 77. 77.

AS with gladness men of old
    Did the guiding star behold,
As with joy they hailed its light,
Leading onward, beaming bright,—
So, most gracious Lord, may we
Evermore be led to Thee.

2 As with joyful steps they sped,
Saviour, to Thy lowly bed,
There to bend the knee before
Thee, whom heaven and **earth**
    adore,—
So may we with willing feet
Ever seek Thy mercy-seat.

3 As they offered gifts most rare
At Thy cradle rude and bare,—
So may we with holy joy,
Pure, and free from sin's alloy,
All our costliest treasures bring,
Christ, to Thee, our heavenly King.

4 Holy Jesus, every day
  Keep us in the narrow way ;
And, when earthly things are past,
  Bring our ransomed souls at last
Where they need no star to guide,
Where no clouds Thy glory hide.

5 In the heavenly country bright
  Need they no created light ;
Thou its light, its joy, its crown,
  Thou its sun which goes not down ;
There for ever may we sing
Hallelujahs to our King.

        WILLIAM CHATTERTON DIX,
                  1837–98.

64
          II 10. 11 10. Dactylic.

BRIGHTEST and best of the sons
  of the morning,
  Dawn on our darkness, and lend us
    thine aid ;
Star of the east, the horizon adorning,
  Guide where our infant Redeemer
  is laid.

2 Cold on His cradle the dew-drops are
    shining ;
  Low lies His head with the beasts
    of the stall ;
Angels adore Him in slumber reclin-
    ing,
  Maker and Monarch and Saviour
  of all.

3 Say, shall we yield Him, in costly de-
    votion,
  Odours of Edom, and offerings
    divine,
Gems of the mountain and pearls of
    the ocean,
  Myrrh from the forest or gold from
  the mine ?

4 Vainly we offer each ample oblation,
  Vainly with gifts would His favour
    secure ;
Richer by far is the heart's adoration ;
  Dearer to God are the prayers of
  the poor.

5 Brightest and best of the sons of the
    morning,
  Dawn on our darkness, and lend
    us thine aid ;
Star of the east, the horizon adorning,
  Guide where our infant Redeemer
  is laid.

        REGINALD HEBER, 1783–1826.

65
               87. 87. 47.

ANGELS from the realms of glory,
  Wing your flight o'er all the
    earth ;
Ye who sang creation's story,
  Now proclaim Messiah's birth :
    Come and worship,
  Worship Christ, the new-born
    King.

2 Shepherds, in the fields abiding,
  Watching o'er your flock by night,
God with man is now residing,
  Yonder shines the Infant Light :
    Come and worship,
  Worship Christ, the new-born
    King.

3 Sages, leave your contemplations ;
  Brighter visions beam afar ;
Seek the great Desire of nations ;
  Ye have seen His natal star ;
    Come and worship,
  Worship Christ, the new-born
    King.

4 Saints, before the altar bending,
  Waiting long in hope and fear,
Suddenly the Lord, descending,
  In His temple shall appear ;
    Come and worship,
  Worship Christ, the new-born
    King.

        JAMES MONTGOMERY, 1771–1854.

66
               65. 65. D.

FROM the eastern mountains,
  Pressing on, they come,
Wise men in their wisdom,
  To His humble home,
Stirred by deep devotion,
  Hasting from afar,
Ever journeying onward,
  Guided by a star.

2 There their Lord and Saviour
  Meek and lowly lay,
Wondrous Light that led them
  Onward on their way,
Ever now to lighten
  Nations from afar,
As they journey homeward
  By that guiding Star.

3 Thou who in a manger
  Once hast lowly lain,
Who dost now in glory
  O'er all kingdoms reign,

HIS INCARNATION

Gather in the heathen,
Who in lands afar
Ne'er have seen the brightness
Of Thy guiding star.

4 Gather in the outcasts,
All who've gone astray,
Throw Thy radiance o'er them,
Guide them on their way ;
Those who never knew Thee,
Those who've wandered far,
Guide them by the brightness
Of Thy guiding star.

5 Onward through the darkness
Of the lonely night,
Shining still before them
With Thy kindly light,
Guide them, Jew and Gentile,
Homeward from afar,
Young and old together,
By Thy guiding star.

GODFREY THRING, 1823–1903.

THE LORD JESUS CHRIST
HIS LIFE AND EXAMPLE

67   Irr.

THOU didst leave Thy throne
And Thy kingly crown
When Thou camest to earth for me,
But in Bethlehem's home
Was there found no room
For Thy holy nativity :
O come to my heart, Lord Jesus ;
There is room in my heart for Thee.

2 Heaven's arches rang
When the angels sang,
Proclaiming Thy royal degree ;
But of lowly birth
Cam'st Thou, Lord, on earth,
And in great humility :
O come to my heart, Lord Jesus ;
There is room in my heart for Thee.

3 The foxes found rest,
And the bird its nest,
In the shade of the forest tree ;
But Thy couch was the sod,
O Thou Son of God,
In the deserts of Galilee :
O come to my heart, Lord Jesus ;
There is room in my heart for Thee.

4 Thou camest, O Lord,
With the living word
That should set Thy people free
But, with mocking scorn,
And with crown of thorn,
They bore Thee to Calvary :
O come to my heart, Lord Jesus
Thy Cross is my only plea.

5 When heaven's arches ring,
And her choirs shall sing,
At Thy coming to victory,
Let Thy voice call me home,
Saying, ' Yet there is room,
There is room at My side for thee ! '
And my heart shall rejoice, Lord
Jesus,
When Thou comest and callest for me.

EMILY ELIZABETH STEELE ELLIOTT,
1836–97.

68   Irr.

THERE came a little Child to earth
Long ago ;
And the angels of God proclaimed
His birth,
High and low.
Out on the night, so calm and still,
Their song was heard :
For they knew that the Child on
Bethlehem's hill
Was Christ the Lord.

2 Far away in a goodly land,
Fair and bright,
Children with crowns of glory stand,
Robed in white,
In white more pure than the spotless
snow ;
And their tongues unite
In the psalm which the angels sang
long ago
On that still night.

3 They sing how the Lord of that world
so fair
A child was born,
And, that they might a crown of
glory wear,
Wore a crown of thorn,
And in mortal weakness, in want and
pain,
Came forth to die,
That the children of earth might for
ever reign
With Him on high.

23

4 He has put on His kingly apparel now,
　　In that goodly land ;
And He leads, to where fountains of
　　water flow,
　　　That chosen band ;
And for evermore, in their robes most
　　fair
　　　And undefiled,
Those ransomed children His praise
　　declare
　　　Who was once a child.

EMILY ELIZABETH STEELE ELLIOTT,
1836–97.

69　　　　　　　　　87. 87. 77.

ONCE in royal David's city
　　Stood a lowly cattle-shed,
Where a mother laid her Baby
　　In a manger for His bed.
Mary was that mother mild,
Jesus Christ her little Child.

2 He came down to earth from heaven
　　Who is God and Lord of all,
And His shelter was a stable,
　　And His cradle was a stall.
With the poor and mean and lowly
Lived on earth our Saviour holy.

3 And through all His wondrous child-
　　hood
　　He would honour and obey,
Love, and watch the lowly maiden
　　In whose gentle arms He lay.
Christian children all must be
Mild, obedient, good as He.

4 For He is our childhood's pattern :
　　Day by day like us He grew ;
He was little, weak, and helpless
　　Tears and smiles like us He knew ;
And He feeleth for our sadness,
And He shareth in our gladness.

5 And our eyes at last shall see Him,
　　Through His own redeeming love ;
For that Child so dear and gentle
　　Is our Lord in heaven above ;
And He leads His children on
To the place where He is gone.

6 Not in that poor lowly stable,
　　With the oxen standing by,
We shall see Him, but in heaven,
　　Set at God's right hand on high,
When, like stars, His children crowned
All in white shall wait around.

CECIL FRANCES ALEXANDER, 1818–95.

70　　　　　　　　　76. 76. D.

COME, praise your Lord and
　　Saviour
　　In strains of holy mirth ;
Give thanks to Him, O children,
　　Who lived a child on earth.
He loved the little children,
　　And called them to His side ;
His loving arms embraced them,
　　And for their sake He died.

Boys only.

2 O Jesus, we would praise Thee
　　With songs of holy joy,
For Thou on earth didst sojourn,
　　A pure and spotless boy.
Make us like Thee, obedient,
　　Like Thee from sin-stains free,
Like Thee in God's own temple,
　　In lowly home like Thee.

Girls only.

3 O Jesus, we too praise Thee,
　　The lowly maiden's Son ;
In Thee all gentlest graces
　　Are gathered into one.
O give that best adornment
　　That Christian maid can wear,
The meek and quiet spirit
　　Which shone in Thee so fair.

All.

4 O Lord, with voices blended
　　We sing our songs of praise ;
Be Thou the light and pattern
　　Of all our childhood's days ;
And lead us ever onward,
　　That, while we stay below,
We may, like Thee, O Jesus,
　　In grace and wisdom grow.

WILLIAM WALSHAM HOW,
1823–97.

71　　　　　　　　　76. 76. D.

I LOVE to hear the story
　　Which angel voices tell,
How once the King of Glory
　　Came down on earth to dwell.
I am both weak and sinful,
　　But this I surely know,
The Lord came down to save me,
　　Because He loved me so.

2 I'm glad my blessèd Saviour
　　Was once a child like me,
To show how pure and holy
　　His little ones might be ;

And, if I try to follow
  His footsteps here below,
He never will forsake me,
  Because He loves me so.

3 To sing His love and mercy
  My sweetest songs I'll raise,
And, though I cannot see Him,
  I know He hears my praise;
For He has kindly promised
  That even I may go
To sing among His angels,
  Because He loves me so.

EMILY HUNTINGTON MILLER,
1833–1913.

72   88. 88. 88.

WE saw Thee not when Thou didst
    come
  To this poor world of sin and death,
Nor e'er beheld Thy cottage home
  In that despisèd Nazareth;
But we believe Thy footsteps trod
  Its streets and plains, Thou Son of
    God.

2 We did not see Thee lifted high
  Amid that wild and savage crew,
Nor heard Thy meek, imploring cry,
  'Forgive, they know not what they
    do';
Yet we believe the deed was done
Which shook the earth, and veiled the
  sun.

3 We stood not by the empty tomb
  Where late Thy sacred body lay,
Nor sat within that upper room,
  Nor met Thee in the open way;
But we believe that angels said,
'Why seek the living with the dead?'

4 We did not mark the chosen few,
  When Thou didst through the
    clouds ascend,
First lift to heaven their wondering
  view,
  Then to the earth all prostrate bend;
Yet we believe that mortal eyes
Beheld that journey to the skies.

5 And now that Thou dost reign on
  high,
  And thence Thy waiting people
    bless,
No ray of glory from the sky
  Doth shine upon our wilderness;
But we believe Thy faithful word,
And trust in our redeeming Lord.

JOHN HAMPDEN GURNEY, 1802–62:
based on ANNE RICHTER, 1792–1857.

73   87. 87. D.

WHO is this, so weak and helpless,
    Child of lowly Hebrew maid,
Rudely in a stable sheltered,
  Coldly in a manger laid?
'Tis the Lord of all creation,
  Who this wondrous path hath trod;
He is God from everlasting,
  And to everlasting God.

2 Who is this, a Man of Sorrows,
  Walking sadly life's hard way,
Homeless, weary, sighing, weeping
  Over sin and Satan's sway?
'Tis our God, our glorious Saviour,
  Who above the starry sky
Now for us a place prepareth,
  Where no tear can dim the eye.

3 Who is this? behold Him shedding
  Drops of blood upon the ground!
Who is this, despised, rejected,
  Mocked, insulted, beaten, bound?
'Tis our God, who gifts and graces
  Poureth on His Church below,
Now, in royal might victorious,
  Triumphing o'er every foe.

4 Who is this that hangeth dying
  While the rude world scoffs and
    scorns,
Numbered with the malefactors,
  Pierced with nails, and crowned
    with thorns?
'Tis the God who ever liveth
  'Mid the shining ones on high,
In the glorious golden city
  Reigning everlastingly.

WILLIAM WALSHAM HOW,
1823–97.

74   D. C. M.

O SING a song of Bethlehem,
    Of shepherds watching there,
And of the news that came to them
  From angels in the air:
The light that shone on Bethlehem
  Fills all the world to-day;
Of Jesus' birth and peace on earth
  The angels sing alway.

2 O sing a song of Nazareth,
  Of sunny days of joy;
O sing of fragrant flowers' breath,
  And of the sinless Boy:

THE LORD JESUS CHRIST

For now the flowers of Nazareth
In every heart may grow ;
Now spreads the fame of His dear
Name
On all the winds that blow.

3 O sing a song of Galilee,
Of lake and woods and hill,
Of Him who walked upon the sea,
And bade its waves be still :
For though, like waves on Galilee,
Dark seas of trouble roll,
When faith has heard the Master's
word,
Falls peace upon the soul.

4 O sing a song of Calvary,
Its glory and dismay ;
Of Him who hung upon the Tree,
And took our sins away :
For He who died on Calvary
Is risen from the grave,
And Christ, our Lord, by heaven
adored,
Is mighty now to save.

LOUIS FITZGERALD BENSON,
1855–1930.

75
88. 88. 88.

YE fair green hills of Galilee,
That girdle quiet Nazareth,
What glorious vision did ye see,
When He who conquered sin and
death
Your flowery slopes and summits
trod,
And grew in grace with man and
God ?

2 ' We saw no glory crown His head,
As childhood ripened into youth ;
No angels on His errands sped ;
He wrought no sign ; but meek-
ness, truth,
And duty marked each step He trod,
And love to man, and love to God.'

3 Jesus ! my Saviour, Master, King,
Who didst for me the burden bear,
While saints in heaven Thy glory
sing,
Let me on earth Thy likeness wear ;
Mine be the path Thy feet have
trod,—
Duty, and love to man and God.

EUSTACE ROGERS CONDER,
1820–92.

76
66. 66. 88.

BEHOLD a little Child,
Laid in a manger bed ;
The wintry blasts blow wild
Around His infant head.
But who is this, so lowly laid ?
'Tis He by whom the worlds were
made.

2 Alas ! in what poor state
The Son of God is seen ;
Why doth the Lord so great
Choose out a home so mean ?
That we may learn from pride to flee,
And follow His humility.

3 Where Joseph plies his trade,
Lo, Jesus labours too ;
The hands that all things made
An earthly craft pursue,
That weary men in Him may rest,
And faithful toil through Him be
blest.

4 Among the doctors see
The Boy so full of grace ;
Say, wherefore taketh He
The scholar's lowly place ?
That Christian boys, with reverence
meet,
May sit and learn at Jesus' feet.

5 Christ, once Thyself a boy !
Our boyhood guard and guide :
Be Thou its light and joy,
And still with us abide,
That Thy dear love, so great and free,
May draw us evermore to Thee.

WILLIAM WALSHAM HOW,
1823–97.

77
77. and refrain.

WHO is He, in yonder stall,
At whose feet the shepherds
fall ?
'Tis the Lord ! O wondrous story !
'Tis the Lord, the King of Glory !
At His feet we humbly fall ;
Crown Him, crown Him Lord
of all.

2 Who is He, in yonder cot,
Bending to His toilsome lot ?

3 Who is He, in deep distress,
Fasting in the wilderness ?

4 Who is He that stands and weeps
At the grave where Lazarus sleeps ?

26

5 Lo ! at midnight, who is He
  Prays in dark Gethsemane ?

6 Who is He, in Calvary's throes,
  Asks for blessings on His foes ?

7 Who is He that from the grave
  Comes to heal and help and save ?

8 Who is He that on yon throne
  Rules the world of light alone ?
        BENJAMIN RUSSELL HANBY,
         1833–67.

78
            L. M.

ON Jordan's bank the Baptist's cry
  Announces that the Lord is
    nigh ;
Come then and hearken, for he brings
Glad tidings from the King of kings.

2 Then cleansed be every breast from
    sin ;
  Make straight the way for God within ;
  Prepare we in our hearts a home,
  Where such a mighty Guest may
    come.

3 For Thou art our salvation, Lord,
  Our refuge, and our great reward ;
  Without Thy grace we waste away,
  Like flowers that wither and decay.

4 Stretch forth Thine hand, to heal our
    sore,
  And make us rise to fall no more ;
  Once more upon Thy people shine,
  And fill the world with love divine.

5 To Him who left the throne of heaven
  To save mankind, all praise be given ;
  Like praise be to the Father done,
  And Holy Spirit, Three in One.
        CHARLES COFFIN, 1676–1749 ;
        tr. by JOHN CHANDLER, 1806–76.

79
           77· 77·

FORTY days and forty nights
  Thou wast fasting in the wild,
Forty days and forty nights
Tempted, and yet undefiled,—

2 Sunbeams scorching all the day,
  Chilly dewdrops nightly shed,
Prowling beasts about Thy way,
  Stones Thy pillow, earth Thy bed.

3 Shall we not Thy sorrow share,
  And from earthly joys abstain,
Fasting with unceasing prayer,
  Glad with Thee to suffer pain ?

4 And if Satan, vexing sore,
  Flesh or spirit should assail,
Thou, his Vanquisher before,
  Grant we may not faint nor fail.

5 So shall we have peace divine ;
  Holier gladness ours shall be ;
Round us too small angels shine,
  Such as ministered to Thee.
      GEORGE HUNT SMYTTAN, 1822–70 ;
        and FRANCIS POTT, 1832–1909.

80
           88. 86.

IT fell upon a summer day,
  When Jesus walked in Galilee,
The mothers from a village brought
  Their children to His knee.

2 He took them in His arms, and laid
His hands on each remembered head ;
' Suffer these little ones to come
  To Me,' He gently said.

3 ' Forbid them not ; unless ye bear
  The childlike heart your hearts
    within,
Unto My Kingdom ye may come,
  But may not enter in.'

4 Master, I fain would enter there ;
O let me follow Thee, and share
Thy meek and lowly heart, and be
  Freed from all worldly care.

5 Of innocence, and love, and trust,
Of quiet work, and simple word,
Of joy, and thoughtlessness of self,
  Build up my life, good Lord.

6 All happy thoughts, and gentle ways,
And loving-kindness daily given,
And freedom through obedience
    gained,
  Make in my heart Thy heaven.

7 O happy thus to live and move !
And sweet this world, where I shall
    find
God's beauty everywhere, His love,
  His good in all mankind.

8 Then, Father, grant this childlike
heart,
   That I may come to Christ, and feel
His hands on me in blessing laid,
   Love-giving, strong to heal.
      STOPFORD AUGUSTUS BROOKE,
        1832–1916.

81
76. 76. D.

GOD, who hath made the daisies,
   And every lovely thing,
He will accept our praises,
   And hearken while we sing.
He says, though we are simple,
   Though ignorant we be,
' Suffer the little children,
   And let them come to Me.'

2 Though we are young and simple,
   In praise we may be bold :
The children in the temple
   He heard in days of old ;
And if our hearts are humble,
   He says to you and me,
' Suffer the little children,
   And let them come to Me.'

3 He sees the bird that wingeth
   Its way o'er earth and sky ;
He hears the lark that singeth
   Up in the heaven so high ;
He sees the heart's low breathings,
   And says, well pleased to see,
' Suffer the little children,
   And let them come to Me.'

4 Therefore we will come near Him,
   And joyfully we'll sing ;
No cause to shrink or fear Him,
   We'll make our voices ring ;
For in our temple speaking,
   He says to you and me,
' Suffer the little children,
   And let them come to Me.'
      EDWIN PAXTON HOOD, 1820–85.

82
Irr.

I THINK, when I read that sweet
   story of old,
When Jesus was here among men,
How He called little children as lambs
   to His fold,
   I should like to have been with
     them then ;

I wish that His hands had been placed
     on my head,
   That His arm had been thrown
     around me,
And that I might have seen His kind
   look when He said,
   ' Let the little ones come unto
     Me.'

2 Yet still to His footstool in prayer I
     may go,
   And ask for a share in His love ;
And, if I now earnestly seek Him be-
     low,
   I shall see Him and hear Him
     above,
In that beautiful place He is gone to
     prepare
   For all who are washed and for-
     given ;
And many dear children are gather-
     ing there,
   For of such is the Kingdom of
     heaven.

3 But thousands and thousands, who
     wander and fall,
   Never heard of that heavenly
     home ;
I should like them to know there is
     room for them all,
   And that Jesus has bid them to
     come.
I long for the joy of that glorious
     time,
   The sweetest and brightest and
     best,
When the dear little children of every
     clime
   Shall crowd to His arms and be
     blest.

      JEMIMA LUKE, 1813–1906.

83
88. 83.

FIERCE raged the tempest o'er the
     deep,
Watch did Thine anxious servants
     keep,
But Thou wast wrapt in guileless
     sleep,
     Calm and still.

2 ' Save, Lord, we perish,' was their
     cry,
' O save us in our agony ! '
Thy word above the storm rose high,
     ' Peace, be still.'

HIS LIFE AND EXAMPLE

3 The wild winds hushed, the angry
       deep
  Sank like a little child to sleep,
  The sullen billows ceased to leap,
       At Thy will.

4 So, when our life is clouded o'er,
  And storm-winds drift us from the
       shore,
  Say, lest we sink to rise no more,
       ' Peace, be still.'
            GODFREY THRING, 1823–1903.

84
64. 64. D.

FIERCE was the wild billow,
     Dark was the night ;
  Oars laboured heavily,
     Foam glimmered white ;
  Trembled the mariners,
     Peril was nigh :
  Then said the God of God,
     ' Peace ! It is I.'

2 Ridge of the mountain-wave,
     Lower thy crest !
  Wail of Euroclydon,
     Be thou at rest !
  Sorrow can never be,
     Darkness must fly,
  Where saith the Light of Light,
     ' Peace ! It is I.'

3 Jesus, Deliverer,
     Come Thou to me :
  Soothe Thou my voyaging
     Over life's sea :
  Thou, when the storm of death
     Roars, sweeping by,
  Whisper, O Truth of Truth,
     ' Peace ! It is I.'
            8th century ;
  tr. by JOHN MASON NEALE, 1818–66.

85
775. 775.

WHEN the Lord of Love was here,
  Happy hearts to Him were dear,
Though His heart was sad ;
Worn and lonely for our sake,
Yet He turned aside to make
  All the weary glad.

2 Meek and lowly were His ways ;
From His loving grew His praise,
  From His giving, prayer :
All the outcasts thronged to hear ;
All the sorrowful drew near
  To enjoy His care.

3 When He walked the fields, He drew
From the flowers, and birds, and dew,
     Parables of God ;
For within His heart of love
All the soul of man did move,
     God had His abode.

4 Lord, be ours Thy power to keep,
In the very heart of grief,
     And in trial, love ;
In our meekness to be wise,
And through sorrow to arise
     To our God above.

5 Fill us with Thy deep desire
All the sinful to inspire
     With the Father's life ;
Free us from the cares that press
On the heart of worldliness,
     From the fret and strife.

6 And, when in the fields and woods
We are filled with Nature's moods,
     May the grace be given
With Thy faithful heart to say,
' All I see and feel to-day
     Is my Father's heaven.'
            STOPFORD AUGUSTUS BROOKE,
                 1832–1916.

86
D. C. M.

THINE arm, O Lord, in days of old,
  Was strong to heal and save ;
It triumphed o'er disease and death,
  O'er darkness and the grave.
To Thee they went—the blind, the
     dumb,
  The palsied, and the lame,
The leper with his tainted life,
  The sick with fevered frame.

2 And, lo ! Thy touch brought life and
     health,
  Gave speech, and strength, and
     sight ;
And youth renewed and frenzy
     calmed
  Owned Thee, the Lord of light.
And now, O Lord, be near to bless,
  Almighty as of yore,
In crowded street, by restless couch,
  As by Gennesaret's shore.

3 Be Thou our great Deliverer still,
  Thou Lord of life and death ;
Restore and quicken, soothe and
     bless,
  With Thine almighty breath ;

THE LORD JESUS CHRIST

To hands that work and eyes that see
  Give wisdom's heavenly lore,
That whole and sick, and weak and
    strong,
  May praise Thee evermore.
                EDWARD HAYES PLUMPTRE,
                        1821-91.

87
                                    C. M.

WHAT grace, O Lord, and beauty
    shone
  Around Thy steps below!
What patient love was seen in all
  Thy life and death of woe!

2 For ever on Thy burdened heart
    A weight of sorrow hung,
  Yet no ungentle, murmuring word
    Escaped Thy silent tongue.

3 Thy foes might hate, despise, revile,
    Thy friends unfaithful prove:
  Unwearied in forgiveness still,
    Thy heart could only love.

4 O give us hearts to love like Thee,
    Like Thee, O Lord, to grieve
  Far more for others' sins than all
    The wrongs that we receive.

5 One with Thyself, may every eye
    In us, Thy brethren, see
  That gentleness and grace that spring
    From union, Lord, with Thee.
                EDWARD DENNY, 1796-1889.

88
                                 D. L. M.

O MASTER, it is good to be
    High on the mountain here
      with Thee,
  Where stand revealed to mortal gaze
  The great old saints of other days,
  Who once received, on Horeb's
      height,
  The eternal laws of truth and right,
  Or caught the still small whisper,
      higher
  Than storm, than earthquake, or than
      fire.

2 O Master, it is good to be
  With Thee and with Thy faithful
      three:
  Here, where the apostle's heart of
      rock
  Is nerved against temptation's shock;

Here, where the Son of Thunder
      learns
  The thought that breathes, the word
      that burns;
  Here, where on eagle's wings we move
  With him whose last, best creed is
      love.

3 O Master, it is good to be
  Entranced, enwrapt, alone with Thee;
  Watching the glistering raiment glow,
  Whiter than Hermon's whitest snow,
  The human lineaments that shine
  Irradiant with a light divine:
  Till we too change from grace to
      grace,
  Gazing on that transfigured face.

4 O Master, it is good to be
  Here on the holy mount with Thee;
  When darkling in the depths of night,
  When dazzled with excess of light,
  We bow before the heavenly voice
  That bids bewildered souls rejoice,
  Though love wax cold and faith be
      dim,
  'This is My Son! O hear ye Him!'
                ARTHUR PENRHYN STANLEY,
                        1815-81.

89
                                    L. M.

O WONDROUS type, O vision
    fair
  Of glory that the Church shall share,
  Which Christ upon the mountain
      shows,
  Where brighter than the sun He
      glows!

2 With shining face and bright array,
  Christ deigns to manifest to-day
  What glory shall be theirs, above,
  Who joy in God with perfect love.

3 And faithful hearts are raised on high
  By this great vision's mystery,
  For which, in joyful strains, we raise
  The voice of prayer, the hymn of
      praise.

4 O Father, with the eternal Son
  And Holy Spirit ever One,
  Vouchsafe to bring us, by Thy grace,
  To see Thy glory face to face.
                        15th century;
  tr. by JOHN MASON NEALE, 1818-66.

90 C. M.

LORD, as to Thy dear Cross we flee,
  And plead to be forgiven,
So let Thy life our pattern be,
  And form our souls for heaven.

2 Help us, through good report and ill,
    Our daily cross to bear,
  Like Thee, to do our Father's will,
    Our brethren's griefs to share.

3 Let grace our selfishness expel,
    Our earthliness refine,
  And kindness in our bosoms dwell,
    As free and true as Thine.

4 If joy shall at Thy bidding fly,
    And grief's dark day come on,
  We, in our turn, would meekly cry,
    'Father, Thy will be done.'

5 Should friends misjudge, or foes defame,
    Or brethren faithless prove,
  Then, like Thine own, be all our aim
    To conquer them by love.

6 Kept peaceful in the midst of strife,
    Forgiving and forgiven,
  O may we lead the pilgrim's life,
    And follow Thee to heaven.

JOHN HAMPDEN GURNEY,
1802–62.

91 76. 76. D.

ALL glory, laud, and honour
    To Thee, Redeemer King,
To whom the lips of children
    Made sweet hosannas ring !
  Thou art the King of Israel,
    Thou David's royal Son,
  Who in the Lord's Name comest,
    The King and Blessèd One.

2 All glory, etc.
  The company of angels
    Are praising Thee on high,
  And mortal men and all things
    Created make reply.

3 All glory, etc.
  The people of the Hebrews
    With palms before Thee went ;
  Our praise and prayer and anthems
    Before Thee we present.

4 All glory, etc.
  To Thee before Thy passion
    They sang their hymns of praise ;
  To Thee now high exalted
    Our melody we raise.

5 All glory, etc.
  Thou didst accept their praises ;
    Accept the prayers we bring,
  Who in all good delightest,
    Thou good and gracious King.
      All glory, etc.
ST. THEODULPH OF ORLEANS,
c. 821 ; tr. by JOHN MASON
NEALE, 1818–66.

92 L. M.

RIDE on ! ride on in majesty !
  Hark ! all the tribes 'Hosanna !' cry ;
O Saviour meek, pursue Thy road
With palms and scattered garments strowed.

2 Ride on ! ride on in majesty !
  In lowly pomp ride on to die ;
  O Christ, Thy triumphs now begin
  O'er captive death and conquered sin.

3 Ride on ! ride on in majesty !
  The wingèd squadrons of the sky
  Look down with sad and wondering eyes
  To see the approaching sacrifice.

4 Ride on ! ride on in majesty !
  Thy last and fiercest strife is nigh ;
  The Father on His sapphire throne
  Awaits His own anointed Son.

5 Ride on ! ride on in majesty !
  In lowly pomp ride on to die ;
  Bow Thy meek head to mortal pain,
  Then take, O God, Thy power, and reign.

HENRY HART MILMAN,
1791–1868.

93 76. 76. D

HOSANNA, loud hosanna,
    The little children sang ;
Through pillared court and temple
    The joyful anthem rang ;
  To Jesus, who had blessed them
    Close folded to His breast,
  The children sang their praises,
    The simplest and the best.

THE LORD JESUS CHRIST

2 From Olivet they followed,
  'Mid an exultant crowd,
The victor palm-branch waving,
  And chanting clear and loud ;
Bright angels joined the chorus,
  Beyond the cloudless sky,—
' Hosanna in the highest !
  Glory to God on high ! '

3 Fair leaves of silvery olive
  They strowed upon the ground,
While Salem's circling mountains
  Echoed the joyful sound ;
The Lord of men and angels
  Rode on in lowly state,
Nor scorned that little children
  Should on His bidding wait.

4 ' Hosanna in the highest ! '
  That ancient song we sing,
For Christ is our Redeemer,
  The Lord of heaven our King.
O may we ever praise Him
  With heart and life and voice,
And in His blissful presence
  Eternally rejoice.

JENNETTE THRELFALL,
1821–80.

THE LORD JESUS CHRIST

HIS SUFFERINGS AND DEATH

94   C. M.

WEEP not for Him who onward
  bears
His Cross to Calvary ;
He does not ask man's pitying tears,
Who wills for man to die.

2 The awful sorrow of His face,
  The bowing of His frame,
Come not from torture nor disgrace :
He fears not cross nor shame.

3 There is a deeper pang of grief,
  An agony unknown,
In which His love finds no relief—
He bears it all alone.

4 He sees the souls for whom He dies
Yet clinging to their sin,
And heirs of mansions in the skies
Who will not enter in.

5 O may I in Thy sorrow share,
  And mourn that sins of mine
Should ever wound with grief or
  care
That loving heart of Thine.

THOMAS BENSON POLLOCK,
1836–96.

95   11 10. 11 10.

MY Lord, my Master, at Thy feet
  adoring,
  I see Thee bowed beneath Thy load
    of woe :
For me, a sinner, is Thy life-blood
    pouring ;
  For Thee, my Saviour, scarce my
    tears will flow.

2 Thine own disciple to the Jews has
    sold Thee ;
  With friendship's kiss and loyal
    word he came :
How oft of faithful love my lips have
    told Thee,
  While Thou hast seen my false-
    hood and my shame !

3 With taunts and scoffs they mock
    what seems Thy weakness,
  With blows and outrage adding
    pain to pain :
Thou art unmoved and steadfast in
    Thy meekness ;
  When I am wronged, how quickly
    I complain !

4 My Lord, my Saviour, when I see
    Thee wearing
  Upon Thy bleeding brow the
    crown of thorn,
Shall I for pleasure live, or shrink
    from bearing
  Whate'er my lot may be of pain or
    scorn ?

5 O victim of Thy love ! O pangs most
    healing !
  O saving death ! O fruitful agonies !
I pray Thee, Christ, before Thee
    humbly kneeling,
  For ever keep Thy Cross before
    mine eyes.

JACQUES BRIDAINE, 1701–67 ;
tr. by THOMAS BENSON POLLOCK,
1836–96.

32

96   L. M.

O COME and mourn with me
   awhile;
O come ye to the Saviour's side;
O come, together let us mourn:
   Jesus, our Lord, is crucified!

2 Have we no tears to shed for Him,
   While soldiers scoff and Jews
      deride?
Ah! look how patiently He hangs:
   Jesus, our Lord, is crucified!

3 Seven times He spake, seven words of
      love;
And all three hours His silence
   cried
For mercy on the souls of men:
   Jesus, our Lord, is crucified!

4 O break, O break, hard heart of mine!
   Thy weak self-love and guilty
      pride
His Pilate and His Judas were:
   Jesus, our Lord, is crucified!

5 A broken heart, a fount of tears,
   Ask, and they will not be denied;
A broken heart love's cradle is:
   Jesus, our Lord, is crucified!

6 O love of God! O sin of man!
   In this dread act your strength is
      tried,
And victory remains with love:
   Jesus, our Lord, is crucified!

FREDERICK WILLIAM FABER,
   1814–63.

97   11 10. 11 10

*'Father, forgive them; for they know
   not what they do.'*

O WORD of pity, for our pardon
      pleading,
   Breathed in the hour of loneliness
      and pain;
O voice, which, through the ages in-
      terceding,
   Calls us to fellowship with God
      again.

2 O word of comfort, through the
      silence stealing,
   As the dread act of sacrifice began;
O infinite compassion, still revealing
   The infinite forgiveness won for
      man.

3 O word of hope, to raise us nearer
      heaven,
   When courage fails us, and when
      faith is dim;
The souls for whom Christ prays to
      Christ are given,
   To find their pardon and their joy
      in Him.

4 O Intercessor, who art ever living
   To plead for dying souls that they
      may live,
Teach us to know our sin which needs
      forgiving,
   Teach us to know the love which
      can forgive.

ADA RUNDALL GREENAWAY,
   1861–1937.

98   10 10. 10 10.

*'Verily I say unto thee, To-day thou
   shalt be with Me in Paradise.'*

'LORD, when Thy Kingdom comes,
      remember me!'
   Thus spake the dying lips to dying
      ears.
O faith, which in that darkest hour
      could see
   The promised glory of the far-off
      years!

2 No kingly sign declares that glory
      now;
   No ray of hope lights up that
      awful hour;
A thorny crown surrounds the bleed-
      ing brow;
   The hands are stretched in weak-
      ness, not in power.

3 Hark! through the gloom the dying
      Saviour saith,
   'Thou too shalt rest in Paradise
      to-day';
O words of love to answer words of
      faith!
   O words of hope for those who live
      to pray!

4 Lord, when with dying lips my
      prayer is said,
   Grant that in faith Thy Kingdom
      I may see,
And, thinking on Thy Cross and
      bleeding head,
   May breathe my parting words,
      'Remember me.'

THE LORD JESUS CHRIST

5 Remember me, but not my shame or
    sin ;
    Thy cleansing blood hath washed
      them all away ;
    Thy precious death for me did
      pardon win ;
    Thy blood redeemed me in that
      awful day.

6 Remember me ; and, ere I pass
    away,
    Speak Thou the assuring word
      that sets us free,
    And make Thy promise to my heart,
      ' To-day
    Thou too shalt rest in Paradise
      with Me.'

      WILLIAM DALRYMPLE MACLAGAN,
                1826–1910.

99
887. D.

' *Woman, behold thy son . . . Behold
thy mother.*'

AT the Cross, her station keeping,
    Stood the mournful mother
      weeping,
    Where He hung, the dying Lord ;
For her soul, of joy bereavèd,
Bowed with anguish, deeply grievèd,
    Felt the sharp and piercing sword.

2 O, how sad and sore distressèd
Now was she, that mother blessèd
    Of the sole-begotten One ;
Deep the woe of her affliction,
When she saw the crucifixion
    Of her ever-glorious Son.

3 Who, on Christ's dear mother gazing,
Pierced by anguish so amazing,
    Born of woman, would not weep ?
Who, on Christ's dear mother think-
    ing,
Such a cup of sorrow drinking,
    Would not share her sorrows deep ?

4 For His people's sins chastisèd,
She beheld her Son despisèd,
    Scourged, and crowned with thorns
      entwinèd ;
Saw Him then from judgment taken,
And in death by all forsaken,
    Till His spirit He resigned.

5 Jesus, may her deep devotion
Stir in me the same emotion,
    Fount of love, Redeemer kind,
That my heart, fresh ardour gaining,
And a purer love attaining,
    May with Thee acceptance find.

      13th century ; *tr.* by EDWARD
      CASWALL, 1814–78, and others.

100
77. 77. 77.

' *My God, My God, why hast Thou
forsaken Me ?*'

THRONED upon the awful Tree,
    King of grief, I watch with Thee.
Darkness veils Thine anguished face :
None its lines of woe can trace :
None can tell what pangs unknown
Hold Thee silent and alone,—

2 Silent through those three dread
    hours,
Wrestling with the evil powers,
Left alone with human sin,
Gloom around Thee and within,
Till the appointed time is nigh,
Till the Lamb of God may die.

3 Hark, that cry that peals aloud
Upward through the whelming
    cloud !
Thou, the Father's only Son,
Thou, His own anointed One,
Thou dost ask Him—can it be ?—
' Why hast Thou forsaken Me ?'

4 Lord, should fear and anguish roll
Darkly o'er my sinful soul,
Thou, who once wast thus bereft
That Thine own might ne'er be left,
Teach me by that bitter cry
In the gloom to know Thee nigh.

      JOHN ELLERTON, 1826–93.

101
' *I thirst.*'
88. 86.

HIS are the thousand sparkling
    rills
    That from a thousand fountains
      burst,
And fill with music all the hills ;
    And yet He saith, ' I thirst.'

2 All fiery pangs on battle-fields,
    On fever beds where sick men toss,
Are in that human cry He yields
    To anguish on the Cross.

3 But more than pains that racked Him
   then
Was the deep longing thirst divine
That thirsted for the souls of men ;
   Dear Lord ! and one was mine.

4 O Love most patient, give me grace ;
   Make all my soul athirst for
      Thee ;
That parched dry lip, that fading
      face,
   That thirst, were all for me.

CECIL FRANCES ALEXANDER,
1818–95.

---

102 S. M.

'*It is finished.*'

O PERFECT life of love !
   All, all is finished now,
All that He left His throne above
   To do for us below.

2 No work is left undone
   Of all the Father willed ;
His toils and sorrows, one by one,
   The Scripture have fulfilled.

3 No pain that we can share
   But He has felt its smart ;
All forms of human grief and care
   Have pierced that tender heart.

4 And on His thorn-crowned head,
   And on His sinless soul,
Our sins in all their guilt were laid,
   That He might make us whole.

5 In perfect love He dies ;
   For me He dies, for me !
O all-atoning Sacrifice,
   I cling by faith to Thee.

6 In every time of need,
   Before the judgment throne,
Thy work, O Lamb of God, I'll
      plead,
   Thy merits, not my own.

7 Yet work, O Lord, in me,
   As Thou for me hast wrought ;
And let my love the answer be
   To grace Thy love has brought.

HENRY WILLIAMS BAKER,
1821–77.

---

103 11 10. 11 10.

'*Father, into Thy hands I commend
My spirit.*'

A ND now, belovèd Lord, Thy
      soul resigning
Into Thy Father's arms with con-
      scious will,
Calmly, with reverend grace, Thy
      head inclining,
   The throbbing brow and labouring
      breast grow still.

2 Freely Thy life Thou yieldest,
      meekly bending
Even to the last beneath our
      sorrows' load,
Yet strong in death, in perfect peace
      commending
   Thy spirit to Thy Father and Thy
      God.

3 My Saviour, in mine hour of mortal
      anguish,
When earth grows dim, and round
      me falls the night,
O breathe Thy peace, as flesh and
      spirit languish ;
   At that dread eventide let there be
      light.

4 To Thy dear Cross turn Thou mine
      eyes in dying ;
Lay but my fainting head upon
      Thy breast ;
Thine outstretched arms receive my
      latest sighing ;
   And then, O then, Thine ever-
      lasting rest !

ELIZA SIBBALD ALDERSON,
1818–89.

---

104 887. D.

B Y the Cross of Jesus standing,
   Love our straitened souls ex-
      panding,
Taste we now the peace and grace !
Health from yonder Tree is flow-
      ing,
Heavenly light is on it glowing,
   From the blessed Sufferer's face.

THE LORD JESUS CHRIST

2 Here is pardon's pledge and token,
   Guilt's strong chain for ever broken,
      Righteous peace securely made ;
   Brightens now the brow once shaded,
   Freshens now the face once faded,
      Peace with God now makes us glad.

3 All the love of God is yonder,
   Love above all thought and wonder,
      Perfect love that casts out fear !
   Strength, like dew, is here distilling,
   Glorious life our souls is filling—
      Life eternal, only here !

4 Here the living water welleth ;
   Here the Rock, now smitten, telleth
      Of salvation freely given :
   This the fount of love and pity,
   This the pathway to the city,
      This the very gate of heaven.
                  HORATIUS BONAR, 1808–89.

105
                                  C. M.

THERE is a green hill far away,
   Without a city wall,
Where the dear Lord was crucified,
Who died to save us all.

2 We may not know, we cannot tell
   What pains He had to bear ;
But we believe it was for us
He hung and suffered there.

3 He died that we might be forgiven,
   He died to make us good,
That we might go at last to heaven,
Saved by His precious blood.

4 There was no other good enough
   To pay the price of sin ;
He only could unlock the gate
Of heaven, and let us in.

5 O dearly, dearly has He loved,
   And we must love Him too,
And trust in His redeeming blood,
And try His works to do.
          CECIL FRANCES ALEXANDER,
                              1818–95.

106
                                  L. M.

WHEN I survey the wondrous Cross
   On which the Prince of Glory died,
My richest gain I count but loss,
   And pour contempt on all my pride.

2 Forbid it, Lord, that I should boast,
      Save in the death of Christ, my God ;
All the vain things that charm me most,
      I sacrifice them to His blood.

3 See ! from His head, His hands, His feet,
      Sorrow and love flow mingled down ;
Did e'er such love and sorrow meet,
      Or thorns compose so rich a crown ?

4 Were the whole realm of Nature mine,
      That were an offering far too small ;
Love so amazing, so divine,
      Demands my soul, my life, my all.
                  ISAAC WATTS, 1674–1748.

107
                              76. 76. D.

O SACRED Head, sore wounded,
   With grief and shame weighed down !
O Kingly Head, surrounded
   With thorns, Thine only crown !
How pale art Thou with anguish,
   With sore abuse and scorn !
How does that visage languish,
   Which once was bright as morn !

2 O Lord of life and glory,
   What bliss till now was Thine !
I read the wondrous story ;
   I joy to call Thee mine.
Thy grief and bitter passion
   Were all for sinners' gain ;
Mine, mine was the transgression,
   But Thine the deadly pain.

3 What language shall I borrow
   To praise Thee, heavenly Friend,
For this Thy dying sorrow,
   Thy pity without end ?
O make me Thine for ever,
   And, should I fainting be,
Lord, let me never, never
   Outlive my love to Thee.

4 Be near me, Lord, when dying ;
   O show Thy Cross to me ;
And, for my succour flying,
   Come, Lord, to set me free ,

36

HIS SUFFERINGS AND DEATH

These eyes, new faith receiving,
From Thee shall never move ;
For he who dies believing
Dies safely through Thy love.
PAUL GERHARDT, 1607–76 ;
tr. by JAMES WADDELL
ALEXANDER, 1804–59.

108
87. 87. 87.

SING, my tongue, how glorious
battle
Glorious victory became ;
And above the Cross, His trophy,
Tell the triumph and the fame :
Tell how He, the earth's Redeemer,
By His death for man o'ercame.

2 Thirty years fulfilled among us—
Perfect life in low estate—
Born for this, and self-surrendered,
To His passion dedicate,
On the Cross the Lamb is lifted,
For His people immolate.

3 His the nails, the spear, the spitting,
Reed and vinegar and gall ;
From His patient body pierced
Blood and water streaming fall :
Earth and sea and stars and mankind
By that stream are cleansèd all.

4 Faithful Cross, above all other,
One and only noble Tree,
None in foliage, none in blossom,
None in fruit compares with thee :
Sweet the wood and sweet the iron,
And thy Load how sweet is He.

5 Unto God be laud and honour :
To the Father, to the Son,
To the mighty Spirit, glory—
Ever Three and ever One :
Power and glory in the highest
While eternal ages run. Amen.

VENANTIUS HONORIUS CLEMENTIANUS
FORTUNATUS, *c.* 530–609 ; *tr.* by
WILLIAM MAIR, 1830–1920 ; and
ARTHUR WELLESLEY WOTHER-
SPOON, 1853–1936 ; and *v.* 4 JOHN
MASON NEALE, 1818–66.

109
L. M.

WE sing the praise of Him who
died,
Of Him who died upon the Cross :
The sinner's hope let men deride,
For this we count the world but
loss.

2 Inscribed upon the Cross we see,
In shining letters, ' God is love ' ;
He bears our sins upon the Tree ;
He brings us mercy from above.

3 The Cross ! it takes our guilt away ;
It holds the fainting spirit up ;
It cheers with hope the gloomy day,
And sweetens every bitter cup ;

4 It makes the coward spirit brave,
And nerves the feeble arm for
fight ;
It takes its terror from the grave,
And gilds the bed of death with
light ;

5 The balm of life, the cure of woe,
The measure and the pledge of
love,
The sinner's refuge here below,
The angels' theme in heaven above.
THOMAS KELLY, 1769–1854.

110
88. 88. 88.

AND can it be, that I should gain
An interest in the Saviour's
blood ?
Died He for me, who caused His
pain—
For me, who Him to death pur-
sued ?
Amazing love ! how can it be
That Thou, my God, shouldst die
for me ?

2 'Tis mystery all ! The Immortal
dies :
Who can explore His strange
design ?
In vain the first-born seraph tries
To sound the depths of love divine.
'Tis mercy all ! let earth adore,
Let angel minds inquire no more.

3 He left His Father's throne above,—
So free, so infinite His grace—
Emptied Himself of all but love,
And bled for Adam's helpless race :
'Tis mercy all, immense and free ;
For, O my God, it found out me !

37

THE LORD JESUS CHRIST

4 Long my imprisoned spirit lay
     Fast bound in sin and nature's
        night;
  Thine eye diffused a quickening
        ray,—
     I woke, the dungeon flamed with
        light;
  My chains fell off, my heart was free,
  I rose, went forth, and followed Thee.

5 No condemnation now I dread;
     Jesus, and all in Him, is mine!
  Alive in Him, my living Head,
     And clothed in righteousness
        divine,
  Bold I approach the eternal throne,
  And claim the crown, through Christ
     my own.

CHARLES WESLEY, 1707–88.

III   86. 886.

O SAVIOUR, where shall guilty
     man
  Find rest, except in Thee?
Thine was the warfare with his foe,
The Cross of pain, the cup of woe,
  And Thine the victory.

2 How came the everlasting Son,
     The Lord of Life, to die?
Why didst Thou meet the tempter's
     power?
Why, Jesus, in Thy dying hour,
  Endure such agony?

3 To save us by Thy precious blood,
     To make us one in Thee,
That ours might be Thy perfect life,
Thy thorny crown, Thy Cross, Thy
     strife,
  And ours the victory.

4 O make us worthy, gracious Lord,
     Of all Thy love to be;
To Thy blest will our wills incline,
That unto death we may be Thine,
  And ever live in Thee.

CAROLINE ELIZABETH MAY,
1808–73.

112   77. 77. 77.

DARK the day on Calvary's Cross
     Where in pain Thou diedst for
        me,
Choosing bitterness and loss,
     From my sins to set me free.
Help me, every passing hour,
By Love's power
     To live for Thee.

2 Faith and Hope through fear did
        fail—
     Heaven's high stars they could
        not see;
Yet even Death could not prevail,
     Sealing Thy captivity:
Thou didst leave its darksome place:
Give me grace
     To live in Thee.

3 Often we have weary feet,
     Many a heavy cross have we;
Yet Thy sacrifice complete
     Gives us faith that Thine we be:
Through the dark day's dragging
     length
Give me strength
     To live to Thee.

4 Saviour, who didst win Love's
        crown,
     Just to pass it on to me,
Help me, those in sin bowed down
     To uplift and bring to Thee,
That together we may climb
Up through Time
     To live with Thee.

LAUCHLAN MACLEAN WATT,
1867–1957.

113   87. 87.

IN the Cross of Christ I glory,
     Towering o'er the wrecks of
        Time;
All the light of sacred story
     Gathers round its head sublime.

2 When the woes of life o'ertake me,
     Hopes deceive and fears annoy,
Never shall the Cross forsake me;
     Lo! it glows with peace and joy.

3 When the sun of bliss is beaming
     Light and love upon my way,
From the Cross the radiance stream-
        ing
     Adds more lustre to the day.

4 Bane and blessing, pain and pleasure,
     By the Cross are sanctified;
Peace is there that knows no measure,
     Joys that through all time abide.

5 In the Cross of Christ I glory,
     Towering o'er the wrecks of Time.
All the light of sacred story
     Gathers round its head sublime.

JOHN BOWRING, 1792–1872.

HIS SUFFERINGS AND DEATH

114 888.

BY Jesus' grave on either hand,
While night is brooding o'er the
land,
The sad and silent mourners stand.

2 At last the weary life is o'er,
The agony and conflict sore
Of Him who all our suffering bore.

3 Deep in the rock's sepulchral shade
The Lord, by whom the worlds were
made,
The Saviour of mankind, is laid.

4 O hearts bereaved and sore distressed,
Here is for you a place of rest ;
Here leave your griefs on Jesus'
breast.

5 So, when the dayspring from on high
Shall chase the night and fill the
sky,
Then shall the Lord again draw
nigh.

ISAAC GREGORY SMITH,
1826–1920.

THE LORD JESUS CHRIST

HIS RESURRECTION

115 11 11. 11 11. and refrain.

' WELCOME, happy morning ! '
—age to age shall say :
' Hell to-day is vanquished, heaven
is won to-day.'
Lo ! the Dead is living, God for
evermore :
Him, their true Creator, all His
works adore.
' *Welcome, happy morning !* '—age to
age shall say.

2 Earth with joy confesses, clothing
her for spring,
All good gifts return with her returning King :
Bloom in every meadow, leaves on
every bough,
Speak His sorrows ended, hail His
triumph now.

3 Thou, of life the Author, death didst
undergo,
Tread the path of darkness, saving
strength to show.
Come then, True and Faithful, now
fulfil Thy word ;
'Tis Thine own third morning : rise,
O buried Lord !

4 Loose the souls long prisoned,
bound with Satan's chain :
All that now is fallen raise to life
again :
Show Thy face in brightness, bid the
nations see :
Bring again our daylight : day returns with Thee.

VENANTIUS HONORIUS CLEMENTIANUS
FORTUNATUS, *c.* 530–609 ; *tr.* by
JOHN ELLERTON, 1826–93.

116 C. M.

BLEST morning, whose first
dawning rays
Beheld the Son of God
Arise triumphant from the grave,
And leave His dark abode !

2 Wrapt in the silence of the tomb
The great Redeemer lay,
Till the revolving skies had brought
The third, the appointed day.

3 Hell and the grave combined their
force
To hold our Lord, in vain ;
Sudden the Conqueror arose,
And burst their feeble chain.

4 To Thy great Name, Almighty Lord,
We sacred honours pay,
And loud hosannas shall proclaim
The triumphs of the day.

5 Salvation and immortal praise
To our victorious King !
Let heaven and earth, and rocks and
seas,
With glad hosannas ring.

6 To Father, Son, and Holy Ghost,
The God whom we adore,
Be glory, as it was, and is,
And shall be evermore.

ISAAC WATTS, 1674–1748.

39

THE LORD JESUS CHRIST

117

66. 66. and refrain.

ON wings of living light,
　　At earliest dawn of day,
Came down the angel bright,
　　And rolled the stone away.
　　　Your voices raise
　　　With one accord,
　　　To bless and praise
　　　Your risen Lord.

2 The keepers watching near,
　　At that dread sight and sound,
Fell down with sudden fear,
　　Like dead men, to the ground.

3 Then rose from death's dark gloom,
　　Unseen by mortal eye,
Triumphant o'er the tomb,
　　The Lord of earth and sky.

4 Ye children of the light,
　　Arise with Him, arise;
See how the Daystar bright
　　Is burning in the skies!

5 Leave in the grave beneath
　　The old things passed away;
Buried with Him in death,
　　O live with Him to-day.

6 We sing Thee, Lord Divine,
　　With all our hearts and powers;
For we are ever Thine,
　　And Thou art ever ours.

WILLIAM WALSHAM HOW,
1823–97.

118

77. 77. D.

'CHRIST the Lord is risen to-
　　day,'
Sons of men and angels say;
Raise your joys and triumphs high;
Sing, ye heavens, and, earth, reply.
Love's redeeming work is done,
Fought the fight, the battle won;
Lo! our Sun's eclipse is o'er;
Lo! He sets in blood no more.

2 Vain the stone, the watch, the seal;
Christ has burst the gates of hell:
Death in vain forbids His rise;
Christ has opened Paradise.
Lives again our glorious King;
Where, O Death, is now thy sting?
Once He died, our souls to save;
Where thy victory, O grave?

3 Soar we now where Christ has led,
Following our exalted Head;
Made like Him, like Him we rise;
Ours the Cross, the grave, the skies.
Hail, the Lord of earth and heaven!
Praise to Thee by both be given;
Thee we greet triumphant now;
Hail, the Resurrection Thou!

CHARLES WESLEY, 1707–88.

119

77. 77. and Hallelujahs.

JESUS CHRIST is risen to-day,
　　　　　　Hallelujah!
Our triumphant holy day,
　　　　　　Hallelujah!
Who did once, upon the Cross,
　　　　　　Hallelujah!
Suffer to redeem our loss.
　　　　　　Hallelujah!

2 Hymns of praise, then, let us sing
Unto Christ, our heavenly King,
Who endured the Cross and grave,
Sinners to redeem and save.

3 But the anguish He endured
Our salvation hath procured;
Now above the sky He 's King,
Where the angels ever sing.

4 Sing we to our God above
Praise eternal as His love;
Praise Him, all ye heavenly host,
Father, Son, and Holy Ghost.

Lyra Davidica, 1708.

120

S. M.

'THE Lord is risen indeed';
　　Now is His work performed;
Now is the mighty Captive freed,
　　And Death's strong castle stormed.

2 'The Lord is risen indeed':
　　The grave has lost his prey;
With Him is risen the ransomed seed,
　　To reign in endless day.

3 'The Lord is risen indeed';
　　He lives, to die no more;
He lives, the sinner's cause to plead,
　　Whose curse and shame He bore.

4 Then, angels, tune your lyres,
　　And strike each cheerful chord;
Join, all ye bright celestial choirs,
　　To sing our risen Lord!

THOMAS KELLY, 1769–1854.

HIS RESURRECTION

121 *78. 78. and Hallelujah.*

JESUS lives ! thy terrors now
Can, O Death, no more appal us ;
Jesus lives ! by this we know
Thou, O grave, canst not enthral
us.   *Hallelujah !*

2 Jesus lives ! henceforth is death
But the gate of life immortal ;
This shall calm our trembling breath
When we pass its gloomy portal.

3 Jesus lives ! for us He died ;
Then, alone to Jesus living,
Pure in heart may we abide,
Glory to our Saviour giving.

4 Jesus lives ! our hearts know well
Nought from us His love shall
sever ;
Life, nor death, nor powers of hell
Part us from His keeping ever.

5 Jesus lives ! to Him the throne
High o'er heaven and earth is
given ;
May we go where He is gone,
Rest and reign with Him in
heaven.
CHRISTIAN FÜRCHTEGOTT GELLERT,
1715–69; *tr.* by FRANCES
ELIZABETH COX, 1812–97.

122   *888. and Alleluias.*

ALLELUIA !   ALLELUIA !   ALLELUIA !

THE strife is o'er, the battle done ;
Now is the Victor's triumph
won ;
Now be the song of praise begun,—
' Alleluia ! '

2 The powers of death have done their
worst,
But Christ their legions hath dis-
persed ;
Let shouts of holy joy outburst,—
' Alleluia ! '

3 The three sad days have quickly
sped ;
He rises glorious from the dead ;
All glory to our risen Head !
Alleluia !

4 He brake the age-bound chains of
hell ;
The bars from heaven's high portals
fell ;
Let hymns of praise His triumph tell.
Alleluia !

5 Lord, by the stripes which wounded
Thee,
From death's dread sting Thy ser-
vants free,
That we may live, and sing to Thee,
' Alleluia ! '
Tr. by FRANCIS POTT, 1832–1909.

123   *76. 76. D.*

THE day of resurrection !
Earth, tell it out abroad ;
The passover of gladness,
The passover of God !
From death to life eternal,
From earth unto the sky,
Our Christ hath brought us over
With hymns of victory.

2 Our hearts be pure from evil,
That we may see aright
The Lord in rays eternal
Of resurrection light,
And, listening to His accents,
May hear, so calm and plain,
His own ' All hail ! ' and, hearing,
May raise the victor strain.

3 Now let the heavens be joyful ;
Let earth her song begin ;
Let the round world keep triumph,
And all that is therein ;
Let all things seen and unseen
Their notes of gladness blend,
For Christ the Lord hath risen,
Our Joy that hath no end.
ST. JOHN OF DAMASCUS, 8th century ;
tr. by JOHN MASON NEALE, 1818–66.

124   *888. and Alleluias.*

ALLELUIA !   ALLELUIA !   ALLELUIA !

O SONS and daughters, let us
sing !
The King of heaven, the glorious
King,
O'er death to-day rose triumphing.
Alleluia !

THE LORD JESUS CHRIST

2 That Easter morn, at break of day,
   The faithful women went their way
   To seek the tomb where Jesus lay.

3 An angel clad in white they see,
   Who sat, and spake unto the three,
   ' Your Lord doth go to Galilee.'

4 That night the apostles met in fear;
   Amidst them came their Lord most
      dear,
   And said, ' My peace be on all here.'

5 When Thomas first the tidings heard,
   He doubted if it were their Lord,
   Until He came and spake the word :

6 ' My piercèd side, O Thomas, see ;
   Behold My hands, My feet,' said
      He,
   ' Not faithless, but believing be.'

7 No longer Thomas then denied ;
   He saw the feet, the hands, the
      side ;
   ' Thou art my Lord and God,' he
      cried.

8 How blest are they who have not
      seen,
   And yet whose faith hath constant
      been,
   For they eternal life shall win.

9 On this most holy day of days,
   To God your hearts and voices raise
   In laud and jubilee and praise.

      JEAN TISSERAND, ? –1494 ; *tr.* by
      JOHN MASON NEALE, 1818–66.

---

125   11 11. 12 11 11.

OUR Lord Christ hath risen !
    The tempter is foiled ;
  His legions are scattered,
    His strongholds are spoiled.
O sing Hallelujah ! O sing Hallelujah !
  O sing Hallelujah ! Be joyful and
    sing,
Our great foe is baffled—Christ Jesus
  is King !

   2 O death, we defy thee !
      A stronger than thou
    Hath entered thy palace ;
      We fear thee not now !

O sing Hallelujah ! O sing Hallelujah !
  O sing Hallelujah ! Be joyful and
    sing,
Death cannot affright us—Christ Jesus
  is King !

   3 O sin, thou art vanquished,
      Thy long reign is o'er ;
    Though still thou dost vex us,
      We dread thee no more.

O sing Hallelujah ! O sing Hallelujah !
  O sing Hallelujah ! Be joyful and
    sing,
Who now can condemn us ? Christ
  Jesus is King !

   4 Our Lord Christ hath risen !
      Day breaketh at last ;
    The long night of weeping
      Is now well-nigh past.

O sing Hallelujah ! O sing Hallelujah !
  O sing Hallelujah ! Be joyful and
    sing,
Our foes are all conquered—Christ
  Jesus is King !

      WILLIAM CONYNGHAM PLUNKET,
              1828–97.

---

126   87. 87. D.

HALLELUJAH ! hallelujah !
    Hearts to heaven and voices
    raise ;
Sing to God a hymn of gladness,
  Sing to God a hymn of praise ;
He who on the Cross a victim
    For the world's salvation bled,
Jesus Christ, the King of Glory,
  Now is risen from the dead.

2 Christ is risen ; we are risen ;
    Shed upon us heavenly grace,
Rain and dew, and gleams of glory
    From the brightness of Thy face,
That we, with our hearts in heaven,
  Here on earth may fruitful be,
And by angel hands be gathered,
  And be ever, Lord, with Thee.

3 Hallelujah ! hallelujah !
    Glory be to God on high ;
Hallelujah to the Saviour,
  Who has gained the victory ;
Hallelujah to the Spirit,
  Fount of love and sanctity :
Hallelujah ! hallelujah
    To the Triune Majesty !

      CHRISTOPHER WORDSWORTH,
              1807–85.

127   65. 65. D.

JESUS, Lord, Redeemer,
    Once for sinners slain,
Crucified in weakness,
    Raised in power, to reign,
Dwelling with the Father,
    Endless in Thy days,
Unto Thee be glory,
    Honour, blessing, praise.

2 Faithful ones, communing,
    Towards the close of day,
Desolate and weary,
    Met Thee in the way.
So, when sun is setting,
    Come to us, and show
All the truth ; and in us
    Make our hearts to glow.

3 In the upper chamber,
    Where the ten, in fear,
Gathered sad and troubled,
    There Thou didst appear.
So, O Lord, this evening,
    Bid our sorrows cease ;
Breathing on us, Saviour,
    Say, ' I give you peace.'
                PATRICK MILLER KIRKLAND,
                        1857–1943.

THE LORD JESUS CHRIST

HIS ASCENSION AND
EXALTATION

128   D. L. M.

OUR Lord is risen from the dead,
    Our Jesus is gone up on high !
The powers of hell are captive led,
    Dragged to the portals of the sky.
There His triumphal chariot waits,
    And angels chant the solemn lay :
' Lift up your heads, ye heavenly
        gates,
    Ye everlasting doors, give way ! '

2 Loose all your bars of massy light,
    And wide unfold the ethereal
        scene :
He claims these mansions as His
        right ;
    Receive the King of Glory in !

Who is this King of Glory ? Who ?
    The Lord, that all our foes o'er-
        came,
The world, sin, death and hell
        o'erthrew ;
    And Jesus is the Conqueror's name.

3 Lo ! His triumphal chariot waits,
    And angels chant the solemn lay :
' Lift up your heads, ye heavenly
        gates ;
    Ye everlasting doors, give way ! '
Who is this King of Glory ? Who ?
    The Lord, of glorious power
        possessed,
The King of saints, and angels too,
    God over all, for ever blest !
                CHARLES WESLEY, 1707–88.

129   77. 77. D.

HE is gone—beyond the skies !
    A cloud receives Him from our
        eyes :
Gone beyond the highest height
Of mortal gaze or angel's flight,
Through the veils of time and space
Passed into the holiest place,—
All the toil, the sorrow done,
All the battle fought and won.

2 He is gone : and we remain
In this world of sin and pain ;
In the void which He has left
On this earth, of Him bereft,
We have still His work to do,
We can still His path pursue,
Seek Him both in friend and foe,
In ourselves His image show.

3 He is gone : we heard Him say,
    ' Good that I should go away.'
Gone is that dear form and face,
But not gone His present grace ;
Though Himself no more we see,
Comfortless we cannot be :
No ! His Spirit still is ours,
Quickening, freshening all our
        powers.

4 He is gone : but we once more
Shall behold Him as before,
In the heaven of heavens the same
As on earth He went and came :
In the many mansions there
Place for us He will prepare ;
In that world unseen, unknown,
He and we shall yet be one.
                ARTHUR PENRHYN STANLEY,
                        1815–81.

THE LORD JESUS CHRIST

130
C. M.

THE golden gates are lifted up,
　The doors are opened wide;
The King of Glory is gone in
　Unto His Father's side.

2 Thou art gone up before us, Lord,
　To make for us a place,
That we may be where now Thou art,
　And look upon God's face.

3 And ever on our earthly path
　A gleam of glory lies;
A light still breaks behind the cloud
　That veiled Thee from our eyes.

4 Lift up our hearts, lift up our minds;
　Let Thy dear grace be given,
That, while we wander here below,
　Our treasure be in heaven;

5 That where Thou art, at God's right hand,
　Our hope, our love may be.
Dwell Thou in us, that we may dwell
　For evermore in Thee.

CECIL FRANCES ALEXANDER,
1818–95.

131
C. M.

THE Head that once was crowned
　with thorns
Is crowned with glory now;
A royal diadem adorns
　The mighty Victor's brow.

2 The highest place that heaven affords
　Is His, is His by right,
The King of kings, and Lord of lords,
　And heaven's eternal Light.

3 The joy of all who dwell above,
　The joy of all below
To whom He manifests His love,
　And grants His Name to know.

4 To them the Cross, with all its shame,
　With all its grace, is given,
Their name an everlasting name,
　Their joy the joy of heaven.

5 They suffer with their Lord below,
　They reign with Him above,
Their profit and their joy to know
　The mystery of His love.

6 The Cross He bore is life and health,
　Though shame and death to Him,
His people's hope, His people's wealth,
　Their everlasting theme.

THOMAS KELLY, 1769–1854.

132
887. 887.

THE Lord ascendeth up on high,
　The Lord hath triumphed gloriously,
In power and might excelling;
The grave and hell are captive led,
Lo! He returns, our glorious Head,
　To His eternal dwelling.

2 The heavens with joy receive their Lord,
By saints, by angel hosts adored;
　O day of exultation!
O earth, adore thy glorious King!
His rising, His ascension sing
　With grateful adoration!

3 Our great High Priest hath gone before,
Now on His Church His grace to pour,
　And still His love He giveth:
O may our hearts to Him ascend;
May all within us upward tend
　To Him who ever liveth!

ARTHUR TOZER RUSSELL,
1806–74.

133
65. 65. D. and refrain.

GOLDEN harps are sounding,
　Angel voices ring,
Pearly gates are opened,
　Opened for the King.
Christ, the King of Glory,
　Jesus, King of Love,
Is gone up in triumph
　To His throne above.
　　' All His work is ended,'
　　　Joyfully we sing:
　　' Jesus hath ascended!
　　　Glory to our King!'

2 He who came to save us,
　He who bled and died,
Now is crowned with glory
　At His Father's side.
Never more to suffer,
　Never more to die,
Jesus, King of Glory,
　Is gone up on high.

44

3 Praying for His children,
    In that blessèd place,
  Calling them to glory,
    Sending them His grace,
  His bright home preparing,
    Faithful ones, for you,
  Jesus ever liveth,
    Ever loveth too.
        FRANCES RIDLEY HAVERGAL,
            1836-79.

134   87. 87. 87.

LOOK, ye saints! the sight is
    glorious;
  See the Man of Sorrows now;
  From the fight returned victorious,
    Every knee to Him shall bow:
        Crown Him! crown Him!
  Crowns become the Victor's brow.

2 Crown the Saviour! angels, crown
    Him!
  Rich the trophies Jesus brings;
  In the seat of power enthrone Him,
    While the vault of heaven rings:
        Crown Him! crown Him!
  Crown the Saviour King of kings!

3 Sinners in derision crowned Him,
    Mocking thus the Saviour's claim;
  Saints and angels crowd around Him,
    Own His title, praise His Name:
        Crown Him! crown Him!
  Spread abroad the Victor's fame.

4 Hark, those bursts of acclamation!
    Hark, those loud triumphant
        chords!
  Jesus takes the highest station:
    O what joy the sight affords!
        Crown Him! crown Him
  King of kings, and Lord of lords!
        THOMAS KELLY, 1769-1854.

135   66. 66. 88.

REJOICE, the Lord is King;
    Your Lord and King adore;
  Mortals, give thanks and sing
    And triumph evermore:
  Lift up your heart, lift up your voice;
  Rejoice; again I say, 'Rejoice.'

2 Jesus, the Saviour, reigns,
    The God of truth and love;
  When He had purged our stains,
    He took His seat above:
  Lift up your heart, lift up your voice!
  Rejoice; again I say, 'Rejoice.'

3 His Kingdom cannot fail;
    He rules o'er earth and heaven;
  The keys of death and hell
    Are to our Jesus given:
  Lift up your heart, lift up your voice;
  Rejoice; again I say, 'Rejoice.'

4 He sits at God's right hand
    Till all His foes submit,
  And bow to His command,
    And fall beneath His feet:
  Lift up your heart, lift up your voice;
  Rejoice; again I say, 'Rejoice.'

5 Rejoice in glorious hope;
    Jesus, the Judge, shall come,
  And take His servants up
    To their eternal home:
  We soon shall hear the archangel's
    voice;
  The trump of God shall sound,
    'Rejoice.'
        CHARLES WESLEY, 1707-88.

136   D. S. M.

CROWN Him with many
    crowns,
  The Lamb upon His throne:
  Hark how the heavenly anthem
        drowns
    All music but its own.
  Awake, my soul, and sing
  Of Him who died for thee,
  And hail Him as thy matchless King
    Through all eternity.

2 Crown Him the Lord of life,
    Who triumphed o'er the grave,
  And rose victorious in the strife
    For those He came to save.
  His glories now we sing
  Who died and rose on high,
  Who died eternal life to bring,
    And lives that death may die.

3 Crown Him the Lord of peace,
    Whose power a sceptre sways
  From pole to pole, that wars may
        cease,
    Absorbed in prayer and praise.

His reign shall know no end ;
  And round His piercèd feet
Fair flowers of Paradise extend
  Their fragrance ever sweet.

4 Crown Him the Lord of love :
  Behold His hands and side,
Rich wounds yet visible above,
  In beauty glorified.
All hail, Redeemer, hail !
  For Thou hast died for me :
Thy praise shall never, never fail
  Throughout eternity.

        MATTHEW BRIDGES, 1800–94 ; and
          GODFREY THRING, 1823–1903.

137 *From 1 St. Peter i. 3–5.*   C. M.

BLEST be the everlasting God,
  The Father of our Lord !
Be His abounding mercy praised,
  His majesty adored !

2 When from the dead He raised His
      Son,
    And called Him to the sky,
He gave our souls a lively hope
    That they should never die.

3 To an inheritance divine
    He taught our hearts to rise ;
'Tis uncorrupted, undefiled,
    Unfading in the skies.

4 Saints by the power of God are kept,
    Till the salvation come :
We walk by faith as strangers here :
    But Christ shall call us home.

        ISAAC WATTS, 1674–1748, and
        WILLIAM CAMERON, 1751–1811,
        as in *Scottish Paraphrases*, 1781.

138   87. 87. D.

ALLELUIA ! sing to Jesus !
  His the sceptre, His the throne ;
Alleluia ! His the triumph,
  His the victory alone.
Hark ! the songs of peaceful Zion
  Thunder like a mighty flood :
' Jesus, out of every nation,
  Hath redeemed us by His blood.'

2 Alleluia ! not as orphans
  Are we left in sorrow now
Alleluia ! He is near us,
  Faith believes, nor questions how

Though the cloud from sight received
      Him
  When the forty days were o'er,
Shall our hearts forget His promise,
  ' I am with you evermore ' ?

3 Alleluia ! Bread of angels,
  Thou on earth our Food, our
      Stay ;
Alleluia ! here the sinful
  Flee to Thee from day to day.
Intercessor, Friend of sinners,
  Earth's Redeemer, plead for me,
Where the songs of all the sinless
  Sweep across the crystal sea.

4 Alleluia ! sing to Jesus !
  His the sceptre, His the throne ;
Alleluia ! His the triumph,
  His the victory alone.
Hark ! the songs of peaceful Zion
  Thunder like a mighty flood :
' Jesus, out of every nation,
  Hath redeemed us by His blood.'

        WILLIAM CHATTERTON DIX,
                      1837–98.

139   C. M.

ALL hail, the power of Jesus'
  Name !
  Let angels prostrate fall ;
Bring forth the royal diadem,
  To crown Him Lord of all.

2 Crown Him, ye martyrs of your God,
  Who from His altar call ;
Extol Him in whose path ye trod,
  And crown Him Lord of all.

3 Ye seed of Israel's chosen race,
  Ye ransomed of the fall,
Hail Him who saves you by His grace,
  And crown Him Lord of all.

4 Sinners, whose love can ne'er forget
  The wormwood and the gall,
Go, spread your trophies at His feet,
  And crown Him Lord of all.

5 Let every tongue and every tribe,
  Responsive to the call,
To Him all majesty ascribe,
  And crown Him Lord of all.

6 O that, with yonder sacred throng,
  We at His feet may fall,
Join in the everlasting song,
  And crown Him Lord of all !

        EDWARD PERRONET, 1726–92.

HIS SYMPATHY AND INTERCESSION

THE LORD JESUS CHRIST

HIS SYMPATHY AND INTERCESSION

140 *From Heb. iv. 14–16.*　L. M.

WHERE high the heavenly temple
　　stands,
The house of God not made with
　　hands,
A great High Priest our nature
　　wears,
The Guardian of mankind appears.

2 He who for men their surety stood,
And poured on earth His precious
　　blood,
Pursues in heaven His mighty plan,
The Saviour and the Friend of man.

3 Though now ascended up on high,
He bends on earth a brother's eye ;
Partaker of the human name,
He knows the frailty of our frame.

4 Our fellow-sufferer yet retains
A fellow-feeling of our pains ;
And still remembers in the skies
His tears, His agonies, and cries.

5 In every pang that rends the heart
The Man of Sorrows had a part ;
He sympathizes with our grief,
And to the sufferer sends relief.

6 With boldness, therefore, at the
　　throne,
Let us make all our sorrows known ;
And ask the aids of heavenly power
To help us in the evil hour.

MICHAEL BRUCE, 1746–67;
as in *Scottish Paraphrases*, 1781.

141　　C. M.

IMMORTAL Love, for ever full,
　For ever flowing free,
For ever shared, for ever whole,
A never-ebbing sea !

2 Blow, winds of God, awake and blow
　The mists of earth away :
Shine out, O Light Divine, and show
How wide and far we stray.

3 We may not climb the heavenly
　　steeps
　To bring the Lord Christ down ;
In vain we search the lowest deeps,
For Him no depths can drown.

4 And not for signs in heaven above,
　Or earth below, they look
Who know with John His smile of
　　love,
　With Peter His rebuke.

5 In joy of inward peace, or sense
　Of sorrow over sin,
He is His own best evidence ;
　His witness is within.

6 And, warm, sweet, tender, even yet
　A present help is He ,
And faith has still its Olivet,
　And love its Galilee.

7 The healing of His seamless dress
　Is by our beds of pain ;
We touch Him in life's throng and
　　press,
　And we are whole again.

JOHN GREENLEAF WHITTIER,
1807–92.

142　　L. M.

STRONG Son of God, immortal
　　Love,
Whom we, that have not seen
　　Thy face,
By faith, and faith alone, embrace,
Believing where we cannot prove ;

2 Thou wilt not leave us in the dust ;
Thou madest man, he knows not
　　why ;
He thinks he was not made to die :
And Thou hast made him ; Thou
　　art just.

3 Thou seemest human and divine,
　The highest, holiest manhood,
　　Thou :
Our wills are ours, we know not
　　how :
Our wills are ours, to make them
　　Thine.

4 Our little systems have their day ;
　They have their day and cease
　　to be :
They are but broken lights of
　　Thee,
And Thou, O Lord, art more than
　　they.

5 We have but faith : we cannot know ;
　For knowledge is of things we see ;
　And yet we trust it comes from
　　Thee,
A beam in darkness : let it grow.

6 Let knowledge grow from more to
   more,
   But more of reverence in us dwell ;
   That mind and soul, according
   well,
   May make one music as before,

7 But vaster : we are fools and slight,
   We mock Thee when we do not
   fear :
   But help Thy foolish ones to bear ;
   Help Thy vain worlds to bear Thy
   light.
                ALFRED TENNYSON, 1809-92.

143   L. M.

O LOVE Divine ! that stooped to
   share
   Our sharpest pang, our bitterest
   tear,
On Thee we cast each earth-born
   care,
We smile at pain while Thou art
   near.

2 Though long the weary way we
   tread,
   And sorrow crown each lingering
   year,
No path we shun, no darkness dread,
   Our hearts still whispering, ' Thou
   art near.'

3 When drooping pleasure turns to
   grief,
   And trembling faith is changed
   to fear,
The murmuring wind, the quiver-
   ing leaf,
   Shall softly tell us Thou art near.

4 On Thee we fling our burdening woe,
   O Love Divine, for ever dear ;
Content to suffer, while we know,
   Living and dying, Thou art near !
                OLIVER WENDELL HOLMES,
                            1809-94.

144   10 10. 10 6.

A ND didst Thou love the race that
   loved not Thee ?
   And didst Thou take to heaven a
   human brow ?
Dost plead with man's voice by the
   marvellous sea ?
   Art Thou his kinsman now ?

2 O God, O Kinsman loved, but not
   enough,
   O Man, with eyes majestic after
   death,
Whose feet have toiled along our
   pathways rough,
   Whose lips drawn human breath !—

3 By that one likeness which is ours
   and Thine,
   By that one nature which doth
   hold us kin,
By that high heaven where, sinless,
   Thou dost shine
   To draw us sinners in ;

4 By Thy last silence in the judgment
   hall,
   By long foreknowledge of the
   deadly Tree,
By darkness, by the wormwood and
   the gall,
   I pray Thee visit me.

5 Come, lest this heart should, cold
   and cast away,
   Die ere the Guest adored she
   entertain—
Lest eyes which never saw Thine
   earthly day
   Should miss Thy heavenly reign.
                JEAN INGELOW, 1820-97.

145   87. 87. 77.

O NE there is, above all others,
   Well deserves the name of
   Friend ;
His is love beyond a brother's,
   Costly, free, and knows no end :
They who once His kindness prove
Find it everlasting love.

2 When He lived on earth abasèd,
   Friend of sinners was His name ;
Now, above all glory raisèd,
   He rejoices in the same ;
Still He calls them brethren, friends,
And to all their wants attends.

3 Could we bear from one another
   What He daily bears from us ?
Yet this glorious Friend and Brother
   Loves us though we treat Him
   thus ;
Though for good we render ill,
He accounts us brethren still.

4 O for grace our hearts to soften !
  Teach us, Lord, at length to love :
We, alas ! forget too often
  What a Friend we have above ;
But, when home our souls are brought,
We will love Thee as we ought.

JOHN NEWTON, 1725–1807.

146
II 10. II 10.

O SON of Man, our Hero strong and tender,
  Whose servants are the brave in all the earth,
Our living sacrifice to Thee we render,
  Who sharest all our sorrows, all our mirth.

2 O feet so strong to climb the path of duty,
  O lips divine that taught the words of truth,
Kind eyes that marked the lilies in their beauty,
  And heart that kindled at the zeal of youth ;

3 Lover of children, boyhood's inspiration,
  Of all mankind the Servant and the King ;
O Lord of joy and hope and consolation,
  To Thee our fears and joys and hopes we bring.

4 Not in our failures only and our sadness
  We seek Thy presence, Comforter and Friend ;
O rich man's Guest, be with us in our gladness,
  O poor man's Mate, our lowliest tasks attend.

FRANK FLETCHER, 1870–1954.

147
66 10. 66 10.

THOU who didst stoop below
  To drain the cup of woe,
Wearing the form of frail mortality,
  Thy blessèd labours done,
  Thy crown of victory won,
Hast passed from earth, passed to Thy home on high.

2 Our eyes behold Thee not,
  Yet hast Thou not forgot

Those who have placed their hope, their trust in Thee ;
  Before Thy Father's face
  Thou hast prepared a place,
That, where Thou art, there they may also be.

3 O Thou who art our life,
  Be with us through the strife :
Thy holy head by earth's fierce storms was bowed ;
  Raise Thou our eyes above,
  To see a Father's love
Beam, like the bow of promise, through the cloud.

4 And O, if thoughts of gloom
  Should hover o'er the tomb,
That light of love our guiding star shall be ;
  Our spirits shall not dread
  The shadowy way to tread,
Friend, Guardian, Saviour, which doth lead to Thee.

SARAH ELIZABETH MILES, 1807–77.

148
C. M.

THERE is no sorrow, Lord, too light
  To bring in prayer to Thee ;
There is no anxious care too slight
  To wake Thy sympathy.

2 Thou, who hast trod the thorny road,
  Wilt share each small distress ;
The love which bore the greater load
  Will not refuse the less.

3 There is no secret sigh we breathe
  But meets Thine ear divine ;
And every cross grows light beneath
  The shadow, Lord, of Thine.

4 Life's ills without, sin's strife within,
  The heart would overflow,
But for that love which died for sin,
  That love which wept with woe.

JANE CREWDSON, 1809–63.

THE LORD JESUS CHRIST
HIS COMING IN POWER

149
88. 88. and refrain.

O COME, O come, Immanuel,
  And ransom captive Israel,
That mourns in lonely exile here
Until the Son of God appear.
  Rejoice ! rejoice ! Immanuel
  Shall come to thee, O Israel.

THE LORD JESUS CHRIST

2 O come, O come, Thou Lord of
    might,
   Who to Thy tribes, on Sinai's height,
   In ancient times didst give the law
   In cloud and majesty and awe.

3 O come, Thou Rod of Jesse, free
   Thine own from Satan's tyranny ;
   From depths of hell Thy people save,
   And give them victory o'er the grave.

4 O come, Thou Dayspring, come and
    cheer
   Our spirits by Thine advent here ;
   Disperse the gloomy clouds of night,
   And death's dark shadows put to
    flight.

5 O come, Thou Key of David, come,
   And open wide our heavenly home ;
   Make safe the way that leads on high,
   And close the path to misery.

                    12th century;
   tr. by JOHN MASON NEALE, 1818–66.

150   87. 87.

COME, Thou long-expected Jesus,
    Born to set Thy people free ;
From our fears and sins release us ;
    Let us find our rest in Thee.

2 Israel's Strength and Consolation,
    Hope of all the earth Thou art,
Dear Desire of every nation,
    Joy of every longing heart.

3 Born Thy people to deliver,
    Born a Child and yet a King,
Born to reign in us for ever,
    Now Thy gracious Kingdom bring.

4 By Thine own eternal Spirit
    Rule in all our hearts alone ;
By Thine all-sufficient merit
    Raise us to Thy glorious throne.
                    CHARLES WESLEY, 1707–88.

151   *From Psalms* lxxxv, lxxxii,
              lxxxvi.   D. C. M.

THE Lord will come and not be
    slow,
   His footsteps cannot err ;
Before Him righteousness shall go,
   His royal harbinger.
Truth from the earth, like to a flower,
   Shall bud and blossom then ;
And justice, from her heavenly bower,
   Look down on mortal men.

2 Surely to such as do Him fear
    Salvation is at hand !
And glory shall ere long appear
    To dwell within our land.
Rise, God, judge Thou the earth in
    might,
    This wicked earth redress ;
For Thou art He who shall by
    right
    The nations all possess.

3 The nations all whom Thou hast
    made
Shall come, and all shall frame
To bow them low before Thee,
    Lord,
    And glorify Thy Name.
For great Thou art, and wonders
    great
By Thy strong hand are done :
Thou in Thy everlasting seat
Remainest God alone.
                    JOHN MILTON, 1608–74.

152   66. 66.

THY Kingdom come, O God ;
    Thy rule, O Christ, begin ;
Break with Thine iron rod
    The tyrannies of sin.

2 Where is Thy reign of peace
    And purity and love ?
When shall all hatred cease,
    As in the realms above ?

3 When comes the promised time
    That war shall be no more,
And lust, oppression, crime,
    Shall flee Thy face before ?

4 We pray Thee, Lord, arise,
    And come in Thy great might ;
Revive our longing eyes,
    Which languish for Thy sight.

5 Men scorn Thy sacred Name,
    And wolves devour Thy fold ;
By many deeds of shame
    We learn that love grows cold.

6 O'er heathen lands afar
    Thick darkness broodeth yet ;
Arise, O Morning Star,
    Arise, and never set.
                    LEWIS HENSLEY, 1824–1905.

153
C. M.

1 'THY Kingdom come!'—on bended knee
The passing ages pray;
And faithful souls have yearned to see
On earth that Kingdom's day.

2 But the slow watches of the night
Not less to God belong;
And for the everlasting right
The silent stars are strong.

3 And lo! already on the hills
The flags of dawn appear;
Gird up your loins, ye prophet souls,
Proclaim the day is near:

4 The day in whose clear-shining light
All wrong shall stand revealed,
When justice shall be throned with might,
And every hurt be healed:

5 When knowledge, hand in hand with peace,
Shall walk the earth abroad,—
The day of perfect righteousness,
The promised day of God.

FREDERICK LUCIAN HOSMER,
1840–1929.

154
From Psalm lxxii.
76. 76. D.

1 HAIL to the Lord's Anointed,
Great David's greater Son!
Hail, in the time appointed,
His reign on earth begun!
He comes to break oppression,
To let the captive free,
To take away transgression,
And rule in equity.

2 He comes with succour speedy
To those who suffer wrong,
To help the poor and needy,
And bid the weak be strong,
To give them songs for sighing,
Their darkness turn to light
Whose souls, condemned and dying,
Were precious in His sight.

3 He shall come down like showers
Upon the fruitful earth,
And love, joy, hope, like flowers,
Spring in His path to birth.
Before Him, on the mountains,
Shall peace, the herald, go;
And righteousness in fountains
From hill to valley flow.

4 For Him shall prayer unceasing
And daily vows ascend,
His Kingdom still increasing,
A Kingdom without end.
The mountain dews shall nourish
A seed, in weakness sown,
Whose fruit shall spread and flourish
And shake like Lebanon.

5 O'er every foe victorious,
He on His throne shall rest,
From age to age more glorious,
All blessing and all-blest.
The tide of time shall never
His covenant remove;
His Name shall stand for ever;
That Name to us is Love.

JAMES MONTGOMERY, 1771–1854.

155
Irr.

1 MINE eyes have seen the glory of the coming of the Lord:
He is trampling out the vintage where the grapes of wrath are stored;
He hath loosed the fatal lightning of His terrible swift sword:
His truth is marching on.

2 He hath sounded forth the trumpet that shall never call retreat;
He is sifting out the hearts of men before His judgment-seat:
O, be swift, my soul, to answer Him; be jubilant, my feet!
Our God is marching on.

3 In the beauty of the lilies Christ was born across the sea,
With a glory in His bosom that transfigures you and me:
As He died to make men holy, let us live to make men free,
While God is marching on.

4 He is coming like the glory of the morning on the wave;
He is wisdom to the mighty; He is succour to the brave;
So the world shall be His footstool, and the soul of time His slave:
Our God is marching on!

JULIA WARD HOWE, 1819–1910,
and others.

156
S. M.

YE servants of the Lord,
Each in his office wait,
Observant of His heavenly word,
And watchful at His gate.

THE LORD JESUS CHRIST

2 Let all your lamps be bright,
    And trim the golden flame ;
Gird up your loins, as in His sight,
    For awful is His Name.

3 Watch : 'tis your Lord's com-
      mand,
    And while we speak He 's near ;
Mark the first signal of His hand,
    And ready all appear.

4 O happy servant he,
    In such a posture found !
He shall his Lord with rapture see,
    And be with honour crowned.

5 Christ shall the banquet spread
    With His own royal hand,
And raise that faithful servant's head
    Amid the angelic band.

          PHILIP DODDRIDGE, 1702–51.

157
            87. 887. 77. 77.

THOU art coming, O my Saviour,
    Thou art coming, O my King,
In Thy beauty all-resplendent,
    In Thy glory all-transcendent ;
Well may we rejoice and sing.
    Coming ! in the opening east
      Herald brightness slowly swells ;
    Coming ! O my glorious Priest,
    Hear we not Thy golden bells ?

2 Thou art coming, Thou art coming ;
    We shall meet Thee on Thy way.
We shall see Thee, we shall know
      Thee,
We shall bless Thee, we shall show
      Thee
    All our hearts could never say.
What an anthem that will be,
    Ringing out our love to Thee,
    Pouring out our rapture sweet
    At Thine own all-glorious feet !

3 Thou art coming ; at Thy table
    We are witnesses for this,
While remembering hearts Thou
      meetest
In communion clearest, sweetest,
    Earnest of our coming bliss ;
    Showing not Thy death alone
      And Thy love exceeding great,
    But Thy coming and Thy throne,
    All for which we long and wait.

4 O the joy to see Thee reigning,
    Thee, my own belovèd Lord !
Every tongue Thy name confessing,
Worship, honour, glory, blessing
    Brought to Thee with glad
      accord,—
    Thee, my Master and my Friend,
    Vindicated and enthroned,
    Unto earth's remotest end
    Glorified, adored, and owned.
        FRANCES RIDLEY HAVERGAL,
                1836–79.

158
            86. 85. and refrain.

WHEN He cometh, when He
    cometh
To make up His jewels,
All His jewels, precious jewels,
    His loved and His own,
    Like the stars of the morning,
    His bright crown adorning,
    They shall shine in their beauty,
    Bright gems for His crown.

2 He will gather, He will gather
    The gems for His Kingdom,
All the pure ones, all the bright ones,
    His loved and His own.

3 Little children, little children
    Who love their Redeemer,
Are the jewels, precious jewels,
    His loved and His own.
        WILLIAM ORCUTT CUSHING,
              1823–1903.

159
              77. 75.

LORD of mercy and of might,
    Of mankind the Life and Light,
Maker, Teacher infinite,
    Jesus, hear and save.

2 Strong Creator, Saviour mild,
Humbled to a mortal child,
Captive, beaten, bound, reviled,
    Jesus, hear and save.

3 Throned above celestial things,
Borne aloft on angels' wings,
Lord of lords and King of kings,
    Jesus, hear and save.

4 Soon to come to earth again,
Judge of angels and of men,
Hear us now, and hear us then,
    Jesus, hear and save.
        REGINALD HEBER, 1783–1826.

HIS COMING IN POWER

160
87. 87. 47

LO! He comes, with clouds descending,
Once for favoured sinners slain;
Thousand thousand saints attending
Swell the triumph of His train;
Hallelujah!
God appears on earth to reign.

2 Every eye shall now behold Him,
Robed in dreadful majesty;
Those who set at nought and sold Him,
Pierced, and nailed Him to the Tree,
Deeply wailing,
Shall the true Messiah see.

3 Now redemption, long expected,
See in solemn pomp appear;
All His saints, by man rejected,
Now shall meet Him in the air;
Hallelujah!
See the day of God appear!

4 Yea, Amen! let all adore Thee,
High on Thine eternal throne;
Saviour, take the power and glory,
Claim the kingdom for Thine own:
O come quickly!
Hallelujah! come, Lord, come!

JOHN CENNICK, 1718–55;
CHARLES WESLEY, 1707–88;
MARTIN MADAN, 1726–90.

161
L. M.

THAT day of wrath, that dreadful day,
When heaven and earth shall pass away,
What power shall be the sinner's stay?
How shall he meet that dreadful day?

2 When, shrivelling like a parchèd scroll,
The flaming heavens together roll;
When, louder yet, and yet more dread,
Swells the high trump that wakes the dead!

3 O, on that day, that wrathful day,
When man to judgment wakes from clay,
Be Thou the trembling sinner's stay,
Though heaven and earth shall pass away!

WALTER SCOTT, 1771–1832.

162
898. 898. 664. 88.

'WAKE, awake! for night is flying,'
The watchmen on the heights are crying,
'Awake, Jerusalem, at last!'
Midnight hears the welcome voices,
And at the thrilling cry rejoices:
'Come forth, ye virgins, night is past!
The Bridegroom comes; awake,
Your lamps with gladness take;
Hallelujah!
And for His marriage feast prepare,
For ye must go to meet Him there.'

2 Zion hears the watchmen singing,
And all her heart with joy is springing;
She wakes, she rises from her gloom;
For her Lord comes down all-glorious,
The strong in grace, in truth victorious,
Her Star is risen, her Light is come!
Ah come, Thou blessèd One,
God's own belovèd Son;
Hallelujah!
We follow till the halls we see
Where Thou hast bid us sup with Thee.

3 Now let all the heavens adore Thee,
And men and angels sing before Thee,
With harp and cymbal's clearest tone;
Of one pearl each shining portal,
Where we are with the choir immortal
Of angels round Thy dazzling throne;
Nor eye hath seen, nor ear
Hath yet attained to hear
What there is ours;
But we rejoice, and sing to Thee
Our hymn of joy eternally.

PHILIPP NICOLAI, 1556–1608; tr. by
CATHERINE WINKWORTH, 1827–78.

53

THE LORD JESUS CHRIST

163
87. 87. 87.

CHRIST is coming! let creation
    From her groans and travail
cease;
Let the glorious proclamation
    Hope restore and faith increase:
        Christ is coming!
Come, Thou blessèd Prince of
    Peace.

2 Earth can now but tell the story
    Of Thy bitter Cross and pain;
She shall yet behold Thy glory,
    When Thou comest back to reign:
        Christ is coming!
Let each heart repeat the strain.

3 Long Thine exiles have been pining,
    Far from rest, and home, and
    Thee:
But, in heavenly vestures shining,
    They their loving Lord shall see:
        Christ is coming!
Haste the joyous jubilee.

4 With that blessèd hope before us,
    Let no harp remain unstrung;
Let the mighty advent chorus
    Onward roll from tongue to
    tongue:
        'Christ is coming!
Come, Lord Jesus, quickly come!'
            JOHN ROSS MACDUFF, 1818-95.

THE LORD JESUS CHRIST
HIS PRAISE

164
87. 87. 87.

TO the Name of our Salvation
    Laud and honour let us pay,
Which for many a generation
    Hid in God's foreknowledge lay,
But with holy exultation
    We may sing aloud to-day.

2 Jesus is the Name we treasure,
    Name beyond what words can tell,
Name of gladness, Name of pleasure,
    Ear and heart delighting well;
Name of sweetness passing measure,
    Saving us from sin and hell.

3 'Tis the Name that whoso preacheth
    Speaks like music to the ear;
Who in prayer this Name beseecheth
    Sweetest comfort findeth near;
Who its perfect wisdom reacheth
    Heavenly joy possesseth here.

4 Jesus is the Name exalted
    Over every other name;
In this Name, whene'er assaulted,
    We can put our foes to shame;
Strength to them who else had halted,
    Eyes to blind, and feet to lame.

5 Therefore we, in love adoring,
    This most blessèd Name revere,
Holy Jesus, Thee imploring
    So to write it in us here
That hereafter, heavenward soaring,
    We may sing with angels there.

            15th century; tr. by
        JOHN MASON NEALE, 1818-66.

165
66. 66. 88.

JOIN all the glorious names
    Of wisdom, love, and power,
That ever mortals knew,
    That angels ever bore:
All are too mean to speak His worth,
Too mean to set my Saviour forth.

2   Great Prophet of my God,
        My tongue would bless Thy
        Name;
    By Thee the joyful news
        Of our salvation came,—
The joyful news of sins forgiven,
Of hell subdued, and peace with
    heaven.

3   Jesus, my great High Priest,
        Offered His blood and died;
    My guilty conscience seeks
        No sacrifice beside:
His powerful blood did once atone,
And now it pleads before the throne.

4   My dear Almighty Lord,
        My Conqueror and my King,
    Thy sceptre and Thy sword,
        Thy reigning grace, I sing:
Thine is the power: behold, I sit
In willing bonds before Thy feet.

5   Now let my soul arise,
        And tread the tempter down:
    My Captain leads me forth
        To conquest and a crown:
A feeble saint shall win the day,
Though death and hell obstruct the
    way.

            ISAAC WATTS, 1674-1748.

166

C. M.

O FOR a thousand tongues, to
sing
My great Redeemer's praise,
The glories of my God and King,
The triumphs of His grace !

2 My gracious Master and my God,
Assist me to proclaim,
To spread through all the earth
abroad
The honours of Thy Name.

3 Jesus ! the Name that charms our
fears,
That bids our sorrows cease ;
'Tis music in the sinner's ears,
'Tis life, and health, and peace.

4 He breaks the power of cancelled
sin,
He sets the prisoner free ;
His blood can make the foulest clean,
His blood availed for me.

5 He speaks, and, listening to His
voice,
New life the dead receive,
The mournful, broken hearts rejoice,
The humble poor believe.

6 Hear Him, ye deaf ; His praise, ye
dumb,
Your loosened tongues employ ;
Ye blind, behold your Saviour come
And leap, ye lame, for joy !

7 Glory to God, and praise, and love
Be ever, ever given
By saints below and saints above,
The Church in earth and heaven.

CHARLES WESLEY, 1707–88.

167

666. 666.

WHEN morning gilds the skies,
My heart awaking cries,
' May Jesus Christ be praised ! '
Alike at work and prayer
To Jesus I repair :
' May Jesus Christ be praised ! '

2 Whene'er the sweet church bell
Peals over hill and dell,
' May Jesus Christ be praised ! '
O hark to what it sings,
As joyously it rings,
' May Jesus Christ be praised ! '

3 When sleep her balm denies,
My silent spirit sighs,
' May Jesus Christ be praised ! '
When evil thoughts molest,
With this I shield my breast,
' May Jesus Christ be praised ! '

4 Does sadness fill my mind ?
A solace here I find,
' May Jesus Christ be praised ! '
Or fades my earthly bliss ?
My comfort still is this,
' May Jesus Christ be praised ! '

5 Let earth's wide circle round
In joyful notes resound,
' May Jesus Christ be praised ! '
Let air and sea and sky,
From depth to height, reply,
' May Jesus Christ be praised ! '

6 Be this, while life is mine,
My canticle divine,
' May Jesus Christ be praised ! '
Be this the eternal song
Through all the ages long,
' May Jesus Christ be praised ! '

Tr. by EDWARD CASWALL,
1814–78.

168

10 10. 11 11.

YE servants of God, your Master
proclaim,
And publish abroad His wonderful
Name ;
The Name all-victorious of Jesus
extol ;
His Kingdom is glorious, and rules
over all.

2 God ruleth on high, almighty to save ;
And still He is nigh, His presence we
have ;
The great congregation His triumph
shall sing,
Ascribing salvation to Jesus our King.

3 Salvation to God, who sits on the
throne !
Let all cry aloud, and honour the
Son :
The praises of Jesus the angels
proclaim,
Fall down on their faces, and worship
the Lamb.

4 Then let us adore, and give Him His
right,
All glory and power, all wisdom and
might,

THE LORD JESUS CHRIST

All honour and blessing, with angels
 above,
And thanks never-ceasing, and infinite love.

    CHARLES WESLEY, 1707-88.

169
    10 10. 10 10. Dactylic.

BLESSING and honour and glory
 and power,
Wisdom and riches and strength
 evermore
Give ye to Him who our battle hath
 won,
Whose are the Kingdom, the crown,
 and the throne.

2 Into the heaven of the heavens hath
 He gone ;
Sitteth He now in the joy of the
 throne ;
Weareth He now of the Kingdom the
 crown ;
Singeth He now the new song with
 His own.

3 Soundeth the heaven of the heavens
 with His Name ;
Ringeth the earth with His glory and
 fame ;
Ocean and mountain, stream, forest,
 and flower
Echo His praises and tell of His
 power.

4 Ever ascendeth the song and the joy ;
Ever descendeth the love from on
 high ;
Blessing and honour and glory and
 praise,—
This is the theme of the hymns that
 we raise.

5 Give we the glory and praise to the
 Lamb ;
Take we the robe and the harp and
 the palm ;
Sing we the song of the Lamb that
 was slain,
Dying in weakness, but rising to reign.

    HORATIUS BONAR, 1808-89.

170
    77. 77.

SWEETER sounds than music
 knows
 Charm me in Immanuel's Name ;
All her hopes my spirit owes
 To His birth, and Cross, and
 shame.

2 When He came, the angels sung
 ' Glory be to God on high ! '
Lord, unloose my stammering
 tongue :
 Who should louder sing than I ?

3 Did the Lord a man become,
 That He might the law fulfil,
Bleed and suffer in my room,—
 And canst thou, my tongue, be
 still ?

4 No ! I must my praises bring,
 Though they worthless are, and
 weak ;
For, should I refuse to sing,
 Sure the very stones would
 speak.

5 O my Saviour, Shield, and Sun,
 Shepherd, Brother, Husband,
 Friend—
Every precious name in one—
 I will love Thee without end.

    JOHN NEWTON, 1725-1807.

171
    11 6. 11 6.

LIGHT of the world ! for ever, ever
 shining.
 There is no change in Thee ;
True Light of Life, all joy and health
 enshrining,
 Thou canst not fade nor flee.

2 Thou hast arisen, but Thou descend-
 est never ;
 To-day shines as the past ;
All that Thou wast Thou art, and
 shalt be ever,
 Brightness from first to last.

3 Night visits not Thy sky, nor storm,
 nor sadness ;
 Day fills up all its blue,—
Unfailing beauty, and unfaltering
 gladness,
 And love for ever new.

4 Light of the world, undimming and
 unsetting !
 O shine each mist away ;
Banish the fear, the falsehood, and the
 fretting ;
 Be our unchanging Day.

    HORATIUS BONAR, 1808-89.

172   88. 88. 88.

O LIGHT, whose beams illumine
    all
  From twilight dawn to perfect day,
Shine Thou before the shadows fall
  That lead our wandering feet
    astray :
At morn and eve Thy radiance pour,
That youth may love, and age adore.

2 O Way, through whom our souls
    draw near
  To yon eternal home of peace,
Where perfect love shall cast out fear,
  And earth's vain toil and wander-
    ing cease,
In strength or weakness may we see
Our heavenward path, O Lord,
    through Thee.

3 O Truth, before whose shrine we
    bow,
  Thou priceless pearl for all who
    seek,
To Thee our earliest strength we
    vow ;
  Thy love will bless the pure and
    meek ;
When dreams or mists beguile our
    sight,
Turn Thou our darkness into light.

4 O Life, the well that ever flows
  To slake the thirst of those that
    faint,
Thy power to bless, what seraph
    knows ?
  Thy joy supreme, what words can
    paint ?
In earth's last hour of fleeting breath,
Be Thou our Conqueror over death.

5 O Light, O Way, O Truth, O Life,
  O Jesus, born mankind to save,
Give Thou Thy peace in deadliest
    strife,
  Shed Thou Thy calm on stormiest
    wave ;
Be Thou our hope, our joy, our
    dread,
Lord of the living and the dead.
      EDWARD HAYES PLUMPTRE, 1821–91.

173   C. M.

THOU art the Way : to Thee alone
  From sin and death we flee ;
And he who would the Father seek
  Must seek Him, Lord, by Thee.

2 Thou art the Truth : Thy word alone
    True wisdom can impart ;
Thou only canst inform the mind,
    And purify the heart.

3 Thou art the Life : the rending
      tomb
    Proclaims Thy conquering arm ;
And those who put their trust in
      Thee
    Nor death nor hell shall harm.

4 Thou art the Way, the Truth, the
      Life :
    Grant us that way to know,
That truth to keep, that life to win,
    Whose joys eternal flow.
      GEORGE WASHINGTON DOANE,
            1799–1859.

174   54. 54. D.

REST of the weary,
    Joy of the sad,
  Hope of the dreary,
    Light of the glad,
Home of the stranger,
    Strength to the end,
Refuge from danger,
    Saviour and Friend !

2 Pillow where, lying,
    Love rests its head,
  Peace of the dying,
    Life of the dead,
Path of the lowly,
    Prize at the end,
Breath of the holy,
    Saviour and Friend !

3 When my feet stumble,
    I to Thee cry,
  Crown of the humble,
    Cross of the high ;
When my steps wander,
    Over me bend,
Truer and fonder,
    Saviour and Friend.

4 Ever confessing
    Thee, I will raise
  Unto Thee blessing,
    Glory, and praise,—
All my endeavour,
    World without end,
Thine to be ever,
    Saviour and Friend.
      JOHN SAMUEL BEWLEY MONSELL,
            1811–75.

175
C. M.

COME, let us join our cheerful
    songs
With angels round the throne ;
Ten thousand thousand are their
    tongues,
But all their joys are one.

2 ' Worthy the Lamb that died,' they
    cry,
    ' To be exalted thus ' ;
    ' Worthy the Lamb,' our lips reply,
    ' For He was slain for us.'

3 Jesus is worthy to receive
    Honour and power divine ;
And blessings, more than we can
    give,
Be, Lord, for ever Thine.

4 The whole creation join in one
    To bless the sacred Name
Of Him that sits upon the throne,
    And to adore the Lamb.
                ISAAC WATTS, 1674–1748.

176
76. 76. D.

O JESUS, ever present,
    O Shepherd, ever kind,
Thy very Name is music
    To ear, and heart, and mind.
It woke our wondering childhood
    To muse on things above ;
It drew our harder manhood
    With cords of mighty love.

2 How oft to sure destruction
    Our feet had gone astray,
Hadst Thou not, patient Shepherd,
    Been Guardian of our way.
How oft, in darkness fallen,
    And wounded sore by sin,
Thy hand has gently raised us,
    And healing balm poured in.

3 O Shepherd good ! we follow
    Wherever Thou wilt lead :
No matter where the pasture,
    With Thee at hand to feed.
Thy voice, in life so mighty,
    In death shall make us bold :
O bring our ransomed spirits
    To Thine eternal fold.
            LAWRENCE TUTTIETT, 1825–97.

177
66. 66. D.

COME, children, join to sing—
            Hallelujah ! Amen !—
Loud praise to Christ our King ;
            Hallelujah ! Amen !
Let all, with heart and voice,
Before His throne rejoice ;
Praise is His gracious choice :
            Hallelujah ! Amen !

2 Come, lift your hearts on high ;
            Hallelujah ! Amen !
Let praises fill the sky ;
            Hallelujah ! Amen !
He is our Guide and Friend ;
To us He'll condescend ;
His love shall never end :
            Hallelujah ! Amen !

3 Praise yet the Lord again ;
            Hallelujah ! Amen !
Life shall not end the strain ;
            Hallelujah ! Amen !
On heaven's blissful shore
His goodness we'll adore,
Singing for evermore,
            ' Hallelujah ! Amen !'
            CHRISTIAN HENRY BATEMAN,
                1813–89.

178
65. 65. D.

IN the Name of Jesus
    Every knee shall bow,
Every tongue confess Him
    King of Glory now ;
'Tis the Father's pleasure
    We should call Him Lord,
Who from the beginning
    Was the mighty Word.

2 Humbled for a season,
    To receive a name
From the lips of sinners,
    Unto whom He came,
Faithfully He bore it
    Spotless to the last ;
Brought it back victorious,
    When from death He passed.

3 Name Him, brothers, name Him
    With love strong as death,
But with awe and wonder
    And with bated breath !
He is God the Saviour,
    He is Christ the Lord,
Ever to be worshipped,
    Trusted, and adored.

HIS PRAISE

4 In your hearts enthrone Him;
   There let Him subdue
All that is not holy,
   All that is not true:
Crown Him as your Captain
   In temptation's hour;
Let His will enfold you
   In its light and power.

5 Brothers, this Lord Jesus
   Shall return again,
With His Father's glory,
   With His angel train;
For all wreaths of empire
   Meet upon His brow,
And our hearts confess Him
   King of Glory now.
                CAROLINE MARIA NOEL,
                          1817–77.

179   76. 76. D.

CHRIST is the world's Redeemer,
   The lover of the pure,
The fount of heavenly wisdom,
   Our trust and hope secure;
The armour of His soldiers,
   The Lord of earth and sky;
Our health while we are living,
   Our life when we shall die.

2 Christ hath our host surrounded
   With clouds of martyrs bright,
Who wave their palms in triumph,
   And fire us for the fight.
Christ the red Cross ascended
   To save a world undone,
And, suffering for the sinful,
   Our full redemption won.

3 Down in the realm of darkness
   He lay a captive bound,
But at the hour appointed
   He rose, a victor crowned;
And now, to heaven ascended,
   He sits upon the throne,
In glorious dominion,
   His Father's and His own.

4 All glory to the Father,
   The unbegotten One;
All honour be to Jesus,
   His sole-begotten Son;
And to the Holy Spirit—
   The Perfect Trinity.
Let all the worlds give answer,
   ' Amen—so let it be.'
                ST. COLUMBA, 521–97; *tr.* by
                DUNCAN MACGREGOR, 1854–1923.

THE HOLY SPIRIT

180   86. 84.

OUR blest Redeemer, ere He
      breathed
His tender last farewell,
A Guide, a Comforter bequeathed,
   With us to dwell.

2 He came in tongues of living flame,
   To teach, convince, subdue;
All-powerful as the wind He came,
   As viewless too.

3 He came sweet influence to impart,
   A gracious, willing Guest,
While He can find one humble heart
   Wherein to rest.

4 And His that gentle voice we hear,
   Soft as the breath of even,
That checks each fault, that calms
      each fear,
   And speaks of heaven.

5 And every virtue we possess,
   And every victory won,
And every thought of holiness,
   Are His alone.

6 Spirit of purity and grace,
   Our weakness, pitying, see;
O make our hearts Thy dwelling-
      place,
      And worthier Thee.
                HARRIET AUBER, 1773–1862.

181   C. M.

WHEN God of old came down
      from heaven,
In power and wrath He came;
Before His feet the clouds were riven,
   Half darkness and half flame.

2 But, when He came the second time,
   He came in power and love;
Softer than gale at morning prime
   Hovered His holy Dove.

3 The fires that rushed on Sinai down
   In sudden torrents dread,
Now gently light, a glorious crown,
   On every sainted head.

THE HOLY SPIRIT

4 And, as on Israel's awe-struck ear
    The voice exceeding loud,
The trump that angels quake to hear,
    Thrilled from the deep, dark cloud,

5 So, when the Spirit of our God
    Came down His flock to find,
A voice from heaven was heard
    abroad,
    A rushing mighty wind.

6 It fills the Church of God ; it fills
    The sinful world around ;
Only in stubborn hearts and wills
    No place for it is found.

7 Come, Lord ; come, Wisdom, Love,
    and Power ;
Open our ears to hear ;
Let us not miss the accepted hour ;
    Save, Lord, by love or fear.
            JOHN KEBLE, 1792–1866.

182
               L. M.

COME, Holy Ghost, our souls
    inspire
And lighten with celestial fire ;
Thou the anointing Spirit art,
Who dost Thy sevenfold gifts impart.

2 Thy blessèd unction from above
Is comfort, life, and fire of love ;
Enable with perpetual light
The dulness of our blinded sight :

3 Anoint and cheer our soilèd face
With the abundance of Thy grace ;
Keep far our foes ; give peace at
    home :
Where Thou art Guide no ill can
    come.

4 Teach us to know the Father, Son,
And Thee of Both, to be but One,
That through the ages all along
This may be our endless song,
    ' Praise to Thine eternal merit,
Father, Son, and Holy Spirit.'
                Amen.
        9th century ; tr. by
      JOHN COSIN, 1594–1672

183
               C. M.

SPIRIT Divine, attend our
    prayers,
    And make this house Thy home ;
Descend with all Thy gracious
    powers ;
    O come, great Spirit, come !

2 Come as the light : to us reveal
    Our emptiness and woe ;
And lead us in those paths of life
    Where all the righteous go.

3 Come as the fire : and purge our
    hearts
    Like sacrificial flame ;
Let our whole soul an offering be
    To our Redeemer's Name.

4 Come as the dew : and sweetly bless
    This consecrated hour ;
May barrenness rejoice to own
    Thy fertilizing power.

5 Come as the dove : and spread Thy
    wings,
    The wings of peaceful love ;
And let Thy Church on earth become
    Blest as the Church above.

6 Come as the wind, with rushing
    sound
    And Pentecostal grace,
That all of woman born may see
    The glory of Thy face.

7 Spirit Divine, attend our prayers ;
    Make a lost world Thy home ;
Descend with all Thy gracious
    powers ;
    O come, great Spirit, come !
          ANDREW REED, 1787–1862.

184
            88. 88. 88.

CREATOR Spirit ! by whose aid
    The world's foundations first
    were laid,
Come, visit every pious mind,
Come, pour Thy joys on human kind ;
From sin and sorrow set us free,
And make Thy temples worthy Thee.

2 O Source of uncreated light,
The Father's promised Paraclete,
Thrice holy Fount, thrice holy Fire,
Our hearts with heavenly love inspire ;
Come, and Thy sacred unction bring
To sanctify us while we sing.

THE HOLY SPIRIT

3 Plenteous of grace, descend from
        high,
    Rich in Thy sevenfold energy ;
    Thou Strength of His almighty hand
    Whose power does heaven and earth
        command,
    Give us Thyself, that we may see
    The Father and the Son by Thee.

4 Immortal honour, endless fame
    Attend the Almighty Father's Name ;
    The Saviour Son be glorified,
    Who for lost man's redemption
        died ;
    And equal adoration be,
    Eternal Paraclete, to Thee.

                9th century ; *tr.* by
            JOHN DRYDEN, 1631–1700.

185   L. M.

SPIRIT of God, that moved of old
        Upon the waters' darkened face,
    Come, when our faithless hearts are
        cold,
        And stir them with an inward
        grace.

2 Thou that art power and peace com-
        bined,
        All highest strength, all purest
        love,
    The rushing of the mighty wind,
    The brooding of the gentle dove,

3 Come, give us still Thy powerful aid,
        And urge us on, and keep us
        Thine ;
    Nor leave the hearts that once were
        made
        Fit temples for Thy grace divine ;

4 Nor let us quench Thy sevenfold
        light ;
        But still with softest breathings
        stir
    Our wayward souls, and lead us
        right,
        O Holy Ghost, the Comforter.
            CECIL FRANCES ALEXANDER,
                        1818–95.

186   777.

COME, Thou Holy Paraclete,
        And from Thy celestial seat
    Send Thy light and brilliancy.

2 Father of the poor, draw near ;
    Giver of all gifts, be here ;
        Come, the soul's true radiancy.

3 Come, of comforters the best,
    Of the soul the sweetest guest,
        Come in toil refreshingly.

4 Thou in labour rest most sweet,
    Thou art shadow from the heat,
        Comfort in adversity.

5 O Thou Light, most pure and blest,
    Shine within the inmost breast
        Of Thy faithful company.

6 Where Thou art not, man hath
        nought ;
    Every holy deed and thought
        Comes from Thy Divinity.

7 What is soilèd make Thou pure ;
    What is wounded, work its cure ;
        What is parchèd fructify ;

8 What is rigid gently bend ;
    What is frozen warmly tend ;
        Straighten what goes erringly.

9 Fill Thy faithful, who confide
    In Thy power to guard and guide,
        With Thy sevenfold mystery.

10 Here Thy grace and virtue send ;
        Grant salvation in the end,
        And in heaven felicity.

            13th century ; *tr.* by
        JOHN MASON NEALE, 1818–66.

187   77. 77. 77.

GRACIOUS Spirit, dwell with
        me !
    I myself would gracious be ;
    And, with words that help and heal,
    Would Thy life in mine reveal ;
    And, with actions bold and meek,
    Would for Christ, my Saviour, speak.

2 Truthful Spirit, dwell with me !
    I myself would truthful be ;
    And, with wisdom kind and clear,
    Let Thy life in mine appear ;
    And, with actions brotherly,
    Speak my Lord's sincerity.

3 Tender Spirit, dwell with me !
    I myself would tender be ;
    Shut my heart up like a flower
    In temptation's darksome hour ;
    Open it when shines the sun,
    And His love by fragrance own.

4 Holy Spirit, dwell with me !
I myself would holy be ;
Separate from sin, I would
Choose and cherish all things good,
And whatever I can be
Give to Him who gave me Thee.

THOMAS TOKE LYNCH,
1818–71.

188
L. M.

COME, gracious Spirit, heavenly
Dove,
With light and comfort from above ;
Be Thou our Guardian, Thou our
Guide ;
O'er every thought and step preside.

2 The light of truth to us display,
And make us know and choose Thy
way ;
Plant holy fear in every heart,
That we from God may ne'er depart.

3 Lead us to Christ, the living Way ;
Nor let us from His pastures stray :
Lead us to holiness, the road
That we must take to dwell with God.

4 Lead us to heaven, that we may share
Fulness of joy for ever there ;
Lead us to God, our final rest,
To be with Him for ever blest.
Amen.

SIMON BROWNE, 1680–1732.

189
65. 65.

HOLY Spirit, hear us ;
Help us while we sing ;
Breathe into the music
Of the praise we bring.

2 Holy Spirit, prompt us
When we kneel to pray ;
Nearer come, and teach us
What we ought to say.

3 Holy Spirit, shine Thou
On the book we read ;
Gild its holy pages
With the light we need.

4 Holy Spirit, give us
Each a lowly mind ;
Make us more like Jesus,
Gentle, pure, and kind.

5 Holy Spirit, brighten
Little deeds of toil ;
And our playful pastimes
Let no folly spoil.

6 Holy Spirit, help us
Daily, by Thy might,
What is wrong to conquer,
And to choose the right.

WILLIAM HENRY PARKER,
1845–1929.

190
S. M.

COME, Holy Spirit, come !
Let Thy bright beams arise ;
Dispel the darkness from our minds,
And open all our eyes.

2 Cheer our desponding hearts,
Thou heavenly Paraclete ;
Give us to lie with humble hope
At our Redeemer's feet.

3 Revive our drooping faith ;
Our doubts and fears remove ;
And kindle in our breasts the flame
Of never-dying love.

4 Convince us of our sin ;
Then lead to Jesus' blood,
And to our wondering view reveal
The secret love of God.

5 'Tis Thine to cleanse the heart,
To sanctify the soul,
To pour fresh life on every part,
And new create the whole.

6 Dwell, therefore, in our hearts ;
Our minds from bondage free ;
Then shall we know and praise and
love
The Father, Son, and Thee.

JOSEPH HART, 1712–68.

191
66. 11. D.

COME down, O Love Divine,
Seek Thou this soul of mine,
And visit it with Thine own ardour
glowing ;
O Comforter, draw near,
Within my heart appear,
And kindle it, Thy holy flame be-
stowing.

THE HOLY SPIRIT

2   O let it freely burn,
    Till earthly passions turn
To dust and ashes, in its heat con-
    suming ;
    And let Thy glorious light
    Shine ever on my sight,
And clothe me round, the while my
    path illuming.

3   Let holy charity
    Mine outward vesture be,
And lowliness become mine inner
    clothing ;
    True lowliness of heart,
    Which takes the humbler part,
And o'er its own shortcomings weeps
    with loathing.

4   And so the yearning strong,
    With which the soul will long,
Shall far outpass the power of human
    telling ;
    For none can guess its grace,
    Till he become the place
Wherein the Holy Spirit makes His
    dwelling.

BIANCO DA SIENA, ?–1434 ; *tr.* by
RICHARD FREDERICK LITTLEDALE,
1833–90.

192
88. 88. 88.

SPIRIT of Grace, Thou Light of
   Life
    Amidst the darkness of the dead !
Bright Star, whereby through worldly
    strife,
    The patient pilgrim still is led ;
Thou Dayspring in the deepest
    gloom,
Wildered and dark, to Thee I come !

2 Pure Fire of God, burn out my sin,
    Cleanse all the earthly dross from
    me ;
Refine my secret heart within,
    The golden streams of love set
    free !
Live Thou in me, O Life divine,
Until my deepest love be Thine.

3 O Breath from far Eternity,
    Breathe o'er my soul's unfertile
    land ;

So shall the pine and myrtle-tree
    Spring up amidst the desert sand ;
And where Thy living water flows,
My heart shall blossom as the rose.

GERHARD TERSTEEGEN, 1697–1769 ; *tr.*
by EMMA FRANCES BEVAN, 1827–
1909, and BENJAMIN HALL KEN-
NEDY, 1804–89.

193
77. 77.

HOLY Spirit, Truth Divine,
   Dawn upon this soul of mine ;
Word of God, and inward Light,
Wake my spirit, clear my sight.

2 Holy Spirit, Love Divine,
Glow within this heart of mine ;
Kindle every high desire ;
Perish self in Thy pure fire.

3 Holy Spirit, Power Divine,
Fill and nerve this will of mine ;
By Thee may I strongly live,
Bravely bear, and nobly strive.

4 Holy Spirit, Right Divine,
King within my conscience reign ;
Be my law, and I shall be
Firmly bound, for ever free.

5 Holy Spirit, Peace Divine,
Still this restless heart of mine ;
Speak to calm this tossing sea,
Stayed in Thy tranquillity.

6 Holy Spirit, Joy Divine,
Gladden Thou this heart of mine ;
In the desert ways I sing,
' Spring, O Well, for ever spring !'

SAMUEL LONGFELLOW, 1819–92.

194
S. M.

BREATHE on me, Breath of
   God ;
Fill me with life anew,
That I may love what Thou dost love,
  And do what Thou wouldst do.

2 Breathe on me, Breath of God,
Until my heart is pure,
Until with Thee I will one will,
  To do and to endure.

3 Breathe on me, Breath of God,
Till I am wholly Thine,
Until this earthly part of me
  Glows with Thy fire divine.

4   Breathe on me, Breath of God ;
    So shall I never die,
But live with Thee the perfect life
  Of Thine eternity.

               EDWIN HATCH, 1835–89.

195
                  10. 10. 10. 10.

SPIRIT of God, descend upon my
    heart ;
  Wean it from earth ; through all
    its pulses move ;
Stoop to my weakness, mighty as
    Thou art,
  And make me love Thee as I
    ought to love.

2 I ask no dream, no prophet-ecstasies,
  No sudden rending of the veil of
    clay,
No angel-visitant, no opening skies ;
  But take the dimness of my soul
    away.

3 Hast Thou not bid me love Thee,
    God and King—
  All, all Thine own, soul, heart, and
    strength, and mind ?
I see Thy Cross—there teach my
    heart to cling :
  O let me seek Thee, and O let me
    find !

4 Teach me to feel that Thou art
    always nigh ;
  Teach me the struggles of the soul
    to bear,
To check the rising doubt, the rebel
    sigh ;
  Teach me the patience of un-
    answered prayer.

5 Teach me to love Thee as Thine
    angels love,
  One holy passion filling all my
    frame—
The baptism of the heaven-descended
    Dove,
  My heart an altar, and Thy love
    the flame.

             GEORGE CROLY, 1780–1860.

196
                      C. M.

COME, Holy Ghost, our hearts
    inspire ;
  Let us Thine influence prove,
Source of the old prophetic fire,
  Fountain of life and love.

2 Come, Holy Ghost, for moved by
    Thee
  The prophets wrote and spoke ;
Unlock the truth, Thyself the
    key ;
  Unseal the sacred book.

3 Expand Thy wings, celestial Dove ;
  Brood o'er our nature's night ;
On our disordered spirits move,
  And let there now be light.

4 God through Himself we then shall
    know,
  If Thou within us shine,
And sound, with all Thy saints
    below,
  The depths of love divine.

             CHARLES WESLEY, 1707–88.

THE HOLY SCRIPTURES

197
                      C. M.

THE Spirit breathes upon the word,
  And brings the truth to sight ;
Precepts and promises afford
  A sanctifying light.

2 A glory gilds the sacred page,
  Majestic, like the sun :
It gives a light to every age ;
  It gives, but borrows none.

3 The hand that gave it still supplies
  The gracious light and heat ;

His truths upon the nations rise ;
  They rise, but never set.

4 Let everlasting thanks be Thine,
  For such a bright display
As makes a world of darkness shine
  With beams of heavenly day.

5 My soul rejoices to pursue
  The steps of Him I love,
Till glory breaks upon my view
  In brighter worlds above.

            WILLIAM COWPER, 1731–1800

THE HOLY SCRIPTURES

198   76. 76. D.

O WORD of God Incarnate,
   O Wisdom from on high,
O Truth unchanged, unchanging,
   O Light of our dark sky,
We praise Thee for the radiance
   That from the hallowed page,
A lantern to our footsteps,
   Shines on from age to age.

2 The Church from her dear Master
   Received the gift divine,
And still that light she lifteth,
   O'er all the earth to shine ;
It is the golden casket
   Where gems of truth are stored ;
It is the heaven-drawn picture
   Of Christ, the living Word ;

3 It floateth like a banner
   Before God's host unfurled ;
It shineth like a beacon,
   Above the darkling world ;
It is the chart and compass
   That, o'er life's surging sea,
'Mid mists and rocks and quicksands,
   Still guides, O Christ, to Thee.

4 O make Thy Church, dear Saviour,
   A lamp of purest gold,
To bear before the nations
   Thy true light, as of old ;
O teach Thy wandering pilgrims
   By this their path to trace,
Till, clouds and darkness ended,
   They see Thee face to face.

          WILLIAM WALSHAM HOW,
                1823–97.

199   66. 66. Trochaic.

LORD, Thy word abideth,
   And our footsteps guideth
Who its truth believeth
   Light and joy receiveth.

2 When our foes are near us,
   Then Thy word doth cheer us,
Word of consolation,
   Message of salvation.

3 When the storms are o'er us,
   And dark clouds before us,
Then its light directeth,
   And our way protecteth.

4 Who can tell the pleasure,
   Who recount the treasure,
By Thy word imparted
   To the simple-hearted ?

5 Word of mercy, giving
   Succour to the living ;
Word of life, supplying
   Comfort to the dying !

6 O that we, discerning
   Its most holy learning,
Lord, may love and fear Thee,
   Evermore be near Thee !

          HENRY WILLIAMS BAKER,
                1821–77.

200   86. 84.

TO Thee, O God, we render thanks,
   That Thou to us hast given
A light that shineth on our path,
   A light from heaven :

2 That Thou into the hearts of men
   Didst breathe Thy Breath Divine,
And mad'st their lips the source from
      whence
   Flowed words of Thine :

3 The words that speak of lives that
      live,
   And life beyond the grave,
Of Him who came that life to give,
   Those lives to save :

4 Of Him who lowly came as man,
   To come as man again
On clouds of glory throned on high,
   As Judge of men :

5 Who lived on earth, on earth who
      died,
   To set His servants free,
And left this message as their guide,
   ' Remember Me.'

6 Then teach us humbly so to tread
   The path that Saviour trod,
That we may ever stand prepared
   To meet our God.

          GODFREY THRING, 1823–1903.

201   C. M.

LAMP of our feet, whereby we
    trace
   Our path when wont to stray ;
Stream from the fount of heavenly
    grace,
   Brook by the traveller's way ;

2 Bread of our souls, whereon we feed,
   True manna from on high ;
Our guide and chart, wherein we
    read
   Of realms beyond the sky ;

3 Pillar of fire through watches dark,
　Or radiant cloud by day ;
When waves would whelm our toss-
　　ing bark,
　Our anchor and our stay ;

4 Word of the ever-living God,
　Will of His glorious Son,—
Without thee how could earth be
　　trod,
　Or heaven itself be won ?

5 Lord, grant that we aright may learn
　The wisdom it imparts,
And to its heavenly teaching turn
　With simple, childlike hearts.
　　　　BERNARD BARTON, 1784–1849.

202
10 10. 10 10.

BREAK Thou the bread of life,
　Dear Lord, to me,
As Thou didst break the loaves
　Beside the sea ;
Beyond the sacred page
　I seek Thee, Lord ;
My spirit pants for Thee,
　O living Word.

2 Bless Thou the truth, dear Lord,
　To me, to me,
As Thou didst bless the bread
　By Galilee ;
Then shall all bondage cease,
　All fetters fall ;
And I shall find my peace,
　My all in all.
　　　　MARY ARTEMISIA LATHBURY,
　　　　　　　　1841–1913.

203
78. 78. 88.

LOOK upon us, blessèd Lord,
　Take our wandering thoughts
　　and guide us :
We have come to hear Thy word :
With Thy teaching now provide us,
　That, from earth's distractions
　　　turning,
We Thy message may be learning.

2　For Thy Spirit's radiance bright
We, assembled here, are hoping :
　If Thou shouldst withhold the
　　light,
In the dark our souls were groping :
　In word, deed, and thought direct
　　us :
　Thou, none other, canst correct us.

3　Brightness of the Father's face,
Light of Light, from God proceeding,
　Make us ready in this place :
Ear and heart await Thy leading.
　In our study, prayers, and praising,
　May our souls find their uprising.
　　　TOBIAS CLAUSNITZER, 1619–84 ; tr.
　　　by ROBERT ALEXANDER STEWART
　　　MACALISTER, 1870–1950.

204
77. 77. 77.

HOLY Father, Thou hast given
　Holy truth from highest heaven ;
Words of counsel wise and pure,
Words of promise bright and sure ;
Light that guides us back to Thee,
Back to peace and purity.

2 Clearer than the sun at noon,
Fairer than the silver moon,
Through the clouds and through the
　　night
Shineth aye this heavenly light ;
Help us, Lord, to lift our eyes,
Take its guidance, and be wise.

3 Here the wisdom from above,
Beaming holiness and love,
Stirring hope, dispelling fear,
Shines to save ; for Christ is here :
Knowing, trusting Him, we come
From our wanderings gladly home.

4 Blessèd Saviour, Light Divine,
Thou hast bid us rise and shine ;
Grant Thy grace, and we shall be
Children of the day in Thee,
Showing all around the road
Back to life, and love, and God.
　　　　　WILLIAM BRUCE, 1812–82.

THE CHURCH

THE COMMUNION OF SAINTS

205
76. 76. D.

THE Church's one foundation
   Is Jesus Christ her Lord:
She is His new creation
   By water and the word;
From heaven He came and sought
      her
   To be His holy bride;
With His own blood He bought her,
   And for her life He died.

2 Elect from every nation,
   Yet one o'er all the earth,
Her charter of salvation
   One Lord, one faith, one birth:
One holy Name she blesses,
   Partakes one holy food,
And to one hope she presses,
   With every grace endued.

3 Though with a scornful wonder
   Men see her sore oppressed,
By schisms rent asunder,
   By heresies distressed,
Yet saints their watch are keeping,
   Their cry goes up, 'How long?'
And soon the night of weeping
   Shall be the morn of song.

4 'Mid toil and tribulation,
   And tumult of her war,
She waits the consummation
   Of peace for evermore,
Till with the vision glorious
   Her longing eyes are blest,
And the great Church victorious
   Shall be the Church at rest.

5 Yet she on earth hath union
   With God the Three in One,
And mystic sweet communion
   With those whose rest is won.
O happy ones and holy!
   Lord, give us grace that we,
Like them, the meek and lowly,
   On high may dwell with Thee.

SAMUEL JOHN STONE,
1839-1900.

206
87. 87. D.

GLORIOUS things of thee are
      spoken,
   Zion, city of our God;
He whose word cannot be broken
   Formed thee for His own abode.
On the Rock of Ages founded,
   What can shake thy sure repose?
With salvation's walls surrounded,
   Thou mayst smile at all thy foes.

2 See! the streams of living waters,
   Springing from eternal love,
Well supply thy sons and daughters,
   And all fear of want remove.
Who can faint while such a river
   Ever flows their thirst to assuage,—
Grace, which, like the Lord the
      Giver,
   Never fails from age to age?

3 Round each habitation hovering,
   See! the cloud and fire appear,
For a glory and a covering,
   Showing that the Lord is near.
Blest inhabitants of Zion,
   Washed in the Redeemer's blood,
Jesus, whom their souls rely on,
   Makes them kings and priests to
      God.

4 Saviour, if of Zion's city
   I, through grace, a member am,
Let the world deride or pity,
   I will glory in Thy Name.
Fading is the worldling's pleasure,
   All his boasted pomp and show;
Solid joys and lasting treasure
   None but Zion's children know.

JOHN NEWTON, 1725-1807.

207
87. 87. 87.

CHRIST is made the sure founda-
      tion,
   Christ the head and corner-stone,
Chosen of the Lord, and precious,
   Binding all the Church in one,
Holy Zion's help for ever,
   And her confidence alone.

67

2 To this temple, where we call Thee,
   Come, O Lord of hosts, to-day :
With Thy wonted loving-kindness,
   Hear Thy servants as they pray,
And Thy fullest benediction
   Shed within its walls alway.

3 Here vouchsafe to all Thy servants
   What they ask of Thee to gain,
What they gain from Thee for
     ever
With the blessèd to retain,
And hereafter in Thy glory
   Evermore with Thee to reign.

4 Laud and honour to the Father,
   Laud and honour to the Son,
Laud and honour to the Spirit,
   Ever Three and ever One,
One in might, and One in glory,
   While unending ages run.

     Latin, 7th or 8th century ; *tr.* by
     JOHN MASON NEALE, 1818–66.

208   77. 76.

JESUS, with Thy Church abide ;
  Be her Saviour, Lord, and Guide,
While on earth her faith is tried :
  We beseech Thee, hear us.

2 Keep her life and doctrine pure ;
  Grant her patience to endure,
Trusting in Thy promise sure :
  We beseech Thee, hear us.

3 All her fettered powers release ;
  Bid our strife and envy cease ;
Grant the heavenly gift of peace :
  We beseech Thee, hear us.

4 May she one in doctrine be,
  One in truth and charity,
Winning all to faith in Thee :
  We beseech Thee, hear us.

5 May she guide the poor and blind,
  Seek the lost until she find,
And the broken-hearted bind :
  We beseech Thee, hear us.

6 May her scattered children be
  From reproach of evil free,
Blameless witnesses for Thee :
  We beseech Thee, hear us.

7 May her lamp of truth be bright ;
  Bid her bear aloft its light
Through the realms of heathen
     night :
  We beseech Thee, hear us.

8 May she thus all glorious be,
Spotless and from wrinkle free,
Pure and bright, and worthy Thee :
  We beseech Thee, hear us.

     THOMAS BENSON POLLOCK,
               1836–96.

209   C. M.

CITY of God, how broad and far
  Outspread thy walls sublime !
The true thy chartered freemen are,
  Of every age and clime.

2 One holy Church, one army strong,
  One steadfast, high intent ;
One working band, one harvest-song,
  One King omnipotent.

3 How purely hath thy speech come
     down
  From man's primeval youth !
How grandly hath thine empire
     grown,
  Of freedom, love and truth !

4 How gleam thy watch-fires through
     the night
  With never-fainting ray !
How rise thy towers, serene and
     bright,
  To meet the dawning day !

5 In vain the surge's angry shock,
  In vain the drifting sands :
Unharmed upon the eternal Rock
  The eternal City stands.

     SAMUEL JOHNSON, 1822–82.

210 *From Psalm* cxxxvii.   S. M.

I LOVE Thy Kingdom, Lord,
  The house of Thine abode,
The Church our blest Redeemer
     saved
  With His own precious blood.

2 I love Thy Church, O God :
  Her walls before Thee stand,
Dear as the apple of Thine eye,
  And graven on Thy hand.

3 For her my tears shall fall,
  For her my prayers ascend,
To her my cares and toils be given,
  Till toils and cares shall end.

4 Beyond my highest joy
  I prize her heavenly ways,
Her sweet communion, solemn vows,
  Her hymns of love and praise.

5   Jesus, Thou Friend Divine,
      Our Saviour and our King,
   Thy hand from every snare and foe
      Shall great deliverance bring.

6   Sure as Thy truth shall last,
      To Zion shall be given
   The brightest glories earth can yield,
      And brighter bliss of heaven.
        TIMOTHY DWIGHT, 1752–1817.

211   87. 87. 887.

WE come unto our fathers' God ;
   Their Rock is our Salvation ;
The eternal arms, their dear abode,
  We make our habitation ;
We bring Thee, Lord, the praise they
    brought ;
We seek Thee as Thy saints have
    sought
   In every generation.

2 The fire divine their steps that led
   Still goeth bright before us ;
The heavenly shield around them
    spread
Is still high holden o'er us ;
The grace those sinners that sub-
    dued,
The strength those weaklings that
    renewed,
  Doth vanquish, doth restore us.

3 Their joy unto their Lord we bring ;
   Their song to us descendeth ;
The Spirit who in them did sing
   To us His music lendeth ;
His song in them, in us, is one ;
We raise it high, we send it on,—
   The song that never endeth.

4 Ye saints to come, take up the strain,
   The same sweet theme endeavour ;
Unbroken be the golden chain ,
   Keep on the song for ever ;
Safe in the same dear dwelling-place,
Rich with the same eternal grace,
   Bless the same boundless Giver.
        THOMAS HORNBLOWER GILL,
                 1819–1906.

212   Anapaestic irr.

FOR the might of Thine arm we
  bless Thee, our God, our fathers'
  God ;
Thou hast kept Thy pilgrim people
  by the strength of Thy staff and
  rod ;

Thou hast called us to the journey
  which faithless feet ne'er trod ;
For the might of Thine arm we bless
  Thee, our God, our fathers'
  God.

2 For the love of Christ constraining,
  that bound their hearts as
  one ;
For the faith in truth and freedom
  in which their work was done ;
For the peace of God's evangel
  wherewith their feet were shod ;
For the might of Thine arm we bless
  Thee, our God, our fathers'
  God.

3 We are watchers of a beacon whose
  light must never die ;
We are guardians of an altar that
  shows Thee ever nigh ;
We are children of Thy freemen who
  sleep beneath the sod ;
For the might of Thine arm we bless
  Thee, our God, our fathers'
  God.

4 May the shadow of Thy presence
  around our camp be spread ;
Baptize us with the courage Thou
  gavest to our dead ;
O keep us in the pathway their saintly
  feet have trod ;
For the might of Thine arm we bless
  Thee, our God, our fathers'
  God.

        CHARLES SILVESTER HORNE,
              1865–1914.

213   88. 84.

FATHER of all, from land and sea
  The nations sing, 'Thine, Lord,
  are we,
Countless in number, but in Thee
    May we be one.'

2 O Son of God, whose love so free
For men did make Thee Man to be,
United to our God, in Thee
    May we be one.

3 Join high with low, join young with
  old,
In love that never waxes cold ;
Under one Shepherd, in one fold,
    Make us all one.

THE CHURCH

4 O Spirit blest, who from above
Cam'st gently gliding like a dove,
Calm all our strife, give faith and love ;
    O make us one.

5 So, when the world shall pass away,
We shall awake with joy and say,
' Now in the bliss of endless day
    We all are one.'
            CHRISTOPHER WORDSWORTH,
                    1807–85.

214
87. 87.

THROUGH the night of doubt
    and sorrow
Onward goes the pilgrim band,
Singing songs of expectation,
Marching to the promised land.

2 Clear before us, through the darkness,
    Gleams and burns the guiding light ;
Brother clasps the hand of brother,
    Stepping fearless through the night ;

3 One the light of God's own presence,
    O'er His ransomed people shed,
Chasing far the gloom and terror,
    Brightening all the path we tread ;

4 One the object of our journey,
    One the faith which never tires,
One the earnest looking forward,
    One the hope our God inspires ;

5 One the strain that lips of thousands
    Lift as from the heart of one ;
One the conflict, one the peril,
    One the march in God begun ;

6 One the gladness of rejoicing
    On the far eternal shore,
Where the one Almighty Father
    Reigns in love for evermore.
BERNHARDT SEVERIN INGEMANN, 1789–
    1862 ; tr. by SABINE BARING-
    GOULD, 1834–1924.

215
76. 76. D.

THY hand, O God, has guided
    Thy flock, from age to age ;
The wondrous tale is written,
    Full clear, on every page ;

Our fathers owned Thy goodness,
    And we their deeds record ;
And both of this bear witness,
    One Church, one Faith, one Lord.

2 Thy heralds brought glad tidings
    To greatest, as to least ;
They bade men rise, and hasten
    To share the great King's feast ;
And this was all their teaching,
    In every deed and word,
To all alike proclaiming
    One Church, one Faith, one Lord.

3 Through many a day of darkness,
    Through many a scene of strife,
The faithful few fought bravely
    To guard the nation's life.
Their Gospel of redemption,
    Sin pardoned, man restored,
Was all in this enfolded,
    One Church, one Faith, one Lord.

4 Thy mercy will not fail us,
    Nor leave Thy work undone ;
With Thy right hand to help us,
    The victory shall be won ;
And then, by men and angels,
    Thy Name shall be adored,
And this shall be their anthem,
    One Church, one Faith, one Lord.
            EDWARD HAYES PLUMPTRE,
                    1821–91.

216
11 11. 11 5.

LORD of our life, and God of our salvation,
Star of our night, and Hope of every nation,
Hear and receive Thy Church's supplication,
    Lord God Almighty.

2 See round Thine ark the hungry billows curling ;
See how Thy foes their banners are unfurling ;
Lord, while their darts envenomed they are hurling,
    Thou canst preserve us.

3 Lord, Thou canst help when earthly armour faileth ;
Lord, Thou canst save when deadly sin assaileth ;
Lord, o'er Thy rock nor death nor hell prevaileth ;
    Grant us Thy peace, Lord.

4 Grant us Thy help till foes are backward driven;
Grant them Thy truth that they may be forgiven;
Grant peace on earth, and, after we have striven,
Peace in Thy heaven.

PHILIP PUSEY, 1799–1855; based on MATTHÄUS APELLES VON LÖWENSTERN, 1594–1648.

217

887. 887. D.

FEAR not, thou faithful Christian flock;
God is thy shelter and thy rock;
Fear not for thy salvation.
Though fierce the foe and dark the night,
The Lord of hosts shall be thy might,
Christ thine illumination.
Arise! Arise! thy foe defy!
Call on the Name of God most high,
With heavenly succour arm you!
'Gainst world and flesh and powers of hell,
Now for His honour quit you well.
Lo! there is nought can harm you.

2 From drear oblivion's shades ye came,
Through idol shrines of earthly shame,
From brutish terror savèd;
Ye, who the chains of tyrants broke,
Ye, who cast off the priestly yoke,
Ye shall not be enslavèd.
Arise! Arise! the foe defy!
Call on the Name of God most high,
That He with might endue you:
And Christ, your everlasting Priest,
In all your conflicts shall assist,
From strength to strength renew you.

Yattendon Hymnal, No. 72, 1899; based on JOHANN MICHAEL ALTENBURG, 1584–1640.

218

88. 84.

FOR those we love within the veil,
Who once were comrades of our way,
We thank Thee, Lord; for they have won
To cloudless day;

2 And life for them is life indeed,
The splendid goal of earth's strait race;
And where no shadows intervene
They see Thy face.

3 Not as we knew them any more,
Toilworn, and sad with burdened care,—
Erect, clear-eyed, upon their brows
Thy Name they bear.

4 Free from the fret of mortal years,
And knowing now Thy perfect will,
With quickened sense and heightened joy
They serve Thee still.

5 O fuller, sweeter is that life,
And larger, ampler is the air:
Eye cannot see nor heart conceive
The glory there;

6 Nor know to what high purpose Thou
Dost yet employ their ripened powers,
Nor how at Thy behest they touch
This life of ours.

7 There are no tears within their eyes;
With love they keep perpetual tryst;
And praise and work and rest are one,
With Thee, O Christ.

WILLIAM CHARTER PIGGOTT, 1872–1943.

219

88. 88. 88.

THE saints of God! their conflict past,
And life's long battle won at last,
No more they need the shield or sword;
They cast them down before their Lord:
O happy saints, for ever blest,
At Jesus' feet how safe your rest!

2 The saints of God! their wanderings done,
No more their weary course they run,
No more they faint, no more they fall,
No foes oppress, no fears appal:
O happy saints, for ever blest,
In that dear home how sweet your rest!

3 The saints of God! life's voyage o'er,
Safe landed on that blissful shore,
No stormy tempests now they dread,
No roaring billows lift their head:
O happy saints, for ever blest
In that calm haven of your rest!

4 O God of saints, to Thee we cry;
O Saviour, plead for us on high;
O Holy Ghost, our Guide and Friend,
Grant us Thy grace till life shall end,
That with all saints our rest may be,
In that bright Paradise with Thee.
WILLIAM DALRYMPLE MACLAGAN,
1826–1910.

220
10 10. 10 4.

FOR all the saints who from their labours rest,
Who Thee by faith before the world confessed,
Thy Name, O Jesus, be for ever blest.
Hallelujah!

2 Thou wast their Rock, their Fortress, and their Might;
Thou, Lord, their Captain in the well-fought fight;
Thou, in the darkness drear, their one true Light.
Hallelujah!

3 O may Thy soldiers, faithful, true, and bold,
Fight as the saints who nobly fought of old,
And win, with them, the victor's crown of gold.
Hallelujah!

4 O blest communion, fellowship divine!
We feebly struggle, they in glory shine;
Yet all are one in Thee, for all are Thine.
Hallelujah!

5 And when the strife is fierce, the warfare long,
Steals on the ear the distant triumph song,
And hearts are brave again, and arms are strong.
Hallelujah!

6 The golden evening brightens in the west;
Soon, soon to faithful warriors cometh rest;
Sweet is the calm of Paradise the blest.
Hallelujah!

7 But, lo! there breaks a yet more glorious day;
The saints triumphant rise in bright array;
The King of Glory passes on His way.
Hallelujah!

8 From earth's wide bounds, from ocean's farthest coast,
Through gates of pearl streams in the countless host,
Singing to Father, Son, and Holy Ghost,
'Hallelujah!'
WILLIAM WALSHAM HOW,
1823–97.

221
76. 86. D.

TEN thousand times ten thousand,
In sparkling raiment bright,
The armies of the ransomed saints
Throng up the steeps of light;
'Tis finished, all is finished,
Their fight with death and sin;
Fling open wide the golden gates,
And let the victors in.

2 What rush of hallelujahs
Fills all the earth and sky!
What ringing of a thousand harps
Bespeaks the triumph nigh!
O day for which creation
And all its tribes were made!
O joy, for all its former woes
A thousandfold repaid!

3 O then what raptured greetings
On Canaan's happy shore,
What knitting severed friendships up,
Where partings are no more!
Then eyes with joy shall sparkle
That brimmed with tears of late;
Orphans no longer fatherless,
Nor widows desolate.

4 Bring near Thy great salvation,
    Thou Lamb for sinners slain ;
Fill up the roll of Thine elect,
    Then take Thy power and reign;
    Appear, Desire of nations,—
        Thine exiles long for home ;
Show in the heaven Thy promised
        sign ;
    Thou Prince and Saviour, come.
        HENRY ALFORD, 1810–71.

222
                    87. 87. 77.

WHO are these, like stars appear-
     ing,
These, before God's throne who
     stand ?
Each a golden crown is wearing :
    Who are all this glorious band ?
      Alleluia ! hark, they sing,
      Praising loud their heavenly
        King.

2 Who are these, of dazzling bright-
     ness,
    These in God's own truth arrayed,
Clad in robes of purest whiteness,
    Robes whose lustre ne'er shall
     fade,
      Ne'er be touched by time's rude
       hand—
      Whence comes all this glorious
       band ?

3 These are they who have contended
For their Saviour's honour long,
Wrestling on till life was ended,
    Following not the sinful throng ;
    These, who well the fight sus-
     tained,
      Triumph through the Lamb have
       gained.

4 These are they whose hearts were
     riven,
Sore with woe and anguish tried,
Who in prayer full oft have striven
    With the God they glorified :
      Now, their painful conflict o'er,
      God has bid them weep no more.

5 These like priests have watched and
     waited,
    Offering up to Christ their will,
Soul and body consecrated,
    Day and night to serve Him still :
      Now in God's most holy place,
      Blest they stand before His face.

HEINRICH THEOBALD SCHENCK, 1656–
    1727 ; tr. by FRANCES ELIZABETH
    COX, 1812–97.

223 *From Rev.* vii. 13–17.   D. C. M.

HOW bright these glorious spirits
    shine !
    Whence all their white array ?
How came they to the blissful seats
    Of everlasting day ?

2 Lo ! these are they, from sufferings
    great
    Who came to realms of light,
And in the blood of Christ have
    washed
    Those robes which shine so bright.

3 Now, with triumphal palms, they
    stand
    Before the throne on high,
And serve the God they love, amidst
    The glories of the sky.

4 His presence fills each heart with joy,
    Tunes every mouth to sing :
By day, by night, the sacred courts
    With glad hosannas ring.

5 Hunger and thirst are felt no more,
    Nor suns with scorching ray ;
God is their sun, whose cheering
    beams
    Diffuse eternal day.

6 The Lamb which dwells amidst the
    throne
    Shall o'er them still preside :
Feed them with nourishment divine,
    And all their footsteps guide.

7 'Mong pastures green He'll lead His
    flock,
    Where living streams appear ;
And God the Lord from every eye
    Shall wipe off every tear.

ISAAC WATTS, 1674–1748, and WILLIAM
    CAMERON (?), 1751–1811, as in
    Scottish Paraphrases, 1781.

224
             10. 10. 10. 10. Dactylic.

O WHAT their joy and their glory
    must be,
Those endless Sabbaths the blessèd
    ones see !
Crown for the valiant ; to weary ones
    rest ;
God shall be all; and in all ever blest.

2 What are the Monarch, His court,
    and His throne ?
What are the peace and the joy that
    they own ?

Tell us, ye blest ones, that in it have
   share,
If what ye feel ye can fully declare.

3 Truly Jerusalem name we that shore,
  'Vision of peace,' that brings joy
    evermore !
Wish and fulfilment can severed be
   ne'er,
  Nor the thing prayed for come short
    of the prayer.

4 We, where no trouble distraction can
   bring,
Safely the anthems of Zion shall sing;
While for Thy grace, Lord, their
    voices of praise
  Thy blessèd people shall evermore
    raise.

5 Low before Him with our praises
   we fall,
Of whom, and in whom, and through
    whom are all ;
Of whom, the Father ; and through
    whom, the Son ;
In whom, the Spirit, with these ever
    One.

    PIERRE ABELARD, 1079–1142 ; tr. by
      JOHN MASON NEALE, 1818–66.

225
                            L. M.

HE wants not friends that hath
  Thy love,
  And may converse and walk with
    Thee,
And with Thy saints here and above,
  With whom for ever I must be.

2 In the communion of the saints
  Is wisdom, safety and delight ;
And, when my heart declines and
    faints,
  It 's raisèd by their heat and light !

3 As for my friends, they are not lost ;
  The several vessels of Thy fleet,
Though parted now, by tempests tost,
  Shall safely in the haven meet.

4 Still we are centred all in Thee,
  Members, though distant, of one
    Head ;
In the same family we be,
  By the same faith and spirit led.

5 Before Thy throne we daily meet,
  As joint-petitioners to Thee ;
In spirit we each other greet,
  And shall again each other see.

6 The heavenly hosts, world without
   end,
  Shall be my company above ;
And Thou, my best and surest
    Friend,
  Who shall divide me from Thy
    love ?

         RICHARD BAXTER, 1615–91.

226
                       2. 88. 88. 8.

O BLEST
   Communion with the saints at
   rest !
O joy excelling this world's best !
All undistressed
   In light they dwell !
Close is the bond that binds us here :
'Twill grow more dear
   Than, tongue can tell.

2 Our Lord,
From out His sacred wounds hath
   poured
Rich blessings from His bounteous
   hoard.
He doth afford
   Us from above
Refreshing streams our souls to guide
To His full tide
   Of boundless love.

3 Delight
Hath dawned on those gone from
   earth's night :
Death was to them but life and light :
In pastures bright
   Serene they rest,
Around the Lamb who once was
   slain,
Untouched by pain,
   For ever blest.

    JOHN ROBERTS, 1731–1806; tr. by
    EVELINE MARTHA LEWIS, b. 1871.

227
                           C. M.

LET saints on earth in concert sing
  With those whose work is done ;
For all the servants of our King
  In earth and heaven are one.

THE COMMUNION OF SAINTS

2 One family, we dwell in Him,
  One Church, above, beneath ;
Though now divided by the stream,
  The narrow stream of death.

3 One army of the living God,
  To His command we bow ;
Part of His host hath crossed the
  flood,
  And part is crossing now.

4 Even now to their eternal home
  There pass some spirits blest,
While others to the margin come,
  Waiting their call to rest.

5 Jesus, be Thou our constant Guide ;
  Then, when the word is given,
Bid Jordan's narrow stream divide,
  And bring us safe to heaven.
        CHARLES WESLEY, 1707-88.

WORSHIP

THE SANCTUARY

228 *From Psalm cxvii.*
            88. 88. and Hallelujahs.

FROM all that dwell below the
  skies
Let the Creator's praise arise :
        Hallelujah !
Let the Redeemer's Name be sung
Through every land, in every tongue.
        Hallelujah !

2 Eternal are Thy mercies, Lord :
Eternal truth attends Thy word :
        Hallelujah !
Thy praise shall sound from shore
  to shore
Till suns shall rise and set no more.
        Hallelujah !
        ISAAC WATTS, 1674-1748.

229 *From Psalm c.*   L. M.

ALL people that on earth do dwell,
  Sing to the Lord with cheerful
  voice.
Him serve with mirth, His praise
  forth tell ;
Come ye before Him and rejoice.

2 Know that the Lord is God indeed ;
  Without our aid He did us make ;
We are His folk, He doth us feed,
  And for His sheep He doth us take.

3 O enter then His gates with praise,
  Approach with joy His courts
  unto ;
Praise, laud, and bless His Name
  always,
  For it is seemly so to do.

4 For why the Lord our God is good ;
  His mercy is for ever sure ;
His truth at all times firmly stood,
  And shall from age to age endure.
        WILLIAM KETHE, c. 1593, as in
              Scottish Psalter, 1650.

230 *From Psalm c.*   L. M.

BEFORE Jehovah's awful throne,
  Ye nations, bow with sacred joy ;
Know that the Lord is God alone ;
  He can create, and He destroy.

2 His sovereign power, without our aid,
  Made us of clay, and formed us
  men ;
And, when like wandering sheep we
  strayed,
  He brought us to His fold again.

3 We are His people, we His care,—
  Our souls and all our mortal frame :
What lasting honours shall we rear,
  Almighty Maker, to Thy Name ?

4 We'll crowd Thy gates with thankful
  songs,
  High as the heavens our voices
  raise ;
And earth, with her ten thousand
  tongues,
  Shall fill Thy courts with sounding
  praise.

5 Wide as the world is Thy command,
  Vast as eternity Thy love ;
Firm as a rock Thy truth must stand,
  When rolling years shall cease to
  move.
        ISAAC WATTS, 1674-1748, and
              JOHN WESLEY, 1703-91.

THE CHURCH

231 *From Psalms* c, xxiii, &c.
87. 87. 66. 667.

ALL lands and peoples, all the
earth,
Put off the night of sadness;
Make cheer and music and high
mirth,
And praise the Lord with gladness!
    Serve Him with joyful heart,
    All kingdoms do their part,
    And let immortal song
    Before His presence throng,
    For ever and for ever!

2 O surely He is God alone,
The earth is mute before Him:
And He is ours, and we His own,
His people who adore Him.
    We are His flock; our feet
    Walk in His pastures sweet;
    And, by cool brooks, the sleep
    Is soft He gives His sheep,
    For ever and for ever!

3 O enter then His temple courts
With trumpet-tongued thanks-
giving:
Praise Him in dances and in sports,
Our Lord, the ever-living!
    With incense to the skies
    Our thankfulness arise;
    His glory wide proclaim,
    Speak good of His great
    Name,
    For ever and for ever!

4 For gracious is the Lord our God:
He hears our dull complaining;
His mercy has a sure abode
And everlasting reigning;
    And times and times roll by,
    And nations fade and die;
    But God's majestic truth
    Leads on an eager youth,
    For ever and for ever.

STOPFORD AUGUSTUS BROOKE,
1832–1916.

232
12 10. 12 10.

WORSHIP the Lord in the beauty
of holiness;
Bow down before Him, His glory
proclaim;
Gold of obedience and incense of lowliness
Bring, and adore Him; the Lord
is His Name!

2 Low at His feet lay thy burden of
carefulness;
    High on His heart He will bear it
    for thee,
Comfort thy sorrows, and answer thy
prayerfulness,
    Guiding thy steps as may best for
    thee be.

3 Fear not to enter His courts, in the
slenderness
    Of the poor wealth thou canst
    reckon as thine;
Truth in its beauty and love in its
tenderness,
    These are the offerings to lay on
    His shrine.

4 These, though we bring them in
trembling and fearfulness,
    He will accept for the Name that
    is dear,
Mornings of joy give for evenings of
tearfulness,
    Trust for our trembling, and hope
    for our fear.

5 Worship the Lord in the beauty of
holiness;
    Bow down before Him, His glory
    proclaim;
Gold of obedience and incense of
lowliness
    Bring, and adore Him; the Lord
    is His Name!

JOHN SAMUEL BEWLEY MONSELL,
1811–75.

233
S. M.

STAND up, and bless the Lord,
Ye people of His choice;
Stand up, and bless the Lord your
God
    With heart and soul and voice.

2 Though high above all praise,
Above all blessing high,
Who would not fear His holy Name,
    And laud and magnify?

3 O for the living flame
From His own altar brought,
To touch our lips, our minds inspire,
    And wing to heaven our thought!

4 God is our strength and song,
And His salvation ours;
Then be His love in Christ pro-
claimed
    With all our ransomed powers.

76

5   Stand up, and bless the Lord ;
The Lord your God adore ;
Stand up, and bless His glorious Name
Henceforth for evermore.
      JAMES MONTGOMERY, 1771–1854.

234   668. 668. 33. 66.

GOD reveals His presence :
  Let us now adore Him,
And with awe appear before Him.
God is in His temple :
  All within keep silence,
Prostrate lie with deepest reverence.
    Him alone
      God we own,
  Him our God and Saviour :
  Praise His Name for ever.

2   God reveals His presence :
    Hear the harps resounding,
See the crowds the throne surround-ing ;
  Holy, holy, holy !
    Hear the hymn ascending,
Angels, saints, their voices blending.
    Bow Thine ear
      To us here ;
  Hearken, O Lord Jesus,
  To our meaner praises.

3   O Thou Fount of blessing,
    Purify my spirit,
Trusting only in Thy merit :
  Like the holy angels
    Who behold Thy glory,
May I ceaselessly adore Thee.
    Let Thy will
      Ever still
  Rule Thy Church terrestrial,
  As the hosts celestial.

GERHARD TERSTEEGEN, 1697–1769; tr.
  by FREDERICK WILLIAM FOSTER,
  1760–1835; JOHN MILLER, 1756–
  90; WILLIAM MERCER, 1811–73.

235   *From Psalm lxxxiv.*   77. 77. D.

PLEASANT are Thy courts above,
  In the land of light and love
Pleasant are Thy courts below,
  In this land of sin and woe.
O my spirit longs and faints
For the converse of Thy saints,
For the brightness of Thy face,
King of glory, God of grace !

2   Happy birds that sing and fly
Round Thy altars, O Most High !
Happier souls that find a rest
In a heavenly Father's breast !
Like the wandering dove that found
No repose on earth around,
They can to their ark repair,
And enjoy it ever there.

3   Happy souls ! their praises flow
Even in this vale of woe ;
Waters in the desert rise,
Manna feeds them from the skies ;
On they go from strength to strength,
Till they reach Thy throne at length,
At Thy feet adoring fall,
Who hast led them safe through all.

4   Lord, be mine this prize to win :
Guide me through a world of sin ;
Keep me by Thy saving grace ;
Give me at Thy side a place.
Sun and shield alike Thou art ;
Guide and guard my erring heart.
Grace and glory flow from Thee ;
Shower, O shower them, Lord, on me.

      HENRY FRANCIS LYTE,
        1793–1847.

236   66. 66.

WE love the place, O God,
  Wherein Thine honour dwells ;
The joy of Thine abode
  All earthly joy excels.

2   It is the house of prayer,
    Wherein Thy servants meet ;
And Thou, O Lord, art there,
    Thy chosen flock to greet.

3   We love the word of life,
    The word that tells of peace,
Of comfort in the strife,
    And joys that never cease.

4   We love to sing below
    For mercies freely given ;
But O we long to know
    The triumph song of heaven !

5   Lord Jesus, give us grace,
    On earth to love Thee more,
In heaven to see Thy face,
    And with Thy saints adore.
      WILLIAM BULLOCK, 1798–1874,
      and HENRY WILLIAMS BAKER,
          1821–77.

THE CHURCH

237
76. 76. D. and refrain.

AGAIN the morn of gladness,
　The morn of light, is here,
And earth itself looks fairer,
　And heaven itself more near :
The bells, like angel voices,
　Speak peace to every breast ;
And all the land lies quiet,
　To keep the day of rest.
　　' *Glory be to Jesus !* '
　　　Let all His children say ;
　　' *He rose again, He rose again,*
　　　On this glad day ! '

2 Again, O loving Saviour,
　The children of Thy grace
Prepare themselves to seek Thee
　Within Thy chosen place.
Our song shall rise to greet Thee,
　If Thou our hearts wilt raise ;
If Thou our lips wilt open,
　Our mouth shall show Thy praise.

3 The shining choir of angels
　That rest not day or night,
The crowned and palm - decked
　　martyrs,
The saints arrayed in white,
The happy lambs of Jesus
　In pastures fair above,—
These all adore and praise Him
　Whom we too praise and love.

4 The Church on earth rejoices
　To join with these to-day ;
In every tongue and nation
　She calls her sons to pray ;
Across the Northern snow-fields,
　Beneath the Indian palms,
She makes the same pure offering,
　And sings the same sweet psalms.

5 Tell out, sweet bells, His praises !
　Sing, children, sing His Name !
Still louder and still farther
　His mighty deeds proclaim,
Till all whom He redeemèd
　Shall own Him Lord and King,
Till every knee shall worship,
　And every tongue shall sing.
　　' *Glory be to Jesus !* '
　　　Let all creation say ;
　　' *He rose again, He rose again*
　　　On this glad day ! '

JOHN ELLERTON, 1826–93.

238
77. 77.

LORD, this day Thy children meet
　In Thy courts with willing feet ;
Unto Thee this day they raise
Grateful hearts in hymns of praise.

2 Not alone the day of rest
With Thy worship shall be blest ;
In our pleasure and our glee,
Lord, we would remember Thee.

3 Help us unto Thee to pray,
Hallowing our happy day,
From Thy presence thus to win
Hearts all pure and free from sin.

4 All our pleasures here below,
Saviour, from Thy mercy flow :
Little children Thou dost love ;
Draw our hearts to Thee above.

5 Make, O Lord, our childhood shine
With all lowly grace, like Thine ;
Then through all eternity
We shall live in heaven with Thee.
　　WILLIAM WALSHAM HOW, 1823–97.

239
From Psalm cxxii.　L. M.

SWEET is the solemn voice that
　calls
　The Christian to the house of
　　prayer ;
I love to stand within its walls,
　For Thou, O Lord, art present
　　there.

2 I love to tread the hallowed courts
　Where two or three for worship
　　meet,
For thither Christ Himself resorts,
　And makes the little band com-
　　plete.

3 'Tis sweet to raise the common song,
　To join in holy praise and love,
And imitate the blessèd throng
　That mingle hearts and songs
　　above.

4 Within these walls may peace abound ;
　May all our hearts in one agree ;
Where brethren meet, where Christ
　　is found,
May peace and concord ever be.
　　HENRY FRANCIS LYTE,
　　　1793–1847.

78

240 77. 75.

GOD of pity, God of grace,
  When we humbly seek Thy face,
Bend from heaven, Thy dwelling-
    place ;
  Hear, forgive, and save.

2 When we in Thy temple meet,
  Spread our wants before Thy feet,
Pleading at Thy mercy-seat,
  Look from heaven and save.

3 When Thy love our hearts shall fill,
  And we long to do Thy will,
Turning to Thy holy hill,
  Lord, accept and save.

4 Should we wander from Thy fold,
  And our love to Thee grow cold,
With a pitying eye behold ;
  Lord, forgive and save.

5 Should the hand of sorrow press,
  Earthly care and want distress,
May our souls Thy peace possess ;
  Jesus, hear and save.

6 And, whate'er our cry may be,
  When we lift our hearts to Thee,
From our burden set us free ;
  Hear, forgive, and save.
        ELIZA FANNY MORRIS, 1821–74

241 L. M.

COMMAND Thy blessing from
  above,
O God, on all assembled here ;
Behold us with a Father's love,
  While we look up with filial fear.

2 Command Thy blessing, Jesus, Lord ;
  May we Thy true disciples be ;
Speak to each heart the mighty word ;
  Say to the weakest, 'Follow Me.'

3 Command Thy blessing in this hour,
  Spirit of truth, and fill this place
With humbling and exalting power,
  With quickening and confirming
    grace.

4 O Thou, our Maker, Saviour, Guide,
  One true eternal God confessed,
May nought in life or death divide
  The saints in Thy communion
    blest.

5 With Thee and these for ever bound,
  May all who here in prayer unite,
With harps and songs Thy throne
    surround,
  Rest in Thy love, and reign in
    light.
        JAMES MONTGOMERY,
          1771–1854.

242 C. M.

BEHOLD us, Lord, a little space
  From daily tasks set free,
And met within Thy holy place
  To rest awhile with Thee.

2 Around us rolls the ceaseless tide
  Of business, toil, and care,
And scarcely can we turn aside
  For one brief hour of prayer.

3 Yet these are not the only walls
  Wherein Thou mayst be sought ;
On homeliest work Thy blessing falls,
  In truth and patience wrought.

4 Thine is the loom, the forge, the
    mart,
  The wealth of land and sea,
The worlds of science and of art,
  Revealed and ruled by Thee.

5 Then let us prove our heavenly birth
  In all we do and know,
And claim the kingdom of the earth
  For Thee, and not Thy foe.

6 Work shall be prayer, if all be
    wrought
  As Thou wouldst have it done,
And prayer, by Thee inspired and
    taught,
  Itself with work be one.
        JOHN ELLERTON, 1826–93.

243 10. 10. 10. 10.

FATHER, again in Jesus' Name we
    meet,
And bow in penitence before Thy
    feet ;
Again to Thee our feeble voices raise,
To sue for mercy, and to sing Thy
    praise.

2 O we would bless Thee for Thy
    ceaseless care,
And all Thy work from day to day
    declare ;
Is not our life with hourly mercies
    crowned ?
Does not Thine arm encircle us
    around ?

3 Alas ! unworthy of Thy boundless
    love,
  Too oft our feet from Thee, our
    Father, rove ;
  But now, encouraged by Thy voice,
    we come,
  Returning sinners, to a Father's
    home.

4 O by that Name in whom all fulness
    dwells,
  O by that love which every love
    excels,
  O by that blood so freely shed for sin,
  Open blest mercy's gate, and take
    us in !

        LUCY ELIZABETH GEORGINA
          WHITMORE, 1792–1840.

244
                  87. 87.

O BE with us, gracious Father,
   While before Thy feet we bow ;
Let thy presence
  Hover o'er Thy temple now.

2 Here are hearts that Thou canst
    soften,
  Earthly dross to purge away ;
  Darkened minds, on which Thy
    Spirit
  Yet may pour celestial day.

3 From the world's entrancing vision,
  From the spirit's sullen night,
  From the tempter's dark dominion,
  Free us, by Thy saving might.

4 Let Thy Spirit's glad communion
  Waken thoughts of peace and love,
  And prepare us for Thy presence
  In the nobler courts above.

5 There to join in perfect worship,
  There to swell the angels' song,
  And in higher, sweeter measure,
  Earth's imperfect praise prolong.

        ALFRED ROOKER, 1814–75.

245
               86. 886.

D EAR Lord and Father of man-
   kind,
  Forgive our foolish ways ;
Reclothe us in our rightful mind ;
  In purer lives Thy service find,
    In deeper reverence, praise.

2 In simple trust like theirs who heard,
  Beside the Syrian sea,
The gracious calling of the Lord,
  Let us, like them, without a word
    Rise up and follow Thee.

3 O Sabbath rest by Galilee !
  O calm of hills above,
Where Jesus knelt to share with
   Thee
  The silence of eternity,
    Interpreted by love !

4 With that deep hush subduing all
  Our words and works that drown
The tender whisper of Thy call,
  As noiseless let Thy blessing fall
    As fell Thy manna down.

5 Drop Thy still dews of quietness,
  Till all our strivings cease ;
Take from our souls the strain and
   stress,
  And let our ordered lives confess
    The beauty of Thy peace.

6 Breathe through the heats of our
   desire
  Thy coolness and Thy balm ;
Let sense be dumb, let flesh retire ;
  Speak through the earthquake, wind,
   and fire,
    O still small voice of calm !

        JOHN GREENLEAF WHITTIER,
                1807–92.

246
                  C. M.

D EAR Shepherd of Thy people,
   hear ;
  Thy presence now display ;
As Thou hast given a place for
   prayer,
  So give us hearts to pray.

2 Within these walls let holy peace
  And love and concord dwell ;
Here give the troubled conscience
   ease,
  The wounded spirit heal.

3 May we in faith receive Thy word,
  In faith present our prayers,
And in the presence of our Lord
  Unbosom all our cares.

4 The hearing ear, the seeing eye,
  The humbled mind bestow ;
And shine upon us from on high,
  To make our graces grow.

       JOHN NEWTON, 1725–1807.

247   L. M.

JESUS, where'er Thy people meet,
  There they behold Thy mercy-
    seat;
Where'er they seek Thee Thou art
    found,
And every place is hallowed ground.

2 For Thou, within no walls confined,
  Inhabitest the humble mind;
Such ever bring Thee where they
    come,
And, going, take Thee to their home.

3 Dear Shepherd of Thy chosen few,
  Thy former mercies here renew;
Here to our waiting hearts proclaim
  The sweetness of Thy saving Name.

4 Here may we prove the power of
    prayer
To strengthen faith and sweeten care,
To teach our faint desires to rise,
And bring all heaven before our eyes.

5 Lord, we are few, but Thou art near,
  Nor short Thine arm, nor deaf Thine
    ear,
O rend the heavens, come quickly
    down,
And make a thousand hearts Thine
    own.
        WILLIAM COWPER, 1731–1800.

248   65. 65.

JESUS, stand among us
  In Thy risen power;
Let this time of worship
  Be a hallowed hour.

2 Breathe the Holy Spirit
  Into every heart;
Bid the fears and sorrows
  From each soul depart.

3 Thus with quickened footsteps
  We pursue our way,
Watching for the dawning
  Of eternal day.
        WILLIAM PENNEFATHER,
                  1816–73.

249   S. M.

LIGHT of the anxious heart,
  Jesus, Thou dost appear,
To bid the gloom of guilt depart,
  And shed Thy sweetness here.

2 Joyous is he with whom,
  God's Word, Thou dost abide,
Sweet Light of our eternal home,
  To fleshly sense denied.

3 Brightness of God above,
  Unfathomable grace,
Thy presence be a fount of love
  Within Thy chosen place.

Attributed to ST. BERNARD OF CLAIR-
    VAUX, 1091–1153; *tr.* by JOHN
    HENRY NEWMAN, 1801–90.

250   84. 86. D.

ENTER Thy courts, Thou Word
  of life,
  My joy and peace;
Let the glad sound therein be heard,
  Bid plaintive sadness cease.
Comfort my heart, Thou Truth most
    fair;
  O enter in,
Chasing despair and earthborn care,
  My woe and slothful sin.

2 Glad was the time when I would sing
    Thy heavenly praise;
Happy my heart when Thou wert
    nigh,
  Directing all my ways.
O let Thy light, Thy joy again
  Return to me
Nor in disdain from me refrain,
  Who lift my soul to Thee.

3 In heaven and earth Thy law endures,
    Thy word abides:
My troubled flesh trembleth in awe,
  My heart in terror hides.
Yet still on Thee my hope is set;
  On Thee, O Lord,
I will await and not forget
  The promise of Thy word.
      Yattendon Hymnal, No. 98, 1899.

251   66. 66. 88.

HUSHED was the evening
  hymn,
  The temple courts were dark,
The lamp was burning dim
  Before the sacred ark,
When suddenly a voice Divine
Rang through the silence of the
    shrine.

THE CHURCH

2 The old man, meek and mild,
      The priest of Israel, slept ;
   His watch the temple child,
      The little Levite, kept ;
And what from Eli's sense was sealed
The Lord to Hannah's son revealed.

3 O give me Samuel's ear,
      The open ear, O Lord,
   Alive and quick to hear
      Each whisper of Thy word,—
Like him to answer at Thy call,
And to obey Thee first of all.

4 O give me Samuel's heart,
      A lowly heart, that waits
   Where in Thy house Thou art,
      Or watches at Thy gates
By day and night,—a heart that still
Moves at the breathing of Thy will.

5 O give me Samuel's mind,
      A sweet unmurmuring faith,
   Obedient and resigned
      To Thee in life and death,
That I may read, with childlike eyes,
Truths that are hidden from the wise.

                    JAMES DRUMMOND BURNS,
                              1823–64.

252

                              85. 85. 84. 3.

ANGEL voices, ever singing
      Round Thy throne of light,
Angel harps, for ever ringing,
      Rest not day nor night ;
Thousands only live to bless Thee,
      And confess Thee
            Lord of might.

2 Yea, we know that Thou rejoicest
      O'er each work of Thine ;
Thou didst ears and hands and voices
      For Thy praise design ;
Craftsman's art and music's measure
      For Thy pleasure
            All combine.

3 In Thy house, great God, we offer
      Of Thine own to Thee,
And for Thine acceptance proffer,
      All unworthily,
Hearts and minds and hands and
            voices,
      In our choicest
            Psalmody.

4 Honour, glory, might, and merit
      Thine shall ever be,
Father, Son, and Holy Spirit,
      Blessèd Trinity.
Of the best that Thou hast given,
      Earth and heaven
            Render Thee.

                    FRANCIS POTT, 1832–1909.

253   Laying foundation-stone
              of a Church.   L. M.

THIS stone to Thee in faith we lay ;
   We build the temple, Lord, to
            Thee :
Thine eye be open, night and day,
   To guard this house and sanctuary.

2 Here, when Thy people seek Thy
            face,
   And dying sinners pray to live,
Hear Thou, in heaven Thy dwelling-
            place,
   And when Thou hearest, O for-
            give !

3 Here, when Thy messengers proclaim
   The blessèd Gospel of Thy Son,
Still, by the power of His great Name,
   Be mighty signs and wonders done.

4 ' Hosanna ! ' to their heavenly King
      When children's voices raise that
            song,
   ' Hosanna ! ' let their angels sing,
   And heaven, with earth, the strain
            prolong.

5 But will indeed Jehovah deign
      Here to abide, no transient guest ?
   Here will the world's Redeemer
            reign,
   And here the Holy Spirit rest ?

6 That glory never hence depart !
      Yet choose not, Lord, this house
            alone ;
   Thy Kingdom come to every heart :
   In every bosom fix Thy throne.

                    JAMES MONTGOMERY,
                              1771–1854.

254   Dedication of a Church.   L. M.

ALL things are Thine ; no gift
      have we,
Lord of all gifts, to offer Thee :
And hence with grateful hearts to-
            day,
Thine own before Thy feet we lay.

82

WORSHIP—THE SANCTUARY

2 Thy will was in the builders'
    thought;
Thy hand unseen amidst us wrought;
Through mortal motive, scheme and
    plan,
Thy wise eternal purpose ran.

3 In weakness and in want we call
On Thee for whom the heavens are
    small;
Thy glory is Thy children's good,
Thy 'oy Thy tender Fatherhood.

4 O Father, deign these walls to bless;
Fill with Thy love their emptiness;
And let their door a gateway be
To lead us from ourselves to Thee.

JOHN GREENLEAF WHITTIER,
1807–92.

255
75. 75. 75. 75. 88.

WHEN the weary, seeking rest,
    To Thy goodness flee;
When the heavy-laden cast
    All their load on Thee;
When the troubled, seeking peace,
    On Thy Name shall call;
When the sinner, seeking life,
    At Thy feet shall fall;
Hear then in love, O Lord, the cry,
In heaven, Thy dwelling-place on
    high.

2 When the child, with grave fresh
    lip,
    Youth, or maiden fair,
When the agèd, weak and grey,
    Seek Thy face in prayer;
When the widow weeps to Thee,
    Sad and lone and low;
When the orphan brings to Thee
    All his orphan woe;
Hear then in love, O Lord, the cry,
In heaven, Thy dwelling-place on
    high.

3 When the stranger asks a home,
    All his toils to end;
When the hungry craveth food,
    And the poor a friend;
When the sailor on the wave
    Bows the fervent knee;
When the soldier on the field
    Lifts his heart to Thee;
Hear then in love, O Lord, the cry,
In heaven, Thy dwelling-place on
    high.

4 When the man of toil and care,
    In the city crowd,
When the shepherd on the moor,
    Names the Name of God;
When the learnèd and the high,
    Tired of earthly fame,
Upon higher joys intent,
    Name the blessèd Name;
Hear then in love, O Lord, the cry,
In heaven, Thy dwelling-place on
    high.

5 When the worldling, sick at heart,
    Lifts his soul above;
When the prodigal looks back
    To his Father's love;
When the proud man from his
    pride
    Stoops to seek Thy face;
When the burdened brings his
    guilt
    To Thy throne of grace;
Hear then in love, O Lord, the cry,
In heaven, Thy dwelling-place on
    high.

HORATIUS BONAR, 1808–80.

MORNING

256
L. M.

AWAKE, my soul, and with the
    sun
Thy daily stage of duty run;
Shake off dull sloth, and joyful rise,
To pay thy morning sacrifice.

2 Thy precious time misspent redeem;
Each present day thy last esteem;
Improve thy talent with due care;
For the great day thyself prepare.

3 In conversation be sincere;
Keep conscience as the noontide
    clear;
Think how all-seeing God thy ways
And all thy secret thoughts surveys.

4 Wake, and lift up thyself, my heart,
And with the angels bear thy part,
Who all night long unwearied sing
High praise to the eternal King.

5 I wake, I wake, ye heavenly choir!
May your devotion me inspire,
That I, like you, my age may spend,
Like you, may on my God attend.

THE CHURCH

6 Praise God, from whom all blessings
    flow;
  Praise Him, all creatures here below;
  Praise Him above, ye heavenly host;
  Praise Father, Son, and Holy Ghost.
            THOMAS KEN, 1637–1711.

257
                                    L. M.

ALL praise to Thee who safe hast
    kept,
And hast refreshed me while I slept!
Grant, Lord, when I from death
    shall wake,
I may of endless light partake.

2 Lord, I my vows to Thee renew;
  Disperse my sins as morning dew;
  Guard my first springs of thought
      and will,
  And with Thyself my spirit fill.

3 Direct, control, suggest, this day,
  All I design, or do, or say,
  That all my powers, with all their
      might,
  In Thy sole glory may unite.

4 Praise God, from whom all blessings
    flow;
  Praise Him, all creatures here below;
  Praise Him above, ye heavenly host;
  Praise Father, Son, and Holy Ghost.
            THOMAS KEN, 1637–1711.

258
                                    L. M.

NOW that the daylight fills the sky,
    We lift our hearts to God on high,
That He, in all we do or say,
  Would keep us free from harm
      to-day:

2 Would guard our hearts and tongues
      from strife,
  From anger's din would hide our life,
  From all ill sights would turn our
      eyes,
  Would close our ears from vanities:

3 Would keep our inmost conscience
      pure,
  Our souls from folly would secure,
  Would bid us check the pride of
      sense
  With due and holy abstinence.

4 So we, when this new day is gone
  And night in turn is drawing on,
  With conscience by the world un-
      stained,
  Shall praise His Name for victory
      gained.

            8th century; tr. by
      JOHN MASON NEALE, 1818–66.

259
                                    L. M.

O TIMELY happy, timely wise,
    Hearts that with rising morn
      arise,
Eyes that the beam celestial view
  Which evermore makes all things
      new!

2 New every morning is the love
  Our wakening and our uprising prove,
  Through sleep and darkness safely
      brought,
  Restored to life, and power, and
      thought.

3 New mercies, each returning day,
  Hover around us while we pray,—
  New perils past, new sins forgiven,
  New thoughts of God, new hopes of
      heaven.

4 If, on our daily course, our mind
  Be set to hallow all we find,
  New treasures still, of countless price,
  God will provide for sacrifice.

5 We need not bid, for cloistered cell,
  Our neighbour and our work farewell,
  Nor strive to wind ourselves too high
  For sinful man beneath the sky;

6 The trivial round, the common task,
  Will furnish all we ought to ask,—
  Room to deny ourselves, a road
  To bring us daily nearer God.

7 Seek we no more; content with
      these,
  Let present rapture, comfort, ease,
  As Heaven shall bid them, come and
      go:
  The secret this of rest below.

8 Only, O Lord, in Thy dear love,
  Fit us for perfect rest above;
  And help us, this and every day,
  To live more nearly as we pray.
            JOHN KEBLE, 1792–1866.

84

260
C. M.

NOW that the daystar glimmers bright,
  We suppliantly pray
That He, the uncreated Light,
  May guide us on our way.

2 No sinful word, nor deed of wrong,
  Nor thoughts that idly rove,
But simple truth be on our tongue,
  And in our hearts be love.

3 And while the hours in order flow,
  O Christ, securely fence
Our gates, beleaguered by the foe,—
  The gate of every sense.

4 And grant that to Thine honour, Lord,
  Our daily toil may tend:
That we begin it at Thy word,
  And in Thy blessing end.

8th century; *tr.* by
JOHN HENRY NEWMAN, 1801–90.

261
77. 77. 77.

CHRIST, whose glory fills the skies,
  Christ, the true, the only Light,
Sun of Righteousness, arise,
  Triumph o'er the shades of night.
Dayspring from on high, be near;
Daystar, in my heart appear.

2 Dark and cheerless is the morn
  Unaccompanied by Thee;
Joyless is the day's return,
  Till Thy mercy's beams I see,
Till they inward light impart,
Glad my eyes, and warm my heart.

3 Visit, then, this soul of mine,
  Pierce the gloom of sin and grief;
Fill me, Radiancy Divine,
  Scatter all my unbelief;
More and more Thyself display,
Shining to the perfect day.

CHARLES WESLEY, 1707–88.

262
77. 77. 73.

JESUS, Sun of Righteousness,
  Brightest Beam of love divine,
With the early morning rays
  Do Thou on our darkness shine,
And dispel with purest light
  All our night.

2 As on drooping herb and flower
  Falls the soft, refreshing dew,
Let Thy Spirit's grace and power
  All our weary souls renew,
Showers of blessing over all
  Softly fall.

3 Like the sun's reviving ray,
  May Thy love, with tender glow,
All our coldness melt away,
  Warm and cheer us forth to go,
Gladly serve Thee and obey,
  All the day.

4 O, our only Hope and Guide,
  Never leave us nor forsake;
Keep us ever at Thy side
  Till the eternal morning break,
Moving on to Zion hill,
  Homeward still.

5 Lead us all our days and years
  In Thy straight and narrow way;
Lead us through the vale of tears
  To the land of perfect day,
Where Thy people, fully blest,
  Safely rest.

CHRISTIAN KNORR VON ROSENROTH,
1636–89; *tr.* by JANE LAURIE
BORTHWICK, 1813–97.

263
11 11. 11 5.

FATHER, we praise Thee, now the night is over;
Active and watchful, stand we all before Thee;
Singing, we offer prayer and meditation:
    Thus we adore Thee.

2 Monarch of all things, fit us for Thy mansions;
Banish our weakness, health and wholeness sending;
Bring us to heaven, where Thy saints united
    Joy without ending.

3 All-holy Father, Son and equal Spirit,
Trinity blessèd, send us Thy salvation;
Thine is the glory, gleaming and resounding
    Through all creation.

Attributed to ST. GREGORY THE GREAT,
540–604; *tr.* by PERCY DEARMER,
1867–1936.

264 C. M.

O LORD of life, Thy quickening
voice
Awakes my morning song !
In gladsome words I would rejoice
That I to Thee belong.

2 I see Thy light, I feel Thy wind ;
The world, it is Thy word ;
Whatever wakes my heart and mind
Thy presence is, my Lord.

3 Therefore I choose my highest part,
And turn my face to Thee ;
Therefore I stir my inmost heart
To worship fervently.

4 Lord, let me live and will this day—
Keep rising from the dead ;
Lord, make my spirit good and gay—
Give me my daily bread.

5 Within my heart speak, Lord, speak
on,
My heart alive to keep,
Till comes the night, and, labour
done,
In Thee I fall asleep.

GEORGE MACDONALD,
1824–1905.

265 77. 77. 77.

AT Thy feet, O Christ, we lay
Thine own gift of this new day ;
Doubt of what it holds in store
Makes us crave Thine aid the more ;
Lest it prove a time of loss,
Mark it, Saviour, with Thy Cross.

2 If it flow on calm and bright,
Be Thyself our chief delight ;
If it bring unknown distress,
Good is all that Thou canst bless ;
Only, while its hours begin,
Pray we, keep them clear of sin.

3 We in part our weakness know,
And in part discern our foe ;
Well for us, before Thine eyes
All our danger open lies ;
Turn not from us, while we plead
Thy compassions and our need.

4 Fain would we Thy word embrace,
Live each moment on Thy grace,
All our selves to Thee consign,
Fold up all our wills in Thine,
Think, and speak, and do, and be
Simply that which pleases Thee.

5 Hear us, Lord, and that right soon ;
Hear, and grant the choicest boon
That Thy love can e'er impart,
Loyal singleness of heart ;
So shall this and all our days,
Christ our God, show forth Thy
praise.

WILLIAM BRIGHT, 1824–1901.

266 77. 77. 77.

HAIL, thou bright and sacred
morn,
Risen with gladness in thy beams !
Light, which not of earth is born,
From thy dawn in glory streams ;
Airs of heaven are breathed around,
And each place is holy ground.

2 Great Creator, who this day
From Thy perfect work didst rest,
By the souls that own Thy sway
Hallowed be its hours and blest ;
Cares of earth aside be thrown,
This day given to heaven alone.

3 Saviour, who this day didst break
The dark prison of the tomb,
Bid my slumbering soul awake,
Shine through all its sin and gloom ;
Let me, from my bonds set free,
Rise from sin, and live to Thee.

4 Blessèd Spirit, Comforter,
Sent this day from Christ on high,
Lord, on me Thy gifts confer,
Cleanse, illumine, sanctify ;
All Thine influence shed abroad ;
Lead me to the truth of God.

JULIA ANNE ELLIOTT,
1809–41.

267 S. M.

THIS is the day of light :
Let there be light to-day ;
O Dayspring, rise upon our night,
And chase its gloom away.

2 This is the day of rest :
Our failing strength renew ;
On weary brain and troubled breast
Shed Thou Thy freshening dew.

3 This is the day of peace :
Thy peace our spirits fill ;
Bid Thou the blasts of discord cease,
The waves of strife be still.

4 This is the day of prayer :
Let earth to heaven draw near ;
Lift up our hearts to seek Thee there,
Come down to meet us here.

5   This is the first of days :
    Send forth Thy quickening breath,
And wake dead souls to love and
    praise,
    O Vanquisher of death !

             JOHN ELLERTON, 1826–93.

268
76. 76. D.

O DAY of rest and gladness,
   O day of joy and light,
O balm of care and sadness,
   Most beautiful, most bright !
On thee the high and lowly,
   Before the eternal throne,
Sing ' Holy, holy, holy,'
   To the great Three in One.

2 On thee, at the creation,
   The light first had its birth ;
On thee, for our salvation,
   Christ rose from depths of earth ;
On thee our Lord victorious
   The Spirit sent from heaven :
And thus on thee most glorious
   A triple light was given.

3 To-day on weary nations
   The heavenly manna falls ;
To holy convocations
   The silver trumpet calls,
Where gospel light is glowing
   With pure and radiant beams,
And living water flowing
   With soul-refreshing streams.

4 New graces ever gaining
   From this our day of rest,
We reach the rest remaining
   To spirits of the blest.
To Holy Ghost be praises,
   To Father, and to Son ;
The Church her voice upraises
   To Thee, blest Three in One.

        CHRISTOPHER WORDSWORTH,
             1807–85.

269
86. 84.

HAIL, sacred day of earthly rest,
   From toil and trouble free !
Hail, quiet spirit, bringing peace
   And joy to me !

2 A holy stillness, breathing calm
   On all the world around,
Uplifts my soul, O God, to Thee,
   Where rest is found.

3 No sound of jarring strife is heard,
   As weekly labours cease,
No voice but those that sweetly
   sing
      Sweet songs of peace.

4 On all I think or say or do
   A ray of light divine
Is shed, O God, this day by Thee,
   For it is Thine.

5 All earthly things appear to fade
   As, rising high and higher,
The yearning voices strive to join
     The heavenly choir.

6 Accept, O God, my hymn of praise
   That Thou this day hast given,
Sweet foretaste of that endless day
    Of rest in heaven.

         GODFREY THRING,
           1823–1903.

270
76. 76.

THE darkness now is over,
   And all the world is bright ;
Praise be to Christ, who keepeth
   His children safe at night !

2 We cannot tell what gladness
   May be our lot to-day,
What sorrow or temptation
   May meet us on our way ;

3 But this we know most surely,
   That, through all good or ill,
God's grace can always help us
   To do His holy will.

4 Then, Jesus, let the angels,
   Who watched us through the
    night,
Be all day long beside us,
   To guide our steps aright

5 And help us to remember,
   In thought and deed and word,
That we are heirs of heaven,
   And children of the Lord.

6 Then, when the evening cometh,
   We'll kneel again to pray,
And thank Thee for the blessings
   Bestowed throughout the day.

     The Children's Hymn Book, 1881.

EVENING

271　　　　　　　　　　98. 98.

BEFORE the day draws near its
　　ending,
　　And evening steals o'er earth and
　　　sky,
Once more to Thee our hymns
　　ascending
　　Shall speak Thy praises, Lord
　　　Most High.

2 Thy Name is blessed by countless
　　numbers
　　In vaster worlds unseen, unknown,
Whose duteous service never slum-
　　bers,
　　In perfect love and faultless tone.

3 Yet Thou wilt not despise the weakest
　　Who here in spirit bend the knee;
Thy Christ hath said, 'Thou, Father,
　　seekest
　　For such as these to worship Thee.'

4 And through the swell of chanting
　　voices,
　　The blended notes of age and
　　　youth,
Thine ear discerns, Thy love rejoices,
　　When hearts rise up to Thee in
　　　truth.

5 O Light all clear, O Truth most holy,
　　O boundless Mercy pardoning all,
Before Thy feet, abashed and lowly,
　　With one last prayer Thy children
　　　fall :—

6 When we no more on earth adore
　　Thee,
　　And others worship here in turn,
O may we sing that song before Thee,
　　Which none but Thy redeemed
　　　can learn.

JOHN ELLERTON,
1826-93.

272　　　　　　　　　　64. 66.

THE sun is sinking fast,
　　The daylight dies;
Let love awake, and pay
　　Her evening sacrifice.

2 As Christ upon the Cross
　　His head inclined,
And to His Father's hands
　　His parting soul resigned,

3 So now herself my soul
　　Would wholly give
Into His sacred charge
　　In whom all spirits live;

4 So now beneath His eye
　　Would calmly rest—
Without a wish or thought
　　Abiding in the breast,

5 Save that His will be done,
　　Whate'er betide—
Dead to herself, and dead
　　In Him to all beside.

6 Thus would I live; yet now
　　Not I, but He
In all His power and love
　　Henceforth alive in me :

7 One sacred Trinity,
　　One Lord Divine;
Myself for ever His,
　　And He for ever mine.

Tr. by EDWARD CASWALL,
1814-78.

273　　　　　　　　　　84. 84. D.

THE sun declines; o'er land and
　　sea
　　Creeps on the night;
The twinkling stars come one by one
　　To shed their light;
With Thee there is no darkness,
　　Lord;
　　With us abide,
And 'neath Thy wings we rest secure,
　　This eventide.

2 Forgive the wrong this day we've
　　done,
　　Or thought, or said;
Each moment with its good or ill
　　To Thee has fled;
O Father, in Thy mercy great
　　Will we confide;
Thy benediction now bestow,
　　This eventide.

3 And when with morning light we rise,
　　Kept by Thy care,
We'll lift to Thee, with grateful
　　hearts,
　　Our morning prayer.
Be Thou through life our Strength
　　and Stay,
　　Our Guard and Guide
To that dear home where there will
　　be
　　No eventide.

ROBERT WALMSLEY.
1831-1905.

274　　　　　　　　　　　　　　　C. M.

AS now the sun's declining rays
　　At eventide descend,
Even so our years are sinking down
　　To their appointed end.

2 Lord, on the Cross Thine arms were
　　　stretched
　　To draw the nations nigh;
O grant us then that Cross to love,
　　And in those arms to die.

3 To God the Father, God the Son,
　　And God the Holy Ghost,
All glory be from saints on earth,
　　And from the angel host.

　　　CHARLES COFFIN, 1676–1749;
　　　tr. by JOHN CHANDLER, 1806–76.

275　　　　　　　　　　　　　　　L. M.

AGAIN, as evening's shadow falls,
　　We gather in these hallowed
　　　walls;
And vesper hymn and vesper prayer
Rise mingling on the holy air.

2 May struggling hearts that seek
　　　release
Here find the rest of God's own
　　　peace,
And, strengthened here by hymn and
　　　prayer,
Lay down the burdens and the care.

3 O God, our Light, to Thee we bow;
Within all shadows standest Thou:
Give deeper calm than night can
　　　bring;
Give sweeter songs than lips can sing.

4 Life's tumult we must meet again;
We cannot at the shrine remain;
But in the spirit's secret cell
May hymn and prayer for ever dwell.

　　　　　SAMUEL LONGFELLOW,
　　　　　1819–92.

276　　　　　　　　　　　　　　　C. M.

AS darker, darker fall around
　　The shadows of the night,
We gather here, with hymn and
　　　prayer,
To seek the eternal light.

2 Father in heaven, to Thee are known
　　Our many hopes and fears,
Our heavy weight of mortal toil,
　　Our bitterness of tears.

3 We pray Thee for all absent friends,
　　Who have been with us here;
And in our secret heart we name
　　The distant and the dear.

4 For weary eyes, and aching hearts,
　　And feet that from Thee rove,
The sick, the poor, the tried, the
　　　fallen,
　　We pray Thee, God of love.

5 We bring to Thee our hopes and
　　　fears,
　　And at Thy footstool lay;
And, Father, Thou who lovest all
　　Wilt hear us when we pray.

　　　　　　　　　　　　　　　Anon.

277　　　　　　　　　　　　　　　L. M.

AT even, when the sun was set,
　　The sick, O Lord, around Thee
　　　lay;
O in what divers pains they met!
O with what joy they went away!

2 Once more 'tis eventide, and we,
　　Oppressed with various ills, draw
　　　near;
What if Thy form we cannot see,
　　We know and feel that Thou art
　　　here.

3 O Saviour Christ, our woes dispel:
　　For some are sick, and some are
　　　sad,
And some have never loved Thee
　　　well,
　　And some have lost the love they
　　　had;

4 And some are pressed with worldly
　　　care,
　　And some are tried with sinful
　　　doubt;
And some such grievous passions
　　　tear,
　　That only Thou canst cast them
　　　out;

5 And some have found the world is
　　　vain,
　　Yet from the world they break not
　　　free;
And some have friends who give
　　　them pain,
　　Yet have not sought a friend in
　　　Thee;

6 And none, O Lord, have perfect rest,
    For none are wholly free from sin ;
And they who fain would serve Thee
        best
    Are conscious most of wrong with-
        in.

7 O Saviour Christ, Thou too art Man ;
    Thou hast been troubled, tempted,
        tried ;
Thy kind but searching glance can
        scan
    The very wounds that shame
        would hide ;

8 Thy touch has still its ancient power ;
    No word from Thee can fruitless
        fall :
Hear in this solemn evening hour,
    And in Thy mercy heal us all.

HENRY TWELLS, 1823–1900.

278   L. M.

NOW cheer our hearts this even-
    tide,
Lord Jesus Christ, and with us bide ;
Thou that canst never set in night,
Our heavenly Sun, our glorious Light.

2 May we and all who bear Thy Name
By gentle love Thy Cross proclaim,
Thy gift of peace on earth secure,
And for Thy truth the world endure.

Yattendon Hymnal, No. 13, 1899 ;
    based on NICOLAUS SELNECKER,
    1532–92.

279   88. 84.

THE radiant morn hath passed
    away,
    And spent too soon her golden
        store ;
The shadows of departing day
        Creep on once more.

2 Our life is but an autumn day,
    Its glorious noon how quickly past !
Lead us, O Christ, Thou living Way,
    Safe home at last.

3 O by Thy soul-inspiring grace
    Uplift our hearts to realms on high :
Help us to look to that bright place,
        Beyond the sky,

4 Where light, and life, and joy, and
        peace
    In undivided empire reign,
And thronging angels never cease
        Their deathless strain ;

5 Where saints are clothed in spotless
        white,
    And evening shadows never fall ;
Where Thou, Eternal Light of light,
        Art Lord of all.

GODFREY THRING, 1823–1903.

280   11 11. 11 5.

NOW God be with us, for the night
    is closing ;
The light and darkness are of His
    disposing,
And 'neath His shadow here to rest
    we yield us,
        For He will shield us.

2 Let evil thoughts and spirits flee
    before us :
Till morning cometh, watch, Pro-
    tector, o'er us ;
In soul and body Thou from harm
    defend us ;
        Thine angels send us.

3 Let holy thoughts be ours when sleep
    o'ertakes us ;
Our earliest thoughts be Thine when
    morning wakes us ;
All day serve Thee, in all that we are
    doing
        Thy praise pursuing.

4 We have no refuge, none on earth
    to aid us,
Save Thee, O Father, who Thine
    own hast made us ;
But Thy dear Presence will not leave
    them lonely
        Who seek Thee only.

5 Father, Thy Name be praised, Thy
    Kingdom given,
Thy will be done on earth as 'tis in
    heaven ;
Keep us in life, forgive our sins,
    deliver
        Us now and ever.

PETRUS HERBERT, ?–1571 ; *tr.* by
    CATHERINE WINKWORTH, 1827–78.

281   Irr.

HAIL, gladdening Light, of His
    pure glory pour'd
    Who is the immortal Father,
        heavenly, blest,
Holiest of Holies, Jesus Christ, our
    Lord !
    Now we are come to the sun's
        hour of rest,

The lights of evening round us
    shine,
We hymn the Father, Son, and Holy
    Spirit Divine.
Worthiest art Thou at all times to be
    sung
    With undefilèd tongue,
Son of our God, Giver of life,
    alone :
Therefore in all the world Thy
    glories, Lord, they own.
        4th century ; *tr.* by
        JOHN KEBLE, 1792–1866.

282
             77. 75.

HOLY Father, cheer our way
    With Thy love's perpetual ray ;
Grant us, every closing day,
    Light at evening time.

2 Holy Saviour, calm our fears
When earth's brightness disappears ;
Grant us in our latter years
    Light at evening time.

3 Holy Spirit, be Thou nigh
When in mortal pains we lie ;
Grant us, as we come to die,
    Light at evening time.

4 Holy, blessèd Trinity,
Darkness is not dark to Thee ;
Those Thou keepest always see
    Light at evening time.
        RICHARD HAYES ROBINSON,
                  1842–92.

283
            887. 887.

FATHER, in high heaven dwelling,
    May our evening song be telling
Of Thy mercy large and free ;
Through the day Thy love has fed us,
Through the day Thy care has led us,
    With divinest charity.

2 This day's sins O pardon, Saviour,
Evil thoughts, perverse behaviour,
    Envy, pride, and vanity ;
From the world, the flesh, deliver,
Save us now, and save us ever,
    O Thou Lamb of Calvary.

3 From enticements of the devil,
From the might of spirits evil,
    Be our shield and panoply ;
Let Thy power this night defend us,
And a heavenly peace attend us,
    And angelic company.

4 While the night-dews are distilling,
Holy Ghost, each heart be filling
    With Thine own serenity.
Softly let our eyes be closing,
Loving souls on Thee reposing,
    Ever-blessèd Trinity.
        GEORGE RAWSON, 1807–89.

284
            776. 778.

THE duteous day now closeth,
    Each flower and tree reposeth,
    Shade creeps o'er wild and wood :
Let us, as night is falling,
On God our Maker calling,
    Give thanks to Him, the Giver
    good.

2 Now all the heavenly splendour
Breaks forth in starlight tender
    From myriad worlds unknown ;
And man, the marvel seeing,
Forgets his selfish being,
    For joy of beauty not his own.

3 His care he drowneth yonder,
Lost in the abyss of wonder ;
    To heaven his soul doth steal :
This life he disesteemeth,
The day it is that dreameth,
    That doth from truth his vision
    seal.

4 Awhile his mortal blindness
May miss God's loving-kindness,
    And grope in faithless strife :
But, when life's day is over,
Shall death's fair night discover
    The fields of everlasting life.
        Yattendon Hymnal, No. 83,
        1899 ; based on PAUL GERHARDT,
                  1607–76.

285
            87. 87. D.

SAVIOUR, breathe an evening
    blessing
    Ere repose our spirits seal ;
Sin and want we come confessing :
    Thou canst save, and Thou canst
    heal.
Though destruction walk around us,
    Though the arrow past us fly,
Angel guards from Thee surround
    us ;
    We are safe if Thou art nigh.

2 Though the night be dark and dreary,
   Darkness cannot hide from Thee ;
Thou art He who, never weary,
   Watchest where Thy people be.
Should swift death this night o'ertake
   us,
   And our couch become our tomb,
May the morn in heaven awake us,
   Clad in light and deathless bloom.
          JAMES EDMESTON, 1791–1867.

286

10 10. 10 10.

ABIDE with me : fast falls the
   eventide ;
The darkness deepens ; Lord, with
   me abide :
When other helpers fail, and comforts flee,
Help of the helpless, O abide with
   me.

2 Swift to its close ebbs out life's little
   day
Earth's joys grow dim, its glories pass
   away :
Change and decay in all around I see :
O Thou who changest not, abide
   with me.

3 I need Thy presence every passing
   hour ;
What but Thy grace can foil the
   tempter's power ?
Who like Thyself my guide and stay
   can be ?
Through cloud and sunshine, O
   abide with me.

4 I fear no foe, with Thee at hand to
   bless ;
Ills have no weight, and tears no
   bitterness :
Where is death's sting ? where,
   grave, thy victory ?
I triumph still if Thou abide with
   me.

5 Hold Thou Thy Cross before my
   closing eyes,
Shine through the gloom, and point
   me to the skies ;
Heaven's morning breaks, and
   earth's vain shadows flee :
In life and death, O Lord, abide
   with me.
          HENRY FRANCIS LYTE,
              1793–1847.

287

76. 76. 88.

THE day is past and over ;
   All thanks, O Lord, to Thee ;
I pray Thee now that sinless
   The hours of dark may be.
O Jesus, keep me in Thy sight,
And guard me through the coming
     night.

2 The joys of day are over :
   I lift my heart to Thee,
And pray Thee that offenceless
   The hours of dark may be.
O Jesus, keep me in Thy sight,
And guard me through the coming
     night.

3 The toils of day are over :
   I raise the hymn to Thee,
And pray that free from peril
   The hours of dark may be.
O Jesus, keep me in Thy sight,
And guard me through the coming
     night.

4 Be Thou my soul's Preserver,
   O God, for Thou dost know
How many are the perils
   Through which I have to go.
Lover of men, O hear my call,
And guard and save me from them
     all.
         6th century ; tr. by
     JOHN MASON NEALE, 1818–66.

288

65. 65.

NOW the day is over,
   Night is drawing nigh,
Shadows of the evening
   Steal across the sky.

2 Now the darkness gathers,
   Stars begin to peep,
Birds, and beasts, and flowers
   Soon will be asleep.

3 Jesus, give the weary
   Calm and sweet repose ;
With Thy tender blessing
   May mine eyelids close.

4 Grant to little children
   Visions bright of Thee ;
Guard the sailors tossing
   On the deep blue sea.

5 Comfort every sufferer
   Watching late in pain ;
Those who plan some evil
   From their sin restrain.

6 Through the long night-watches,
  May Thine angels spread
  Their white wings above me,
  Watching round my bed.

7 When the morning wakens,
  Then may I arise
  Pure, and fresh, and sinless
  In Thy holy eyes.

8 Glory to the Father,
  Glory to the Son,
  And to Thee, blest Spirit,
  Whilst all ages run.

SABINE BARING-GOULD,
1834–1924.

289

98. 98.

THE day Thou gavest, Lord, is
  ended ;
The darkness falls at Thy behest ;
To Thee our morning hymns
  ascended,
Thy praise shall sanctify our rest.

2 We thank Thee that Thy Church
  unsleeping,
While earth rolls onward into light,
Through all the world her watch is
  keeping,
And rests not now by day or night.

3 As o'er each continent and island
The dawn leads on another day,
The voice of prayer is never silent,
Nor dies the strain of praise away.

4 The sun that bids us rest is waking
Our brethren 'neath the western
  sky,
And hour by hour fresh lips are
  making
Thy wondrous doings heard on
  high.

5 So be it, Lord ! Thy throne shall
  never,
Like earth's proud empires, pass
  away ;
Thy Kingdom stands and grows for
  ever,
Till all Thy creatures own Thy
  sway.

JOHN ELLERTON, 1826–93.

290

S. M.

OUR day of praise is done ;
  The evening shadows fall ;
But pass not from us with the sun,
True Light, that lightenest all !

2 Around the throne on high,
  Where night can never be,
The white-robed harpers of the sky
  Bring ceaseless hymns to Thee.

3 Too faint our anthems here ;
  Too soon of praise we tire ;
But O the strains, how full and clear,
  Of that eternal choir !

4 Yet, Lord, to Thy dear will
  If Thou attune the heart,
We in Thine angels' music still
  May bear our lower part.

5 'Tis Thine each soul to calm,
  Each wayward thought reclaim,
And make our life a daily psalm
  Of glory to Thy Name.

6 A little while, and then
  Shall come the glorious end,
And songs of angels and of men
  In perfect praise shall blend.

JOHN ELLERTON, 1826–93.

291

L. M.

ALL praise to Thee, my God, this
  night,
For all the blessings of the light !
Keep me, O keep me, King of kings,
Beneath Thy own almighty wings.

2 Forgive me, Lord, for Thy dear Son,
The ill that I this day have done,
That with the world, myself, and
  Thee,
I, ere I sleep, at peace may be.

3 Teach me to live, that I may dread
The grave as little as my bed ;
Teach me to die, that so I may
Rise glorious at the awful day.

4 O may my soul on Thee repose,
And may sweet sleep mine eyelids
  close,—
Sleep that may me more vigorous
  make
To serve my God when I awake.

5 When in the night I sleepless lie,
My soul with heavenly thoughts
  supply ;
Let no ill dreams disturb my rest,
No powers of darkness me molest.

6 Praise God, from whom all blessings
  flow ;
Praise Him, all creatures here below ;
Praise Him above, ye heavenly host ;
Praise Father, Son, and Holy Ghost.

THOMAS KEN, 1637–1711.

292   L. M.

SUN of my soul, Thou Saviour
    dear,
It is not night if Thou be near;
O may no earth-born cloud arise
To hide Thee from Thy servant's
    eyes.

2 When the soft dews of kindly sleep
My wearied eyelids gently steep,
Be my last thought, how sweet to rest
For ever on my Saviour's breast.

3 Abide with me from morn till eve,
For without Thee I cannot live;
Abide with me when night is nigh,
For without Thee I dare not die.

4 If some poor wandering child of
    Thine
Have spurned to-day the voice divine,
Now, Lord, the gracious work begin;
Let him no more lie down in sin.

5 Watch by the sick; enrich the poor
With blessings from Thy boundless
    store;
Be every mourner's sleep to-night,
Like infant's slumbers, pure and
    light.

6 Come near and bless us when we
    wake,
Ere through the world our way we
    take,
Till in the ocean of Thy love
We lose ourselves in heaven above.

    JOHN KEBLE, 1792–1866.

293   84. 84. 8884.

GOD, that madest earth and
    heaven,
    Darkness and light,
Who the day for toil hast given,
    For rest the night:
May Thine angel guards defend us,
Slumber sweet Thy mercy send us,
Holy dreams and hopes attend us,
    This livelong night.

2 Guard us waking, guard us sleeping;
    And, when we die,
May we, in Thy mighty keeping,
    All peaceful lie.

When the last dread trump shall
    wake us,
Do not Thou, our Lord, forsake us,
But to reign in glory take us
    With Thee on high.

    1 v. REGINALD HEBER, 1783–1826.
    2 v. RICHARD WHATELY, 1787–1863.

294   8. 33. 6.

ERE I sleep, for every favour
    This day showed
    By my God,
I will bless my Saviour.

2 O my Lord, what shall I render
    To Thy Name,
    Still the same,
Gracious, good, and tender?

3 Thou hast ordered all my goings
    In Thy way,
    Heard me pray,
Sanctified my doings.

4 Leave me not, but ever love me:
    Let Thy peace
    Be my bliss,
Till Thou hence remove me.

5 Visit me with Thy salvation;
    Let Thy care
    Now be near,
Round my habitation.

6 Thou my Rock, my Guard, my
    Tower,
    Safely keep,
    While I sleep,
Me, with all Thy power.

7 So, whene'er in death I slumber,
    Let me rise
    With the wise,
Counted in their number.

    JOHN CENNICK, 1718–55.

CLOSE OF WORSHIP

295   C. M.

ALMIGHTY God, Thy word is
    cast
Like seed into the ground,
Now let the dew of heaven descend,
And righteous fruits abound.

2 Let not the foe of Christ and man
    This holy seed remove,
But give it root in every heart
To bring forth fruits of love.

3 Let not the world's deceitful cares
　　The rising plant destroy,
　But let it yield a hundredfold
　　The fruits of peace and joy.

4 Oft as the precious seed is sown,
　　Thy quickening grace bestow,
　That all whose souls the truth receive
　　Its saving power may know.

　　　　　　　JOHN CAWOOD, 1775–1852.

296　　　　　　　　　　　C. M.

AND now the wants are told that
　　brought
　Thy children to Thy knee ;
Here lingering still, we ask for
　　nought,
　But simply worship Thee.

2 For Thou art God, the One, the
　　Same,
　　O'er all things high and bright ;
　And round us, when we speak Thy
　　Name,
　　There spreads a heaven of light.

3 O wondrous peace, in thought to
　　dwell
　　On excellence divine,
　To know that nought in man can tell
　　How fair Thy beauties shine !

4 O Thou, above all blessing blest,
　　O'er all things exalted far,
　Thy very greatness is a rest
　　To weaklings as we are ;

5 For when we feel the praise of Thee
　　A task beyond our powers,
　We say, ' A perfect God is He,
　　And He is fully ours.'

6 All glory to the Father be,
　　All glory to the Son,
　All glory, Holy Ghost, to Thee,
　　While endless ages run.

　　　　　　　WILLIAM BRIGHT, 1824–1901.

297　　　　　　　　　　　L. M.

COME, dearest Lord, descend and
　　dwell
　By faith and love in every breast ;
Then shall we know, and taste, and
　　feel
　The joys that cannot be expressed.

2 Come, fill our hearts with inward
　　strength,
　Make our enlargèd souls possess
And learn the height and breadth and
　　length
　Of Thine unmeasurable grace

3 Now to the God whose power can do
　　More than our thoughts or wishes
　　　know,
　Be everlasting honours done
　By all the Church, through Christ
　　His Son.

　　　　　　　ISAAC WATTS, 1674–1748.

298　　　　　　　　87. 87. 77 8 77.

OF Thy love some gracious token
　　Grant us, Lord, before we go ;
Bless Thy word which has been
　　spoken ;
　Life and peace on all bestow.
When we join the world again,
Let our hearts with Thee remain ;
　　O direct us,
　　And protect us,
Till we gain the heavenly shore,
Where Thy people want no more.

　　　　　　　THOMAS KELLY, 1769–1854.

299　　　　　　　　　　87. 87. 87.

LORD, dismiss us with Thy blessing ;
　　Fill our hearts with joy and peace ;
Let us each, Thy love possessing,
　　Triumph in redeeming grace ;
　　　O refresh us,
　　Travelling through this wilderness.

2 Thanks we give and adoration
　　For Thy Gospel's joyful sound ;
May the fruits of Thy salvation
　　In our hearts and lives abound ;
　　　May Thy presence
　　With us evermore be found.

　　　　　　　JOHN FAWCETT, 1740–1817.

300　　　　　　　　　　　77. 77.

NOW may He who from the dead
　　Brought the Shepherd of the
　　　sheep,
Jesus Christ, our King and Head,
　　All our souls in safety keep.

2 May He teach us to fulfil
  What is pleasing in His sight,
Perfect us in all His will,
  And preserve us day and night.

3 To that dear Redeemer's praise,
  Who the covenant sealed with
    blood,
Let our hearts and voices raise
  Loud thanksgivings to our God.
                JOHN NEWTON, 1725–1807.

301   10 10. 10 10.

SAVIOUR, again to Thy dear
  Name we raise
With one accord our parting hymn of
    praise ;
We stand to bless Thee ere our
    worship cease,
Then, lowly kneeling, wait Thy word
    of peace.

2 Grant us Thy peace upon our home-
    ward way ;
With Thee began, with Thee shall
    end the day ;
Guard Thou the lips from sin, the
    hearts from shame,
That in this house have called upon
    Thy Name.

3 Grant us Thy peace through this
    approaching night ;
Turn Thou for us its darkness into
    light ;
From harm and danger keep Thy
    children free,
For dark and light are both alike to
    Thee.

4 Grant us Thy peace throughout our
    earthly life,
Our balm in sorrow, and our stay in
    strife ;
Then, when Thy voice shall bid our
    conflict cease,
Call us, O Lord, to Thine eternal
    peace.

                JOHN ELLERTON, 1826–93.

302   88. 88. and refrain.

O SAVIOUR, bless us ere we go ;
  Thy word into our minds instil ;
And make our lukewarm hearts to
    glow
With lowly love and fervent will.
  *Through life's long day and
      death's dark night,
  O gentle Jesus, be our light !*

2 The day is done, its hours have run,
  And Thou hast taken count of
    all,—
The scanty triumphs grace hath
    won,
  The broken vow, the frequent fall.

3 Grant us, dear Lord, from evil ways
  True absolution and release ;
And bless us, more than in past days,
  With purity and inward peace.

4 Do more than pardon : give us joy,
  Sweet fear, and sober liberty,
And loving hearts without alloy,
  That only long to be like Thee.

5 Labour is sweet, for Thou hast toiled,
  And care is light, for Thou hast
    cared ;
Let not our works with self be soiled,
  Nor in unsimple ways ensnared.

6 For all we love, the poor, the sad,
  The sinful, unto Thee we call ;
O let Thy mercy make us glad ;
  Thou art our Jesus and our All.
            FREDERICK WILLIAM FABER,
                            1814–63.

303   77. 77.

PART in peace : Christ's life was
    peace,
Let us live our life in Him ;
Part in peace : Christ's death was
    peace,
Let us die our death in Him.

2 Part in peace : Christ promise gave
Of a life beyond the grave,
Where all mortal partings cease ;
Brethren, sisters, part in peace.
                SARAH FLOWER ADAMS,
                            1805–48.

BAPTISM

304
88. 88. and refrain.

LORD Jesus Christ, our Lord most dear,
As Thou wast once an infant here,
So give this child of Thine, we pray,
Thy grace and blessing day by day.
O holy Jesus, Lord Divine,
We pray Thee guard this child of
Thine.

2 As in Thy heavenly Kingdom, Lord,
All things obey Thy sacred word,
Do Thou Thy mighty succour give,
And shield this child by morn and
eve.

3 Their watch let angels round *him*
keep
Where'er *he* be, awake, asleep;
Thy holy Cross now let *him* bear,
That *he* Thy crown with saints may
wear.
HEINRICH VON LAUFENBERG, 15th cent.;
tr. by CATHERINE WINKWORTH,
1827–78.

305
L. M.

A LITTLE child the Saviour
came,
The Mighty God was still His Name,
And angels worshipped as He lay
The seeming infant of a day.

2 He who, a little child, began
The life divine to show to man,
Proclaims from heaven the message
free,
' Let little children come to Me.'

3 We bring them, Lord, and with the
sign
Of sprinkled water name them Thine:
Their souls with saving grace endow;
Baptize them with Thy Spirit now.

4 O give Thine angels charge, good
Lord,
Them safely in Thy way to guard;
Thy blessing on their lives command,
And write their names upon Thy
hand.

5 O Thou who by an infant's tongue
Dost hear Thy perfect glory sung,
May these, with all the heavenly host,
Praise Father, Son, and Holy Ghost.
WILLIAM ROBERTSON, 1820–64.

306
C. M.

OUR children, Lord, in faith and
prayer,
We now devote to Thee;
Let them Thy covenant mercies
share,
And Thy salvation see.

2 Such helpless babes Thou didst
embrace,
While dwelling here below;
To us and ours, O God of grace,
The same compassion show.

3 In early days their hearts secure
From worldly snares, we pray;
O let them to the end endure
In every righteous way.
THOMAS HAWEIS, 1734–1820.

307
78. 78. 88.

BLESSED Jesus, here we stand,
Met to do as Thou hast spoken;
And this child, at Thy command,
Now we bring to Thee in token
That to Christ it here is given,
For of such shall be His heaven.

2 Therefore hasten we to Thee;
Take the pledge we bring, O take it;
Let us here Thy glory see,
And in tender pity make it
Now Thy child, and leave it
never—
Thine on earth, and Thine for ever.

3 Make it, Head, Thy member now;
Shepherd, take Thy lamb and feed
it;
Prince of Peace, its peace be Thou;
Way of life, to heaven O lead it;
Vine, this branch may nothing
sever,
Grafted firm in Thee for ever.

4 Now upon Thy heart it lies,
What our hearts so dearly treasure;
Heavenward lead our burdened
sighs;
Pour Thy blessing without mea-
sure;
Write the name we now have given,
Write it in the book of heaven.
BENJAMIN SCHMOLK, 1672–1737;
tr. by CATHERINE WINKWORTH,
1827–78.

308

10 6. 10 6. 884.

O FATHER, Thou who hast
created all
In wisest love, we pray,
Look on this babe, who at Thy
gracious call
Is entering on life's way;
Bend o'er *him* in Thy tenderness,
Thine image on *his* soul impress;
O Father, hear.

2 O Son of God, who diedst for us,
behold,
We bring our child to Thee;
Thou tender Shepherd, take *him* to
Thy fold,
Thine own for aye to be;
Defend *him* through this earthly
strife,
And lead *him* on the path of life,
O Son of God.

3 O Holy Ghost, who broodedst o'er
the wave,
Descend upon this child;
Give *him* undying life, *his* spirit lave
With waters undefiled;
Grant *him*, while yet a babe, to be
A child of God, a home for Thee,
O Holy Ghost.

4 O Triune God, what Thou com-
mand'st is done;
We speak, but Thine the might;
This child hath scarce yet seen our
earthly sun,
Yet pour on *him* Thy light,
In faith and hope, in joy and love,
Thou Sun of all below, above,
O Triune God.
ALBERT KNAPP, 1798–1864;
tr. by CATHERINE WINKWORTH,
1827–78.

309

C. M.

BY cool Siloam's shady rill
How sweet the lily grows!
How sweet the breath, beneath the
hill,
Of Sharon's dewy rose!

2 Lo! such the child whose early feet
The paths of peace have trod,
Whose secret heart with influence
sweet
Is upward drawn to God.

3 O Thou whose infant feet were found
Within Thy Father's shrine,
Whose years, with changeless virtue
crowned,
Were all alike divine,

4 Dependent on Thy bounteous
breath,
We seek Thy grace alone,
In childhood, manhood, age, and
death,
To keep us still Thine own.
REGINALD HEBER, 1783–1826.

310

87. 87. 87.

GRACIOUS Saviour, gentle
Shepherd,
Little ones are dear to Thee;
Gathered with Thine arms and
carried
In Thy bosom, may they be
Sweetly, fondly, safely tended,
From all want and danger free.

2 Tender Shepherd, never leave them
From Thy fold to go astray;
By Thy look of love directed,
May they walk the narrow way;
Thus direct them, and protect them,
Lest they fall an easy prey.

3 Let Thy holy word instruct them;
Fill their minds with heavenly
light;
Let Thy love and grace constrain
them
To approve whate'er is right,
Take Thine easy yoke and wear it,
And to prove Thy burden light.

4 Taught to lisp the holy praises
Which on earth Thy children sing,
Both with lips and hearts unfeigned
Glad thank-offerings may they
bring;
Then, with all the saints in glory,
Join to praise their Lord and King.
JANE ELIZA LEESON, 1807–82,
and JOHN KEBLE, 1792–1866.

THE LORD'S SUPPER

311

L. M.

MY God, and is Thy table spread?
And does Thy cup with love
o'erflow?
Thither be all Thy children led,
And let them all its sweetness
know.

2 Hail, sacred feast, which Jesus makes,
   Rich banquet of His flesh and
     blood
Thrice happy he who here partakes
   That sacred stream, that heavenly
     food !

3 Let crowds approach with hearts
   prepared ;
   With hearts inflamed let all attend,
Nor, when we leave our Father's
   board,
   The pleasure or the profit end.

4 O let Thy table honoured be,
   And furnished well with joyful
     guests ;
And may each soul salvation see
   That here its sacred pledges tastes.

       PHILIP DODDRIDGE, 1702-51.

312 *From St. Matthew*
    xxvi. 26-29.   L. M.

'TWAS on that night when doomed
   to know
The eager rage of every foe,
That night in which He was betrayed,
The Saviour of the world took bread ;

2 And, after thanks and glory given
   To Him that rules in earth and
     heaven,
That symbol of His flesh He broke,
And thus to all His followers spoke :

3 ' My broken body thus I give
For you, for all ; take, eat, and live :
And oft the sacred rite renew
That brings My wondrous love to
   view.'

4 Then in His hands the cup He
   raised,
And God anew He thanked and
   praised,
While kindness in His bosom glowed,
And from His lips salvation flowed.

5 ' My blood I thus pour forth,' He
   cries,
' To cleanse the soul in sin that lies ;
In this the covenant is sealed,
And Heaven's eternal grace revealed.

6 ' With love to man this cup is
   fraught,
Let all partake the sacred draught ;
Through latest ages let it pour
In memory of My dying hour.'

     JOHN MORISON, 1750-98, as in
    Scottish Paraphrases, 1781.

313   C. M.

ACCORDING to Thy gracious
   word,
   In meek humility,
This will I do, my dying Lord,
   I will remember Thee.

2 Thy body, broken for my sake,
   My bread from heaven shall be ;
Thy testamental cup I take,
   And thus remember Thee.

3 Gethsemane can I forget ?
   Or there Thy conflict see,
Thine agony and bloody sweat,
   And not remember Thee ?

4 When to the Cross I turn mine eyes
   And rest on Calvary,
O Lamb of God, my sacrifice,
   I must remember Thee,—

5 Remember Thee, and all Thy pains,
   And all Thy love to me ;
Yea, while a breath, a pulse remains,
   Will I remember Thee.

6 And when these failing lips grow
   dumb,
   And mind and memory flee,
When Thou shalt in Thy Kingdom
   come,
   Jesus, remember me.

       JAMES MONTGOMERY,
          1771-1854.

314   777.

JESUS, to Thy table led,
   Now let every heart be fed
With the true and living Bread.

2 When we taste the mystic wine,
Of Thine outpoured blood the sign,
Fill our hearts with love divine.

3 While upon Thy Cross we gaze,
Mourning o'er our sinful ways,
Turn our sadness into praise.

4 Draw us to Thy wounded side,
Whence there flowed the healing
   tide ;
There our sins and sorrows hide.

5 From the bonds of sin release ;
Cold and wavering faith increase ;
Lamb of God, grant us Thy peace.

6 Lead us by Thy piercèd hand,
Till around Thy throne we stand,
In the bright and better land.

       ROBERT HALL BAYNES,
          1831-95.

315
76. 76.

THOU standest at the altar,
  Thou offerest every prayer ;
In faith's unclouded vision
  We see Thee ever there.

2 Out of Thy hand the incense
    Ascends before the throne,
  Where Thou art interceding,
    Lord Jesus, for Thine own.

3 And, through Thy blood accepted,
    With Thee we keep the feast :
  Thou art alone the Victim ;
    Thou only art the Priest.

4 We come, O only Saviour ;
    On Thee, the Lamb, we feed :
  Thy flesh is bread from heaven ;
    Thy blood is drink indeed.

5 To Thee, Almighty Father ;
    Incarnate Son, to Thee ;
  To Thee, Anointing Spirit,—
    All praise and glory be.
                EDWARD WILTON EDDIS,
                      1825–1905.

316
C. M.

I AM not worthy, holy Lord,
  That Thou shouldst come to me ;
Speak but the word ; one gracious
      word
  Can set the sinner free.

2 I am not worthy ; cold and bare
    The lodging of my soul ;
  How canst Thou deign to enter
      there ?
  Lord, speak, and make me whole.

3 I am not worthy ; yet, my God,
    How can I say Thee nay,—
  Thee, who didst give Thy flesh and
      blood
    My ransom price to pay ?

4 O come, in this sweet morning[1] hour,
    Feed me with food divine ;
  And fill with all Thy love and power
    This worthless heart of mine.
              [1] Or evening.
                HENRY WILLIAMS BAKER,
                        1821–77.

317
66. 66. 88.

AUTHOR of life divine,
  Who hast a table spread,
Furnished with mystic wine
  And everlasting bread,
Preserve the life Thyself hast given,
And feed and train us up for heaven.

2   Our needy souls sustain
      With fresh supplies of love,
  Till all Thy life we gain,
      And all Thy fulness prove,
  And, strengthened by Thy perfect
      grace,
  Behold without a veil Thy face.
              CHARLES WESLEY, 1707–88.

318
98. 98. D.

BREAD of the world, in mercy
      broken,
  Wine of the soul, in mercy shed,
By whom the words of life were spoken,
  And in whose death our sins are dead :
Look on the heart by sorrow broken,
  Look on the tears by sinners shed ;
And be Thy feast to us the token
  That by Thy grace our souls are fed.
              REGINALD HEBER, 1783–1826.

319
10 10. 10 10.

THEE we adore, O hidden Saviour,
      Thee,
Who in Thy sacrament dost deign
      to be :
Both flesh and spirit at Thy presence
      fail,
Yet here Thy presence we devoutly
      hail.

2 O blest memorial of our dying Lord !
  Thou living Bread, who life dost
      here afford,
  O may our souls for ever live by
      Thee,
  And Thou to us for ever precious be.

3 Fountain of goodness, Jesus, Lord,
      and God,
  Cleanse us, unclean, with Thy most
      cleansing blood ;
  Make us in Thee devoutly to believe,
  In Thee to hope, to Thee in love to
      cleave.

THE LORD'S SUPPER

4 Ŏ Christ, whom nŏw beneath a veil
      we see,
   Măy what we thĭrst for soon our
      portion be,
   There ĭn the glŏry of Thy dwelling-
      place
   Tŏ gaze on Thee unveiled, and see
      Thy face. Ȁmen.
      ST. THOMAS AQUINAS, 1227–74
         tr. by JAMES RUSSELL WOODFORD,
            1820–85.

320
                    10 10. 10 10. 10 10.

AND now, O Father, mindful of the
   love
   That bought us, once for all, on
      Calvary's Tree,
   And having with us Him that pleads
      above,
   We here present, we here spread
      forth to Thee
   That only offering perfect in Thine
      eyes,
   The one true, pure, immortal
      sacrifice.

2 Look, Father, look on His anointed
      face,
   And only look on us as found in
      Him ;
   Look not on our misusings of Thy
      graces,
   Our prayer so languid, and our
      faith so dim :
   For lo ! between our sins and their
      reward
   We set the passion of Thy Son our
      Lord.

3 And then for those, our dearest and
      our best,
   By this prevailing presence we
      appeal ;
   O fold them closer to Thy mercy's
      breast,
   O do Thine utmost for their souls'
      true weal ;
   From tainting mischief keep them
      white and clear,
   And crown Thy gifts with strength
      to persevere.

4 And so we come : O draw us to Thy
      feet,
   Most patient Saviour, who canst
      love us still ;
   And by this food, so awful and so
      sweet,
   Deliver us from every touch of ill :
   In Thine own service make us glad
      and free,
   And grant us never more to part with
      Thee.
      WILLIAM BRIGHT, 1824–1901.

321
                            77. 77. 77.

'TILL He come !' O let the words
   Linger on the trembling chords ;
   Let the little while between
   In their golden light be seen ;
   Let us think how heaven and home
   Lie beyond that ' Till He come '.

2 When the weary ones we love
   Enter on their rest above,
   Seems the earth so poor and vast,
   All our life-joy overcast ?
   Hush, be every murmur dumb ;
   It is only till He come.

3 Clouds and conflicts round us press ;
   Would we have one sorrow less ?
   All the sharpness of the cross,
   All that tells the world is loss,
   Death, and darkness, and the tomb
   Only whisper ' Till He come '.

4 See, the feast of love is spread ;
   Drink the wine, and break the
      bread—
   Sweet memorials,—till the Lord
   Call us round His heavenly board,
   Some from earth, from glory some,
   Severed only till He come.
      EDWARD HENRY BICKERSTETH,
         1825–1906.

322
                                88. 84.

BY Christ redeemed, in Christ
   restored,
   We keep the memory adored,
   And show the death of our dear Lord
               Until He come.

2 His body, broken in our stead,
   Is here in this memorial bread,
   And so our feeble love is fed
               Until He come.

3 The drops of His dread agony,
His life-blood shed for us, we see ;
The wine shall tell the mystery
          Until He come.

4 And thus that dark betrayal night
With the last advent we unite,
By one blest chain of loving rite,
          Until He come.

5 O blessèd hope ! with this elate,
Let not our hearts be desolate,
But, strong in faith, in patience wait
          Until He come.

                    GEORGE RAWSON, 1807–89.

323
10 10. 10 10.

HERE, O my Lord, I see Thee
     face to face ;
  Here would I touch and handle
     things unseen,
  Here grasp with firmer hand the
     eternal grace,
  And all my weariness upon Thee
     lean.

2 Here would I feed upon the bread
     of God,
  Here drink with Thee the royal
     wine of heaven ;
  Here would I lay aside each earthly
     load,
  Here taste afresh the calm of sin
     forgiven.

3 This is the hour of banquet and of
     song ;
  This is the heavenly table spread
     for me ;
  Here let me feast, and, feasting, still
     prolong
  The brief, bright hour of fellow-
     ship with Thee.

4 Too soon we rise ; the symbols
     disappear ;
  The feast, though not the love, is
     past and gone ;
  The bread and wine remove, but
     Thou art here,
  Nearer than ever, still my Shield
     and Sun.

5 I have no help but Thine ; nor do
     I need
  Another arm save Thine to lean
     upon ;
  It is enough, my Lord, enough
     indeed ;
  My strength is in Thy might, Thy
     might alone.

6 Mine is the sin, but Thine the right-
     eousness ;
  Mine is the guilt, but Thine the
     cleansing blood ;
  Here is my robe, my refuge, and my
     peace ;—
  Thy blood, Thy righteousness, O
     Lord my God.

7 Feast after feast thus comes and
     passes by,
  Yet, passing, points to the glad feast
     above,
  Giving sweet foretaste of the festal joy,
  The Lamb's great bridal feast of
     bliss and love.

                    HORATIUS BONAR, 1808–89.

324
88. 88. D. Trochaic.

DECK thyself, my soul, with glad-
     ness,
Leave the gloomy haunts of sadness,
Come into the daylight's splendour,
There with joy thy praises render
Unto Him whose grace unbounded
Hath this wondrous banquet founded ;
High o'er all the heavens He reigneth,
Yet to dwell with thee He deigneth.

2 Hasten as a bride to meet Him,
And with loving reverence greet
     Him,
For with words of life immortal
Now He knocketh at thy portal ;
Haste to ope the gates before Him,
Saying, while thou dost adore Him,
' Suffer, Lord, that I receive Thee,
And I never more will leave Thee.'

3 Sun, who all my life dost brighten ;
Light, who dost my soul enlighten ;
Joy, the sweetest man e'er knoweth ;
Fount, whence all my being floweth :
At Thy feet I cry, my Maker,
Let me be a fit partaker
Of this blessèd food from heaven,
For our good, Thy glory, given.

4 Jesus, Bread of Life, I pray Thee,
Let me gladly here obey Thee ;
Never to my hurt invited,
Be Thy love with love requited :
From this banquet let me measure,
Lord, how vast and deep its treasure ;
Through the gifts Thou here dost
     give me,
As Thy guest in heaven receive me.

                    JOHANN FRANCK, 1618–77 ; tr. by
                    CATHERINE WINKWORTH, 1827–78.

325

88. 86.

O GOD of Love, to Thee we bow,
And pray for these before Thee
now,
That, closely knit in holy vow,
They may in Thee be one.

2 When days are filled with pure
delight,
When paths are plain and skies are
bright,
Walking by faith and not by sight,
May they in Thee be one.

3 When stormy winds fulfil Thy will,
And all their good seems turned to
ill,
Then, trusting Thee completely, still
May they in Thee be one.

4 Whate'er in life shall be their share
Of quickening joy or burdening care,
In power to do and grace to bear,
May they in Thee be one.

5 Eternal Love, with them abide ;
In Thee for ever may they hide,
For even death cannot divide
Those whom Thou makest one.

WILLIAM VAUGHAN JENKINS,
1868–1920.

326

76. 76. D.

O FATHER, all creating,
Whose wisdom, love, and power
First bound two lives together
In Eden's primal hour,
To-day to these Thy children
Thine earliest gifts renew,—
A home by Thee made happy,
A love by Thee kept true.

2 O Saviour, Guest most bounteous
Of old in Galilee,
Vouchsafe to-day Thy presence
With these who call on Thee ;
Their store of earthly gladness
Transform to heavenly wine,
And teach them, in the tasting,
To know the gift is Thine.

3 O Spirit of the Father,
Breathe on them from above,
So mighty in Thy pureness,
So tender in Thy love ;
That, guarded by Thy presence,
From sin and strife kept free,
Their lives may own Thy guidance,
Their hearts be ruled by Thee.

4 Except Thou build it, Father,
The house is built in vain ;
Except Thou, Saviour, bless it,
The joy will turn to pain ;
But nought can break the union
Of hearts in Thee made one ;
And love Thy Spirit hallows
Is endless love begun.

JOHN ELLERTON, 1826–93.

327

11 10. 11 10.

O PERFECT Love, all human
thought transcending,
Lowly we kneel in prayer before
Thy throne,
That theirs may be the love which
knows no ending
Whom Thou for evermore dost
join in one.

2 O perfect Life, be Thou their full
assurance
Of tender charity and steadfast
faith,
Of patient hope, and quiet brave
endurance,
With childlike trust that fears nor
pain nor death.

3 Grant them the joy which brightens
earthly sorrow ;
Grant them the peace which calms
all earthly strife,
And to life's day the glorious unknown morrow
That dawns upon eternal love and
life.

DOROTHY FRANCES GURNEY,
1858–1932.

328   77. 77. D.

SAFELY, safely gathered in,
  No more sorrow, no more sin,
No more childish griefs or fears,
No more sadness, no more tears ;
For the life, so young and fair,
  Now hath passed from earthly
        care ;
God Himself the soul will keep,
  Giving His belovèd sleep.

2 Safely, safely gathered in,
  Free from sorrow, free from sin,
Passed beyond all grief and pain,
Death for thee is truest gain :
For our loss we must not weep,
Nor our loved one long to keep
From the home of rest and peace,
Where all sin and sorrow cease.

3 Safely, safely gathered in,
  No more sorrow, no more sin ;
God has saved from weary strife,
In its dawn, this young fresh life,
Which awaits us now above,
Resting in the Saviour's love.
Jesus, grant that we may meet
There, adoring at Thy feet.

          HENRIETTA OCTAVIA DE LISLE
                    DOBREE, 1831–94.

329   77. 77.

WHEN our heads are bowed with
        woe,
When our bitter tears o'erflow,
When we mourn the lost, the dear,
Jesus, Son of Mary, hear !

2 Thou our throbbing flesh hast worn :
Thou our mortal griefs hast borne :
Thou hast shed the human tear :
Jesus, Son of Mary, hear !

3 When the sullen death-bell tolls
For our own departing souls,
When our final doom is near,
Jesus, Son of Mary, hear !

4 Thou hast bowed the dying head :
Thou the blood of life hast shed :
Thou hast filled a mortal bier :
Jesus, Son of Mary, hear !

5 When the heart is sad within
With the thought of all its sin,
When the spirit shrinks with fear,
Jesus, Son of Mary, hear !

6 Thou the shame, the grief, hast
        known,
  Though the sins were not Thine
        own :
  Thou hast deigned their load to
        bear :
  Jesus, Son of Mary, hear !

          HENRY HART MILMAN,
                    1791–1868.

330   77. 77. and refrain.

NOW the labourer's task is o'er,
  Now the battle-day is past ;
Now upon the farther shore
  Lands the voyager at last.
    Father, in Thy gracious keeping
    Leave we now Thy servant sleep-
        ing.

2 There the tears of earth are dried ;
    There its hidden things are clear :
  There the work of life is tried
    By a juster Judge than here.

3 There the penitents that turn
    To the Cross their dying eyes
  All the love of Jesus learn
    At His feet in Paradise.

4 ' Earth to earth, and dust to dust,'
    Calmly now the words we say ;
  Leaving *him* to sleep, in trust,
    Till the resurrection day.

          JOHN ELLERTON, 1826–93.

Alternative last verse for USE AT SEA :—

5 ' Till the sea gives up its dead,'—
    Calmly now the words we say,—
  Laid in ocean's quiet bed
    Till the resurrection day.
      Father, in Thy gracious keeping
      Leave we now Thy servant sleep-
          ing.

331   88. 84.

O LORD of life, where'er they be,
  Safe in Thine own eternity,
Our dead are living unto Thee.
          Hallelujah !

2 All souls are Thine, and, here or
        there,
  They rest within Thy sheltering care ;
  One providence alike they share.
          Hallelujah !

BURIAL OF THE DEAD

3 Thy word is true, Thy ways are just ;
Above the requiem, ' Dust to dust,'
Shall rise our psalm of grateful trust,
Hallelujah !

4 O happy they in God who rest,
No more by fear and doubt op-
pressed ;
Living or dying, they are blest.
Hallelujah !

FREDERICK LUCIAN HOSMER,
1840–1929.

332   88. 88. 88.

GOD of the living, in whose eyes
Unveiled Thy whole creation
lies,
All souls are Thine ; we must not
say
That those are dead who pass away ;
From this our world of flesh set
free,
We know them living unto Thee.

2 Released from earthly toil and strife,
With Thee is hidden still their life ;
Thine are their thoughts, their works,
their powers,
All Thine, and yet most truly ours ;
For well we know, where'er they be,
Our dead are living unto Thee.

3 Thy word is true, Thy will is just ;
To Thee we leave them, Lord, in
trust ;
And bless Thee for the love which
gave
Thy Son to fill a human grave,
That none might fear that world to
see,
Where all are living unto Thee.

4 O Giver unto man of breath,
O Holder of the keys of death,
O Quickener of the life within,
Save us from death, the death of sin ;
That body, soul, and spirit be
For ever living unto Thee.

JOHN ELLERTON, 1826–93.

THE SERVICE OF THE KINGDOM

333   *Ordination* (333–334).
                                L. M.

POUR out Thy Spirit from on
high ;
Lord, Thine ordainèd servants
bless ;
Graces and gifts to each supply,
And clothe Thy priests with
righteousness.

2 Within Thy temple when they stand,
To teach the truth, as taught by
Thee,
Saviour, like stars in Thy right hand
The angels of the churches be !

3 Wisdom and zeal and faith impart,
Firmness with meekness, from
above,
To bear Thy people on their heart,
And love the souls whom Thou
dost love ;

4 To watch and pray, and never faint ;
By day and night strict guard to
keep ;
To warn the sinner, cheer the saint,
Nourish Thy lambs, and feed Thy
sheep ;

5 Then, when their work is finished
here,
In humble hope their charge
resign.
When the Chief Shepherd shall
appear,
O God, may they and we be Thine.
JAMES MONTGOMERY,
1771–1854.

334   L. M.

O THOU who makest souls to
shine
With light from brighter worlds
above,
And droppest glistening dew divine
On all who seek a Saviour's love,

2 Do Thou Thy benediction give
On all who teach, on all who learn,
That all Thy Church may holier live,
And every lamp more brightly burn.

3 Give those that teach pure hearts and
wise,
Faith, hope, and love, all warmed
by prayer ;
Themselves first training for the
skies,
They best will raise their people
there.

105

4 Give those that learn the willing ear,
    The spirit meek, the guileless
        mind ;
Such gifts will make the lowliest here
    Far better than a kingdom find.

5 O bless the shepherd, bless the sheep,
    That guide and guided both be
        one,
One in the faithful watch they keep,
    Until this hurrying life be done.

6 If thus, good Lord, Thy grace be
        given,
    Our glory meets us ere we die ;
Before we upward pass to heaven,
    We taste our immortality.

                    JOHN ARMSTRONG,
                        1813–56.

Consecration of Church-workers
                (335–339)
335   76. 76. D.

LORD of the living harvest
    That whitens o'er the plain,
Where angels soon shall gather
    Their sheaves of golden grain,
Accept fresh hands to labour,
    Fresh hearts to trust and love,
And deign with them to hasten
    Thy Kingdom from above.

2 As labourers in Thy vineyard,
    Lord, send them out to be,
Content to bear the burden
    Of weary days for Thee,
Content to ask no wages
    When Thou shalt call them home,
But to have shared the travail
    That makes Thy Kingdom come.

3 Be with them, God the Father,
    Be with them, God the Son,
Be with them, God the Spirit,
    Eternal Three in One !
Make them a royal priesthood,
    Thee rightly to adore,
And fill them with Thy fulness
    Now and for evermore.
        JOHN SAMUEL BEWLEY MONSELL,
                        1811–75.

336   66. 66. D.

SHINE Thou upon us, Lord,
    True Light of men, to-day,
And through the written word
    Thy very self display ;

That so, from hearts which burn
    With gazing on Thy face,
Thy little ones may learn
    The wonders of Thy grace.

2 Breathe Thou upon us, Lord,
    Thy Spirit's living flame,
That so, with one accord,
    Our lips may tell Thy Name ;
Give Thou the hearing ear,
    Fix Thou the wandering thought,
That those we teach may hear
    The great things Thou hast
        wrought.

3 Speak Thou for us, O Lord,
    In all we say of Thee ;
According to Thy word
    Let all our teaching be ;
That so Thy lambs may know
    Their own true Shepherd's voice,
Where'er He leads them go,
    And in His love rejoice.

4 Live Thou within us, Lord ;
    Thy mind and will be ours ;
Be Thou beloved, adored,
    And served with all our powers ;
That so our lives may teach
    Thy children what Thou art,
And plead, by more than speech,
    For Thee, with every heart.
                    JOHN ELLERTON, 1826–93.

337   87. 87. D.

LORD of light, whose Name out-
        shineth
    All the stars and suns of space,
Deign to make us Thy co-workers
    In the Kingdom of Thy grace ;
Use to fulfil Thy purpose
    In the gift of Christ Thy Son :
Father, as in highest heaven,
    So on earth Thy will be done.

2 By the toil of lowly workers
    In some far outlying field ;
By the courage where the radiance
    Of the Cross is still revealed ;
By the victories of meekness,
    Through reproach and suffering
        won,—
Father, as in highest heaven,
    So on earth Thy will be done.

3 Grant that knowledge, still increasing,
    At Thy feet may lowly kneel ;
With Thy grace our triumphs hallow,
    With Thy charity our zeal ;

THE SERVICE OF THE KINGDOM

Lift the nations from the shadows
    To the gladness of the sun :
Father, as in highest heaven,
    So on earth Thy will be done.

4 By the prayers of faithful watch-
        men,
    Never silent day or night ;
By the Cross of Jesus bringing
    Peace to men, and healing light ;
By the love that passeth knowledge,
    Making all Thy children one :
Father, as in highest heaven,
    So on earth Thy will be done.
                HOWELL ELVET LEWIS,
                    1860-1953.

338   L. M.

LORD, speak to me, that I may
        speak
    In living echoes of Thy tone ;
As Thou hast sought, so let me seek
    Thy erring children lost and lone.

2 O lead me, Lord, that I may lead
    The wandering and the wavering
        feet ;
O feed me, Lord, that I may feed
    Thy hungering ones with manna
        sweet.

3 O strengthen me, that, while I stand
    Firm on the rock, and strong in
        Thee,
I may stretch out a loving hand
    To wrestlers with the troubled sea.

4 O teach me, Lord, that I may teach
    The precious things Thou dost
        impart ;
And wing my words, that they may
        reach
    The hidden depths of many a
        heart.

5 O give Thine own sweet rest to me,
    That I may speak with soothing
        power
A word in season, as from Thee,
    To weary ones in needful hour.

6 O fill me with Thy fulness, Lord,
    Until my very heart o'erflow
In kindling thought and glowing
        word,
    Thy love to tell, Thy praise to
        show.

7 O use me, Lord, use even me,
    Just as Thou wilt, and when, and
        where,
Until Thy blessèd face I see,
    Thy rest, Thy joy, Thy glory share.
        FRANCES RIDLEY HAVERGAL,
                    1836-79.

339   L. M.

O MASTER, let me walk with
        Thee
In lowly paths of service free ;
Thy secret tell ; help me to bear
The strain of toil, the fret of care.

2 Help me the slow of heart to move
By some clear winning word of love ;
Teach me the wayward feet to stay,
And guide them in the homeward
    way.

3 Teach me Thy patience ; still with
        Thee
In closer, dearer company,
In work that keeps faith sweet and
    strong,
In trust that triumphs over wrong,

4 In hope that sends a shining ray
Far down the future's broadening
    way,
In peace that only Thou canst give,
With Thee, O Master, let me live.
            WASHINGTON GLADDEN,
                    1836-1918.

Home Missions (340-346).

340   L. M.

LOOK from the sphere of endless
        day,
    O God of mercy and of might,
In pity look on those who stray,
    Benighted in this land of light.

2 In peopled vale, in lonely glen,
    In crowded mart, by stream or sea,
How many of the sons of men
    Hear not the message sent from
        Thee !

3 Send forth Thy heralds, Lord, to call
    The thoughtless young, the
        hardened old,
A wandering flock, and bring them
        all
    To the Good Shepherd's peaceful
        fold.

4 Send them Thy mighty word to speak,
　Till faith shall dawn and doubt depart,
To awe the bold, to stay the weak,
　And bind and heal the broken heart.

5 Then all these wastes, a dreary scene,
　On which, with sorrowing eyes, we gaze,
Shall grow, with living waters, green,
　And lift to heaven the voice of praise.

WILLIAM CULLEN BRYANT,
1794–1878.

341
77. 77.

SOLDIERS of the Cross, arise !
　Gird you with your armour bright ;
Mighty are your enemies,
　Hard the battle ye must fight.

2 O'er a faithless fallen world
　Raise your banner in the sky ;
Let it float there wide unfurled ;
　Bear it onward ; lift it high.

3 'Mid the homes of want and woe,
　Strangers to the living word,
Let the Saviour's herald go,
　Let the voice of hope be heard.

4 Where the shadows deepest lie,
　Carry truth's unsullied ray ;
Where are crimes of blackest dye,
　There the saving sign display.

5 To the weary and the worn
　Tell of realms where sorrows cease ;
To the outcast and forlorn
　Speak of mercy and of peace.

6 Guard the helpless ; seek the strayed ;
　Comfort troubles ; banish grief ;
In the might of God arrayed,
　Scatter sin and unbelief.

7 Be the banner still unfurled,
　Still unsheathed the Spirit's sword,
Till the kingdoms of the world
　Are the Kingdom of the Lord.

WILLIAM WALSHAM HOW,
1823–97.

342
76. 76.

BOWED low in supplication,
　We come, O Lord, to Thee ;
Thy grace alone can save us ;
　To Thee alone we flee.

2 We come for this our parish
　Thy mercy to implore ;
On church, and homes, and people,
　O Lord, Thy blessing pour.

3 Blot out our sins, O Father ;
　Forgive the guilty past ;
Loose from their chains the captives
　Whom Satan holdeth fast.

4 Wake up the slumbering conscience
　To listen to Thy call ;
The weak and wavering strengthen,
　And raise up them that fall.

5 Our crying sin drive from us
　With Thy chastising rod,
That we may be a people
　Fearing and loving God.

6 O be Thy house, Lord, hallowed,
　And hallowed be Thy day ;
Let sin-stained souls find pardon,
　And learn to love and pray.

7 With heavenly food supported,
　O be they firm and strong
To follow all things holy,
　To flee from all things wrong.

8 Lord, banish strife and variance ;
　Knit sundered hearts in one ;
And bind us all together
　In love to Thy dear Son.

WILLIAM WALSHAM HOW,
1823–97.

343
65. 65.

CHRISTIAN, work for Jesus,
　Who on earth for thee
Laboured, wearied, suffered,
　Died upon the Tree.

2 Work, with lips so fervid
　That thy words may prove
Thou hast brought a message
　From the God of love.

3 Work, with heart that burneth
　Humbly at His feet
Priceless gems to offer,
　For His crown made meet.

4 Work, with prayer unceasing,
　Borne on faith's strong wing,
Earnestly beseeching
　Trophies for the King.

5 Work, with strength endureth,
　Until death draw near ;
Then thy Lord's sweet welcome
　Thou in heaven shalt hear.

MARY HASLOCH, 1816–92.

344   S. M.

RISE up, O men of God !
Have done with lesser things ;
Give heart and soul and mind and
                                strength
To serve the King of kings.

2 Rise up, O men of God !
His Kingdom tarries long ;
Bring in the day of brotherhood,
And end the night of wrong.

3 Rise up, O men of God !
The Church for you doth wait,
Her strength unequal to her task ;
Rise up and make her great.

4 Lift high the Cross of Christ !
Tread where His feet have trod ;
As brothers of the Son of Man
Rise up, O men of God !
WILLIAM PIERSON MERRILL,
1867–1954.

345   C. M.

FOUNTAIN of good, to own Thy
                                love
Our thankful hearts incline ;
What can we render, Lord, to Thee,
When all the worlds are Thine ?

2 But Thou hast needy brethren here,
Partakers of Thy grace,
Whose names Thou wilt Thyself
                                confess
Before the Father's face.

3 And in their accents of distress
Thy pleading voice is heard ;
In them Thou mayst be clothed and
                                fed,
And visited and cheered.

4 Thy face, with reverence and with
                                love,
We in Thy poor would see ;
O may we minister to them,
And in them, Lord, to Thee.
PHILIP DODDRIDGE, 1702–51.

346   S. M.

WE give Thee but Thine own,
Whate'er the gift may be ;
All that we have is Thine alone,
A trust, O Lord, from Thee.

2 May we Thy bounties thus
As stewards true receive,
And gladly, as Thou blessest us,
To Thee our first-fruits give.

3 O hearts are bruised and dead,
And homes are bare and cold,
And lambs for whom the Shepherd
                                bled
Are straying from the fold.

4 To comfort and to bless,
To find a balm for woe,
To tend the lone and fatherless,
Is angels' work below.

5 The captive to release,
To God the lost to bring,
To teach the way of life and peace,
It is a Christ-like thing.

6 And we believe Thy word,
Though dim our faith may be,—
Whate'er for Thine we do, O Lord,
We do it unto Thee.
WILLIAM WALSHAM HOW,
1823–97.

347 *Flower Service.*   11 10. 11 10.

HERE, Lord, we offer Thee all
that is fairest,
Bloom from the garden and flowers
from the field,
Gifts for the stricken ones, knowing
Thou carest
More for the love than the wealth
that we yield.

2 Send, Lord, by these to the sick and
the dying,
Speak to their hearts with a
message of peace ;
Comfort the sad who in weakness
are lying,
Grant the departing a gentle
release.

3 Raise, Lord, to health again those
who have sickened ;
Fair be their lives as the roses in
bloom ;
Give, of Thy grace, to the souls Thou
hast quickened,
Gladness for sorrow and brightness for gloom.
ABEL GERALD WILSON BLUNT,
1827–1902.

348

Temperance Work (348–349).
76. 76. D.

O THOU, before whose presence
Nought evil may come in,
Yet who dost look in mercy
Down on this world of sin,
O give us noble purpose
To set the sin-bound free,
And Christ-like tender pity
To seek the lost for Thee.

2 Fierce is our subtle foeman :
The forces at his hand,
With woes that none can number,
Despoil the pleasant land ;
All they who war against them,
In strife so keen and long,
Must in their Saviour's armour
Be stronger than the strong.

3 So hast Thou wrought among us
The great things that we see !
For things that are, we thank
Thee,
And for the things to be :
For bright hope is uplifting
Faint hands and feeble knees,
To strive, beneath Thy blessing,
For greater things than these.

4 Lead on, O Love and Mercy,
O Purity and Power,
Lead on till peace eternal
Shall close this battle-hour ;
Till all who prayed and struggled
To set their brethren free,
In triumph meet to praise Thee,
Most Holy Trinity.

SAMUEL JOHN STONE,
1839–1900.

349

88. 87.

FATHER, who on man dost
shower
Gifts of plenty from Thy dower,
To Thy people give the power
All Thy gifts to use aright.

2 Give pure happiness in leisure,
Temperance in every pleasure,
Holy use of earthly treasure,
Bodies clear and spirits bright.

3 Lift from this and every nation
All that brings us degradation ;
Quell the forces of temptation ;
Put Thine enemies to flight.

4 Be with us, Thy strength supplying,
That with energy undying,
Every foe of man defying,
We may rally to the fight.

5 Thou who art our Captain ever,
Lead us on to great endeavour ;
May Thy Church the world deliver :
Give us wisdom, courage, might.

6 Father, who hast sought and found
us,
Son of God, whose love has bound
us,
Holy Ghost, within us, round us—
Hear us, Godhead infinite.
PERCY DEARMER, 1867–1936.

350

Dumb creatures.   88. 88. 88.

MAKER of earth and sea and sky,
Creation's Sovereign, Lord
and King,
Who hung the starry worlds on high
With hands that shaped the spar-
row's wing :
Bless the dumb creatures in our care,
And listen to their voiceless prayer.

2 For us they toil, for us they die,
These humble creatures Thou hast
made ;
How shall we dare their rights deny,
On whom Thy seal of love is laid ?
Teach Thou our hearts to heed their
plea,
As Thou dost man's in prayer to
Thee.

EMILY BRYANT LORD,
1839–86.

Medical Work (351–353).

351

C. M.

FROM Thee all skill and science
flow,
All pity, care, and love,
All calm and courage, faith and hope ;
O pour them from above.

2 And part them, Lord, to each and all,
As each and all shall need,
To rise like incense, each to Thee,
In noble thought and deed.

3 And hasten, Lord, that perfect day
When pain and death shall cease,
And Thy just rule shall fill the earth
With health, and light, and peace ;

4 When ever blue the sky shall gleam,
    And ever green the sod ;
And man's rude work deface no more
    The Paradise of God.
                CHARLES KINGSLEY, 1819–75.

352   87. 87. 77.

THOU to whom the sick and dying
    Ever came, nor came in vain,
Still with healing words replying
    To the wearied cry of pain,
        Hear us, Jesus, as we meet,
        Suppliants at Thy mercy-seat.

2 Still the weary, sick, and dying
    Need a brother's, sister's care ;
On Thy higher help relying,
    May we now their burden share,
        Bringing all our offerings meet,
        Suppliants at Thy mercy-seat.

3 May each child of Thine be willing,
    Willing both in hand and heart,
All the law of love fulfilling,
    Ever comfort to impart,
        Ever bringing offerings meet,
        Suppliant, to Thy mercy-seat.

4 So may sickness, sin, and sadness
    To Thy healing virtue yield,
Till the sick and sad, in gladness,
    Rescued,   ransomed,   cleansèd,
        healed,
        One in Thee together meet,
        Pardoned at Thy judgment-seat.
                GODFREY THRING, 1823–1903.

Medical Missions.

353   C. M.

FATHER, whose will is life and
        good
    For all of mortal breath,
Bind strong the bond of brotherhood
    Of those who fight with death.

2 Empower the hands and hearts and
        wills
    Of friends in lands afar,
Who battle with the body's ills,
    And wage Thy holy war.

3 Where'er they heal the maimed and
        blind,
    Let love of Christ attend :
Proclaim the good Physician's mind,
    And prove the Saviour friend.

4 For still His love works wondrous
        charms,
    And, as in days of old,
He takes the wounded to His arms,
    And bears them to the fold.

5 O Father, look from heaven and bless,
    Where'er Thy servants be,
Their works of pure unselfishness,
    Made consecrate to Thee !
            HARDWICKE DRUMMOND RAWNSLEY,
                        1851–1920.

354   86. 86. 86.

DISMISS me not Thy service,
        Lord,
    But train me for Thy will :
For even I, in fields so broad,
    Some duties may fulfil ;
And I will ask for no reward,
    Except to serve Thee still.

2 How many serve, how many more
    May to the service come !
To tend the vines, the grapes to store,
    Thou dost appoint for some ;
Thou hast Thy young men at the
        war,
    Thy little ones at home.

3 All works are good, and each is best
    As most it pleases Thee ;
Each worker pleases when the rest
    He serves in charity ;
And neither man nor work unblest
    Wilt Thou permit to be.

4 Our Master all the work hath done
    He asks of us to-day ;
Sharing His service, every one
    Share too His sonship may :
Lord, I would serve and be a son ;
    Dismiss me not, I pray.
                THOMAS TOKE LYNCH, 1818–71.

355   D. C. M.

O LORD of life, and love, and
        power,
    How joyful life would be,
If in Thy service every hour
    We lived and moved with Thee !
If youth in all its bloom and might
    By Thee were sanctified,
And manhood found its chief delight
    In working at Thy side !

2 'Tis ne'er too late, while life shall
        last,
    A new life to begin ;
  'Tis ne'er too late to leave the past,
    And break with self and sin :
  And we this day, both old and young,
    Would earnestly aspire
  For hearts to nobler purpose strung,
    And purified desire.

3 Nor for ourselves alone we plead,
    But for all faithful souls
  Who serve Thy cause by word or
        deed,
    Whose names Thy book enrols.
  O speed Thy work, victorious King,
    And give Thy workers might,
  That through the world Thy truth
        may ring,
    And all men see Thy light.
        ELLA SOPHIA ARMITAGE, 1841–1931.

356   L. M.

GO, labour on : spend and be
        spent,
    Thy joy to do the Father's will ;
  It is the way the Master went ;
    Should not the servant tread it
        still ?

2 Go, labour on while it is day :
    The world's dark night is hasten-
        ing on ;
  Speed, speed thy work ; cast sloth
        away ;
    It is not thus that souls are won.

3 Men die in darkness at thy side,
    Without a hope to cheer the tomb ;
  Take up the torch and wave it wide,
    The torch that lights time's thick-
        est gloom.

4 Toil on, faint not, keep watch, and
        pray ;
    Be wise the erring soul to win ;
  Go forth into the world's highway,
    Compel the wanderer to come in.

5 Toil on, and in thy toil rejoice
    For toil comes rest, for exile home ;
  Soon shalt thou hear the Bride-
        groom's voice,
    The midnight peal, ' Behold, I
        come ! '
        HORATIUS BONAR, 1808–89.

357   76. 75. D.

WORK, for the night is coming !
    Work through the morning
        hours ;
  Work while the dew is sparkling ;
    Work 'mid springing flowers ;
  Work while the day grows brighter,
    Under the glowing sun ;
  Work, for the night is coming,
    When man's work is done.

2 Work, for the night is coming !
    Work through the sunny noon ;
  Fill brightest hours with labour ;
    Rest comes sure and soon.
  Give to each flying minute
    Something to keep in store ;
  Work, for the night is coming,
    When man works no more.

3 Work, for the night is coming !
    Under the sunset skies,
  While their bright tints are glowing,
    Work, for daylight flies.
  Work till the last beam fadeth,
    Fadeth to shine no more ;
  Work while the night is darkening,
    When man's work is o'er.
        Adapted from ANNA LOUISA COGHILL,
                            1836–1907.

358   888.

O YE who taste that love is sweet,
    Set waymarks for all doubtful
        feet
  That stumble on in search of it.

2 Sing notes of love : that some who
        hear
  Far off, inert, may lend an ear,
  Rise up and wonder and draw near.

3 Lead lives of love ; that others who
  Behold your life may kindle too
  With love, and cast their lot with you.
        CHRISTINA GEORGINA ROSSETTI,
                            1830–94.

359   87. 87. D.

SON of God, eternal Saviour,
    Source of life and truth and
        grace,
  Son of Man, whose birth incarnate
    Hallows all our human race ;

Thou, our Head, who, throned in glory,
  For Thine own dost ever plead,
Fill us with Thy love and pity,
  Heal our wrongs, and help our need.

2 As Thou, Lord, hast lived for others,
    So may we for others live ;
  Freely have Thy gifts been granted,
    Freely may Thy servants give.
  Thine the gold and Thine the silver,
    Thine the wealth of land and sea,
  We but stewards of Thy bounty,
    Held in solemn trust for Thee.

3 Come, O Christ, and reign among us,
    King of love, and Prince of peace ;
  Hush the storm of strife and passion,
    Bid its cruel discords cease.
  Ah, the past is dark behind us,
    Strewn with wrecks and stained with blood ;
  But before us gleams the vision
    Of the coming brotherhood.

4 See the Christlike host advancing,
    High and lowly, great and small,
  Linked in bonds of common service
    For the common Lord of all.
  Thou who prayedst, Thou who willest
    That Thy people should be one,
  Grant, O grant our hope's fruition :
    Here on earth Thy will be done.

SOMERSET CORRY LOWRY,
1855–1932.

360
11 10. 11 10.

O SON of God, our Captain of salvation,
    Thyself by suffering schooled to human grief,
  We bless Thee for Thy sons of consolation,
    Who follow in the steps of Thee their Chief ;

2 Those whom Thy Spirit's dread vocation severs
    To lead the vanguard of Thy conquering host ;
  Whose toilsome years are spent in brave endeavours
    To bear Thy saving Name from coast to coast ;

3 Those whose bright faith makes feeble hearts grow stronger,
    And sends fresh warriors to the great campaign,
  Bids the lone convert feel estranged no longer,
    And wins the sundered to be one again ;

4 And all true helpers, patient, kind, and skilful,
    Who shed Thy light across our darkened earth,
  Counsel the doubting, and restrain the wilful,
    Soothe the sick-bed, and share the children's mirth.

5 Thus, Lord, Thy blessèd saints in memory keeping,
    Still be Thy Church's watchword,
    ' Comfort ye,'—
  Till in our Father's house shall end our weeping,
    And all our wants be satisfied in Thee.

JOHN ELLERTON, 1826–93.

361
88. 84.

DEAR Master, what can children do ?
    The angels came from heaven above
  To comfort Thee ; may children too
    Give Thee their love ?

2 No more, as on that night of shame,
    Art Thou in dark Gethsemane,
  Where worshipping, an angel came
    To strengthen Thee.

3 But Thou hast taught us that Thou art
    Still present in the crowded street,
  In every lonely, suffering heart
    That there we meet :

4 And not one simple, loving deed,
    That lessens gloom, or lightens pain,
  Or answers some unspoken need,
    Is done in vain :

5 Since every passing joy we make
    For men and women that we see,
  If it is offered for Thy sake,
    Is given to Thee.

6 O God, our Master, help us then
　To bless the weary and the sad,
And, comforting our fellow-men,
　To make Thee glad.
ANNIE MATHESON, 1853–1924.

362
56. 659.

THE fields are all white,
　And the reapers are few;
We children are willing,
　But what can we do
To work for our Lord in His harvest?

2　Our hands are so small,
　And our words are so weak:
We cannot teach others;
　How then shall we seek
To work for our Lord in His harvest?

3　We'll work by our prayers,
　By the offerings we bring,
By small self-denials;
　The least little thing
May work for our Lord in His harvest:

4　Until by and by
　As the years pass, at length
We too may be reapers,
　And go forth in strength,
To work for our Lord in His harvest.
The Book of Praise for Children, 1881.

363
76. 76. D.

THE wise may bring their learning,
　The rich may bring their wealth,
And some may bring their greatness,
　And some bring strength and health;
We too would bring our treasures
　To offer to the King;
We have no wealth or learning:
　What shall we children bring?

2　We'll bring Him hearts that love Him;
　We'll bring Him thankful praise,
And young souls meekly striving
　To walk in holy ways:
And these shall be the treasures
　We offer to the King,
And these are gifts that even
　The poorest child may bring.

3　We'll bring the little duties
　We have to do each day;
We'll try our best to please Him,
　At home, at school, at play:
And better are these treasures
　To offer to our King,
Than richest gifts without them;
　Yet these a child may bring.
Congregational Church Hymnal, 1887.

MISSIONS

364
664. 6664.

THOU whose almighty word
　Chaos and darkness heard
　　And took their flight,
Hear us, we humbly pray,
And, where the gospel day
Sheds not its glorious ray,
　　Let there be light.

2 Thou who didst come to bring,
On Thy redeeming wing,
　　Healing and sight,
Health to the sick in mind,
Sight to the inly blind,
O now to all mankind
　　Let there be light.

3 Spirit of truth and love,
Life-giving, holy Dove,
　　Speed forth Thy flight;
Move o'er the waters' face,
Bearing the lamp of grace,
And in earth's darkest place
　　Let there be light.

4 Blessèd and holy Three,
Glorious Trinity,
　　Wisdom, Love, Might,
Boundless as ocean's tide
Rolling in fullest pride,
Through the world far and wide
　　Let there be light.
JOHN MARRIOTT,
1780–1825.

365　From Isaiah ii. 2–6.
C. M.

BEHOLD! the mountain of the Lord
　In latter days shall rise
On mountain tops above the hills,
　And draw the wondering eyes.

2 To this the joyful nations round,
　All tribes and tongues, shall flow;
Up to the hill of God, they'll say,
　And to His house we'll go.

3 The beam that shines from Zion hill
    Shall lighten every land ;
  The King who reigns in Salem's
      towers
    Shall all the world command.

4 Among the nations He shall judge ;
    His judgments truth shall guide ;
  His sceptre shall protect the just,
    And quell the sinner's pride.

5 No strife shall rage, nor hostile feuds
    Disturb those peaceful years ;
  To ploughshares men shall beat their
      swords,
    To pruning-hooks their spears.

6 No longer hosts encountering hosts
    Shall crowds of slain deplore :
  They hang the trumpet in the hall,
    And study war no more.

7 Come then, O house of Jacob ! come
    To worship at His shrine ;
  And, walking in the light of God,
    With holy beauties shine.
          MICHAEL BRUCE, 1746–67 ;
          as in *Scottish Paraphrases*.

Jewish Missions (366–369).

366
L. M.

GREAT God of Abraham, hear
  our prayer :
Let Abraham's seed Thy mercy
  share ;
O may they now at length return,
And look on Him they pierced, and
  mourn !

2 Remember Jacob's flock of old,
  Bring home the wanderers to Thy
    fold ;
Remember, too, Thy promised word,
' Israel at last shall seek the Lord.'

3 Lord, put Thy law within their
  hearts,
And write it in their inward parts ;
The veil of darkness rend in two,
Which hides Messiah from their view.

4 O haste the day, foretold so long,
  When Jew and Greek, a glorious
    throng,
One house shall seek, one prayer shall
    pour,
And one Redeemer shall adore.
      THOMAS COTTERILL, 1779–1823.

367
L. M.

WHEN Israel, of the Lord
  beloved,
Out of the land of bondage came,
Her fathers' God before her moved,
  An awful guide, in smoke and
    flame.

2 By day, along the astonished lands
  The cloudy pillar glided slow ;
By night, Arabia's crimsoned sands
  Returned the fiery column's glow.

3 There rose the choral hymn of praise,
  And trump and timbrel answered
    keen,
And Zion's daughters poured their
    lays,
  With priest's and warrior's voice
    between.

4 No portents now their foes amaze ;
  Forsaken Israel wanders lone ;
Their fathers would not know Thy
    ways,
  And Thou hast left them to their
    own.

5 But, present still, though now un-
    seen,
  When brightly shines the pros-
    perous day,
Be thoughts of Thee a cloudy screen
  To temper the deceitful ray.

6 And O, when stoops on Judah's path,
  In shade and storm, the frequent
    night,
Be Thou, long-suffering, slow to
    wrath,
  A burning and a shining light !
      WALTER SCOTT, 1771–1832.

368 *From Psalm xiv.*
76. 76.

O THAT the Lord's salvation
  Were out of Zion come,
To heal His ancient nation,
  To lead His outcasts home !

2 Let fall Thy rod of terror ;
  Thy saving grace impart ;
Roll back the veil of error ;
  Release the fettered heart.

3 Let Israel, home returning,
  Her lost Messiah see ;
Give oil of joy for mourning,
  And bind Thy Church to Thee.
      HENRY FRANCIS LYTE,
          1793–1847.

369　　　　　　　　　L. M.

ARM of the Lord, awake, awake !
　　Put on Thy strength, the
　　　　nations shake,
And let the world, adoring, see
Triumphs of mercy wrought by
　　　Thee.

2 Say to the heathen from Thy throne,
　' I am Jehovah, God alone ' ;
Thy voice their idols shall confound,
And cast their altars to the ground.

3 Let Zion's time of favour come ;
　O bring the tribes of Israel home ;
And let our wondering eyes behold
Gentiles and Jews in Jesus' fold.

4 Almighty God, Thy grace proclaim
　In every clime of every name ;
Let adverse powers before Thee fall,
And crown the Saviour Lord of all.
　　　WILLIAM SHRUBSOLE, 1759–1829.

370　　　　　　　　　87. 87. D.

' FOR My sake and the Gospel's,
　　　go
　And tell redemption's story ' ;
His heralds answer, ' Be it so,
　And Thine, Lord, all the glory ! '
They preach His birth, His life, His
　　　Cross,
　The love of His atonement
For whom they count the world but
　　　loss,
　His Easter, His enthronement.

2 Hark ! hark ! the trump of jubilee
　　Proclaims to every nation,
From pole to pole, by land and sea,
　　Glad tidings of salvation ;
As nearer draws the day of doom,
　While still the battle rages,
The heavenly dayspring, through the
　　　gloom,
　Breaks on the night of ages.

3 Still on and on the anthems spread,
　　Of hallelujah voices ;
In concert with the holy dead,
　　The warrior Church rejoices ;
Their snow-white robes are washed
　　in blood,
　Their golden harps are ringing ;
Earth and the Paradise of God
　One triumph song are singing.

4 He comes whose advent-trumpet
　　drowns
　The last of time's evangels,
Immanuel, crowned with many
　　crowns,
　The Lord of saints and angels.
O Life, Light, Love, the great I AM
　Triune, who changest never,
The throne of God and of the Lamb
　Is Thine, and Thine for ever.
　　　EDWARD HENRY BICKERSTETH,
　　　　　　　1825–1906.

371　　　　　　　　　76. 76. D.

FROM Greenland's icy mountains,
　　From India's coral strand,
Where Afric's sunny fountains
　Roll down their golden sand,
From many an ancient river,
　From many a palmy plain,
They call us to deliver
　Their land from error's chain.

2 Can we, whose souls are lighted
　　With wisdom from on high,
Can we to men benighted
　The lamp of life deny ?
Salvation ! O salvation !
　The joyful sound proclaim
Till each remotest nation
　Has learnt Messiah's Name.

3 Waft, waft, ye winds, His story,
　And you, ye waters, roll,
Till, like a sea of glory,
　It spreads from pole to pole ;
Till o'er our ransomed nature
　The Lamb for sinners slain,
Redeemer, King, Creator,
　In bliss returns to reign.
　　　REGINALD HEBER, 1783–1826.

372　　　　　　　　　66. 66. 88.

HILLS of the North, rejoice !
　　River and mountain-spring,
Hark to the advent voice !
　　Valley and lowland, sing !
Though absent long, your Lord is
　　nigh,
He judgment brings, and victory.

2　　Isles of the Southern seas,
　　　Deep in your coral caves
Pent be each warring breeze,
　　　Lulled be your restless waves :
He comes to reign with boundless
　　sway,
And make your wastes His great
　　highway.

MISSIONS

3 Lands of the East, awake !
   Soon shall your sons be free,
The sleep of ages break,
   And rise to liberty :
On your far hills, long cold and grey,
Has dawned the everlasting day.

4 Shores of the utmost West,
   Ye that have waited long,
Unvisited, unblest,
   Break forth to swelling song ;
High raise the note, that Jesus died,
Yet lives and reigns—the Crucified !

5 Shout while ye journey home !
   Songs be in every mouth !—
Lo, from the North we come,
   From East, and West, and
    South :
City of God, the bond are free ;
We come to live and reign in thee.

CHARLES EDWARD OAKLEY,
1832–65.

373   10 10. 10 10.

FAR round the world Thy children
   sing their song :
From East and West their voices
   sweetly blend,
Praising the Lord in whom young
   lives are strong,
Jesus our Guide, our Hero, and our
   Friend.

2 Where Thy wide ocean, wave on
   rolling wave,
Beats through the ages, on each
   island shore,
They praise their Lord, whose hand
   alone can save,
Whose sea of love surrounds them
   evermore.

3 Thy sun-kissed children on earth's
   spreading plain,
Where Asia's rivers water all the land,
Sing, as they watch Thy fields of
   glowing grain,
Praise to the Lord who feeds them
   with His hand.

4 Still there are lands where none have
   seen Thy face,
Children whose hearts have never
   shared Thy joy ;
Yet Thou wouldst pour on these Thy
   radiant grace,
Give Thy glad strength to every girl
   and boy.

5 All round the world let children sing
   Thy song :
From East and West their voices
   sweetly blend,
Praising the Lord in whom young
   lives are strong,
Jesus our Guide, our Hero, and our
   Friend.

BASIL JOSEPH MATHEWS,
1879–1951.

374   77. 77.

ONCE again, dear Lord, we pray
   For the children far away,
Who have never even heard
Name of Jesus, sweetest word.

2 Little lips that Thou hast made,
'Neath the far-off temples' shade
Give to gods of wood and stone
Praise that should be all Thine own.

3 Little hands, whose wondrous skill
Thou hast given to do Thy will,
Offerings bring, and serve with fear
Gods that cannot see or hear.

4 Teach them, O Thou heavenly King,
All their gifts and praise to bring
To Thy Son, who died to prove
Thy forgiving, saving love.

MARY JANE WILLCOX,
1835–1919.

375   87. 87.

GOD of heaven, hear our singing ;
   Only little ones are we,
Yet, a great petition bringing,
Father, now we come to Thee.

2 Let Thy Kingdom come, we pray
   Thee ;
Let the world in Thee find rest ;
Let all know Thee, and obey Thee,
Loving, praising, blessing, blest.

3 Let the sweet and joyful story,
   Of the Saviour's wondrous love,
Wake on earth a song of glory,
Like the angels' song above.

4 Father, send the glorious hour,
   Every heart be Thine alone,
For the Kingdom, and the power,
And the glory are Thine own.

FRANCES RIDLEY HAVERGAL,
1836–79.

376
S. M.

O LORD our God, arise !
　　The cause of truth maintain,
And wide o'er all the peopled world
　　Extend her blessèd reign.

2　Thou Prince of Life, arise !
　　Nor let Thy glory cease ;
Far spread the conquests of Thy grace,
　　And bless the earth with peace.

3　Thou Holy Ghost, arise !
　　Expand Thy quickening wing,
And o'er a dark and ruined world
　　Let light and order spring.

4　All on the earth, arise !
　　To God the Saviour sing ;
From shore to shore, from earth to heaven,
　　Let echoing anthems ring.

RALPH WARDLAW, 1779–1853.

377
9 10. 9 10. 10 10.

WAKE, Spirit, who in times now olden
Didst fire the watchmen of the Church's youth,
　　And 'gainst their every foe embolden,
To witness day and night the eternal truth ;
Whose voices through the world are ringing still,
And bringing hosts to know and do Thy will.

2　Soon may that fire from heaven be lent us,
That swift from land to land its flame may leap !
　　Soon, Lord, that priceless boon be sent us,
Of faithful servants, fit for Thee to reap
The harvest of the soul ; look down and view
How great the harvest, but the labourers few.

3　Lord, to our earnest prayer now hearken,
The prayer we offer at Thy Son's command ;
For, lo ! while storms around us darken,
Thy children's hearts are stirred in every land,

To cry for help, with fervent soul, to Thee ;
O hear us, Lord, and speak : ' Thus let it be ! '

4　O speedily that help be granted !
Send forth evangelists, in spirit strong,
　　Armed with Thy word, a host undaunted,
Bold to attack the rule of ancient wrong ;
And let them all the earth for Thee reclaim,
To be Thy Kingdom and to know Thy Name !

CARL HEINRICH BOGATZKY, 1690–1774 ;
　　tr. by CATHERINE WINKWORTH,
　　　　　　　　　　　　1827–78.

378
87. 87 D.

LORD, her watch Thy Church is keeping ;
When shall earth Thy rule obey ?
When shall end the night of weeping,
　　When shall break the promised day ?
See the whitening harvest languish,
　　Waiting still the labourers' toil ;
Was it vain, Thy Son's deep anguish ?
　　Shall the strong retain the spoil ?

2　Tidings, sent to every creature,
　　Millions yet have never heard ;
Can they hear without a preacher ;
　　Lord Almighty, give the word.
Give the word ; in every nation
　　Let the gospel trumpet sound,
Witnessing a world's salvation,
　　To the earth's remotest bound.

3　Then the end,—Thy Church completed,
　　All Thy chosen gathered in,
With their King in glory seated,
　　Satan bound, and banished sin,
Gone for ever parting, weeping,
　　Hunger, sorrow, death, and pain.
Lo ! her watch Thy Church is keeping ;
　　Come, Lord Jesus, come to reign.

HENRY DOWNTON, 1818–85.

379
From Psalm lxvii.
77. 77. 77.

GOD of mercy, God of grace,
　　Show the brightness of Thy face ;
Shine upon us, Saviour, shine,
Fill Thy Church with light divine,

And Thy saving health extend
Unto earth's remotest end.

2 Let the people praise Thee, Lord ;
Be by all that live adored ;
Let the nations shout and sing
Glory to their Saviour King,
At Thy feet their tribute pay,
And Thy holy will obey.

3 Let the people praise Thee, Lord ;
Earth shall then her fruits afford,
God to man His blessing give,
Man to God devoted live—
All below and all above,
One in joy and light and love.

HENRY FRANCIS LYTE,
1793–1847.

380 Irr.

GOD is working His purpose out,
as year succeeds to year :
God is working His purpose out, and
the time is drawing near—
Nearer and nearer draws the time—
the time that shall surely be,
When the earth shall be filled with
the glory of God, as the waters
cover the sea.

2 From utmost east to utmost west,
where'er man's foot hath trod,
By the mouth of many messengers
goes forth the voice of God ;
Give ear to Me, ye continents—ye
isles, give ear to Me,
That the earth may be filled with the
glory of God, as the waters
cover the sea.

3 What can we do to work God's work,
to prosper and increase
The brotherhood of all mankind—
the reign of the Prince of
Peace ?
What can we do to hasten the time—
the time that shall surely be,
When the earth shall be filled with
the glory of God, as the waters
cover the sea ?

4 March we forth in the strength of
God, with the banner of Christ
unfurled,
That the light of the glorious Gospel
of truth may shine throughout
the world ;

Fight we the fight with sorrow and
sin, to set their captives free,
That the earth may be filled with
the glory of God, as the waters
cover the sea.

5 All we can do is nothing worth,
unless God blesses the deed ;
Vainly we hope for the harvest-tide,
till God gives life to the seed ;
Yet nearer and nearer draws the
time—the time that shall surely
be,
When the earth shall be filled with
the glory of God, as the waters
cover the sea.

ARTHUR CAMPBELL AINGER,
1841–1919.

381 C. M.

LIGHT of the lonely pilgrim's
heart,
Star of the coming day,
Arise, and with Thy morning beams
Chase all our griefs away.

2 Come, blessèd Lord, bid every shore
And answering island sing
The praises of Thy royal Name,
And own Thee as their King.

3 Bid the whole earth, responsive now
To the bright world above,
Break forth in rapturous strains of
joy,
In memory of Thy love.

4 Lord, Lord, Thy fair creation
groans—
The air, the earth, the sea—
In unison with all our hearts,
And calls aloud for Thee.

5 Thine was the Cross, with all its
fruits
Of grace and peace divine ;
Be Thine the crown of glory now,
The palm of victory Thine.

EDWARD DENNY, 1796–1889.

382 87. 87. D.

SAVIOUR, sprinkle many nations,
Fruitful let Thy sorrows be ;
By Thy pains and consolations
Draw the Gentiles unto Thee.
Of Thy Cross the wondrous story,
Be it to the nations told ;
Let them see Thee in Thy glory
And Thy mercy manifold.

THE CHURCH

2 Far and wide, though all unknowing,
   Pants for Thee each mortal breast ;
Human tears for Thee are flowing,
   Human hearts in Thee would rest.
Thirsting, as for dews of even,
   As the new-mown grass for rain,
Thee they seek as God of heaven,
   Thee as Man for sinners slain.

3 Saviour, lo ! the isles are waiting,
   Stretched the hand and strained
      the sight,
For Thy Spirit, new-creating,
   Love's pure flame and wisdom's
      light ;
Give the word, and of the preacher
   Speed the foot and touch the
      tongue,
Till on earth by every creature
   Glory to the Lamb be sung.
                  ARTHUR CLEVELAND COXE,
                           1818–96.

383
L. M.

FLING out the banner ! let it
   float
Skyward and seaward, high and
   wide ;
The sun that lights its shining folds,
   The Cross on which the Saviour
      died.

2 Fling out the banner ! angels bend
   In anxious silence o'er the sign,
And vainly seek to comprehend
   The wonder of the love divine.

3 Fling out the banner ! heathen lands
   Shall see from far the glorious
      sight,
And nations, crowding to be born,
   Baptize their spirits in its light.

4 Fling out the banner ! let it float
   Skyward and seaward, high and
      wide,
Our glory, only in the Cross,
   Our only hope, the Crucified.

5 Fling out the banner ! wide and
      high,
   Seaward and skyward let it shine :
Nor skill, nor might, nor merit ours ;
   We conquer only in that sign.
                  GEORGE WASHINGTON DOANE,
                           1799–1859.

384
87. 87. D.

ONWARD march, all-conquering
      Jesus,
   Gird Thee on Thy mighty sword !
Sinful earth can ne'er oppose Thee ;
   Hell itself quails at Thy word.
Thy great Name is so exalted,
   Every foe shrinks back in fear ;
Terror creeps through all creation,
   When it knows that Thou art near.

2 Free my soul from sin's foul bondage ;
   Hasten now the glorious dawn ;
Break proud Babel's gates in sunder ;
   Let the massive bolts be drawn.
Forth, like ocean's heaving surges,
   Bring in myriads ransomed slaves,
Host on host, with shouts of triumph,
   Endless, countless as the waves.

3 Even to-day I hear sweet music,
   Praises of a blood-freed throng :
Full deliverance, glorious freedom,
   Are their themes for endless song ;
Whiter than the snow their raiment,
   Victor palms they wave on high,
As they pass, with fullest glory,
   Into life's felicity.

4 How my raptured soul rejoices
   That the jubilee is near ;
Every word will be accomplished,
   Spoken by our Saviour here.
North and South, in countless
      myriads,
   From earth's darkest ends they
      come,
With the dance and gladsome music,
   Into heaven's eternal home.
                  WILLIAM WILLIAMS, 1717–91 ;
         tr. by WILLIAM HOWELLS, 1855–1932.

385
C. M.

LIFT up your heads, ye gates of
      brass,
   Ye bars of iron, yield,
And let the King of Glory pass ;
   The Cross is in the field.

2 Ye armies of the living God,
   His sacramental host,
Where hallowed footstep never trod,
   Take your appointed post.

3 Follow the Cross ; the ark of peace
   Accompany your path,
To slaves and rebels bring release
   From bondage and from wrath.

120

4 Though few and small and weak
     your bands,
     Strong in your Captain's strength,
  Go to the conquest of all lands ;
     All must be His at length.

5 O fear not, faint not, halt not now ;
     Quit you like men, be strong ;
  To Christ shall every nation bow,
     And sing with you this song :

6 ' Uplifted are the gates of brass ;
     The bars of iron yield ;
  Behold the King of Glory pass !
     The Cross hath won the field.'
          JAMES MONTGOMERY, 1771–1854.

386   L. M.

O SPIRIT of the living God,
     In all Thy plenitude of grace,
Where'er the foot of man hath trod,
  Descend on our apostate race.

2 Give tongues of fire and hearts of
     love,
  To preach the reconciling word ;
  Give power and unction from above,
     Whene'er the joyful sound is
          heard.

3 Be darkness, at Thy coming, light ;
     Confusion order, in Thy path ;
  Souls without strength inspire with
     might ;
  Bid mercy triumph over wrath.

4 O Spirit of the Lord, prepare
     All the round earth her God to
          meet ;
  Breathe Thou abroad like morning
     air,
  Till hearts of stone begin to beat.

5 Baptize the nations ; far and nigh
     The triumphs of the Cross record ;
  The Name of Jesus glorify,
     Till every kindred call Him Lord.
          JAMES MONTGOMERY, 1771–1854.

387   87. 87. 47.

O'ER those gloomy hills of dark-
     ness
Look, my soul ; be still, and gaze ;
All the promises do travail
  With a glorious day of grace :
     Blessèd jubilee !
Let thy glorious morning dawn.

2 Kingdoms wide that sit in darkness,
     Let them have the glorious light ;
  And from eastern coast to western
     May the morning chase the night,
          And redemption,
     Freely purchased, win the day.

3 Fly abroad, eternal Gospel !
     Win and conquer, never cease ;
  May thy lasting wide dominions
     Multiply and still increase ;
          May thy sceptre
     Sway the enlightened world
          around.
          WILLIAM WILLIAMS, 1717–91.

388 *From Psalm lxxii.*   L. M.

JESUS shall reign where'er the sun
     Does his successive journeys run ;
His Kingdom stretch from shore to
     shore,
Till moons shall wax and wane no
     more.

2 For Him shall endless prayer be
     made,
  And praises throng to crown His
     head ;
  His Name like sweet perfume shall
     rise
  With every morning sacrifice.

3 People and realms of every tongue
  Dwell on His love with sweetest song ;
  And infant voices shall proclaim
  Their early blessings on His Name.

4 Blessings abound where'er He reigns :
  The prisoner leaps to lose his chains,
  The weary find eternal rest,
  And all the sons of want are blest.

5 Let every creature rise and bring
  Peculiar honours to our King,
  Angels descend with songs again,
  And earth repeat the long Amen.
          ISAAC WATTS, 1674–1748.

389   77. 77. D.

HARK ! the song of jubilee,
     Loud as mighty thunders' roar,
Or the fulness of the sea
     When it breaks upon the shore.
Hallelujah ! for the Lord
     God omnipotent shall reign ;
Hallelujah ! let the word
     Echo round the earth and main.

THE CHURCH

2 Hallelujah ! hark, the sound,
   From the depths unto the skies,
Wakes above, beneath, around,
   All creation's harmonies :
See Jehovah's banner furled,
   Sheathed His sword ; He speaks—
      'tis done,
And the kingdoms of this world
   Are the kingdoms of His Son.

3 He shall reign from pole to pole
   With illimitable sway ;
He shall reign when, like a scroll,
   Yonder heavens have passed away ;
Then the end ; beneath His rod
   Man's last enemy shall fall ;
Hallelujah ! Christ in God,
   God in Christ, is all in all.

JAMES MONTGOMERY, 1771–1854.

THE CHRISTIAN LIFE

THE GOSPEL CALL

390
76. 76. D.

'COME unto Me, ye weary,
And I will give you rest.'
O blessèd voice of Jesus,
Which comes to hearts oppressed !
It tells of benediction,
Of pardon, grace, and peace,
Of joy that hath no ending,
Of love which cannot cease.

2 'Come unto Me, ye wanderers,
And I will give you light.'
O loving voice of Jesus,
Which comes to cheer the night !
Our hearts were filled with sadness,
And we had lost our way ;
But morning brings us gladness,
And songs the break of day.

3 'Come unto Me, ye fainting,
And I will give you life.'
O peaceful voice of Jesus,
Which comes to end our strife !
The foe is stern and eager,
The fight is fierce and long ;
But Thou hast made us mighty,
And stronger than the strong.

4 'And whosoever cometh,
I will not cast him out.'
O patient voice of Jesus,
Which drives away our doubt,
Which calls us—very sinners,
Unworthy though we be
Of love so free and boundless—
To come, dear Lord, to Thee !

WILLIAM CHATTERTON DIX,
1837–98.

391
85. 83.

ART thou weary, art thou languid,
Art thou sore distressed ?
'Come to Me,' saith One, ' and,
coming,
Be at rest.'

2 Hath He marks to lead me to Him
If He be my Guide ?
In His feet and hands are wound-
prints,
And His side !

3 Is there diadem, as Monarch,
That His brow adorns ?
Yea, a crown in very surety,
But of thorns !

4 If I find Him, if I follow,
What His guerdon here ?
Many a sorrow, many a labour,
Many a tear !

5 If I still hold closely to Him,
What hath He at last ?
Sorrow vanquished, labour ended,
Jordan passed !

6 If I ask Him to receive me,
Will He say me nay ?
Not till earth and not till heaven
Pass away !

7 Finding, following, keeping, strug-
gling,
Is He sure to bless ?
Angels, martyrs, saints, and prophets
Answer, Yes !

JOHN MASON NEALE, 1818–66 ; based
on ST. STEPHEN of MAR SABA,
8th cent.

392
87. 87. 47.

COME, ye souls by sin afflicted,
Bowed with fruitless sorrow
down,
By the broken law convicted,
Through the Cross behold the
crown ;
Look to Jesus ;
Mercy flows through Him alone.

2 Blessèd are the eyes that see Him,
Blest the ears that hear His voice ;
Blessèd are the souls that trust Him
And in Him alone rejoice ;
His commandments
Then become their happy choice.

3 Take His easy yoke and wear it ;
Love will make obedience sweet ;
Christ will give you strength to bear
it,
While His wisdom guides your feet
Safe to glory,
Where His ransomed captives meet.

4 Sweet as home to pilgrims weary,
    Light to newly opened eyes,
Or full springs in deserts dreary,
    Is the rest the Cross supplies ;
        All who taste it
    Shall to rest immortal rise.
        JOSEPH SWAIN, 1761–96.

393   87. 87. 47.

COME, ye sinners, poor and
    wretched,
    Weak and wounded, sick and sore ;
Jesus ready stands to save you,
    Full of pity joined with power :
        He is able,
    He is willing ; doubt no more.

2 Ho ! ye needy, come and welcome ;
    God's free bounty glorify ;
True belief and true repentance,
    Every grace that brings us nigh,
        Without money
    Come to Jesus Christ and buy.

3 Come, ye weary, heavy laden,
    Bruised and broken by the fall ;
If you tarry till you're better,
    You will never come at all :
        Not the righteous—
    Sinners Jesus came to call.

4 Let not conscience make you linger,
    Nor of fitness fondly dream ;
All the fitness He requireth
    Is to feel your need of Him :
        This He gives you ;
    'Tis the Spirit's rising beam.

5 Lo ! the Incarnate God, ascended,
    Pleads the merit of His blood ;
Venture on Him, venture wholly ;
    Let no other trust intrude :
        None but Jesus
    Can do helpless sinners good.
        JOSEPH HART, 1712–68.

394   77. 77. 77.

SINNERS Jesus will receive :
    Tell this word of grace to all
Who the heavenly pathway leave,
    All who linger, all who fall ;
This can bring them back again :
' Christ receiveth sinful men.'

2 Shepherds seek their wandering sheep
    O'er the mountains bleak and cold ;
Jesus such a watch doth keep
    O'er the lost ones of His fold,
Seeking them o'er moor and fen :
Christ receiveth sinful men.

3 Sick and sorrowful and blind,
    I with all my sins draw nigh ;
O my Saviour, Thou canst find
    Help for sinners such as I ;
Speak that word of love again :
' Christ receiveth sinful men.'

4 Christ receiveth sinful men,
    Even me with all my sin,
Openeth to me heaven again ;
    With Him I may enter in.
Death hath no more sting nor pain :
Christ receiveth sinful men.
    ERDMANN NEUMEISTER, 1671–1756 ;
        tr. by EMMA FRANCES BEVAN,
            1827–1909.

395   87. 87.

SOULS of men ! why will ye
    scatter
Like a crowd of frightened sheep ?
Foolish hearts ! why will ye wander
From a love so true and deep ?

2 Was there ever kindest shepherd
    Half so gentle, half so sweet,
As the Saviour who would have us
    Come and gather round His feet ?

3 There 's a wideness in God's mercy,
    Like the wideness of the sea ;
There 's a kindness in His justice,
    Which is more than liberty.

4 There is no place where earth's
      sorrows
    Are more felt than up in heaven :
There is no place where earth's
      failings
    Have such kindly judgment given.

5 For the love of God is broader
    Than the measures of man's mind ;
And the heart of the Eternal
    Is most wonderfully kind.

6 There is plentiful redemption
    In the blood that has been shed ;
There is joy for all the members
    In the sorrows of the Head.

7 Pining souls ! come nearer Jesus,
   And O come, not doubting thus,
But with faith that trusts more
       bravely
   His huge tenderness for us.

8 If our love were but more simple,
   We should take Him at His word ;
And our lives would be all sunshine,
   In the sweetness of our Lord.

FREDERICK WILLIAM FABER,
1814–63.

396
76. 76. D.

THE King of Glory standeth
   Beside that heart of sin ;
His mighty voice commandeth
   The raging waves within ;
The floods of deepest anguish
   Roll backward at His will,
As o'er the storm ariseth
   His mandate, ' Peace, be still.'

2 At times, with sudden glory,
   He speaks, and all is done ;
Without one stroke of battle
   The victory is won,
While we, with joy beholding,
   Can scarce believe it true
That even our kingly Jesus
   Can form such hearts anew.

3 O Christ, Thy love is mighty ;
   Long-suffering is Thy grace ;
And glorious is the splendour
   That beameth from Thy face.
Our hearts up-leap in gladness
   When we behold that love,
As we go singing onward,
   To dwell with Thee above.

CHARITIE LEES DE CHENEZ,
b. 1841.

397
76. 76. D.

O JESUS, Thou art standing
   Outside the fast-closed door,
In lowly patience waiting
   To pass the threshold o'er.
Shame on us, Christian brothers,
   His Name and sign who bear,
O shame, thrice shame upon us,
   To keep Him standing there !

2 O Jesus, Thou art knocking ;
   And, lo ! that hand is scarred,
And thorns Thy brow encircle,
   And tears Thy face have marred.
O love that passeth knowledge,
   So patiently to wait !
O sin that hath no equal,
   So fast to bar the gate !

3 O Jesus, Thou art pleading
   In accents meek and low,
' I died for you, My children,
   And will ye treat Me so ? '
O Lord, with shame and sorrow
   We open now the door ;
Dear Saviour, enter, enter,
   And leave us nevermore.

WILLIAM WALSHAM HOW,
1823–97.

398
D. C. M.

THE Lord is rich and merciful ;
   The Lord is very kind ;
O come to Him, come now to Him,
   With a believing mind.
His comforts, they shall strengthen
       thee,
   Like flowing waters cool ;
And He shall for thy spirit be
   A fountain ever full.

2 The Lord is glorious and strong ;
   Our God is very high ;
O trust in Him, trust now in Him,
   And have security.
He shall be to thee like the sea,
   And thou shalt surely feel
His wind, that bloweth healthily
   Thy sicknesses to heal.

3 The Lord is wonderful and wise,
   As all the ages tell ;
O learn of Him, learn now of Him,
   Then with thee it is well.
And with His light thou shalt be
       blest,
   Therein to work and live ;
And He shall be to thee a rest
   When evening hours arrive.

THOMAS TOKE LYNCH,
1818–71.

399   77. 76.

JESUS, we are far away
  From the light of heavenly day;
Lost in paths of sin we stray:
  Lord, in mercy hear us.

2 Help us to bewail our sin,
And, in heavenly strength, begin
Daily victories to win:
  Lord, in mercy hear us.

3 Keep us lowly, that we may,
Ever watchful, turn away
From the snares our tempters lay:
  Lord, in mercy hear us.

4 On our darkness shed Thy light;
Lead our wills to what is right;
Wash our evil nature white:
  Lord, in mercy hear us.

5 May Thy wisdom be our guide,
Comfort, rest, and peace provide
Near to Thy protecting side:
  Lord, in mercy hear us.

6 Fix our hearts on things on high;
Let no evil thoughts come nigh;
Purge from sin our memory:
  Lord, in mercy hear us.

7 May Thy grace within the soul
Nature's waywardness control,
Guiding towards the heavenly goal:
  Lord, in mercy hear us.
          THOMAS BENSON POLLOCK,
                    1836–96.

400 *From Hosea* vi. 1–4.   C. M.

COME, let us to the Lord our God
  With contrite hearts return;
Our God is gracious, nor will leave
  The desolate to mourn.

2 His voice commands the tempest
    forth,
  And stills the stormy wave;
And though His arm be strong to
    smite,
  'Tis also strong to save.

3 Long hath the night of sorrow
    reigned,
  The dawn shall bring us light:
God shall appear, and we shall rise
  With gladness in His sight.

4 Our hearts, if God we seek to know,
  Shall know Him, and rejoice;
His coming like the morn shall be,
  Like morning songs His voice.

5 As dew upon the tender herb,
  Diffusing fragrance round;
As showers that usher in the spring,
  And cheer the thirsty ground:

6 So shall His presence bless our souls,
  And shed a joyful light;
That hallowed morn shall chase away
  The sorrows of the night.
          JOHN MORISON, 1750–98;
          as in *Scottish Paraphrases*, 1781.

401   C. M.

O LORD, turn not away Thy face
  From him that lies prostrate,
Lamenting sore his sinful life,
  Before Thy mercy-gate;

2 Which gate Thou openest wide to
    those
  That do lament their sin:
Shut not that gate against me, Lord,
  But let me enter in.

3 And call me not to mine account,
  How I have lived here;
For then I know right well, O Lord,
  How vile I shall appear.

4 So come I to Thy mercy-gate,
  Where mercy doth abound,
Requiring mercy for my sin,
  To heal my deadly wound.

5 Mercy, good Lord, mercy I ask,
  This is the total sum;
For mercy, Lord, is all my suit:
  Lord, let Thy mercy come.
          JOHN MARCKANT, 1562.

402   68. 86.

O THOU, my Judge and King—
  My broken heart, my voiceless
    prayer,
My poverty, and blind despair,
  To Thee, O Christ, I bring.

2 O Thou, my Judge and King—
  My treason to Thy love most sweet,
My pride that pierced Thy weary
    feet,
  To Thee, O Christ, I bring.

3 O Thou, my Judge and King—
  My tearful hope, my faith's distress,
For Thee to pardon and to bless,
To Thee, O Christ, I bring.

4 O Thou, my Judge and King—
  With no excuse, for Thou art just,
My sins, that set me in the dust,
To Thee, O Christ, I bring.

O Thou, my Judge and King—
  My soul, from depths of my disgrace,
To seek for mercy at Thy face,
To Thee, O Christ, I bring.

LAUCHLAN MACLEAN WATT,
1867-1957.

403   S. M.

LORD Jesus, think on me,
  And purge away my sin ;
From earthborn passions set me free,
And make me pure within.

2 Lord Jesus, think on me,
  With care and woe opprest ;
Let me Thy loving servant be,
And taste Thy promised rest.

3 Lord Jesus, think on me,
  Amid the battle's strife ;
In all my pain and misery
Be Thou my health and life.

4 Lord Jesus, think on me,
  Nor let me go astray ;
Through darkness and perplexity
Point Thou the heavenly way.

5 Lord Jesus, think on me,
  When flows the tempest high :
When on doth rush the enemy,
O Saviour, be Thou nigh.

6 Lord Jesus, think on me,
  That, when the flood is past,
I may the eternal brightness see,
And share Thy joy at last.

SYNESIUS OF CYRENE, 375-430 ;
tr. by ALLEN WILLIAM CHATFIELD,
1808-96.

404   87. 87.

LORD, Thy mercy now entreating,
  Low before Thy throne we fall :
Our misdeeds to Thee confessing,
On Thy Name we humbly call.

2 Sinful thoughts and words unloving
    Rise against us one by one :
Acts unworthy, deeds unthinking,
    Good that we have left undone ;

3 Hearts that far from Thee were straying,
    While in prayer we bowed the knee ;
Lips that, while Thy praises sounding,
    Lifted not the soul to Thee ;

4 Precious moments idly wasted,
    Precious hours in folly spent ;
Christian vow and fight unheeded ;
    Scarce a thought to wisdom lent.

5 Lord, Thy mercy still entreating,
    We with shame our sins would own ;
From henceforth, the time redeeming,
    May we live to Thee alone.

6 Heavenly Father, bless Thy children ;
    Hearken from Thy throne on high ;
Loving Saviour, Holy Spirit,
    Hear and heed our humble cry.

MARY ANN SIDEBOTHAM,
1833-1913.

405   777.

LORD, in this Thy mercy's day,
  Ere it wholly pass away,
On our knees we fall and pray.

2 Holy Jesus, grant us tears,
  Fill us with heart-searching fears,
Ere that awful doom appears.

3 Lord, on us Thy Spirit pour,
  Kneeling lowly at Thy door,
Ere it close for evermore.

4 By Thy night of agony,
  By Thy supplicating cry,
By Thy willingness to die,

5 By Thy tears of bitter woe
  For Jerusalem below,
Let us not Thy love forgo.

6 Judge and Saviour of our race,
  When we see Thee face to face,
Grant us 'neath Thy wings a place.

ISAAC WILLIAMS, 1802-65.

406   C. M.

ONE who is all unfit to count
  As scholar in Thy school,
Thou of Thy love hast named a friend—
  O kindness wonderful !

THE CHRISTIAN LIFE

2 So weak am I, O gracious Lord,
  So all unworthy Thee,
That even the dust upon Thy feet
  Outweighs me utterly.

3 Thou dwellest in unshadowed light,
  All sin and shame above—
That Thou shouldst bear our sin
    and shame,
  How can I tell such love ?

4 Ah, did not He the heavenly throne
  A little thing esteem,
And not unworthy for my sake
  A mortal body deem ?

5 When in His flesh they drove the
    nails,
  Did He not all endure ?
What name is there to fit a life
  So patient and so pure ?

6 So, Love itself in human form,
  For love of me He came ;
I cannot look upon His face
  For shame, for bitter shame.

7 If there is aught of worth in me,
  It comes from Thee alone ;
Then keep me safe, for so, O Lord,
  Thou keepest but Thine own.

From the Marathi of NARAYAN VAMAN
  TILAK, 1862–1919 ; tr. by NICOL
  MACNICOL, 1870–1952.

---

407 *From Psalm cxxx.*   87. 87. 887.

FROM depths of woe I raise to
    Thee
  The voice of lamentation ;
Lord, turn a gracious ear to me,
  And hear my supplication :
If Thou shouldst be extreme to
    mark
Each secret sin and misdeed dark,
  O who could stand before Thee ?

2 To wash away the crimson stain,
  Grace, grace alone availeth ;
Our works, alas ! are all in vain ;
  In much the best life faileth :
No man can glory in Thy sight,
All must alike confess Thy might,
  And live alone by mercy.

3 Therefore my trust is in the Lord,
  And not in mine own merit ;
On Him my soul shall rest, His word
  Upholds my fainting spirit :
His promised mercy is my fort,
  My comfort and my sweet support ;
I wait for it with patience.

---

4 What though I wait the livelong
    night,
  And till the dawn appeareth,
My heart still trusteth in His might ;
  It doubted not, nor feareth :
So let the Israelite in heart,
  Born of the Spirit, do his part,
  And wait till God appeareth.

5 Although our sin is great indeed,
  God's mercies far exceed it ;
His hand can give the help we need,
  However much we need it :
He is the Shepherd of the sheep
Who Israel doth guard and keep,
  And shall from sin redeem him.
      MARTIN LUTHER, 1483–1546 ;
      tr. by RICHARD MASSIE, 1800–87.

---

408   88. 84.

THERE is a holy sacrifice
  Which God in heaven will not
    despise,
Yea, which is precious in His eyes,
      The contrite heart.

2 That lofty One, before whose throne
  The countless hosts of heaven bow
    down,
Another dwelling-place will own,
      The contrite heart.

3 The Holy One, the Son of God,
  His pardoning love will shed abroad,
And consecrate as His abode
      The contrite heart.

4 The Holy Spirit from on high
  Will listen to its faintest cry,
And cheer and bless and purify
      The contrite heart.

5 Saviour, I cast my hopes on Thee ;
  Such as Thou art, I fain would be ;
In mercy, Lord, bestow on me
      The contrite heart.
      CHARLOTTE ELLIOTT, 1789–1871.

---

409   88. 88. 88.

O JESUS, full of pardoning grace,
  More full of grace than I of sin,
Yet once again I seek Thy face ;
  Open Thine arms and take me in,
And freely my backslidings heal,
And love the faithless sinner still.

2 Thou know'st the way to bring me
    back,
  My fallen spirit to restore ;
O, for Thy truth and mercy's sake,
  Forgive, and bid me sin no more ;
The ruins of my soul repair,
  And make my heart a house of
    prayer.

3 Ah ! give me, Lord, the tender heart
  That trembles at the approach of
    sin ;
A godly fear of sin impart,
  Implant, and root it deep within,
That I may dread Thy gracious
    power,
  And never dare offend Thee more.

CHARLES WESLEY, 1707-88.

410   D. C. M.

I HEARD the voice of Jesus say,
    ' Come unto Me and rest ' ;
Lay down, thou weary one, lay down
    Thy head upon My breast ' :
I came to Jesus as I was,
    Weary, and worn, and sad ;
I found in Him a resting-place,
    And He has made me glad.

2 I heard the voice of Jesus say,
    ' Behold, I freely give
The living water ; thirsty one,
    Stoop down and drink, and live ' :
I came to Jesus, and I drank
    Of that life-giving stream ;
My thirst was quenched, my soul
    revived,
    And now I live in Him.

3 I heard the voice of Jesus say,
    ' I am this dark world's Light ;
Look unto Me, thy morn shall rise,
    And all thy day be bright ' :
I looked to Jesus, and I found
    In Him my Star, my Sun ;
And in that light of life I'll walk,
    Till travelling days are done.

HORATIUS BONAR, 1808-89.

411   88. 86.

J UST as I am, without one plea
    But that Thy blood was shed for
    me,
And that Thou bidd'st me come to
    Thee,
    O Lamb of God, I come.

2 Just as I am, and waiting not
  To rid my soul of one dark blot,
  To Thee, whose blood can cleanse
    each spot,
    O Lamb of God, I come.

3 Just as I am, though tossed about
  With many a conflict, many a doubt,
  Fightings and fears within, without,
    O Lamb of God, I come.

4 Just as I am, poor, wretched, blind,—
  Sight, riches, healing of the mind,
  Yea, all I need, in Thee to find,
    O Lamb of God, I come.

5 Just as I am, Thou wilt receive,
  Wilt welcome, pardon, cleanse, re-
    lieve ;
  Because Thy promise I believe,
    O Lamb of God, I come.

6 Just as I am—Thy love unknown
  Has broken every barrier down—
  Now to be Thine, yea, Thine alone,
    O Lamb of God, I come.

7 Just as I am, of that free love
  The breadth, length, depth, and
    height to prove,
  Here for a season, then above,—
    O Lamb of God, I come.

CHARLOTTE ELLIOTT, 1789-1871.

412   8 10. 10 4.

N ONE other Lamb, none other
    Name,
  None other Hope in heaven or
    earth or sea,
  None other Hiding-place from guilt
    and shame,
      None beside Thee.

2 My faith burns low, my hope burns
    low ;
  Only my heart's desire cries out
    in me,
  By the deep thunder of its want and
    woe,
      Cries out to Thee.

3 Lord, Thou art Life, though I be
    dead ;
  Love's Fire Thou art, however
    cold I be :
  Nor heaven have I, nor place to lay
    my head,
      Nor home, but Thee.

CHRISTINA GEORGINA ROSSETTI,
                              1830-94.

413   77. 77. 77.

ROCK of Ages, cleft for me,
    Let me hide myself in Thee;
Let the water and the blood,
From Thy riven side which flowed,
Be of sin the double cure,
Cleanse me from its guilt and power.

2 Not the labours of my hands
    Can fulfil Thy law's demands;
Could my zeal no respite know,
Could my tears for ever flow,
All for sin could not atone:
Thou must save, and Thou alone.

3 Nothing in my hand I bring,
    Simply to Thy Cross I cling;
Naked, come to Thee for dress;
Helpless, look to Thee for grace;
Foul, I to the fountain fly;
Wash me, Saviour, or I die.

4 While I draw this fleeting breath,
    When mine eyelids close in death,
When I soar through tracts unknown,
See Thee on Thy judgment throne,
Rock of Ages, cleft for me,
Let me hide myself in Thee.

                AUGUSTUS MONTAGUE TOPLADY,
                        1740–78.

414   77. 77. D.

JESUS, Lover of my soul,
    Let me to Thy bosom fly,
While the nearer waters roll,
    While the tempest still is high;
Hide me, O my Saviour, hide,
    Till the storm of life is past;
Safe into the haven guide;
    O receive my soul at last!

2 Other refuge have I none;
    Hangs my helpless soul on Thee;
Leave, ah! leave me not alone;
    Still support and comfort me.
All my trust on Thee is stayed;
    All my help from Thee I bring;
Cover my defenceless head
    With the shadow of Thy wing.

3 Thou, O Christ, art all I want;
    More than all in Thee I find;
Raise the fallen, cheer the faint,
    Heal the sick, and lead the blind.
Just and holy is Thy Name,
    I am all unrighteousness;
False and full of sin I am,
    Thou art full of truth and grace.

4 Plenteous grace with Thee is found,
    Grace to cover all my sin;
Let the healing streams abound;
    Make and keep me pure within.
Thou of life the fountain art,
    Freely let me take of Thee;
Spring Thou up within my heart,
    Rise to all eternity.

                    CHARLES WESLEY, 1707–88.

415   664. 6664.

MY faith looks up to Thee,
    Thou Lamb of Calvary,
        Saviour Divine:
Now hear me while I pray;
Take all my guilt away;
O let me from this day
        Be wholly Thine.

2 May Thy rich grace impart
    Strength to my fainting heart,
        My zeal inspire;
As Thou hast died for me,
O may my love to Thee
Pure, warm, and changeless be,
        A living fire.

3 While life's dark maze I tread,
    And griefs around me spread,
        Be Thou my Guide;
Bid darkness turn to day,
Wipe sorrow's tears away,
Nor let me ever stray
        From Thee aside.

4 When ends life's transient dream,
    When death's cold, sullen stream
        Shall o'er me roll,
Blest Saviour, then, in love,
Fear and distrust remove;
O bear me safe above,
        A ransomed soul.

                    RAY PALMER, 1808–87.

416   88. 88. 88.

COME, O Thou Traveller un-
        known,
Whom still I hold but cannot see ;
My company before is gone,
    And I am left alone with Thee ;
With Thee all night I mean to stay,
And wrestle till the break of day.

2 I need not tell Thee who I am,
    My misery or sin declare ;
Thyself hast called me by my name ;
    Look on Thy hands, and read it
        there.
But who, I ask Thee, who art Thou ?
Tell me Thy Name, and tell me now.

3 Yield to me now, for I am weak,
    But confident in self-despair ;
Speak to my heart, in blessings speak ;
    Be conquered by my instant prayer.
Speak, or Thou never hence shalt
        move,
And tell me if Thy Name is Love.

4 'Tis Love ! 'tis Love ! Thou diedst
        for me !
    I hear Thy whisper in my heart ;
The morning breaks, the shadows
        flee ;
    Pure universal Love Thou art ;
To me, to all, Thy mercies move ;
Thy nature and Thy Name is Love.

5 I know Thee, Saviour, who Thou art,
    Jesus, the feeble sinner's Friend ;
Nor wilt Thou with the night depart,
    But stay and love me to the end :
Thy mercies never shall remove ;
Thy nature and Thy Name is Love.
                    CHARLES WESLEY, 1707-88.

417   77. 77.

HARK, my soul ! it is the Lord ;
    'Tis thy Saviour, hear His word ;
Jesus speaks, and speaks to thee :
    'Say, poor sinner, lov'st thou Me ?

2 'I delivered thee when bound,
    And, when bleeding, healed thy
        wound ;
Sought thee wandering, set thee
        right ;
Turned thy darkness into light.

3 'Can a woman's tender care
    Cease towards the child she bare ?

Yes, she may forgetful be,
Yet will I remember thee.

4 ' Mine is an unchanging love,
Higher than the heights above,
Deeper than the depths beneath,
Free and faithful, strong as death.

5 'Thou shalt see My glory soon,
When the work of grace is done ;
Partner of My throne shalt be ;
Say, poor sinner, lov'st thou Me ? '

6 Lord, it is my chief complaint
That my love is weak and faint ;
Yet I love Thee, and adore ;
O for grace to love Thee more !
            WILLIAM COWPER, 1731-1800.

418   C. M.

JESUS, these eyes have never seen
    That radiant form of Thine ;
The veil of sense hangs dark between
    Thy blessèd face and mine.

2 I see Thee not, I hear Thee not,
    Yet art Thou oft with me ;
And earth hath ne'er so dear a spot
    As where I meet with Thee.

3 Like some bright dream that comes
        unsought,
    When slumbers o'er me roll,
Thine image ever fills my thought,
    And charms my ravished soul.

4 Yet, though I have not seen, and still
    Must rest in faith alone,
I love Thee, dearest Lord, and will,
    Unseen but not unknown.

5 When death these mortal eyes shall
        seal,
    And still this throbbing heart,
The rending veil shall Thee reveal
    All glorious as Thou art.
                    RAY PALMER, 1808-87.

419   C. M.

HOW sweet the Name of Jesus
        sounds
    In a believer's ear !
It soothes his sorrows, heals his
        wounds,
    And drives away his fear.

2 It makes the wounded spirit whole,
    And calms the troubled breast ;
'Tis manna to the hungry soul,
    And to the weary rest.

3 Dear Name! the rock on which I
    build,
  My shield and hiding-place,
My never-failing treasury, filled
  With boundless stores of grace.

4 Jesus, my Shepherd, Husband,
    Friend,
  My Prophet, Priest, and King,
My Lord, my Life, my Way, my
    End,
  Accept the praise I bring.

5 Weak is the effort of my heart,
  And cold my warmest thought;
But, when I see Thee as Thou art,
  I'll praise Thee as I ought.

6 Till then I would Thy love proclaim
  With every fleeting breath;
And may the music of Thy Name
  Refresh my soul in death.

        JOHN NEWTON, 1725-1807.

420
                  L. M.

JESUS, Thou Joy of loving hearts,
  Thou Fount of life, Thou Light
    of men,
From the best bliss that earth imparts
  We turn unfilled to Thee again.

2 Thy truth unchanged hath ever
    stood;
  Thou savest those that on Thee
    call:
To them that seek Thee Thou art
    good,
  To them that find Thee, all in all.

3 We taste Thee, O Thou living Bread,
  And long to feast upon Thee still;
We drink of Thee, the Fountain-
    head,
  And thirst our souls from Thee
    to fill.

4 Our restless spirits yearn for Thee,
  Where'er our changeful lot is
    cast,—
  Glad when Thy gracious smile we
    see,
  Blest when our faith can hold Thee
    fast.

5 O Jesus, ever with us stay;
  Make all our moments calm and
    bright;
Chase the dark night of sin away;
  Shed o'er the world Thy holy light.

Attributed to ST. BERNARD OF CLAIR-
    VAUX, 1091-1153; *tr.* by RAY
        PALMER, 1808-87.

421
                  L. M.

JESUS! the very thought is sweet,
  In that dear Name all heart-joys
    meet;
But sweeter than the honey far
  The glimpses of His presence are.

2 No word is sung more sweet than
    this,
No name is heard more full of bliss,
No thought brings sweeter comfort
    nigh
Than Jesus, Son of God most high.

3 Jesus, Thou sweetness pure and blest,
Truth's fountain, Light of souls
    distressed,
Surpassing all that heart requires,
Exceeding all that soul desires!

4 No tongue of mortal can express,
No pen can write the blessedness;
He only who hath proved it knows
What bliss from love for Jesus flows.

5 Jesus, the hope of souls forlorn,
How good to them for sin that
    mourn!
To them that seek Thee, O how
    kind!
But what art Thou to them that find!

6 We follow Jesus now, and raise
The voice of prayer, the hymn of
    praise,
That He at last may make us meet
With Him to gain the heavenly seat.
                  Amen.

Attributed to ST. BERNARD OF CLAIR-
    VAUX, 1091-1153; *tr.* by JOHN
    MASON NEALE, 1818-66.

422
                  C. M.

JESUS, the very thought of Thee
  With sweetness fills my breast;
But sweeter far Thy face to see,
  And in Thy presence rest.

2 Nor voice can sing, nor heart can
    frame,
    Nor can the memory find
A sweeter sound than Thy blest
    Name,
    O Saviour of mankind !

3 O Hope of every contrite heart,
    O Joy of all the meek,
To those who fall how kind Thou
    art !
    How good to those who seek !

4 But what to those who find ? Ah,
    this,
    Nor tongue nor pen can show ;
The love of Jesus, what it is
    None but His loved ones know.

5 Jesus, our only joy be Thou,
    As Thou our prize wilt be ;
Jesus, be Thou our glory now,
    And through eternity.
Attributed to St. Bernard of Clair-
    vaux, 1091–1153 ; *tr.* by Edward
    Caswall, 1814–78.

423   C. M.

O JESUS, King most wonderful,
    Thou Conqueror renowned,
Thou Sweetness most ineffable,
    In whom all joys are found !

2 When once Thou visitest the heart,
    Then truth begins to shine,
Then earthly vanities depart,
    Then kindles love divine.

3 O Jesus, Light of all below,
    Thou Fount of life and fire,
Surpassing all the joys we know,
    And all we can desire,—

4 May every heart confess Thy Name,
    And ever Thee adore,
And, seeking Thee, itself inflame
    To seek Thee more and more.

5 Thee may our tongues for ever bless ;
    Thee may we love alone,
And ever in our lives express
    The image of Thine own.
Attributed to St. Bernard of Clair-
    vaux, 1091–1153 ; *tr.* by Edward
    Caswall, 1814–78.

424   88. 88. 6.

O LOVE that wilt not let me go,
    I rest my weary soul in Thee :
I give Thee back the life I owe,
That in Thine ocean depths its flow
      May richer, fuller be.

2 O Light that followest all my way,
    I yield my flickering torch to Thee :
My heart restores its borrowed ray,
That in Thy sunshine's blaze its day
      May brighter, fairer be.

3 O Joy that seekest me through pain,
    I cannot close my heart to Thee :
I trace the rainbow through the rain,
And feel the promise is not vain,
      That morn shall tearless be.

4 O Cross that liftest up my head,
    I dare not ask to fly from Thee :
I lay in dust life's glory dead,
And from the ground there blossoms
    red
      Life that shall endless be.
      George Matheson, 1842–1906.

425   88. 86.

O SAVIOUR, I have nought to
    plead,
    In earth beneath or heaven above,
But just my own exceeding need,
    And Thy exceeding love.

2 The need will soon be past and gone,
    Exceeding great, but quickly o'er ;
The love unbought is all Thine own,
    And lasts for evermore.
      Jane Crewdson, 1809–63.

426   76. 76.

O THOU, whose mercy found me,
    From bondage set me free,
And then for ever bound me
    With three-fold cords to Thee !

2 Though all the world deceive me,
    I know that I am Thine,
And Thou wilt never leave me,
    O blessèd Saviour, mine !

3 O for a heart to love Thee
    More truly as I ought,
And nothing place above Thee,
    In deed, or word, or thought !

4 O for that choicest blessing
Of living in Thy love,
And thus on earth possessing
The peace of heaven above !
JOHN SAMUEL BEWLEY MONSELL,
1811–75.

427   64. 64. 10 10.

I LIFT my heart to Thee,
    Saviour Divine ;
For Thou art all to me,
    And I am Thine.
Is there on earth a closer bond than
    this,
That my Belovèd's mine, and I am
    His ?

2 Thine am I by all ties ;
    But chiefly Thine,
That through Thy sacrifice
    Thou, Lord, art mine.
By Thine own cords of love, so
    sweetly wound
Around me, I to Thee am closely
    bound.

3 To Thee, Thou bleeding Lamb,
    I all things owe ;
All that I have and am,
    And all I know.
All that I have is now no longer
    mine,
And I am not mine own ; Lord, I
    am Thine.

4 I pray Thee, Saviour, keep
    Me in Thy love,
Until death's holy sleep
    Shall me remove
To that fair realm where, sin and
    sorrow o'er,
Thou and Thine own are one for
    evermore.
CHARLES EDWARD MUDIE,
1818–90.

428   886. 886.

O LOVE Divine, how sweet thou
    art !
When shall I find my willing heart
    All taken up by thee ?
I thirst, I faint, I die to prove
The greatness of redeeming love,
    The love of Christ to me.

2 Stronger His love than death or hell :
    Its riches are unsearchable :
        The first-born sons of light
Desire in vain its depth to see ;
They cannot reach the mystery,
    The length, and breadth, and
        height.

3 God only knows the love of God :
    O that it now were shed abroad
        In this poor stony heart !
For love I sigh, for love I pine ;
This only portion, Lord, be mine,
    Be mine this better part.

4 O that I could for ever sit
    Like Mary at the Master's feet !
        Be this my happy choice :
My only care, delight, and bliss,
My joy, my heaven on earth be this,
    To hear the Bridegroom's voice.
CHARLES WESLEY, 1707–88.

429   10 10. 10 10.

N OT what I am, O Lord, but what
    Thou art !
    That, that alone can be my soul's
        true rest ;
Thy love, not mine, bids fear and
    doubt depart,
    And stills the tempest of my toss-
        ing breast.

2 It blesses now, and shall for ever
    bless,
    It saves me now, and shall for ever
        save,
It holds me up in days of helpless-
    ness,
    It bears me safely o'er each swell-
        ing wave.

3 'Tis what I know of Thee, my Lord
    and God,
    That fills my soul with peace, my
        lips with song ;
Thou art my health, my joy, my
    staff, my rod ;
    Leaning on Thee, in weakness I
        am strong.

4 I am all want and hunger ; this
    faint heart
    Pines for a fulness which it finds
        not here :
Dear ones are leaving, and, as they
    depart,
    Make room within for something
        yet more dear.

5 More of Thyself, O shew me hour by
    hour,
  More of Thy glory, O my God and
    Lord ;
  More of Thyself, in all Thy grace and
    power,
  More of Thy love and truth,
    Incarnate Word !

    HORATIUS BONAR, 1808–89.

430   88. 88. 88.

JESUS, my Lord, my God, my All,
    Hear me, blest Saviour, when I
  call ;
Hear me, and from Thy dwelling-
  place
Pour down the riches of Thy grace.
  Jesus, my Lord, I Thee adore ;
  O make me love Thee more and more.

2 Jesus, too late I Thee have sought ;
  How can I love Thee as I ought ?
  And how extol Thy matchless love,
  The glorious beauty of Thy Name ?

3 Jesus, what didst Thou find in me
  That Thou hast dealt so lovingly ?
  How great the joy that Thou hast
    brought,
  So far exceeding hope or thought !

4 Jesus, of Thee shall be my song ;
  To Thee my heart and soul belong ;
  All that I have or am is Thine,
  And Thou, blest Saviour, Thou art
    mine.

    HENRY COLLINS, 1827–1919.

431   88. 88. 88.

THEE will I love, my Strength,
    my Tower ;
  Thee will I love, my Joy, my
    Crown ;
Thee will I love with all my power,
  In all Thy works, and Thee alone ;
Thee will I love, till sacred fire
Fill my whole soul with pure desire.

2 I thank Thee, uncreated Sun,
    That Thy bright beams on me
    have shined ;
  I thank Thee, who hast overthrown
  My foes, and healed my wounded
    mind ;
  I thank Thee, whose enlivening voice
  Bids my freed heart in Thee rejoice.

3 Uphold me in the doubtful race,
    Nor suffer me again to stray ;
  Strengthen my feet with steady pace
    Still to press forward in Thy way ;
  My soul and flesh, O Lord of might,
  Fill, satiate, with Thy heavenly light.

4 Thee will I love, my Joy, my Crown ;
    Thee will I love, my Lord, my God ;
  Thee will I love, beneath Thy frown
    Or smile, Thy sceptre or Thy rod ;
  What though my flesh and heart
    decay,
  Thee shall I love in endless day.

    JOHANN SCHEFFLER, 1624–77 ;
    tr. by JOHN WESLEY, 1703–91.

432   88. 88. 88.

JESUS, Thy boundless love to me
    No thought can reach, no tongue
  declare ;
O knit my thankful heart to Thee,
    And reign without a rival there :
Thine wholly, Thine alone, I am ;
Lord, with Thy love my heart in-
  flame.

2 O grant that nothing in my soul
    May dwell, but Thy pure love
    alone ;
  O may Thy love possess me whole,
    My joy, my treasure, and my
    crown :
  All coldness from my heart remove ;
  May every act, word, thought, be
    love.

3 O Love, how cheering is Thy ray !
    All pain before Thy presence flies ;
  Care, anguish, sorrow, melt away,
    Where'er Thy healing beams
    arise ;
  O Jesus, nothing may I see,
  Nothing desire, or seek, but Thee.

4 In suffering, be Thy love my peace ;
    In weakness, be Thy love my
    power ;
  And, when the storms of life shall
    cease,
  Jesus, in that tremendous hour,
  In death, as life, be Thou my Guide,
  And save me, who for me hast died.

    PAUL GERHARDT, 1607–76 ;
    tr. by JOHN WESLEY, 1703–91.

433
C. M.

MY God, I love Thee; not be-
cause
I hope for heaven thereby,
Nor yet because who love Thee not
Are lost eternally.

2 Thou, O my Jesus, Thou didst me
Upon the Cross embrace;
For me didst bear the nails and spear,
And manifold disgrace.

3 And griefs and torments numberless,
And sweat of agony,
Even death itself; and all for one
Who was Thine enemy.

4 Then why, most loving Jesus Christ,
Should I not love Thee well,
Not for the sake of winning heaven,
Or of escaping hell?

5 Not with the hope of gaining aught,
Not seeking a reward;
But as Thyself hast lovèd me,
O ever-loving Lord?

6 Even so I love Thee, and will love,
And in Thy praise will sing,
Solely because Thou art my God,
And my eternal King.

Attributed to St. FRANCIS XAVIER,
1506-52; tr. by EDWARD CASWALL,
1814-78.

434
77. 77. D.

LOVED with everlasting love,
Led by grace that love to know;
Spirit, breathing from above,
Thou hast taught me it is so.
O this full and perfect peace!
O this transport all divine!
In a love which cannot cease
I am His, and He is mine.

2 Heaven above is softer blue,
Earth around is sweeter green;
Something lives in every hue,
Christless eyes have never seen.
Birds with gladder songs o'erflow,
Flowers with deeper beauties
shine,
Since I know, as now I know,
I am His, and He is mine.

3 His for ever, only His:
Who the Lord and me shall part?
Ah, with what a rest of bliss
Christ can fill the loving heart!

Heaven and earth may fade and flee,
First-born light in gloom decline;
But, while God and I shall be,
I am His, and He is mine.

GEORGE WADE ROBINSON,
1838-77.

435
87. 87.

COME, Thou Fount of every
blessing,
Tune my heart to sing Thy grace;
Streams of mercy never ceasing
Call for songs of loudest praise.

2 Jesus sought me when a stranger,
Wandering from the fold of God;
He, to rescue me from danger,
Interposed His precious blood.

3 O to grace how great a debtor
Daily I'm constrained to be!
Let that grace now, like a fetter,
Bind my wandering heart to Thee.

4 Prone to wander—Lord, I feel it—
Prone to leave the God I love,
Take my heart, O take and seal it,
Seal it from Thy courts above.

ROBERT ROBINSON, 1735-90.

436
L. M.

IT is a thing most wonderful,
Almost too wonderful to be,
That God's own Son should come
from heaven,
And die to save a child like me.

2 And yet I know that it is true:
He chose a poor and humble lot,
And wept, and toiled, and mourned,
and died,
For love of those who loved Him
not.

3 It is most wonderful to know
His love for me so free and sure;
But 'tis more wonderful to see
My love for Him so faint and poor.

4 And yet I want to love Thee, Lord;
O light the flame within my heart,
And I will love Thee more and more,
Until I see Thee as Thou art.

WILLIAM WALSHAM HOW,
1823-97.

437 77. 77.

SAVIOUR, teach me, day by day,
Love's sweet lesson to obey;
Sweeter lesson cannot be,
Loving Him who first loved me.

2 With a child's glad heart of love
At Thy bidding may I move,
Prompt to serve and follow Thee,
Loving Him who first loved me.

3 Teach me thus Thy steps to trace,
Strong to follow in Thy grace,

Learning how to love from Thee,
Loving Him who first loved me.

4 Love in loving finds employ,
In obedience all her joy;
Ever new that joy will be,
Loving Him who first loved me.

5 Thus may I rejoice to show
That I feel the love I owe;
Singing, till Thy face I see,
Of His love who first loved me.
JANE ELIZA LEESON,
1807–82.

PEACE AND JOY

438 *From Psalm xxiii.* 87. 87.

THE King of Love my Shepherd is,
Whose goodness faileth never;
I nothing lack if I am His
And He is mine for ever.

2 Where streams of living water flow
My ransomed soul He leadeth,
And where the verdant pastures grow
With food celestial feedeth.

3 Perverse and foolish oft I strayed;
But yet in love He sought me,
And on His shoulder gently laid,
And home rejoicing brought me.

4 In death's dark vale I fear no ill,
With Thee, dear Lord, beside me;
Thy rod and staff my comfort still,
Thy Cross before to guide me.

5 Thou spread'st a table in my sight;
Thy unction grace bestoweth;
And O what transport of delight
From Thy pure chalice floweth!

6 And so through all the length of days
Thy goodness faileth never;
Good Shepherd, may I sing Thy
praise
Within Thy house for ever!
HENRY WILLIAMS BAKER.
1821–77.

439 76. 76. D.

SOMETIMES a light surprises
The Christian while he sings;
It is the Lord who rises
With healing in His wings:

When comforts are declining,
He grants the soul again
A season of clear shining,
To cheer it after rain.

2 In holy contemplation,
We sweetly then pursue
The theme of God's salvation,
And find it ever new.
Set free from present sorrow,
We cheerfully can say,
' Even let the unknown to-morrow
Bring with it what it may:

3 ' It can bring with it nothing
But He will bear us through;
Who gives the lilies clothing
Will clothe His people too.
Beneath the spreading heavens,
No creature but is fed;
And He who feeds the ravens
Will give His children bread.'

4 Though vine nor fig-tree neither
Their wonted fruit should bear,
Though all the fields should wither,
Nor flocks nor herds be there,
Yet, God the same abiding,
His praise shall tune my voice;
For, while in Him confiding,
I cannot but rejoice.
WILLIAM COWPER, 1731–1800.

440 C. M.

HAPPY are they, they that love
God,
Whose hearts have Christ confest,
Who by His Cross have found their
life,
And 'neath His yoke their rest.

THE CHRISTIAN LIFE

2 Glad is the praise, sweet are the
songs,
When they together sing ;
And strong the prayers that bow the
ear
Of heaven's eternal King.

3 Christ to their homes giveth His
peace,
And makes their loves His own ;
But ah, what tares the evil one
Hath in His garden sown !

4 Sad were our lot, evil this earth,
Did not its sorrows prove
The path whereby the sheep may
find
The fold of Jesus' love.

5 Then shall they know, they that love
Him,
How all their pain is good ;
And death itself cannot unbind
Their happy brotherhood.

Yattendon Hymnal, No. 34, 1899 ;
based on CHARLES COFFIN, 1676–
1749.

441
84. 84. 84.

MY God, I thank Thee, who hast
made
The earth so bright,
So full of splendour and of joy,
Beauty and light ;
So many glorious things are here,
Noble and right.

2 I thank Thee, too, that Thou hast
made
Joy to abound,
So many gentle thoughts and deeds
Circling us round
That in the darkest spot of earth
Some love is found.

3 I thank Thee more that all our joy
Is touched with pain,
That shadows fall on brightest hours,
That thorns remain,
So that earth's bliss may be our guide,
And not our chain.

4 For Thou, who knowest, Lord, how
soon
Our weak heart clings,
Hast given us joys, tender and true,
Yet all with wings,
So that we see, gleaming on high,
Diviner things.

5 I thank Thee, Lord, that here our
souls,
Though amply blest,
Can never find, although they seek,
A perfect rest,
Nor ever shall, until they lean
On Jesus' breast.

ADELAIDE ANNE PROCTER,
1825–64.

442
76. 76. D.

IN heavenly love abiding,
No change my heart shall fear ;
And safe is such confiding,
For nothing changes here :
The storm may roar without me,
My heart may low be laid ;
But God is round about me,
And can I be dismayed ?

2 Wherever He may guide me,
No want shall turn me back ;
My Shepherd is beside me,
And nothing can I lack.
His wisdom ever waketh,
His sight is never dim :
He knows the way He taketh,
And I will walk with Him.

3 Green pastures are before me,
Which yet I have not seen ;
Bright skies will soon be o'er me,
Where the dark clouds have been.
My hope I cannot measure :
My path to life is free ;
My Saviour has my treasure,
And He will walk with me.

ANNA LAETITIA WARING,
1823–1910.

443
65. 65. D. and refrain.

LIKE a river glorious
Is God's perfect peace,
Over all victorious
In its bright increase ;
Perfect, yet it floweth
Fuller every day,—
Perfect, yet it groweth
Deeper all the way.
*Stayed upon Jehovah,
Hearts are fully blest,
Finding, as He promised,
Perfect peace and rest,*

138

2 Hidden in the hollow
　　Of His blessèd hand,
　Never foe can follow,
　　Never traitor stand ;
　Not a surge of worry,
　　Not a shade of care,
　Not a blast of hurry,
　　Touch the spirit there.

3 Every joy or trial
　　Falleth from above,
　Traced upon our dial
　　By the Sun of Love.
　We may trust Him fully
　　All for us to do ;
　They who trust Him wholly
　　Find Him wholly true.

FRANCES RIDLEY HAVERGAL,
1836–79.

444
10 10.

PEACE, perfect peace, in this dark
　　world of sin ?
The blood of Jesus whispers peace
　within.

2 Peace, perfect peace, by thronging
　　duties pressed ?
To do the will of Jesus, this is rest.

3 Peace, perfect peace, with sorrows
　　surging round ?
On Jesus' bosom nought but calm is
　found.

4 Peace, perfect peace, with loved ones
　　far away ?
In Jesus' keeping we are safe, and
　they.

5 Peace, perfect peace, our future all
　　unknown ?
Jesus we know, and He is on the
　throne.

6 Peace, perfect peace, death shadow-
　　ing us and ours ?
Jesus has vanquished death and all
　its powers.

7 It is enough : earth's struggles soon
　　shall cease,
And Jesus call us to heaven's perfect
　peace.

EDWARD HENRY BICKERSTETH,
1825–1906.

445
87. 87. D.

SPEAK, I pray Thee, gentle Jesus !
　O, how passing sweet Thy words,
Breathing o'er my troubled spirit
　Peace which never earth affords.
All the world's distracting voices,
　All the enticing tones of ill,
At Thy accents mild, melodious,
　Are subdued, and all is still.

2 Tell me Thou art mine, O Saviour,
　　Grant me an assurance clear ;
Banish all my dark misgivings,
　　Still my doubting, calm my fear.
O, my soul within me yearneth
　　Now to hear Thy voice divine ;
So shall grief be gone for ever,
　　And despair no more be mine.

WILLIAM WILLIAMS, 1717–91 ; tr. by
RICHARD MORRIS LEWIS, 1849–
1918.

446
D. C. M.

MY heart is resting, O my God,
　I will give thanks and sing ;
My heart is at the secret source
　Of every precious thing.
I thirst for springs of heavenly life,
　And here all day they rise ;
I seek the treasure of Thy love,
　And close at hand it lies.

2 I have a heritage of joy,
　　That yet I must not see ;
But the hand that bled to make it
　　mine
　Is keeping it for me.
And a new song is in my mouth,
　To long-loved music set :
' Glory to Thee for all the grace
　I have not tasted yet.'

3 My heart is resting, O my God,
　My heart is in Thy care ;
I hear the voice of joy and health
　Resounding everywhere.
' Thou art my portion, saith my
　　soul,'
　Ten thousand voices say,
And the music of their glad Amen
　Will never die away.

ANNA LAETITIA WARING,
1823–1910.

THE CHRISTIAN LIFE

447

S. M.

COME, we that love the Lord,
And let our joys be known :
Join in a song with sweet accord,
And thus surround the throne.

2 Let those refuse to sing
That never knew our God ;
But children of the heavenly King
Must speak their joys abroad.

3 The men of grace have found
Glory begun below ;
Celestial fruits on earthly ground
From faith and hope may grow.

4 The hill of Zion yields
A thousand sacred sweets,
Before we reach the heavenly fields
Or walk the golden streets.

5 There shall we see His face,
And never, never sin ;
There from the rivers of His grace
Drink endless pleasures in.

6 Then let our songs abound,
And every tear be dry ;
We're marching through Immanuel's
ground
To fairer worlds on high.

ISAAC WATTS, 1674–1748.

448

87. 87. 337.

ALL my hope on God is founded ;
He doth still my trust renew.
Me through change and chance He
guideth,

Only good and only true.
God unknown,
He alone
Calls my heart to be His own.

2 Pride of man and earthly glory,
Sword and crown betray his trust ;
What with care and toil he buildeth,
Tower and temple, fall to dust.
But God's power,
Hour by hour,
Is my temple and my tower.

3 God's great goodness aye endureth,
Deep His wisdom passing thought :
Splendour, light, and life attend Him,
Beauty springeth out of nought.
Evermore,
From His store
New-born worlds rise and adore.

4 Daily doth the Almighty Giver
Bounteous gifts on us bestow ;
His desire our soul delighteth,
Pleasure leads us where we go.
Love doth stand
At His hand ;
Joy doth wait on His command.

5 Still from man to God eternal
Sacrifice of praise be done,
High above all praises praising
For the gift of Christ His Son.
Christ doth call
One and all :
Ye who follow shall not fall.

Yattendon Hymnal, No. 69, 1899 ;
based on JOACHIM NEANDER, 1650–80.

PRAYER, ASPIRATION, AND HOLINESS

449

88. 84.

MY God, is any hour so sweet,
From blush of morn to evening
star,
As that which calls me to Thy feet,
The hour of prayer ?

2 Blest is that tranquil hour of morn,
And blest that hour of solemn eve,
When, on the wings of prayer up-
borne,
The world I leave ;

3 For then a dayspring shines on me,
Brighter than morn's ethereal glow,

And richer dews descend from Thee
Than earth can know.

4 Then is my strength by Thee re-
newed ;
Then are my sins by Thee for-
given ;
Then dost Thou cheer my solitude
With hope of heaven.

5 No words can tell what sweet relief
There for my every want I find,
What strength for warfare, balm for
grief,
What peace of mind.

PRAYER, ASPIRATION, AND HOLINESS

6 Hushed is each doubt, gone every
    fear ;
    My spirit seems in heaven to stay ;
And even the penitential tear
    Is wiped away.

7 Lord, till I reach yon blissful shore.
    No privilege so dear shall be
As thus my inmost soul to pour
    In prayer to Thee.
        CHARLOTTE ELLIOTT, 1789–1871.

450
                                    77. 77.

COME, my soul, thy suit prepare ;
    Jesus loves to answer prayer ;
He Himself has bid thee pray,
Therefore will not say thee nay.

2 Thou art coming to a King ;
Large petitions with thee bring ;
For His grace and power are such,
None can ever ask too much.

3 With my burden I begin :
Lord, remove this load of sin ;
Let Thy blood, for sinners spilt,
Set my conscience free from guilt.

4 Lord, I come to Thee for rest ;
Take possession of my breast ;
There Thy blood-bought right main-
    tain,
And without a rival reign.

5 While I am a pilgrim here,
Let Thy love my spirit cheer ;
As my Guide, my Guard, my Friend,
Lead me to my journey's end.
        JOHN NEWTON, 1725–1807.

451
                                    C. M.

APPROACH, my soul, the mercy-
    seat,
    Where Jesus answers prayer ;
There humbly fall before His feet,
    For none can perish there.

2 Thy promise is my only plea ;
    With this I venture nigh :
Thou callest burdened souls to Thee,
    And such, O Lord, am I.

3 Bowed down beneath a load of sin,
    By Satan sorely pressed,
By war without and fears within,
    I come to Thee for rest.

4 Be Thou my Shield and Hiding-
    place,
    That, sheltered near Thy side,
I may my fierce accuser face,
    And tell him Thou hast died.

5 O wondrous love ! to bleed and die,
    To bear the Cross and shame,
That guilty sinners, such as I,
    Might plead Thy gracious Name !
        JOHN NEWTON, 1725–1807.

452
                                    777.

PRESENT with the two or three
    Deign, most gracious God, to be,
While we lift our souls to Thee.

2 Jesus, by Thy blood alone
Who didst for our sins atone,
Dare we come before Thy throne.

3 Thou who knowest all our need,
Grant the prayer of faith to plead,
Teach us how to intercede.

4 Holy Spirit, from on high
Helping our infirmity,
Aid us in our feeble cry.

5 Flesh and heart would faint and fail,
But there stands within the veil
One who ever doth prevail.

6 Glory to the Father, Son,
Holy Spirit, Three in One,
While the endless ages run.
        FANNY FREER, 1801–91.

453
                                    10 10.

O KING of mercy, from Thy
    throne on high
Look down in love, and hear our
    humble cry.

2 Thou tender Shepherd of the blood-
    bought sheep,
Thy feeble wandering flock in safety
    keep.

3 O gentle Saviour, by Thy death we
    live ;
To contrite sinners life eternal give.

4 Thou art the Bread of heaven, on
    Thee we feed ;
Be near to help our souls in time of
    need.

5 Thou art the mourner's Stay, the
    sinner's Friend,
Sweet Fount of joy and blessings
    without end.

THE CHRISTIAN LIFE

6 O come and cheer us with Thy
    heavenly grace ;
  Reveal the brightness of Thy glorious
    face.

7 In cooling cloud by day, in fire by
    night,
  Be near our steps, and make our
    darkness light.

8 Go where we go, abide where we
    abide,
  In life, in death, our Comfort,
    Strength, and Guide.

9 O lead us daily with Thine eye of
    love,
  And bring us safely to our home
    above.

           THOMAS RAWSON BIRKS,
                1810-83.

454
                      76. 76. D.

O GOD, Thou art the Father
    Of all that have believed :
From whom all hosts of angels
  Have life and power received.

2 O God, Thou art the Maker
    Of all created things,
The righteous Judge of judges,
  The Almighty King of kings.

3 High in the heavenly Zion
    Thou reignest God adored ;
And in the coming glory
  Thou shalt be Sovereign Lord.

4 Beyond our ken Thou shinest,
    The everlasting Light ;
Ineffable in loving,
  Unthinkable in might.

5 Thou to the meek and lowly
    Thy secrets dost unfold ;
O God, Thou doest all things,
  All things both new and old.

6 I walk secure and blessèd
    In every clime or coast,
In Name of God the Father,
  And Son, and Holy Ghost.

          ST. COLUMBA, 521-97 ; *tr.* by
      DUNCAN MACGREGOR, 1854-1923.

455
                         C. M.

O HELP us, Lord ; each hour of
    need
  Thy heavenly succour give ;
Help us in thought, and word, and
    deed,
  Each hour on earth we live.

2 O help us when our spirits bleed
    With contrite anguish sore ;
And, when our hearts are cold and
    dead,
  O help us, Lord, the more.

3 O help us, through the prayer of
    faith,
  More firmly to believe ;
For still the more the servant hath
  The more shall he receive.

4 If, strangers to Thy fold, we call,
    Imploring at Thy feet
The crumbs that from Thy table fall,
  'Tis all we dare entreat.

5 But be it, Lord of mercy, all,
    So Thou wilt grant but this ;
The crumbs that from Thy table fall
  Are light and life and bliss.

6 O help us, Saviour, from on high ;
    We know no help but Thee :
O help us so to live and die
  As Thine in heaven to be.

             HENRY HART MILMAN,
                1791-1868.

456
                        66. 66.

MY spirit longs for Thee
    Within my troubled breast,
Though I unworthy be
  Of so Divine a Guest.

2 Of so Divine a Guest
    Unworthy though I be,
Yet has my heart no rest,
  Unless it come from Thee.

3 Unless it come from Thee,
    In vain I look around ;
In all that I can see
  No rest is to be found.

4 No rest is to be found
    But in Thy blessèd love :
O let my wish be crowned,
  And send it from above !

           JOHN BYROM, 1691-1763.

457
                         C. M.

O FOR a closer walk with God,
    A calm and heavenly frame,
A light to shine upon the road
  That leads me to the Lamb !

2 Where is the blessedness I knew
    When first I saw the Lord ?
Where is the soul-refreshing view
  Of Jesus and His word ?

3 What peaceful hours I once enjoyed !
  How sweet their memory still !
But they have left an aching void
  The world can never fill.

4 Return, O Holy Dove ! return,
  Sweet messenger of rest !
I hate the sins that made Thee mourn,
  And drove Thee from my breast.

5 The dearest idol I have known,
  Whate'er that idol be,
Help me to tear it from Thy throne,
  And worship only Thee.

6 So shall my walk be close with God,
  Calm and serene my frame ;
So purer light shall mark the road
  That leads me to the Lamb.

           WILLIAM COWPER, 1731–1800.

458
           66. 66. 88.

O LIGHT that knew no dawn,
   That shines to endless day,
All things in earth and heaven
   Are lustred by Thy ray ;
No eye can to Thy throne ascend,
Nor mind Thy brightness comprehend.

2 Thy grace, O Father, give,
   That I may serve in fear ;
Above all boons, I pray,
   Grant me Thy voice to hear ;
From sin Thy child in mercy free,
And let me dwell in light with Thee :

3 That, cleansed from stain of sin,
   I may meet homage give,
And, pure in heart, behold
   Thy beauty while I live ;
Clean hands in holy worship raise,
And Thee, O Christ my Saviour,
   praise.

4 In supplication meek
   To Thee I bend the knee ;
O Christ, when Thou shalt come,
   In love remember me,
And in Thy Kingdom, by Thy grace,
Grant me a humble servant's place.

5 Thy grace, O Father, give,
   I humbly Thee implore ;
And let Thy mercy bless
   Thy servant more and more.
All grace and glory be to Thee,
From age to age eternally.

    ST. GREGORY NAZIANZEN, 325–390 ;
    tr. by JOHN BROWNLIE, 1859–1925.

459
           88. 88. 88.

THOU hidden Love of God,
   whose height,
  Whose depth unfathomed, no man
   knows,
I see from far Thy beauteous light,
  Inly I sigh for Thy repose ;
My heart is pained, nor can it be
At rest till it finds rest in Thee.

2 Thy secret voice invites me still
   The sweetness of Thy yoke to
   prove ;
And fain I would ; but, though my
   will
  Seem fixed, yet wide my passions
   rove ;
Yet hindrances strew all the way ;
I aim at Thee, yet from Thee stray.

3 'Tis mercy all, that Thou hast
   brought
  My mind to seek her peace in
   Thee ;
Yet, while I seek but find Thee not,
  No peace my wandering soul shall
   see.
O when shall all my wanderings end,
And all my steps to Thee-ward
   tend ?

4 Is there a thing beneath the sun
   That strives with Thee my heart
   to share ?
Ah ! tear it thence, and reign alone,
  The Lord of every motion there ;
Then shall my heart from earth be
   free,
When it has found repose in Thee.

    GERHARD TERSTEEGEN, 1697–1769 ;
    tr. by JOHN WESLEY, 1703–91.

460
           L. M.

DEAR Master, in whose life I see
   All that I would but fail to be,
Let Thy clear light for ever shine,
To shame and guide this life of mine.

2 Though what I dream and what I do
In my weak days are always two,
Help me, oppressed by things undone,
O Thou, whose deeds and dreams
   were one !

       JOHN HUNTER, 1848–1917.

THE CHRISTIAN LIFE

461
88. 84.

ONE thing I of the Lord desire,—
 For all my way hath miry been—
Be it by water or by fire,
  O make me clean !

2 If clearer vision Thou impart,
  Grateful and glad my soul shall
    be ;
But yet to have a purer heart
  Is more to me.

3 Yea, only as the heart is clean
  May larger vision yet be mine,
For mirrored in its depths are seen
    The things divine.

4 I watch to shun the miry way,
  And stanch the spring of guilty
    thought :
But, watch and wrestle as I may,
  Pure I am not.

5 So wash Thou me without, within,
  Or purge with fire, if that must
    be,—
No matter how, if only sin
  Die out in me.

WALTER CHALMERS SMITH,
1824–1908.

462
65. 65.

JESUS, meek and gentle,
 Son of God most high,
Pitying, loving Saviour,
  Hear Thy children's cry.

2 Pardon our offences,
  Loose our captive chains,
Break down every idol
  Which our soul detains.

3 Give us holy freedom,
  Fill our hearts with love,
Draw us, holy Jesus,
  To the realms above.

4 Lead us on our journey,
  Be Thyself the Way
Through terrestrial darkness
  To celestial day.

5 Jesus, meek and gentle,
  Son of God most high,
Pitying, loving Saviour,
  Hear Thy children's cry.

GEORGE RUNDLE PRYNNE,
1818–1903.

463
76. 76. Irr.

MY soul, there is a country
 Afar beyond the stars,
Where stands a wingèd Sentry
  All skilful in the wars.

2 There, above noise, and danger,
  Sweet peace sits, crowned with
    smiles,
And One born in a manger
  Commands the beauteous files.

3 He is thy gracious friend,
  And—O my soul, awake !—
Did in pure love descend,
  To die here for thy sake.

4 If thou canst get but thither,
  There grows the flower of peace,
The rose that cannot wither,
  Thy fortress, and thy ease.

5 Leave then thy foolish ranges ;
  For none can thee secure,
But One, who never changes,
  Thy God, thy Life, thy Cure.

HENRY VAUGHAN,
1621–95.

464
D. S. M.

MAKE me a captive, Lord,
 And then I shall be free ;
Force me to render up my sword,
  And I shall conqueror be.
I sink in life's alarms
  When by myself I stand ;
Imprison me within Thine arms,
  And strong shall be my hand.

2 My heart is weak and poor
  Until it master find ;
It has no spring of action sure—
  It varies with the wind.
It cannot freely move,
  Till Thou hast wrought its chain :
Enslave it with Thy matchless love,
  And deathless it shall reign.

3 My power is faint and low
  Till I have learned to serve ;
It wants the needed fire to glow,
  It wants the breeze to nerve ;
It cannot drive the world,
  Until itself be driven ;
Its flag can only be unfurled
  When Thou shalt breathe from
    heaven.

4 My will is not my own
  Till Thou hast made it Thine;
If it would reach a monarch's throne
  It must its crown resign;
  It only stands unbent,
  Amid the clashing strife,
When on Thy bosom it has leant
  And found in Thee its life.

GEORGE MATHESON, 1842-1906.

465

87. 87.

BLESSÈD Jesus, high in glory,
  Seen of saints and angels fair,
Children's voices now adore Thee;
  Listen to Thy children's prayer.

2 Gentle Jesus, Thou dost love us,
    Thou hast died upon the Tree,
And Thou reignest now above us,
  That we too might reign with
    Thee.

3 Give us grace to trust Thee wholly;
    Give us each a childlike heart;
Make us meek and pure and holy,
  Meet to see Thee as Thou art.

4 Father, Son, and Holy Spirit,
    Bless us all our life below,
Till we each that heaven inherit
  Which the childlike only know.

JOHN MACLEOD, 1840-98.

466

L. M.

O GRANT us light, that we may
    know
  The wisdom Thou alone canst
    give;
That truth may guide where'er we
    go,
  And virtue bless where'er we live!

2 O grant us light, that we may see
    Where error lurks in human lore,
And turn our doubting minds to
    Thee,
  And love Thy simple word the
    more.

3 O grant us light, that we may learn
    How dead is life from Thee apart;
How sure is joy for all who turn
  To Thee an undivided heart.

4 O grant us light, in grief and pain,
    To lift our burdened hearts above,
And count the very cross a gain,
  And bless our Father's hidden love.

5 O grant us light, when, soon or late,
    All earthly scenes shall pass away,
In Thee to find the open gate
  To deathless home and endless
    day.

LAWRENCE TUTTIETT, 1825-97.

467

C. M.

O FOR a heart to praise my God!
    A heart from sin set free;
A heart that always feels Thy blood,
  So freely shed for me;

2 A heart resigned, submissive, meek,
    My great Redeemer's throne,
Where only Christ is heard to speak,
  Where Jesus reigns alone;

3 A humble, lowly, contrite heart,
    Believing, true, and clean,
Which neither life nor death can part
  From Him that dwells within;

4 A heart in every thought renewed,
    And full of love divine,
Perfect and right and pure and good,
  A copy, Lord, of Thine!

5 Thy nature, gracious Lord, impart;
    Come quickly from above;
Write Thy new Name upon my
    heart,
  Thy new, best Name of Love.

CHARLES WESLEY, 1707-88.

468 Children's Litany.

77. 76.

JESUS, Saviour ever mild,
  Born for us a little Child
Of the Virgin undefiled:
      Hear us, Holy Jesus.

2 Jesus, at whose infant feet
Shepherds, coming Thee to greet,
Knelt to pay their worship meet:
      Hear us, Holy Jesus.

3 Jesus, unto whom of yore
Wise men, hastening to adore,
Gold and myrrh and incense bore:
      Hear us, Holy Jesus.

4 From all pride and vain conceit,
From all spite and angry heat,
From all lying and deceit,
      Save us, Holy Jesus.

5 From all sloth and idleness,
From not caring for distress,
From all lust and greediness,
      Save us, Holy Jesus.

THE CHRISTIAN LIFE

6 From refusing to obey,
From the love of our own way,
From forgetfulness to pray,
   Save us, Holy Jesus.

7 By Thy pattern bright and pure,
By the pains Thou didst endure
Our salvation to procure,
   Save us, Holy Jesus.

8 By the Name we bow before,
Human Name, which evermore
All the hosts of heaven adore,
   Save us, Holy Jesus.

9 By Thine own unconquered might,
By Thy glory in the height,
By Thy mercies infinite,
   Save us, Holy Jesus.
   RICHARD FREDERICK LITTLEDALE,
   1833–90, and others.

469
77. 76.

JESUS, from Thy throne on high,
Far above the bright blue sky,
Look on us with loving eye :
   Hear us, Holy Jesus.

2 Be Thou with us every day,
In our work and in our play,
When we learn and when we pray :
   Hear us, Holy Jesus.

3 May our thoughts be undefiled ;
May our words be true and mild ;
Make us each a holy child :
   Hear us, Holy Jesus.

4 Jesus, Son of God most high,
Who didst in the manger lie,
Who upon the Cross didst die,
   Hear us, Holy Jesus.

5 Jesus, from Thy heavenly throne
Watching o'er each little one,
Till our life on earth is done,
   Hear us, Holy Jesus.
   THOMAS BENSON POLLOCK,
   1836–96.

470
76. 76. D.

O LAMB of God, still keep me
Close to Thy piercèd side ;
'Tis only there in safety
And peace I can abide.
What foes and snares surround me,
What lusts and fears within !
The grace that sought and found me
Alone can keep me clean.

2 'Tis only in Thee hiding
I feel myself secure ;
Only in Thee abiding,
The conflict can endure.
Thine arm the victory gaineth
O'er every hateful foe ;
Thy love my heart sustaineth
In all its cares and woe.

3 Soon shall my eyes behold Thee
With rapture face to face ;
One half hath not been told me
Of all Thy power and grace.
Thy beauty, Lord, and glory,
The wonders of Thy love,
Shall be the endless story
Of all Thy saints above.
   JAMES GEORGE DECK, 1802–84.

471
L. M.

O THOU who camest from above,
The pure celestial fire to impart,
Kindle a flame of sacred love
On the mean altar of my heart.

2 There let it for Thy glory burn
With inextinguishable blaze,
And trembling to its source return,
In humble prayer and fervent praise.

3 Jesus, confirm my heart's desire
To work, and speak, and think for Thee ;
Still let me guard the holy fire,
And still stir up Thy gift in me :

4 Ready for all Thy perfect will,
My acts of faith and love repeat,
Till death Thy endless mercies seal,
And make the sacrifice complete.
   CHARLES WESLEY, 1707–88.

472
L. M.

FOR Thee, my God, for Thee alone,
My spirit longs with ardent love ;
On earth beside Thee there is none,
And none but Thee in heaven above.

2 Fulfil, O God, my heart's desires ;
While I look up, look down to bless ;
Each holy wish Thy grace inspires
May I in Thy deep love possess.

3 My soul cleaves heavy to the dust,
    But Thou canst raise and set it
        free ;
And then, in calm and joyful trust,
    It soars from earth to heaven and
        Thee.

4 Now in this stillness, as the breath
    Of prayer steals upward to the
        skies,
O give my soul the wings of faith,
    That it to Thee may gladly rise ;

5 That, breaking through each fleshly
        link
    Which binds its being to the clod,
At life's clear wellspring it may drink,
    Rejoicing in the smile of God.

JAMES DRUMMOND BURNS,
1823–64.

473 *From Psalm* lxiii.   L. M.

O GOD, Thou art my God alone ;
    Early to Thee my soul shall cry,
A pilgrim in a land unknown,
    A thirsty land whose springs are
        dry.

2 O that it were as it hath been
    When, praying in the holy place,
Thy power and glory I have seen,
    And marked the footsteps of Thy
        grace !

3 Yet through this rough and thorny
        maze
    I follow hard on Thee, my God ;
Thine hand unseen upholds my ways ;
    I safely tread where Thou hast
        trod.

4 Thee, in the watches of the night,
    When I remember on my bed,
Thy presence makes the darkness
        light ;
    Thy guardian wings are round my
        head.

5 Better than life itself Thy love,
    Dearer than all beside to me ;
For whom have I in heaven above,
    Or what on earth, compared with
        Thee ?

6 Praise, with my heart, my mind, my
        voice,
    For all Thy mercy I will give ;
My soul shall still in God rejoice ;
    My tongue shall bless Thee while
        I live.

JAMES MONTGOMERY, 1771–1854.

474   C. M.

O FOR a faith that will not shrink,
    Though pressed by many a foe,
That will not tremble on the brink
    Of poverty or woe,

2 That will not murmur nor complain
    Beneath the chastening rod,
But, in the hour of grief or pain,
    Can lean upon its God ;

3 A faith that shines more bright and
        clear
    When tempests rage without,
That when in danger knows no fear,
    In darkness feels no doubt ;

4 A faith that keeps the narrow way
    Till life's last spark is fled,
And with a pure and heavenly ray
    Lights up a dying bed !

5 Lord, give me such a faith as this,
    And then, whate'er may come,
I taste even now the hallowed bliss
    Of an eternal home.

WILLIAM HILEY BATHURST,
1796–1877.

475   64. 64. 664.

NEARER, my God, to Thee,
    Nearer to Thee !
Even though it be a cross
    That raiseth me,
Still all my song would be,
    ' Nearer, my God, to Thee,
    Nearer to Thee ! '

2 Though, like the wanderer,
    The sun gone down,
Darkness be over me,
    My rest a stone,
Yet in my dreams I'd be
    Nearer, my God, to Thee,
    Nearer to Thee !

3 There let the way appear
    Steps unto heaven,
All that Thou send'st to me
    In mercy given,
Angels to beckon me
    Nearer, my God, to Thee,
    Nearer to Thee !

4 Then, with my waking thoughts
    Bright with Thy praise,
Out of my stony griefs
    Bethel I'll raise,
So by my woes to be
    Nearer, my God, to Thee,
    Nearer to Thee !

5 Or if on joyful wing
    Cleaving the sky,
Sun, moon, and stars forgot,
    Upwards I fly,
Still all my song shall be,
    ' Nearer, my God, to Thee,
      Nearer to Thee ! '
            SARAH FLOWER ADAMS,
                 1805-48.

476
                    65. 65. D.

SAVIOUR, blessèd Saviour,
  Listen while we sing,
Hearts and voices raising
    Praises to our King ;
All we have to offer,
    All we hope to be,
Body, soul, and spirit,
    All we yield to Thee.

2 Nearer, ever nearer,
    Christ, we draw to Thee,
Deep in adoration
    Bending low the knee.
Thou for our redemption
    Cam'st on earth to die ;
Thou, that we might follow,
    Hast gone up on high.

3 Clearer still and clearer
    Dawns the light from heaven,
In our sadness bringing
    News of sins forgiven ;
Life has lost its shadows,
    Pure the light within ;
Thou hast shed Thy radiance
    On a world of sin.

4 Onward, ever onward,
    Journeying o'er the road
Worn by saints before us,
    Journeying on to God,
Leaving all behind us,
    May we hasten on,
Backward never looking
    Till the prize is won.

5 Higher then and higher
    Bear the ransomed soul,
Earthly toils forgotten,
    Saviour, to its goal,
Where, in joys unthought of,
    Saints with angels sing,
Never weary raising
    Praises to their King.
            GODFREY THRING,
              1823-1903.

477
              10 10. 10 10.

BE Thou my Vision, O Lord of my
  heart ;
Naught be all else to me, save that
    Thou art,—
Thou my best thought, by day or by
    night,
Waking or sleeping, Thy presence
    my light.

2 Be Thou my Wisdom, Thou my
    true Word ;
I ever with Thee, Thou with me,
    Lord ;
Thou my great Father, I Thy true
    son ;
Thou in me dwelling, and I with
    Thee one.

3 Be Thou my battle-shield, sword for
    the fight,
Be Thou my dignity, Thou my
    delight.
Thou my soul's shelter, Thou my
    high tower :
Raise Thou me heavenward, O
    Power of my power.

4 Riches I heed not, nor man's empty
    praise,
Thou mine inheritance, now and
    always :
Thou and Thou only, first in my
    heart,
High King of heaven, my treasure
    Thou art.

5 High King of heaven, after victory
    won,
May I reach heaven's joys, O bright
    heaven's Sun !
Heart of my own heart, whatever
    befall,
Still be my Vision, O Ruler of all.
               Ancient Irish,
      tr. by MARY BYRNE, 1880-1931;
versified by ELEANOR HULL, 1860-1935.

478
                    S. M.

BLEST are the pure in heart,
  For they shall see their God :
The secret of the Lord is theirs ;
  Their soul is Christ's abode.

2 The Lord, who left the sky
  Our life and peace to bring,
And dwelt in lowliness with men,
  Their Pattern and their King,—

3　Still to the lowly soul
　He doth Himself impart,
And for His dwelling and His throne
　Chooseth the pure in heart.

4　Lord, we Thy presence seek ;
　Ours may this blessing be :
O give the pure and lowly heart,
　A temple meet for Thee.
　　　　　JOHN KEBLE, 1792–1866,
　　　　　　　　and others.

479　　　　　　　　　87. 87. D.

LOVE Divine, all loves excelling,
　Joy of heaven, to earth come
　　　down,
Fix in us Thy humble dwelling,
　All Thy faithful mercies crown.
Jesus, Thou art all compassion,
　Pure, unbounded love Thou art ;
Visit us with Thy salvation,
　Enter every trembling heart.

2　Come, almighty to deliver ;
　Let us all Thy life receive ;
Suddenly return, and never,
　Never more Thy temples leave.
Thee we would be always blessing,
　Serve Thee as Thy hosts above,
Pray, and praise Thee, without
　　　ceasing,
　Glory in Thy perfect love.

3　Finish then Thy new creation :
　Pure and spotless let us be ;
Let us see Thy great salvation,
　Perfectly restored in Thee,
Changed from glory into glory,
　Till in heaven we take our place,
Till we cast our crowns before Thee,
　Lost in wonder, love, and praise.
　　　　　CHARLES WESLEY, 1707–88.

480　　　　　　　　　66. 55. 6.

THERE is a city bright ;
　Closed are its gates to sin ;
Nought that defileth,
Nought that defileth
Can ever enter in.

2　Saviour, I come to Thee ;
　O Lamb of God, I pray,
Cleanse me and save me,
Cleanse me and save me,
Wash all my sins away.

3　Lord, make me, from this hour,
　Thy loving child to be,
　Kept by Thy power,
　Kept by Thy power
From all that grieveth Thee,—

4　Till in the snow-white dress
　Of Thy redeemed I stand,
　Faultless and stainless,
　Faultless and stainless,
Safe in that happy land.
　　　　MARY ANN SANDERSON DECK,
　　　　　　　　1813–1902.

481　*From Heb.* xiii. 20–21.　　c. m.

FATHER of peace, and God of
　love !
We own Thy power to save,
That power by which our Shepherd
　　　rose
　Victorious o'er the grave.

2　Him from the dead Thou brought'st
　　　again,
　When, by His sacred blood,
Confirmed and sealed for evermore,
　The eternal covenant stood.

3　O may Thy Spirit seal our souls,
　And mould them to Thy will,
That our weak hearts no more may
　　　stray,
　But keep Thy precepts still ;

4　That to perfection's sacred height
　We nearer still may rise,
And all we think, and all we do,
　Be pleasing in Thine eyes.
　　　　　PHILIP DODDRIDGE, 1702–51 ;
　　　　　as in *Scottish Paraphrases,* 1781.

482　　　　　　　　　c. m.

WALK in the light : so shalt thou
　know
That fellowship of love
His Spirit only can bestow
　Who reigns in light above.

2　Walk in the light : and sin, abhorred,
　Shall ne'er defile again ;
The blood of Jesus Christ thy Lord
　Shall cleanse from every stain.

3　Walk in the light : and thou shalt
　　　find
　Thy heart made truly His
Who dwells in cloudless light en-
　　　shrined,
　In whom no darkness is.

4 Walk in the light : and thou shalt own
  Thy darkness passed away,
Because that light hath on thee shone
  In which is perfect day.

5 Walk in the light : and even the tomb
  No fearful shade shall wear ;
Glory shall chase away its gloom,
  For Christ hath conquered there.

6 Walk in the light : and thine shall be
  A path, though thorny, bright ;
For God, by grace, shall dwell in thee,
  And God Himself is Light.

BERNARD BARTON, 1784–1849.

483 *From 1 St. John iii. 1–4.*   C. M.

BEHOLD the amazing gift of love
  The Father hath bestowed
On us, the sinful sons of men,
  To call us sons of God !

2 Concealed as yet this honour lies,
  By this dark world unknown,—
A world that knew not when He came,
  Even God's eternal Son.

3 High is the rank we now possess,
  But higher we shall rise,
Though what we shall hereafter be
  Is hid from mortal eyes.

4 Our souls, we know, when He appears,
  Shall bear His image bright ;
For all His glory, full disclosed,
  Shall open to our sight.

5 A hope so great, and so divine,
  May trials well endure ;
And purge the soul from sense and sin,
  As Christ Himself is pure.

Scottish Paraphrases, 1781.

BROTHERLY LOVE

484 *From 1 Corinthians xiii.*   77. 75.

GRACIOUS Spirit, Holy Ghost,
  Taught by Thee, we covet most,
Of Thy gifts at Pentecost,
  Holy, heavenly love.

2 Faith that mountains could remove,
Tongues of earth or heaven above,
Knowledge, all things, empty prove
  Without heavenly love.

3 Though I as a martyr bleed,
Give my goods the poor to feed,
All is vain if love I need ;
  Therefore give me love.

4 Love is kind, and suffers long ;
Love is meek, and thinks no wrong,
Love than death itself more strong ;
  Therefore give us love.

5 Prophecy will fade away,
Melting in the light of day ;
Love will ever with us stay ;
  Therefore give us love.

6 Faith and hope and love we see,
Joining hand in hand, agree ;
But the greatest of the three,
  And the best, is love.

CHRISTOPHER WORDSWORTH,
1807–85.

485   11 10. 11 10.

O BROTHER man, fold to thy heart thy brother !
  Where pity dwells, the peace of God is there ;
To worship rightly is to love each other,
  Each smile a hymn, each kindly deed a prayer.

2 For he whom Jesus loved hath truly spoken :
    The holier worship which He deigns to bless
Restores the lost, and binds the spirit broken,
    And feeds the widow and the fatherless.

3 Follow with reverent steps the great example
    Of Him whose holy work was doing good ;
So shall the wide earth seem our Father's temple,
    Each loving life a psalm of gratitude.

4 Then shall all shackles fall ; the stormy clangour
    Of wild war-music o'er the earth shall cease ;

BROTHERLY LOVE

Love shall tread out the baleful fire
  of anger,
And in its ashes plant the tree of
  peace.
JOHN GREENLEAF WHITTIER,
1807–92.

486
D. C. M.

OUR Father, Thy dear Name doth
  show
  The greatness of Thy love ;
All are Thy children here below,
  As in Thy heaven above.
One family on earth are we,
  Throughout its widest span :
O help us everywhere to see
  The brotherhood of man.

2 Alike we share Thy tender care ;
    We trust one heavenly Friend ;
  Before one mercy-seat, in prayer,
    With confidence we bend ;
  Alike we hear Thy loving call,
    One heavenly vision scan,—
  One Lord, one faith, one hope for all,
    The brotherhood of man.

3 Bring in, we pray, the glorious day
    When warfare shall be stilled,
  And bitter strife be swept away,
    And hearts with love be filled.
  Help us to banish pride and wrong,
    Which, since the world began,
  Have marred its peace ; and so make
    strong
  The brotherhood of man.
CHARLES HERBERT RICHARDS,
1839–1925.

487
88. 86.

O GOD of mercy, God of might,
  In love and pity infinite,
Teach us, as ever in Thy sight,
  To live our life to Thee.

2 And Thou, who cam'st on earth to
    die
  That fallen man might live thereby,
  O hear us, for to Thee we cry,—
    In hope, O Lord, to Thee.

3 Teach us the lesson Thou hast
    taught,
  To feel for those Thy blood hath
    bought,
  That every word and deed and
    thought
  May work a work for Thee.

4 For all are brethren, far and wide,
  Since Thou, O Lord, for all hast
    died ;
  Then teach us, whatsoe'er betide,
    To love them all in Thee.

5 In sickness, sorrow, want, or care,
  Whate'er it be, 'tis ours to share ;
  May we, where help is needed, there
    Give help as unto Thee.

6 And may Thy Holy Spirit move
  All those who live, to live in love,
  Till Thou shalt greet in heaven above
    All those who give to Thee.
GODFREY THRING, 1823–1903.

488
10 10.

BELOVÈD, let us love : love is
  of God ;
In God alone hath love its true abode.

2 Belovèd, let us love : for they who
    love,
  They only, are His sons, born from
    above.

3 Belovèd, let us love : for love is rest,
  And he who loveth not abides un-
    blest.

4 Belovèd, let us love : for love is
    light,
  And he who loveth not dwelleth in
    night.

5 Belovèd, let us love : for only thus
  Shall we behold that God who
    loveth us.
HORATIUS BONAR, 1808–89.

489
10 10. 10 10. 10 10.

ETERNAL Ruler of the ceaseless
  round
  Of circling planets singing on their
    way,
  Guide of the nations from the night
    profound
  Into the glory of the perfect day :
  Rule in our hearts, that we may ever
    be
  Guided and strengthened and up-
    held by Thee.

2 We are of Thee, the children of Thy
    love,
  The brothers of Thy well-belovèd
    Son ;
  Descend, O Holy Spirit, like a dove,
  Into our hearts, that we may be as
    one ;

THE CHRISTIAN LIFE

As one with Thee, to whom we ever
tend ;
As one with Him, our Brother and
our Friend.

3 We would be one in hatred of all
wrong,
One in our love of all things sweet
and fair,
One with the joy that breaketh into
song,
One with the grief that trembleth
into prayer,
One in the power that makes the
children free
To follow truth, and thus to follow
Thee.

4 O clothe us with Thy heavenly
armour, Lord,
Thy trusty shield, Thy sword of
love divine ;
Our inspiration be Thy constant
word ;
We ask no victories that are not
Thine ;
Give or withhold, let pain or pleasure
be
Enough to know that we are serving
Thee.

JOHN WHITE CHADWICK,
1840–1904.

490
S. M.

BLEST be the tie that binds
Our hearts in Jesus' love ;
The fellowship of Christian minds
Is like to that above.

2 Before our Father's throne
We pour our ardent prayers ;
Our fears, our hopes, our aims are
one,
Our comforts, and our cares.

3 When for awhile we part,
This thought will soothe our
pain,
That we shall still be joined in
heart
And one day meet again.

4 This glorious hope revives
Our courage by the way ;
While each in expectation lives,
And longs to see the day,

5 When from all toil and pain
And sin we shall be free,
And perfect love and friendship
reign
Through all eternity.

JOHN FAWCETT, 1740–1817,
and others.

491
L. M.

ALMIGHTY Father, who dost
give
The gift of life to all who live,
Look down on all earth's sin and
strife,
And lift us to a nobler life.

2 Lift up our hearts, O King of kings,
To brighter hopes and kindlier things,
To visions of a larger good,
And holier dreams of brotherhood.

3 Thy world is weary of its pain,
Of selfish greed and fruitless gain,
Of tarnished honour, falsely strong,
And all its ancient deeds of wrong.

4 Hear Thou the prayer Thy servants
pray,
Uprising from all lands to-day,
And o'er the vanquished powers of
sin
O bring Thy great salvation in.

JOHN HOWARD BERTRAM
MASTERMAN, 1867–1933.

492
87. 87. D. Iambic.

O GOD our Father, throned on
high,
Enrobed in ageless splendour,
To Thee, in awe and love and joy,
Ourselves we would surrender—
To live obedient to Thy will
As servants to each other,
And show our faithfulness to Thee
By love to one another.

2 To serve by love ! O teach us how !
Be this our great vocation—
To comfort grief, to seek the lost
With message of salvation ;
In loving may our full hearts beat,
Our words be wise and winning ;
In helping others may our joy
Have ever new beginning.

BROTHERLY LOVE

3 Thee, Lord, for Thy dear Son we
    bless ;
  His heart for us was broken ;
O Love ! upon the bitter Cross
  Thy deepest word was spoken ;
The echo of that word is heard
  In love for every brother ;
So test we, Lord, our love for Thee,
  By loving one another.
        GEORGE THOMAS COSTER,
               1835–1912.

493   888.

FATHER of men, in whom are one
  All humankind beneath Thy sun,
Stablish our work in Thee begun.

2 Except the house be built of Thee,
In vain the builder's toil must be :
O strengthen our infirmity !

3 Man lives not for himself alone,
In others' good he finds his own ;
Life's worth in fellowship is known.

4 We, friends and comrades on life's
    way,
Gather within these walls to pray :
Bless Thou our fellowship to-day.

5 O Christ, our Elder Brother, who
By serving man God's will didst do,
Help us to serve our brethren too.

6 Guide us to seek the things above,
The base to shun, the pure approve,
To live by Thy free law of love.

7 In all our work, in all our play,
Be with us, Lord, our Friend, our
    Stay ;
Lead onward to the perfect day :

8 Then may we know, earth's lesson
    o'er,
With comrades missed or gone be-
    fore,
Heaven's fellowship for evermore.
        HENRY CARY SHUTTLEWORTH,
               1850–1900.

CONSECRATION AND DISCIPLESHIP

494   S. M.

FAIR waved the golden corn
  In Canaan's pleasant land,
When full of joy, some shining morn,
  Went forth the reaper band.

2 To God, so good and great,
  Their cheerful thanks they pour,
Then carry to His temple gate
  The choicest of their store.

3 For thus the holy word,
  Spoken by Moses, ran :
' The first ripe ears are for the Lord,
  The rest He gives to man.'

4 Like Israel, Lord, we give
  Our earliest fruits to Thee,
And pray that, long as we shall live,
  We may Thy children be.

5 Thine is our youthful prime,
  And life and all its powers ;
Be with us in our morning time,
  And bless our evening hours.

6 In wisdom let us grow,
  As years and strength are given,
That we may serve Thy Church
    below,
  And join Thy saints in heaven.
        JOHN HAMPDEN GURNEY,
               1802–62.

495   87. 87.

SAVIOUR, while my heart is
  tender,
  I would yield that heart to Thee,
All my powers to Thee surrender,
  Thine, and only Thine, to be.

2 Take me now, Lord Jesus, take
    me ;
  Let my youthful heart be Thine ;
Thy devoted servant make me ;
  Fill my soul with love divine.

3 Send me, Lord, where Thou wilt
    send me,
  Only do Thou guide my way ;
May Thy grace through life attend
    me,
  Gladly then shall I obey.

4 Let me do Thy will or bear it ;
  I would know no will but Thine ;
Shouldst Thou take my life or spare
    it,
  I that life to Thee resign.

5 Thine I am, O Lord, for ever,
  To Thy service set apart ;
Suffer me to leave Thee never ;
  Seal Thine image on my heart.
        JOHN BURTON, 1803–77.

THE CHRISTIAN LIFE

496   88. 88. 88.

O LOVE, who formedst me to wear
  The image of Thy Godhead
    here ;
Who soughtest me with tender care
Through all my wanderings wild
    and drear :
    O Love, I give myself to Thee,
    Thine ever, only Thine to be.

2 O Love, who ere life's earliest morn
  On me Thy choice hast gently
    laid ;
O Love, who here as Man wast born,
And wholly like to us wast made :

3 O Love, who once in time wast slain,
  Pierced through and through with
    bitter woe ;
O Love, who wrestling thus didst
    gain
  That we eternal joy might know :

4 O Love, who lovest me for aye,
  Who for my soul dost ever plead ;
O Love, who didst my ransom pay,
  Whose power sufficeth in my
    stead :

5 O Love, whose voice shall bid me
    rise
  From out this dying life of ours ;
O Love, whose hand o'er yonder
    skies
  Shall set me in the fadeless bowers :
    O Love, I give myself to Thee,
    Thine ever, only Thine to be.
        JOHANN SCHEFFLER, 1624–77 ;
        tr. by CATHERINE WINKWORTH,
                1827–78.

497   88. 86.

JUST as I am, Thine own to be,
  Friend of the young, who lovest
    me,
To consecrate myself to Thee,
  O Jesus Christ, I come.

2 In the glad morning of my day,
  My life to give, my vows to pay,
With no reserve and no delay,
  With all my heart I come.

3 I would live ever in the light,
  I would work ever for the right,
I would serve Thee with all my
    might,
  Therefore to Thee I come.

4 Just as I am, young, strong and free,
  To be the best that I can be
For truth, and righteousness, and
    Thee,
  Lord of my life, I come.
        MARIANNE FARNINGHAM,
                1834–1909.

498   C. M.

LORD, in the fulness of my might,
  I would for Thee be strong :
While runneth o'er each dear delight,
  To Thee should soar my song.

2 I would not give the world my heart,
  And then profess Thy love ;
I would not feel my strength depart,
  And then Thy service prove.

3 I would not with swift-wingèd zeal
  On the world's errands go,
And labour up the heavenly hill
  With weary feet and slow.

4 O not for Thee my weak desires,
  My poorer, baser part !
O not for Thee my fading fires,
  The ashes of my heart !

5 O choose me in my golden time :
  In my dear joys have part !
For Thee the glory of my prime,
  The fulness of my heart !
        THOMAS HORNBLOWER GILL,
                1819–1906.

499   L. M.

O HAPPY day, that fixed my
    choice
On Thee, my Saviour and my God !
Well may this glowing heart rejoice,
And tell its raptures all abroad.

2 O happy bond, that seals my vows
  To Him who merits all my love !
Let cheerful anthems fill His house,
While to that sacred shrine I move.

3 'Tis done ! the great transaction 's
    done !
  I am my Lord's and He is mine ;
He drew me, and I followed on,
  Charmed to confess the voice
    divine.

4 Now rest, my long-divided heart ;
  Fixed on this blissful centre, rest .
O who with earth would grudge to
    part,
  When called with angels to be blest ?

154

5 High heaven, that heard the solemn vow,
    That vow renewed shall daily hear,
Till in life's latest hour I bow,
    And bless in death a bond so dear.
            PHILIP DODDRIDGE, 1702–51.

500
87. 87.

JESUS calls us ! O'er the tumult
  Of our life's wild restless sea,
Day by day His sweet voice soundeth,
  Saying, ' Christian, follow Me : '

2 As, of old, Saint Andrew heard it
  By the Galilean lake,
Turned from home and toil and kindred,
  Leaving all for His dear sake.

3 Jesus calls us from the worship
  Of the vain world's golden store,
From each idol that would keep us,
  Saying, ' Christian, love Me more.'

4 In our joys and in our sorrows,
  Days of toil and hours of ease,
Still He calls, in cares and pleasures,
  ' Christian, love Me more than these.'

5 Jesus calls us ! By Thy mercies,
  Saviour, make us hear Thy call,
Give our hearts to Thy obedience,
  Serve and love Thee best of all.
        CECIL FRANCES ALEXANDER,
                  1818–95.

501
L. M.

' TAKE up thy cross,' the Saviour said,
  ' If thou wouldst My disciple be ;
Take up thy cross, with willing heart,
  And humbly follow after Me.'

2 Take up thy cross ; let not its weight
  Fill thy weak soul with vain alarm ;
His strength shall bear thy spirit up,
  And brace thy heart, and nerve thine arm.

3 Take up thy cross, nor heed the shame,
  And let thy foolish pride be still :
Thy Lord refused not e'en to die
  Upon a Cross, on Calvary's hill.

4 Take up thy cross, then, in His strength,
  And calmly every danger brave ;
'Twill guide thee to a better home,
  And lead to victory o'er the grave.

5 Take up thy cross, and follow Christ,
  Nor think till death to lay it down ;
For only he who bears the cross
  May hope to wear the glorious crown.
        CHARLES WILLIAM EVEREST,
                 1814–77.

502
87. 87. D.

JESUS, I my cross have taken,
  All to leave, and follow Thee ;
Destitute, despised, forsaken,
  Thou from hence my all shalt be.
Perish every fond ambition,
  All I've sought, and hoped, and known ;
Yet how rich is my condition !
  God and heaven are still my own.

2 Man may trouble and distress me,
  'Twill but drive me to Thy breast ;
Life with trials hard may press me,
  Heaven will bring me sweeter rest.
O 'tis not in grief to harm me,
  While Thy love is left to me !
O 'twere not in joy to charm me,
  Were that joy unmixed with Thee !

3 Take, my soul, thy full salvation ;
  Rise o'er sin and fear and care :
Joy, to find in every station
  Something still to do or bear.
Think what Spirit dwells within thee,
  What a Father's smile is thine,
What thy Saviour died to win thee :
  Child of heaven, shouldst thou repine ?

4 Haste then on from grace to glory,
  Armed by faith, and winged by prayer ;
Heaven's eternal day 's before thee ;
  God's own hand shall guide thee there.
Soon shall close thy earthly mission ;
  Swift shall pass thy pilgrim days,
Hope soon change to glad fruition,
  Faith to sight, and prayer to praise.
        HENRY FRANCIS LYTE,
              1793–1847.

503

10 10. 10 10.

ALMIGHTY Father of all things
that be,
Our life, our work, we consecrate to
Thee,
Whose heavens declare Thy glory
from above,
Whose earth below is witness to Thy
love.

2 For well we know this weary, soilèd
earth
Is yet Thine own by right of its new
birth,
Since that great Cross upreared on
Calvary
Redeemed it from its fault and shame
to Thee.

3 Thine still the changeful beauty of
the hills,
The purple valleys flecked with silver
rills,
The ocean glistening 'neath the
golden rays ;
They all are Thine, and voiceless
speak Thy praise.

4 Thou dost the strength to workman's
arm impart ;
From Thee the skilled musician's
mystic art,
The grace of poet's pen or painter's
hand
To teach the loveliness of sea and
land.

5 Then grant us, Lord, in all things
Thee to own,
To dwell within the shadow of Thy
throne,
To speak and work, to think, and
live, and move,
Reflecting Thine own nature, which
is love ;

6 That so, by Christ redeemed from
sin and shame,
And hallowed by Thy Spirit's
cleansing flame,
Ourselves, our work, and all our
powers may be
A sacrifice acceptable to Thee.

ERNEST EDWARD DUGMORE,
1843–1925.

504

77. 77.

THINE for ever ! God of Love,
Hear us from Thy throne above ;
Thine for ever may we be,
Here and in eternity.

2 Thine for ever ! O how blest
They who find in Thee their rest !
Saviour, Guardian, Heavenly Friend,
O defend us to the end.

3 Thine for ever ! Lord of Life,
Shield us through our earthly strife ,
Thou the Life, the Truth, the Way,
Guide us to the realms of day.

4 Thine for ever ! Shepherd, keep
These, Thy frail and trembling sheep ;
Safe alone beneath Thy care,
Let us all Thy goodness share.

5 Thine for ever ! Thou our Guide,
All our wants by Thee supplied,
All our sins by Thee forgiven,
Lead us, Lord, from earth to
heaven.

MARY FAWLER MAUDE,
1819–1913.

505

Irr.

TO-DAY I arise,
Invoking the Blessèd Trinity,
Confessing the Blessèd Unity,
Creator of all the things that be.

2 To-day I arise,
By strength of Christ and His
mystic Birth,
By His Passion, and Triumph's
saving worth,
By His Coming again to judge
the earth.

3 To-day I arise,
By seraphs serving the Lord
above,
By truths His ancient heralds
prove,
By saints in purity, labour, love.

4 To-day I arise,
By splendour of sun and flaming
brand,
By rushing wind, by lightning
grand,
By depth of sea, by strength of
land.

5 To-day I arise,
    With God my steersman, stay
        and guide,
    To guard, to counsel, to hear,
        to bide,
    His way before, His hosts be-
        side—

6 Protecting me now
    From crafty wiles of demon
        crew,
    From foemen, be they many or
        few,
    From lusts that I can scarce
        subdue.

7 Lord Jesus the Christ,
    To-day surround me with Thy
        might ;
    Before, behind, on left and right,
    Be Thou in breadth, in length,
        in height.

8 Direct and control
    The minds of all who think on
        me,
    The lips of all who speak to me,
    The eyes of all who look on me.

9 To-day I arise,
    Invoking the Blessèd Trinity,
    Confessing the Blessèd Unity :
    Saviour, on us salvation be !
      St. Patrick, 372–466; *tr.* by
      Robert Alexander Stewart
      Macalister, 1870–1950.

506   D. L. M. and refrain.

I BIND unto myself to-day
    The strong Name of the Trinity,
By invocation of the same,
    The Three in One, and One in
        Three.

2 I bind this day to me for ever,
    By power of faith, Christ's In-
        carnation ;
His baptism in the Jordan river ;
    His death on Cross for my salva-
        tion ;
His bursting from the spicèd tomb ;
    His riding up the heavenly way ;
His coming at the day of doom :
    I bind unto myself to-day.

3 I bind unto myself to-day
    The virtues of the star-lit heaven,
The glorious sun's life-giving ray,
    The whiteness of the moon at even,
The flashing of the lightning free,

    The whirling wind's tempestuous
        shocks,
The stable earth, the deep salt sea
    Around the old eternal rocks.

4 I bind unto myself to-day
    The power of God to hold and lead,
His eye to watch, His might to stay,
    His ear to hearken to my need,
The wisdom of my God to teach,
    His hand to guide, His shield to
        ward,
The word of God to give me speech,
    His heavenly host to be my guard.

5 *Christ be with me, Christ within me,*
    Christ behind me, Christ before me,
Christ beside me, Christ to win me,
    Christ to comfort and restore me,
Christ beneath me, Christ above me,
    Christ in quiet, Christ in danger,
Christ in hearts of all that love me,
    Christ in mouth of friend and
        stranger.

6 I bind unto myself the Name,
    The strong Name of the Trinity,
By invocation of the same,
    The Three in One, and One in
        Three,
Of whom all nature hath creation,
    Eternal Father, Spirit, Word.
Praise to the Lord of my salvation :
    Salvation is of Christ the Lord.
      St. Patrick, 372–466 ; version by
      Cecil Frances Alexander,
        1818–95.

507 *From 2 Tim. i. 12.*   C. M.

I'M not ashamed to own my Lord,
    Or to defend His cause,
Maintain the glory of His Cross,
    And honour all His laws.

2 Jesus, my Lord . I know His Name,
    His Name is all my boast ;
Nor will He put my soul to shame,
    Nor let my hope be lost.

3 I know that safe with Him remains,
    Protected by His power,
What I've committed to His trust,
    Till the decisive hour.

4 Then will He own His servant's
        name
Before His Father's face,
    And in the New Jerusalem
      Appoint my soul a place.
      Isaac Watts, 1674–1748, as in
      Scottish Paraphrases, 1781.

508

76. 76. D.

O JESUS, I have promised
To serve Thee to the end;
Be Thou for ever near me,
My Master and my Friend:
I shall not fear the battle
If Thou art by my side,
Nor wander from the pathway
If Thou wilt be my Guide.

2 O let me feel Thee near me:
The world is ever near;
I see the sights that dazzle,
The tempting sounds I hear;
My foes are ever near me,
Around me and within;
But, Jesus, draw Thou nearer,
And shield my soul from sin.

3 O let me hear Thee speaking
In accents clear and still,
Above the storms of passion,
The murmurs of self-will;
O speak to reassure me,
To hasten or control;
O speak, and make me listen,
Thou Guardian of my soul.

4 O Jesus, Thou hast promised,
To all who follow Thee,
That where Thou art in glory
There shall Thy servant be;
And, Jesus, I have promised
To serve Thee to the end;
O give me grace to follow,
My Master and my Friend.

JOHN ERNEST BODE, 1816–74.

509

77. 77. 77.

JESUS, Master, whose I am,
Purchased, Thine alone to be,
By Thy blood, O spotless Lamb,
Shed so willingly for me,
Let my heart be all Thine own,
Let me live to Thee alone.

2 Jesus, Master, I am Thine:
Keep me faithful, keep me near;
Let Thy presence in me shine,
All my homeward way to cheer.
Jesus, at Thy feet I fall,
O be Thou my All in All.

3 Jesus, Master, whom I serve,
Though so feebly and so ill,
Strengthen hand and heart and nerve
All Thy bidding to fulfil;
Open Thou mine eyes to see
All the work Thou hast for me.

4 Jesus, Master, wilt Thou use
One who owes Thee more than all?
As Thou wilt! I would not choose;
Only let me hear Thy call.
Jesus, let me always be
In Thy service glad and free.

FRANCES RIDLEY HAVERGAL,
1836–79.

510

10 10. 10 10.

TEACH me, O Lord, to follow
Him who trod
With loving zeal the pathway to His
God;
Help me to rest my faith on Him
alone
Who died for my transgression to
atone.

2 Wean my rebellious heart from
earthly things,
Show me the Fount whence living
water springs;
Teach me to feel that, when afflictions
come,
They're sent in love, to turn my
thoughts to home.

3 So may I live, that in my daily race
The things of God may hold the
highest place;
So may I die, that death to me may
be
The opening dawn of immortality.

N. LAMBERT.

511

S. M.

TEACH me, my God and King,
In all things Thee to see;
And what I do in anything,
To do it as for Thee!

2 A man that looks on glass,
On it may stay his eye;
Or if he pleaseth, through it pass,
And then the heaven espy.

3 All may of Thee partake;
Nothing can be so mean,
Which with this tincture, 'for Thy
sake',
Will not grow bright and clean.

4 A servant with this clause
Makes drudgery divine:
Who sweeps a room, as for Thy laws,
Makes that and the action fine.

5   This is the famous stone
      That turneth all to gold ;
For that which God doth touch and
      own
    Cannot for less be told.

        GEORGE HERBERT, 1593–1632.

512
77. 77.

TAKE my life, and let it be
   Consecrated, Lord, to Thee.
Take my moments and my days ;
Let them flow in ceaseless praise.

2 Take my hands, and let them move
At the impulse of Thy love.
Take my feet, and let them be
Swift and beautiful for Thee.

3 Take my voice, and let me sing
Always, only, for my King.
Take my lips, and let them be
Filled with messages from Thee.

4 Take my silver and my gold ;
Not a mite would I withhold.
Take my intellect, and use
Every power as Thou shalt choose.

5 Take my will, and make it Thine ;
It shall be no longer mine.
Take my heart—it is Thine own ;
It shall be Thy royal throne.

6 Take my love ; my Lord, I pour
At Thy feet its treasure-store.
Take myself, and I will be
Ever, only, all for Thee.

        FRANCES RIDLEY HAVERGAL,
                1836–79.

513
C. M.

O LORD and Master of us all,
   Whate'er our name or sign,
We own Thy sway, we hear Thy call,
   We test our lives by Thine.

2 Thou judgest us : Thy purity
   Doth all our lusts condemn ;
The love that draws us nearer Thee
   Is hot with wrath to them.

3 Our thoughts lie open to Thy sight ;
   And naked to Thy glance
Our secret sins are, in the light
   Of Thy pure countenance.

4 Yet, weak and blinded though we be,
   Thou dost our service own ;
We bring our varying gifts to Thee,
   And Thou rejectest none.

5 Apart from Thee all gain is loss,
   All labour vainly done ;
The solemn shadow of Thy Cross
   Is better than the sun.

6 Our Friend, our Brother, and our
    Lord,
   What may Thy service be ?
Nor name, nor form, nor ritual word,
   But simply following Thee.

7 We faintly hear ; we dimly see ;
   In differing phrase we pray ;
But, dim or clear, we own in Thee
   The Light, the Truth, the Way.

        JOHN GREENLEAF WHITTIER,
               1807–92.

514
88. 84.

THROUGH good report and evil,
   Lord,
Still guided by Thy faithful word—
Our staff, our buckler, and our
   sword—
      We follow Thee.

2 In silence of the lonely night,
In fullest glow of day's clear light,
Through life's strange windings, dark
   or bright,
      We follow Thee.

3 Strengthened by Thee we forward go,
'Mid smile or scoff of friend or foe ;
Through pain or ease, through joy
   or woe,
      We follow Thee.

4 Great Master, point Thou out the
   way,
Nor suffer Thou our steps to stray ;
Then, in the path that leads to day,
      We follow Thee.

5 Thou hast passed on before our face ;
Thy footsteps on the way we trace :
O keep us, aid us by Thy grace ;
      We follow Thee.

        HORATIUS BONAR, 1808–89.

515
C. M.

THOUGH lowly here our lot may
   be,
   High work have we to do—
In faith and trust to follow Him
   Whose lot was lowly too.

2 Our days of darkness we may bear,
   Strong in our Father's love ;
We lean on His almighty arm,
   And fix our hopes above.

THE CHRISTIAN LIFE

3 Our lives enriched with gentle
        thoughts
    And loving deeds may be,
As streams that still the nobler grow,
    The nearer to the sea.

4 To duty firm, to conscience true,
    However tried and pressed,
In God's clear sight high work we do,
    If we but do our best.

5 Thus may we make the lowliest lot
    With rays of glory bright;
Thus may we turn a crown of thorns
    Into a crown of light.
                    WILLIAM GASKELL, 1805-84.

516   L. M.

WE are but little children weak,
    Nor born in any high estate;
What can we do for Jesus' sake,
    Who is so high and good and
        great?

2 O, day by day, each Christian child
    Has much to do, without, within,—
A life to live for Jesus' sake,
    A constant war to wage with sin.

3 When deep within our swelling
        hearts
    The thoughts of pride and anger
        rise,
When bitter words are on our
        tongues
    And tears of passion in our eyes,

4 Then we may stay the angry blow,
    Then we may check the hasty
        word,
Give gentle answers back again,
    And fight a battle for our Lord.

5 With smiles of peace and looks of
        love
    Light in our dwellings we may
        make,
Bid kind good-humour brighten
        there,
    And still do all for Jesus' sake.

6 There's not a child so small and
        weak
    But has his little cross to take,
His little work of love and praise
    That he may do for Jesus' sake.
                    CECIL FRANCES ALEXANDER,
                                1818-95.

517   L. M.

FIGHT the good fight
    With all thy might;
Christ is thy strength, and Christ thy
        right;
Lay hold on life, and it shall be
Thy joy and crown eternally.

2 Run the straight race
    Through God's good grace,
Lift up thine eyes, and seek His face;
Life with its path before us lies;
Christ is the way, and Christ the
        prize.

3 Cast care aside;
    And on thy Guide
Lean, and His mercy will provide,—
Lean, and the trusting soul shall
        prove
Christ is its life, and Christ its love.

4 Faint not, nor fear;
    His arm is near;
He changeth not, and thou art dear;
Only believe, and thou shalt see
That Christ is all in all to thee.
                    JOHN SAMUEL BEWLEY MONSELL,
                                1811-75.

518   S. M.

A CHARGE to keep I have,
    A God to glorify,
A never-dying soul to save,
    And fit it for the sky:

2 To serve the present age,
    My calling to fulfil:
O may it all my powers engage
    To do my Master's will!

3 Arm me with jealous care,
    As in Thy sight to live;
And O, Thy servant, Lord, prepare
    A strict account to give.

4 Help me to watch and pray,
    And on Thyself rely,
And let me ne'er my trust betray,
    But press to realms on high.
                    CHARLES WESLEY, 1707-88.

519   65. 65. 65. D.

WHO is on the Lord's side?
    Who will serve the King?
Who will be His helpers
    Other lives to bring?

160

Who will leave the world's side ?
Who will face the foe ?
Who is on the Lord's side ?
Who for Him will go ?
    By Thy call of mercy,
    By Thy grace divine,
    We are on the Lord's side ;
    Saviour, we are Thine.

2 Jesus, Thou hast bought us,
    Not with gold or gem,
But with Thine own life-blood,
    For Thy diadem.
With Thy blessing filling
    Each who comes to Thee,
Thou hast made us willing,
    Thou hast made us free.
    By Thy grand redemption,
    By Thy grace divine,
    We are on the Lord's side ;
    Saviour, we are Thine.

3 Fierce may be the conflict,
    Strong may be the foe,
But the King's own army
    None can overthrow.
Round His standard ranging,
    Victory is secure,
For His truth unchanging
    Makes the triumph sure.
    Joyfully enlisting,
    By Thy grace divine,
    We are on the Lord's side ;
    Saviour, we are Thine.

4 Chosen to be soldiers
    In an alien land,
Chosen, called, and faithful,
    For our Captain's band,
In the service royal
    Let us not grow cold ;
Let us be right loyal,
    Noble, true, and bold.
    Master, Thou wilt keep us,
    By Thy grace divine,
    Always on the Lord's side,
    Saviour, always Thine.
            FRANCES RIDLEY HAVERGAL,
                        1836–79.

520   C. M.

WORKMAN of God ! O lose not
    heart,
    But learn what God is like,
And, in the darkest battle-field,
    Thou shalt know where to strike.

2 Thrice blest is he to whom is given
    The instinct that can tell
That God is on the field when He
    Is most invisible.

3 He hides Himself so wondrously,
    As though there were no God ;
He is least seen when all the powers
    Of ill are most abroad.

4 Ah ! God is other than we think ;
    His ways are far above,
Far beyond reason's height, and
        reached
    Only by childlike love.

5 Then learn to scorn the praise of
        men,
    And learn to lose with God ;
For Jesus won the world through
        shame,
    And beckons thee His road.

6 For right is right, since God is God,
    And right the day must win ;
To doubt would be disloyalty,
    To falter would be sin.
            FREDERICK WILLIAM FABER,
                        1814–63.

521   Guild Hymn.   86. 86. D. 88.

BELIEVING fathers oft have told
    What things by God were done,
When faithful men in days of old
    Their lifelong battle won ;
And now when God calls us to life,
    And Satan tempts each man,
We choose our side in the mortal
        strife
    To fight as best we can,—
        Like brothers true, of one accord,
        To hold one faith and serve one
        Lord.

2 Our King has come to claim His own,
    Has paid the debt we owe,
Himself has fought the fight alone,
    In straits we cannot know.
Amid the world's confusèd noise,
    Where we but darkly see,
The Christ appeals, with sweet, clear
        voice,
    ' My brothers, follow Me,'—
        Like brothers true, of one ac-
        cord,
        To hold one faith, to serve one
        Lord.

THE CHRISTIAN LIFE

3 His Church our shelter, He our
    Guide,
  Our strength His healing Cross,
We range ourselves upon His side,
  Where none can suffer loss.
We're safe behind our Saviour's
    shield ;
  He makes us heirs of heaven ;
We claim upon the embattled field
    The victory Christ has given,—
      Like brother true, of one accord,
    To hold one faith and serve one
      Lord.

4 And yet, O Christ, our Saviour King,
  Unless Thou keep us Thine,
Our faith will soon dry at the spring,
  Our love will shrink and pine.
So by Thy Spirit mould us, Lord ;
  Inspire our hearts to pray ;
Our hungry souls feed with Thy
    word,
  Teach all our Guild to say,
    'True brothers we, of one
      accord,
    We hold one faith, we serve one
      Lord.'

5 We fain would do our Master's part,
  And help our fellow-men,
Would cheer some lonely brother's
    heart,
  Some lost one bring again,
Would serve the Church abroad, at
    home,
  With hearts from self set free,
Striving to make Thy Kingdom
    come.
    O God, so may it be,

That, brothers true, with one
    accord
We hold the faith and serve the
    Lord !
      ARCHIBALD HAMILTON CHARTERIS,
      1835–1908.

522   L. M.

HE liveth long who liveth well !
  All other life is short and vain ;
He liveth longest who can tell
  Of living most for heavenly gain.

2 He liveth long who liveth well :
  All else is being flung away ;
He liveth longest who can tell
  Of true things truly done each day.

3 Be what thou seemest ; live thy
    creed ;
  Hold up to earth the torch divine :
Be what thou prayest to be made ;
  Let the great Master's steps be
    thine.

4 Fill up each hour with what will
    last ;
  Buy up the moments as they go
The life above, when this is past,
  Is the ripe fruit of life below.

5 Sow love, and taste its fruitage pure ;
  Sow peace, and reap its harvest
    bright ;
Sow sunbeams on the rock and moor,
  And find a harvest-home of light.
      HORATIUS BONAR, 1808–89.

CONFLICT AND VICTORY

523   77. 73.

CHRISTIAN, seek not yet repose ;
  Hear thy guardian angel say,
'Thou art in the midst of foes :
    Watch and pray.'

2 Principalities and powers,
  Mustering their unseen array,
Wait for thy unguarded hours :
    Watch and pray.

3 Gird thy heavenly armour on ;
  Wear it ever, night and day ;
Ambushed lies the evil one :
    Watch and pray.

4 Hear the victors who o'ercame ;
  Still they mark each warrior's way
All with one sweet voice exclaim,
    'Watch and pray.'

5 Hear, above all, hear thy Lord,
  Him thou lovest to obey ;
Hide within thy heart His word,
    'Watch and pray.'

6 Watch, as if on that alone
  Hung the issue of the day ;
Pray, that help may be sent down :
    Watch and pray.
      CHARLOTTE ELLIOTT, 1789–1871.

524 87. 87. 47.

JESUS, Lord of Life and Glory,
  Bend from heaven Thy gracious
    ear ;
While our waiting souls adore Thee,
  Friend of helpless sinners, hear :
    By Thy mercy,
    O deliver us, good Lord.

2 From the depth of nature's blind-
    ness,
  From the hardening power of sin,
From all malice and unkindness,
  From the pride that lurks within,
    By Thy mercy,
    O deliver us, good Lord.

3 When temptation sorely presses,
  In the day of Satan's power,
In our times of deep distresses,
  In each dark and trying hour,
    By Thy mercy,
    O deliver us, good Lord.

4 When the world around is smiling,
  In the time of wealth and ease,
Earthly joys our hearts beguiling,
  In the day of health and peace,
    By Thy mercy,
    O deliver us, good Lord.

5 In the weary hours of sickness,
  In the times of grief and pain,
When we feel our mortal weakness,
  When the creature's help is vain,
    By Thy mercy,
    O deliver us, good Lord.

6 In the solemn hour of dying,
  In the awful judgment day,
May our souls, on Thee relying,
  Find Thee still our Rock and Stay :
    By Thy mercy,
    O deliver us, good Lord.
          JOHN JAMES CUMMINS,
                1795–1867.

525 65. 65. D.

IN the hour of trial,
  Jesus, pray for me,
Lest by base denial
  I depart from Thee ;
When Thou seest me waver,
  With a look recall,
Nor for fear or favour
  Suffer me to fall.

2 With its witching pleasures
    Would this vain world charm,
  Or its sordid treasures
    Spread to work me harm,—
Bring to my remembrance
    Sad Gethsemane,
Or, in darker semblance,
    Cross-crowned Calvary.

3 If with sore affliction
    Thou in love chastise,
  Pour Thy benediction
    On the sacrifice ;
Then, upon Thine altar
    Freely offered up,
Though the flesh may falter,
    Faith shall drink the cup.

4 When in dust and ashes
    To the grave I sink,
  While heaven's glory flashes
    O'er the shelving brink,
On Thy truth relying
    Through that mortal strife,
Lord, receive me, dying,
    To eternal life.
          JAMES MONTGOMERY,
                1771–1854.

526 *From Psalm* xlvi. 87. 87. 66. 667.

A SAFE stronghold our God is
    still,
  A trusty shield and weapon ;
He'll help us clear from all the ill
  That hath us now o'ertaken.
    The ancient prince of hell
    Hath risen with purpose fell ;
    Strong mail of craft and power
    He weareth in this hour ;
    On earth is not his fellow.

2 With force of arms we nothing can,
  Full soon were we down-ridden ;
But for us fights the proper Man,
  Whom God Himself hath bidden.
    Ask ye who is this same ?
    Christ Jesus is His Name,
    The Lord Sabaoth's Son ;
    He, and no other one,
    Shall conquer in the battle.

3 And were this world all devils o'er,
  And watching to devour us,
We lay it not to heart so sore ;
  Not they can overpower us.
    And let the prince of ill
    Look grim as e'er he will,
    He harms us not a whit ;
    For why his doom is writ ;
    A word shall quickly slay him.

4 God's word, for all their craft and
      force,
  One moment will not linger,
But, spite of hell, shall have its
      course :
  'Tis written by His finger.
    And, though they take our life,
    Goods, honour, children, wife,
    Yet is their profit small :
  These things shall vanish all :
  The city of God remaineth.
            MARTIN LUTHER, 1483–1546 ;
              tr. by THOMAS CARLYLE,
                        1795–1881.

527 *From Psalm* xxvii.   76. 76.

GOD is my strong salvation ;
    What foe have I to fear ?
In darkness and temptation
    My light, my help is near.

2 Though hosts encamp around me,
    Firm to the fight I stand ;
  What terror can confound me,
    With God at my right hand ?

3 Place on the Lord reliance ;
    My soul, with courage wait '
  His truth be thine affiance,
    When faint and desolate.

4 His might thine heart shall strengthen,
    His love thy joy increase ;
  Mercy thy days shall lengthen ;
    The Lord will give thee peace.
              JAMES MONTGOMERY, 1771–1854.

528   D. C. M.

I FEEL the winds of God to-day ;
    To-day my sail I lift,
Though heavy oft with drenching
      spray,
    And torn with many a rift ;
If hope but light the water's crest,
    And Christ my bark will use,
I'll seek the seas at His behest,
    And brave another cruise.

2 It is the wind of God that dries
    My vain regretful tears,
Until with braver thoughts shall rise
    The purer, brighter years ;
  If cast on shores of selfish ease
    Or pleasure I should be,
Lord, let me feel Thy freshening
      breeze,
    And I'll put back to sea.

3 If ever I forget Thy love
    And how that love was shown,
  Lift high the blood-red flag above :
    It bears Thy Name alone.
  Great Pilot of my onward way,
    Thou wilt not let me drift ;
  I feel the winds of God to-day,
    To-day my sail I lift.
                JESSIE ADAMS, 1863–1954.

529   87. 87. D.

COURAGE, brother ! do not
    stumble,
    Though thy path be dark as night ;
  There 's a star to guide the humble :
    ' Trust in God, and do the right.'

2 Let the road be rough and dreary,
    And its end far out of sight,
  Foot it bravely ; strong or weary,
    Trust in God, and do the right.

3 Perish policy and cunning,
    Perish all that fears the light !
  Whether losing, whether winning,
    Trust in God, and do the right.

4 Some will hate thee, some will love
      thee,
    Some will flatter, some will slight ;
  Cease from man, and look above
      thee :
    Trust in God, and do the right.

5 Simple rule, and safest guiding,
    Inward peace, and inward might,
  Star upon our path abiding,—
    Trust in God, and do the right.

6 Courage, brother ! do not stumble,
    Though thy path be dark as
      night ;
  There 's a star to guide the humble :
    ' Trust in God, and do the right.'
                NORMAN MACLEOD, 1812–72.

530   D. C. M.

THE Son of God goes forth to
    war,
    A kingly crown to gain ;
  His blood-red banner streams afar :
    Who follows in His train ?
  Who best can drink his cup of
      woe
    Triumphant over pain,
  Who patient bears his cross below,
    He follows in His train.

2 The martyr first, whose eagle eye
    Could pierce beyond the grave,
Who saw his Master in the sky,
    And called on Him to save ;
Like Him, with pardon on his tongue
    In midst of mortal pain,
He prayed for them that did the
      wrong :
    Who follows in his train ?

3 A glorious band, the chosen few
    On whom the Spirit came,
Twelve valiant saints, their hope
      they knew,
    And mocked the cross and flame ;
They met the tyrant's brandished
      steel,
    The lion's gory mane,
They bowed their necks the death
      to feel :
    Who follows in their train ?

4 A noble army, men and boys,
    The matron and the maid,
Around the Saviour's throne rejoice,
    In robes of light arrayed :
They climbed the steep ascent of
      heaven,
    Through peril, toil, and pain :
O God, to us may grace be given
    To follow in their train.
        REGINALD HEBER, 1783–1826.

531   C. M.

O GOD of truth, whose living
    word
    Upholds whate'er hath breath,
Look down on Thy creation, Lord,
    Enslaved by sin and death.

2 Set up Thy standard, Lord, that we,
    Who claim a heavenly birth,
May march with Thee to smite the
      lies
    That vex Thy groaning earth.

3 Fain would we join the blest array,
    And follow in the might
Of Him, the Faithful and the True,
    In raiment clean and white.

4 Yet who can fight for truth and God,
    Enthralled by lies and sin ?
He who would wage such war on
      earth
    Must first be true within.

5 O God of truth, for whom we long,
    O Thou that hearest prayer,
Do Thine own battle in our hearts,
    And slay the falsehood there.

6 So, tried in Thy refining fire,
    From every lie set free,
In us Thy perfect truth shall dwell,
    And we may fight for Thee.
        THOMAS HUGHES, 1823–96.

532   76. 76. D.

STAND up ! stand up for Jesus,
    Ye soldiers of the Cross !
Lift high His royal banner ;
    It must not suffer loss.
From victory to victory
    His army He shall lead,
Till every foe is vanquished,
    And Christ is Lord indeed.

2 Stand up ! stand up for Jesus !
    The trumpet-call obey ;
Forth to the mighty conflict
    In this His glorious day
Ye that are men, now serve Him
    Against unnumbered foes ;
Your courage rise with danger,
    And strength to strength oppose.

3 Stand up ! stand up for Jesus !
    Stand in His strength alone ;
The arm of flesh will fail you ;
    Ye dare not trust your own.
Put on the gospel armour,
    Each piece put on with prayer ;
Where duty calls, or danger,
    Be never wanting there.

4 Stand up ! stand up for Jesus !
    The strife will not be long ;
This day the noise of battle,
    The next the victor's song.
To him that overcometh
    A crown of life shall be ;
He with the King of Glory
    Shall reign eternally.
        GEORGE DUFFIELD, 1818–88.

533   77. 77.

MUCH in sorrow, oft in woe,
    Onward, Christians, onward
      go !
Fight the fight, maintain the strife,
    Strengthened with the bread of
      life.

2 Onward, Christians, onward go !
    Join the war, and face the foe ;
Faint not ! much doth yet remain,
    Dreary is the long campaign.

THE CHRISTIAN LIFE

3 Shrink not, Christians ! will ye
yield ?
Will ye quit the painful field ?
Will ye flee in danger's hour ?
Know ye not your Captain's power ?

4 Let your drooping hearts be glad ;
March, in heavenly armour clad ;
Fight, nor think the battle long ;
Victory soon shall tune your song.

5 Let not sorrow dim your eye,
Soon shall every tear be dry ;
Let not fears your course impede,
Great your strength, if great your
need.

6 Onward then to battle move ;
More than conquerors ye shall prove ;
Though opposed by many a foe,
Christian soldiers, onward go !

HENRY KIRKE WHITE, 1785–1806 ;
and FRANCES SARA COLQUHOUN,
1809–77.

534
S. M.

SOLDIERS of Christ ! arise,
And put your armour on,
Strong in the strength which God
supplies
Through His eternal Son ;

2 Strong in the Lord of hosts,
And in His mighty power ;
Who in the strength of Jesus trusts
Is more than conqueror.

3 Stand, then, in His great might,
With all His strength endued ;
And take, to arm you for the fight,
The panoply of God.

4 To keep your armour bright
Attend with constant care,
Still walking in your Captain's sight,
And watching unto prayer.

5 From strength to strength go
on ;
Wrestle, and fight, and pray ;
Tread all the powers of darkness
down,
And win the well-fought day,—

6 That, having all things done,
And all your conflicts passed,
Ye may o'ercome through Christ
alone,
And stand complete at last.

CHARLES WESLEY, 1707–88.

535
65. 65. D. and refrain.

ONWARD ! Christian soldiers,
Marching as to war,
With the Cross of Jesus
Going on before.
Christ, the Royal Master,
Leads against the foe ;
Forward into battle,
See ! His banners go.
Onward ! Christian soldiers,
Marching as to war,
With the Cross of Jesus
Going on before.

2 At the sign of triumph
Satan's legions flee ;
On then, Christian soldiers,
On to victory !
Hell's foundations quiver
At the shout of praise ;
Brothers, lift your voices,
Loud your anthems raise.

3 Like a mighty army
Moves the Church of God ;
Brothers, we are treading
Where the saints have trod.
We are not divided,
All one body we,
One in hope, in doctrine,
One in charity.

4 Crowns and thrones may perish,
Kingdoms rise and wane,
But the Church of Jesus
Constant will remain ;
Gates of hell can never
'Gainst that Church prevail ;
We have Christ's own promise,
And that cannot fail.

5 Onward, then, ye people !
Join our happy throng ;
Blend with ours your voices
In the triumph song :
' Glory, laud, and honour
Unto Christ the King ! '
This, through countless ages,
Men and angels sing.

SABINE BARING-GOULD, 1834–1924.

536
98. 98.

SAY not, ' The struggle nought
availeth ;
The labour and the wounds are vain ;
The enemy faints not nor faileth,
And as things have been they
remain.'

166

2 If hopes were dupes, fears may be
    liars :
      It may be, in yon smoke concealed,
Your comrades chase even now the
    fliers,
      And, but for you, possess the field.

3 For while the tired waves, vainly
    breaking,
      Seem here no painful inch to gain,
Far back, through creeks and inlets
    making,
      Comes silent, flooding in, the
      main.

4 And not by eastern windows only,
    When daylight comes, comes in
    the light ;
    In front the sun climbs slow, how
    slowly !
    But westward, look ! the land is
    bright.
           ARTHUR HUGH CLOUGH,
                    1819–61.

537   66. 66. 88.

MARCH on, my soul, with
    strength,
    March forward, void of fear ;
He who hath led will lead,
    While year succeedeth year ;
And as thou goest on thy way,
His hand shall hold thee day by
    day.

2 March on, my soul, with strength,
    In ease thou dar'st not dwell ;
High duty calls thee forth ;
    Then up, and quit thee well !
Take up thy cross, take up thy sword,
And fight the battles of thy Lord !

3 March on, my soul, with strength,
    With strength, but not thine own ;
The conquest thou shalt gain,
    Through Christ thy Lord alone ;
His grace shall nerve thy feeble arm,
His love preserve thee safe from
    harm.

4 March on, my soul, with strength,
    From strength to strength march
    on ;
Warfare shall end at length,
    All foes be overthrown.
Then, O my soul, if faithful now,
The crown of life awaits thy brow.
           WILLIAM WRIGHT, 1859–1924.

538   65. 65. D. and refrain.

BRIGHTLY gleams our banner,
    Pointing to the sky,
Waving on Christ's soldiers
    To their home on high.
Marching through the desert,
    Gladly thus we pray,
Still with hearts united
    Singing on our way.
     Brightly gleams our banner,
      Pointing to the sky,
     Waving on Christ's soldiers
      To their home on high.

2 Jesus, Lord and Master,
    At Thy sacred feet,
Here, with hearts rejoicing,
    See Thy children meet.
Often have we left Thee,
    Often gone astray ;
Keep us, mighty Saviour,
    In the narrow way.

3 Pattern of our childhood,
    Once Thyself a child,
Make our childhood holy,
    Pure, and meek, and mild.
In the hour of danger
    Whither can we flee,
Save to Thee, dear Saviour,
    Only unto Thee ?

4 All our days direct us
    In the way we go ;
Crown us still victorious
    Over every foe ;
When the march is over,
    Then come rest and peace,
Jesus in His beauty,
    Songs that never cease.
          THOMAS JOSEPH POTTER,
              1827–73, and others.

THE CHRISTIAN LIFE

TRUST AND RESIGNATION

539 88. 84.

MY God and Father, while I stray
Far from my home in life's
rough way,
O teach me from my heart to say,
    'Thy will be done.'

2 Though dark my path and sad my
lot,
Let me be still and murmur not,
Or breathe the prayer divinely
taught,
    'Thy will be done.'

3 What though in lonely grief I sigh
For friends beloved, no longer nigh,
Submissive still would I reply,
    'Thy will be done.'

4 If Thou shouldst call me to resign
What most I prize, it ne'er was mine,
I only yield Thee what was Thine:
    Thy will be done.

5 Let but my fainting heart be blest
With Thy sweet Spirit for its guest,
My God, to Thee I leave the rest:
    Thy will be done.

6 Renew my will from day to day;
Blend it with Thine; and take away
All that now makes it hard to say,
    'Thy will be done.'

7 Then, when on earth I breathe no
more
The prayer oft mixed with tears
before,
I'll sing upon a happier shore,
    'Thy will be done.'
        CHARLOTTE ELLIOTT, 1789–1871.

540 87. 87. 888.

WHATE'ER my God ordains is
right:
Holy His will abideth;
I will be still whate'er He doth,
And follow where He guideth:
He is my God:
    Though dark my road,
He holds me that I shall not fall:
Wherefore to Him I leave it all.

2 Whate'er my God ordains is right:
He never will deceive me;
He leads me by the proper path;
I know He will not leave me:
    I take, content,
    What He hath sent;
His hand can turn my griefs away,
And patiently I wait His day.

3 Whate'er my God ordains is right:
Though now this cup, in drinking,
May bitter seem to my faint heart,
I take it all, unshrinking:
    Tears pass away
    With dawn of day;
Sweet comfort yet shall fill my heart,
And pain and sorrow shall depart.

4 Whate'er my God ordains is right:
Here shall my stand be taken;
Though sorrow, need, or death be
mine,
Yet am I not forsaken;
    My Father's care
    Is round me there;
He holds me that I shall not fall:
And so to Him I leave it all.
        SAMUEL RODIGAST, 1649–1708;
        tr. by CATHERINE WINKWORTH,
                1827–78.

541 98. 98. 88.

IF thou but suffer God to guide
thee,
And hope in Him through all thy
ways,
He'll give thee strength, whate'er
betide thee,
And bear thee through the evil
days;
Who trusts in God's unchanging love
Builds on the rock that nought can
move.

2 What can these anxious cares avail
thee,
These never-ceasing moans and
sighs?
What can it help if thou bewail thee
O'er each dark moment as it flies?
Our cross and trials do but press
The heavier for our bitterness.

3 Only be still, and wait His leisure
   In cheerful hope, with heart
      content
To take whate'er thy Father's
     pleasure
   And all-discerning love have sent ;
Nor doubt our inmost wants are
    known
To Him who chose us for His own.

4 Sing, pray, and keep His ways un-
    swerving ;
   So do thine own part faithfully,
And trust His word,—though un-
    deserving,
   Thou yet shalt find it true for
    thee ;
God never yet forsook at need
The soul that trusted Him indeed.

GEORG NEUMARK, 1621–81 ;
tr. by CATHERINE WINKWORTH,
1827–78.

542
65. 65.

O LET him whose sorrow
  No relief can find,
Trust in God, and borrow
  Ease for heart and mind.

2 Where the mourner, weeping,
  Sheds the secret tear,
God His watch is keeping,
  Though none else be near.

3 God will never leave thee ;
  All thy wants He knows,
Feels the pains that grieve thee,
  Sees thy cares and woes.

4 If in grief thou languish,
  He will dry the tear,
Who His children's anguish
  Soothes with succour near.

5 All thy woe and sadness,
  In this world below,
Balance not the gladness
  Thou in heaven shalt know,

6 When thy gracious Saviour,
  In the realms above,
Crowns thee with His favour,
  Fills thee with His love.

HEINRICH SIEGMUND OSWALD, 1751–
1834 ; *tr.* by FRANCES ELIZABETH
COX, 1812–97.

543
886. 886.

O LORD, how happy should we be
  If we could cast our care on
    Thee,
  If we from self could rest,
And feel at heart that One above,
In perfect wisdom, perfect love,
  Is working for the best ;

2 Could we but kneel, and cast our
    load,
Even while we pray, upon our God,
  Then rise with lightened cheer,
Sure that the Father, who is nigh
To still the famished raven's cry,
  Will hear, in that we fear.

3 We cannot trust Him as we should ;
So chafes weak nature's restless mood
  To cast its peace away ;
But birds and flowerets round us
    preach ;
All, all the present evil teach
  Sufficient for the day.

4 Lord, make these faithless hearts of
    ours
Such lessons learn from birds and
    flowers :
  Make them from self to cease,
Leave all things to a Father's will,
And taste, before Him lying still,
  Even in affliction, peace.

JOSEPH ANSTICE, 1808–36.

544
10 10. 10 10. 10 10.

L ONG did I toil, and knew no
  earthly rest,
  Far did I rove, and found no
    certain home ;
At last I sought them in His shelter-
    ing breast,
  Who opes His arms, and bids the
    weary come :
With Him I found a home, a rest
    divine,
And I since then am His, and He is
    mine.

2 The good I have is from His stores
    supplied,
  The ill is only what He deems the
    best ;
He for my Friend, I'm rich with
    nought beside,
  And poor without Him, though of
    all possest :

Changes may come—I take, or I
resign,
Content, while I am His, while He is
mine.

3 Whate'er may change, in Him no
change is seen ;
A glorious Sun that wanes not nor
declines,
Above the clouds and storms He
walks serene,
And on His people's inward darkness shines :
All may depart—I fret not, nor
repine,
While I my Saviour's am, while He
is mine.

4 While here, alas ! I know but half
His love,
But half discern Him, and but half
adore ;
But, when I meet Him in the realms
above,
I hope to love Him better, praise
Him more,
And feel, and tell, amid the choir
divine,
How fully I am His, and He is mine.

JOHN QUARLES, 1624–65 : and
HENRY FRANCIS LYTE, 1793–1847.

545

10 10. 10 10.

O CHRIST, my God, who seest the
unseen,
O Christ, my God, who knowest
the unknown,
Thy mighty blood was poured
forth to atone
For every sin that can be or hath
been.

2 O Thou who seest what I cannot see,
Thou who didst love us all so long
ago,
O Thou who knowest what I must
not know ;
Remember all my hope, remember
me.

CHRISTINA GEORGINA ROSSETTI,
1830–94.

546

S. M.

COMMIT thou all thy griefs
And ways into His hands,
To His sure truth and tender care,
Who earth and heaven commands.

2 Who points the clouds their course,
Whom winds and seas obey,
He shall direct thy wandering feet,
He shall prepare thy way.

3 Thou on the Lord rely,
So safe shalt thou go on ;
Fix on His work thy steadfast eye,
So shall thy work be done.

4 No profit canst thou gain
By self-consuming care ;
To Him commend thy cause : His
ear
Attends the softest prayer.

5 Thy everlasting truth,
Father, Thy ceaseless love,
Sees all Thy children's wants, and
knows
What best for each will prove.

6 Thou everywhere hast sway,
And all things serve Thy might ;
Thy every act pure blessing is,
Thy path unsullied light.

PAUL GERHARDT, 1607–76 ;
tr. by JOHN WESLEY, 1703–91.

547

S. M.

PUT thou thy trust in God,
In duty's path go on ;
Walk in His strength with faith and
hope,
So shall thy work be done.

2 Give to the winds thy fears ;
Hope, and be undismayed ;
God hears thy sighs and counts thy
tears,
God shall lift up thy head.

3 Through waves, and clouds, and
storms
He gently clears thy way ;
Wait thou His time ; so shall this
night
Soon end in joyous day.

4 Leave to His sovereign sway
To choose and to command ;
So shalt thou, wondering, own His
way
How wise, how strong His hand.

5 Thou seest our weakness, Lord ;
Our hearts are known to Thee ;
O lift Thou up the sinking hand,
Confirm the feeble knee.

6   Let us, in life, in death,
      Thy steadfast truth declare,
And publish, with our latest breath,
    Thy love and guardian care.

          PAUL GERHARDT, 1607–76 ;
     tr. by JOHN WESLEY, 1703–91.

548
                  86. 86. 86.

FATHER, I know that all my life
    Is portioned out for me ;
And the changes that are sure to
      come
    I do not fear to see ·
But I ask Thee for a present mind,
    Intent on pleasing Thee.

2 I ask Thee for a thoughtful love,
    Through constant watching wise,
To meet the glad with joyful smiles,
    And to wipe the weeping eyes,
And a heart at leisure from itself,
    To soothe and sympathise.

3 I would not have the restless will
    That hurries to and fro,
Seeking for some great thing to do,
    Or secret thing to know ;
I would be treated as a child,
    And guided where I go.

4 Wherever in the world I am,
    In whatsoe'er estate,
I have a fellowship with hearts
    To keep and cultivate,
And a work of lowly love to do,
    For the Lord on whom I wait.

5 So I ask Thee for the daily strength
    To none that ask denied,
And a mind to blend with outward
      life
While keeping at Thy side,
Content to fill a little space,
    If Thou be glorified.

          ANNA LAETITIA WARING.
              1823–1910,

549
                  C. M.

LORD, it belongs not to my care
    Whether I die or live ·
To love and serve Thee is my share,
    And this Thy grace must give.

2 If life be long, I will be glad,
    That I may long obey ;
If short, yet why should I be sad
    To welcome endless day ?

3 Christ leads me through no darker
      rooms
    Than He went through before ;
He that into God's Kingdom comes
    Must enter by this door.

4 Come, Lord, when grace hath made
      me meet
    Thy blessèd face to see ;
For, if Thy work on earth be sweet,
    What will Thy glory be ?

5 My knowledge of that life is small,
    The eye of faith is dim ;
But 'tis enough that Christ knows all,
    And I shall be with Him.

          RICHARD BAXTER, 1615–91.

550
                  L. M.

GREAT God ! and wilt Thou
    condescend
To be my Father and my Friend ?
I a poor child, and Thou so high,
The Lord of earth and air and sky.

2 Art Thou my Father ? canst Thou
      bear
To hear my poor imperfect prayer ?
Or wilt Thou listen to the praise
That such a little one can raise ?

3 Art Thou my Father ? let me be
A meek obedient child to Thee,
And try, in word and deed and
      thought,
To serve and please Thee as I ought.

4 Art Thou my Father ? I'll depend
Upon the care of such a Friend,
And only wish to do and be
Whatever seemeth good to Thee.

5 Art Thou my Father ? then at last,
When all my days on earth are past,
Send down and take me in Thy love
To be Thy better child above.

          ANN GILBERT, 1782–1866.

551
                  S. M.

MY times are in Thy hand ;
    My God, I wish them there ;
My life, my friends, my soul I leave
    Entirely to Thy care.

2   My times are in Thy hand,
      Whatever they may be,
Pleasing or painful, dark or bright,
    As best may seem to Thee.

THE CHRISTIAN LIFE

3 My times are in Thy hand :
  Why should I doubt or fear ?
My Father's hand will never cause
  His child a needless tear.

4 My times are in Thy hand,
  Jesus, the Crucified ;
Those hands my cruel sins had
    pierced
  Are now my guard and guide.

5 My times are in Thy hand :
  I'll always trust in Thee ;
And, after death, at Thy right hand
  I shall for ever be.
               WILLIAM FREEMAN LLOYD,
                         1791–1853.

552
65. 65. D.

JESUS is our Shepherd,
  His the voice we hear ;
Folded in His bosom,
  What have we to fear ?
Only let us follow
  Whither He doth lead,—
To the thirsty desert,
  Or the dewy mead.

2 Jesus is our Shepherd :
  Well we know His voice ;
How its gentlest whisper
  Makes our heart rejoice !
Even when He chideth,
  Tender is its tone ;
None but He shall guide us ;
  We are His alone.

3 Jesus is our Shepherd :
  For the sheep He bled ;
Every lamb is sprinkled
  With the blood He shed ;
Then on each He setteth
  His own secret sign :
' They that have my Spirit,
  These ', saith He, ' are Mine.'

4 Jesus is our Shepherd :
  Guarded by His arm,
Though the wolves may raven,
  None can do us harm ;
When we tread death's valley,
  Dark with fearful gloom,
We will fear no evil,
  Victors o'er the tomb.
               HUGH STOWELL, 1799–1865.

553
66. 66.

THY way, not mine, O Lord,
  However dark it be !
Lead me by Thine own hand ;
  Choose out the path for me.

2 Smooth let it be or rough,
  It will be still the best ;
Winding or straight, it leads
  Right onward to Thy rest.

3 I dare not choose my lot,
  I would not if I might :
Choose Thou for me, my God,
  So shall I walk aright.

4 The Kingdom that I seek
  Is Thine ; so let the way
That leads to it be Thine,
  Else I must surely stray.

5 Take Thou my cup, and it
  With joy or sorrow fill
As best to Thee may seem :
  Choose Thou my good and ill.

6 Choose Thou for me my friends
  My sickness or my health ;
Choose Thou my cares for me,
  My poverty or wealth.

7 Not mine, not mine the choice
  In things or great or small ;
Be Thou my Guide, my Strength,
  My Wisdom, and my All.
               HORATIUS BONAR, 1808–89.

554
87. 87. 87.

SAVIOUR, like a shepherd lead us,
  Much we need Thy tender care ;
In Thy pleasant pastures feed us ;
  For our use Thy folds prepare :
      Blessèd Jesus !
  Thou hast bought us, Thine we
    are.

2 We are Thine ; do Thou befriend us,
  Be the Guardian of our way ;
Keep from ill ; from sin defend us :
  Seek us when we go astray :
      Blessèd Jesus !
  Hear us children when we pray.

3 Thou hast promised to receive us,
  Poor and sinful though we be ;
Thou hast mercy to relieve us,
  Grace to cleanse, and power to free :
      Blessèd Jesus !
  Early let us turn to Thee.

4 Early let us seek Thy favour;
Early let us do Thy will;
Blessèd Lord and only Saviour,
With Thyself our bosoms fill:
Blessèd Jesus!
Thou hast loved us, love us still.
DOROTHY ANN THRUPP'S
Hymns for the Young, 1836.

555
48. 84.

HOLD Thou my hands!
In grief and joy, in hope and fear,
Lord, let me feel that Thou art near:
Hold Thou my hands!

2 If e'er by doubts
Of Thy good Fatherhood depressed,
I cannot find in Thee my rest,
Hold Thou my hands!

3 Hold Thou my hands,—
These passionate hands too quick to smite,
These hands so eager for delight:
Hold Thou my hands!

4 And when at length,
With darkened eyes and fingers cold,
I seek some last loved hand to hold,
Hold Thou my hands!
WILLIAM CANTON, 1845–1926.

556
10. 10. 10. 10. 10. 10.

BE still, my soul: the Lord is on thy side;
Bear patiently the cross of grief or pain;
Leave to thy God to order and provide;
In every change He faithful will remain.
Be still, my soul: thy best, thy heavenly Friend
Through thorny ways leads to a joyful end.

2 Be still, my soul: thy God doth undertake
To guide the future as He has the past.
Thy hope, thy confidence let nothing shake;
All now mysterious shall be bright at last.

Be still, my soul: the waves and winds still know
His voice who ruled them while He dwelt below.

3 Be still, my soul: when dearest friends depart,
And all is darkened in the vale of tears,
Then shalt thou better know His love, His heart,
Who comes to soothe thy sorrow and thy fears.
Be still, my soul: thy Jesus can repay,
From His own fulness, all He takes away.

4 Be still, my soul: the hour is hastening on
When we shall be forever with the Lord,
When disappointment, grief, and fear are gone,
Sorrow forgot, love's purest joys restored.
Be still, my soul: when change and tears are past,
All safe and blessèd we shall meet at last.
KATHARINA VON SCHLEGEL, 1697–?;
tr. by JANE LAURIE BORTHWICK,
1813–97.

557
C. M.

HE that is down needs fear no fall,
He that is low, no pride;
He that is humble ever shall
Have God to be his guide.

2 I am content with what I have,
Little be it or much;
And, Lord, contentment still I crave,
Because Thou savest such.

3 Fulness to such a burden is
That go on pilgrimage;
Here little, and hereafter bliss,
Is best from age to age.
JOHN BUNYAN, 1628–88.

558
C. M.

WHO fathoms the eternal thought?
Who talks of scheme and plan?
The Lord is God! He needeth not
The poor device of man.

2 Here in the maddening maze of
   things,
   When tossed by storm and flood,
To one fixed ground my spirit clings :
   I know that God is good.

3 I long for household voices gone,
   For vanished smiles I long ;
But God hath led my dear ones on,
   And He can do no wrong.

4 I know not what the future hath
   Of marvel or surprise,
Assured alone that life and death
   His mercy underlies.

5 And if my heart and flesh are weak
   To bear an untried pain,
The bruisèd reed He will not break,
   But strengthen and sustain.

6 And so beside the silent sea
   I wait the muffled oar ;
No harm from Him can come to me
   On ocean or on shore.

7 I know not where His islands lift
   Their fronded palms in air ;
I only know I cannot drift
   Beyond His love and care.
                    JOHN GREENLEAF WHITTIER,
                               1807–92.

559
                                    D. C. M.

'TWIXT gleams of joy and clouds
      of doubt
   Our feelings come and go ;
Our best estate is tossed about
   In ceaseless ebb and flow.
No mood of feeling, form of thought,
   Is constant for a day ;
But Thou, O Lord, Thou changest
      not :
   The same Thou art alway.

2 I grasp Thy strength, make it mine
      own,
   My heart with peace is blest ;
I lose my hold, and then comes down
   Darkness, and cold unrest.
Let me no more my comfort draw
   From my frail hold of Thee,
In this alone rejoice with awe—
   Thy mighty grasp of me.

3 Out of that weak, unquiet drift
   That comes but to depart,
To that pure heaven my spirit lift
   Where Thou unchanging art.

Lay hold of me with Thy strong
      grasp,
   Let Thy almighty arm
In its embrace my weakness clasp,
   And I shall fear no harm.

4 Thy purpose of eternal good
   Let me but surely know ;
On this I'll lean—let changing mood
   And feeling come or go—
Glad when Thy sunshine fills my
      soul,
   Not lorn when clouds o'ercast,
Since Thou within Thy sure control
   Of love dost hold me fast.
                    JOHN CAMPBELL SHAIRP,
                               1819–85.

560
                        88. 88. D. Anapaestic.

A SOVEREIGN Protector I have,
   Unseen, yet for ever at hand,
Unchangeably faithful to save,
   Almighty to rule and command.
He smiles, and my comforts abound ;
   His grace as the dew shall descend,
And walls of salvation surround
   The souls He delights to defend.

2 Inspirer and Hearer of prayer,
   Thou Shepherd and Guardian of
      Thine,
My all to Thy covenant care
   I sleeping and waking resign.
If Thou art my Shield and my Sun,
   The night is no darkness to me ;
And, fast as my moments roll on,
   They bring me but nearer to Thee.
                    AUGUSTUS MONTAGUE TOPLADY,
                               1740–78.

561
                                    S. M.

YOUR harps, ye trembling saints,
   Down from the willows take :
Loud to the praise of love divine
   Bid every string awake.

2 Though in a foreign land,
   We are not far from home ;
And nearer to our house above
   We every moment come.

3 His grace will to the end
   Stronger and brighter shine ;
Nor present things nor things to
      come
   Shall quench the spark divine.

4 When we in darkness walk,
　Nor feel the heavenly flame,
Then is the time to trust our God,
　And rest upon His Name.

5 Soon shall our doubts and fears
　Subside at His control;
His loving-kindness shall break
　through
The midnight of the soul.

6 Wait till the shadows flee;
　Wait thy appointed hour;
Wait till the Bridegroom of thy soul
　Reveals His love with power.

7 Blest is the man, O God,
　That stays himself on Thee:
Who wait for Thy salvation, Lord,
　Shall Thy salvation see.

AUGUSTUS MONTAGUE TOPLADY,
1740–78.

PILGRIMAGE AND REST

562 *From Genesis* xxviii. 20–22.
C. M.

O GOD of Bethel! by whose hand
　Thy people still are fed
Who through this weary pilgrimage
　Hast all our fathers led:

2 Our vows, our prayers, we now
　present
Before Thy throne of grace:
God of our fathers: be the God
　Of their succeeding race.

3 Through each perplexing path of life
　Our wandering footsteps guide;
Give us each day our daily bread,
　And raiment fit provide.

4 O spread Thy covering wings around,
　Till all our wanderings cease,
And at our Father's loved abode
　Our souls arrive in peace.

5 Such blessings from Thy gracious
　hand
Our humble prayers implore;
And Thou shalt be our chosen God,
　And portion evermore.

PHILIP DODDRIDGE, 1702–51; and
MICHAEL BRUCE, 1746–67; as in
Scottish Paraphrases, 1781.

563 87. 87. 87.

LEAD us, heavenly Father, lead us
　O'er the world's tempestuous
　sea;
Guard us, guide us, keep us, feed us,
　For we have no help but Thee;
Yet possessing every blessing
If our God our Father be.

2 Saviour, breathe forgiveness o'er us;
　All our weakness Thou dost know;
Thou didst tread this earth before us,
　Thou didst feel its keenest woe;
Lone and dreary, faint and weary,
　Through the desert Thou didst go.

3 Spirit of our God, descending,
　Fill our hearts with heavenly joy,
Love with every passion blending,
　Pleasure that can never cloy;
Thus provided, pardoned, guided,
　Nothing can our peace destroy.

JAMES EDMESTON, 1791–1867.

564 87. 87. 87.

GUIDE me, O Thou great Jehovah,
　Pilgrim through this barren land;
I am weak, but Thou art mighty;
　Hold me with Thy powerful hand:
Bread of heaven,
　Feed me till my want is o'er.

2 Open now the crystal fountain,
　Whence the healing stream doth
　flow;
Let the fire and cloudy pillar
　Lead me all my journey through:
Strong Deliverer,
　Be Thou still my strength and
　shield.

3 When I tread the verge of Jordan,
　Bid my anxious fears subside!
Death of death, and hell's Destruc-
　tion,
Land me safe on Canaan's side!
　Songs of praises
I will ever give to Thee.

WILLIAM WILLIAMS, 1717–91;
tr. by PETER WILLIAMS, 1727–96.

565

77. 77.

FATHER, lead me, day by day,
  Ever in Thine own sweet way ;
Teach me to be pure and true ;
Show me what I ought to do.

2 When in danger, make me brave ;
Make me know that Thou canst save ;
Keep me safe by Thy dear side ;
Let me in Thy love abide.

3 When I'm tempted to do wrong,
Make me steadfast, wise, and strong ;
And, when all alone I stand,
Shield me with Thy mighty hand.

4 When my heart is full of glee,
Help me to remember Thee,
Happy most of all to know
That my Father loves me so.

5 May I do the good I know,
Be Thy loving child below,
Then at last go home to Thee,
Evermore Thy child to be.
JOHN PAGE HOPPS, 1834–1912.

566

10 10. 10 10.

LEAD us, O Father, in the paths of
  peace :
  Without Thy guiding hand we go
    astray,
And doubts appal, and sorrows still
    increase ;
  Lead us through Christ, the true
    and living Way.

2 Lead us, O Father, in the paths of
    truth :
  Unhelped by Thee, in error's maze
    we grope,
While passion stains and folly dims
    our youth,
  And age comes on uncheered by
    faith or hope.

3 Lead us, O Father, in the paths of
    right :
  Blindly we stumble when we walk
    alone,
Involved in shadows of a darkening
    night ;
  Only with Thee we journey safely
    on.

4 Lead us, O Father, to Thy heavenly
    rest,
  However rough and steep the path-
    way be,
Through joy or sorrow, as Thou
    deemest best,
  Until our lives are perfected in
    Thee.
WILLIAM HENRY BURLEIGH,
1812–71.

567

55. 88. 55.

JESUS, still lead on,
  Till our rest be won,
And, although the way be cheerless,
We will follow, calm and fearless ;
  Guide us by Thy hand
  To our fatherland.

2 If the way be drear,
  If the foe be near,
Let not faithless fears o'ertake us,
Let not faith and hope forsake us ;
  For, through many a foe,
  To our home we go.

3 When we seek relief
  From a long-felt grief,
When oppressed by new temptations,
Lord, increase and perfect patience
  Show us that bright shore
  Where we weep no more.

4 Jesus, still lead on,
  Till our rest be won ;
Heavenly Leader, still direct us,
Still support, console, protect us,
  Till we safely stand
  In our fatherland.
NICOLAUS LUDWIG VON ZINZENDORF,
1700–60 ; tr. by JANE LAURIE
BORTHWICK, 1813–97.

568

10 4. 10 4. 10 10.

LEAD, kindly Light, amid the en-
  circling gloom,
    Lead Thou me on :
The night is dark, and I am far from
  home ;
    Lead Thou me on.
Keep Thou my feet ; I do not ask
  to see
The distant scene,—one step enough
  for me.

2 I was not ever thus, nor prayed that Thou
  Shouldst lead me on;
I loved to choose and see my path, but now
  Lead Thou me on;
I loved the garish day, and, spite of fears,
Pride ruled my will: remember not past years.

3 So long Thy power hath blest me, sure it still
  Will lead me on,
O'er moor and fen, o'er crag and torrent, till
  The night is gone,
And with the morn those angel faces smile,
Which I have loved long since, and lost awhile.

    JOHN HENRY NEWMAN,
     1801–90.

569   76. 76.

LEAD, holy Shepherd, lead us,
 Thy feeble flock, we pray;
Thou King of little pilgrims,
 Safe lead us all the way.

2 In Thy blest footprints guide us
 Along the heavenward road;
Thine age fills all the ages,
 Undying Word of God.

3 That life, O Christ, is noblest
 Which praises God the best,
A life celestial, nourished
 At wisdom's holy breast.

4 By her good nurture let us,
 Thy little ones, be fed,
And by her guidance gentle
 Our wandering steps be led.

5 O fill us with Thy Spirit,
 Like morning dew shed down,
And with our praises loyal
 King Jesus we shall crown.

6 O be our lives our tribute,
 The meed of praise we bring,
When thus we join to honour
 Our Teacher and our King.

CLEMENT OF ALEXANDRIA, c. 170–220;
 tr. by HAMILTON MONTGOMERIE
 MACGILL, 1807–80.

570   76. 76. D.

O LORD, I sing Thy praises
 Who art my strength and stay,
My leader through life's mazes,
 To bring me to Thy way;
Thou didst not leave me straying
 When I afar would go,
With heedless footsteps, playing
 Upon the brink of woe.

2 For Thou, Thy glory showing,
 Mad'st me Thy beauty see;
Thy love has been bestowing
 New life and joy on me.
Thou grace and glory givest,
 Thou art a Sun and Shield,
Thou only ever livest,
 Thy words salvation yield.

3 O Lord, do not forsake me,
 But guide me as a friend;
And strong in heart still make me,
 For what Thy love may send.
Through death's dark vale victorious,
 O let me lean on Thee,
And let me see Thee glorious,
 Through all eternity.

  PETER GRANT, 1783–1867; tr. by
  LACHLAN MACBEAN, 1853–1931.

571   66. 84. D.

THE God of Abraham praise,
 Who reigns enthroned above,
Ancient of everlasting days,
 And God of love.
Jehovah, Great I AM!
 By earth and heaven confessed,
I bow, and bless the sacred Name
 For ever blest.

2 The God of Abraham praise,
 At whose supreme command
From earth I rise, and seek the joys
 At His right hand.
I all on earth forsake—
 Its wisdom, fame, and power—
And Him my only portion make,
 My shield and tower.

3 He by Himself hath sworn,
 I on His oath depend;
I shall, on eagle's wings upborne,
 To heaven ascend :
I shall behold His face,
 I shall His power adore,
And sing the wonders of His grace
 For evermore.

THE CHRISTIAN LIFE

4   There dwells the Lord our King,
       The Lord our Righteousness;
Triumphant o'er the world and sin,
       The Prince of Peace;
On Zion's sacred height
His Kingdom He maintains,
And glorious with His saints in light
       For ever reigns.

5   The whole triumphant host
Give thanks to God on high;
'Hail, Father, Son, and Holy
       Ghost!'
       They ever cry.
Hail, Abraham's God, and mine!—
I join the heavenly lays,—
All might and majesty are Thine,
       And endless praise.

       THOMAS OLIVERS, 1725–99.

572   65. 65. 66. 65.

FAR off I see the goal—
       O Saviour, guide me;
I feel my strength is small—
       Be Thou beside me;
With vision ever clear,
With love that conquers fear,
And grace to persevere,
       O Lord, provide me.

2   When'er Thy way seems strange,
       Go Thou before me;
And, lest my heart should change,
       O Lord, watch o'er me;
But, should my faith prove frail,
And I through blindness fail,
O let Thy grace prevail,
       And still restore me.

3   Should earthly pleasures wane,
       And joy forsake me,
And lonely hours of pain
       At length o'ertake me,—
My hand in Thine hold fast
Till sorrow be o'er-past,
And gentle death at last
       For heaven awake me.

4   There, with the ransomed throng
       Who praise for ever
The love that made them strong
       To serve for ever,
I, too, would see Thy face,
Thy finished work re-trace,
And magnify Thy grace,
       Redeemed for ever.

       ROBERT ROWLAND ROBERTS,
                     1865–1945.

573   87. 87. 87.

WHEN from Egypt's house of
       bondage
Israel marched, a mighty band,
Little children numbered with them
Journeyed to the promised land;
       Little children
Trod the desert's trackless sand.

2   Little children crossed the Jordan,
Landed on fair Canaan's shore,
'Neath the sheltering vine they rested,
Homeless wanderers now no more;
       Little children
Sang sweet praise for perils o'er.

3   Saviour, like those Hebrew children,
Youthful pilgrims would we be;
From the chains of sin and Satan
Thou hast died to set us free;
       We would traverse
All the wilderness with Thee.

4   Guide our feeble, erring footsteps,
Shade us from the heat by day;
Be our light from shadowy nightfall
Till the darkness pass away;
       Jesus, guard us
From the dangers of the way.

5   When we reach the cold, dark river,
Bid us tremble not nor fear;
Be Thou with us in the waters—
We are safe if Thou art near;
       Through the billows
Let the emerald bow appear.

6   Then, our pilgrim journey ended,
All Thy glory we shall see,
Dwell with saints and holy angels,
Rest beneath life's healing tree,—
       Happy children,
Praising, blessing, loving Thee.

       JENNETTE THRELFALL, 1821–80.

574   77. 77.

CHILDREN of the heavenly King,
       As ye journey, sweetly sing;
Sing your Saviour's worthy praise,
Glorious in His works and ways.

2   We are travelling home to God,
In the way the fathers trod;
They are happy now, and we
Soon their happiness shall see.

3 Lift your eyes, you sons of light ;
Zion's city is in sight ;
There our endless home shall be,
There our Lord we soon shall see.

4 Fear not, brethren ; joyful stand
On the borders of your land ;
Jesus Christ, your Father's Son,
Bids you undismayed go on.

5 Lord, obediently we go,
Gladly leaving all below ;
Only Thou our Leader be,
And we still will follow Thee.
JOHN CENNICK, 1718-55.

575
76. 76. 76. 73.

THE world looks very beautiful
And full of joy to me ;
The sun shines out in glory
On everything I see ;
I know I shall be happy
While in the world I stay,
For I will follow Jesus
All the way.

2 I'm but a little pilgrim,
My journey 's just begun ;
They say I shall meet sorrow
Before my journey 's done
' The world is full of sorrow
And suffering,' they say ;
But I will follow Jesus
All the way.

3 Then, like a little pilgrim,
Whatever I may meet,
I'll take it, joy or sorrow,
To lay at Jesus' feet.
He'll comfort me in trouble ;
He'll wipe my tears away
With joy I'll follow Jesus
All the way.

4 Then trials cannot vex me,
And pain I need not fear,
For, when I'm close by Jesus,
Grief cannot come too near ;
Not even death can harm me,
When death I meet one day ;
To heaven I'll follow Jesus
All the way.
ANNA BARTLETT WARNER,
1820-1915.

576
65. 65. 6665.

WHO would true valour see,
Let him come hither ;
One here will constant be,
Come wind, come weather
There 's no discouragement
Shall make him once relent
His first avowed intent
To be a pilgrim.

2 Whoso beset him round
With dismal stories,
Do but themselves confound ;
His strength the more is.
No lion can him fright,
He'll with a giant fight,
But he will have a right
To be a pilgrim.

3 Hobgoblin nor foul fiend
Can daunt his spirit ;
He knows he at the end
Shall life inherit.
Then fancies fly away ;
He'll fear not what men say ;
He'll labour night and day
To be a pilgrim.
JOHN BUNYAN, 1628-88.

577
76. 76.

O HAPPY band of pilgrims,
If onward ye will tread,
With Jesus as your Fellow,
To Jesus as your Head !

2 O happy if ye labour
As Jesus did for men ;
O happy if ye hunger
As Jesus hungered then !

3 The Cross that Jesus carried,
He carried as your due ;
The crown that Jesus weareth,
He weareth it for you.

4 The faith by which ye see Him,
The hope in which ye yearn,
The love that through all troubles
To Him alone will turn,—

5 What are they but vaunt-couriers
To lead you to His sight ?
What are they save the effluence
Of uncreated light ?

6 The trials that beset you,
The sorrows ye endure,
The manifold temptations
That death alone can cure,—

7 What are they but His jewels
   Of right celestial worth?
What are they but the ladder
   Set up to heaven on earth?

8 O happy band of pilgrims,
   Look upward to the skies,
Where such a light affliction
   Shall win you such a prize.

JOHN MASON NEALE, 1818–66; based
   on JOSEPH the Hymnographer,
   9th century.

578   87. 87. 887.

WHITHER, pilgrims, are you
   going,
   Going each with staff in hand?
'We are going on a journey,
   Going at our King's command;
Over hills and plains and valleys,
We are going to His palace,
   Going to the better land.'

2 Fear ye not the way so lonely,
   You a little, feeble band?
'No; for friends unseen are near us,
   Holy angels round us stand;
Christ, our Leader, walks beside us;
He will guard, and He will guide us,
   Guide us to the better land.'

3 Tell us, pilgrims, what you hope for
   In that far-off better land?
'Spotless robes and crowns of glory,
   From a Saviour's loving hand;
We shall drink of life's clear river,
We shall dwell with God for ever,
   In that bright and better land.'

4 Pilgrims, may we travel with you
   To that bright and better land?
'Come and welcome, come and
      welcome,
   Welcome to our pilgrim band.
Come, O come, and do not leave us;
Christ is waiting to receive us
   In that bright and better land.'

Golden Chain,
1861.

579   65. 65. 65. D.

'FORWARD!' be our watch-
   word,
   Steps and voices joined;
Seek the things before us,
   Not a look behind;
Burns the fiery pillar
   At our army's head;

Who shall dream of shrinking,
   By Jehovah led?
   Forward through the desert,
      Through the toil and fight;
   Jordan flows before us,
      Zion beams with light.

2 Glories upon glories
   Hath our God prepared,
By the souls that love Him
   One day to be shared;
Eye hath not beheld them,
   Ear hath never heard,
Nor of these hath uttered
   Thought or speech a word.
      Forward, marching forward,
         Where the heaven is bright,
      Till the veil be lifted,
         Till our faith be sight.

3 Far o'er yon horizon
   Rise the city towers,
Where our God abideth;
   That fair home is ours:
Flash the streets with jasper,
   Shine the gates with gold,
Flows the gladdening river,
   Shedding joys untold.
      Thither, onward thither,
         In Jehovah's might;
      Pilgrims to your country,
         Forward into light!

4 To the Father's glory
   Loudest anthems raise,
To the Son and Spirit
   Echo songs of praise;
To the Lord Jehovah,
   Blessèd Three in One,
Be by men and angels
   Endless honour done.
      Weak are earthly praises,
         Dull the songs of night;
      Forward into triumph,
         Forward into light!

HENRY ALFORD, 1810–71.

580   11 10. 11 10. 9 11.

HARK, hark, my soul! angelic
   songs are swelling
O'er earth's green fields and
   ocean's wave-beat shore:
How sweet the truth those blessèd
   strains are telling
Of that new life when sin shall be
   no more.
   *Angels of Jesus, angels of light,
   Singing to welcome the pilgrims
      of the night!*

PILGRIMAGE AND REST

2 Onward we go, for still we hear them
    singing,
  ' Come, weary souls, for Jesus bids
    you come ' ;
  And through the dark, its echoes
    sweetly ringing,
    The music of the Gospel leads us
    home.

3 Far, far away, like bells at evening
    pealing,
    The voice of Jesus sounds o'er land
    and sea,
  And laden souls, by thousands meekly
    stealing,
    Kind Shepherd, turn their weary
    steps to Thee.

4 Rest comes at length ; though life
    be long and dreary,
    The day must dawn, and dark-
    some night be past ;
  Faith's journey ends in welcomes to
    the weary,
    And heaven, the heart's true home,
    will come at last.

5 Angels, sing on, your faithful watches
    keeping,
    Sing us sweet fragments of the
    songs above,
  Till morning's joy shall end the
    night of weeping,
    And life's long shadows break in
    cloudless love.

FREDERICK WILLIAM FABER,
1814–63.

581

76. 76. 76. 75.

THE sands of time are sinking ;
    The dawn of heaven breaks ;
The summer morn I've sighed for,
  The fair, sweet morn, awakes.
Dark, dark hath been the midnight,
  But dayspring is at hand,
And glory, glory dwelleth
  In Immanuel's land.

2 O Christ ! He is the fountain,
    The deep, sweet well of love ;
The streams on earth I've tasted
  More deep I'll drink above :
There to an ocean fulness
  His mercy doth expand,
And glory, glory dwelleth
  In Immanuel's land.

3 With mercy and with judgment
    My web of time He wove,
And aye the dews of sorrow
    Were lustred by His love ;
I'll bless the hand that guided,
    I'll bless the heart that planned,
When throned where glory dwelleth
    In Immanuel's land.

4 I've wrestled on towards heaven,
    'Gainst storm and wind and tide ;
Now, like a weary traveller
    That leaneth on his guide,
Amid the shades of evening,
    While sinks life's lingering sand,
I hail the glory dawning
    In Immanuel's land.

ANNE ROSS COUSIN, 1824–1906.

582

77. 77. 77.

WHEN this passing world is done,
    When has sunk yon glaring
    sun,
When we stand with Christ in glory,
    Looking o'er life's finished story,
    Then, Lord, shall I fully know,
    Not till then, how much I owe.

2 When I stand before the throne,
    Dressed in beauty not my own,
When I see Thee as Thou art,
    Love Thee with unsinning heart,
    Then, Lord, shall I fully know,
    Not till then, how much I owe.

3 When the praise of heaven I hear,
    Loud as thunders to the ear,
    Loud as many waters' noise,
    Sweet as harp's melodious voice,
    Then, Lord, shall I fully know,
    Not till then, how much I owe.

4 Even on earth, as through a glass,
    Darkly, let Thy glory pass ;
Make forgiveness feel so sweet ;
Make Thy Spirit's help so meet ;
    Even on earth, Lord, make me
    know
    Something of how much I owe.

ROBERT MURRAY McCHEYNE,
1813–43.

583

D. S. M.

FOR ever with the Lord !
    Amen, so let it be :
Life from the dead is in that word,
    'Tis immortality.

Here in the body pent,
Absent from Him I roam,
Yet nightly pitch my moving tent
A day's march nearer home.

2 My Father's house on high,
Home of my soul, how near
At times, to faith's foreseeing eye,
Thy golden gates appear !
Ah ! then my spirit faints
To reach the land I love,
The bright inheritance of saints,
Jerusalem above.

3 For ever with the Lord !
Father, if 'tis Thy will,
The promise of that faithful word
Even here to me fulfil.
Be Thou at my right hand,
Then can I never fail ;
Uphold Thou me, and I shall stand ;
Fight, and I must prevail.

4 So, when my latest breath
Shall rend the veil in twain,
By death I shall escape from death,
And life eternal gain.
Knowing as I am known,
How shall I love that word,
And oft repeat before the throne,
' For ever with the Lord ! '
JAMES MONTGOMERY, 1771–1854.

584
77. 75.

WHEN the day of toil is done,
When the race of life is run,
Father, grant Thy wearied one,
Rest for evermore.

2 When the strife of sin is stilled,
When the foe within is killed,
Be Thy gracious word fulfilled,
' Peace for evermore.'

3 When the darkness melts away
At the breaking of Thy day,
Bid us hail the cheering ray,
Light for evermore.

4 When the heart by sorrow tried
Feels at length its throbs subside,
Bring us, where all tears are dried,
Joy for evermore.

5 When for vanished days we yearn,
Days that never can return,
Teach us in Thy love to learn
Love for evermore.

6 When the breath of life is flown,
When the grave must claim its own,
Lord of life, be ours Thy crown—
Life for evermore.

JOHN ELLERTON, 1826–93.

DEATH, RESURRECTION, AND THE LIFE
EVERLASTING

585
87. 87.

DAYS and moments quickly flying
Blend the living with the dead :
Soon our bodies will be lying
Each within its narrow bed.

2 Jesus, infinite Redeemer,
Maker of this mighty frame,
Teach, O teach us to remember
What we are, and whence we came.

3 As a shadow life is fleeting ;
As a vapour, so it flies ;
For the bygone years retreating,
Pardon grant, and make us wise,—

4 Wise that we our days may number,
Strive and wrestle with our sin,
Stay not in our work, nor slumber,
Till Thy holy rest we win.

5 Jesus, merciful Redeemer,
Rouse dead souls to hear Thy
voice ;
Wake, O wake each idle dreamer
Now to make the eternal choice.

6 Soon before the Judge all glorious
We with all the dead shall stand ;
Saviour over death victorious,
Place us then at Thy right hand.
EDWARD CASWALL, 1814–78,
and others.

586
86.

SOONER or later : yet at last
The Jordan must be past.

2 Sooner or later : yet one day
We all must pass that way.

3 When mysteries shall be revealed,
   All secrets be unsealed :

4 Jesus, most merciful of men,
   Show mercy on us then ;

5 Lord God of mercy and of men,
   Show mercy on us then.
         CHRISTINA GEORGINA ROSSETTI,
                                1830–94.

587   64. 64. 67. 64.

THERE is a happy land,
      Far, far away,
Where saints in glory stand,
      Bright, bright as day.
O how they sweetly sing,
' Worthy is our Saviour King ! '
Loud let His praises ring,
      Praise, praise for aye.

2 Come to this happy land,
      Come, come away ;
Why will ye doubting stand ?
      Why still delay ?
O we shall happy be
When, from sin and sorrow free,
Lord, we shall live with Thee,
      Blest, blest for aye.

3 Bright in that happy land
      Beams every eye ;
Kept by a Father's hand,
      Love cannot die :
On then to glory run ;
Be a crown and kingdom won ;
And, bright above the sun,
      Reign, reign for aye.
                  ANDREW YOUNG, 1807–89.

588   Irr.

SUNSET and evening star,
      And one clear call for me !
And may there be no moaning of the
      bar,
      When I put out to sea,
But such a tide as, moving, seems
      asleep,
Too full for sound and foam,
When that which drew from out the
      boundless deep
      Turns again home.

2 Twilight and evening bell,
      And after that the dark !
And may there be no sadness of fare-
      well
      When I embark ;

For, though from out our bourne of
      time and place
The flood may bear me far,
I hope to see my Pilot face to face
When I have crost the bar.
            ALFRED TENNYSON, 1809–92.

589   11 10. 11 6.

WHEN on my day of life the night
      is falling,
   And in the winds, from unsunned
      spaces blown,
I hear far voices out of darkness
      calling
      My feet to paths unknown,

2 Thou who hast made my home of
      life so pleasant,
   Leave not its tenant when its walls
      decay ;
O Love Divine, O Helper ever
      present,
      Be Thou my strength and stay.

3 Be near me when all else is from me
      drifting,—
   Earth, sky, home's pictures, days
      of shade and shine,
And kindly faces, to my own up-
      lifting
      The love which answers mine.

4 I have but Thee, my Father ; let Thy
      Spirit
   Be with me then to comfort and
      uphold ;
No gate of pearl, no branch of palm I
      merit,
      Nor street of shining gold.

5 Suffice it if—my good and ill un-
      reckoned,
   And both forgiven through Thy
      abounding grace—
I find myself by hands familiar
      beckoned
      Unto my fitting place,

6 Some humble door among Thy many
      mansions,
   Some sheltering shade where sin
      and striving cease,
And flows for ever, through heaven's
      green expansions,
      The river of Thy peace.

7 There, from the music round about
    me stealing,
    I fain would learn the new and holy
      song,
And find at last, beneath Thy trees
    of healing,
      The life for which I long.
        JOHN GREENLEAF WHITTIER,
                1807–92.

590
S. M.

THERE is no night in heaven :
    In that blest world above,
Work never can bring weariness,
    For work itself is love.

2 There is no grief in heaven :
    For all is perfect day ;
And tears are of those former things
    Which all have passed away.

3 There is no sin in heaven,
    Amid that blessèd throng ;
All holy is their spotless robe,
    All holy is their song.

4 There is no death in heaven :
    For they who gain that shore
Have won their immortality,
    And they can die no more.

5 Lord Jesus, be our Guide ;
    O lead us safely on,
Till night and grief and sin and death
    Are past, and heaven is won.
        FRANCIS MINDEN KNOLLIS,
                1815–63.

591
75. 75. 77.

EVERY morning the red sun
    Rises warm and bright ;
But the evening cometh on,
    And the dark, cold night :
There 's a bright land far away,
Where 'tis never-ending day.

2 Every spring the sweet young flowers
    Open bright and gay,
Till the chilly autumn hours
    Wither them away :
There 's a land we have not seen,
Where the trees are always green.

3 Little birds sing songs of praise
    All the summer long,
But in colder, shorter days
    They forget their song :
There 's a place where angels sing
Ceaseless praises to their King.

4 Christ our Lord is ever near
    Those who follow Him ;
But we cannot see Him here,
    For our eyes are dim :
There is a most happy place,
Where men always see His face.

5 Who shall go to that bright land ?
    All who love the right :
Holy children there shall stand
    In their robes of white ;
For that heaven, so bright and blest,
Is our everlasting rest.
        CECIL FRANCES ALEXANDER,
                1818–95.

592
C. M.

THERE is a land of pure delight,
    Where saints immortal reign ;
Infinite day excludes the night,
    And pleasures banish pain ;

2 There everlasting spring abides,
    And never-withering flowers :
Death, like a narrow sea, divides
    This heavenly land from ours.

3 Sweet fields beyond the swelling flood
    Stand dressed in living green ;
So to the Jews old Canaan stood,
    While Jordan rolled between.

4 But timorous mortals start and shrink
    To cross this narrow sea,
And linger, shivering on the brink,
    And fear to launch away.

5 O could we make our doubts re-
      move—
    Those gloomy doubts that rise—
And see the Canaan that we love,
    With unclouded eyes ;

6 Could we but climb where Moses
    stood,
    And view the landscape o'er,
Not Jordan's stream, nor death's
    cold flood,
      Should fright us from the shore.
        ISAAC WATTS, 1674–1748.

593
86. 76. 76. 76.

THERE 's a Friend for little
    children,
    Above the bright blue sky,
A Friend that never changes,
    Whose love will never die.

Unlike our friends by nature,
  Who change with changing years,
This Friend is always worthy
  The precious Name He bears.

2 There's a home for little children
    Above the bright blue sky,
  Where Jesus reigns in glory,
    A home of peace and joy.
  No home on earth is like it,
    Or can with it compare,
  For every one is happy,
    Nor could be happier, there.

3 There's a crown for little children
    Above the bright blue sky,
  And all who look to Jesus
    Shall wear it by and by,—
  A crown of brightest glory,
    Which He will then bestow
  On all who love the Saviour,
    And walk with Him below.

4 There's a song for little children
    Above the bright blue sky,
  And a harp of sweetest music
    And a palm of victory;
  All, all above is pleasure,
    And found in Christ alone;
  O come, dear little children,
    That all may be your own!
          ALBERT MIDLANE, 1825–1909.

594   66. 66. D.

THERE is a blessèd home
    Beyond this land of woe,
  Where trials never come,
    Nor tears of sorrow flow;
  Where faith is lost in sight,
    And patient hope is crowned,
  And everlasting light
    Its glory throws around.

2 There is a land of peace;
    Good angels know it well;
  Glad songs that never cease
    Within its portals swell;
  Around its glorious throne
    Ten thousand saints adore
  Christ, with the Father one
    And Spirit, evermore.

3 O joy all joys beyond!
    To see the Lamb who died,
  For ever there enthroned,
    For ever glorified;
  To give to Him the praise
    Of every triumph won,
  And sing, through endless days,
    The great things He hath done.

4 Look up, ye saints of God!
    Nor fear to tread below,
  The path your Saviour trod,
    Of daily toil and woe;
  Wait but a little while
    In uncomplaining love,
  His own most gracious smile
    Shall welcome you above.
          HENRY WILLIAMS BAKER, 1821–77.

595   C. M.

JERUSALEM, my happy home,
    When shall I come to thee?
  When shall my sorrows have an end?
    Thy joys when shall I see?

2 O happy harbour of the saints!
    O sweet and pleasant soil!
  In thee no sorrow may be found,
    No grief, no care, no toil.

3 Thy walls are made of precious
      stones,
    Thy bulwarks diamonds square;
  Thy gates are of right orient pearl,
    Exceeding rich and rare;

4 Thy gardens and thy gallant walks
    Continually are green;
  There grow such sweet and pleasant
      flowers
    As nowhere else are seen.

5 Quite through the streets, with silver
      sound,
    The flood of life doth flow,
  Upon whose banks on every side
    The wood of life doth grow.

6 Our sweet is mixed with bitter gall,
    Our pleasure is but pain,
  Our joys scarce last the looking on,
    Our sorrows still remain.

7 But there they live in such delight,
    Such pleasure and such play,
  As that to them a thousand years
    Doth seem as yesterday.

8 Jerusalem, my happy home,
    Would God I were in thee!
  Would God my woes were at an end,
    Thy joys that I might see!
        F. B. P.; probably 16th century.

596 *The Saints at Rest.*   98. 98. D.

FROM heavenly Jerusalem's towers,
    The path through the desert they
      trace;
  And every affliction they suffered
    Redounds to the glory of grace;

Their look they cast back on the
    tempests,
On fears, on grim death and the
    grave,
Rejoicing that now they're in safety,
    Through Him that is mighty to
    save.

2 And we, from the wilds of the desert,
    Shall flee to the land of the blest ;
Life's tears shall be changed to
    rejoicing,
Its labours and toil into rest :
There we shall find refuge eternal,
    From sin, from affliction, from
    pain,
And in the sweet love of the Saviour,
    A joy without end shall attain.
        DAVID CHARLES, 1762–1834 ;
        tr. by LEWIS EDWARDS, 1809–87.

597
76. 76.

BRIEF life is here our portion,
    Brief sorrow, short-lived care ;
The life that knows no ending,
    The tearless life, is there.

2 O happy retribution !
    Short toil, eternal rest ;
For mortals and for sinners
    A mansion with the blest !

3 There grief is turned to pleasure,
    Such pleasure as below
No human voice can utter,
    No human heart can know.

4 And now we fight the battle,
    But then shall wear the crown
Of full and everlasting
    And passionless renown.

5 And now we watch and struggle,
    And now we live in hope,
And Zion, in her anguish,
    With Babylon must cope ;

6 But He whom now we trust in
    Shall then be seen and known,
And they that know and see Him
    Shall have Him for their own.

7 The morning shall awaken,
    The shadows shall decay,
And each true-hearted servant
    Shall shine as doth the day.

8 Yes ! God, our King and Portion,
    In fulness of His grace,
We then shall see for ever,
    And worship face to face.

9 O sweet and blessèd country,
    The home of God's elect !
O sweet and blessèd country,
    That eager hearts expect !

10 Jesus, in mercy bring us
    To that dear land of rest,
Who art, with God the Father
    And Spirit, ever blest.
        BERNARD OF CLUNY, 12th cent. ;
    tr. by JOHN MASON NEALE, 1818–66.

598
76. 76. D.

FOR thee, O dear, dear country,
    Mine eyes their vigils keep ;
For very love, beholding
    Thy happy name, they weep ;
The mention of thy glory
    Is unction to the breast,
And medicine in sickness,
    And love, and life, and rest.

2 With jaspers glow thy bulwarks ;
    Thy streets with emeralds blaze ;
The sardius and the topaz
    Unite in thee their rays ;
Thine ageless walls are bonded
    With amethyst unpriced ;
Thy saints build up its fabric,
    And the corner-stone is Christ.

3 The Cross is all thy splendour,
    The Crucified thy praise ;
His laud and benediction
    Thy ransomed people raise.
Upon the Rock of Ages
    They build thy holy tower ;
Thine is the victor's laurel,
    And thine the golden dower.

4 O sweet and blessèd country,
    The home of God's elect !
O sweet and blessèd country,
    That eager hearts expect !
Jesus, in mercy bring us
    To that dear land of rest,
Who art, with God the Father
    And Spirit, ever blest.
        BERNARD OF CLUNY, 12th cent. ;
    tr. by JOHN MASON NEALE, 1818–66.

599
76. 76. D.

JERUSALEM the golden,
    With milk and honey blest,
Beneath thy contemplation
    Sink heart and voice oppressed :

I know not, O I know not
  What social joys are there,
What radiancy of glory,
  What light beyond compare.

2 They stand, those halls of Zion,
  Conjubilant with song,
And bright with many an angel,
  And all the martyr throng:
The Prince is ever in them;
  The daylight is serene;
The pastures of the blessèd
  Are decked in glorious sheen.

3 There is the throne of David,
  And there, from care released,
The shout of them that triumph,
  The song of them that feast;
And they who, with their Leader,
  Have conquered in the fight,
For ever and for ever
  Are clad in robes of white.

4 O sweet and blessèd country,
  The home of God's elect!
O sweet and blessèd country,
  That eager hearts expect!
Jesus, in mercy bring us
  To that dear land of rest,
Who art, with God the Father
  And Spirit, ever blest.
    BERNARD OF CLUNY, 12th cent.;
tr. by JOHN MASON NEALE, 1818–66.

600
                     c. m. and refrain.

AROUND the throne of God in
    heaven
Thousands of children stand,
Children whose sins are all forgiven,
  A holy, happy band,
    Singing, 'Glory, glory, glory!'

2 What brought them to that world
    above,
  That heaven so bright and fair,
Where all is peace and joy and love?
  How came those children there,
    Singing, 'Glory, glory, glory'?

3 Because the Saviour shed His blood
  To wash away their sin;
Bathed in that pure and precious
    flood,
  Behold them white and clean,
    Singing, 'Glory, glory, glory!'

4 On earth they sought the Saviour's
    grace,
  On earth they loved His Name;
So now they see His blessèd face,
  And stand before the Lamb,
    Singing, 'Glory, glory glory!'
        ANNE SHEPHERD, 1809–57.

TIMES AND SEASONS

601 *From Psalm xc.*   C. M.

O GOD, our help in ages past,
  Our hope for years to come,
Our shelter from the stormy blast,
  And our eternal home !

2 Under the shadow of Thy throne
  Thy saints have dwelt secure ;
Sufficient is Thine arm alone,
  And our defence is sure.

3 Before the hills in order stood,
  Or earth received her frame,
From everlasting Thou art God,
  To endless years the same.

4 A thousand ages in Thy sight
  Are like an evening gone ;
Short as the watch that ends the night
  Before the rising sun.

5 Time, like an ever-rolling stream,
  Bears all its sons away ;
They fly forgotten, as a dream
  Dies at the opening day.

6 O God, our help in ages past,
  Our hope for years to come,
Be Thou our guard while troubles
    last
  And our eternal home.

ISAAC WATTS, 1674–1748.

602   76. 76. D.

STILL on the homeward journey
  Across the desert plain,
Beside another landmark,
  We pilgrims meet again.
We meet, in cloud and sunshine,
  Beneath a changeful sky,
With calm and storm before us,
  As in the days gone by.

2 We meet with loving greetings,
  Fond wishes from the heart,
As brothers often parted,
  And soon again to part.
With tender recollections,
  With many a gentle tear
We meet, for some are wanting ;
  All loved ones are not here.

3 Safe in the home of Jesus,
  With Him for ever blest,
How glorious is their portion,
  How undisturbed their rest !
How gladly will they greet us,
  When, all our journey past,
We reach the better country,
  The Father's house, at last !

4 Thus round the silent landmark,
  Here on the desert plain,
We pilgrims meet together,
  With loving hearts, again.
The storm may gather round us,
  But Christ has gone before ;
We follow in His footsteps,
  And doubt and fear no more.

JANE LAURIE BORTHWICK,
1813–97.

603   87. 87. D.

HEAVENLY Father, Thou hast
  brought us
Safely to the present day,
Gently leading on our footsteps,
  Watching o'er us all the way.
Friend and Guide through life's long
    journey,
  Grateful hearts to Thee we bring ;
But for love so true and changeless
  How shall we fit praises sing ?

2 Mercies new and never-failing
  Brightly shine through all the past,
Watchful care and loving-kindness,
  Always near from first to last,
Tender love, divine protection
  Ever with us day and night ;
Blessings more than we can number
  Strew the path with golden light.

3 Shadows deep have crossed our path-
    way ;
  We have trembled in the storm ;
Clouds have gathered so darkly
  That we could not see Thy form ;
Yet Thy love hath never left us
  In our griefs alone to be,
And the help each gave the other
  Was the strength that came from
    Thee.

188

4 Many that we loved have left us,
    Reaching first their journey's end ;
Now they wait to give us welcome—
    Brother, sister, child, and friend.
When at last our journey's over,
    And we pass away from sight,
Father, take us through the darkness
    Into everlasting light.

HESTER PERIAM HAWKINS,
1846–1928.

604
77. 77.

FOR Thy mercy and Thy grace,
    Faithful through another year,
Hear our song of thankfulness ;
    Jesus, our Redeemer, hear.

2 Lo ! our sins on Thee we cast,
    Thee, our perfect sacrifice,
And, forgetting all the past,
    Press towards our glorious prize.

3 Dark the future ; let Thy light
    Guide us, Bright and Morning
        Star ;
Fierce our foes, and hard the fight ;
    Arm us, Saviour, for the war.

4 In our weakness and distress,
    Rock of strength, be Thou our
        stay ;
In the pathless wilderness
    Be our true and living way.

5 Keep us faithful, keep us pure,
    Keep us evermore Thine own ;
Help, O help us to endure ;
    Fit us for the promised crown.

HENRY DOWNTON, 1818–85.

605
87. 87. D.

AT Thy feet, our God and Father,
    Who hast blessed us all our
        days,
We with grateful hearts would gather,
    To begin the year with praise,—
Praise for light so brightly shining
    On our steps from heaven above,
Praise for mercies daily twining
    Round us golden cords of love.

2 Jesus, for Thy love most tender,
    On the Cross for sinners shown,
We would praise Thee, and surrender
    All our hearts to be Thine own.
With so blest a Friend provided,
    We upon our way would go,
Sure of being safely guided,
    Guarded well from every foe.

3 Every day will be the brighter
    When Thy gracious face we see ;
Every burden will be lighter
    When we know it comes from
        Thee.
Spread Thy love's broad banner o'er
        us ;
Give us strength to serve and wait,
    Till the glory breaks before us,
Through the city's open gate.

JAMES DRUMMOND BURNS,
1823–64.

606
75. 75. D.

FATHER, let me dedicate
    All my times to Thee,
In whatever worldly state
    Thou wilt have me be ;
Not from sorrow, pain, or care
    Freedom dare I claim ;
This alone shall be my prayer,
    ' Glorify Thy Name ! '

2 Can a child presume to choose
    Where or how to live ?
Can a father's love refuse
    All the best to give ?
More Thou givest every day
    Than the best can claim
Nor withholdest aught that may
    Glorify Thy Name.

3 If Thou callest to the cross,
    And its shadow come,
Turning all my gain to loss,
    Shrouding heart and home,
Let me think how Thy dear Son
    To His glory came,
And in deepest woe pray on,
    ' Glorify Thy Name.'

4 If in mercy Thou wilt spare
    Joys that yet are mine,
If on life, serene and fair,
    Brighter rays may shine,
Let my glad heart, while it sings,
    Thee in all proclaim,
And, whate'er the future brings,
    Glorify Thy Name.

LAWRENCE TUTTIETT, 1825–97.

607
L. M.

GREAT God, we sing that mighty
    hand
By which supported still we stand ;
The opening year Thy mercy shows,
And mercy crowns its lingering close.

2 By day, by night, at home, abroad,
  Still are we guarded by our God,
  By His incessant bounty fed,
  By His unerring counsel led.

3 With grateful hearts the past we own ;
  The future, all to us unknown,
  We to Thy guardian care commit,
  And peaceful leave before Thy feet.

4 In scenes exalted or depressed
  Thou art our joy, and Thou our rest ;
  Thy goodness all our hopes shall
    raise,
  Adored through all our changing
    days.

5 When death shall interrupt these
    songs,
  And seal in silence mortal tongues,
  Our Helper God, in whom we trust,
  Shall keep our souls and guard our
    dust.

          PHILIP DODDRIDGE, 1702–51.

Spring (608–611).

608
                                   C. M.

THE glory of the spring how sweet !
  The new-born life how glad !
What joy the happy earth to greet,
  In new, bright raiment clad !

2 Divine Renewer, Thee I bless ;
    I greet Thy going forth ;
  I love Thee in the loveliness
    Of Thy renewèd earth.

3 But O these wonders of Thy grace,
    These nobler works of Thine,
  These marvels sweeter far to trace,
    These new births more divine.

4 This new-born glow of faith so
    strong,
    This bloom of love so fair,
  This new-born ecstasy of song,
    And fragrancy of prayer !

5 Creator Spirit, work in me
    These wonders sweet of Thine ;
  Divine Renewer, graciously
    Renew this heart of mine.

        THOMAS HORNBLOWER GILL,
                   1819–1906.

609
                              87. 87. D.

ALL is bright and cheerful round
    us ;
  All above is soft and blue ;
Spring at last hath come and found
    us,
  Spring and all its pleasures too.
Every flower is full of gladness ;
  Dew is bright, and buds are gay ;
Earth, with all its sin and sadness,
  Seems a happy place to-day.

2 If the flowers that fade so quickly,
    If a day that ends in night,
  If the skies that clouds so thickly
      Often cover from our sight—
  If they all have so much beauty,
    What must be God's land of
      rest,
  Where His sons that do their duty,
    After many toils are blest ?

3 There are leaves that never wither ;
  There are flowers that ne'er decay ;
  Nothing evil goeth thither ;
    Nothing good is kept away.
  They that came from tribulation,
    Washed their robes and made
      them white,
  Out of every tongue and nation,
    Now have rest, and peace, and
      light.

            JOHN MASON NEALE,
                   1818–66.

610
                                   Irr.

FOR all Thy love and goodness, so
    bountiful and free,
    Thy Name, Lord, be adored !
  On the wings of joyous praise our
    hearts soar up to Thee :
    Glory to the Lord !

2 The springtime breaks all round
    about, waking from winter's
    night :
    Thy Name, Lord, be adored !
  The sunshine, like God's love, pours
    down in floods of golden light :
    Glory to the Lord !

3 A voice of joy is in all the earth, a
    voice is in all the air :
    Thy Name, Lord, be adored !
  All nature singeth aloud to God ;
    there is gladness everywhere :
    Glory to the Lord !

4 The flowers are strown in field and
      copse, on the hill and on the
      plain :
      Thy Name, Lord, be adored !
The soft air stirs in the tender leaves
      that clothe the trees again :
      Glory to the Lord !

5 The works of Thy hands are very
      fair ; and for all Thy bounteous
      love
      Thy Name, Lord, be adored !
But what, if this world is so fair, is
      the better land above ?
      Glory to the Lord !

6 O to awake from death's short sleep,
      like the flowers from their wintry
      grave—
      Thy Name, Lord, be adored !—
And to rise all glorious in the day
      when Christ shall come to save !
      Glory to the Lord !

7 O to dwell in that happy land where
      the heart cannot choose but sing—
      Thy Name, Lord, be adored !—
And where the life of the blessèd ones
      is a beautiful endless spring !
      Glory to the Lord ! Hallelujah !
                WILLIAM WALSHAM HOW,
                        1823-97.

611   C. M.

LORD, in Thy Name Thy servants
      plead,
      And Thou hast sworn to hear ;
Thine is the harvest, Thine the seed,
      The fresh and fading year.

2 Our hope, when autumn winds blew
      wild,
      We trusted, Lord, with Thee ;
And now, when spring has on us
      smiled,
      We wait on Thy decree.

3 The former and the latter rain,
      The summer sun and air,
The green ear and the golden grain,
      All Thine, are ours by prayer ;

4 Thine too by right, and ours by grace,
      The wondrous growth unseen,
The hopes that soothe, the fears that
      brace,
      The love that shines serene.

5 So grant the precious things brought
      forth
By sun and moon below,
That Thee in Thy new heaven and
      earth
      We never may forgo.
                JOHN KEBLE, 1792-1866.

Summer (612-613).

612   D. C. M.

THE summer days are come again ;
      Once more the glad earth yields
Her golden wealth of ripening grain,
      And breath of clover fields,
And deepening shade of summer
      woods,
      And glow of summer air,
And winging thoughts, and happy
      moods
      Of love and joy and prayer.

2 The summer days are come again ;
      The birds are on the wing ;
God's praises, in their loving strain,
      Unconsciously they sing.
We know who giveth all the good
      That doth our cup o'erbrim ;
For summer joy in field and wood,
      We lift our song to Him.
                SAMUEL LONGFELLOW, 1819-92.

613   65. 65. D.

SUMMER suns are glowing
      Over land and sea ;
Happy light is flowing,
      Bountiful and free.
Everything rejoices
      In the mellow rays ;
All earth's thousand voices
      Swell the psalm of praise.

2 God's free mercy streameth
      Over all the world,
And His banner gleameth,
      Everywhere unfurled.
Broad and deep and glorious,
      As the heaven above,
Shines in might victorious
      His eternal love.

3 Lord, upon our blindness
      Thy pure radiance pour ;
For Thy loving-kindness
      Make us love Thee more.

And, when clouds are drifting
    Dark across our sky,
Then, the veil uplifting,
    Father, be Thou nigh.

4 We will never doubt Thee,
    Though Thou veil Thy light ;
Life is dark without Thee ;
    Death with Thee is bright.
Light of light, shine o'er us
    On our pilgrim way ;
Go Thou still before us,
    To the endless day.

WILLIAM WALSHAM HOW,
1823–97.

Harvest (614–620).

614

98. 98. Dactylic.

NOW sing we a song for the harvest ;
    Thanksgiving and honour and
    praise
For all that the bountiful Giver
    Hath given to gladden our days,

2 For grasses of upland and lowland,
    For fruits of the garden and field,
For gold which the mine and the
    furrow
To delver and husbandman yield ;

3 And thanks for the harvest of beauty,
    For that which the hands cannot
    hold,
The harvest eyes only can gather,
    And only our hearts can enfold.

4 We reap it on mountain and moor-
    land ;
    We glean it from meadow and lea ;
We garner it in from the cloudland ;
    We bind it in sheaves from the sea.

5 But the song it goes deeper and
    higher ;
    There are harvests that eye cannot
    see ;
They ripen on mountains of duty,
    Are reaped by the brave and the
    free.

6 And these have been gathered and
    garnered,
    Some golden with honour and gain,
And some as with heart's blood are
    ruddy,
    The harvests of sorrow and pain.

7 O Thou who art Lord of the harvest,
    The Giver who gladdens our days,
Our hearts are for ever repeating
    Thanksgiving and honour and
    praise.

JOHN WHITE CHADWICK,
1840–1904.

615

88. 88. 88.

LORD of the harvest, once again
    We thank Thee for the ripened
    grain ;
For crops safe carried, sent to cheer
Thy servants through another year ;
For all sweet holy thoughts, supplied
By seed-time, and by harvest-tide.

2 The bare dead grain, in autumn sown,
Its robe of vernal green puts on ;
Glad from its wintry grave it springs,
Fresh garnished by the King of kings :
So, Lord, to those who sleep in Thee
Shall new and glorious bodies be.

3 Daily, O Lord, our prayers be said,
As Thou hast taught, for daily bread ;
But not alone our bodies feed,—
Supply our fainting spirits' need.
O Bread of life, from day to day
Be Thou their comfort, food and
    stay !

JOSEPH ANSTICE, 1808–36.

616

87. 87. D.

TO Thee, O Lord, our hearts we
    raise
    In hymns of adoration,
To Thee bring sacrifice of praise,
    With shouts of exultation.
Bright robes of gold the fields adorn,
    The hills with joy are ringing,
The valleys stand so thick with corn
    That even they are singing.

2 And now, on this our festal day,
    Thy bounteous hand confessing,
Before Thee thankfully we lay
    The first-fruits of Thy blessing.
By Thee the souls of men are fed
    With gifts of grace supernal ;
Thou who dost give us earthly bread,
    Give us the Bread eternal.

3 We bear the burden of the day,
    And often toil seems dreary ;
But labour ends with sunset ray,
    And rest comes for the weary.

May we, the angel-reaping o'er,
  Stand at the last accepted,
Christ's golden sheaves, for evermore
  To garners bright elected.

4 O blessèd is that land of God
  Where saints abide for ever,
Where golden fields spread far and
    broad,
  Where flows the crystal river.
The strains of all its holy throng
  With ours to-day are blending;
Thrice blessèd is that harvest song
  Which never hath an ending.
            WILLIAM CHATTERTON DIX,
                1837-98.

617   C. M.

FOUNTAIN of mercy, God of
    love,
  How rich Thy bounties are!
The rolling seasons, as they move,
  Proclaim Thy constant care.

2 When in the bosom of the earth
  The sower hid the grain,
Thy goodness marked its secret birth,
  And sent the early rain.

3 The spring's sweet influence was
    Thine;
  The plants in beauty grew;
Thou gav'st refulgent suns to shine,
  And mild refreshing dew.

4 These various mercies from above
  Matured the swelling grain;
A yellow harvest crowns Thy love,
  And plenty fills the plain.

5 Seed-time and harvest, Lord, alone
  Thou dost on man bestow;
Let him not then forget to own
  From whom his blessings flow.

6 Fountain of love, our praise is Thine;
  To Thee our songs we'll raise,
And all created nature join
  In sweet harmonious praise.
            ALICE FLOWERDEW, 1759-1830.

618   76. 76. D. and refrain.

WE plough the fields, and scatter
    The good seed on the land,
But it is fed and watered
  By God's almighty hand;

He sends the snow in winter,
  The warmth to swell the grain,
The breezes and the sunshine
  And soft refreshing rain.
    All good gifts around us
      Are sent from heaven above;
    Then thank the Lord, O thank
        the Lord,
      For all His love.

2 He only is the Maker
  Of all things near and far;
He paints the wayside flower,
  He lights the evening star;
The winds and waves obey Him,
  By Him the birds are fed;
Much more to us, His children,
  He gives our daily bread.

3 We thank Thee then, O Father,
  For all things bright and good,
The seed-time and the harvest,
  Our life, our health, our food.
Accept the gifts we offer
  For all Thy love imparts,
And, what Thou most desirest,
  Our humble, thankful hearts.
            MATTHIAS CLAUDIUS, 1740-1815; tr.
                by JANE MONTGOMERY CAMPBELL,
                1817-78.

619   77. 77. D.

COME, ye thankful people, come,
    Raise the song of harvest-home:
All is safely gathered in,
Ere the winter storms begin;
God, our Maker, doth provide
For our wants to be supplied:
Come to God's own temple, come,
Raise the song of harvest-home.

2 All this world is God's own field,
Fruit unto His praise to yield;
Wheat and tares together sown,
Unto joy or sorrow grown;
First the blade, and then the ear,
Then the full corn shall appear:
Lord of harvest, grant that we
Wholesome grain and pure may be.

3 For the Lord our God shall come,
And shall take His harvest home;
From His field shall in that day
All offences purge away;
Give His angels charge at last
In the fire the tares to cast;
But the fruitful ears to store
In His garner evermore.

4 Even so, Lord, quickly come ;
  Bring Thy final harvest home :
  Gather Thou Thy people in,
  Free from sorrow, free from sin ;
  There, for ever purified,
  In Thy garner to abide :
  Come, with all Thine angels, come,
  Raise the glorious harvest-home.
                HENRY ALFORD, 1810–71.

620   77. 77.

PRAISE, O praise our God and
    King ;
Hymns of adoration sing ;
  For His mercies still endure,
  Ever faithful, ever sure.

2 Praise Him that He made the sun
  Day by day his course to run ;—
    For His mercies still endure,
    Ever faithful, ever sure ;—

3 And the silver moon, by night
  Shining with her gentle light ;
    For His mercies still endure,
    Ever faithful, ever sure.

4 Praise Him that He gave the rain
  To mature the swelling grain ;—
    For His mercies still endure,
    Ever faithful, ever sure ;—

5 And hath bid the fruitful field
  Crops of precious increase yield ;
    For His mercies still endure,
    Ever faithful, ever sure.

6 Praise Him for our harvest-store ;
  He hath filled the garner floor ;—
    For His mercies still endure,
    Ever faithful, ever sure ;—

7 And for richer food than this,
  Pledge of everlasting bliss ;
    For His mercies still endure,
    Ever faithful, ever sure.

8 Glory to our bounteous King !
  Glory let creation sing,
    Glory to the Father, Son,
    And blest Spirit, Three in One !
              HENRY WILLIAMS BAKER,
                          1821–77.

621   *Autumn.*   76. 76.

THE year is swiftly waning,
    The summer days are past ;
And life, brief life, is speeding ;
    The end is nearing fast.

2 The ever-changing seasons
    In silence come and go ;
  But Thou, eternal Father,
    No time or change canst know.

3 O pour Thy grace upon us,
    That we may worthier be,
  Each year that passes o'er us,
    To dwell in heaven with Thee.

4 Behold, the bending orchards
    With bounteous fruit are crowned :
  Lord, in our hearts more richly
    Let heavenly fruits abound.

5 O by each mercy sent us,
    And by each grief and pain,
  By blessings like the sunshine,
    And sorrows like the rain,

6 Our barren hearts make fruitful
    With every goodly grace,
  That we Thy Name may hallow,
    And see at last Thy face.
              WILLIAM WALSHAM HOW,
                          1823–97.

Winter (622–623).

622   77. 77.

WINTER reigneth o'er the land,
    Freezing with its icy breath ;
Dead and bare the tall trees stand ;
  All is chill and drear as death.

2 Yet it seemeth but a day
    Since the summer flowers were
      here,
  Since they stacked the balmy hay,
    Since they reaped the golden ear.

3 Sunny days are past and gone ;
    So the years go, speeding fast,
  Onward ever, each new one
    Swifter speeding than the last.

4 Life is waning ; life is brief ;
    Death, like winter, standeth nigh :
  Each one, like the falling leaf,
    Soon shall fade, and fall, and die.

5 But the sleeping earth shall wake ;
    New-born flowers shall burst in
      bloom,
  And all nature, rising, break
    Glorious from its wintry tomb.

6 So the saints, from slumber blest
　　Rising, shall awake and sing,
And our flesh in hope shall rest,
　　Till there breaks the endless spring.
　　　　　WILLIAM WALSHAM HOW,
　　　　　　　　　1823–97.

623

L. M.

'TIS winter now; the fallen snow
　　Has left the heavens all coldly
　　clear;
Through leafless boughs the sharp
　　winds blow,
　　And all the earth lies dead and
　　drear.

2 And yet God's love is not with-
　　drawn;
　　His life within the keen air
　　breathes;

His beauty paints the crimson dawn,
　　And clothes the boughs with
　　glittering wreaths.

3 And though abroad the sharp winds
　　blow,
　　And skies are chill, and frosts are
　　keen,
Home closer draws her circle now,
　　And warmer glows her light
　　within.

4 O God! who giv'st the winter's
　　cold,
　　As well as summer's joyous rays,
Us warmly in Thy love enfold,
　　And keep us through life's wintry
　　days.
　　　　　SAMUEL LONGFELLOW, 1819–92.

624

98. 89.

GOD be with you till we meet again,
By His counsels guide, uphold
you,
With His sheep securely fold you :
God be with you till we meet again.

2 God be with you till we meet again,
'Neath His wings protecting hide
you,
Daily manna still divide you :
God be with you till we meet again.

3 God be with you till we meet again,
When life's perils thick confound
you,
Put His arms unfailing round you :
God be with you till we meet again.

4 God be with you till we meet again,
Keep love's banner floating o'er
you,
Smite death's threatening wave be-
fore you :
God be with you till we meet again.

JEREMIAH EAMES RANKIN,
1828–1904.

Seafarers (625–627).

625

C. M.

O LORD, be with us when we sail
Upon the lonely deep,
Our Guard when on the silent deck
The midnight watch we keep.

2 We need not fear, though all around,
'Mid rising winds, we hear
The multitude of waters surge ;
For Thou, O God, art near.

3 The calm, the breeze, the gale, the
storm,
That pass from land to land,
All, all are Thine—are held within
The hollow of Thy hand.

4 As when on blue Gennesaret
Rose high the angry wave,
And Thy disciples quailed in dread,
One word of Thine could save,

5 So when the fiercer storms arise
From man's unbridled will,
Be Thou, Lord, present in our hearts,
To whisper, 'Peace, be still !'

6 Across this troubled tide of life
Thyself our Pilot be,
Until we reach that better land,
The land that knows no sea.

7 To Thee the Father, Thee the Son,
Whom earth and sky adore,
And Spirit, moving o'er the deep,
Be praise for evermore.

EDWIN ARTHUR DAYMAN,
1807–90.

626

88. 88. 88.

ETERNAL Father, strong to save,
Whose arm hath bound the rest-
less wave,
Who bidd'st the mighty ocean deep
Its own appointed limits keep :
O hear us when we cry to Thee
For those in peril on the sea.

2 O Christ, whose voice the waters
heard,
And hushed their raging at Thy word,
Who walkedst on the foaming deep,
And calm amid the storm didst sleep :
O hear us when we cry to Thee
For those in peril on the sea.

3 O Holy Spirit, who didst brood
Upon the waters dark and rude,
And bid their angry tumult cease,
And give, for wild confusion, peace :
O hear us when we cry to Thee
For those in peril on the sea.

4 O Trinity of love and power,
Our brethren shield in danger's hour ;
From rock and tempest, fire and foe,
Protect them wheresoe'er they go :
Thus evermore shall rise to Thee
Glad hymns of praise from land and
sea.

WILLIAM WHITING, 1825–78.

627

87. 84.

STAR of peace to wanderers weary,
Bright the beams that smile on
me ;
Cheer the pilot's vision dreary,
Far, far at sea.

2 Star of hope, gleam on the billow ;
Bless the soul that sighs for Thee ;
Bless the sailor's lonely pillow,
Far, far at sea.

3 Star of faith, when winds are mocking
All his toil, he flies to Thee ;
Save him on the billows rocking,
Far, far at sea.

4 Star Divine, O safely guide him ;
 Bring the wanderer home to Thee ;
Sore temptations long have tried
    him,
    Far, far at sea.
                    JANE CROSS SIMPSON,
                        1811–86.

628
                                L. M.

WHOM oceans part, O Lord, unite
 To love Thy Name, and seek
    Thy light :
Though from each other far we be,
Let none, O Christ, be far from Thee.

2 On many a distant island shore
Still let men see heaven's opened
    door ;
'Mid silent hills, beneath fresh skies,
Let Bethel's shining ladder rise.

3 Bring thoughts of home and Christian
    ways
To those who miss sweet Sabbath
    days ;
The long-forgotten prayer recall
To those who sin, and mourn their
    fall.

4 Our sons and daughters guide in
    truth ;
Take for Thyself the flower of youth ;
Afar from home, through gain or loss,
Keep them true-hearted to Thy
    Cross.

5 Whom oceans part, O Lord, unite—
One commonwealth for God and
    right,
A ransomed people, strong and free,
To bring the whole wide world to
    Thee !
                    HOWELL ELVET LEWIS,
                        1860–1953.

629
                                85. 83.

HOLY Father, in Thy mercy,
 Hear our anxious prayer ;
Keep our loved ones, now far distant,
    'Neath Thy care.

2 Jesus, Saviour, let Thy presence
Be their light and guide ;
Keep, O keep them, in their weak-
    ness,
    At Thy side.

3 When in sorrow, when in danger,
    When in loneliness,
In Thy love look down and comfort
    Their distress.

4 May the joy of Thy salvation
    Be their strength and stay ;
May they love and may they praise
    Thee
    Day by day.

5 Holy Spirit, let Thy teaching
    Sanctify their life ;
Send Thy grace that they may con-
    quer
    In the strife.

6 Father, Son, and Holy Spirit,
    God the One in Three,
Bless them, guide them, save them,
    keep them
    Near to Thee.
                    ISABEL STEPHANA STEVENSON,
                        1843–90.

630
                            66. 66. 88.

FATHER, who art alone
 Our helper and our stay,
O hear us, as we plead
For loved ones far away,
And shield with Thine almighty hand
Our wanderers by sea and land.

2 For Thou, our Father God,
    Art present everywhere,
And bendest low Thine ear
    To catch the faintest prayer,
Waiting rich blessings to bestow
On all Thy children here below.

3 O compass with Thy love
    The daily path they tread ;
And may Thy light and truth
    Upon their hearts be shed,
That, one in all things with Thy will,
Heaven's peace and joy their souls
    may fill.

4 Guard them from every harm
    When dangers still assail,
And teach them that Thy power
    Can never, never fail ;
We cannot with our loved ones be,
But trust them, Father, unto Thee.

5 We all are travellers here
    Along life's various road,
Meeting and parting oft
    Till we shall mount to God,—
At home at last, with those we love,
Within the fatherland above.
                    EDITH JONES, 1849–1929.

NATIONAL HYMNS

631
664. 6664.

GOD save our gracious Queen,
Long live our noble Queen;
God save the Queen!
Send her victorious,
Happy and glorious,
Long to reign over us :
God save the Queen!

2 Thy choicest gifts in store
On her be pleased to pour;
Long may she reign;
May she defend our laws,
And ever give us cause
To sing with heart and voice,
'God save the Queen!'

632
664. 6664.

GOD bless our native land ;
God's all-protecting hand
Still guard our shore :
May peace her sway extend,
Foe be transformed to friend,
And Britain's power depend
On war no more.

2 Lord God, our monarch bless ;
Girded with righteousness,
Long may she reign !
Her heart inspire and move
With wisdom from above ;
Throned on a nation's love,
Her power maintain.

3 Break, Lord, all lawless might ;
Founded in truth and right,
Stablish our laws ;
God of all equity,
Set Thou the captive free ;
Give the poor liberty,
Judge Thou his cause.

4 Nor on this land alone,
But be Thy mercies known
From shore to shore.
Lord, make the nations see
All men should brothers be,
One league, one family,
One, the world o'er.

WILLIAM EDWARD HICKSON,
1803–70.

633
C. M.

LORD, while for all mankind we
pray,
Of every clime and coast,
O hear us for our native land,
The land we love the most.

2 Our fathers' sepulchres are here,
And here our kindred dwell,
Our children too ; how should we
love
Another land so well ?

3 O guard our shores from every foe ;
With peace our borders bless ;
With prosperous times our cities
crown,
Our fields with plenteousness.

4 Unite us in the sacred love
Of knowledge, truth, and Thee ;
And let our hills and valleys shout
The songs of liberty.

5 Lord of the nations, thus to Thee
Our country we commend ;
Be Thou her refuge and her trust,
Her everlasting Friend.

JOHN REYNELL WREFORD,
1800–81.

634
L. M.

PRAISE to our God, whose
bounteous hand
Prepared of old our glorious land,
A garden fenced with silver sea,
A people prosperous, strong, and
free !

2 Praise to our God ! through all our
past
His mighty arm hath held us fast,
Till wars and perils, toils and tears,
Have brought the rich and peaceful
years.

3 Praise to our God ! the vine He set
Within our coasts is fruitful yet ;
On many a shore her seedlings grow ;
'Neath many a sun her clusters glow.

4 Praise to our God ! His power alone
Can keep unmoved our ancient
throne,
Sustained by counsels wise and just,
And guarded by a people's trust.

5 Praise to our God ! though chasten-
      ings stern
Our evil dross should throughly burn,
His rod and staff, from age to age,
Shall rule and guide His heritage.

JOHN ELLERTON, 1826–93.

635
66. 66. and refrain.

TO Thee our God we fly
    For mercy and for grace ;
O hear our lowly cry,
    And hide not Thou Thy face.
    O Lord, stretch forth Thy mighty
       hand,
      And guard and bless our father-
       land.

2 Arise, O Lord of hosts !
    Be jealous for Thy Name,
And drive from out our coasts
    The sins that put to shame.

3 Give peace, Lord, in our time ;
    O let no foe draw nigh,
Nor lawless deed of crime
    Insult Thy majesty.

4 The powers ordained by Thee
    With heavenly wisdom bless ;
May they Thy servants be,
    And rule in righteousness.

5 The Church of Thy dear Son
    Inflame with love's pure fire ;
Bind her once more in one,
    And life and truth inspire.

6 Thy best gifts from on high
    In rich abundance pour,
That we may magnify
    And praise Thee more and more.

WILLIAM WALSHAM HOW,
1823–97.

636
87. 87. 87.

JUDGE Eternal, throned in splen-
    dour,
    Lord of lords and King of kings,
With Thy living fire of judgment
    Purge this land of bitter things ;
Solace all its wide dominion
    With the healing of Thy wings.

2 Still the weary folk are pining
    For the hour that brings release ;
And the city's crowded clangour
    Cries aloud for sin to cease ;
And the homesteads and the wood-
    lands
    Plead in silence for their peace.

3 Crown, O God, Thine own en-
    deavour ;
    Cleave our darkness with Thy
      sword ;
Feed the faint and hungry heathen
    With the richness of Thy word ;
Cleanse the body of this Empire
    Through the glory of the Lord.

HENRY SCOTT HOLLAND,
1847–1918.

637
Recessional. 88. 88. 88.

GOD of our fathers, known of old,
    Lord of our far-flung battle-line,
Beneath whose awful hand we hold
    Dominion over palm and pine—
Lord God of hosts, be with us yet,
Lest we forget—lest we forget !

2 The tumult and the shouting dies ;
    The captains and the kings depart :
Still stands Thine ancient sacrifice,
    An humble and a contrite heart.
Lord God of hosts, be with us yet,
Lest we forget—lest we forget !

3 Far-called, our navies melt away ;
    On dune and headland sinks the
      fire :
Lo, all our pomp of yesterday
    Is one with Nineveh and Tyre !
Judge of the nations, spare us yet,
Lest we forget—lest we forget !

4 If, drunk with sight of power, we
    loose
    Wild tongues that have not Thee
     in awe,
Such boastings as the Gentiles use,
    Or lesser breeds without the law—
Lord God of hosts, be with us yet,
Lest we forget—lest we forget !

5 For heathen heart that puts her trust
    In reeking tube and iron shard,
All valiant dust that builds on dust,
    And, guarding, calls not Thee to
     guard,
For frantic boast and foolish word—
Thy mercy on Thy people, Lord !

RUDYARD KIPLING, 1865–1936.

638

76. 76. D.

O GOD of earth and altar,
  Bow down and hear our cry ;
Our earthly rulers falter,
  Our people drift and die ;
The walls of gold entomb us,
  The swords of scorn divide,
Take not Thy thunder from us,
  But take away our pride.

2 From all that terror teaches,
  From lies of tongue and pen,
From all the easy speeches
  That comfort cruel men,
From sale and profanation
  Of honour and the sword,
From sleep and from damnation,
  Deliver us, good Lord !

3 Tie in a living tether
  The prince and priest and thrall ;
Bind all our lives together,
  Smite us and save us all ;
In ire and exultation,
  Aflame with faith, and free,
Lift up a living nation,
  A single sword to Thee.
          GILBERT KEITH CHESTERTON,
                1874–1936.

639

L. M.

THESE things shall be : a loftier race
  Than e'er the world hath known,
    shall rise,
With flame of freedom in their souls
  And light of knowledge in their
    eyes.

2 They shall be gentle, brave, and
    strong,
  To spill no drop of blood, but dare
All that may plant man's lordship
    firm
  On earth, and fire, and sea, and air.

3 Nation with nation, land with land,
  Inarmed shall live as comrades free ;
In every heart and brain shall throb
  The pulse of one fraternity.

4 Man shall love man, with heart as
    pure
  And fervent as the young-eyed
    throng
Who chant their heavenly psalms
    before
  God's face with undiscordant song.

5 New arts shall bloom of loftier mould,
  And mightier music thrill the skies,
And every life shall be a song,
  When all the earth is paradise.

6 There shall be no more sin, nor
    shame,
  Though pain and passion may not
    die ;
For man shall be at one with God
  In bonds of firm necessity.
          JOHN ADDINGTON SYMONDS,
                1840–93.

640

D. L. M.

AND did those feet in ancient time
  Walk upon England's mountains
    green ?
And was the Holy Lamb of God
  On England's pleasant pastures
    seen ?
And did the countenance divine
  Shine forth upon our clouded hills ?
And was Jerusalem builded here
  Among these dark satanic mills ?

2 Bring me my bow of burning gold !
  Bring me my arrows of desire !
Bring me my spear ! O clouds, un-
    fold !
  Bring me my chariot of fire !
I will not cease from mental fight,
  Nor shall my sword sleep in my
    hand,
Till we have built Jerusalem
  In England's green and pleasant
    land.
          WILLIAM BLAKE, 1757–1827.

641

11 10. 11 9.

GOD the Omnipotent ! King, who
    ordainest
  Great winds Thy clarions, light-
    nings Thy sword :
Show forth Thy pity on high where
    Thou reignest ;
  Give to us peace in our time, O
    Lord.

2 God the All-merciful ! earth hath
    forsaken
  Meekness and mercy, and slighted
    Thy word ;
Bid not Thy wrath in its terrors
    awaken ;
  Give to us peace in our time, O
    Lord.

3 God the All-righteous One ! man
    hath defied Thee ;
    Yet to eternity standeth Thy word ;
Falsehood and wrong shall not tarry
    beside Thee ;
    Give to us peace in our time, O
        Lord.

4 God the All-wise ! by the fire of Thy
    chastening,
    Earth shall to freedom and truth
        be restored ;
Through the thick darkness Thy
    Kingdom is hastening ;
    Thou wilt give peace in Thy time,
        O Lord.

5 So shall Thy children, with thankful
    devotion,
    Praise Him who saved them from
        peril and sword,
Singing in chorus, from ocean to
    ocean,
    Peace to the nations, and praise to
        the Lord.
            HENRY FOTHERGILL CHORLEY,
                1808–72, and JOHN ELLERTON,
                1826–93.

642   *For use overseas.*   11 10. 11 10.

GOD of Eternity, Lord of the Ages,
    Father and Spirit and Saviour
        of men !
Thine is the glory of time's numbered
    pages ;
Thine is the power to revive us again.

2 Thankful, we come to Thee, Lord of
    the nations,
    Praising Thy faithfulness, mercy, and
        grace,
Shown to our fathers in past genera-
    tions,
    Pledge of Thy love to our people and
        race.

3 Far from our ancient home, sundered
    by oceans,
    Zion is builded, and God is adored :
Lift we our hearts in united devotions !
    Ends of the earth, join in praise to
        the Lord.

4 Beauteous this land of ours, bounti-
    ful Giver !
    Brightly the heavens Thy glory de-
        clare ;

Streameth the sunlight on hill, plain,
    and river,
Shineth Thy Cross over fields rich
    and fair.

5 Pardon our sinfulness, God of all
    pity,
Call to remembrance Thy mercies of
    old ;
Strengthen Thy Church to abide as
    a city
Set on a hill for a light to Thy fold.

6 Head of the Church on earth, risen,
    ascended !
Thine is the honour that dwells in
    this place :
As Thou hast blessed us through
    years that have ended,
Still lift upon us the light of Thy face.
            ERNEST NORTHCROFT MERRINGTON,
                1876–1953.

643   D. C. M.

GREAT King of nations, hear our
    prayer,
    While at Thy feet we fall,
And humbly with united cry
    To Thee for mercy call.
The guilt is ours, but grace is Thine ;
    O turn us not away,
But hear us from Thy lofty throne,
    And help us when we pray.

2 Our fathers' sins were manifold,
    And ours no less we own ;
Yet wondrously from age to age
    Thy goodness hath been shown.
When dangers, like a stormy sea,
    Beset our country round,
To Thee we looked, to Thee we
    cried,
    And help in Thee was found.

3 With one consent we meekly bow
    Beneath Thy chastening hand,
And, pouring forth confession meet,
    Mourn with our mourning land.
With pitying eye behold our need,
    As thus we lift our prayer ;
Correct us with Thy judgments,
    Lord,
    Then let Thy mercy spare.
            JOHN HAMPDEN GURNEY,
                1802–62.

644
D. C. M.

WHAT service shall we render
thee,
O Fatherland we love?
What gift of hand, or heart, or brain
May our devotion prove?
The coming age invokes our aid,
Thy voice of old inspires;
Shall we, its sons and daughters, be
Less worthy than our sires?

2 The service of the commonwealth
Is not in arms alone;
A nobler chivalry shall rise
Than have been known:
Glad rivalries in arts of peace,
True ministries of life,
Shall supersede the arts of war
And calm our feverish strife.

3 Too long the pagan rule of force
Has held the world in thrall;
Too long the clash of arms has
drowned
The higher human call.
O comrades, seek a nobler quest!
O keep a worthier tryst!
The laws of hate have had their day;
Proclaim the laws of Christ!

4 Lord of the nations, far and near,
Send forth Thy quickening breath,
Equip us for the tasks of life,
Save us from deeds of death;
Enlist us in Thy ranks to fight
Fair freedom's holy war,
Whose battle-cry is 'Brotherhood',
Far-flung from shore to shore.

ERNEST JAMES DODGSHUN, 1876–1944.

645
The League of Nations.
11 10. 11 10 10.

FATHER Eternal, Ruler of Crea-
tion,
Spirit of Life, which moved ere
form was made,
Through the thick darkness covering
every nation,
Light to man's blindness, O be
Thou our aid!
*Thy Kingdom come, O Lord, Thy
will be done.*

2 Races and peoples, lo! we stand
divided,
And, sharing not our griefs, no joy
can share;

By wars and tumults Love is mocked,
derided,
His conquering Cross no kingdom
wills to bear;
*Thy Kingdom come, O Lord, Thy
will be done.*

3 Envious of heart, blind-eyed, with
tongues confounded,
Nation by nation still goes un-
forgiven;
In wrath and fear, by jealousies surrounded,
Building proud towers which shall
not reach to heaven.
*Thy Kingdom come, O Lord, Thy
will be done.*

4 Lust of possession worketh desolations;
There is no meekness in the sons
of earth.
Led by no star, the rulers of the
nations
Still fail to bring us to the blissful
birth.
*Thy Kingdom come, O Lord, Thy
will be done.*

5 How shall we love Thee, holy, hidden
Being,
If we love not the world which
Thou hast made?
O, give us brother-love, for better
seeing
Thy Word made flesh and in a
manger laid.
*Thy Kingdom come, O Lord, Thy
will be done.*

LAURENCE HOUSMAN, 1865–1959.

646
L. M.

O GOD of love, O King of peace,
Make wars throughout the world
to cease;
The wrath of sinful man restrain:
Give peace, O God, give peace again.

2 Remember, Lord, Thy works of old,
The wonders that our fathers told;
Remember not our sin's dark stain:
Give peace, O God, give peace again.

3 Whom shall we trust but Thee, O
Lord?
Where rest but on Thy faithful word?
None ever called on Thee in vain:
Give peace, O God, give peace again.

4 Where saints and angels dwell above,
All hearts are knit in holy love ;
O bind us in that heavenly chain :
Give peace, O God, give peace again.

HENRY WILLIAMS BAKER,
1821–77.

647

L. M.

LAND of our Birth, we pledge to thee
Our love and toil in the years to be ;
When we are grown and take our place,
As men and women with our race.

2 Father in heaven, who lovest all,
O help Thy children when they call ;
That they may build from age to age,
An undefilèd heritage.

3 Teach us to bear the yoke in youth,
With steadfastness and careful truth ;
That, in our time, Thy grace may give
The truth whereby the nations live.

4 Teach us to rule ourselves alway,
Controlled and cleanly night and day ;
That we may bring, if need arise,
No maimed or worthless sacrifice.

5 Teach us to look, in all our ends,
On Thee for Judge, and not our friends ;
That we, with Thee, may walk uncowed
By fear or favour of the crowd.

6 Teach us the strength that cannot seek,
By deed or thought, to hurt the weak ;
That, under Thee, we may possess
Man's strength to succour man's distress.

7 Teach us delight in simple things,
And mirth that has no bitter springs :
Forgiveness free of evil done,
And love to all men 'neath the sun !

8 *Land of our Birth, our faith, our pride,*
For whose dear sake our fathers died ;
O Motherland, we pledge to thee,
Head, heart, and hand through the years to be !

RUDYARD JOSEPH KIPLING, 1865–1936.

HOME AND SCHOOL

Family Life (648–650).

648

11 10. 11 10.

O HAPPY home, where Thou art
    loved the dearest,
  Thou loving Friend, and Saviour
    of our race,
And where among the guests there
    never cometh
  One who can hold such high and
    honoured place !

2 O happy home, where two in heart
    united
  In holy faith and blessèd hope are
    one,
Whom death a little while alone
    divideth,
  And cannot end the union here
    begun !

3 O happy home, whose little ones are
    given
  Early to Thee, in humble faith and
    prayer,—
To Thee, their Friend, who from the
    heights of heaven
  Dost guide and guard with more
    than mother's care !

4 O happy home, where each one serves
    Thee, lowly,
  Whatever his appointed work may
    be,
Till every common task seems great
    and holy,
  When it is done, O Lord, as unto
    Thee !

5 O happy home, where Thou art not
    forgotten
  When joy is overflowing, full and
    free :
O happy home, where every wounded
    spirit
  Is brought, Physician, Comforter,
    to Thee :

6 Until at last, when earth's day's-
    work is ended,
  All meet Thee in the blessèd home
    above,
From whence Thou camest, where
    Thou hast ascended,
  Thy everlasting home of peace and
    love !

KARL JOHANN PHILIPP SPITTA, 1801–
    59 ; tr. by SARAH LAURIE FIND-
    LATER, 1823–1907.

649

L. M.

THOU gracious Power, whose
    mercy lends
The light of home, the smile of
    friends,
Our gathered flock Thine arms
    enfold,
As in the peaceful days of old.

2 Wilt Thou not hear us while we raise,
In sweet accord of solemn praise,
The voices that have mingled long
In joyous flow of mirth and song ?

3 For all the blessings life has brought,
For all its sorrowing hours have
    taught,
For all we mourn, for all we keep,
The hands we clasp, the loved that
    sleep,

4 The noontide sunshine of the past,
These brief, bright moments fading
    fast,
The stars that gild our darkening
    years,
The twilight ray from holier spheres,

5 We thank Thee, Father ; let Thy
    grace
Our loving circle still embrace,
Thy mercy shed its heavenly store,
Thy peace be with us evermore.

OLIVER WENDELL HOLMES,
1809–94.

650

6 10. 10 10.

FATHER, our children keep ;
    We know not what is coming
    on the earth ;
Beneath the shadow of Thy
    heavenly wing
O keep them, keep them, Thou who
    gav'st them birth.

2   Father, draw nearer us ;
Draw firmer round us Thy protecting
    arm ;
  O clasp our children closer to Thy
    side,
Uninjured in the day of earth's
    alarm.

3   Them in Thy chambers hide ;
O hide them and preserve them calm
       and safe,
When sin abounds, and error flows
       abroad,
And Satan tempts, and human pas-
       sions chafe.

4   O keep them undefiled,
Unspotted from a tempting world of
       sin,
That, clothed in white, through the
       bright city-gates,
They may with us in triumph enter
       in.

       HORATIUS BONAR, 1808–89.

651   *Daily Work.*   L. M.

FORTH in Thy Name, O Lord,
    I go,
My daily labour to pursue,
Thee, only Thee, resolved to know
In all I think, or speak, or do.

2 The task Thy wisdom hath assigned
    O let me cheerfully fulfil,
In all my works Thy presence find,
    And prove Thy good and perfect
       will.

3 Thee may I set at my right hand,
    Whose eyes mine inmost substance
       see,
And labour on at Thy command,
    And offer all my works to Thee.

4 Give me to bear Thy easy yoke,
    And every moment watch and pray,
And still to things eternal look,
    And hasten to Thy glorious day ;

5 For Thee delightfully employ
    Whate'er Thy bounteous grace
       hath given,
And run my course with even joy,
    And closely walk with Thee to
       heaven.

       CHARLES WESLEY, 1707–88.

652   *A Mother's Prayer.*   87. 87. 87.

LORD of Life and King of Glory,
   Who didst deign a child to be,
Cradled on a mother's bosom,
   Throned upon a mother's knee :
For the children Thou hast given
   We must answer unto Thee.

2 Since the day the blessèd mother
   Thee, the world's Redeemer, bore,
Thou hast crowned us with an
       honour
Women never knew before ;
   And, that we may bear it meetly,
We must seek Thine aid the more.

3 Grant us, then, pure hearts and
       patient,
   That, in all we do or say,
Little souls our deeds may copy,
   And be never led astray :
Little feet our steps may follow
   In a safe and narrow way.

4 When our growing sons and daugh-
       ters
   Look on life with eager eyes,
Grant us then a deeper insight,
   And new powers of sacrifice :
Hope to trust them, faith to guide
       them,
   Love that nothing good denies.

5 May we keep our holy calling
   Stainless in its fair renown,
That, when all the work is over,
   And we lay the burden down,
Then the children Thou hast given
   Still may be our joy and crown.

       CHRISTIAN BURKE, 1859–1944.

For Little Children (653–671).

653   446. D.

THE morning bright,
    With rosy light,
Has waked me up from sleep
    Father, I own,
    Thy love alone
Thy little one doth keep.

2   All through the day,
      I humbly pray,
Be Thou my Guard and Guide ;
    My sins forgive,
    And let me live,
Blest Jesus, near Thy side.

3   O make Thy rest
      Within my breast,
Great Spirit of all grace ;
    Make me like Thee,
    Then shall I be
Prepared to see Thy face.

       THOMAS OSMOND SUMMERS,
               1812–82.

HOME AND SCHOOL

654 87. 87.

JESUS, tender Shepherd, hear me;
Bless Thy little lamb to-night;
Through the darkness be Thou near
me;
Watch my sleep till morning light.

2 All this day Thy hand has led me,
And I thank Thee for Thy care;
Thou hast clothed me, warmed and
fed me;
Listen to my evening prayer.

3 Let my sins be all forgiven;
Bless the friends I love so well;
Take me, when I die, to heaven,
Happy there with Thee to dwell.
MARY LUNDIE DUNCAN,
1814-40.

655 C. M.

LORD, I would own Thy tender
care,
And all Thy love to me;
The food I eat, the clothes I wear,
Are all bestowed by Thee.

2 'Tis Thou preservest me from death
And dangers every hour;
I cannot draw another breath
Unless Thou give me power.

3 Kind angels guard me every night,
As round my bed they stay;
Nor am I absent from Thy sight
In darkness or by day.

4 My health and friends and parents
dear
To me by God are given;
I have not any blessing here
But what is sent from heaven.

5 Such goodness, Lord, and constant
care
A child can ne'er repay;
But may it be my daily prayer
To love Thee and obey.
JANE TAYLOR, 1783-1824.

656 L. M.

BE present at our table, Lord,
Be here and everywhere adored;
These mercies bless, and grant that
we
May feast in Paradise with Thee.
JOHN CENNICK, 1718-55.

657 11 11. 11 11.

AWAY in a manger, no crib for a
bed,
The little Lord Jesus laid down His
sweet head.
The stars in the bright sky looked
down where He lay,
The little Lord Jesus asleep on the
hay.

2 The cattle are lowing, the Baby
awakes,
But little Lord Jesus no crying He
makes.
I love Thee, Lord Jesus! Look down
from the sky,
And stay by my side until morning
is nigh.

3 Be near me, Lord Jesus; I ask Thee
to stay
Close by me for ever, and love me,
I pray.
Bless all the dear children in Thy
tender care,
And fit us for heaven, to live with
Thee there.
Anon.

658 77. 77. and refrain.

CHILDREN of Jerusalem
Sang the praise of Jesus' name:
Children, too, of modern days
Join to sing the Saviour's praise.
*Hark! while infant voices sing
Loud hosannas to our King.*

2 We are taught to love the Lord,
We are taught to read His word,
We are taught the way to heaven:
Praise for all to God be given.

3 Parents, teachers, old and young,
All unite to swell the song;
Higher and yet higher rise,
Till hosannas reach the skies.
JOHN HENLEY, 1800-42.

659 Irr.

WHEN mothers of Salem
Their children brought to
Jesus,
The stern disciples drove them
back and bade them depart;

206

FOR LITTLE CHILDREN

But Jesus saw them ere they fled,
And sweetly smiled, and kindly said,
' Suffer little children
To come unto Me.

2 ' For I will receive them
And fold them to My bosom ;
I'll be a Shepherd to these lambs,
O drive them not away ;
For, if their hearts to Me give,
They shall with Me in glory live :
Suffer little children
To come unto Me.'

3 How kind was our Saviour
To bid these children welcome !
But there are many thousands who
have never learned His name ;
The Bible they have never read ;
They know not that the Saviour said,
' Suffer little children
To come unto Me.'

4 O soon may the heathen,
Of every tribe and nation,
Fulfil Thy blessèd word, and cast
their idols all away ;
O shine upon them from above,
And show Thyself a God of love ;
Teach the little children
To come unto Thee.

WILLIAM MEDLEN HUTCHINGS,
1827–76.

660
77. 77. and refrain.

JESUS loves me ! this I know,
For the Bible tells me so ;
Little ones to Him belong ;
They are weak, but He is strong.
Yes ! Jesus loves me !
The Bible tells me so.

2 Jesus loves me ! He who died
Heaven's gate to open wide ;
He will wash away my sin,
Let His little child come in.

3 Jesus loves me ! He will stay
Close beside me all the way ;
Then His little child will take
Up to heaven, for His dear sake.

ANNA BARTLETT WARNER,
1820–1915.

661
87. 87. D.

LORD, a little band and lowly,
We are come to sing to Thee ;
Thou art great and high and holy ;
O how solemn we should be !

Fill our hearts with thoughts of Jesus,
And of heaven, where He is
gone ;
And let nothing ever please us
He would grieve to look upon.

2 For we know the Lord of glory
Always sees what children do,
And is writing now the story
Of our thoughts and actions too.
Let our sins be all forgiven ;
Make us fear whate'er is wrong :
Lead us on our way to heaven,
There to sing a nobler song.

MARTHA EVANS SHELLY,
1812–1901.

662
77. 77.

GENTLE Jesus, meek and mild,
Look upon a little child,
Pity my simplicity,
Suffer me to come to Thee.

2 Lamb of God, I look to Thee ;
Thou shalt my example be ;
Thou art gentle, meek, and mild :
Thou wast once a little child.

3 Fain I would be as Thou art ;
Give me Thy obedient heart ;
Thou art pitiful and kind ;
Let me have Thy loving mind.

4 Loving Jesus, gentle Lamb,
In Thy gracious hands I am ;
Make me, Saviour, what Thou art ;
Live Thyself within my heart.

5 I shall then show forth Thy praise,
Serve Thee all my happy days ;
Then the world shall always see
Christ, the Holy Child, in me.

CHARLES WESLEY, 1707–88.

663
65. 65.

DO no sinful action ;
Speak no angry word ;
Ye belong to Jesus,
Children of the Lord.

2 Christ is kind and gentle,
Christ is pure and true,
And His little children
Must be holy too.

3 There 's a wicked spirit
Watching round you still
And he tries to tempt you
To all harm and ill.

4 But ye must not hear him,
   Though 't is hard for you
To resist the evil,
   And the good to do.

5 Christ is your own Master ;
   He is good and true,
And His little children
   Must be holy too.

CECIL FRANCES ALEXANDER,
1818–95.

664   65. 75.

GOD is always near me,
   Hearing what I say,
Knowing all my thoughts and deeds,
   All my work and play.

2 God is always near me ;
   In the darkest night
He can see me just the same
   As by mid-day light.

3 God is always near me,
   Though so young and small ;
Not a look or word or thought,
   But God knows it all.

PHILIPP BLISS, 1838–76.

665   77. 77.

JESUS, holy, undefiled,
   Listen to a little child.
Thou hast sent the glorious light,
Chasing far the silent night.

2 Thou hast sent the sun to shine
O'er this glorious world of Thine,
Warmth to give, and pleasant glow,
On each tender flower below.

3 Now the little birds arise,
Chirping gaily in the skies ;
Thee their tiny voices praise
In the early songs they raise.

4 Thou by whom the birds are fed,
Give to me my daily bread ;
And Thy Holy Spirit give,
Without whom I cannot live.

5 Make me, Lord, obedient, mild,
As becomes a little child ;
All day long, in every way,
Teach me what to do and say.

6 Make me, Lord, in work and play,
Thine more truly every day ;
And, when Thou at last shalt come,
Take me to Thy heavenly home.

EMILY MARY SHAPCOTE,
1828–1909.

666   65. 65.

JESUS, high in glory,
   Lend a listening ear ;
When we bow before Thee,
   Children's praises hear.

2 Though Thou art so holy,
   Heaven's almighty King,
Thou wilt stoop to listen
   When Thy praise we sing.

3 We are little children,
   Weak and apt to stray ;
Saviour, guide and keep us
   In the heavenly way.

4 Save us, Lord, from sinning ;
   Watch us day by day ;
Help us now to love Thee ;
   Take our sins away.

5 Then, when Thou shalt call us
   To our heavenly home,
We will gladly answer,
   ' Saviour, Lord, we come.'

HARRIET BURN McKEEVER,
1807–86.

667   85. 83.

JESUS, Friend of little children,
   Be a friend to me ;
Take my hand and ever keep me
   Close to Thee.

2 Teach me how to grow in goodness
   Daily as I grow ;
Thou hast been a child, and surely
   Thou dost know.

3 Never leave me nor forsake me,
   Ever be my Friend ;
For I need Thee from life's dawning
   To its end.

WALTER JOHN MATHAMS,
1853–1931.

668   77. 77.

LOVING Shepherd of Thy sheep,
   Keep me, Lord, in safety
   keep ;
Nothing can Thy power withstand ;
None can pluck me from Thy hand.

2 Loving Shepherd, Thou didst give
Thine own life that I might live ;
May I love Thee day by day,
Gladly Thy sweet will obey.

FOR LITTLE CHILDREN

3 Loving Shepherd, ever near,
  Teach me still Thy voice to hear;
  Suffer not my feet to stray
  From the straight and narrow way.

4 Where Thou leadest may I go,
  Walking in Thy steps below;
  Then, before Thy Father's throne,
  Jesus, claim me for Thine own.
  JANE ELIZA LEESON, 1807–82.

669
65. 65. and refrain.

IF I come to Jesus,
  He will make me glad;
He will give me pleasure
  When my heart is sad.
    If I come to Jesus,
    Happy shall I be;
    He is gently calling
    Little ones like me.

2 If I come to Jesus,
    He will hear my prayer;
  He will love me dearly;
    He my sins did bear.

3 If I come to Jesus,
    He will take my hand,
  He will kindly lead me
    To a better land.

4 There with happy children,
    Robed in snowy white,
  I shall see my Saviour
    In that world so bright.
  FRANCES JANE VAN ALSTYNE,
  1820–1915.

670
76. 887.

O WHAT can little hands do
  To please the King of heaven?
The little hands some work may try,
  To help the poor in misery:
    Such grace to mine be given.

2 O what can little lips do
    To please the King of heaven?
  The little lips can praise and pray,
  And gentle words of kindness say:
    Such grace to mine be given.

3 O what can little eyes do
    To please the King of heaven?
  The little eyes can upward look,
  Can learn to read God's holy book:
    Such grace to mine be given.

4 O what can little hearts do
    To please the King of heaven?
  Young hearts, if God His Spirit send,
  Can love their Maker, Saviour,
    Friend:
    Such grace to mine be given.
    Anon.

671
55. 65. 64. 64.

JESUS bids us shine
  With a pure, clear light,
Like a little candle
  Burning in the night.
In this world is darkness;
  So let us shine,
You in your small corner,
  And I in mine.

2 Jesus bids us shine,
  First of all for Him;
Well He sees and knows it,
  If our light grows dim:
He looks down from heaven
  To see us shine,
You in your small corner,
  And I in mine.

3 Jesus bids us shine,
  Then, for all around
Many kinds of darkness
  In the world are found—
Sin, and want, and sorrow;
  So we must shine,
You in your small corner,
  And I in mine.
  SUSAN WARNER, 1819–85.

672
Facing the World.   L. M.

GO forth to life, O child of earth,
  Still mindful of thy heavenly
    birth:
Thou art not here for ease or sin,
But manhood's noble crown to win.

2 Though passion fires are in thy soul,
  Through Christ thou canst their
    flames control:
Though tempters strong beset thy
    way,
Through Christ thou art more strong
    than they.

3 Go on from innocence of youth
  To manly pureness, manly truth:
God's angels still are near to save,
And God Himself doth help the
    brave.

209

HOME AND SCHOOL

4 Then forth to life, O child of earth ;
Be worthy of thy heavenly birth :
For noble service thou art here ;
Thy neighbour help, thy God revere.
SAMUEL LONGFELLOW, 1819–92.

673 *A Boy's Prayer.* 66. 66. D.

GOD, who created me
Nimble and light of limb,
In three elements free,
To run, to ride, to swim ;
Not when the sense is dim,
But now from the heart of joy,
I would remember Him :
Take the thanks of a boy.

2 Jesus, King and Lord,
Whose are my foes to fight,
Gird me with Thy sword,
Swift and sharp and bright.
Thee would I serve if I might,
And conquer if I can :
From day-dawn till night,
Take the strength of a man.

3 Spirit of love and truth,
Breathing, in grosser clay,
The light and flame of youth,
Delight of men in the fray,
Wisdom in strength's decay :
From pain, strife, wrong to be free,
This best gift I pray—
Take my spirit to Thee.
HENRY CHARLES BEECHING,
1859–1919.

674 76. 76. Trochaic.

LOOKING upward every day,
Sunshine on our faces ;
Pressing onward every day
Toward the heavenly places ;

2 Growing every day in awe,
For Thy Name is holy ;
Learning every day to love
With a love more lowly ;

3 Walking every day more close
To our Elder Brother ;
Growing every day more true
Unto one another ;

4 Leaving every day behind
Something which might hinder ;
Running swifter every day ;
Growing purer, kinder,—

5 Lord, so pray we every day :
Hear us in Thy pity,
That we enter in at last
To the holy city.
MARY BUTLER, 1841–1916.

675 *A School Hymn.* C. M.

O JESUS, strong and pure and
true,
Before Thy feet we bow ;
The grace of earlier years renew,
And lead us onward now.

2 The joyous life that year by year
Within these walls is stored,
The golden hope, the gladsome cheer,
We bring to Thee, O Lord.

3 Our faith endow with keener powers,
With warmer glow our love ;
And draw these halting hearts of ours
From earth to things above.

4 In paths our bravest ones have trod,
O make us strong to go,
That we may give our lives to God,
In serving man below.

5 Scorn we the selfish aim or choice,
And love's high precept keep,
' Rejoice with those that do rejoice,
And weep with those that weep.'

6 So hence shall flow fresh strength
and grace,
As from a full-fed spring,
To make the world a better place,
And life a worthier thing.
WILLIAM WALSHAM HOW,
1823–97.

676 *Commemoration.*
11 10. 11 10. Dactylic.

PRAISE to our God, who with
love never swerving
Guides our endeavours, enfolds us
from harm,
Peace and prosperity, past our
deserving,
Showering upon us with bountiful
arm.

2 Gone are the labours, the joy, and
the sorrow ;
Lo, at the end we draw near to
adore,
Ere our full life is begun on the
morrow,
Childhood behind us and manhood before.

210

3 Shepherd of souls, O Door of salva-
    tion,
    Keep Thou Thy flock in Thine
      infinite care,
  Fold them as one in their last
    adoration,
    Ere in the distance divided they
      fare.

4 Though nevermore in one place all
    may gather,
    Though in life's battle we struggle
      apart,
  One be our Saviour, and One be our
    Father,
    Bind us together in faith and in
      heart.

          HERBERT BRANSTON GRAY,
              1851–1929.

677 *Beginning of Term.*   87. 87. 47.

L ORD, behold us with Thy blessing,
    Once again assembled here ;
  Onward be our footsteps pressing,
    In Thy love, and faith, and fear ;
      Still protect us
    By Thy presence ever near.

2 For Thy mercy we adore Thee,
    For this rest upon our way ;
  Lord, again we bow before Thee,
    Speed our labours day by day ;
      Mind and spirit
    With Thy choicest gifts array.

3 Keep the spell of home affection
    Still alive in every heart ;
  May its power, with mild direction,
    Draw our love from self apart,
      Till Thy children
    Feel that Thou their Father art.

4 Break temptation's fatal power,
    Shielding all with guardian care,
  Safe in every careless hour,
    Safe from sloth and sensual snare
      Thou, our Saviour,
    Still our failing strength repair.

          HENRY JAMES BUCKOLL,
              1803–71.

678 *End of Term.*   87. 87. 47.

L ORD, dismiss us with Thy blessing,
    Thanks for mercies past receive ;
  Pardon all, their faults confessing ;
    Time that 's lost may all retrieve ;
      May Thy children
    Ne'er again Thy Spirit grieve.

2 Bless Thou all our days of leisure ;
    Help us selfish lures to flee ;
  Sanctify our every pleasure ;
    Pure and blameless may it be ;
      May our gladness
    Draw us evermore to Thee.

3 By Thy kindly influence cherish
    All the good we here have gained ;
  May all taint of evil perish,
    By Thy mightier power restrained;
      Seek we ever
    Knowledge pure and love un-
      feigned.

4 Let Thy Father-hand be shielding
    All who here shall meet no more ;
  May their seed-time past be yielding
    Year by year a richer store ;
      Those returning
    Make more faithful than before.

          HENRY JAMES BUCKOLL,
              1803–71.

679

S. M.

REVIVE Thy work, O Lord :
  Thy mighty arm make bare ;
Speak with the voice which wakes
    the dead,
And make Thy people hear.

2 Revive Thy work, O Lord :
Create soul-thirst for Thee ;
And hungering for the Bread of Life
O may our spirits be.

3 Revive Thy work, O Lord :
Exalt Thy precious Name ;
And, by the Holy Ghost, our love
For Thee and Thine inflame.

4 Revive Thy work, O Lord :
Give power unto Thy word ;
Grant that Thy blessèd Gospel may
In living faith be heard.

5 Revive Thy work, O Lord :
And give refreshing showers :
The glory shall be all Thine own,
The blessing, Lord, be ours.

ALBERT MIDLANE, 1825-1909.

680

73. 73. 77. 73.

WE have heard a joyful sound,—
    ' Jesus saves ! '
Spread the gladness all around :
    ' Jesus saves ! '
Bear the news to every land,
  Climb the steeps and cross the
    waves ;
Onward !—'tis our Lord's com-
    mand.
      Jesus saves !

2 Waft it on the rolling tide :
    ' Jesus saves ! '
Tell to sinners far and wide,
    ' Jesus saves ! '
Sing, ye islands of the sea ;
  Echo back, ye ocean caves ;
Earth shall keep her jubilee :
      Jesus saves !

3 Sing above the battle's strife
    ' Jesus saves ! '
By His death and endless life
    Jesus saves ! '

Sing it softly through the gloom,
  When the heart for mercy craves ;
Sing in triumph o'er the tomb,
      ' Jesus saves ! '

4 Give the winds a mighty voice,
      ' Jesus saves ! '
Let the nations now rejoice :
      Jesus saves !
Shout salvation full and free
  To every strand that ocean laves,—
This our song of victory,
      ' Jesus saves ! '

PRISCILLA JANE OWENS,
1829-1907.

681

11 10. 11 10. and refrain,
Dactylic.

RESCUE the perishing, care for
    the dying ;
  Snatch them in pity from sin and
    the grave ;
Weep o'er the erring one, lift up the
    fallen ;
  Tell them of Jesus, the mighty to
    save.
    *Rescue the perishing, care for the
        dying ;*
    Jesus is merciful, Jesus will save.

2 Though they are slighting Him, still
      He is waiting,
  Waiting the penitent child to
    receive ;
Plead with them earnestly, plead with
      them gently ;
  He will forgive, if they only believe.

3 Down in the human heart, crushed
      by the tempter,
  Feelings lie buried that grace can
    restore ;
Touched by a loving hand, wakened
      by kindness,
  Chords that were broken will
    vibrate once more.

4 Rescue the perishing—duty demands
      it ;
  Strength for thy labour the Lord
    will provide ;

Back to the narrow way patiently win
  them ;
  Tell the poor wanderer a Saviour
  has died.
FRANCES JANE VAN ALSTYNE,
1820–1915.

682
76. 76.

TELL me the old, old story
  Of unseen things above,
Of Jesus and His glory,
  Of Jesus and His love.

2 Tell me the story simply,
  As to a little child ;
For I am weak and weary,
  And helpless, and defiled.

3 Tell me the story slowly,
  That I may take it in,—
That wonderful redemption,
  God's remedy for sin.

4 Tell me the story often,
  For I forget so soon ;
The early dew of morning
  Has passed away at noon.

5 Tell me the story softly,
  With earnest tones and grave ;
Remember, I'm the sinner
  Whom Jesus came to save.

6 Tell me the story always,
  If you would really be,
In any time of trouble,
  A comforter to me.

7 Tell me the same old story
  When you have cause to fear
That this world's empty glory
  Is costing me too dear.

8 Yes, and, when that world's glory
  Shall dawn upon my soul,
Tell me the old, old story,
  ' Christ Jesus makes thee whole.'
ARABELLA CATHERINE HANKEY,
1834–1911.

683
87. 87. and refrain.

I WILL sing the wondrous story
  Of the Christ who died for me,—
How He left the realms of glory,
  For the Cross on Calvary.
  Yes, I'll sing the wondrous story
  Of the Christ who died for me,—
  Sing it with His saints in glory,
  Gathered by the crystal sea.

2 I was lost : but Jesus found me,
  Found the sheep that went astray,
Raised me up and gently led me
  Back into the narrow way.

3 Faint was I, and fears possessed me,
  Bruised was I from many a fall ;
Hope was gone, and shame distressed
  me :
  But His love has pardoned all.

4 Days of darkness still may meet me,
  Sorrow's paths I oft may tread ;
But His presence still is with me,
  By His guiding hand I'm led.

5 He will keep me till the river
  Rolls its waters at my feet :
Then He'll bear me safely over,
  Made by grace for glory meet.
FRANCIS HAROLD ROWLEY,
1854–1952.

684
76. 76. D.

TO-DAY Thy mercy calls us
  To wash away our sin,
However great our trespass,
  Whatever we have been ;
However long from mercy
  We may have turned away,
Thy blood, O Christ, can cleanse us,
  And make us white to-day.

2 To-day Thy gate is open,
  And all who enter in
Shall find a Father's welcome,
  And pardon for their sin ;
The past shall be forgotten,
  A present joy be given,
A future grace be promised,
  A glorious crown in heaven.

3 O all-embracing Mercy,
  Thou ever-open Door,
What should we do without Thee
  When heart and eyes run o'er ?
When all things seem against us,
  To drive us to despair,
We know one gate is open,
  One ear will hear our prayer.
OSWALD ALLEN, 1816–78.

685
97. 97. 99. Irr.

THERE were ninety and nine that
  safely lay
  In the shelter of the fold ;
But one was out on the hills away,
  Far off from the gates of gold ;

Away on the mountains wild and
    bare,
Away from the tender Shepherd's
    care.

2 'Lord, Thou hast here Thy ninety
    and nine ;
Are they not enough for Thee ? '
But the Shepherd made answer,
    ' This of Mine
Has wandered away from Me ;
And although the road be rough and
    steep,
I go to the desert to find My sheep.'

3 But none of the ransomed ever knew
    How deep were the waters crossed,
Nor how dark was the night that the
    Lord passed through,
Ere He found His sheep that was
    lost.
Out in the desert He heard its cry,
Sick and helpless and ready to die.

4 ' Lord, whence are those blood-drops
    all the way,
    That mark out the mountain's
      track ? '
' They were shed for one who had
    gone astray,
    Ere the Shepherd could bring him
      back.'
' Lord, whence are Thy hands so rent
    and torn ? '
' They are pierced to-night by many
    a thorn.'

5 And all through the mountains,
    thunder-riven,
And up from the rocky steep,
There rose a cry to the gate of heaven,
    ' Rejoice, I have found My sheep.'
And the angels echoed around the
    throne,
' Rejoice, for the Lord brings back
    His own.'

ELIZABETH CECILIA CLEPHANE,
1830–69.

686
64. 64.

TO-DAY the Saviour calls :
    Ye wanderers, come ;
O, ye benighted souls,
    Why longer roam ?

2 To-day the Saviour calls :
    O hear Him now ;
Within these sacred walls
    To Jesus bow.

3 The Spirit calls to-day :
    Yield to His power ;
O grieve Him not away ;
    'Tis mercy's hour.

SAMUEL FRANCIS SMITH,
1808–95.

687
87. 87. 3.

LORD, I hear of showers of bless-
    ing
Thou art scattering, full and free,—
Showers, the thirsty land refreshing ;
    Let some drops descend on me,
        Even me.

2 Pass me not, O gracious Father,
    Sinful though my heart may be !
Thou might'st leave me, but the
    rather
    Let Thy mercy light on me,
        Even me.

3 Pass me not, O tender Saviour !
    Let me love and cling to Thee ;
I am longing for Thy favour ;
    When Thou comest, call for me,
        Even me.

4 Pass me not, O mighty Spirit !
    Thou canst make the blind to see ;
Witnesser of Jesus' merit,
    Speak the word of power to me,
        Even me.

5 Have I long in sin been sleeping,
    Long been slighting, grieving
    Thee ?
Has the world my heart been keep-
    ing ?
    O forgive and rescue me,
        Even me.

6 Love of God, so pure and changeless,
    Blood of Christ, so rich and free,
Grace of God, so strong and bound-
    less,—
    Magnify them all in me,
        Even me.

ELIZABETH CODNER, 1824–1919.

688
11 10. 11 10. Dactylic.

COME, ye disconsolate, where'er
    ye languish,
Come to the mercy-seat, fervently
    kneel ;
Here bring your wounded hearts,
    here tell your anguish ;
Earth has no sorrows that heaven
    cannot heal.

2 Joy of the desolate, Light of the
  straying,
    Hope of the penitent, fadeless and
    pure !
Here speaks the Comforter, tenderly
  saying,
    Earth has no sorrows that heaven
    cannot cure.

3 Here see the Bread of Life ; see
  waters flowing
    Forth from the throne of God, pure
    from above :
Come to the feast of love ; come,
  ever knowing
    Earth has no sorrows but heaven
    can remove.

    THOMAS MOORE, 1779–1852, and
      THOMAS HASTINGS, 1784–1872.

689
                    S. M. and refrain.

I HEAR Thy welcome voice
  That calls me, Lord, to Thee,
For cleansing in Thy precious blood
  That flowed on Calvary.
    I am coming, Lord,
      Coming now to Thee ;
    Wash me, cleanse me in the blood
      That flowed on Calvary.

2 'Tis Jesus calls me on
    To perfect faith and love,
To perfect hope and peace and trust,
    For earth and heaven above.

3 'Tis Jesus who confirms
    The blessèd work within,
By adding grace to welcomed grace,
    Where reigned the power of sin.

4 All hail, atoning blood !
    All hail, redeeming grace !
All hail, the gift of Christ our Lord,
    Our Strength and Righteousness !
    LEWIS HARTSOUGH, 1828–72.

690
                            77. 75.

THOU who didst on Calvary
  bleed,
Thou who dost for sinners plead,
Help me in my time of need ;
    Jesus, hear my cry.

2 In my darkness and my grief,
With my heart of unbelief,
I, who am of sinners chief,
    Lift to Thee mine eye.

3 Foes without and fears within,
With no plea Thy grace to win
But that Thou canst save from sin,
    To Thy Cross I fly.

4 Others, long in fetters bound,
There deliverance sought and found,
Heard the voice of mercy sound ;
    Surely so may I.

5 There on Thee I cast my care ;
There to Thee I raise my prayer ;
Jesus, save me from despair,—
    Save me, or I die.

6 When the storms of trial lower,
When I feel temptation's power,
In the last and darkest hour,
    Jesus, be Thou nigh.
        JAMES DRUMMOND BURNS,
                        1823–64.

691
                        76. 86. 86. 86.

BENEATH the Cross of Jesus
  I fain would take my stand—
The shadow of a mighty rock
  Within a weary land ;
A home within a wilderness,
  A rest upon the way,
From the burning of the noontide
    heat
  And the burden of the day.

2 O safe and happy shelter,
  O refuge tried and sweet,
O trysting-place where heaven's love
  And heaven's justice meet !
As to the exiled patriarch
  That wondrous dream was given,
So seems my Saviour's Cross to me—
  A ladder up to heaven.

3 Upon that Cross of Jesus,
  Mine eye at times can see
The very dying form of One
  Who suffered there for me ;
And from my smitten heart, with
    tears,
  Two wonders I confess—
The wonder of His glorious love,
  And my own worthlessness.

4 I take, O Cross, thy shadow
  For my abiding-place ;
I ask no other sunshine than
  The sunshine of His face :

Content to let the world go by,
To know no gain nor loss—
My sinful self my only shame,
My glory all, the Cross.
ELIZABETH CECILIA CLEPHANE,
1830–69.

692
C. M.

THERE is a fountain filled with
blood
Drawn from Immanuel's veins ;
And sinners, plunged beneath that
flood,
Lose all their guilty stains.

2 The dying thief rejoiced to see
That fountain in his day ;
And there have I, as vile as he,
Washed all my sins away.

3 Dear dying Lamb, Thy precious
blood
Shall never lose its power
Till all the ransomed Church of God
Be saved, to sin no more.

4 E'er since, by faith, I saw the stream
Thy flowing wounds supply,
Redeeming love has been my theme,
And shall be till I die.

5 Then, in a nobler, sweeter song,
I'll sing Thy power to save,
When this poor lisping, stammering
tongue
Lies silent in the grave.

6 Lord, I believe Thou hast prepared,
Unworthy though I be,
For me a blood-bought free reward,
A golden harp for me ;

7 'Tis strung and tuned for endless
years,
And formed, by power divine,
To sound in God the Father's ears
No other name but Thine.
WILLIAM COWPER, 1731–1800.

693
77. 78.

MAN of Sorrows ! wondrous
Name
For the Son of God, who came
Ruined sinners to reclaim !
Hallelujah ! what a Saviour !

2 Bearing shame and scoffing rude,
In my place condemned He stood,
Sealed my pardon with His blood :
Hallelujah ! what a Saviour !

3 Guilty, vile, and helpless we ;
Spotless Lamb of God was He :
Full atonement,—can it be ?
Hallelujah ! what a Saviour !

4 Lifted up was He to die,
' It is finished ' was His cry ;
Now in heaven exalted high :
Hallelujah ! what a Saviour !

5 When He comes, our glorious King,
All His ransomed home to bring,
Then anew this song we'll sing,
' Hallelujah ! what a Saviour ! '
PHILIPP BLISS, 1838–76.

694
76. 76. D.

I LAY my sins on Jesus,
The spotless Lamb of God ;
He bears them all, and frees us
From the accursèd load.
I bring my guilt to Jesus,
To wash my crimson stains
White in His blood most precious,
Till not a spot remains.

2 I lay my wants on Jesus ;
All fulness dwells in Him ;
He heals all my diseases,
He doth my soul redeem.
I lay my griefs on Jesus,
My burdens, and my cares ;
He from them all releases,
He all my sorrows shares.

3 I rest my soul on Jesus,
This weary soul of mine ;
His right hand me embraces,
I on His breast recline.
I love the Name of Jesus,
Immanuel, Christ, the Lord ;
Like fragrance on the breezes,
His Name abroad is poured.

4 I long to be like Jesus,
Meek, loving, lowly, mild ;
I long to be, like Jesus,
The Father's holy child.
I long to be with Jesus,
Amid the heavenly throng,
To sing with saints His praises,
To learn the angels' song.
HORATIUS BONAR, 1808–89.

695
85. 83.

I AM trusting Thee, Lord Jesus,
Trusting only Thee,
Trusting Thee for full salvation,
Great and free.

2 I am trusting Thee for pardon :
  At Thy feet I bow,
For Thy grace and tender mercy
    Trusting now.

3 I am trusting Thee to guide me ;
    Thou alone shalt lead,
Every day and hour supplying
    All my need.

4 I am trusting Thee for power :
    Thine can never fail ;
Words which Thou Thyself shalt
    give me
      Must prevail.

5 I am trusting Thee, Lord Jesus ;
    Never let me fall ;
I am trusting Thee for ever,
    And for all.
          FRANCES RIDLEY HAVERGAL,
                    1836–79.

696
65. 65. D.

JESUS, I will trust Thee,—
    Trust Thee with my soul ;
Guilty, lost, and helpless,
    Thou canst make me whole.
There is none in heaven
    Or on earth like Thee ;
Thou hast died for sinners—
    Therefore, Lord, for me.

2 Jesus, I will trust Thee ;
    Name of matchless worth,
Spoken by the angel
    At Thy wondrous birth,
Written, and for ever,
    On Thy Cross of shame :
Sinners read and worship,
    Trusting in that Name.

3 Jesus, I will trust Thee,
    Pondering Thy ways
Full of love and mercy
    All Thine earthly days.
Sinners gathered round Thee,
    Lepers sought Thy face,
None too vile or loathsome
    For a Saviour's grace.

4 Jesus, I will trust Thee,
    Trust without a doubt ;
Whosoever cometh
    Thou wilt not cast out.
Faithful is Thy promise ;
    Precious is Thy blood ;
These my soul's salvation,
    Thou my Saviour God !
          MARY JANE WALKER, 1816–78.

697
L. M. and refrain.

MY hope is built on nothing less
    Than Jesus' blood and right-
      eousness ;
I dare not trust my sweetest frame,
But wholly lean on Jesus' Name.
    On Christ, the solid rock, I stand ;
    All other ground is sinking sand.

2 When darkness seems to veil His face,
I rest on His unchanging grace ;
In every high and stormy gale,
My anchor holds within the veil.

3 His oath, His covenant, and blood,
Support me in the whelming flood ;
When all around my soul gives way,
He then is all my hope and stay.
          EDWARD MOTE, 1797–1874.

698
88. 87.

I AM not skilled to understand
    What God hath willed, what God
      hath planned ;
I only know at His right hand
    Stands One who is my Saviour.

2 I take God at His word and deed :
  ' Christ died to save me ', this I read ;
And in my heart I find a need
    Of Him to be my Saviour.

3 And was there then no other way
For God to take ?—I cannot say ;
I only bless Him, day by day,
    Who saved me through my Saviour.

4 That He should leave His place on
    high
And come for sinful man to die,
You count it strange ?—so do not I,
    Since I have known my Saviour.

5 And O that He fulfilled may see
The travail of His soul in me,
And with His work contented be,
    As I with my dear Saviour !

6 Yea, living, dying, let me bring
My strength, my solace, from this
    spring,
That He who lives to be my King,
    Once died to be my Saviour.
          DORA GREENWELL, 1821–82.

699   C. M. and refrain.

O CHRIST, in Thee my soul hath
found,
And found in Thee alone,
The peace, the joy, I sought so long,
The bliss till now unknown.
Now none but Christ can satisfy,
None other Name for me !
There's love, and life, and lasting
joy,
Lord Jesus, found in Thee.

2 I sighed for rest and happiness,
I yearned for them, not Thee ;
But, while I passed my Saviour by,
His love laid hold on me.

3 I tried the broken cisterns, Lord,
But, ah, the waters failed :
Even as I stooped to drink they fled,
And mocked me as I wailed.

4 The pleasures lost I sadly mourned,
But never wept for Thee,
Till grace the sightless eyes received,
Thy loveliness to see.
B. E.

700   64. 64. and refrain.

I NEED Thee every hour,
Most gracious Lord ;
No tender voice but Thine
Can peace afford.
I need Thee, O I need Thee ;
Every hour I need Thee ;
O bless me now, my Saviour ;
I come to Thee.

2 I need Thee every hour ;
Stay Thou near by ;
Temptations lose their power
When Thou art nigh.

3 I need Thee every hour,
In joy or pain ;
Come quickly and abide,
Or life is vain.

4 I need Thee every hour,
Teach me Thy will ;
And Thy rich promises
In me fulfil.
ANNIE SHERWOOD HAWKS,
1835-1918. Refrain added.

701   87. 87. D.

WHAT a Friend we have in Jesus,
All our sins and griefs to bear !
What a privilege to carry
Everything to God in prayer !
O what peace we often forfeit,
O what needless pain we bear,
All because we do not carry
Everything to God in prayer !

2 Have we trials and temptations ?
Is there trouble anywhere ?
We should never be discouraged :
Take it to the Lord in prayer.
Can we find a friend so faithful,
Who will all our sorrows share ?
Jesus knows our every weakness :
Take it to the Lord in prayer.

3 Are we weak and heavy-laden,
Cumbered with a load of care ?
Jesus only is our refuge :
Take it to the Lord in prayer.
Do thy friends despise, forsake thee ?
Take it to the Lord in prayer ;
In His arms He'll take and shield
thee ;
Thou wilt find a solace there.
JOSEPH SCRIVEN, 1820-86.

702   84. 84. 8884.

THROUGH the love of God our
Saviour
All will be well.
Free and changeless is His favour ;
All, all is well.
Precious is the blood that healed us,
Perfect is the grace that sealed us,
Strong the hand stretched forth to
shield us ;
All must be well.

2 Though we pass through tribulation,
All will be well.
Ours is such a full salvation,
All, all is well.
Happy, still in God confiding,
Fruitful, if in Christ abiding,
Holy, through the Spirit's guiding ;
All must be well.

3 We expect a bright to-morrow ;
All will be well.
Faith can sing through days of
sorrow,
' All, all is well.'

On our Father's love relying,
Jesus every need supplying,
Or in living or in dying,
   All must be well.
        MARY PETERS, 1813–56.

703   88. 88. D. Anapaestic.

A DEBTOR to mercy alone,
  Of covenant mercy I sing;
Nor fear, with Thy righteousness on,
  My person and offering to bring.
The terrors of law and of God
  With me can have nothing to do;
My Saviour's obedience and blood
  Hide all my transgressions from
    view.

2 The work which His goodness began,
  The arm of His strength will com-
    plete;
His promise is Yea and Amen,
  And never was forfeited yet.
Things future, nor things that are
    now,
  Nor all things below or above,
Can make Him His purpose forgo,
  Or sever my soul from His love.

3 My name from the palms of His
    hands
  Eternity will not erase;
Impressed on His heart it remains,
  In marks of indelible grace.
Yes, I to the end shall endure,
  As sure as the earnest is given;
More happy, but not more secure,
  The glorified spirits in heaven.
    AUGUSTUS MONTAGUE TOPLADY,
                 1740–78.

704   11 11. 11 12. and refrain.

Y IELD not to temptation, for
  yielding is sin;
Each victory will help you some other
  to win;
Fight manfully onward; dark passions subdue;
Look ever to Jesus, He will carry you
  through.
    Ask the Saviour to help you,
    Comfort, strengthen, and keep you;
    He is willing to aid you;
    He will carry you through.

2 Shun evil companions; bad language disdain;
God's Name hold in reverence, nor
  take it in vain;
Be thoughtful and earnest, kind-
  hearted and true;
Look ever to Jesus, He will carry you
  through.

3 To him that o'ercometh God giveth
  a crown;
Through faith we shall conquer,
  though often cast down;
He who is our Saviour our strength
  will renew;
Look ever to Jesus, He will carry you
  through.
    HORATIO RICHMOND PALMER,
                1834–1907.

705   87. 87. D.

I 'VE found a Friend; O such a
  Friend!
  He loved me ere I knew Him;
He drew me with the cords of love,
  And thus He bound me to Him;
And round my heart still closely
    twine
  Those ties which nought can sever,
For I am His, and He is mine,
  For ever and for ever.

2 I've found a Friend; O such a
  Friend!
  He bled, He died to save me;
And not alone the gift of life,
  But His own self He gave me.
Nought that I have mine own I'll call,
  I'll hold it for the Giver;
My heart, my strength, my life, my
    all,
  Are His, and His for ever.

3 I've found a Friend; O such a
  Friend!
  All power to Him is given,
To guard me on my onward course,
  And bring me safe to heaven.
The eternal glories gleam afar,
  To nerve my faint endeavour;
So now to watch, to work, to war,
  And then to rest for ever.

4 I've found a Friend; O such a
  Friend!
  So kind, and true, and tender!
So wise a Counsellor and Guide,
  So mighty a Defender!

From Him who loves me now so
    well
  What power my soul shall sever ?
Shall life or death, shall earth or
    hell ?
  No ! I am His for ever.
JAMES GRINDLAY SMALL,
1817–88.

706
77. 77. 77.

JESUS, Saviour, pilot me
  Over life's tempestuous sea ;
Unknown waves before me roll,
Hiding rock and treacherous shoal ;
Chart and compass come from Thee :
Jesus, Saviour, pilot me.

2 As a mother stills her child,
  Thou canst hush the ocean wild ;
Boisterous waves obey Thy will,
When Thou say'st to them, ' Be
    still ! '.
Wondrous Sovereign of the sea,
Jesus, Saviour, pilot me.

3 When at last I near the shore,
  And the fearful breakers roar
'Twixt me and the peaceful rest,
Then, while leaning on Thy breast,
May I hear Thee say to me,
' Fear not, I will pilot thee.'
EDWARD HOPPER, 1818–88.

707
76. 76. D. and refrain.

SAFE in the arms of Jesus,
  Safe on His gentle breast,
There, by His love o'ershaded,
  Sweetly my soul shall rest.
Hark ! 'tis the voice of angels,
  Borne in a song to me,
Over the fields of glory,
  Over the crystal sea !
    Safe in the arms of Jesus,
      Safe on His gentle breast,
    There, by His love o'ershaded,
      Sweetly my soul shall rest.

2 Safe in the arms of Jesus,
  Safe from corroding care,
Safe from the world's temptations,
  Sin cannot harm me there,—
Free from the blight of sorrow,
  Free from my doubts and fears,
Only a few more trials,
  Only a few more tears.

3 Jesus, my heart's dear refuge,
  Jesus has died for me ;
Firm on the Rock of Ages
  Ever my trust shall be.
Here let me wait with patience,
  Wait till the night is o'er,
Wait till I see the morning
  Break on the golden shore.
FRANCES JANE VAN ALSTYNE,
1820–1915.

DOXOLOGIES

708   87. 87. 447.

NOW to Him who loved us, gave us
    Every pledge that love could
                  give,
Freely shed His blood to save us,
Gave His life that we might live,
      Be the Kingdom
      And dominion
And the glory evermore.
          SAMUEL MILLER WARING,
                  1792–1827.

709   L. M.

PRAISE God, from whom all bless-
    ings flow ;
Praise Him, all creatures here below ;
Praise Him above, ye heavenly host ;
Praise Father, Son, and Holy Ghost.
          THOMAS KEN, 1637–1711.

710   66. 66. 88.

NOW to the King of heaven
    Your cheerful voices raise ;
To Him be glory given,
    Power, majesty, and praise ;

Wide as He reigns
    His Name be sung
    By every tongue,
In endless strains.
      PHILIP DODDRIDGE, 1702–51,
    and ISAAC WATTS, 1674–1748.

711   C. M.

TO Him who sits upon the throne,
    The God whom we adore,
And to the Lamb that once was slain,
    Be glory evermore.
      ISAAC WATTS, 1674–1748.

712

GLORY be to the Father, and to the
    Son, and to the Holy Ghost :
As it was in the beginning, is now,
and ever shall be, world without end.
                     Amen.

713

HOLY, holy, holy, Lord God of
    hosts :
Heaven and earth are full of Thy glory.
    Glory be to Thee, O Lord most high!

ANCIENT HYMNS AND CANTICLES

The Canticles are pointed for Anglican chanting only.

714

BENEDICTUS

St. Luke i. 68–79.

FIRST FORM

BLESSÈD be the | Lord · God of | Isra-el : || for He hath | visited · and re- | deemed His | people ; ||

2 And hath raised up an horn of sal- | vation | for us || in the | house of His | servant | David ; ||

3 As He spake by the mouth of His | holy | prophets : || which have | been · since the | world be- | gan ; ||

4 That we should be | saved · from our | ene-mies, || and from the | hand of | all that | hate us ; ||

5 To perform the mercy promised to our fathers * and to remember His | holy | cove-nant ; ||

6 The oath which He sware to our father | Abra-ham that | He would · grant | unto · us, ||

7 That we, being delivered out of the hand of our enemies, might | serve Him with-out | fear ; ||

8 In holiness and righteousness be- fore Him, | all the | days of our | life. ||

9 And thou, child, shalt be called the | prophet · of the | Highest : || for thou shalt go before the face of the | Lord · to pre- | pare His | ways ; ||

10 To give knowledge of salvation | unto His | people || by | the re- | mission · of their | sins, ||

11 Through the tender | mercy · of our | God : || whereby the | dayspring · from on | high hath | visited · us, ||

12 To give light to them that sit in darkness and in the | shadow of | death : || to guide our | feet in-to the | way of | peace. ||

Glory | be · to the | Father, || and to the | Son, | and · to the | Holy | Ghost ; ||

As it | was in · the be- | ginning, || is now, and ever shall be : | world with-out | end. A- | men. ||

SECOND FORM

BLESSÈD be the | Lord · God of | Isra-el : || for He hath | visited · and re- | deemed His | people ; ||

2 And hath raised up a mighty sal- | vation | for us || in the | house of His | servant | David ; ||

3 As He spake by the mouth of His | holy | prophets : || which have | been · since the | world be- | gan ; ||

4 That we should be | saved · from our | ene-mies, || and from the | hands of | all that | hate us ; ||

5 To perform the mercy promised to our forefathers * and to remember His | holy | cove-nant ; ||

6 To perform the oath which He sware to our forefather | Abra-ham that | He would | give us, ||

7 That we, being delivered out of the hands of our enemies, might | serve Him with-out | fear ; ||

8 In holiness and righteousness be- fore Him, | all the | days of our | life. ||

9 And thou, child, shalt be called the | prophet · of the | Highest : || for thou shalt go before the face of the | Lord · to pre- | pare His | ways ; ||

10 To give knowledge of salvation unto His | people : || for | the re- | mission · of their | sins, ||

11 Through the tender | mercy · of our | God : || whereby the | dayspring · from on | high hath | visited · us, ||

12 To give light to them that sit in darkness and in the | shadow of | death : || and to guide our | feet in-to the | way of | peace. ||

Glory | be · to the | Father, || and to the | Son, | and · to the | Holy | Ghost ; ||

As it | was in · the be- | ginning, || is now, and ever shall be : | world with-out | end. A- | men. ||

715

MAGNIFICAT

St. Luke i. 46–55.

FIRST FORM

MY soul doth magnify the Lord,* and my spirit hath rejoiced in | God my | Saviour. ||

2 For He hath regarded the | low es-tate | of His | hand-maiden : ||

3 For, be- | hold, from | henceforth ǁ all gener- | ations · shall | call me | blessèd. ǁ

4 For He that is mighty hath | done to me | great things ; ǁ and | holy | is His | Name. ǁ

5 And His mercy is on | them that | fear Him ǁ from gener- | ation to | gener- | ation. ǁ

6 He hath shewed | strength · with His | arm ; ǁ He hath scattered the proud in the imagi- | nation | of their | hearts. ǁ

7 He hath put down the | mighty · from their | seats, ǁ and ex- | alted them of | low de- | gree. ǁ

8 He hath filled the | hungry with | good things ; ǁ and the | rich He · hath sent | empty a- | way. ǁ

{ 9 He hath holpen His servant Israel in re- | membrance · of His | mercy ; ǁ
10 As He spake to our fathers, to { Abraham · and to his | seed for | ever. ǁ

Glory | *be · to the* | *Father,* ǁ *and to the Son,* | *and · to the* | *Holy* | *Ghost ;* ǁ

As it | *was in · the be-* | *ginning,* ǁ *is now, and ever shall be :* | *world with-out* | *end. A-* | *men.* ǁ

SECOND FORM

{ MY soul doth magnify the Lord,* and my spirit hath rejoiced in | God my | Saviour. ǁ

2 For He hath regarded the | lowliness | of His | hand-maiden. ǁ

3 For be- | hold from | henceforth ǁ all gener- | ations · shall | call me | blessèd. ǁ

4 For He that is | mighty · hath magnified · me ; ǁ and | holy · is His | Name. ǁ

5 And His mercy is on | them that | fear Him ǁ through- | out all | gener- | ations. ǁ

6 He hath shewed | strength · with His | arm ; ǁ He hath scattered the proud in the imagi- | nation | of their | hearts. ǁ

7 He hath put down the | mighty · from their | seat, ǁ and hath ex- | alted the | humble and | meek. ǁ

8 He hath filled the | hungry with | good things ; ǁ and the | rich He · hath sent | empty a- | way. ǁ

9 He remembering His mercy hath holpen His | servant | Isra-el : ǁ as He promised to our forefathers, | Abraham · and his | seed for | ever. ǁ

Glory | *be · to the* | *Father,* ǁ *and to the Son,* | *and · to the* | *Holy* | *Ghost ;* ǁ

As it | *was in · the be-* | *ginning,* ǁ *is now, and ever shall be :* | *world with-out* | *end. A-* | *men.* ǁ

716

NUNC DIMITTIS

St. Luke ii. 29–32.

FIRST FORM

{ LORD, now lettest Thou Thy servant depart in peace,* ac- | cording · to Thy | word. ǁ

2 For mine | eyes have | seen Thy | sal- | vation, ǁ

3 Which Thou hast prepared before the | face of · all | people ; ǁ

4 A light to lighten the Gentiles, and the | glory · of Thy | people | Isra-el. ǁ

Glory | *be · to the* | *Father,* ǁ *and to the Son,* | *and · to the* | *Holy* | *Ghost ;* ǁ

As it | *was in · the be-* | *ginning,* ǁ *is now, and ever shall be :* | *world with-out* | *end. A-* | *men.* ǁ

SECOND FORM

{ LORD, now lettest Thou Thy servant depart in peace,* ac- | cording · to Thy | word ; ǁ

2 For mine | eyes have | seen Thy | sal- | vation, ǁ

3 Which Thou hast prepared before the | face of · all | people ; ǁ

4 To be a light to lighten the Gentiles, and to be the | glory · of Thy | people | Isra-el. ǁ

Glory | *be · to the* | *Father,* ǁ *and to the Son,* | *and · to the* | *Holy* | *Ghost ;* ǁ

As it | *was in · the be-* | *ginning,* ǁ *is now, and ever shall be :* | *world with-out* | *end. A-* | *men.* ǁ

717

GLORIA IN EXCELSIS

GLORY be to | God on | high, ǁ and in earth | peace, good- | will towards | men. ǁ

2 We | praise Thee · we | bless Thee, | we | worship · Thee, we | glorify | Thee. ǁ

{ 3 We give thanks to Thee for | Thy great | glory. ǁ

4 O Lord God, heavenly King, | God the | Father Al- | mighty. ǁ

5 O Lord, the only begotten Son, | Jesus | Christ ; ||
6 O Lord God, | Lamb of · God, | Son of the | Father, ||

7 That takest away the sins of the world, have | mer-cy up- | on us. ||
8 Thou that takest away the sins of the | world, have | mer-cy up- | on us. ||
9 Thou that takest away the sins of the world, re- | ceive our | prayer. ||
10 Thou that sittest at the right hand of God the | Father · have | mer-cy up- | on us. ||
11 For Thou only art holy, Thou only | art the | Lord ; ||
12 Thou only, O Christ, with the Holy Ghost, art most high in the | glory of | God the | Father. ||

718

TE DEUM LAUDAMUS

WE praise | Thee, O | God ; || we ac- | knowledge · Thee to | be the | Lord. ||
2 All the | earth doth | worship | Thee, || the | Father ever- | lasting. ||
3 To Thee all angels | cry a- | loud ; || the | heavens · and | all the | powers there-in. ||
4 To Thee | cheru-bin and | seraph-in || con- | tinu-al- | ly do | cry, ||
5 'Holy, holy, holy ; Lord | God of Sa- | baoth ; ||
6 Heaven and earth are full of the | majesty | of Thy | glory.' ||
7 The glorious company of the a-postles | praise Thee. ||
8 The goodly | fellowship · of the | prophets | praise Thee. ||
9 The noble army of | martyrs | praise Thee. ||
10 The holy Church throughout | all the | world · doth ac- | knowledge · Thee ; ||
11 The Father of an | infinite | majes-ty ; ||
12 Thine honourable, true, and only | Son ; *(13) Also the | Holy | Ghost the | Comfort-er. ||
14 Thou art the King of | Glory · O | Christ ; ||
15 Thou art the ever- | lasting | Son · of the | Father. ||
16 When Thou tookest upon Thee to de- | liver | man, || Thou didst not ab- | hor the | Virgin's | womb. ||

17 When Thou hadst overcome the | sharpness · of | death, || Thou didst open the Kingdom of | heaven to | all be- | lievers. ||
18 Thou sittest at the | right · hand of | God, || in the | glory | of the | Father. ||
19 We believe that Thou shalt | come to · be our | Judge. ||
20 We therefore pray Thee, help Thy servants, whom Thou hast re- | deemed · with Thy | precious | blood. ||
21 Make them to be | numbered · with Thy | saints || in | glory ever- | lasting. ||
22 O Lord, save Thy people, and | bless Thine | herit-age. ||
23 Govern them and | lift them | up for | ever. ||
24 Day by | day we | magnify · Thee ; ||
25 And we worship Thy | Name · ever | world with-out | end. ||
26 Vouchsafe, O Lord, to keep us this | day with-out | sin. ||
27 O Lord, have mercy up- | on us · have | mer-cy up- | on us. ||
28 O Lord, let Thy mercy lighten upon us, as our | trust · is in | Thee. ||
29 O Lord, in Thee have I trusted : let me | never | be con- | founded. ||

719

BENEDICITE, OMNIA OPERA

Daniel iii. (Greek Version.)

O ALL ye works of the Lord, | bless ye the | Lord : ||
Praise Him, and | magnify | Him for | ever. ||
2 O ye angels of the Lord, | bless ye the | Lord : ||
Praise Him, and | magnify | Him for | ever. ||
3 O ye heavens, | bless ye the | Lord : ||
Praise Him, and | magnify | Him for | ever. ||
4 O ye waters that be above the firma-ment, | bless ye the | Lord : ||
Praise Him, and | magnify | Him for | ever. ||
5 O all ye powers of the Lord, | bless ye the | Lord : ||
Praise Him, and | magnify | Him for | ever. ||

ANCIENT HYMNS AND CANTICLES

6 O ye sun and moon, | bless ye the | Lord : ||
Praise Him, and | magnify | Him for | ever. ||

7 O ye stars of heaven, | bless ye the | Lord : ||
Praise Him, and | magnify | Him for | ever. ||

8 O ye showers and dew, | bless ye the | Lord : ||
Praise Him, and | magnify | Him for | ever. ||

9 O ye winds of God, | bless ye the | Lord : ||
Praise Him, and | magnify | Him for | ever. ||

10 O ye fire and heat, | bless ye the | Lord : ||
Praise Him, and | magnify | Him for | ever. ||

11 O ye winter and summer, | bless ye the | Lord : ||
Praise Him, and | magnify | Him for | ever. ||

12 O ye dews and frosts, | bless ye the | Lord : ||
Praise Him, and | magnify | Him for | ever. ||

13 O ye frost and cold, | bless ye the | Lord : ||
Praise Him, and | magnify | Him for | ever. ||

14 O ye ice and snow, | bless ye the | Lord : ||
Praise Him, and | magnify | Him for | ever. ||

15 O ye nights and days, | bless ye the | Lord : ||
Praise Him, and | magnify | Him for | ever. ||

16 O ye light and darkness, | bless ye the | Lord : ||
Praise Him, and | magnify | Him for | ever. ||

17 O ye lightnings and clouds, | bless ye the | Lord : ||
Praise Him, and | magnify | Him for | ever. ||

18 O let the earth | bless the | Lord : ||
Yea, let it praise Him, and | magnify | Him for | ever. ||

19 O ye mountains and hills, | bless ye the | Lord : ||
Praise Him, and | magnify | Him for | ever. ||

20 O all ye green things upon the earth, | bless ye the | Lord : ||

21 O ye wells, | bless ye the | Lord : ||
Praise Him, and | magnify | Him for | ever. ||

22 O ye seas and floods, | bless ye the | Lord : ||
Praise Him, and | magnify | Him for | ever. ||

23 O ye whales, and all that move in the waters, | bless ye the | Lord : ||
Praise Him, and | magnify | Him for | ever. ||

24 O all ye fowls of the air, | bless ye the | Lord : ||
Praise Him, and | magnify | Him for | ever. ||

25 O all ye beasts and cattle, | bless ye the | Lord : ||
Praise Him, and | magnify | Him for | ever. ||

26 O ye children of men, | bless ye the | Lord : ||
Praise Him, and | magnify | Him for | ever. ||

27 O let Israel | bless the | Lord : ||
Praise Him, and | magnify | Him for | ever. ||

28 O ye priests of the Lord, | bless ye the | Lord : ||
Praise Him, and | magnify | Him for | ever. ||

29 O ye servants of the Lord, | bless ye the | Lord : ||
Praise Him, and | magnify | Him for | ever. ||

30 O ye spirits and souls of the righteous, | bless ye the | Lord : ||
Praise Him, and | magnify | Him for | ever. ||

31 O ye holy and humble men of heart, | bless ye the | Lord : ||
Praise Him, and | magnify | Him for | ever. ||

32 O Ananias, Azarias, and Misael, | bless ye the | Lord : ||
Praise Him, and | magnify | Him for | ever. ||

Glory be to the Father, | and to the | Son : || and to the | Ho-ly | Ghost ; ||
As it was in the beginning, | is now, and ev-er | shall be : || world without | end. A- | men. ||

720

THE TEN COMMANDMENTS

Exodus xx.

GOD spake all these words, saying, I am the Lord thy God, which have brought thee out of the land of Egypt, out of the house of bondage.

Thou shalt have no other gods before Me.

Lord, have mercy upon us, and incline our hearts to keep this law.

Thou shalt not make unto thee any graven image, or any likeness of any thing that is in heaven above, or that is in the earth beneath, or that is in the water under the earth : thou shalt not bow down thyself to them, nor serve them : for I the Lord thy God am a jealous God, visiting the iniquity of the fathers upon the children unto the third and fourth generation of them that hate Me ; and shewing mercy unto thousands of them that love Me, and keep My commandments.

Lord, have mercy upon us, and incline our hearts to keep this law.

Thou shalt not take the Name of the Lord thy God in vain ; for the Lord will not hold him guiltless that taketh His Name in vain.

Lord, have mercy upon us, and incline our hearts to keep this law.

Remember the sabbath day, to keep it holy. Six days shalt thou labour, and do all thy work : but the seventh day is the sabbath of the Lord thy God : in it thou shalt not do any work, thou, nor thy son, nor thy daughter, thy manservant, nor thy maidservant, nor thy cattle, nor thy stranger that is within thy gates : for in six days the Lord made heaven and earth, the sea, and all that in them is, and rested the seventh day : wherefore the Lord blessed the sabbath day, and hallowed it.

Lord, have mercy upon us, and incline our hearts to keep this law.

Honour thy father and thy mother : that thy days may be long upon the land which the Lord thy God giveth thee.

Lord, have mercy upon us, and incline our hearts to keep this law.

Thou shalt not kill.

Lord, have mercy upon us, and incline our hearts to keep this law.

Thou shalt not commit adultery.

Lord, have mercy upon us, and incline our hearts to keep this law.

Thou shalt not steal.

Lord, have mercy upon us, and incline our hearts to keep this law.

Thou shalt not bear false witness against thy neighbour.

Lord, have mercy upon us, and incline our hearts to keep this law.

Thou shalt not covet thy neighbour's house, thou shalt not covet thy neighbour's wife, nor his manservant, nor his maidservant, nor his ox, nor his ass, nor any thing that is thy neighbour's.

Lord, have mercy upon us, and write all these Thy laws in our hearts, we beseech Thee.

721

THE COMMANDMENTS OF THE LORD JESUS

St. Matthew xxii ; St. Mark xii ; St. John xiii.

JESUS said : The first of all the commandments is : The Lord our God is one Lord : and thou shalt love the Lord thy God with all thy heart, and with all thy soul, and with all thy mind, and with all thy strength. This is the first and great commandment.

Lord, have mercy upon us, and incline our hearts to keep this law.

And the second is like unto it, namely this : Thou shalt love thy neighbour as thyself.

Lord, have mercy upon us, and incline our hearts to keep this law.

A new commandment I give unto you, That ye love one another ; as I have loved you, that ye also love one another.

Lord, have mercy upon us, and write all these Thy laws in our hearts, we beseech Thee.

722

THE BEATITUDES

St. Matthew v.

BLESSED are the poor in spirit : for theirs is the Kingdom of heaven.

Grant us this grace, we beseech Thee, O Lord.

THE BEATITUDES

Blessed are they that mourn : for they shall be comforted.

Grant us this grace, we beseech Thee, O Lord.

Blessed are the meek : for they shall inherit the earth.

Grant us this grace, we beseech Thee, O Lord.

Blessed are they which do hunger and thirst after righteousness : for they shall be filled.

Grant us this grace, we beseech Thee, O Lord.

Blessed are the merciful : for they shall obtain mercy.

Grant us this grace, we beseech Thee, O Lord.

Blessed are the pure in heart : for they shall see God.

Grant us this grace, we beseech Thee, O Lord.

Blessed are the peacemakers : for they shall be called the children of God.

Grant us this grace, we beseech Thee, O Lord.

Blessed are they which are persecuted for righteousness' sake : for theirs is the Kingdom of heaven.

Write these words in our hearts, we beseech Thee, O Lord.

723
THE LORD'S PRAYER

St. Matthew vi. 9–13.

FIRST FORM

OUR Father which art in heaven, Hallowed be Thy Name.
Thy Kingdom come.
Thy will be done in earth, as it is in heaven.
Give us this day our daily bread.
And forgive us our debts, as we forgive our debtors.
And lead us not into temptation, but deliver us from evil :
For Thine is the Kingdom, and the power, and the glory, for ever. Amen.

SECOND FORM

OUR Father, which art in heaven, Hallowed be Thy Name.
Thy Kingdom come.
Thy will be done, in earth as it is in heaven.
Give us this day our daily bread.

And forgive us our trespasses, as we forgive them that trespass against us.
And lead us not into temptation, but deliver us from evil :
For Thine is the Kingdom, the power, and the glory, for ever and ever. Amen.

724
THE APOSTLES' CREED

I BELIEVE in God the Father Almighty, Maker of heaven and earth ;
And in Jesus Christ His only Son our Lord, Who was conceived by the Holy Ghost, Born of the Virgin Mary, Suffered under Pontius Pilate, Was crucified, dead, and buried ; He descended into hell ; The third day He rose again from the dead ; He ascended into heaven, And sitteth on the right hand of God the Father Almighty ; From thence He shall come to judge the quick and the dead.

I believe in the Holy Ghost ; The holy Catholic Church ; The Communion of Saints ; The Forgiveness of sins ; The Resurrection of the body ; And the Life everlasting. Amen.

725
THE NICENE CREED

I BELIEVE in one God the Father Almighty, Maker of heaven and earth, And of all things visible and invisible :
And in one Lord Jesus Christ, the only-begotten Son of God, Begotten of His Father before all worlds, God of God, Light of Light, Very God of Very God, Begotten, not made, Being of one substance with the Father, By whom all things were made : Who for us men, and for our salvation, came down from heaven, And was incarnate by the Holy Ghost of the Virgin Mary, And was made man, And was crucified also for us under Pontius Pilate. He suffered and was buried, And the third day He rose again according to the Scriptures, And ascended into heaven, And sitteth on the right hand of the Father. And He shall come again with glory to judge both the quick and the dead : Whose Kingdom shall have no end.

227

THE NICENE CREED

And I believe in the Holy Ghost, The Lord and Giver of Life, Who proceedeth from the Father and the Son, Who with the Father and the Son together is worshipped and glorified, Who spake by the Prophets. And I believe one Holy Catholic and Apostolic Church. I acknowledge one Baptism for the remission of sins. And I look for the Resurrection of the dead, And the Life of the world to come. Amen.

COUNCIL OF NICÆA, A.D. 325.

---

726 Πατέρων ὕμνος.

Ecclesiasticus xliv.

LET us now praise | famous | men : ‖ and our | fathers | that be- | gat us. ‖

2 The Lord hath wrought great glory | by them : ‖ through His great power | from the be- | ginning. ‖

3 Such as did bear rule in their kingdoms, men re- | nowned · for their | power : ‖

4 Giving counsel by their under- standing · and de- | claring | pro- phe-cies : ‖

5 Leaders of the people by their counsels, and by their knowledge of learning | meet for the | people : ‖ wise and | eloquent | in their in- structions : ‖

6 Such as found out | musical tunes : ‖ and re- | cited | verses in | writing : ‖

7 Rich men | furnished · with a- bility : ‖ living | peaceably | in their · habi- | tations : ‖

8 All these were honoured in their generations, and were the | glory · of their | times. ‖

9 There be of them that have left a name behind them that their | praises | might be re- | ported : ‖

And some there be which | have no me- | morial ; ‖

Who are perished, as | though · they had | never | been, ‖

10 And are become as though they had | never been | born : ‖ and their | children | after | them. ‖

11 But these were | merciful | men : ‖ whose righteousness | hath not | been for- | gotten. ‖

12 With their seed shall continually remain a | good in- | herit-ance : ‖ their | children · are with- | in the | cove-nant. ‖

13 Their | seed · standeth | fast : ‖ and their | children | for their | sakes. ‖

14 Their seed shall re- | main for ever : ‖ and their | glory shall · not be | blotted | out. ‖

15 Their bodies are | buried in | peace : ‖ but their name | liveth for ever- | more. ‖

16 The people will | tell of their | wisdom : ‖ and the congre- | gation · will shew | forth their | praise. ‖

727

Numbers vi.

THE Lord bless thee, and keep thee : the Lord make His face to shine upon thee, and be gracious unto thee : the Lord lift up His countenance upon thee, and give thee peace. **Amen.**

728

Amen.

HYMNS FOR THE YOUNG

THE following hymns are suggested as suitable for use as Hymns for the Young in Public Worship, and in Sunday Schools, Bible Classes, Guilds, and other meetings for the young. Hymns marked * are more suitable for Children, those marked † for Adolescents.

The Holy Trinity

1 Holy, holy, holy, Lord God Almighty
2 †Round the Lord in glory seated
7 Glory be to God the Father

God in Creation, Providence, and Redemption

9 O worship the King all-glorious above
10 †The spacious firmament on high
11 Let us with a gladsome mind
12 †Immortal, invisible, God only wise
13 All creatures of our God and King
14 The strain upraise of joy and praise
15 Let all the world in every corner sing
16 Praise the Lord, His glories show
17 For the beauty of the earth
18 *All things bright and beautiful
19 †O Lord of heaven and earth and sea
20 *God who made the earth
21 Praise, my soul, the King of heaven
22 Praise to the Lord, the Almighty, the King of creation
23 Sing to the Lord a joyful song
28 A gladsome hymn of praise we sing
29 Now thank we all our God
35 Praise the Lord! ye heavens, adore Him
37 *Above the clear blue sky
38 Songs of praise the angels sang

The Lord Jesus Christ
His Incarnation

40 Hark, the glad sound! the Saviour comes
41 All my heart this night rejoices
42 While humble shepherds watched their flocks
43 In the field with their flocks abiding
44 *Little children, wake and listen
45 The first Nowell the angel did say

46 Hark! the herald angels sing
47 It came upon the midnight clear
48 O little town of Bethlehem
49 Still the night, holy the night
50 In the bleak mid-winter
51 See! in yonder manger low
53 Child in the manger
55 O come, all ye faithful
56 From heaven above to earth I come
57 The race that long in darkness pined
58 Good Christian men, rejoice
63 As with gladness men of old
64 Brightest and best of the sons of the morning
65 Angels from the realms of glory
66 From the eastern mountains

His Life and Example

67 Thou didst leave Thy throne
68 *There came a little Child to earth
69 *Once in royal David's city
70 *Come, praise your Lord and Saviour
71 *I love to hear the story
74 O sing a song of Bethlehem
75 †Ye fair green hills of Galilee
76 *Behold a little Child
77 Who is He, in yonder stall
80 †It fell upon a summer day
81 *God, who hath made the daisies
82 *I think, when I read that sweet story of old
85 When the Lord of Love was here
86 Thine arm, O Lord, in days of old
87 †What grace, O Lord, and beauty shone
90 †Lord, as to Thy dear Cross we flee
91 All glory, laud, and honour
93 *Hosanna, loud hosanna

His Sufferings and Death

105 There is a green hill far away
106 †When I survey the wondrous Cross

HYMNS FOR THE YOUNG

His Resurrection

115 'Welcome, happy morning!'—age to age shall say
116 Blest morning, whose first dawning rays
117 On wings of living light
118 'Christ the Lord is risen to-day'
119 Jesus Christ is risen to-day
120 'The Lord is risen indeed'
122 The strife is o'er, the battle done
124 O sons and daughters, let us sing

His Ascension and Exaltation

130 The golden gates are lifted up
131 †The Head that once was crowned with thorns
133 *Golden harps are sounding
134 †Look, ye saints! the sight is glorious
135 Rejoice, the Lord is King
136 Crown Him with many crowns
137 Blest be the everlasting God

His Sympathy and Intercession

145 One there is, above all others
146 †O Son of Man, our Hero strong and tender

His Coming in Power

149 O come, O come, Immanuel!
150 Come, Thou long-expected Jesus
151 †The Lord will come and not be slow
153 †'Thy Kingdom come!'—on bended knee
154 †Hail to the Lord's Anointed
155 †Mine eyes have seen the glory of the coming of the Lord
158 *When He cometh, when He cometh

His Praise

167 When morning gilds the skies
168 Ye servants of God, your Master proclaim
177 *Come, children, join to sing
178 †In the Name of Jesus

The Holy Spirit

180 Our blest Redeemer, ere He breathed
182 Come, Holy Ghost, our souls inspire
187 †Gracious Spirit, dwell with me
188 Come, gracious Spirit, heavenly Dove
189 *Holy Spirit, hear us
193 Holy Spirit, Truth Divine

The Holy Scriptures

198 †O Word of God Incarnate
199 Lord, Thy Word abideth
204 Holy Father, Thou hast given

The Church
The Communion of Saints

220 †For all the saints who from their labours rest
221 †Ten thousand times ten thousand
223 How bright these glorious spirits shine

Worship
The Sanctuary

228 From all that dwell below the skies
229 All people that on earth do dwell
230 †Before Jehovah's awful throne
231 †All lands and peoples, all the earth
233 †Stand up, and bless the Lord
236 We love the place, O God
237 Again the morn of gladness
238 *Lord, this day Thy children meet
248 Jesus, stand among us
251 *Hushed was the evening hymn

Morning

256 †Awake, my soul, and with the sun
257 †All praise to Thee who safe hast kept
258 Now that the daylight fills the sky
263 †Father, we praise Thee, now the night is over
264 O Lord of life, Thy quickening voice
268 O day of rest and gladness
270 The darkness now is over

Evening

273 The sun declines ; o'er land and sea
278 Now cheer our hearts this eventide
280 †Now God be with us, for the night is closing
288 *Now the day is over
289 The day Thou gavest, Lord, is ended
291 All praise to Thee, my God, this night
292 Sun of my soul, Thou Saviour dear
294 Ere I sleep, for every favour

Close of Worship

300 †Now may He who from the dead
301 †Saviour, again to Thy dear Name we raise

HYMNS FOR THE YOUNG

The Service of the Kingdom

341 †Soldiers of the Cross, arise
344 †Rise up, O men of God
345 †Fountain of good, to own Thy love
346 †We give Thee but Thine own
347 †Here, Lord, we offer Thee all that is fairest
349 †Father, who on man dost shower
351 †From Thee all skill and science flow
352 †Thou to whom the sick and dying
353 †Father, whose will is life and good
361 *Dear Master, what can children do
362 *The fields are all white
363 *The wise may bring their learning

Missions

364 Thou whose almighty word
365 Behold ! the mountain of the Lord
371 From Greenland's icy mountains
372 †Hills of the North, rejoice
373 †Far round the world Thy children sing their song
374 *Once again, dear Lord, we pray
375 *God of heaven, hear our singing
380 †God is working His purpose out
388 Jesus shall reign where'er the sun

The Christian Life
The Gospel Call

398 †The Lord is rich and merciful

Love and Gratitude

423 O Jesus, King most wonderful
436 *It is a thing most wonderful
437 *Saviour, teach me day by day

Peace and Joy

438 †The King of Love my Shepherd is

Prayer, Aspiration, and Holiness

454 †O God, Thou art the Father
460 †Dear Master, in whose life I see
462 Jesus, meek and gentle
465 *Blessèd Jesus, high in glory
468 *Jesus, Saviour ever mild
469 *Jesus, from Thy throne on high
476 †Saviour, blessèd Saviour
477 †Be Thou my Vision, O Lord of my heart
478 Blest are the pure in heart
480 *There is a city bright
481 Father of peace, and God of love
483 Behold the amazing gift of love

Brotherly Love

485 †O brother man, fold to thy heart thy brother
486 Our Father, Thy dear Name doth show
487 †O God of mercy, God of might
489 †Eternal Ruler of the ceaseless round
491 †Almighty Father, who dost give
492 †O God our Father, throned on high
493 †Father of men, in whom are one

Consecration and Discipleship

494 Fair waved the golden corn
495 *Saviour, while my heart is tender
497 †Just as I am, Thine own to be
498 †Lord, in the fulness of my might
506 †I bind unto myself to-day
507 I'm not ashamed to own my Lord
508 †O Jesus, I have promised
509 †Jesus, Master, whose I am
512 †Take my life, and let it be
514 †Through good report and evil, Lord
516 *We are but little children weak
517 †Fight the good fight

Conflict and Victory

519 †Who is on the Lord's side
521 †Believing fathers oft have told
527 †God is my strong salvation
529 †Courage, brother ! do not stumble
530 †The Sonᵗ of God goes forth to war
531 †O God of Truth, whose living word
532 †Stand up ! stand up for Jesus
534 †Soldiers of Christ, arise
535 †Onward ! Christian soldiers
537 †March on, my soul, with strength
538 *Brightly gleams our banner

Trust and Resignation

550 *Great God ! and wilt Thou condescend
552 *Jesus is our Shepherd
554 *Saviour, like a shepherd lead us

Pilgrimage and Rest

562 O God of Bethel, by whose hand
565 *Father, lead me day by day
569 *Lead, holy Shepherd, lead us
573 *When from Egypt's house of bondage
574 Children of the heavenly King
575 *The world looks very beautiful

231

HYMNS FOR THE YOUNG

576 †Who would true valour see
577 †O happy band of pilgrims
578 *Whither, pilgrims, are you going
579 Forward ! be our watchword

*Death, Resurrection, and the Life
Everlasting*

587 *There is a happy land
591 *Every morning the red sun
593 *There 's a Friend for little children
600 *Around the throne of God in
heaven

Times and Seasons

605 At Thy feet, our God and Father
612 The summer days are come again
613 Summer suns are glowing
617 Fountain of mercy, God of love
618 We plough the fields, and scatter
620 Praise, O praise our God and King

Travellers and the Absent

626 Eternal Father, strong to save
629 Holy Father, in Thy mercy

National Hymns

631 God save our gracious Queen
632 God bless our native land
640 †And did those feet in ancient time
647 Land of our Birth, we pledge to
thee

Home and School

651 †Forth in Thy Name, O Lord, I go
653 *The morning bright
654 *Jesus, tender Shepherd, hear me
655 *Lord, I would own Thy tender
care
656 Be present at our table, Lord
657 *Away in a manger, no crib for a
bed
658 *Children of Jerusalem
659 *When mothers of Salem

660 *Jesus loves me ! this I know
661 *Lord, a little band and lowly
662 *Gentle Jesus, meek and mild
663 *Do no sinful action
664 *God is always near me
665 *Jesus, holy, undefiled
666 *Jesus, high in glory
667 *Jesus, Friend of little children
668 *Loving Shepherd of Thy sheep
669 *If I come to Jesus
670 *O what can little hands do
671 *Jesus bids us shine
672 †Go forth to life, O child of earth
673 God, who created me
674 *Looking upward every day
675 †O Jesus, strong and pure and true
676 †Praise to our God, who with love
never swerving
677 †Lord, behold us with Thy blessing
678 †Lord, dismiss us with Thy blessing

Ancient Hymns and Canticles

714 Blessed be the Lord God of Israel
715 My soul doth magnify the Lord
716 Lord, now lettest Thou Thy servant depart in peace
717 Glory be to God on high
718 We praise Thee, O God
719 O all ye works of the Lord, bless
ye the Lord
720 God spake all these words, saying
721 Jesus said : The first of all the
commandments is
722 Blessed are the poor in spirit
723 Our Father which art in heaven
724 I believe in God the Father Almighty
725 I believe in one God the Father
Almighty
726 Let us now praise famous men
727 The Lord bless thee, and keep thee

INDEX OF FIRST WORDS

Brackets indicate that the first line in some collections begins thus.

518 A CHARGE to keep I have,
703 A debtor to mercy alone,
28 A gladsome hymn of praise we sing,
305 A little child the Saviour came,
526 A safe stronghold our God is still
560 A Sovereign Protector I have,
286 Abide with me ;
37 Above the clear blue sky,
313 According to Thy gracious word,
275 Again, as evening's shadow falls,
237 Again the morn of gladness,
13 All creatures of our God and King,
91 All glory, laud, and honour
139 All hail, the power of Jesus' Name !
609 All is bright and cheerful round us ;
231 All lands and peoples, all the earth,
41 All my heart this night rejoices,
448 All my hope on God is founded ;
229 All people that on earth do dwell,
291 All praise to Thee, my God,
257 All praise to Thee who safe hast kept,
254 All things are Thine ;
18 All things bright and beautiful,
138 Alleluia ! sing to Jesus !
503 Almighty Father of all things
491 Almighty Father, who dost give
295 Almighty God, Thy word is cast
728 Amen
110 And can it be, that I should gain
640 And did those feet in ancient time
144 And didst Thou love the race
103 And now, belovèd Lord,
320 And now, O Father,
296 And now the wants are told
252 Angel voices, ever singing
65 Angels from the realms of glory,
451 Approach, my soul, the mercy-seat,
369 Arm of the Lord, awake, awake !
600 Around the throne of God
391 Art thou weary, art thou languid,
276 As darker, darker fall around
274 As now the sun's declining rays
63 As with gladness men of old
277 At even, when the sun was set,
99 At the Cross, her station keeping,
178 (At the Name of Jesus)
265 At Thy feet, O Christ, we lay
605 At Thy feet, our God and Father
317 Author of life divine,

256 Awake, my soul, and with the sun
657 Away in a manger, no crib for a bed,

656 BE present at our table, Lord,
556 Be still, my soul : the Lord
477 Be Thou my Vision, O Lord
230 Before Jehovah's awful throne,
271 Before the day draws near its ending,
76 Behold a little Child,
483 Behold the amazing gift of love
365 Behold ! the mountain of the Lord
242 Behold us, Lord, a little space
521 Believing fathers oft have told
488 Belovèd, let us love : love is of God :
691 Beneath the Cross of Jesus
722 Blessed are the poor in spirit :
714 Blessed be the Lord God of Israel :
307 Blessèd Jesus, here we stand,
465 Blessèd Jesus, high in glory,
169 Blessing and honour and glory
478 Blest are the pure in heart,
137 Blest be the everlasting God,
490 Blest be the tie that binds
116 Blest morning, whose first dawning rays
342 Bowed low in supplication,
318 Bread of the world, in mercy broken
202 Break Thou the bread of life,
194 Breathe on me, Breath of God ;
597 Brief life is here our portion,
2 (Bright the vision that delighted)
64 Brightest and best of the sons
538 Brightly gleams our banner,
322 By Christ redeemed,
309 By cool Siloam's shady rill
114 By Jesus' grave on either hand,
104 By the Cross of Jesus standing,

53 CHILD in the manger,
658 Children of Jerusalem
574 Children of the heavenly King,
163 Christ is coming ! let creation
207 Christ is made the sure foundation,
179 Christ is the world's Redeemer,
118 Christ the Lord is risen to-day,
261 Christ, whose glory fills the skies,
523 Christian, seek not yet repose :
343 Christian, work for Jesus,
54 Christians, awake,

233

INDEX OF FIRST WORDS

209 City of God, how broad and far
177 Come, children, join to sing
297 Come, dearest Lord, descend
191 Come down, O Love Divine,
188 Come, gracious Spirit, heavenly Dove,
196 Come, Holy Ghost, our hearts
182 Come, Holy Ghost, our souls
190 Come, Holy Spirit, come ;
175 Come, let us join our cheerful songs
400 Come, let us to the Lord our God
450 Come, my soul, thy suit prepare ;
416 Come, O Thou Traveller unknown,
70 Come, praise your Lord
435 Come, Thou Fount of every blessing,
186 Come, Thou Holy Paraclete,
150 Come, Thou long-expected Jesus,
390 Come unto Me, ye weary,
447 Come, we that love the Lord,
688 Come, ye disconsolate,
393 Come, ye sinners,
392 Come, ye souls by sin afflicted,
619 Come, ye thankful people, come,
241 Command Thy blessing from above,
546 Commit thou all thy griefs
529 Courage, brother ! do not stumble,
184 Creator Spirit ! by whose aid
136 Crown Him with many crowns,

112 DARK the day on Calvary's Cross
585 Days and moments quickly flying
245 Dear Lord and Father of mankind,
460 Dear Master, in whose life I see
361 Dear Master, what can children do?
246 Dear Shepherd of Thy people, hear;
324 Deck thyself, my soul, with gladness
354 Dismiss me not Thy service, Lord,
663 Do no sinful action ;

250 ENTER Thy courts, Thou Word
294 Ere I sleep, for every favour
626 Eternal Father, strong to save,
36 Eternal Light ! eternal Light !
489 Eternal Ruler of the ceaseless round
591 Every morning the red sun

494 FAIR waved the golden corn
572 Far off I see the goal
373 Far round the world Thy children sing their song
243 Father, again in Jesus' Name
645 Father Eternal, Ruler of Creation,
548 Father, I know that all my life
647 (Father in heaven, who lovest all,)
283 Father, in high heaven dwelling,
565 Father, lead me, day by day,
606 Father, let me dedicate

213 Father of all, from land and sea
5 Father of heaven, whose love
493 Father of men, in whom are one
481 Father of peace, and God of love
650 Father, our children keep ;
263 Father, we praise Thee,
630 Father, who art alone
349 Father, who on man dost shower
353 Father, whose will is life and good
217 Fear not, thou faithful Christian flock
83 Fierce raged the tempest
84 Fierce was the wild billow,
517 Fight the good fight
383 Fling out the banner ! let it float
220 For all the saints who from their labours rest,
610 For all Thy love and goodness,
583 For ever with the Lord !
370 For My sake and the Gospel's, go
17 For the beauty of the earth,
212 For the might of Thine arm we bless Thee
472 For Thee, my God, for Thee alone,
508 For thee, O dear, dear country
218 For those we love within the veil,
604 For Thy mercy and Thy grace,
651 Forth in Thy Name, O Lord, I go,
79 Forty days and forty nights
579 'Forward !' be our watchword,
345 Fountain of good, to own Thy love
617 Fountain of mercy, God of love,
228 From all that dwell below the skies
407 From depths of woe I raise to Thee
371 From Greenland's icy mountains,
56 From heaven above to earth I come,
596 From heavenly Jerusalem's towers,
66 From the eastern mountains,
351 From Thee all skill and science flow,

662 GENTLE Jesus, meek and mild
547 (Give to the winds thy fears ;)
206 Glorious things of thee are spoken,
717 Glory be to God on high :
7 Glory be to God the Father,
712 Glory be to the Father,
672 Go forth to life, O child of earth,
356 Go, labour on : spend and be spent,
59 God and Father, we adore Thee
624 God be with you till we meet again,
632 God bless our native land ;
664 God is always near me,
33 God is love : His mercy brightens
527 God is my strong salvation ;
380 God is working His purpose out,
31 God moves in a mysterious way,

234

INDEX OF FIRST WORDS

642 God of Eternity, Lord of the Ages
375 God of heaven, hear our singing ;
379 God of mercy, God of grace,
637 God of our fathers, known of old,
240 God of pity, God of grace,
332 God of the living, in whose eyes
234 God reveals His presence
631 God save our gracious King,
720 God spake all these words,
293 God, that madest earth and heaven,
641 God the Omnipotent !
673 God, who created me
81 God, who hath made the daisies,
20 God, who made the earth,
133 Golden harps are sounding
58 Good Christian men, rejoice
310 Gracious Saviour, gentle Shepherd,
187 Gracious Spirit, dwell with me !
484 Gracious Spirit, Holy Ghost,
550 Great God ! and wilt Thou condescend
366 Great God of Abraham,
607 Great God, we sing that mighty hand
643 Great King of nations,
246 (Great Shepherd of Thy people, hear)
564 Guide me, O Thou great Jehovah,

281 HAIL, gladdening Light,
269 Hail, sacred day of earthly rest,
266 Hail, thou bright and sacred morn,
154 Hail to the Lord's Anointed,
126 Hallelujah ! hallelujah !
440 Hallelujah ! hallelujah !
580 Hark, hark, my soul !
417 Hark, my soul ! it is the Lord ;
40 Hark, the glad sound !
46 Hark, the herald angels sing,
389 Hark ! the song of jubilee,
129 He is gone—beyond the skies !
522 He liveth long who liveth well :
557 He that is down needs fear no fall,
225 He wants not friends that hath Thy love,
576 (He who would valiant be)
603 Heavenly Father, Thou hast brought us
347 Here Lord, we offer Thee
323 Here, O my Lord, I see Thee
372 Hills of the North, rejoice !
101 His are the thousand sparkling rills
555 Hold Thou my hands
282 Holy Father, cheer our way
629 Holy Father, in Thy mercy,
204 Holy Father, Thou hast given
1 Holy, holy, holy, Lord God Almighty !

713 Holy, holy, holy, Lord God of hosts :
49 (Holy night, peaceful night)
189 Holy Spirit, hear us :
193 Holy Spirit, Truth Divine,
93 Hosanna, loud hosanna,
223 How bright these glorious spirits shine !
419 How sweet the Name of Jesus sounds
251 Hushed was the evening hymn,

698 I AM not skilled to understand
316 I am not worthy, holy Lord,
695 I am trusting Thee, Lord Jesus,
724 I believe in God the Father Almighty,
725 I believe in one God the Father Almighty,
506 I bind unto myself to-day
528 I feel the winds of God to-day
689 I hear Thy welcome voice
410 I heard the voice of Jesus say
694 I lay my sins on Jesus
427 I lift my heart to Thee
210 I love Thy kingdom, Lord,
71 I love to hear the story
700 I need Thee every hour,
82 I think, when I read that sweet story of old,
683 I will sing the wondrous story
669 If I come to Jesus,
541 If thou but suffer God to guide thee,
507 I'm not ashamed to own my Lord,
12 Immortal, invisible, God only wise,
141 Immortal Love, for ever full,
442 In heavenly love abiding
50 In the bleak mid-winter,
113 In the Cross of Christ I glory,
43 In the fields with their flocks abiding
525 In the hour of trial,
178 In the Name of Jesus
47 It came upon the midnight clear,
80 It fell upon a summer day,
436 It is a thing most wonderful,
705 I've found a Friend ;

595 JERUSALEM, my happy home,
599 Jerusalem the golden,
671 Jesus bids us shine
500 Jesus calls us ! O'er the tumult
119 Jesus Christ is risen to-day,
667 Jesus, Friend of little children,
469 Jesus, from Thy throne on high,
666 Jesus, high in glory,
665 Jesus, holy, undefiled,
502 Jesus, I my cross have taken,

235

INDEX OF FIRST WORDS

696 Jesus, I will trust Thee,
552 Jesus is our Shepherd,
121 Jesus lives ! thy terrors now
524 Jesus, Lord of life and glory,
127 Jesus, Lord, Redeemer,
414 Jesus, Lover of my soul
660 Jesus loves me ! this I know,
509 Jesus, Master, whose I am,
462 Jesus, meek and gentle,
430 Jesus, my Lord, my God, my All,
62 ' Jesus ! ' Name of wondrous love ;
721 Jesus said : The first of all the commandments is :
468 Jesus, Saviour ever mild,
706 Jesus, Saviour, pilot me
388 Jesus shall reign where'er the sun
248 Jesus, stand among us
567 Jesus, still lead on,
262 Jesus, Sun of Righteousness,
654 Jesus, tender Shepherd, hear me ;
421 Jesus ! the very thought is sweet,
422 Jesus, the very thought of Thee
418 Jesus, these eyes have never seen
420 Jesus, Thou Joy of loving hearts,
432 Jesus, Thy boundless love to me
314 Jesus, to Thy table led,
399 Jesus, we are far away
247 Jesus, where'er Thy people meet,
208 Jesus, with Thy Church abide ;
165 Join all the glorious names
636 Judge Eternal, throned in splendour,
497 Just as I am, Thine own to be
411 Just as I am, without one plea

201 LAMP of our feet, whereby we trace
647 Land of our Birth, we pledge to thee
569 Lead, holy Shepherd, lead us,
568 Lead, kindly Light,
563 Lead us, heavenly Father, lead us
566 Lead us, O Father, in the paths
15 Let all the world in every corner sing,
227 Let saints on earth in concert sing
726 Let us now praise famous men :
11 Let us with a gladsome mind
385 Lift up your heads, ye gates
249 Light of the anxious heart,
381 Light of the lonely pilgrim's heart,
171 Light of the world !
443 Like a river glorious
44 Little children, wake and listen !
160 Lo ! He comes, with clouds descending
544 Long did I toil, and knew no earthly rest,
340 Look from the sphere of endless day,
203 Look upon us, blessèd Lord,

134 Look, ye saints ! the sight is glorious ;
674 Looking upward every day,
661 Lord, a little band and lowly,
90 Lord, as to Thy dear Cross we flee,
677 Lord, behold us with Thy blessing
299 Lord, dismiss us with Thy blessing ;
678 Lord, dismiss us with Thy blessing
378 Lord, her watch Thy Church
687 Lord, I hear of showers of blessing
655 Lord, I would own Thy tender care,
498 Lord, in the fulness of my might,
405 Lord, in this Thy mercy's day,
611 Lord, in Thy Name Thy servants
549 Lord, it belongs not to my care
304 Lord, Jesus Christ, our Lord
403 Lord Jesus, think on me,
716 Lord, now lettest Thou Thy servant depart in peace:
24 Lord of all being, throned afar,
652 Lord of Life and King of Glory,
337 Lord of light, whose Name
159 Lord of mercy and of might,
216 Lord of our life, and God
615 Lord of the harvest, once again
335 Lord of the living harvest
338 Lord, speak to me,
238 Lord, this day Thy children meet
404 Lord, Thy mercy now entreating,
199 Lord, Thy word abideth,
98 Lord, when Thy Kingdom comes,
633 Lord, while for all mankind we pray,
52 Love came down at Christmas,
479 Love Divine, all loves excelling
434 Loved with everlasting love
668 Loving Shepherd of Thy sheep,

464 MAKE me a captive, Lord,
350 Maker of earth and sea and sky,
693 Man of Sorrows ! wondrous Name
537 March on, my soul, with strength,
155 Mine eyes have seen the glory
533 Much in sorrow, oft in woe,
415 My faith looks up to Thee,
539 My God and Father, while I stray
311 My God, and is Thy table spread ?
27 My God, how wonderful Thou art,
433 My God, I love Thee ; not because
441 My God, I thank Thee,
449 My God, is any hour so sweet,
446 My heart is resting, O my God,
697 My hope is built on nothing less
95 My Lord, my Master, at Thy feet
715 My soul doth magnify the Lord ;
463 My soul, there is a country
456 My spirit longs for Thee
551 My times are in Thy hand :

INDEX OF FIRST WORDS

99 (NEAR the Cross was)
475 Nearer, my God, to Thee,
259 (New every morning is the love)
412 None other Lamb, none other Name,
429 Not what I am, O Lord,
278 Now cheer our hearts this eventide,
280 Now God be with us, for the night
300 Now may He who from the dead
614 Now sing we a song for the harvest:
29 Now thank we all our God,
258 Now that the daylight fills the sky,
260 Now that the daystar glimmers
288 Now the day is over,
330 Now the labourer's task is o'er,
708 Now to Him who loved us, gave us
710 Now to the King of heaven

719 O ALL ye works of the Lord,
244 O be with us, gracious Father,
226 O blest communion with the saints
485 O brother man, fold to thy heart
699 O Christ, in Thee my soul
545 O Christ, my God, who seest
55 O come, all ye faithful,
96 O come and mourn with me awhile;
149 O come, O come, Immanuel,
268 O day of rest and gladness,
326 O Father, all creating,
308 O Father, Thou who hast created all
457 O for a closer walk with God,
474 O for a faith that will not shrink
467 O for a heart to praise my God !
166 O for a thousand tongues, to sing
562 O God of Bethel ! by whose hand
638 O God of earth and altar,
646 O God of love, O King of peace
325 O God of Love, to Thee we bow,
487 O God of mercy, God of might,
531 O God of truth, whose living word
492 O God our Father, throned on high,
601 O God, our help in ages past,
473 O God, Thou art my God alone ;
454 O God, Thou art the Father
466 O grant us light, that we may know
577 O happy band of pilgrims,
499 O happy day, that fixed my choice
648 O happy home, where Thou art loved the dearest,
455 O help us, Lord ; each hour of need
520 (O it is hard to work for God)
176 O Jesus, ever present,
409 O Jesus, full of pardoning grace,
508 O Jesus, I have promised
423 O Jesus, King most wonderful,
675 O Jesus, strong and pure and true,
397 O Jesus, Thou art standing
6 O King of kings, before whose throne
453 O King of mercy, from Thy throne
470 O Lamb of God, still keep me
542 O let him whose sorrow
458 O Light that knew no dawn,
172 O Light, whose beams illumine all
48 O little town of Bethlehem,
513 O Lord and Master of us all,
625 O Lord, be with us when we sail
543 O Lord, how happy should we be
570 O Lord, I sing Thy praises
19 O Lord of heaven and earth and sea,
355 O Lord of life, and love, and power,
264 O Lord of life, Thy quickening voice
331 O Lord of life, where'er they be,
376 O Lord our God, arise !
401 O Lord, turn not away Thy face
428 O Love Divine, how sweet thou art!
143 O Love Divine ! that stooped to share
424 O Love that wilt not let me go,
496 O Love, who formedst me to wear
88 O Master, it is good to be
339 O Master, let me walk with Thee
102 O perfect life of love !
327 O perfect Love, all human thought
107 O sacred Head, sore wounded,
302 O Saviour, bless us ere we go ;
425 O Saviour, I have nought to plead,
111 O Saviour, where shall guilty man
74 O sing a song of Bethlehem,
360 O Son of God, our Captain of salvation,
146 O Son of Man, our Hero strong
124 O sons and daughters, let us sing
386 O Spirit of the living God,
368 O that the Lord's salvation
348 O Thou, before whose presence
402 O Thou, my Judge and King
471 O Thou who camest from above,
334 O Thou who makest souls to shine
426 O Thou, whose mercy found me,
259 O timely happy, timely wise,
4 O Trinity, O blessèd Light,
670 O what can little hands do
224 O what their joy and their glory must be,
89 O wondrous type, O vision fair,
198 O Word of God Incarnate,
97 O word of pity, for our pardon
9 O worship the King all-glorious
358 O ye who taste that love is sweet,
387 O'er those gloomy hills of darkness
60 Of the Father's love begotten,

INDEX OF FIRST WORDS

298 Of Thy love some gracious token
78 On Jordan's bank the Baptist's cry
117 On wings of living light,
374 Once again, dear Lord, we pray
69 Once in royal David's city
145 One there is, above all others,
461 One thing I of the Lord desire,
406 One who is all unfit to count
535 Onward ! Christian soldiers,
384 Onward march, all-conquering Jesus,
80 Our blest Redeemer, ere He breathed
306 Our children, Lord, in faith and prayer,
290 Our day of praise is done ;
486 Our Father, Thy dear Name doth show
723 Our Father which art in heaven,
601 (Our God, our help in ages past,)
125 Our Lord Christ hath risen !
128 Our Lord is risen from the dead,

303 PART in peace : Christ's life was peace,
444 Peace, perfect peace,
235 Pleasant are Thy courts above,
333 Pour out Thy Spirit from on high ;
709 Praise God, from whom all blessings flow ;
21 Praise, my soul, the King of heaven ;
620 Praise, O praise our God and King;
16 Praise the Lord, His glories show,
35 Praise the Lord ! ye heavens,
634 Praise to our God, whose bounteous hand
676 Praise to our God, who with love
32 Praise to the Holiest in the height,
22 Praise to the Lord, the Almighty,
34 Praise ye Jehovah, praise the Lord
452 Present with the two or three
547 Put thou thy trust in God,

135 REJOICE, the Lord is King;
681 Rescue the perishing, care for the dying;
174 Rest of the weary,
679 Revive Thy work, O Lord :
92 Ride on ! ride on in majesty !
61 Ring out, ye crystal spheres !
344 Rise up, O men of God !
413 Rock of Ages, cleft for me,
2 Round the Lord in glory seated,

707 SAFE in the arms of Jesus,
328 Safely, safely gathered in,
301 Saviour, again to Thy dear Name

476 Saviour, blessèd Saviour,
285 Saviour, breathe an evening blessing
554 Saviour, like a shepherd lead us,
382 Saviour, sprinkle many nations,
437 Saviour, teach me, day by day,
495 Saviour, while my heart is tender,
536 Say not, ' The struggle nought availeth ;
51 See ! in yonder manger low,
336 Shine Thou upon us, Lord,
108 Sing, my tongue, how glorious battle
23 Sing to the Lord a joyful song,
394 Sinners Jesus will receive :
534 Soldiers of Christ ! arise,
341 Soldiers of the Cross, arise !
439 Sometimes a light surprises
359 Son of God, eternal Saviour,
38 Songs of praise the angels sang,
586 Sooner or later : yet at last
395 Souls of men ! why will ye scatter
445 Speak, I pray Thee, gentle Jesus !
183 Spirit Divine, attend our prayers,
195 Spirit of God, descend upon my heart ;
185 Spirit of God, that moved of old
192 Spirit of Grace, Thou Light
233 Stand up, and bless the Lord,
532 Stand up ! stand up for Jesus,
627 Star of peace to wanderers weary,
602 Still on the homeward journey
49 Still the night, holy the night !
142 Strong Son of God, immortal Love,
613 Summer suns are glowing
292 Sun of my soul, Thou Saviour dear,
588 Sunset and evening star,
239 Sweet is the solemn voice that calls
170 Sweeter sounds than music knows

512 TAKE my life, and let it be
501 ' Take up thy cross,' the Saviour said,
511 Teach me, my God and King,
510 Teach me, O Lord, to follow Him
682 Tell me the old, old story
221 Ten thousand times ten thousand,
161 That day of wrath, that dreadful day,
205 The Church's one foundation
270 The darkness now is over,
287 The day is past and over :
123 The day of resurrection !
289 The day Thou gavest, Lord,
284 The duteous day now closeth,
362 The fields are all white,
45 The first Nowell the angel did say
608 The glory of the spring how sweet !

INDEX OF FIRST WORDS

571 The God of Abraham praise,
130 The golden gates are lifted up,
131 The Head that once was crowned
396 The King of Glory standeth
438 The King of Love my Shepherd is,
132 The Lord ascendeth up on high,
727 The Lord bless thee, and keep thee:
25 The Lord is King! lift up thy voice,
398 The Lord is rich and merciful;
120 The Lord is risen indeed;
151 The Lord will come and not be slow,
653 The morning bright,
57 The race that long in darkness pined
279 The radiant morn hath passed
219 The saints of God!
581 The sands of time are sinking;
530 The Son of God goes forth to war,
10 The spacious firmament on high,
197 The Spirit breathes upon the word,
14 The strain upraise of joy and praise,
122 The strife is o'er, the battle done;
612 The summer days are come again:
273 The sun declines; o'er land and sea
272 The sun is sinking fast,
363 The wise may bring their learning,
575 The world looks very beautiful
621 The year is swiftly waning,
319 Thee we adore, O hidden Saviour,
431 Thee will I love, my Strength,
68 There came a little Child to earth
594 There is a blessèd home
8 There is a book, who runs may read,
480 There is a city bright;
692 There is a fountain filled with blood
105 There is a green hill far away,
587 There is a happy land,
408 There is a holy sacrifice
592 There is a land of pure delight,
590 There is no night in heaven:
148 There is no sorrow, Lord, too light
593 There 's a Friend for little children,
685 There were ninety and nine that safely lay
639 These things shall be :
86 Thine arm, O Lord, in days of old,
504 Thine for ever ! God of Love,
267 This is the day of light :
253 This stone to Thee in faith we lay ;
157 Thou art coming, O my Saviour,
173 Thou art the Way : to Thee alone
67 Thou didst leave Thy throne
649 Thou gracious Power, whose mercy
459 Thou hidden Love of God,
315 Thou standest at the altar,
352 Thou to whom the sick and dying

690 Thou who didst on Calvary bleed,
147 Thou who didst stoop below
364 Thou whose almighty word
515 Though lowly here our lot may be,
30 Though troubles assail and dangers
100 Throned upon the awful Tree,
514 Through good report and evil,
702 Through the love of God
214 Through the night of doubt
215 Thy hand, O God, has guided
152 Thy Kingdom come, O God ;
153 'Thy Kingdom come !' on bended knee
553 Thy way, not mine, O Lord,
321 'Till He come !' O let the words
623 'Tis winter now ; the fallen snow
505 To-day I arise,
686 To-day the Saviour cails :
684 To-day Thy mercy calls us
711 To Him, who sits upon the throne,
164 To the Name of our Salvation
200 To Thee, we render thanks,
616 To Thee, O Lord, our hearts we raise
635 To Thee our God we fly
312 'Twas on that night when doomed to know
559 'Twixt gleams of joy and clouds

162 WAKE, awake ! for night is flying,
377 Wake, Spirit, who in times
482 Walk in the light :
516 We are but little children weak,
211 We come unto our fathers' God ;
346 We give Thee but Thine own,
680 We have heard a joyful sound,
236 We love the place, O God,
141 (We may not climb the heavenly steeps)
618 We plough the fields, and scatter
718 We praise Thee, O God :
3 We praise, we worship Thee,
72 We saw Thee not
109 We sing the praise of Him
409 (Weary of wandering from my God)
94 Weep not for Him
115 'Welcome, happy morning !'
701 What a Friend we have in Jesus,
87 What grace, O Lord,
644 What service shall we render thee,
540 Whate'er my God ordains is right :
26 When all Thy mercies, O my God !
573 When from Egypt's house
181 When God of old came down
158 When He cometh, when He cometh
106 When I survey the wondrous Cross
367 When Israel, of the Lord beloved
167 When morning gilds the skies,

INDEX OF FIRST WORDS

659 When mothers of Salem
589 When on my day of life
329 When our heads are bowed
584 When the day of toil is done,
85 When the Lord of Love was here,
255 When the weary, seeking rest,
582 When this passing world is done,
140 Where high the heavenly temple
42 While humble shepherds watched
578 Whither, pilgrims, are you going,
222 Who are these, like stars appearing,
558 Who fathoms the eternal thought ?
77 Who is He, in yonder stall,
519 Who is on the Lord's side ?

73 Who is this, so weak and helpless,
576 Who would true valour see,
628 Whom oceans part, O Lord, unite
622 Winter reigneth o'er the land,
357 Work, for the night is coming !
520 Workman of God !
232 Worship the Lord in the beauty

75 YE fair green hills of Galilee,
39 Ye holy angels bright,
168 Ye servants of God, your Master
156 Ye servants of the Lord,
704 Yield not to temptation,
561 Your harps, ye trembling saints,